Understanding Deaf Culture

MULTILINGUAL MATTERS

Please contact us for the latest book information:
Multilingual Matters, Frankfurt Lodge, Clevedon Hall,
Victoria Road, Clevedon, BS21 7HH, England
http://www.multilingual-matters.com

Understanding Deaf Culture

In Search of Deafhood

Paddy Ladd

'The critical ontology of ourselves has to be considered ... as an attitude, an ethos, a philosophical life in which the critique of what we are is at one and the same time the historical analysis of the limits that are imposed on us and an experiment in going beyond them.'

Michel Foucault

'You don't see anything unless you have the right metaphor to let you perceive it.'

Robert Shaw

'Let me be known as the man who told you something you already know.'

Woody Guthrie

MULTILINGUAL MATTERS LTD
Clevedon • Buffalo • Toronto • Sydney

Library of Congress Cataloging in Publication Data
Ladd, Paddy
Understanding Deaf Culture: In Search of Deafhood/Paddy Ladd
Includes bibliographical references and index.
1. Deaf. 2. Deaf–Great Britain. 3. Subculture. 4. Sociology of disability. I. Title.
HV2380.L26 2002
305.9′08162–dc21   2001056804

British Library Cataloguing in Publication Data
A catalogue entry for this book is available from the British Library.

ISBN 1-85359-546-2 (hbk)
ISBN 1-85359-545-4 (pbk)

Multilingual Matters Ltd
UK: Frankfurt Lodge, Clevedon Hall, Victoria Road, Clevedon BS21 7HH.
USA: UTP, 2250 Military Road, Tonawanda, NY 14150, USA.
Canada: UTP, 5201 Dufferin Street, North York, Ontario M3H 5T8, Canada.
Australia: Footprint Books, PO Box 418, Church Point, NSW 2103, Australia.

Typeset by Archetype-IT Ltd (http://www.archetype-it.com).
Printed and bound in the United States of America.

Dedication

This study is dedicated to three Deaf women
who, embodying as they do true Deafhood wisdom,
inspired and taught me more than even Signs can show:

Dorothy Miles – whose vision of Deafhood
will only be realised in the years to come.

Marie Philip – who showed that a comrade-in-arms
can also be a hero to their peers.

Gloria Pullen – for insisting both that this work should be undertaken,
and that I should be the one to devote my energies to it.

I hope I have lived up to the standards you have set ...

Contents

Acknowledgements

This decade-long journey into Deaf culture owes its beginnings to Carol Erting and Harlan Lane, who sowed the original seeds by suggesting that I present a plenary paper on that subject at the 'Deaf Way' conference in 1989 in Washington DC. Important groundwork was laid during my tenure in the Powrie V. Doctor Chair of Deaf Studies at Gallaudet University in 1992–3, and my thanks are extended to Mike Karchmer, Carol Erting and those whose efforts funded the Chair, for helping to make this possible. Thanks are also due to so many Deaf and hearing people for their contributions during this time – unfortunately I cannot yet name you all yet since many of you have made contributions to the ongoing document from this period which forms part of the next volume of the series. Your interest in and recognition of me was more valuable than you may ever know. Finally, I would like to thank my companion during those years, Bren Marshall, and wave my hands in salute to her parents, Marvin and Tessa.

My personal journey in search of self and Deafhood has been assisted or supported by so many people that it would be unthinkable not to name then. Some have passed on, but a true Deaf history must mark their names for the generations to come. As Black communities insist on emphasising, our own elevated position comes from standing on the shoulders of those who have gone before us.

There is almost nothing I can say about my first lost 18 years, but some people helped keep me alive back then: so a doff of the hat to Roger K., Malcolm S., Mick A, Sandy W., Steve H., and Dave W., and a hug to my brother Nick for living through it with me.

Concerning the three years at Reading University which followed, and also our sixties-inspired anarchist/community action group ADE, there are so many who could be thanked for their support and friendship towards me as a deaf person. I can see even from the list in front of me that for each I name there are ten who also played their part and it would be stretching the reader's tolerance to go that far. So if you are not here, know nonetheless that I remember and am grateful: Rob R., Phil S., Terry Mc-B., Paul R., Jill P., Ginge, Val L., Sue T., Miriam B., Gill A., Paul H., Pogle,

Matthew G., Ken Mc-G., Rob G., Jane C., Robin S., Oliver R., Phil F., Sue S., Mick D., Maggie P., Rosy E., Phill S., Hilary T., Sandy M., Al W., Mark F., Viv E., Chris M., Mark F. and the Toc H folks.

At the end of that time, it was Des Fagan and Mary Bowes who encouraged me to take all that I had learned from our time in the 'sixties', as it were, to bring that into the Deafworld, and to return to them for support whenever the long haul got too much. That 25 year-long mission culminated in the first ever FDP (Federation of Deaf People) march to Trafalgar Square in July 1999, and the torch is now in the hands of young Deaf people who remind me so much of the people we once were all those years ago. Thank Goodness for the strength to persevere long enough to see that happen.

For the opportunity to enter the Deafworld in 1974 as a social worker with Deaf children, young people and their parents I am grateful to the foresight of Betty Langford who saw something in me worth developing. (I was offered the job at that interview with a proviso – that 'the Labour Party wins the Greater London Council elections', so that funding for the post would then be possible. What a contrast between then and now!) Thanks also to Caroline Taylor, and to the members of the Hillingdon Deaf Youth Club and Hillingdon Deaf Rangers FC, who gave me my name sign and thus my first acceptance in Deaf society. And thanks too for personal support to enlightened 'liberals' such as Ruth Cook, Claire Brooke-Hughes, Hamish Bozon, Joan Turner, Allan Hayhurst, Ken Carter and Dennis Uttley, who showed that, despite what some may think, there was back then a genuine core of hearing people who were itching to see some young Deaf people emerge and create change.

When I and my supportive partner of those years, Angela White, realised that shocking state of affairs in West London was mirrored, not only across the UK but most of the world, I could not rest til we found others who wanted to do something about it. Of those many important comrades in arms who set up the National Union of the Deaf in 1976, I would like to thank Raymond Lee, Maggie Woolley, Linda Richards, Chris Marsh, John Lawler and the late Emil Stryker. Didn't we do well for an international organisation carried out from spare bedrooms? A bow too to my 'Deaf parents' Arthur and Jean Dimmock who exemplified what proud Deaf people from the 'Golden Age' of Deafhood (before sign languages were banned) might have been like. Of those with whom we allied in the disability movement back then, I also tip the hat to Peter Townsend, Rosalie Wilkins, Allan Sutherland, Nabil Shaban, Chris Davies and the inspiring leaders of the TUC-affiliated National League of the Blind.

During the era of the Deaf resurgence which followed, in my work with sign linguistics, with the British Deaf Association and then at BBC TV's *See*

Hear, there are many to whom my cap is respectfully doffed. I must, however single out as a colleague and friend Arthur Verney who in his BDA administration (and ever since) was congenitally disinclined to let the outrageousness of a vision get in the way of trying to achieve it. In enabling our setting up of the London Deaf Video Project (LDVP) as part of the Deaf creative revival, I must thank Ken Livingstone's administration at the Greater London Council in 1985. Thatcher may have closed you down, but I note that our own and many of the other types of projects you inaugurated were of such undeniable value, all £30 million pounds per annum worth of them, that they are still funded today. Quite some legacy . . . And I must also thank all my colleagues at the LDVP between then and 1992; we were almost the only Deaf-run workplace in the UK, and you all did such pioneering work in envisioning and carrying out ideas about what Deafhood in film might mean.

Speaking of which, I would like to thank all those who have worked on or facilitated the other ongoing major project in my life – creating videos of signed songs which are written from inside the Deaf experience. One day, that vision will finally be realised. Many of us have cause to thank Nigel Evans for his own creative nous in realising my proposal which led to that (shamefully not yet surpassed) Deaf docu-drama for Channel 4 in 1988, *Pictures in the Mind.* And this leads me neatly into paying tribute to a special person whose vision, friendship and courage has done so much to transform our worlds in the most positive ways – Harlan Lane.

Throughout the past 27 years, there have been so many other wonderful and valuable Deaf and hearing people who have participated both in earnest, vision-clarifying debates and in life-changing actions. To name you all as you indeed deserve would literally take a couple of pages. Special thanks however are due to Dot Miles, to my then-partner Sheila Cragg for her integrity, to Gloria Pullen, Clark Denmark, Lorna Allsop, Mika Brojer, Wendy Daunt, Billy Burt, Lesley McGilp, Clive Mason, Gerry Hughes, Bob Duncan, George Montgomery and Reuben Conrad. And I am sure most of us would agree that without Doug Alker's guts, persistence and all-round talent, we would not be where we are today.

On the global scene there are even more to thank, but I would like to focus on some of the pioneers or colleagues who inspired or befriended me – Fred Schreiber, Bill Stokoe, Marie Philip, Linwood Smith, Manfa Suwanarat, Liisa Kaupinnen, Gary Malkowski, Jean-Francois Mercurio, Carol-Lee Aquilane, Breda Carty, Ben Bahan, Al Barwiolek and Chuck McKinney.

One of the downsides of being a member of an international intergenerational community, in knowing so many people, is that one has to experience a disproportionate amount of pain when members pass on, not least when some do so from pressures and circumstances in which, had they been hearing people, they might probably still be alive. Some of you know to whom I am referring; the rest of you might like to join me in a moment's silence for their unique contributions.

Every word of this text and my life has been infused by some special sources largely hidden from view – the Black activists of the 1960s (and beyond) in the USA, the many Afro-Caribbean contributions to our lives, the Black Consciousness Movement in South Africa and the American Indian Movement. Speaking across from one minority group to another, they helped me to recognise crucial parallels as they arose and assisted me in sensing deeper levels of kinship which existed. I trust that when their Deaf sisters and brothers, both across the 'third world' and here at home, receive the treatment and support they deserve, they will feel pleasure at knowing their work and example was still effective so many decades hence. Fortunately the next volume will see these sources become more visible as we journey deeper.

A similar sense of inspiration and gratitude dates back to that moment in 1973 when I first saw a poster advertising the existence of something called the Centre for Contemporary Cultural Studies. The work of one of their major figures, Stuart Hall, has inspired much of what I have thought and written ever since. On a personal level, his exhortations to pursue this project and to 'hunt the Snark' were also gratifying. I trust it has not turned out to be a Boojum in the end!

And so we come back to the starting point of the Deaf Culture Project itself. Between leaving Gallaudet in 1993 and finishing the work you now hold, deepest thanks are also due for support throughout to Alys Young, who was a wonderful source of insights, suggestions and support, as were my other graduate colleagues, notably Mary Griggs, Helen Reed and Sally Reynolds. Jan Branson and Don Miller provided key insights at an important time. The interest, support and encouragement of the staff and students at the Centre for Deaf Studies was and is very much appreciated and I must also thank my advisor Jim Kyle and my upgrading referee Liz Bird for numerous useful contributions.

This study would be nothing without the many wonderful responses from my Deaf and hearing informants and conversationalists – unfortunately most of you have chosen to remain anonymous, but you know who you are! Special thanks then to Albert, Barry, Bonnie, Clara, Colin, Dorothy, Emma, Frances, Florence, Frank, Gefilte, Jade, James, Jim, Lorna Allsop, Ken, Liz, Maria, Mark, Martha, Michael, Olivia, Peggy, Queenie, Ralph, Raymond Lee, Renata, Sally, Sean, Stefan, and Ursula. Thanks are also due to Bristol Deaf Centre's Senior Citizens Group, and to David Kingdon and Len Wyatt for their support there.

For helpful feedback on parts or all of Chapters 4 and 5, I am grateful to Carol Erting, Stuart Allen and Allen Abramson. Any weaknesses which remain are of course my own. Many thanks are also due to Kay Alexander for valuable feedback in several key places. The whole of this text and much else over the years owes an immense debt to my good friend from the valleys who one day no doubt will reveal herself. Other helpful feedback came from Jordan Eickman and Philip Waters. I am also grateful to the Economic and Social Research Council for their funding in the form of award number R0042934173, which made this study possible.

This book itself could not have become what it is without the remarkable and heartening support from my editor, Colin Baker, his own vision of its significance, and his determination that this initial text should serve as a long-term resource.

Much gratitude is also extended to publishers Mike and Marjukka Grover, to my patient editor Ken Hall, and our publicists Kathryn King and Jon Booth. For important help with the photographs used in the book, many thanks to Janie Goncalves and Maria Gascon-Ramos.

For recognition and support in life outside this study, without which it can be hard to find the strength to persevere, I must thank Jo Smith, Lori Abrams, Jake Frost, Judi Derisley, Steve Knapp, Kay Alexander, Elaine Heller, Sue Edgley and the 'Reverend Godmother' Alice Stephens. Furthermore, at a time of severe crisis, a chain of helping hands relayed me back to safety; without them I would not be here now. Blessings then to you, Kathy and Steve, Mary, Alys, Olin, Larry F., Lorrie-Beth and Larry, Fen, David D, Ann, Jen, Steve and Helen, Carolyn, Val and Sue, Sheila, Kate, Ben Steiner, Anna, Martin, Sarah and John.

This book was finished on the day that Ken Kesey departed this earth – the pain of his leaving cannot outweigh the importance of his inspiration and personal example. In a very real sense then, this book echoes and continues his life-long motto – 'Further'.

And so the 25-year journey arrives at this plateau. Hopefully the momentum of Deaf cultural research is established now, so that we can move on to the next stages at a swifter pace. May this text, then, serve simply as a staging post on the journey from deafness to Deafhood, for those alive now and for the Deaf children and parents of the generations to come.

Paddy Ladd, Bristol

Glossary of Terms and Abbreviations

Many of the terms and abbreviations used in this study are explained within the text. Comprehension, however, will be easier if some are clarified from the start. These are grouped thematically rather than alphabetically for easier assimilation.

Conceptual Glossary

deaf/Deaf: The lowercase 'deaf' refers to those for whom deafness is primarily an audiological experience. It is mainly used to describe those who lost some or all of their hearing in early or late life, and who do not usually wish to have contact with signing Deaf communities, preferring to try and retain their membership of the majority society in which they were socialised.

'Deaf' refers to those born Deaf or deafened in early (sometimes late) childhood, for whom the sign languages, communities and cultures of the Deaf collective represents their primary experience and allegiance, many of whom perceive their experience as essentially akin to other language minorities.

Deaf culture: This term was developed in the 1970s to give utterance to the belief that Deaf communities contained their own ways of life mediated through their sign languages. Belief in the existential accuracy of this terminology has greatly outstripped research into it, leaving its users vulnerable when required to explain or defend its tenets. Lack of research has also made it hard to enact cultural norms and values within various important domains such as Deaf education. Nevertheless, the important task of understanding Deaf communities cannot be

	said even to have begun whilst Deaf cultural research remains unrecognised and unfunded.
Deafhood:	This term was developed in 1990 by the present author in order to begin the process of defining the existential state of Deaf 'being-in- the-world'. Hitherto, the medical term 'deafness' was used to subsume that experience within the larger category of 'hearing- impaired', the vast majority of whom were elderly 'hard of hearing' people, so that the true nature of Deaf collective existence was rendered invisible. Deafhood is not seen as a finite state but as a process by which Deaf individuals come to actualise their Deaf identity, positing that those individuals construct that identity around several differently ordered sets of priorities and principles, which are affected by various factors such as nation, era and class.
hearing/Hearing:	The lowercase 'hearing' is a term originating in the Deaf community to describe non-Deaf people (including 'deaf' people). I have sometimes capitalised this to indicate an additional dimension expressed by Deaf people – for example, 'Hearing world' or 'Hearing ways', akin to the capitalisation of 'White' or 'Male' by Black and feminist theoreticians.
oralist/Oralism:	Oralism can be defined as the educational system imposed on Deaf communities worldwide during the last 120 years which removed Deaf educators, Deaf communities and their sign languages from the Deaf education system. By replacing it with an exclusively Hearing-led system promoting the use of speech, lipreading and hearing aids only, and advocating no fraternisation between Deaf children and Deaf adults, they hoped to remove the 'need for' Deaf communities to exist at all. I have capitalised the concept itself to reflect the additional dimensions of meaning given to the term by Deaf people.
Total Communication:	Growing concern about the poor educational results of Oralism led in the 1970s to the first attempts to re-introduce sign language to the edu-

cation system. Total Communication was launched as a philosophy which encouraged the use of whichever forms of communication were deemed appropriate for the individual Deaf child.

This led to the development of signed systems, using signs (either taken from indigenous sign languages or invented), designed to be used in conjunction with speech – that is, spoken language word order. In some countries, such as the USA, these approaches have become the main method of education. Although they had the benefit of freeing Deaf children and their parents from the atmosphere of fear and suppression that characterised Oralism, they represented a compromise in which Deaf teachers and *bona fide* sign languages were still constructed as objects – as 'educational tools', rather than bearers of an organic, holistic approach to the lives and experiences of Deaf children and Deaf communities. In these circumstances, it is unsurprising that these educational theories have achieved less than its proponents had hoped for.

'Bi–Bi' education: This term was coined to describe the bilingual bicultural approach to Deaf education developed in the 1980s. This philosophy accepted many of the Deaf communities' arguments about their linguistic minority status and some of their cultural arguments, and placed its emphasis on teaching the children in their perceived first language of signs, and from that base moving to the national written language. Scandinavian countries have pioneered its use as a national policy; elsewhere its introduction has been more *ad hoc*. The limited number of Deaf teachers and headteachers, the limited signing skills (and Bi–Bi training) of hearing teachers, and the very limited understanding of Deaf culture, all indicate that the Bi–Bi approach is still far from a truly Deaf-centred educational praxis.

Mainstreaming: Since the 1960s, several terms have been used to describe the (initially oralist) strategy of assimilating Deaf children into hearing schools, for example 'integration' and 'inclusion'. This strategy, with its concomitant closing of many Deaf schools, has been widely opposed by Deaf communities. The term 'mainstreaming' has proved to be the most enduring, in part due to the popularity of its signed translation which combines two BSL signs to visually represent the suppression of the individual Deaf child by a more powerful overarching system.

Cochlear Implants (CI): From the 1980s onwards, growing numbers of Deaf children have been surgically implanted with an electro-magnetic device intended to directly stimulate the auditory nerve. In so doing, any residual hearing is destroyed. The medical establishment claims that significant benefits in speech, lipreading and hearing skills have taken place. However, Deaf communities and their allies are aware that CI proponents have sought (so far, successfully), to prevent independent research and evaluation of the results. They view CIs as unethical experiments on non- consenting Deaf children, whose parents have been either misled by distorted information or subjected to forms of emotional blackmail. The CI debate perfectly illustrates the power of the media to control discourses around deafness and Deaf people. Instead of conducting investigative journalism into this widespread breach of medical ethics, they have chosen to advertise it, against all evidence, as a 'miracle cure'.

Linguistic Glossary

ASL: American Sign Language – the official language of Deaf communities in the USA.

BSL: British Sign Language. As above in respect of the UK. Other sign languages are represented in the text by similar acronyms – e.g. LSF, Language de Sourdes des France, etc.

'DEAF-HIS':   British Sign Language (BSL) orthography requires that the quotation of key phrases be rendered in capitals, hyphenated when appropriate, as in this example.

Organisational Glossary

BDA/BDDA: The British Deaf (formerly Deaf and Dumb) Association, formed in 1890 is the nationally structured and elected organisation *of* Deaf people in the UK.

BDHS: The British Deaf History Society was formed in the 1990s as part of a strategy for community and cultural regeneration, and at present is the only 'academic' domain run by Deaf people themselves.

BDSC: The British Deaf Sports Council, formed in the 1950s, is the official representative of British Deaf sport. It is also seen as the first sustained attempt by the missioners to control Deaf sporting activities.

FDP: The Federation of Deaf People was established in the UK in 1998 to re-develop and sustain a political dimension within Deaf life. They have been responsible for the first ever marches for BSL recognition which began in 1999.

HMFD: Hearing children of Deaf parents have a unique status within Deaf communities. The abbreviation refers to the BSL term used to describe them – 'HEARING, MOTHER–FATHER DEAF'. In the USA, they term themselves 'CODAs' – 'Children of Deaf Adults'.

LDVP: London Deaf Video Project, later known as the LDAP (Access Project), was formed in 1985 with a grant from the then Greater London Council to establish the language minority principle by translating official information into BSL via videotapes. In doing so, it gave numerous Deaf people their first training in film and television skills.

MHGS: The apex of the UK's oralist system, the Mary Hare Grammar School, has had a significant effect on the post-war Deaf community, and is often represented by this abbreviation.

NAD: The National Association of the Deaf was formed in 1880 as the official organisation of the USA Deaf community. Similar acronyms are used for other national Deaf organisations around the world – cf. SDR (Sveriges Dovas Riksforbund) in Sweden.

NUD: The National Union of the Deaf was formed by a group of Deaf radicals in the UK in 1976, and during its 12 year existence played a major role in transforming the UK situation.

SDASA: The Southern (Region) Deaf Athletics and Sports Association was one of the regional bodies established and run by Deaf subaltern prior to the establishment of the BDSC.

SHED: The Society for Higher Education of the Deaf was a campaign group established in the later 1940s to campaign for
Deaf access to higher education, which culminated in the
establishment of the MHGS (see earlier).

SWD: The Scottish Workshop with the Deaf was formed in 1975
as a a progressive coalition between Deaf and hearing people. It has published numerous books and pamphlets and
maintained an important informal alliance with the NUD.

WOD: An abbreviation of 'Welfare Officers to the Deaf', and a
generic term used here to describe the missioners and later
the welfare officers who took control of Deaf local and
national affairs in the post-oralist era.

Introduction

People with disabilities, Deaf people, and others who might not even consider themselves as having a disability have been relegated to the margins by
the very people who have celebrated and championed the emergence of
multiculturalism, class consciousness, feminism and queer studies, from the
margins.

(Lennard Davis, 1997 : xi)

Without a proper understanding of history, those who practise in the disciplines of applied social sciences operate in a vacuum, thereby merely
perpetuating . . . ongoing neocolonialism.

(Eduardo & Bonnie Duran, 1995: 1)

Walking the Tight Trope

What is Deaf culture? Why is it of such importance in the Deaf liberation
struggle? Does it have anything to offer to majority societies, anything to
teach them? And why has the world heard so little about it hitherto?

Deaf communities too might ask these questions. But they would also
ask: 'Why does the burden of proof fall upon us? Why is it we who must
strive to raise funds in order to accumulate evidence which "proves" that
our sign languages are bona fide languages, and that the collective lives of
Deaf people are *bona fide* cultures?' These questions represent a major challenge, which this book directly addresses, and which, by its close should
have come into sharper focus.

However, I also face another challenge – an extremely wide-ranging
audience. For this book is not only aimed at Deaf people, parents of Deaf
children and those who work with Deaf communities, but is also virtually
the first ever attempt to reach the radical sectors of our societies and their
progressive academic disciplines in order that we can come in from the
margins that Davis describes. If the project is successful, Deaf communities
may at last be admitted to those progressive agendas. In order to attain this,
however, these sectors have to be convinced that Deaf communities, far

1

from being the objects of pity and benevolence, actually have much to teach them.

Thus this book has to walk a tightrope, to operate on several levels and I have tried to design it in order to accomplish that task. First and foremost then, it is intended as a *resource*, in which different chapters may be of use to different people at different times. These various levels can be found within this introduction itself, and you are encouraged to focus on whichever sections draw your attention and to set aside the other sections for a later reading.

Let us begin this journey, then, with the kind of extended metaphor that lies at the heart of Deaf peoples' sign language discourses.

Inside the Museums, Deafness Goes on Trial

When a Deaf friend asked me to explain what it is that I have created here, my response in British Sign Language (referred to hereafter as 'BSL') was to reply by use of a metaphor, a cultural feature very dear to those who call themselves 'strong Deaf', which I will share with you.

Reader, place yourself at the door of a building above which the sign 'Deafness' is displayed. Entering the room, you will see all around a display of the various totems placed there by its curators – ear trumpets from the 17th century, hearing aids from the 20th century, models of the ear and diagrams of its tiniest parts. Drawings of Deaf children being operated on by 18th century dignitaries who called themselves doctors, photographs of 19th century children, their mouths forced open with silver tools in order to bring forth sounds, and of children in the 20th century weighed under by headphones half the size of their heads. On the walls are paintings in gilded frames of doctors and benefactors in impressive robes modelling the honours laid on them by a grateful society. And in a corner marked 'The Future' are more models, of scintillating operations carried out close to the brain itself, and of the human genome project, illustrating the genetic mutations of deafness due for honour-bestowing removal in the not-so-distant decades.

At the very back of the hall there is a wall, behind which is a room whose existence is under dispute. Deaf people and their friends have asserted that there *is* in fact a room behind the wall, whilst those with vested interests (and considerable control over the lives of the Deaf community) decry this as wishful thinking and demand irrefutable proof. (Perhaps, one might say, like those who make similar demands on the subject of global warming before feeling the need to take any action at all.)

My task is to locate a door in that wall and to draw attention to its existence by affixing a sign upon it. The demands of the vested interests described here can only be met by requiring that we assess concepts of culture, on their own terms and in their many guises, and apply these to the Deaf community. If that task is successfully conducted here, then we may conclusively affix the words 'Deaf Culture' to that notice. Of course, this process requires me to enter that room and attempt to map out its structure and contents – to provide a framework if you like. Such a challenge is an essential first step, in order that others may later use this guide to explore the room in more detail and depth, and perhaps in time, who knows, to even re-arrange the furniture.

Once I located, entered and began to examinine this room, I could not help but notice some of the paintings therein, which had all been turned to face the wall. On righting them, I noticed that each embodied themes which had not previously been recognised. These themes seemed to run in complete contrast to the way in which the professional world had defined issues relating to Deaf people. The paintings spoke of communities all across the world who were experiencing joy in their collective existence, a defiant pride in their sign languages and deep pleasure at the sight of new generations of small children taking the first steps to reproduce their thoughts and feelings on their hands. They spoke of people whose lives were not motivated by a sadness in not being able to hear birds singing or who were not primarily motivated to come together by any sense of loneliness or exclusion, although, being human, such emotions could still be recognised. They spoke of oppression of these communities by those supposedly charged with responsibility for their welfare. But they also portrayed a clear sense of the ingenuity, determination and humour by which they struggled to resist that oppression. Their tales, as represented by their language illustrated in the paintings, were so inspiring that it became clear that beneath them lay an even deeper set of themes.

As I absorbed these stories and emotions, I found myself coining a new label of 'Deafhood'. Deafhood is not, however, a 'static' medical condition like 'deafness'. Instead, it represents a process – the struggle by each Deaf child, Deaf family and Deaf adult to explain to themselves and each other their own existence in the world. In sharing their lives with each other as a community, and enacting those explanations rather than writing books about them, Deaf people are engaged in a daily praxis, a continuing internal and external dialogue. This dialogue not only acknowledges that existence as a Deaf person is actually a process of *becoming* and maintaining 'Deaf', but also reflects different interpretations of Deafhood, of what being a Deaf person in a Deaf community might mean.

Such evidence appeared to contribute answers to questions that in the recent years which I have termed the 'Deaf Resurgence', people have found the psycho-cultural space to begin to ask: What could a Deaf person, and a

Deaf community *become*? What could we have been had not sign language and Deaf teachers been removed from Deaf education after the Milan 'Congress' of 1880, a date as pregnant with meaning for us as 1492 is for Native Americans. What could we have been had we not been forced to endure more than a century of English illiteracy, self-shame and stigma? Who and what *were* we in the centuries before such prohibitions descended, when Deaf professionals and Deaf pride was reputedly much stronger? And what can we bring forward from those times which might inform the fledgling steps we must take in this 21st century?

The drive to answer these questions, the process of becoming – these I have called *Deafhood*. Deafhood affirms that how we have been these past 120 years is not all that we truly are. It affirms the existence of a Deaf sense of *being*, both within the individual and throughout the collective, which, like a river surging against a dam, cannot rest until it can find a way through that will take it down to a sea of life, where all human souls are enabled both to find their fullest self-expression and to interpenetrate each other.

Deaf communities contend that without a knowledge or understanding of the existence of this collective sense of Deaf *Weltanshauung*, all the pieces of paper, medals or white coats one might possess are not only worthless, but actively dangerous.

Although almost none of this is news to Deaf peoples, a century of linguistic oppression has left very few of the communities able to (or inclined to) present their beliefs in written form, so it was very much my duty to present and structurally represent them to the rest of the world. Thus with a deepened appreciation that the tales so passionately conveyed by the figures in the paintings could not be adequately translated into mere English prose, I had determined that the notice on the door should be amended to 'Deaf Culture and Deafhood'.

However, I then noticed that the paintings had been arranged in a particular pattern. The hand movements in them pointed towards the far wall, where a metal shutter hung. On looking more closely, I discovered that behind the shutter lay a door directly leading to the world outside. The message became clear – the way to enter this building was not via the door I had just prised open – instead, the task was to re-open that door in the external wall, so that all who were interested in Deaf peoples could now enter from that direction – without having to have their perceptions mediated by the 'miracles' on display in the room of *deafness*.

At this moment, it occurred to me with no little amusement, that the deafness room itself was perhaps more properly regarded as a kind of annexe to the one I found myself in – an exhibition of curios belonging to another tribe of beings who had sought to remake Deaf people in their own image – or, perhaps more appropriately, in their own limited image of themselves.

As for more detailed description of the paintings and the other contents – ah, such interpretations would have to wait their turn in a later volume. I could but hope that those who finally gained entrance would construct a new sign to affix on the door of that 'annexe', a sign which described those curios and their tribes of practitioners more appropriately – as 'Colonialist Relics'.

This thought caused me to look back at the paintings, and I noticed that many of the Deaf people of old had included those who could hear amongst their company. Some were able to sign with them, some stood on the conversation fringe admiringly, and some were going about their lives simply respecting that relationship. The paintings seemed to encompass virtually the entire history of humankind, across the whole planet. Some revealed the high prestige of sign language and Deaf people at the Ottoman court. Others illustrated the cooperation between hearing and Deaf people during the French Revolution. One set showed Queen Victoria signing with a Deaf servant. Others illustrated societies from Mexico to Martha's Vineyard to the Bedouin nomads to Bali, where all its members, both Deaf and hearing, could communicate in Sign.

These paintings made it clear that large numbers of Hearing people had indeed once passed through that door – indeed several faces in the paintings seemed to look expectantly towards it, some with an expression of puzzlement that the flow of visitors through that external door appeared to dwindled during much of the 20th century.

Suddenly I realised why for so many years, expressions like 'the public' or 'society' had irritated me so much when used in respect of Deaf people. They were anonymous terms somehow, meaning everything and therefore nothing at all. The figures portrayed in the paintings were not 'professionals'. These were living and breathing 'lay people' – lay as in the sense of 'non-expert', whose reality needed to be distinguished from the 'experts' in the annexe. Numbers of such 'lay people' existed in the past. Numbers also exist within the pages of this book. And, it became clear once more, the multitudes of the Future wait beyond that door – if one chooses to recognise them.

For we are all at times lay people – except for that privileged few whose self-proclaimed 'experthood' blinds them to that reality. Moreover, at many different times and in many different ways across the globe, the coming together of lay people and oppressed groups has enabled the downfall of many bigger buildings than the one earlier. In less unfashionable times this used to be known as 'solidarity'. Now, instead of the movie adage, 'If you build it, they will come', it seemed to be more a case of 'If you believe it, and demonstrate it, they will return'.

And at that moment, the portraits of Desloges, Berthier and Deseine, of Massieu, Clerc, Burns and Kirk, of Foster, Suwanarat and Mercurio, of Miles, Philip and Woodhouse, of Barwiolek, McKinney and de Fay seemed to move their hands in turn – 'If lay people are able to behold us here, we too will return'. I realised then my duty was not only to the Deaf and lay peoples of the 21st century, but to those pioneers of the past, whose works illustrated the exciting larger dimensions that Deafhood offered to the future. Surely, I thought, the achievements of these people deserved not only to be recognised and respected, but also admitted to the range of discourses taking place within and across other oppressed groups, as located in the works of Du Bois and Said, Biko and Black Elk, Benedict and Geertz, Fanon and Marcuse, Foucault and Freire, Williams, Thompson and Hall?

As I left the Deaf room and walked back past the exhibits, this exalted reverie gave way to a grimmer realism. It was clear that one could not harbour any illusions that those who maintained the deafness defences would give up their power quietly. However, as I closed the main door behind me, and walked down the long luxurious driveway towards the gates, I passed rows of statues erected to revere those who had colonised other peoples and other languages. It was impossible not to notice that most of those subject peoples had attained a degree of freedom which would have caused those figures to turn in their graves. Thus, with a renewed hope that people in our own societies would, if properly directed, be able once again to listen to the signs and tales told by the hands in the paintings, I let myself out through the gates. It was only later that I realised I had forgotten to ask the man at the ticket booth in his white coat for my money back . . .

This extended BSL metaphor is presented here as a stylistic bridge to Chapters 7, 8 and 9 in which Deaf people gave their views in sign languages, for which the English translation can only be a crude approximation. Indeed, it would be inappropriate for a book which formally initiates the search for Deaf epistemologies to ignore all questions of Deaf 'style' – ideally the book's style would mirror the implications of its contents. Yet to do so at this point in history would be to risk the continuation of neglect or disdain by those who control 'knowledge', and who therefore man the media gates through which such information must flow; thus for now we must indeed render unto the academic Caesar that which is 'his'. This volume must therefore walk a tightrope, making it both like and unlike other academic publications. Hopefully, later works will not need to make that compromise.

Unpeeling the Mask of Benevolence

Deaf communities around the world have devoted much energy during the past 250 years towards recognition of the true nature of their being-in-the-world. However, only in Scandinavia during the past decade has there been sustained governmental recognition of their linguistic minority status, recognition that has also been enshrined in policy and equipped with appropriate resources.

Such a situation may surprise the reader, but there are others in store. On looking more closely, they will be puzzled to learn that across the world for the last 120 years, Deaf children and their parents have been subjugated to an all-encompassing set of policies and discourses aimed at preventing them from learning or using sign languages to communicate, referred to hereafter by the term '*Oralism*'. They will be astonished to know that Deaf teachers were first removed and then effectively banned from working with Deaf children.[1] And they will be shocked to find that, as a consequence, Deaf children have left schools for over a century with a reading age averaging eight – enough only to comprehend the headlines of a tabloid newspaper, with speech virtually incomprehensible to anyone but their own teachers, and with lipreading skills no better than those of a hearing child who has never had so much as a day's practice of this in their lives (Conrad, 1979).[2] Furthermore, although experiencing the same percentage of 'genetic' psychiatric disorder as the rest of the population, there is a distressing difference in the percentages of 'life-induced' emotional/behavioural problems – 20–25% for the population and 45–50% for Deaf people (Hindley & Kitson, 2000). In the light of what has been said earlier, the reader will not be surprised to find that the Deaf community lays these shocking statistics at the door of Oralism.

The second surprise I am sure many of you will be experiencing even as you read. You will be asking yourselves why this has not come to public notice before and why someone [else] isn't doing something about it. One of the aims of this book is to find answers to both questions. For in order to understand how something like this has escaped notice on such a planet-wide, century-long scale, one has to be able to understand the true nature of the society in which we live; how political power, medical and educational dominance and media information strategies interact and reinforce each other to create an overarching form of what is effectively thought control. In other words, to understand how one's own cultures really operate.

It is at this point that I invite the reader to begin the process of unravelling the cultural web. If you now reflect on what you know about 'the Deaf and Dumb', as you have traditionally named them, you will see a succession of images flash through your minds: images of people in whose name charities raise money, supposedly to 'help them' (for who might dare to think that such benevolence towards poor unfortunates is, as Harlan Lane has termed it, only a mask?); images of scientists producing 'miracle cures', and of tabloid newspapers beating the drum to raise money for Deaf children to be subjected to them (never stopping to think that perhaps such operations might be against the wishes of the children themselves).

The most insidious quality of these images is indeed that of benevolence. This construction of Deaf communities is deeply woven into patterns of ideas and ideologies placed in your head by people you have never met. Those ideas and images, have not come from the users of these global sign languages or from the communities they have built and maintained in the face of all the odds.

At this point you might yourself responding, 'Yes, but . . .' This is also an important moment. For in your next sentences you will find the next level of social conditioning upon which your construction is built. Fascinating though it would be to know your thoughts, there are two factors it is helpful to be aware of. One is that Deaf people have heard them before; they have experienced over a century of just such 'Yes Buts'. The other is that there is a bottom line – one either respects Deaf communities enough to accept that they have a consistent and collective view of their own as language users which should be granted acceptance such as would be given to any other language. Or . . . there is something which holds one back from being able to accede to this. And from where Deaf people reside, they intepret this as an inability to transcend one's social conditioning and to be able to perceive them as fully human; that you construct them, not as collectives of language users, but as medically, karmically or intellectually damaged beings.

These words are frank, but they are not complacently so. Nor do they intend to push you away – in fact the opposite is the case. This book attempts to describe and deal with as many of those 'Yes Buts' as possible, to form that vital bridge between your cultural understanding and theirs. It is the first to be published outside of the United States (and only the third in all),[3] which attempts to bring you inside the Deaf experience by means of a focus on a subject which many speak of but few understand – culture.

For culture is the key held in common with other colonised peoples and linguistic minorities. Political and economic power may or may not be the driving forces behind language oppression. But both the key and the lock in which it turns is culture. A people may exist without a living language unique to themselves, but without a culture there is no 'people'.

Similarly, a battle fought to retain one's own language may be countered with attempted political, linguistic or economic resistance – but the key to that resistance resides within, and is conducted through, the culture.

Members of language majorities cannot effectively participate in opposing the actions of those holding power in their own societies unless they are willing to understand how that power is mediated and implemented throughout the cultural workings of their own societies. No matter from which position one approaches these subjects, it is the concept of culture which is the key to resistance and change.

However, this book is not intended to be a dry academic account. For cultural experience, even amongst oppressed cultures, is constituted of rich, vibrant and exciting modes of being – not merely the sinews and bones of human existence, but the flesh upon them, the colour in their clothes and the creative activities of those minds and bodies. The cultural lives of the world's sign-language-using communities are no less rich. Like other cultures they have the power to speak to us about the beauty of human diversity. Unlike other cultures, they have been living right under your noses all this time, unrecognised.

In the past 20 years, the repression of sign languages has slowed or halted, so that in numerous countries they have become visible once more. In the stories that these languages have to tell, of the different ways in which the human eye, hand and body can operate, they also have the power to confront us with questions not only exciting but disturbing. How is it that Deaf communities not only rejoice whenever another Deaf child is born, but actively devote their energies towards creating a cultural future for those children? How can it be that these communities dare to suggest that people who have *not* developed these abilities of eye, face, hand and body might not be justified in considering themselves to be fully evolved as human beings?

This may seem astonishing questions. However, as will later be seen, they are ones which have been covertly or overtly raised by Deaf communities and their hearing friends across different countries and times during the past few hundred years. If we are able to listen to their cultural stories, we might come to believe, in the words of Victor Hugo that 'What matters deafness of the ear, when the mind hears? The one true deafness . . . is of the mind'. Thus it may well prove to be the case that in proceeding on this journey towards an understanding of Deaf culture, we may actually be embarking on a trail towards understanding – ourselves. In this respect then, the journey in search of the meanings of Deafhood might well constitute mankind's final frontier.

Signposts for the Journey

Chapter 1 thus begins with an introductory account of Deaf communities, and the forms and activities which characterise them at the present time, both in the UK and elsewhere. There have been very few descriptions written by Deaf people themselves, and so this one can be used as a useful contrast to those assembled by outside 'experts'.

Chapters 2 and 3 introduce the key terminology for analysing the history of Deaf communities and the ways in which they have been constructed by those holding power over them. The central analytical tool is that of discourse analysis, where traditionally privileged narratives are brought down from their lofty gaze and repositioned simply as discourses. In this manner, Chapter 2 presents the first sustained Deaf counter-narrative of Deaf history, from 5000 BC to the beginnings of the anti-sign language hegemony in 1880.

Chapter 3 continues this counter-narrative through the 20th century to the present day. Reaching that point, it then introduces the 'subaltern' concept in order to frame the changes in the structure of the discourses which have taken place in the last 250 years, and to identify who the Deaf subaltern might be. From this position it then examines the barriers which Deaf communities face in gaining academic recognition and acceptance for their Deaf subaltern discourses.

The events of the 11 September 2001 have brought home to many of us just how little we understand of the complexities of differing cultures, indeed of 'culture' itself. Thus, before we can examine Deaf culture, it is useful to know precisely how others have studied and theorised about culture. Chapter 4 therefore examines nine disciplines and, in the process, identifies theories, tools and strategies which might prove of most use when coming to analyse Deaf culture. In so doing it is able to make the case that Deaf culture not only exists but is a fully fledged culture rather than a subculture.

It is then possible for Chapter 5 to examine and critique what has been recorded about Deaf culture itself and to identify four domains. One is the discourse in the printed media, chiefly academic texts and journals. Another is the printed media within Deaf communities themselves, whilst the other two exist mainly in sign language forms, in workshops conducted by Deaf subalterns and professionals, and in the discourses which take place between Deaf subalterns themselves. This background being established, we are able to utilise the most relevant aspects of its data or theories in our own study.

However, one more vital step remains. In order to allow the reader to bring their own judgement to bear on the quality, the validity of the evidence presented in this book, it is necessary for me to problematicise my own status as a Deaf researcher and to render myself as transparent as possible. Chapter 6 therefore initiates that process and outlines the methodologies utilised in this study of Deaf culture.

The next three chapters present some of the findings in the words of Deaf informants themselves. Chapters 7 and 8 are concerned with identifying the roots and traditions of Deaf cultures, locating them in the Deaf residential schools and Deaf clubs respectively. Chapter 7 focuses on the cultural strategies developed by Deaf children to resist Oralism, and on the positive and negative cultural features which those strategies produced. Chapter 8 examines the power structure within Deaf clubs, the role of the (mainly hearing) Missioner to the Deaf and identifies two polarised positions taken by Deaf club members. These positions are initially identified as class-based but the chapter proceeds to re-define them both within the subaltern terminology and within the Deafhood concept.

Chapter 9 examines the situation of those Deaf club members who re-belled against the ethos of 'mission control' and gives examples of how young school-leavers sought out Deaf elders in order to develop their Deafhood. It identifies the pub as the site around which Deaf rebellion co-alesced, and how relationships with lay hearing people informed that Deafhood, before illustrating the contrasting interpretations of Deafhood held by the rebels and those who remained in the club. The narration then focuses on the British Deaf Association (BDA), and the national post-war contestation between the deafness narrative and the varying Deafhood readings. It then moves forward to 1996 in order to examine the changes (or absence thereof) during this time. Throughout these three chapters, the significance of Deaf relationships with lay people are outlined, and Deaf cultural patterns are identified as having existed and mutated over a period of a century. Thus one is able to conclude that Deaf culture, in the UK at least, exhibits qualities that confirm its status as a *bona fide* culture.

Chapter 10 then draws all these threads together, and describes the powerful implications of such cultural recognition for those administering Deaf colonies, and for those lay people who wish to assist in their liberation. The interviews and narratives together enable us to posit numerous important implications for social scientists, in general, and cultural theory, in particular. It is then suggested that these hypotheses offer a springboard from which to develop cultural typologies that help us to get to grips with that most omnipresent, yet elusive of creatures, the cultures of nation states themselves.

Finally Chapter 11 brings news of other important discoveries and events which have taken place since 1996, and describes how these reinforce what we have learned so far. They culminate in the crucial contemporary battle for recognition of sign languages as official minority languages, and the resistance presently found both within governments and within organisations of minority languages. The chapter also identifies a dozen other important Deaf cultural themes which will form the next volumes of published research, and emphasises the need for those volumes to examine other minority cultures in order to widen, deepen and refine the parallels which have been suggested.

There are few opportunities for colonised peoples to present accounts of their own cultural experiences; moreover in order for them even to do so, they must often use a language other than their own. It is factors such as these which create pressure for those few accounts to then become all things to all people, to lay reader and professional alike. This pressure also holds true for the Deaf experience; furthermore the majority of my Deaf audience will only gain true access to what has been written in their name if this book can be published in a visual medium. To counterbalance these various pressures and forces, the journey on which we are embarked upon here has been designated as a 'Deaf Cultural Project' taking several forms, and this book is designed as the first of a series of three texts and one DVD.

Succeeding volumes *(Journeying through Deafhood)* will explore present-day Deaf cultural manifestations and patterns. However, the task of the second volume *(Conversations in Deafhood)* is to correct immediately some of the inevitable imbalance created by the existence of a single study; whether the researcher be Deaf or hearing, the material presented must, by definition, be selective. The many wonderful Deaf accounts deserve to be presented in their own right, so that you can listen directly to what Deaf communities are saying without my own editing and I am confident that they will prove to be fascinating for any reader.

Likewise, Deaf audiences have the right not only to consider what their colleagues are saying, but also to access the wider theoretical material presented in this book. Hence the DVD. This will also become a text which non-Deaf people can use to engage with us in our own language, for with the best will in the world, written translations of sign languages are the palest shadow of the power and beauty that lies therein.

The Relevance of Deaf Culture for Diverse Audiences

Before outlining these, it is necessary to enlarge on what has already been said about 'lay people', since this is one of the seven concepts which underpins this project. As a result of my experiences, not only in the decade in which this work has been directly researched, but also over the three decades preceding them, I have concluded that the concept of the *lay person* is central to the entire process by which we must all approach Deaf issues. I define such a person as anyone who is neither directly employed within Deaf-related domains, nor within adjacent professional domains.

Such a lay person is also essentially someone who has been politically and/or culturally disenfranchised. For a century or more, the views of lay people (and in this context it is crucial to make clear that there are situations and domains in which most of us are 'lay people'), have counted for nothing when set against the overarching structure which links beliefs, policies and practices of different groups of professionals (so-called 'experts'). We are used to forming analyses in terms of class, industry and politics. However (as we are coming to realise in our dealings with the medical, legal, media and educational professions to name but four), our disenfranchisement in these domains can damage the physical and/or mental health of ourselves or those for whom we care.

Many Deaf people have long known that the views and attitudes of ordinary people are either more positive or less damaging than those held by the professions which hold power over our communities. There exists a virtually unbroken line of thought within Deaf cultures that many 'hearing' people have exhibited a covert or overt fascination with the power and beauty of sign languages. Furthermore, numbers of Deaf people also feel that, were lay people to be properly informed of what takes place behind the mask of professional benevolence, their subsequent anger or revulsion would lead them to become allies.

Thus one finds what can be seen as a triangular, two-tier relationship existing between Deaf and lay communities, where learning to see what has been enacted on us, proceeding hand-in-hand with an existing appreciation that has never been allowed its voice, provides the lay person not only with the ability to understand how societies have disenfranchised us, but a set of tools by which to understand their own disenfranchisement, not only from important sectors of their own societies, but even from their own bodies.

This is why the initial responsibility of this volume must be to disrupt the discourses which shape the lay reader's perceptions of Deaf communities. Once that has been accomplished, new Deaf-centred 'spaces' can then be created within a range of majority cultural discourses from lay to academia. This disruption can then be translated into positive action and change on as many levels as possible, and it is because of the vast range of discourses involved that this volume is intended first and foremost as a *resource, where you are encouraged to use the index to its fullest extent.*

One of the problems which bedevils minority groups is the way majority societies administer them in a piecemeal, departmental manner, so that a full presentation of the total range of their culture is never available to the lay person. Thus particular chapters here may be of varying interest or usefulness at differing times but *in toto* the full scope of the issues surrounding Deaf cultures are present within the text for the reader to explore.

Thus I welcome the general lay reader to this resource. However, this counter-narrative has especial significance for other lay readers, those engaged in multilingual and multicultural studies, in Black Studies, Post-Colonial Studies and minority studies in general, in anthropology, Cultural and Media Studies and for ethnographic theorists. Because of the way knowledge about Deaf communities has been ring-fenced, gatekeepered and submerged, these domains have never had the opportunity to consider how the Deaf experience might inform their own work. If these volumes are able to initiate new discourses between these domains, that might almost be achievement enough, for the ensuing dialogues will challenge and reform those other 'expert' domains which directly affect Deaf people's lives, whether they be medicine, education, psychology, social policy or even religion.

The Other Central Concepts for the Deaf Cultural Project

Deafhood

The Deafhood concept was illustrated earlier; however, more needs to be said. Some of you may have been puzzled, challenged even, by the apparent celebration of 'deafness'. Indeed, if by deafness one means the loss of one's hearing in adult life (a fate or rather a destiny that lies ahead for as many as 10% of the population), then one can appreciate why the idea of Deaf pride is confusing.

However, sign language users are those who were born Deaf or became so at an early age. For them, the issue of loss has no meaningful reality. By creating their own communities and utilising their beautiful languages, they have created a linguistic and cultural environment in which they take both comfort and pride. Moreover, as will later be seen, Deaf people are easily able to adapt from one sign language to another and, as a result, to form a global 'language' of communication, to become, in effect, Citizens of the entire planet. Such a powerful experience cannot continue to be constrained by the feeble diminutive of 'deafness'; hence the concept of Deafhood seeks to encompass those larger dimensions.

In order to convey the all-pervasiveness of the deafness term, comparison may fruitfully made between Deaf and blind people. As Alker (2000) has illustrated, no one would suggest that spectacle wearers and blind people inhabit the same conceptual space. One would not consider the millions of people in the UK who wear glasses to be blind – that designation is reserved for the 10,000 or so who are officially registered as such.

Yet the distinction between the nine million hard-of-hearing, mostly elderly people and the Deaf signing communities has been skilfully blurred. The counter-narrative presented in this volume proposes that this blurring was a deliberate tactic, forming part of the array of tools that were used to suppress sign languages in Deaf education over the past 120 years.

A culturo-linguistic model

This third concept concerns the belief widely held among signing Deaf communities – that their existential situation is primarily that of a language minority, rather than as a disabled group. Disability theory achieved a breakthrough in the 1980s when disabled people identified attitudes towards them as originating in a belief that they were not full human beings because of the absence of, or damage to, a physical faculty and termed this a *medical model* of disability which in effect 'blamed the victims' for their inability to achieve equality.

The disability movement inverted this pattern, pointing out that societies were constructed solely for the benefit of non-disabled people, so that any attempt to gain equal access and rights was seen as an 'adding-on' process, which left them at the mercy of benevolence, munificience and charity. They proposed instead a radical *social model* which asserted their fundamental equality as human beings with entitlement to full citizenship. Societies should, they contended, be built and managed with all its members in mind, taking collective responsibility to ensure equal access and full citizenship for all, and refusal to do so should be seen as social and political discrimination.

This radical approach has made considerable progress, being adopted in numerous domains, and the 1990s have seen the beginnings of processes to ensure comprehensive legislation to enforce this model. It should be noted however, that the powerful medical and scientific sectors continue to pursue their own model, as can be seen in the current genetic engineering discourses.

Deaf communities have been swept along with the social model movement largely because they lacked the power to make their own views known. In so doing, they have received a (limited) number of benefits from this association, which has also compromised their ability to express their reservations. Many are uncomfortable with their inclusion in the disability social model because, however it might try to construct itself to assimilate them, the criterion used for including Deaf communities in their ranks is that of physical deafness – in other words, the medical concept. Thus social-model legislation is suitable for needs arising out of *individual hearing impairment,* such as flashing light doorbells, text telephones and TV subtitles, and applies to Deaf and deafened people alike – these are not specific to Deaf communities, nor does it address their own deeper needs.

Deaf communities, therefore, find that such an approach does not address the true nature of their being-in-the-world, the issues which arise from this or the politics and policies needed to embrace it. Instead, they see themselves as having far more in common with language minorities. However, not only is this argument new, but it is one that society, 'brain-washed' as it is by the medical model, cannot easily grasp because it requires that Deaf communities are seen as intrinsic 'dual-category members' – that is, that some of their issues might relate to issues of non-hearing, whilst others relate to language and culture. Thus, one has not only to contend with suspicion from language minorities, but with governments who seek simple categorisation for administrative ease.

For all of these reasons, the Deaf case has not been comprehensively constructed and presented, so it becomes the task of this book on Deaf culture to explain in detail how sign language-using communities in fact constitute a third model, a *culturo-linguistic model*. The essence of this model is rooted in ideas about individualism and collectivism in Western societies. Deaf cultures are not cultures of individualism, but of *collectivism*, a trait which they share with 70% of the global population (Mindess, 2000).

Were a disabled child to receive a shamefully poor education, any resultant lack of access to majority society can be seen as a crime enacted upon that individual, whose primary focus is to achieve a 'home' within that society. Sign language users, by contrast, know that they cannot find 'home' within a majority society until the day when that society is able to use their language. For them, home is the Deaf community, and over the past 250 years they have put their efforts into building strong communities, ones that will sustain them through the daily effort to co-exist alongside majority culture members who do not understand them. Yet throughout that time and despite all the setbacks, they have never given up the hope that they can persuade majority societies to learn sign languages, so that both communities can move in and out of each others' worlds.

Thus when Deaf children receive such a shamefully oppressive education, it is *not only the individual who is damaged, but the community in which s/he will grow up to become an active participant*. If Deaf children leave school not only unable to read or write, but unaware of their Deaf community, unaware too of how society works, how can they hope to run the clubs, sports, cultural events and poitical organisations which characterise Deaf community life? Seen from this position, therefore, we can observe that oppression visited on Deaf children is in fact a *double oppression*.

In this it has much in common with other oppressed language minorities, where damage enacted upon their own children affects the quality of life of those communities. Such double oppression can also be observed in the experiences of indigenous, enslaved and colonised peoples. The clinching factor in this argument is that the primary battleground for those communities, for the quality of their future lives, is education. And so it is with Deaf communities. Their priorities are not focused on gaining increased disability allowances, or access to buildings and so on, but for Deaf children to receive an appropriate Deaf-centred education in their own language, so that the quality of life within the collective culture can be maintained and enhanced. At the same time they continue to make the case for majority societies to include sign languages on their national curricula, in the hopes that those children will grow up to become bilingual adults, and thus the two sets of communities will be able to collectively interact for the first time.

This new model which I propose has in its earlier formulations met with resistance from all the parties previously mentioned. Thus one of the central aims of this book is to provide evidence to firm up understanding of this model so that its proponents can finally be heard.

Colonialism

This position leads to the fourth concept, the need to locate modern tools which will help us to appropriately frame the Deaf situation. The culturo-linguistic model thus leads to the situating of Deaf community experiences within the rubric of *colonialism*. Although most people conceive colonialism as formed around economic power visited upon cultures less able to defend themselves, there is undeniably a case to be made for the concept of *linguistic colonialism* and it is this which provides a bridge across which discourses between signing and other colonised communities can begin.

Moreover, given what has been explained about the tropes of charity and benevolence, there is another dimension which has to be considered. Attwood and Marcus (1999), when discussing the forms by which colonisation of Australian Aborigines was carried out, refer to *welfare colonialism*, and the applicability of this to Deaf communities will be examined in Chapter 2.

Both linguistic and welfare colonialism point us once again in the direction of culture, for in essence this is what colonialism set out to achieve – *the destruction and replacement of indigenous cultures by Western cultures*. Thus, by proceeding along this path we arrive at the fifth concept, one which is focused on cultural theory itself.

Minority cultures

Cultural theories, unlike most other academic theories, span a wide range of different disciplines. Anthropology has traditionally built its theories around the examination of small-scale tribal cultures (ironically, and uncoincidentally, cultures in the process of being colonised). Cultural Studies has focused on majority societies, and the ways in which we are manipulated by, give consent to or rebel against the hidden cultural values and belief systems of the ruling classes. Post-colonialism has centred itself around an investigation of the colonial process, sometimes in cultural terms. But as yet there have been very few attempts at rapprochement, to bring together cultural theories which encompass both small tribal and huge post-industrial societies.

This volume takes the first step towards such rapprochement by positing the concept of *minority cultures*, establishing a fundamental distinction between the experiences of members of majority and minority cultures, a distinction that, by comparison of the various literature and discourses, can be raised into the beginnings of a fruitful networking leading to a fully-fledged frameworking. Thus the experiences of sign-language-using communities can be seen to have far more in common with Black or 'First Nation' minority cultures, than with French, German, Chinese or American cultures, so that an analysis of Deaf culture has resonance for cultural theories right across the board.

Deaf epistemologies

This leads us to the sixth concept. If these volumes are able to demonstrate clearly that sign languages are *bona fide* languages, and that Deaf culture is therefore a *bona fide* culture, then one is confronted with the inescapable conclusion that there exists a 'Deaf Way', or ways, of thinking, of viewing the world; in short, Deaf epistemologies. On arriving at that conclusion, it is then a relatively easier task to make the case for those values and beliefs to be accepted by majority societies. It is to be expected that the medical and scientific domains will continue to maintain their reactionary positions. But in the course of this journey through these volumes, Deaf communities may pick up valuable allies to assist in the struggle. And with the age of genetic manipulation around the corner, with its aim to eradicate signing communities from the planet, these allies will be sorely needed.

At this point I need to insert a cautionary paragraph for the post-modernists among my readers. Although it is undeniably true that human beings contain complex and shifting 'multiple identities', it is also unfortunate for minority cultures that post-modernism has emerged in Western thought at this time. Having spent decades or centuries struggling for the right to be able to define themselves on their own terms, and not on those created by their rulers, they now find their initial attempts to locate their own 'authenticity' denigrated by some post-modernists.

Whilst it is undoubtedly the case that one is not simply 'Black', 'Native American' or a 'Woman', and that class, age and gender do produce identities which intersect with these categories, it is also important for these minorities' process of re-emergence to try to locate groups of features which their members hold in common. It is the rejection of any validity being granted to these attempts that has led many minority members to see post-modernism itself as simply another tool of Western thought-control.

The subaltern and the subaltern researcher

The seventh concept seems on the surface to be a methodological one. What constitutes knowledge; how is it 'obtained' by the process of re-search; and what are its fundamental weaknesses when it applies its gaze to minority cultures? Given the reification of the trope of 'objectivity', when are researchers from minority cultures admitted to the academy, and how might they situate themselves? Until very recently they have been ex-cluded, and the theoretical basis for their exclusion has been centred around the supposed impossibility of obtaining 'objective' data by re-searching in their own communities. Much valuable work has taken place within Women's Studies around these issues – however theoretical termi-nology seems not to have progressed beyond that the use of the phrase 'insider-researcher'.

But is being an 'insider' enough? In order to become such a researcher one must spend years learning to think and feel in ways and methods designed by white, middle-class, able-bodied males within majority society academic structures. Thus an inevitable question arises – how rep-resentative of minority communities is such a person, and how does that affect the nature of their research? I attempt to problematicise that relation-ship by developing the concept of *subaltern researcher,* using the term subaltern to distinguish between what we might call 'grass-roots' and 'in-tellectual' members of minority cultures. In applying that concept to myself as stringently as possible, I aim to model a form of self-examination and transparency which, I submit, should be a requirement for any aca-demic or scientist.

If this concept can be followed through one should be able to enact a crucial disruption in the relationship between professionals and lay people, because, as has been shown earlier, there are situations when many of us are lay people, are subaltern.

Thus these seven central concepts return us to the starting point, where the lay person concept is central to any overturning of the oppressive cul-tural patterns we have all internalised. Moreover, the centrality of cultural analysis as the tool by which this process can be achieved becomes ever clearer. In this respect, then, the process of understanding Deaf culture and of 'proving' its existence, the search for Deafhood itself, may enrich us all.

Demystifying the Author – An Invitation to Participate

I must re-emphasise that, notwithstanding the academic nature of some of the language used here, the overriding ethos is one of exploration – a journey, an odyssey for all types of readers. In making myself as transparent as possible, and attempting to render Deaf cultural patterns similarly transparent, I hope to encourage you in turn to reflect and begin to render yourselves more transparent to others. On that basis, I hope you may take this work-in-progress to be a series of interlocking questions and to feel able not only to question what I have written but to actively engage in dialogue about it.

Now such a sentence, on the few occasions when an author uses it in a book, is usually offered as a distant ideal. That is not my intention, and I am happy to break with tradition in this way. Perhaps it is the part of me, which as a member of a collectively oriented Deaf culture, regards each person as essentially equal and thus capable of dialogue. Perhaps it comes from growing up in a village where one must communicate with every member one passes in the street, whether we like each other or not. Or perhaps it is simply an axiom of my socialist / anarchist / hippie / Deadhead subcultural memberships and subjectivities.

Throughout the last century, readers and writers became ever further removed from the opportunity for dialogue (outside of specialised journals). I know for my part that, despite the numerous times I have wished to write to an author, I could never overcome the emotions engendered by ideas about the disparity in our cultural status. And I placed no more trust in the idea that letters to a publisher would reach the author than one would place in a letter sent to a rockstar via their record company or agent. Now, with the advent of the Internet, it is actually possible for us to engage in dialogue, and I welcome you to make contact via my email address (deafhood1@yahoo.co.uk – with all its Swiftian ironies) or to the website *www.deafhood.com* as part of de-mystifying the roles of writer and reader.

Similarly I must acknowledge my different audiences with their own priorities. Thus for the Deaf reader who feels daunted by the language used, I suggest that Chapters 7, 8 and 9 are read first. If they ring true, the others are worthy of your attention. If they do not, you owe it to us all to tell me so. For those involved in multicultural issues or with a political bent, Chapters 1–3, 10 and 11 will indicate to you whether the rest is of use. For my other readers, I trust that you will use your own judgement in deciding which chapters you will explore and when.

After all, we are all of us explorers, and we all have much to bring to each other from our own journeyings. Since this book is the first volume, what you are able to share might become an essential part of the rest. For, in its assertion that Deaf cultures have an important contribution to make to human life, a very special and exciting period of cross-fertilisation between all aspects of multilingual and multicultural development is now becoming an active possibility. And that, like so much else in life, is a journey best shared.

The Importance of 'Culture' in Achieving Recognition and Change

At this point, some readers may like to move on to the main text. Others, intrigued by the central role of culture in our lives, may wish to ponder further before taking that journey.

As I have indicated throughout, learning about other people's cultures is challenging, since the process makes one aware that some cherished beliefs may simply be cultural norms and values that have been unquestioningly inherited. This disruption, however, is often the key to political change. Description and explication of minority peoples' cultures requires considerable resources and patience, but if those communities demanded that the same standards be applied to our own white Western majority communities, we would struggle to be able to provide serious answers.

What is 'English culture'? What does the phrase 'French culture' actually mean? Can anyone actually describe 'American culture' in any meaningful and comprehensive way? However, therein lies the crucial distinction between majority and minority cultures – the former are under no obligation either to make explicit the beliefs which drive their actions, let alone to have to justify their actual existence. The latter, by contrast, are not only required to do so, but operate under a double yoke. There is the extent to which they lack (or are denied) the material resources to accomplish this justification, whilst majority cultural dominance ensures that is *they* who investigate and analyse the 'Other', who file the reports which collectively constitute what the West defines as 'knowledge'.

Over the last 40 years, various previously colonised minorities have managed to break free, to create some cultural 'spaces' for their own representations to percolate around majority societies. In so doing, they have challenged those in the West to question their own cultural assumptions and practices, and to take some responsibility for righting imbalances of justice. However, people have become skilled in dealing with the challenge, focusing on small-scale examples and make minor adjustments to how 'We' treat 'Them'. It is also convenient for Western purposes if these small examples can be ones which achieve high visibility, since they assist in obscuring the fact that one might have set aside deeper and more disturbing challenges; challenges which may have a higher priority for the minority cultures themselves. A simple example – the 'feelgood' visibility of Black television newsreaders when contrasted with the barely visible challenges posed by institutionalised racism.

On a more positive note, Western engagement with those cultural spaces has enabled people to widen and deepen their own cultures. In the past 30 years they have absorbed a multitude of different cuisines, musics, medicines, clothes, artefacts, even drugs and philosophies. They are less aware, however, in their post-modern splendour, that the cultures from which they have extracted these features are less than enamoured of these activities, so long as the West continues to fail to admit the totality of their cultures and thus the true implications of those features, into genuinely equal economic and political relationships. One may have succeeded in *adding* to Western cultures, yet still remain unwilling to really concede that 'They' might have anything of a more fundamental nature to teach 'Us', anything that might be used to radically transform Western societies into less oppressive machines of destruction.

Traditional theorists have stressed the central analytical concept underlying societies' actions as political or economical. There is much truth in this. However it is through *culture* that values, beliefs and actions are mediated. It is relatively easy to identify how oppression operates through power and finance. It is far harder to unravel the densely tangled web of cultural histories in order to understand how those with power and money have shaped what one thinks of as 'our own' beliefs and values.

Moreover, any attempt to do so is deeply threatening to the sense of self and identity which has been constructed, for one is not simply confronted with our knowledge of past wrongs, but with the realisation of how one has been led to give assent to them in present lives. It is only partly a matter of, as the Black writer bell hooks has it, of identifying and relinquishing privileges. Once one has gazed that deeply into one's own culture, one is then confronted with the fearful task of reconstructing new forms of self and identity. And, being human, there are also psychological as well as cultural factors involved in how people have constructed ourselves from childhood onwards. It would be unfortunate for anyone to simply assume that a mental understanding of one's role in oppressing others is the be-all and end-all of the self-changing process.

As one stands at the beginning of a new century and millennium, it is clear that there is a long way to go before people understand their psychological selves. And if one gazes even briefly around European majority cultures, it has to be admitted that one knows very little about them or, rather, very little that we can put into expressive words beyond the stale nationalistic cliches that pass for media discourse.

This is not unremarkable; indeed it is all too human, for one of the givens of culture is that almost by definition it operates at an unconscious level. All societies, white, Black, yellow, red or brown, construct themselves over historical time through agreements concerning behaviour or belief, the rationale for which may have either been long forgotten or manipulated by the more powerful members of those tribes, societies and nations.

Thus it is understandable that people have far to go in bringing cultural patterns to the surface for the necessary examination. And as for developing the much-needed interface between psychology and culture, wherein we might be enabled not simply to learn, but thence to understand how we might proceed – ah that interdisciplinary challege has barely begun.

However, the reader should not be dismayed, for there is another way to gaze upon this. Where human beings stand right now at this point in history is simply and exactly that – the place where they stand, the point we humans have evolved to in our long journey through historical understanding. This journey through life, not simply through our own lives but historical lifetimes as well, is all we have. If we are able to grasp the full implications of this, we can transcend feelings of guilt and hopelessness and know that an exciting journey still lies ahead, one in which we can play our part and lay down our own markers for future generations to walk upon.

Multiculturalism and all its challenges are increasingly set before us, through migration, the global media village, the Internet, and now through the events of 11 September 2001. Thus we are able to appreciate that *'cultural literacy'*, as it were, *will become an ever more important tool for a richer and more harmonious existence*. In all these respects, then, the concept of culture is the key to effective change, acting as both verb and noun; it is simultaneously the object of our gaze, the process through which challenges to our identity must be examined, and the 'medium' by which we make our reports and carry out changes.

Whilst we resist the process of self-examination, destruction of minority cultures continues apace. Visualise yourself as a member of such a minority people, and try to imagine the frustration or despair that you might feel when one multinational after another invades, uproots and damages the economy and culture of your people as effectively as if overt war had been declared on them. And yet the Geneva Convention has not been broken – for the war that is global capitalism does not figure within its strictures. If, as Metternich said, 'War is diplomacy by other means', then colonialism in the 21st century is also effectively 'war by other means' – a cultural war. This of course is not news to colonised peoples and cultures, but we have (been) managed to ignore it until the events of September 2001 forced upon our awareness that other peoples are seriously angry at the 'Coca-colonisation' of their cultures.

We have slowly become aware of the extent to which the past 400 years of Western history, viewed not from our narrow vantage point, but from a global perspective, is one of colonialism, and how the violence of colonialism operated through the subjugating of indigenous peoples. However, violence takes many forms, and the destruction of a people's language and culture is perhaps the most insidious (and effective) kind of all. The imposition of alien education systems, and the enforced enrolment of their children in these systems has, in many cases, brought those languages and cultures to the brink of extinction. And the belief systems and language that we use in our media and our universities to help us ignore or justify these latter strategies continue a process of what has rightly been called *epistemic violence*.

One need not look outside the West for examples of linguistic and cultural oppression. The attempts by the English to erase Welsh and Gaelic are notable, whilst the struggles of Catalan and Basque peoples to maintain their own languages are brought to our attention by radical, news-making activities. With the disintegration of the Eastern bloc we are now seeing a proliferation of attempts by majority languages and cultures to assert dominance over, rather than to live in harmony with, their own minorities. Despite the grand 'advances' of Western science and knowledge, linguistic and cultural oppression continues apace. One might be forgiven for wondering when we will finally prioritise our resources to attempt a serious understanding of what it is about our cultures and societies that drives us to behave the way we do.

The events of September 2001 have hurled us bodily into a new era, where we now have to redefine such long established concepts as 'war' and 'terrorism', and strive to come to grips with acts of violence whose rationale is more deeply bound up with cultural conflict than any we have known for centuries. Not only this, but we are also slowly becoming aware of the extent to which this cultural conflict is intertwined with the economic thrusts of capitalism. These are early days in this new era of 'a war by other means'. Is it possible to rise to this new challenge to all the beliefs upon which Western cultures have been constructed? And can one turn a response born from a defensive position into a process which is positive, excited and interested, one which is willing to continue that exploration into other hidden aspects of Western lives?

This crisis-become-opportunity may well turn out to be the defining feature of the 21st century, even of the millennium itself. We have the chance now to become culturally literate, to emotionally inhabit the whole of our planet in deeper, richer ways. We have the chance to truly appreciate our amazing cultural diversity which stands as a much truer testament of what human beings can accomplish than the media-trumpeted rockets to the moon, smart bombs to Afghanistan or genetic manipulation.

In taking these steps, one does not have to cross oceans to locate models of what humans might become. Before one's eyes, hitherto unnoticed, stand those Deaf communities and their sign languages, each with their own skills and abilities to embrace the planet by communicating through those *very parts of our own bodies which we ourselves are afraid to utilise*. Through the unique plasticity of sign languages, they move in and out of each other's very different cultures like shoals of fish, eagerly seeking out new information about different ways of living in this world of ours.

Perhaps instead of continuing to see them as objects to be pitied or 'cured', we might begin taking our first baby steps in the process of developing our new cultural literacy by actively seeking out what it is they have to teach us.

Notes

1. In order to convey the scale of what has been enacted on Deaf communities, generalisations are necessary. There are some exceptions to this description, but in the global context of Deaf education, these patterns are overwhelmingly the norm.

2. Although later chapters explore these themes in greater detail, some words are necessary here to describe ways in which the USA situation differs. Although Oralism held sway for the majority of the 20th century, it has, to a large extent, been superseded by the introduction of artificial sign systems, which were designed so that one can (in theory) speak in English and use some signs to support that English. Although a degree of improvement has been noted in educational and social outcomes, the results have not been what their proponents hoped for. In no small part this is due to the unwieldy nature of the systems themselves, to the educators' failure to utilise the 'visual logic' of natural sign language grammar which is so important to the small Deaf child, and to the teachers' inability to understand the children's responses which are couched in that same visual logic.

   The US Deaf community has become increasingly concerned that instead of using Deaf people's own sign languages, cultures and epistemologies at the core of the Deaf education process, many professionals in the field still cling to what is known as a 'Hearing' perception of deafness, where artificial sign systems and Deaf staff are seen as no more than 'educational tools' towards 'achieving normalcy'.

   This contrast between such an individualistic assimilationist strategy and the holistic, collective view of Deaf peoples, can be read as colonialism in the same way as Oralism, that is, where the colonisers language (in this case English) is imposed on the colonised, no matter whether it is enacted by 'overt' oralists or 'covert' users of artificial signed English systems.

3. The other two texts are *Deaf in America – Voices from a Culture* (Padden and Humphries, 1988) and *Journey into the Deaf World* (Lane *et al.*, 1996). Other sociological accounts exist, but are not focused on Deaf culture – some are given in the list of Further Reading at the end of the book.

Chapter 1

Deaf Communities

> Anthropologists have a number of advantages when addressing the general public, one of them being that hardly anyone in their audience has much in the way of independent knowledge of the supposed facts being retailed. This allows one to get away with a great deal. But it is, as most things, something of a disadvantage. If a literary critic discourses on *King Lear*, a philosopher on Kant, or a historian on Gibbon he [*sic*] can begin more or less with the presentation of his views, quoting only here and there to drive matters home. He need not inform them who Gloucester is, what epistemology is about, or where and when the Roman Empire was. This is usually not the case for the anthropologist, who is faced with the unattractive choice of boring his audiences with a great deal of exotic information, or attempting to make his argument in an empirical vaccuum.
>
> (Clifford Geertz, 1983: 36)

Introduction

This first chapter presents an overview of Deaf communities and is one of the first sustained 'insider readings' of these communities. It incorporates the perceived priorities of those communities in respect of the Deaf domains selected for presentation. Likewise, the terminology and the language registers used reflect the strong and positive self-image these communities embody, as well as illustrating the scale by which they measure some of the damage that has been wrought upon them. Thus, all told, the reading represents the beginnings of a Deaf counter-narrative, established here to counterbalance the medical and social welfare narratives which have served to 'explain' those communities to others for so many centuries.

Because the chapter serves as an introduction for those new to Deaf issues, and because it has to generalise across different nation states, the presentation is kept at a relatively simple level. Likewise, because of the radical differences in Deaf realities across the planet, and because my primary audience is a Western one, this counter-narrative is focused on the Deaf communities of the Western world. Although examples are drawn

26

from across those nations, the 'baseline' accounts are of the UK and USA Deaf communities. This enables those from other countries to make comparisons and identify important differences that can be used to develop a more sophisticated overall narrative.

What did *you* do in the Deaf Wars, Daddy?

From our vantage point here at the beginning of the 21st century, most of us will have noticed that over the past 20 years, Deaf people themselves have become more visible. Those who have not known a Deaf person, or had a Deaf friend at some point in their lives, will nonetheless be aware of the existence of sign-language-using Deaf people from the television media. Many will have said to themselves at some point *'It's nice to see that they're doing more for those people nowadays'* and consigned the matter to the back of their minds, assuming that their taxes or charity donations had paid for some distant, well-meaning people to look after and do their best for 'them'.

But others, attracted by some indefinable quality in the languages of sign, will have taken courses to learn them. In the UK, British Sign Language (BSL) is the second most popular course at Further Education level. In the USA, American Sign Language (ASL) is now estimated to be the third most widely-used language in the country (after English and Spanish). And through the process of learning these languages, many of these novitiates have now begun to realise that behind this 'mask of benevolence' (Lane, 1993a) lies another tale entirely.

But still the traces of our early indoctrination remain – when we think about what we call 'physical handicap', we assume benign intent. Black and First Nation peoples' struggles, feminism, Gay and Lesbian issues even environment and animal rights issues, all have taken on new forms during the last 30 years, are acknowledged as political issues, and admitted to the liberal and Left pantheon of 'causes'. Indeed, possessing a degree of awareness of them has, in some quarters, become a badge of hipness. Nobody would now suggest that support for these causes was based on ideas about charitability or kindness.

For Deaf and disabled people, however, a long march still lies ahead. The blindfold of benevolence still informs perceptions that these cannot really be political issues. There has been some progress made towards acceptance of the existence of a disability movement. But that there could be a Deaf movement, with a radically different agenda, and with something of its own to offer and enhance one's own world? This still seems a bridge too far and too rickety to cross with a blindfold on.[1]

This perception is perhaps understandable. Looking back through the literature on deafness, I arrive at the mid-1970s. In the writings there I find us, Deaf and hearing alike, timorously suggesting as if for the first time, that such a thing as a 'Deaf community' exists. Trying to prove it, with an air of daring in the enterprise. I smile at the recollection of how far we have come since then, the many years of duelling with the labels of 'extremism' and what a long strange trip it has all been.

For back in 1974, Deaf people were in the grip of a system of education known to us as Oralism, which outlawed the use of sign language and Deaf educators (who had once constituted up to 40% of the teaching staff). Although it had been steadily encroaching for decades, this system was formally instituted at the Congress of Milan in 1880, whose proceedings were closely followed day-by-day by the London Times, and who at the end pronounced the extraordinary message 'Deafness is Abolished'. Oralism then proceeded to hold sway across the entire planet for almost a century. In stark contrast to that early media attention, the actual results of Oralism's practices were then discreetly ignored. In the ensuing century and across the entire world, they were never subjected to professional research on a national scale by anybody, whether inside or outside the profession – an extraordinary wall of silence.

Unknown to us in 1974, a research team from Oxford University led by Reuben Conrad begin to consider undertaking just this project. Hints of their findings began to seep out over the next few years, before their eventual publication literally a century after Milan, producing a spectrum of reactions – shock from well-meaning liberals and a grim 'we've told you so for a hundred years' from Deaf people.

The English literacy level of the profoundly Deaf school-leaver was 8¾ years, enough to comprehend a tabloid headline, but little more. In most cases, their speech – the very *raison d'être* of Oralism – was unintelligible to all but their teachers and families. Even their ability to lipread was found to be no better than that of hearing people who had never been exposed to it before. The study did not examine mental or psychological health, but it did not take much imagination to envisage the scale of the damage wreaked on that score alone. These results were published in 1979 – to a deafening media silence.

But at least the 'truth was out there somewhere' – and not in a file marked 'X'. And in the years following Conrad, surveys in other countries revealed uncannily almost exactly the same 'achievement' thresholds. Deaf people's growing anger at the worldwide nature of these figures saw them begin to describe Oralism as a 'Deaf Holocaust'. This 'larger' language, stemming from growing global awareness among Deaf communities, scandalised numbers of people, as much for its use of political vocabulary as for its comparison with the incomparable. To this came a Deaf response – 'One destroyed bodies; the other destroyed minds'.

The exchanges between these two discourses is of great importance if we are to understand what Deaf communities really are, and over the course of this book we will come to see how the Deaf response is actually a reasonable one, however much we might end up edging it with qualifications. At this point, two issues must be clarified. In the last 300 years, the Western sectors of the human race have carried out other widesweeping policies which have resulted in other holocausts – enslavement which, it is often forgotten, brought estimated millions of African deaths in the 'Middle Passage', witchburning, with the death of half a million women, and virtual extermination of several First Nations. All these can fairly be considered holocausts – if the meaning of the word is understood as a sense of *scale and magnitude* – and each deserves equal recognition, which is as yet not the case.[2]

It would appear that holocausting is something at which certain groups of humans are rather good. So if we look into the mirror, we might grimly concede that there might be others which we have perpetuated which might not have been brought to our unwilling attention. And each time, through tiny cracks in the media, new stories emerge, usually the result of lone journalists persevering in the face of decades of refusal. Each time we see the words 'Armenia', East Timor', 'South Africa', 'Rwanda', 'Bosnia', we flinch. How much more might we have to acknowledge in that mirror? How much of what is occurring now between Israel and Palestine is also of our own making? To paraphrase Faulkner, 'the past isn't past – it hasn't even ended yet'.

Deaf peoples' mirrors contain these images too, though with minimal access to the media they might be forgiven in not comprehending the magnitude of some of these revelations. But in that mirror they also see, reflected back at them, the faces of other Deaf people, of all colours, races and ages. They know that in every country in the world, in every tribe in the farthest-flung Amazonian rainforests, there are people like themselves. They know that if they met any of those people, they could, despite their very different sign languages, fall into conversation and learn about each others' cultures and ways of life, as viewed from the inside outwards. This self-image is not always as rosy as it seems. In everyday life, Deaf people are as prone to discriminatory thoughts and practices as anyone else. But in some deep, almost unfathomable way, they are linked to each other as citizens of a global Deaf community, that is now coming to style itself as a global Deaf Nation.

It is from this vista of awareness that Deaf people come to take a global perspective of the scale and magnitude of what has been visited upon them. They see, indeed they know all too well from their own experiences, exactly what it feels like for a Deaf person in Russia, the United States,

Australia, Japan, Argentina, South Africa, India and China to have undergone this experience. They count up the hundreds of thousands, perhaps even millions, (who is keeping records anyway?) subjected to the oralist regime over that 100 years. And from that standpoint, they assert holocaust status.

This book could have been written without mentioning in any depth these two polarising positions – this global citizenship and the scale of the damage wreaked upon it. It would have been all too easy to do so, judging from the discourses on deafness that do get published, and the limited dimensions and terms in which even the most liberal of writers confine themselves to. But whether or not I had written so overtly, every word of the book would nevertheless have been seeped in that unspoken knowledge. Every word from every Deaf informant or conversationalist, and most of the quotations from Deaf people of past centuries too, is likewise suffused by a sense of one or both of these two realities. It is time, once and for all, to render them visible.

Silence, cunning and exile

Let us move forward in time now to 1999, skipping past 25 years of the Deaf Resurgence. Something which is now so bold as to call itself the 'British Deaf Community' has undertaken its first-ever political march. Initiated and led by the newly formed radical group, the Federation of Deaf People, (FDP), 4000 Deaf and hearing people have marched to Trafalgar Square. Stopping off at Downing Street (now there's a delicious irony),[3] young Deaf children deliver 30,000 petitions calling for official government recognition of BSL, the language of that community. In the speeches given at the Square, once more the call goes up for the return of that language in education, and an end to Oralism and the artificial sign systems which are its offshoots.

Yet, as we shall learn in the next two chapters, despite all the gains made in Deaf-related domains, despite the numerous appearances of sign language on television, despite the beginnings of bicultural education movements, Oralism is alive and continuing to be visited upon Deaf children and their parents right across the globe. Only in Scandinavian countries has the rebellion become a revolution, and bilingualism installed at the heart of (sign) language-planning policies and education.

In the days that follow, the marchers find out just how pervasive the mask of benevolence is. In vain, they search the media for film or printed evidence of the historical nature of their achievement. Instead they are confronted with the same media images they have had to tolerate on almost a daily basis for the last 10 years. 'New Miracle Cure for Deaf Baby' they read. 'Wonder Cochlear Implant Operation Abolishes Deafness.' But unlike the 1880 Milan Congress, now it is not only the London _Times_ which broadcasts these tidings, but every other news publication. Once again Deaf stomachs churn with the anger of knowing that their own point of view on these implants (that these are actually medical experiments on non-consenting Deaf children, that the true results are hidden from public view, and that funding to expose these facts is systematically rejected by those who, also hidden from sight, control the public purse strings), will never be seriously admitted to media discourses. Those who ignore history are condemned to repeat it, the saying goes. It does not mention that those who ignore history also condemn its victims to repeat it.

It is one of the premises of this book that the lay person, brought face to face with the truth of what is visited on Deaf communities, has and will continue to be shocked by these revelations. There is enough evidence of a change of heart for one to feel a small degree of optimism. It is what does *not* happen that gives one pause for thought. Shock is not carried over into political action. We know that changes in the apartheid system owe much to white support, boycotts and actions. We know that other political struggles of necessity involve the concepts of alliance and coalition. Yet somewhere the mask of benevolence still holds us back from applying those concepts to Deaf struggles and campaigns. 'Surely', we seem to think, 'This can't all be a deliberate policy'.

Yet passivity of this kind does not, in the end, excuse us. Millions of Germans had only a dim idea of what was taking place in their countries, in their name. Millions of Britons like to pretend that something like *that* could 'never happen here'. Yet millions of Europeans knew a little of what was being enacted across oceans and continents in their name. Millions of Americans had only a partial picture of what was taking place a few hundred miles from where they lived. But all that vague knowledge, hurriedly pushed aside whenever it raised its head, added up to an enabling of what we now shamefacedly recognise as *real* extremism. For evil to triumph, as the saying goes, it indeed requires only that good men and women do nothing.

Thus it might be understood that Deaf communities view the notion that 'They' will 'make things better for Deaf people' with considerable scepticism. But something else is indubitably awakening across discourses both private and public. Sign languages, if not yet their users, are becoming sexy. Here a former Spice Girl has a number one hit using sign language on national TV (where the whole song is signed, rather than a token chorus). There entities as diverse as Boyzone, U2 and Sinead O'Connor bring sign language to the performing stage. And over there a new American TV serial brings Marlee Marlin as a signing Deaf political professional into the White House itself. Cultural hipness apparently awaits. But political hipness – ah that is not yet in sight.[4]

A few people are aware that this continuing acceptance of benevolence is partly why the gulf between awareness and action exists. Some might fairly say that 'until Deaf organisations take an aggressive political lead and then specifically ask for our support, we do not really know what our place should be in this struggle'. This response is understandable. Optimism among Deaf radicals is situated not least around the public and media response to the events which took place in 1988 at Gallaudet University (the world's only Deaf university), Washington DC. The 2000 students occupied the university in a 10 day long campaign to achieve their first ever 'Deaf President Now'. They gained extensive media coverage, and attracted tremendous public support across the entire spectrum, from being loaned Martin Luther King's 'We Still Have a Dream' banner, to receiving donations from unions, to simply involving hearing volunteers in manning the phones. Clearly lay support can be found – if Deaf communities select the right leadership which will take the 'right' kind of action which will unlock the editorial doors of the media.

But few realise the extent to which those Deaf community organisations have been decimated by decades of Oralism or the extent to which their conventional leadership is still timorous and fearful, whether in the mighty USA or the humblest new post-Cold War nation. Fewer still are aware that in some countries, leadership (or the channels to the ears of governments) is still in the hands of hearing people who wish at any cost to suppress these Deaf subaltern voices. Even the names of the very offices assigned to deal with sign language communities tell their own tale – in Russia, the Ministry of Defectology and even in the USA, the Department of Communication Disorders (the latter amounting to a quite Orwellian twist!).Were we more aware of these factors, we might feel more inclined to take the first step forwards.

But still a nagging voice holds us back. 'What exactly *are* Deaf communities? What exactly are the salient facts of their existence? Individual hearing-impaired people, that we can comprehend. But communities? And Deaf nations?' Thus before we can begin the process of journeying in search of this mythical landscape called 'Deaf Culture', and the mythical inhabitants of 'Deafhood', we must first understand in which direction we must set out, and why all those millions of people walking around with hearing aids, some of them our own grandparents, are as far removed from the realities of Deaf community as Camelot is from Shangri La.

Towards Deafinitions

Deafness, commonly understood as the partial or total absence of the faculty of hearing, has been estimated to affect approximately 16% of the population, that is, 10 million people in the UK (Institute of Hearing

Research, DHSS, 1988), although this figure has been challenged as being too high (Alker, 1998). Of these, the vast majority are people whose hearing has become impaired later in life, who are traditionally referred to in lay discourse as 'hard of hearing'. A much smaller number who suffer total or near total loss of hearing during their working lives are described as 'deafened'. All these are administered by social policies under the appellation (in English-using countries) of 'hearing-impaired'. From the Deaf cultural perspective, these are 'hearing people who have lost some of their hearing'. With that loss of hearing comes a loss of status in mainstream societies and a loss of the opportunity to continue to acquire 'cultural capital'. In these respects, whether hearing impairment is interpreted through the medical or social model, the fundamental reality is one of loss. When referring to such people, the book will use the term 'deaf', that is, with a small 'd'.

Their reality is totally different from those who grow up with 'severe' deafness as their everyday childhood reality, who experience a fundamental language barrier standing between them and meaningful relationships with hearing children and who experience scorn, pity and mockery as a consequence. Their closest friends are other Deaf children, with whom they communicate in sign language despite all attempts to prevent them from doing so. On leaving school, they seek out local, regional, national and international groups of Deaf people, and thus become fully enculturated into Deaf communities. All these interactions over the past 200-plus years, all these worldviews, values, norms and beliefs, are situated in and mediated through, sign languages.

These communities have come to adopt Woodward's (1972) formulation of 'Deaf' with a capital 'D' and to refer to themselves (in English) as 'culturally Deaf'. Deaf communities have found it difficult to estimate their numbers, because of traditional governmental disinterest in undertaking a census. This is compounded by use of different critieria by the few studies in existence. Estimates therefore vary from 'one in a thousand' with 'a major hearing loss' (Taylor & Gregory, 1991: 17) to 1.4 per 1000 (Institute of Hearing Research, 1992 in Kyle, 1996: 23), to approximately two per thousand 'pre-vocationally deaf' (Schein, 1989: 9).[5]

Thus the *potential* size of a British community consisting of such people ranges from 60–120,000. The figure most widely used at the present time is 50–70,000. In the United States, similar percentages result in a potential community of a quarter of a million, whilst in China and India, numbers are a million or more. When applied across the globe, therefore, this becomes an estimated figure of 4–5 million sign language users. Clearly a large number of compatriots for an 'imagined community'. Yet somehow these numbers have not become part of public discourse. Why might that be?

Medical and cultural confusions

Ascertaining the size of the community has also been affected by the confusion of medical and cultural criteria. Prior to the mid-20th century there appears to have been a higher incidence of deafness during childhood, thereby offering a larger pool of potential community membership. This pool was likewise enlarged by the absence of hearing aids in earlier eras; more children who were later classified as partially deaf in the audiological sense were also placed within the Deaf education system. The widespread use of the term 'semi-mute' in an era of 'deaf-mutes' appears to confirm this – Deaf communities embraced both and each was able to bring their own special skills to bear to support the other.

Upon the advent of hearing aids, oralists began to isolate the partially deaf from their former compatriots and, from the 1960s onwards, most were moved into mainstream schools. Numbers of them have 'found their way back home' (as they often term it) into the Deaf community in their late teens or young adult life (Ladd, 1979; Lawson, 1981). Others, however, especially those with more hearing, continue to aspire to assimilation in majority society. To these can be added a tiny minority of those educated in Deaf schools (usually the most stringently oral ones). Both resist association with Deaf communities, a rejection which Deaf people attribute to the feelings of shame engendered by Oralism (Dodds, 1998: Walker, 2001). These people use varying nouns to describe themselves, but for ease of comprehension I will refer to them also as 'deaf', that is, with a small 'd'.

It is important for the reader to grasp certain basic principles of 'deaf' interaction with majority society, especially since these have rarely been set down anywhere before. If one has a partial or even a severe hearing loss from birth, interaction with hearing people can take place slowly and patiently on a one-to-one basis. However, given the necessity of lipreading in this process, and the inability of hearing aids to discriminate and isolate individual sounds in noisy places, interaction with *groups* of people is virtually impossible. The reader might take a moment to introspect here. What would your lives be like if you did not interact with groups of people? What would school life, family life, teenage social life, working life, and so on be like if such interaction was problematic? One finds one's self in one-to-one situations often during those lives. But the process of arriving at one-to-one discourse requires, in the first instance, socialising within groups in order to find those individuals that one wishes to engage with more closely. Whichever way one looks at these situations, meaningful cultural membership is unavoidably centred around understanding the language and culture of these groups.

Now approach this from a different angle. Imagine that all children with a hearing loss on a scale that inhibits meaningful interaction with mainstream societies were brought up bilingually and biculturally; that they were told throughout their childhood *'By learning both spoken and sign languages, you can learn to navigate your life path in and around two cultures and two communities, selecting whatever you wish for from either in order to build your own lives.'* Is this not culturally-centred perspective a more healthy social philosophy than the medical one which stresses the shamefulness of association with signing communities?

It is this very confusion of medical and cultural models which renders the Deaf situation hard for the lay person to grasp. And it is one of the tasks of this book to illustrate the extent to which this confusion has been deliberately constructed.

Culture and disability confusions

These confusions are augmented by another clash of discourses. Over the last 100 years, 'medical' and 'social' models of deafness have viewed Deaf people as disabled and situated them accordingly within its practices. However, the very recent 'culturo-linguistic model' has produced a contemporary Deaf discourse which refuses this categorisation and denies that degree of hearing impairment has relevance for cultural membership. (We will explore this discourse in Chapter 3.) It is important to note that the culturo-linguistic discourse has been led by Deaf children of Deaf parents, for whom the degree of deafness is very much secondary to their hereditary cultural influences.

As the previous section has suggested, this is an eminently reasonable model. However, 90% of deaf and Deaf (hereafter abbreviated to d/Deaf) children are born to hearing parents. Of the many factors which affect Deaf communities and cultures, this is perhaps the most significant of all. Although 10% of Deaf children inherit their sign languages and cultures and are able to pass them onto other d/Deaf children, the process of enculturation for the majority is always vulnerable to ideological interventions from external power blocs. Put simply, to achieve success in those interventions (such as Oralism, cochlear implants and genetic manipulation), its proponents need only to ensure that they control access to the parents of the other 90% and use that access to put across an intensively biased account of deafness. Playing on those parents' fears of 'abnormality' and their desire to achieve 'normality', they then present their medical model which claims that normality can only be achieved by denying the realities of deafness and keeping their children away from Deaf communities lest they be 'contaminated' by them.

This profoundly anti-democratic policy has been enacted throughout the world for the 120 years and shows little sign of waning in power. It has created immense psychic damage for both children and parents, in family-bonding, social relationships and even marital relationships. And inevitably (as it was designed to do), it has severely impaired linguistic minority recognition, for in the cases of language minorities who have won their rights, it is of course the parents of minority children who fought those battles.

As previously described, adherence to the medical or social models leaves Deaf communities vulnerable to an audiological 'grey area', in which the degree of difficulty in accessing majority societies will be unclear. Thus a partially deaf child can give the appearance of 'coping' in mainstream childhood and thus seeming to rock no boats with regard to educational policy (Ladd, 1979). It is only in teenagehood or later life that the truth begins to emerge – that many are simply left without meaningful membership of any community, whether that be Deaf or hearing. These outcomes persist because of the unwillingness by relevant funding bodies to examine the ways in which young children's socialisation patterns differ from those of teenagers and adults – the power to consider these differences resides, of course, with the latter.

The culturally Deaf discourse constructs those degrees of hearing loss as unimportant within the culture. However, this model does not directly confront the problem that external forces base their constructions on just that issue. And, since Conrad's (1979) illustration of deaf school-leavers' differing levels of achievement with regard to speech clarity, lipreading ability and English literacy, concludes that degree of hearing loss *is* a statistically significant variable, it is not hard to imagine that if external forces apply pressure to just those grey areas, then Deaf cultural membership will be affected by the degree to which those with a smaller hearing loss attempt to get by, to 'pass' in majority societies. And whilst those forces construct their beliefs around a disability model, whether medical or social, then it is upon this very terrain that resistance must be founded. For the culturally Deaf discourse to refuse such categorisation is understandable; however, to turn its back on the disability discourse is to continue to surrender that terrain to the hegemonic forces.

Ethnocentric confusions

Another reason for the difficulty hearing people have when trying to grasp the concept of a Deaf community stems from ethnocentricity. Lane (1993b: 481) summarises this well:

> It is not hard to see how a disinterested observer ... might arrive at the stereotypes with which we stigmatise Deaf people, and the conclusion that their plight is therefore desperate. It comes from an extrapolative leap: to imagine what deafness is like, I will imagine my world without

sound. A terrifying prospect, and one that conforms quite well with the stereotype we project onto those in the Deaf community. I would be isolated, disoriented, uncommunicative and unreceptive to communication.

To attempt to empathise is laudable. But empathy should not be mistaken for projection. It is a central position in modern Deaf discourses that community members do not wish to 'become hearing' and that to give birth to and raise Deaf children is a positive, even desirable goal. For those who have made liberal ethnocentric projections, the idea seems scandalous. 'How dare you wish more Deaf children into the world?', they cry.

To which the response is 'If by "deaf" you mean people who were born hearing but whose daily reality is now one of forever being condemned to live on the margins of existence, where, to adapt an old advertisement, *"the edge of a conversation is the loneliest place in the world"*; who have to cling to the coat-tails of the hearing world and numbly accept being reduced to imbecilic status in the eyes of the media, by cartoonists and comedians', yes indeed, who would wish that isolated and unhappy existence on anyone?

But if, like us, you mean 'Deaf' as a national and international community of people with their own beautiful languages, their own organisations, history, arts and humour, their own lifelong friends whom otherwise we would not have met, then perhaps you will understand our pride in what we have created, our desire to pass this on to future generations of Deaf children. And if you can comprehend this pride, then you will understand the longstanding Deaf belief that if societies learn these languages and become able to participate in what we have created, barriers can come down, and all may benefit from the unique skills of Deaf existence.

This discourse goes on to point out that suffering oppression does not entice Black people to wish to become white (with the occasional notable exception), Jewish people to become Gentiles, nor women to become men. In each case, what is wished for is simply the removal of oppression. And so it is with Deaf people. It is having a *cultural community*, a high quality *collective life*, that marks the difference. And it is this struggle between the differing cultural values and concepts of *individualism* and *collectivism* which informs all the actions we shall observe throughout this book.[6]

Contesting community authenticity

These confusions take on greater significance when they are manipulated in discourses within the academic and political domains surrounding the Deaf community. Whenever culturally Deaf groups present their views to those in authority over them, their assertion of a Deaf community is challenged by oralists and their protegés as untypical of all Deaf people.

Presented with such striking differences of opinion, liberal administrators are unable to decide which position to accept, and the consequent
tendency is to fall back on the status quo. Bahan (1997) gives a telling illustration.

In 1993, the Smithsonian musuem decided to create an exhibition
around the theme of the American Deaf community. The more radical of
community leaders insisted that the realities of Oralism be considered
central to the exhibit, provoking an outcry from the leading oralist body,
the Alexander Graham Bell Society (AGBS). Because the AGBS also contained a small number of deaf people, it was able to make the remarkable
claim that the exhibition was 'unrepresentative of the majority of deaf
people' who 'did not belong to a Deaf community'. As we will learn in
Chapter 2, this position is usually adopted by those with wealthy parents
(and of course initiated by the parents themselves). Easy and speedy access
to political influence was possible, Congressmen's ears were bent, and this
medically-oriented lobby, powerful far beyond its numerical size, brought
pressure to bear on the Smithsonian from above. Confused by what was occurring, the musuem abandoned its plans, and thus the very rare
opportunity for public exposure of Oralism comparable to that created by
Jewish Holocaust museums was lost.

Reflecting on the centrality of arguments around deafness which contributed to this defeat, Bahan proposed that Deaf people need to elevate a
position already in existence within Deaf discourse to the public domain.
Noting that no matter how much the external labels have changed during
the past century, Deaf people still describe themselves by an ASL noun
which can be translated as 'DEAF-MUTE', he pointed out that were the exhibition to have been flagged in English as 'the American Deaf-Mute
Community', the AGBS and others would have actually shied from associating themselves with it, and thus it could have succeeded in being
mounted. Alas, he noted, Deaf discourse was still unconfident and fearful
of any negative backlash that might have occurred in such a change of
name. Lesbians may now be unafraid to call themselves 'dykes' and Gays
have begun to develop an unashamed 'Queer Theory'. But Deaf people
were not ready to become 'Deaf-Mutes' once more in public debate.

This debate also points up a further confusion between the differing discourses. Although the culturally Deaf groups claim that the ability (not) to
speak is unimportant for cultural membership, the 'dumb' lexeme in the
ASL sign above carries an unspecified cultural weight with American
hearing people, and it is this very weight which informs Bahan's suggestion, marking the Deaf community out from those 'other deaf who value
speech'. Although he may well be right in hypothesising that his argument

might have solved the problem of the Smithsonian, in other domains the problem remains.

This is particularly relevant in educational discourses/domains. Assertion by Deaf people of the validity of 'the views of the British Deaf and Dumb Community' are thus still academically and ideologically vulnerable to an oralist lobby similar to that described here. This claims that there is no such thing as a 'Deaf and Dumb' person, only someone who has failed to try hard enough whilst at school to speak, and who, instead of wishing to slip unnoticed into society's mainstream, perversely wishes to visibly associate with others so 'afflicted'. Whilst (very recently and reluctantly) acknowledging that such a community of the afflicted exists, they defend their practices by challenging the actual size of that community and asserting that the majority of deaf children exist outside of it. (That they do not need to provide independently verifiable data for their assertions tells us much about the power of their lobby and the general disinterest in academic discussions around Deaf people.)

The basis for that position is situated around the larger numbers of schoolchildren who have a small degree of hearing loss. *Despite needing very little input from the oralist professions*, these numbers are claimed within the general 'hearing-impaired' rubric as 'treated' by their philosophy. Thus in all matters educational where they have inserted themselves into the discourse, oralists are able to claim that 'profoundly hearing-impaired' children form a tiny minority within the overall total, and thus a similar minority when it comes to assessing success or failure. It would be stretching the truth too far to describe this as a clever argument, but it has certainly been a successful one for them, though of course not for Deaf children.

Deafinitions of Community

The problems of defining 'community' are not unique to the Deaf situation, although it is arguable that minority communities suffer more from the lack of consensus. Cohen (1985: 7) points out that

[T]he concept of community has been one of the most compelling and attractive themes in modern social science, and at the same time one of the most elusive to define.

He further suggests (p. 11) that:

it has proved to be highly resistant to satisfactory definition in anthropology and sociology, perhaps for the simple reason that all definitions contain or imply theories, and the theory of community [itself] has been very contentious.

Although in many circumstances this resistance would not seem too significant, later chapters will reveal some of the problems created by such elusiveness.

Williams (1976: 66) traces the theoretical difficulties in part to differing historical tendencies:

> on the one hand, the sense of direct common concern; on the other hand the materializations of various forms of common organization, which may or may not adequately express this.

To give but one example of this conceptual discontinuity in the Deaf domain, Padden (1980: 3), basing her definitions of community on Hillery (1974), states:

> A community has some degree of freedom to organise the social life and responsibilities of its members. Institutions such as prisons and mental hospitals bring together groups of people in one locality, but the people have no power to make decisions about their daily lives and routines. Thus we cannot call these types of groups 'communities'.

Such a definition would appear not to suit minority communities – for example a slave group could not under these terms be called a community. However, since this was written, colloquial and informal academic use of the term has developed to the point where such groups are indeed called 'communities', for better or worse. Viewing this from the perspective of discourse theory, the term is clearly a manifestation of belief systems within certain groups of people, and used in reference to the collective identity of their group. From this perspective, geographical or other boundaries are thus less significant than the actual discourses which take place within and without the communities themselves as to how best they should be described.

For example, when do hundreds of communities scattered across a country become a 'national community'? Anderson (1983) developes the concept of 'imagined communities' to describe the way in which a huge nation state, spread across tens of thousands of square miles and encompassing hundreds of millions of people, can imagine itself to be one national community. It is this concept that can help to give us as a working frame of reference for this study.

Williams identifies five senses of the use of the term community. Three are geographically based, but two, 'the quality of holding something in common, as in *community of interests*', and 'a particular quality of relationship (as in *communitas*)' are of particular use for identifying the Deaf community, and these can also be utilised within the previous frame of reference.

With regard to 'Deaf community' itself, although this term is currently the most widely used appellation for Deaf collective life, Deaf people have only just moved away from the use of an earlier sign-trope 'DEAF-WORLD' during the last 15 years. This term has a slightly different semantic field which has yet to be analysed (Bahan [1994] begins that process) but it is placed in a binary relationship with another term, 'HEARING-WORLD'.

The modern signed term 'DEAF-COMMUNITY' can be seen to imply acknowledgement of a more pluralistic view of society (one that is made up of many communities), thus lessening the impact of the binary opposition. Nevertheless, users of the language retain a historical sense of the old signs, so that 'DEAF' is therefore still set in opposition to 'HEARING'. Thus there is still one 'Deaf Community' faced with many 'Hearing Communities'. For convenience, this study will work with the more recent term, whilst acknowledging the importance of the previous one, and utilising it where appropriate.

With regard to a definition of 'Deaf community' from within or in sympathy with Deaf discourse, perhaps the most concise and useful working definition is provided by Baker and Padden (1978: 4):

> The deaf community comprises those deaf and hard of hearing individuals who share a common language, common experiences and values, and a common way of interacting with each other, and with hearing people.

This definition is, in some respects, circular as Chapter 5 illustrates, but it is nevertheless utilisable for this study.

There has been some doubt cast on this use of the singular form, especially in the USA, where it has been argued that white and Black Deaf people, having experienced similar forms of segregation to those found within the hearing community, might have formed two separate Deaf communities. However, there as in the UK, minority Deaf communities are usually given an appellation like 'Black Deaf community' and to consider political issues regarding the subsuming of such minorities under the overall term would complicate this study too early in its life.

Resolving questions around the size and range of the community are of great importance – *inability to construct and defend its borders and boundaries means that the community cannot begin to establish policies and services centred within its own collective values*, as the Smithsonian example showed; thus the study must aim to reach some working conclusions on this subject.

Deaf community membership

Similarly intricate discourses obtain around definitions of membership of the Deaf community. Baker and Padden (1978: 4) offer the most succinct definition (we should note that their work pre-dates the acceptance of the 'big D' appellation):

> The most basic factor determining who is a member of the deaf community seems to be what is called 'attitudinal deafness'. This occurs when a person identifies him/herself as a member of the deaf community, and other members accept that person as part of the community.

This definition takes as read the necessity of having a hearing loss, as previously explained. With regard to the confusions arising from the opposing discourses we have noted, I would suggest a slight refinement of the Deaf discourse – it is not that degree of hearing loss or the ability to speak does not matter, but that it does not *have* to matter. It only becomes an issue if the would-be Deaf person makes an issue of it.

There are three fundamental routes to membership. The first is being among the 5% of Deaf people born to Deaf parents (a further 5% have one parent Deaf, but remain a group that has never been studied.) Of those 10%, an unknown percentage are multi-generational, that is, they have a lineage of as many as nine generations in some instances, which sometimes contain an extensive kinship network of great-aunts, uncles and cousins. The second route consists of those who have graduated from Deaf schools. In the last 30 years, however, those numbers of mainstreamed Deaf children placed in hearing schools and belatedly finding their way to the Deaf community after their schooldays constitute a growing third route.

Partial membership, however, may be designated to hearing children of Deaf parents. These are referred to in the UK by a title which reflects the BSL construction – 'Hearing, Mother–Father Deaf' (HMFD hereafter), and in the USA as 'Children of Deaf Adults' (CODA). Their numbers are at least equal to the number of Deaf signers, since only 10% of Deaf marriages at most produce Deaf children. Their identification as a conscious group is very recent (20 years or so), and their cultural membership is the subject of heated debate both within their own discourse and that of Deaf communities. To some extent this membership can be related to the degree to which they sign or socialise in Deaf environments.[7]

More rarely, partial membership can also be granted to hearing people who marry a Deaf person, who parent a Deaf child, who become deaf in their early working lives or who have worked in the community for a number of years. Each example is much debated at the present time.[8]

Other membership criteria

Membership of the community is also characterised and strengthened by endogamous marriage – of those Deaf people who marry, 90% marry other Deaf people, a figure which compares favourably with most ethnic minorities, and is higher than many others.

The other key characteristic is, of course, the use of the national sign language, BSL in UK, ASL in the United States, LSF in France and so on. This is learned by members from the first two routes either from birth as their first language or covertly at school, where it also becomes their first language. Members from a third route, that is, from schools which resisted using the national sign languages and constructed variants of their own (a philosophy from the 1970s known as 'Total Communication') adapt those variants into the linguistic grammars of BSL, ASL, LSF etc. in later childhood.

Education and socialisation

As explained earlier, Deaf communities differ from other linguistic minorities in one crucial respect – their language and culture can be transmitted down the generations only by the 5–10% with Deaf parents. For the other 90% of Deaf children, born to hearing parents, access to a sophisticated language and its traditions can only be gained by attending Deaf schools. As Chapter 2 describes, Deaf schools socialised newly entering Deaf children, enabling Deaf norms, values and traditions to develop and be passed down from generation to generation. In pre-oralist times, this transmission was effected by Deaf teachers and adults; since then, because of their exclusion from Deaf childrens' lives, peer group transmission has been the norm.

The crucial importance of those schools (some of which have existed since the 18th century) for community membership is reflected in the regular formal reunions which take place, and which have continued even when some schools were closed following mainstreaming. Similarly, education has been placed at the head of almost every Deaf agenda for as long as there have been Deaf organisations. Since this issue does not benefit adult Deaf individuals directly, its place at the top of their agenda is in striking contrast to the natural self-interest of the political agendas and campaigns of most other groups, and speaks volumes about the deeply held belief of the importance of Deaf schools to Deaf children.

It is important to realise, however, that many countries in the Southern hemisphere and elsewhere do not yet provide anywhere near universal Deaf education. Many which did make a beginning had Oralism foisted upon them as part of their colonial inheritance, which is only now beginning to be removed.

Conclusion

Baker and Padden's (1978) definitions are useful in outlining the general conceptual field, and the statistics quoted earlier give us a similarly approximate image of the numbers of people involved. However, because of the rapid changes visited upon the community in recent years, this general picture is becoming less clear. It therefore seems necessary to build the historical dimension into the picture by emphasising the idea of the *traditional Deaf community*, so that modern variations have something to be measured against.

This traditional community therefore consists of Deaf people who attended Deaf schools and met either in Deaf clubs or at other Deaf social activities. As for the modern Deaf community – this is something which will be explored in depth in later volumes.

We should also note the slippage that takes place between the use of 'Deaf community' as referring to one nation, and its use as an international term of reference. Although ideally one should use the full phrase 'International Deaf community', in reality, due to the Deaf global vision mentioned earlier, it is often used the other way around – i.e. that 'Deaf community' signifies the global Deaf population, and specific national communities are the ones to be marked – thus ' the Sri Lankan Deaf community' etc. Although Deaf people can slip easily back and forth between these two readings, it may take the lay reader a little while to adjust to this global perspective.

Deaf Community Practices

Attempting an overview of worldwide Deaf communities, especially in an introduction of this nature, means that much detail, difference and subtlety has to be omitted. To give but one dramatic example – the World Federation of the Deaf estimates that at least 80% of all Deaf children on the planet receive no education whatsoever. This alone suggests radically different histories and practices in those Deaf communities. I will therefore centre the narrative around the UK and USA Deaf communities. Broadly speaking, the patterns found in the UK also apply throughout Western Europe and possibly to Japan. I will highlight differences where they appear significant.

In approaching the narrative, the reader should attempt to don an important pair of lenses – ones which enable them to consider the extent to which the communities have been damaged by Oralism. There are different ways of conceptualising this, of which perhaps the most powerful is to conduct an exercise in imagining what they would be like had Oralism never happened. The results are extremely powerful.

Not only would there be far greater numbers of healthy Deaf individuals, many achieving positions of power and influence, and far fewer requiring social welfare help or support, but Deaf schools and community organisations themselves would be far more Deaf-centred, literate, confident and effective. Sign language interpreters would have been visible for much of the century, and Deaf people far more noticeable in the local and national communities, in the media, in the arts and so on. And the numbers of hearing people who would have learned sign language at school and gone on to engage fruitfully with Deaf communities would have been so much greater that we might even have been looking at a significant degree of biculturality in that respect alone.

The other way to approach Deaf community praxis can be found in the dynamics captured by these two quotations. Widell (1993: 464), speaking of the Danish Deaf situation states:

> One could say that in the Deaf clubs, a socialisation has taken place . . . This socialisation has literally protected the life of the Deaf community from failure.

What he says applies right across the world, and thus we have a basis for cultural survival. Dimmock (1993: 12), writing of the UK situation, relates that:

> These [the 1920s to 1940s] were great days for Deaf club members. During one . . . AGM at Acton, twelve names were nominated for the post of unpaid club secretary! Nowadays the declining club communities have to go on their knees and plead with anyone to take up the position, even with perks offered.

Dimmock is drawing attention to a post specifically connected to English literacy, a comparison which, in itself, marks the decline of Deaf literacy over the century. But in providing an anchor for collecting and maintaining views and decisions, this post also acts as a springboard for higher level organisation – if one does not record decisions, then meetings cannot take them forward into combat.

Thus the two quotations summarise a century of Deaf praxis. The effect of Oralism therefore was to reduce Deaf communities to a kind of 'subsistence level', where certain social activities were organised quite effectively, but where there was no longer a significant ability to resist anything imposed on them. Thus we find Deaf sporting domains to be relatively unhampered (at least until mainstreaming was introduced), but considerable damage incurred in the political and artistic domains. With these general points understood, we can now proceed to the details.

Schein (1989) makes the telling observation that 'the Deaf community is highly organised'. Indeed there are thousands of small, Deaf-run organisations concerned both with local, regional and national issues, and artistic, leisure, sporting and minority interests. Almost all of these have been traditionally sited around the Deaf club network. Underpinning this is the Deaf school network; many schools drew pupils from around the country, who after returning home kept in touch via the activities and networks described here.

From these activities and networks, new friendships were developed, some of which led to marriages, and these in turn extended the friendship networks. Additionally, when people moved to work in different parts of the country in question, they plugged into the local Deaf club network and thus extended their contacts. After a century of such activity, an impressively complex and sophisticated national community network exists in most Western countries.

Deaf clubs

Most Deaf people choose not to live in close geographical communities, or are unable to achieve this and it is, for the most part, impracticable for them to share the same workplaces (although we should note that in formerly communist countries, formidable numbers of Deaf people worked in 'their own' factories and lived in their own 'Deaftowns', a whole discourse with which the West has not yet engaged).

Thus, the traditional cornerstones of the community are the Deaf clubs, many of which were founded in the 19th century and thus have their own history and traditions. In the UK, for example, there are currently over 250 local clubs, and in the early 1990s there were over 50 in the London area alone. As Kyle (1991b) puts it: 'although the Deaf Club was not absolutely vital to community membership, it was absolutely vital to community life', since it serves not only as a focus, but as a multi-generational entity within which Deaf values and norms are passed down through the history of the club.

Traditionally, clubs were open two or three times a week; once or twice for social activities, and once for church, although in some this was supplemented by nights allocated to trade workshops, drama groups or visiting lectures, and in others, by a residential facility for retired or infirm Deaf or single women. Nowadays many open several times a week for meetings of special interest sections like youth groups, senior citizens' activities, sporting activities and women's groups, as well as regional and national Deaf meetings. In the last decade, a significant number have established nights for hard of hearing groups and sign language teaching classes, whilst the current Deaf resurgence has seen clubs used much more frequently for workshops and training days than before.

This is not to suggest that all Deaf people within the community attend the club. Although there has been little research, in Jackson's (1986) study, 86% of those interviewed were either current or former members of a Deaf club, a statistic which was congruent with Kyle and Allsop (1982), where 58% attended the club once a week or more, whilst 29% attended very rarely. Of those not attending at all, the most common reasons given were inability 'to relate to the people and / or the activities of the club' (Jackson, 1986: 18), or disagreements with other members or with the Welfare Officer, which persisted even after those concerned had died or left the club. However, as this study reveals, research has not picked up an over-looked minority of 'rebels', who meet in pubs and whose social network overlaps and interrelates with sections of the sports and leisure groupings described later.

Since most of the clubs were developed as part of a mission or diocese, the issue of control of the club or the board of management is an important and often overlooked issue. Essentially a two-tier colonial structure existed – Deaf people had some say in the running of their social commit-tee, but none in the management committee. In the last 20 years, they have gained more control of the former, but the latter is still effectively out of their hands. These themes are examined in the data of Chapter 8. The role of the missioner was crucial as the link between the two committees and one example of the extent of the colonialism is the fight to establish bars in the clubs – it was not until 1967 in Coventry that the first Deaf club bar in the UK was won. This opened the floodgates, and now almost all clubs have bars – an important factor in attracting and keeping younger Deaf people within the network.

In the last 15 years in the USA, and the last 5 years elsewhere, there has been a significant decline in the numbers attending clubs. Reasons given include mainstreaming in education which cuts young deaf and Deaf chil-dren off from the traditional entry route, technological developments such as the textphone and captioned television, as well as changing social pat-terns based on greater mobility.

Deaf sport

Of those activities which take place outside the club, sport has tradition-ally been the main focus of Deaf people's interest. Indeed, it has been an underrated source of community pride and unity for a century. As Jordan states 'Nowhere in the Deaf community is the sense of Deaf people taking charge of their own lives as strong as it is in Deaf sport' (in Stewart, 1991).

These sporting activities can be defined as intra-club, local (mostly within hearing leagues), inter-club, regional, national and international. Initially, these were informally organised (although Deaf international soccer, for example, is over 100 years old, and the first of the [now four-yearly] World Games for the Deaf took place in 1924). Formal UK regional bodies were established from the 1930s onwards, and in the 1950s, the

British Deaf Sports Council were said to have drawn these together into a national organisation, thus (in theory) establishing a structured route for the young Deaf school-leaver from club to Olympics. In recent years with the growth of mainstreaming, Deaf sport has assumed an even more vital role as a community recruitment point for those young Deaf who have been discouraged by Oralism from joining Deaf club activities (Eickman, forthcoming).

Deaf sport differs from mainstream sporting activity in that matches against other clubs see sizable numbers of Deaf club members travelling with the teams, not so much for the games themselves as for the opportunity to network with other Deaf people on a regional and national basis, to exchange information, look for potential partners, meet with old schoolfriends or to develop their networks further still (Kyle, 1996). Deaf sport is also an important contact point for a number of those Deaf who do not wish to attend their local club, like the rebels described earlier.

Other social activities

The concept of Deaf sport also embraces leisure and hobby activities, and there are national Deaf clubs and organisations for such varied activities as mountain-climbing, yachting, chess, caravanning and camping, film-making and motor-biking. These also attract Deaf people who do not otherwise attend their local clubs and together with the sporting network described earlier forms secondary networks which weave in and out of the Deaf club structure without being confined to it.

Although most Deaf dances are held in Deaf clubs, numerous private parties, dinners and receptions are held either in people's homes or in hired premises. These events are characterised by party games and rituals, either Deaf-developed or adapted from hearing equivalents. Amongst younger people, there has been a greater move towards socialising on 'hearing' terrain, either in pubs or at dances and other similar events.

International activities provide a further dimension to Deaf life. Several organizations arrange regular visits abroad, and considerable numbers of younger Deaf people travel either to sporting events or carry out *ad hoc* touring plans. Most of these visits differ from majority society ideas about holidaying abroad in that the prime aim of the journey is to meet up with or to seek out Deaf people from those countries, in order to exchange information about Deaf life as well as to socialise.

Deaf Artistic Practices

Deaf communities embrace a wide range of artforms, some of which originate from specific attributes of their language and culture, whilst others mirror the forms used in majority society. It is difficult to give an accurate historical overview due to the virtual absence of research, whilst, since artforms based on sign language could not of course be easily recorded, few examples have survived.

Folk arts

The most prevalent artforms in the community are the 'folk arts', that is, those most closely integrated into everyday Deaf life, of which storytelling is the most notable example. Sign languages appear to be especially suited to storytelling (there is evidence that Native Americans used the medium for this purpose), which was nurtured in the residential schools despite all the attempts to stop it. With the advent of video, there has been further development of the form, particularly in the USA. However, since story-telling is not confined to formal occasions, but a fundamental part of everyday Deaf social and cultural life, Deaf people have found it unnecessary to remark upon it, and so there has been little study of its history and development, especially as a medium for transmitting historical and cultural information.

Similarly Deaf games, Deaf humour and Deaf jokes appear to have been a part of the community since its inception, again so central to Deaf life that there has been almost no attempt to study them. Everyday creative sign-play has also been unrecorded, though there have been suggestions that in the UK, though not in the USA, this was severely damaged by Oralism and only really re-emerged in the mid-1980s. (The intervening period seems to be characterised by sign-play based on English puns, which were not accessible to many Deaf people.) By contrast, creative sign has been part of the American residential school experience for many more years (Rutherford, 1993), and may not have ceased even at the height of Oralism.

Deaf visual arts

Miles (1974) classifies Deaf art into three categories. The first consists of Deaf works which bear no obvious trace of the creator's deafness, whilst the second treats conventional subjects in a way that reveals a Deaf perspective. The third category consists of art on subjects which are specifically Deaf-related. Unless otherwise stated, the works described here belong to the latter two categories.

The importance of Deaf visual arts within different communities has varied widely during history. Chapter 2 indicates their prevalence at certain important historical moments and discussed their significance in influencing majority society's views of Deaf people's humanity. Mirzoeff's (1995) research suggests that many Deaf painters, sculptors and photographers were aware of this deeper discourse behind their work and suggests that much Deaf visual art thus contained a political agenda.

He notes, however, that once Oralism gained ascendancy in Deaf education, the number of known Deaf artists declined and remained minimal until the start of the Deaf Resurgence in the early 1970s. Significantly, many of the first works from this period are specifically aimed at Oralism, as if to clear the decks (cf. Miller in Gannon, 1981). Since that time, there has been an outpouring of Deaf paintings, sculptures and photography across all three categories, in the UK as well as abroad, and several organisations of Deaf artists have been formed to further their collective Deaf-oriented perspectives.

Deaf performing arts

Deaf theatre has existed formally since the late 19th century, although little is known of its audiences and practitioners. Deaf clubs have a tradition of informal performance, usually around festive dates, comparable to those of village dramatic societies. In the UK, the BDDA established a triennial national drama competition, but the choice of subject matter and the signing styles were strongly influenced by the hearing missioners to the Deaf, and it has been suggested that Deaf people attended these performances more for social reasons than for artistic ones (Ladd, 1985). In the 1960s the National Theatre of the Deaf (later the Interim Theatre) was formed and lasted til the early 1980s, but its choice of material and signing styles were also strongly influenced by its hearing directors, and Deaf audiences often complained that its works were unintelligible, leading to hearing people forming the majority of its paying customers.

In the USA, a similar pattern obtains, although their own National Theatre of the Deaf is much more established, and has brought an impressive number of high quality performers through its ranks, even though it has been subject to the same criticisms as Interim.

In the former communist countries, government sponsorship of Deaf arts led to a particularly strong tradition of Deaf stage performance. Here, however, Oralism also gained influence, and many of these have specialised in mime rather than in use of their own sign languages.

The Deaf Resurgence saw the first known plays written and directed by Deaf people on Deaf themes emerge in the USA in the early 1970s, in the UK in the late 1980s and elsewhere in the 1990s (Handtheater, 1997). However, with the demise of the BDA's drama competition, and with fewer young people joining the clubs, Deaf theatre in the UK has seriously declined; the occasional group being formed to tour the clubs and then disband again. Another reason for this decline has been the growth of 'integrated theatre', where hearing groups have taken on a 'token' Deaf person, learned some basic signs and presented this as signed theatre. With their knowledge of the grant allocation systems, they are able to win money that might otherwise have gone to sustaining Deaf drama groups with Deaf-centred themes.

It is not known whether sign language poetry existed in the last century; the first mentions of anything resembling this in the UK came with the BDDA's Signed Poetry competitions. These were, however, competing renderings of the missioners' favourite poems and were judged on how well they used Signed English. A more Deaf-oriented Sign poetry emerged in the early 1970s and became an important part of the resurgence, especially in the USA, with the pioneering work of British-born Dorothy Miles. Miles' work combined English and ASL (later BSL), but her example inspired other Deaf people, both in the UK and in the USA, to develop purely visually oriented sign poetry which used no English at all. Since Miles' untimely death in 1993, growing numbers of Deaf people have started to produce their own work to fill the vacuum (cf. Emmerick, 1995; Lentz, 1995; Valli, 1995).

Deaf Cabaret appears to have existed for as long as Deaf clubs themselves, usually with an 'open stage' policy, where anyone could get up and perform skits or jokes or tell stories. However, it was not until the mid 1980s and the advent of the Deaf Comedians in the UK and CHALB in the USA that there was a concerted effort to develop Deaf-oriented material. Their successful reception, has influenced other Deaf drama groups to turn away from theatre and towards similar 'Deaf cultural' skits and mini plays.

The earliest examples of signed songs were developed in the Christian church and therefore hymn-oriented and in the UK perhaps a score of clubs developed a Deaf choir guided or controlled by various hearing missioners. In the late 1970s, a number of Deaf individuals began to develop their own interpretations of pop songs (in the USA, several groups formed and toured), but it is only in the 1990s that they have adapted the lyrics of hearing songs to fit the Deaf situation or composed their own material (Ladd, 1991) around these themes. This artform is a controversial one since, in many cases, only those Deaf with some hearing can gain a full appreciation of the work, leading those with no hearing to feel alienated from it.

In many societies, these four artforms are highly important; each enables a mirror to be held up to contemporary culture, creating domains where members of these communities can speak to each other and discuss cultural, political and ontological issues of pressing importance. Each creates an environment in which language use within cultures can be refined and transmuted; often the 'new' language styles can be found in dialectical relationship with the kinds of cultural issues that are newly emerging. The absence of these characteristics in Deaf performing arts for most of the 20th century speaks volumes about the degree of linguistic and cultural oppression visited on the Deaf community by Oralism. In these circumstances it is perhaps understandable that only the folk arts flourished.

Deaf Communication Media

Printed media

Deaf written literature seems to be confined to poetry – there are very few Deaf novels, although Deaf magazines do contain some short stories. In several countries, notably the USA, Deaf schools contained print workshops which thereby trained Deaf people in the range of skills associated with print, whether typesetting, bookbinding or journalism itself. The schools printed newspapers for local communities also, and within their own community formed a network for considerable discourse.

In the UK, many Deaf magazines which were inaugurated in the later 1800s closed during the 20th century, apparently because of the lack of English-literate contributors and a similar decline in the numbers of literate readers, although in the UK, one survived to be taken over by the BDA's *British Deaf News* (*BDN*). Dominated by the missioners, its subject matter consisted of reports on social activities written by hearing people; almost the only section by Deaf people was the club news, which was particularly popular because of the community's nationwide interconnectivity – significant numbers of Deaf people had an active interest in the doings of their friends and acquaintances around the country.

Following pressure from BSL activists, BDN became easier to read from the 1980s and most of the articles were written by Deaf people themselves. However, the discourse was until recently still strongly focused on *activities* – there is much about what Deaf people do but very little about what Deaf people *think* outside of a small letters page.

Numbers of 'parish magazines' also existed during the 20th century, but these were dominated by the missioners and were mostly confined to reports from the local diocesan, and have since declined. During those years, occasional 'rebel' magazines like *The Argonaut* and *ABC Deaf Sports* have had a limited lifespan, but it was not until the rise of the *National Union of the Deaf Newsletter* in 1976 that a ten year forum existed for alternative subaltern discourse. This forum has been re-established by the Federation of Deaf People's *The Voice* in 1998.

In the 1990s there has been a rise in the number of specialist Deaf magazines stimulating new discourses on Deaf arts, film, TV, history, and so on, and the beginnings of cyberspace discourses (such as DeafUK), whilst the development of teletext saw weekly magazines begin on BBC 2 and Channel 4. The latter point up important questions about the concept of

Deaf community discourse. The discussion pages offered the most frequent, extensive and public forum ever for UK Deaf discourse. However, these pages are also shared by hard of hearing and deafened people, and the arguments which rage back and forth concerning the merits and validity of BSL, Deaf schools, Deaf culture and so on reveal two sets of discourses talking at cross purposes to each other, indicating the degree of confusion resulting from subsuming two culturally differing groups under one medical category.

This is further complicated by two degrees of overlap. One is that the forum's other pages (events, workshops, job adverts etc.) are of equal value to both groups. Another is that certain technological developments (the textphone, visual alarms and doorbells etc.) are also of use to both groups, lending support to the idea that deafness is medical, not cultural. In addition, very few subalterns in the Deaf community are willing to risk their English skills in public, and the debates are thus conducted by those more fluent, who are therefore not necessarily representative of the subaltern view. This is also an important factor when considering the cyberspace discourses.

In the USA, Deaf newpapers have a more sustained history – the *Silent Worker*, now the *Deaf American*, has existed for over 100 years, and there are at least four other national newspapers/magazines. It is noticeable, however, that these too tend to focus on what Deaf people do rather than what they think, except on 'obvious' topics such as Oralism or cochlear implants. Political and cultural discourse, here and elsewhere, it appears is confined to sign language domains.

Deaf film and video media

Deaf communities made little use of film in the silent movie era; although several Deaf performers were prominent (Chaplin's relationship with his Deaf friend Granville Redmond was formerly thought to have influenced his own style – Schumann, 1988), only one Deaf movie is known to exist (*His Busy Hour*, 1926). The most significant use of film occurred in 1913, when, alarmed by the spread of Oralism, the American National Association of the Deaf made several films of sign language oratory in order to preserve the language for future generations. Chapter 4 illustrates the level and style of that discourse.

However, up until the Deaf resurgence, very few formal films were made and of those which exist, few focus on the sign language content. The neglect of such a perfect medium for recording sign language is puzzling, until one takes into account the damage done to Deaf creativity under Oralism, which took off as the film medium emerged.

Even now, despite the resurgence, there are few Deaf films and videos of an artistic nature. In the USA there have, however, been concerted attempts to film Deaf storytelling and poetry, theatre and cabaret, as well as recording old people's memories and important lectures and workshops. In the UK, the main thrust of Deaf film creativity has been directed towards making Deaf documentary items within the existing Deaf television programmes, and in making information videos which translate English text for those unable to read it into the visual medium. In Scandinavia, these two routes have been combined – Deaf drama and art are filmed but they are also used as broadcast material.

Perhaps the most notable aspect of the video medium has been the extent to which it serves to exchange what might be termed instructional information. Talks, lectures and seminars, conferences and festivals seem to be the video modes which carry Deaf discourses, though it is unclear how often they are watched or by by how many. In the UK, the London Deaf Video Project (LDVP) was established in 1985 specifically to force government bodies to translate their information into BSL. This has proved to be very effective, with numerous spin-offs to other bodies, and the LDVP also ended up training numbers of Deaf people who were later to go on to work in Deaf television. Chase Productions took off in the 1990s, mainly to create material for children, and has since developed a huge catalogue of broader educational material, often incorporating particularly artistic aspects of Deaf culture into those programmes.

In the USA there are a handful of companies which also have an extensive video catalogue. Much of this material is either instructional, or used as such by those learning to sign. Between them they carry some impressive programming, since video serves as a major vehicle for sign discourse. Thus one finds stories, folklore, history, biography, humour and poetry, for example.

In Scandinavia, the achievements in Denmark and Sweden have also been impressive. Government funding for video services has enabled a healthy nationwide industry to develop, containing the same range as that of the USA.

Although these recent developments are heartening, very few entertainment or artistic videos have yet been developed other than for Deaf children and little use has been made of the CDRom or DVD formats. Nevertheless, national networks of Deaf film-makers are beginning to emerge, and the future looks brighter.

Televisual media

In order to appreciate the importance of this media, it must be understood that Deaf people place huge cultural weight both on visually presented information and discussion, and on being able to observe and digest other Deaf people's sign language. In additional, as we have seen, they have little access to written English discourse, and no access to voice discourses such as the radio or everyday majority conversation. Television programming therefore takes on huge significance for drawing Deaf discourses into the creation of a potentially powerful Deaf discursive system.

In the UK, two attempts in the 1950s and 1960s to provide programmes for Deaf childen and adults came to an end because of campaigns to remove sign language from the screen, in the first case by oralists and in the second by hearing-impaired people.

Deaf campaigns in the late 1970s resulted in _See Hear_, the BBC's first magazine programme for the Deaf community, and this was followed by programmes on other channels. Deaf activists hoped that _See Hear_ would provide a forum to enable the community to speak to each other face-to-face once a week, to revive and extend Deaf discourses around injustice and power, culture and history, to demonstrate Deaf arts and accomplishments, all these helping to unify the community and take it forward (NUD, 1977).

Unfortunately this (essentially cultural) perspective was not shared by the hearing people set in charge of the programme, and the 20 years of the programme's existence have been characterised by fierce debates between its makers and its Deaf audience across a wide range of subjects. One of the most longstanding criticisms was the patronising tone – it was nicknamed 'Blue Peter' for its earliest years – whilst more recent distress was expressed when the show had to be shared with hearing-impaired people, with the cross-purpose conflict of interests already described. In the last 3 years, it has moved back to addressing its Deaf audience, and has developed a number of innovative styles of Deaf television. Nevertheless, after 20 years, little use is made of the golden opportunity to develop investigative journalism or to accept that it carries such powerful primary responsibility for leading the way by representing Deaf political issues (such as cochlear implantation) appropriately onscreen.

Thus, although the sheer presence of sign language and Deaf people on TV for the first time has had many beneficial effects, the loss of the opportunity to control the direction and progress of one's own discourses has proved to be very distressing to many.

Listening Eye (later _Sign On_), Channel 4's Deaf programme, began in the early 1980s with a strong culturally Deaf focus and began to explore what that implied for production values. However, despite enjoying great popularity and continuing to improve, it was scaled down and then axed, for no apparent reason, in 1998, and replaced by a programme for Deaf children, despite widespread Deaf protest. The replacement issue in itself sent a disturbing message; rather than ensuring that it was the responsibility of Channel 4's Children's Department to make and broadcast such a programme, the company was asserting that there existed but a single slot for Deaf television, and it was for them alone to decide which section of the Deaf community was going to gain their favour at any one time. In additional, by closing *Sign On*, they had single-handedly dismantled 15 years' worth of experience and expertise in Deaf broadcasting which the community badly needed.

Channel 4's actions incurred further outrage when the post of Deaf Advisor became vacant. This had been held for a decade or so by a hearing person and, upon their departure, significant numbers of very experienced Deaf people applied for the post. Perhaps mindful of the battles held over *Sign On's* closure, Channel 4 decided that a 21 year old, TV-inexperienced Deaf secretary was the person for the job. In so doing, they could not have made their fear of genuine accountability to the Deaf community any clearer.

Situating both programmes within the Educational TV departments also sends a clear message that the hierarchy's view of the Deaf community is that of a people who, above all, should be educated. This is very interesting in the light of the identification of the 'pedagogical conditional' in the next chapter, and helps to explain why the scope of the Deaf TV discourses has been so constrained.

In the USA, there was a flurry of Deaf programming between the late 1970s and the mid 1990s, which was usually given restricted broadcasting access and easily lost amidst the numerous channels. Although the best known was *Deaf Mosaic*, broadcasting out of Gallaudet, its mode of presentation was often of a kind that produced similar criticisms to those made of the BBC's *See Hear*. Perhaps the most culturally memorable work was created by those involved in the Deaf children's programme, *Rainbow's End*.

It is difficult to summarise the situation in other countries, since programming is so diverse. Some countries give a healthy percentage of time to news programmes with sign language, whilst others, particularly in Scandinavia, are beginning to broadcast programmes actually made by the national Deaf associations. This owes much to the principle of direct Government funding.

Dear Participation in Majority Society

Overall participation

There are few studies of the ways in which Deaf people interact with majority society, either individually or collectively. How they relate to their neighbours, their neighbourhood, their villages, towns and cities, how they negotiate in public territories like streets and shops, with officialdom (other than through the welfare services) and how they utilise the media and other sources to collect and circulate information for themselves and their community – all these subjects have rarely been examined. One consequence of this is to reinforce what might be called 'welfare colonialism' – that meaningful Deaf activity can only be measured by the degree of interaction with those bodies charged with their welfare – and independent individual and collective initiatives therefore are not considered to have their own existence.

Deaf working lives

Apart from the Deaftowns of Eastern Europe, the majority of Deaf-hearing interaction (such as exists) occurs at the 'hearing' workplace, and research findings make depressing reading.

For the UK, Kyle and Allsop (1982) found that 46% in their local study worked as unskilled manual labour, whilst Kyle and Pullen (1985) found 61% to be so employed. This compares with 5% in the general population. Semi-skilled and personal service accounted for 40% and 23% respectively (the national figure being 16%). Those in skilled manual and professional positions numbered 14% and 15% respectively, contrasting with the national figure of 79%.

Thus, since unemployment rates for Deaf and hearing are similar, the major characteristic of Deaf working lives is under-employment. In the pre-oralist era when Deaf schools emphasised trade training, the skilled manual and professional figures are thought to have been higher, but otherwise the patterns were similar.

Whether one argues that these statistics reflect Oralism or the attitudes of employers and missioners, the consequences for the community as a whole remain the same – less disposable income to spend within the community, less access to life experience that comes from responsible employment positions and a reinforced sense of the inferiority developed during Oralism, among other factors. Few of these consequences are favourable to establishing a community climate of self-belief and independence.

Deaf higher education

Outside the USA, the number of Deaf people attending universities during the 20th century was close to zero. To use the UK as an example, a few attended Further Education colleges to obtain Higher National Certificates and the like – these are, by definition, trade-training courses. There was little or no access to the curricula via sign language interpretation, so that those who took on the system did so alone.

Certain professions of great relevance to Deaf people, such as teacher training, actively disqualified them on medical grounds. The one avenue of access to a higher education was through the welfare worker training courses run by the missioners and later the social work course of the North London Polytechnic.

In the last 10 years, following the Deaf resurgence, with increasing numbers of Deaf children exposed once again to sign language, the numbers entering universities, mostly via Deaf Studies courses, have mushroomed, and the number of graduates approaches three figures.

The US situation is rather different, mainly due to the foresight and determination of the (hearing) Gallaudet family. The National Deaf-Mutes College (later Gallaudet University) was founded in the 1860s, and produced a steady stream of graduates and professionals for the pre-oralist education system, and indeed public life generally. This process continued after Oralism – indeed it remained the one place where sign language could not be outlawed, since the students were effectively adults who could not be browbeaten in this way. Thus there has never been an oralist president of Gallaudet, and throughout the century it remained the one lighthouse beacon that illuminated the darkness which had fallen across the Deaf world.

It is difficult to speak of its importance as the only Deaf university in the world, with 2000 students from many countries, without becoming emotional. Quite apart from anything else, it probably maintained the value of sign language art and aesthetics in ASL. But it also served as the fount from which the whole resurgence could be mounted. The first research into sign linguistics was based here, and for two decades was almost the only place it existed. The various waves of campaigns to reintroduce sign language to education naturally had their roots in the one place which never stopped using it.

However, we must be wary of painting too romantic a picture. Until the 1970s there were only a handful of Deaf faculty (there are many more now) and it took until 1988 and a profound international campaign to achieve the first Deaf president; even then he was a man deafened in adulthood. It took even longer to agree to establish a Deaf Studies department – there was considerable fearfulness that this might prove a rallying point for a Deaf or Deaf-centred takeover of the university. Sectors of the American Deaf community also resent the amount of power and influence its alumni have had, and their perceived attitudes towards subaltern Deaf (cf. the play *Tales from a Clubroom*, Bergmann & Bragg, 1981). We might be surprised that the professional classes should *not* be considered natural leaders. But as we shall learn throughout this book, in Deaf communities, with their strong belief in cultural collectivism, *attitude* is, or can be, all. And there is a consistent perception that, in submitting to Hearing mores and influences, together with forms of 'career anxiety', numbers of its alumni in leading political positions are wary of 'upsetting' majority society by fighting for Deaf issues. In short, leadership which does not initiate powerful subaltern campaigning simply becomes authority held over others.

From the 1950s onwards, two other large centres for Deaf tertiary education have emerged, the National Technical Institute for the Deaf at Rochester and California State University, Northridge, both of which are attached to large hearing universities, while numerous Deaf students enter other colleges – at the time of writing, for example, there are over 60 PhD holders in the USA.

Deaf Minority Groups

There has been little research into Deaf minority groups until recent years; thus the summary following is necessarily incomplete and attempts only to sketch a basic picture.

This is an appropriate moment to re-introduce of one of our first key themes. As we have seen, one major Deaf discourse insists on the commonality between all Deaf people, no matter where they live. In reality there also exists another discourse, one in which Deaf people are also influenced by the majority culture with which they grew up, and whose discriminatory views they have to some extent imbibed. An interesting situation is thus created where one can observe the tensions between the two discourses within each person.

Deaf minorities therefore do perceive discrimination to exist, but it is also tempered by the Deaf commonality; thus if one wished to explore the issue, it would be a case of needing to explore the many different domains, fields and situations occurring in community life in which these two discourses contend, before being able to state with certainty that there was less or more Deaf discrimination than elsewhere.

We do know that it is generally said that in Northern Ireland, Deaf Protestant and Catholic differences are much less pronounced, and my own experiences in the Balkan states confirm a similar impression. But at the moment, that is all that they are – impressions.

It is also important to note that within Western societies where there is significant immigration, or within linguistic minorities inside a single nation-state, there are Deaf people who are, in effect, minorities within minorities. Given the oralist hegemony, most of these Deaf people have been cut off not only from mainstream culture, but from also their own 'native' cultures, a form of double oppression immensely damaging to them even without factoring in oppression from the Deaf communities themselves.

Deaf women

Little is known as to whether the status of Deaf women within the communities is different from elsewhere in majority societies. From what we know of Deaf club roles, the divisions of labour and responsibilities followed traditional patterns, and few Deaf women were able to attain important posts within the community, at either local or national level. This does not mean that other sets of values did not exist concerning the 'psychological' status of male–female relationships, but we know little about them. When it comes to Deaf history, we are even further disadvantaged – most of the accounts we have are of Deaf men. An example which highlights this is that of Thomas and Sophie Gallaudet. The latter was known as the 'Queen of the Deaf Community' – but we know almost nothing else about her.

In recent years, as in the general population, there has been a great increase in the numbers of Deaf women in active community positions, so the imbalance is in the process of being corrected. In the UK, a particular growth area has been in the number of Deaf women's health groups and projects. Another point of comparison can be made across two decades with the two radical Deaf groups in the UK, the NUD and the FDP. During the NUD's existence it was male dominated. The present FDP committee, by comparison, has women very much in the majority.

In the USA, far higher percentages of Deaf women now occupy important professional positions (possibly a higher percentage pro rata to men than with hearing women) and a national organisation exists. Perhaps surprisingly it was only the third to be formed – India and New Zealand Deaf women being the first two off the mark. Certainly a Deaf Women's International is a very real possibility within the next decade.

Deaf religious minorities

This is a subject which has received little attention, and indeed it would be impossible to summarise the global picture, since a majority in one country might be a minority in another. I will, however, give UK examples so that readers may begin their own comparisons.

The first Deaf minority groups to emerge in the UK were religious ones. Roman Catholic Deaf schools were established in Yorkshire and Glasgow in the early 20th century, and their own clubs in towns like Liverpool, Newcastle, Manchester, London and Glasgow. As with their hearing equivalents, Irish influence is strong, and this is perhaps even more noticeable because it naturally involves different sign languages. In that respect, use of the Catholic sign variant in the UK might properly be regarded as the UK's only minority (sign) language, though all of its members can use BSL with ease. The National Deaf Catholic Association is the organisation through which networking is still conducted. All this is not only unresearched but also little known to the mainstream Deaf community even though some of its members are nationally known for other work – it would appear that religious difference is no longer an issue in that respect.

Traditionally serious tensions existed in some of these cities between 'Protestant' and Catholic clubs from time to time; the situation is now much calmer. The effect on the overall community has not been measured, but it is interesting to note that the NUD was (wrongly) perceived by some as a 'Catholic' organisation because of the degree of mixed membership. Similarly, the numbers of highly able Catholic Deaf people who have emerged into wider community life after the renaissance suggests that the community was hitherto unsupportive of their involvement and all the weaker for their absence.

Deaf ethnic minorities

This is an even more difficult topic to explicate, as the situation varies so widely from country to country. Again I will use the UK and the USA as two examples for readers to make their own self-assessments.

The only Deaf ethnic minority group to be organised on an international basis is the Jewish Deaf community. Interestingly the first UK oral school was also Jewish, and from this basis the community has developed its own clubs (in London) and network, which appears mostly confined to the South of England.

From the 1950s onwards, Deaf offspring of Commonwealth migrants began to appear, and at the present time there are substantial numbers of Deaf Black and Asian people, mostly young, with the oldest being in their forties. Their relationship with the majority Deaf community is problematic (Taylor & Bishop, 1991) and feelings of discrimination and exclusion have often been expressed, yet without much overt discourse in white Deaf circles. Recently that they have begun to establish their own clubs and organisations, and there appears to be a strong informal national network, espcially amongst Deaf Asians.

Analysing this situation is difficult because, although the numbers of Black Deaf young people involved in local or national committees is miniscule, the same is true for their white equivalents. Both grew up during the most intense period of Oralism, when the introduction of hearing aids and mainstreaming produced particularly strong divisions between Deaf and deaf, and both have been reluctant to come forward whenever Deaf leaders have tried to locate and encourage their involvement and taking of responsibility. Thus, frustrations expressed by the BDA at not being able to set up programmes for Black members because of lack of participation have been expressed in virtually the same terms for Deaf youth programmes.

The wider historical picture has only recently begun to come clear. When the radical FDP was set up in 1998, young Deaf people appeared on the scene in numbers for the first time in two decades. On examining FDP membership and the wider situation, it was realised that, broadly speaking, the activist Deaf people are those in their mid 40s to mid 50s, and they have been active for around 20 years. There are comparatively few activists between the ages of 30 and 45. _It appears that almost an entire generation has been lost to Oralism_. And it is precisely this generation which contained the first Black British Deaf people.

One must also point out that some oppressed peoples are so caught up with trying to survive that they do not have the psychic time and space to campaign on behalf of others (witness the small numbers of hearing Black people involved with Left activism). This dynamic undoubtedly plays a part in white Deaf discourse.

Nonetheless, until white Deaf discourse seriously addresses (as opposed to wringing its hands about) the issue of why many Black Deaf are reluctant to participate in community activities, and until academic resources are made available for meaningful interventionist and support studies and projects, the shadow of racism will rightly continue to hang over the community.

In the USA the situation is even more pronounced, since under the apartheid system, there were separate Black and white Deaf schools, with very different 'Black ASL' dialects. Racism is therefore even more common. Aramburo (1988) found that the majority of Black Deaf Americans considered themselves to be Black first and Deaf second, although for those coming from the residential schools of the Northern states, this tended to be reversed. Gallaudet's first Black student did not register until 1951, and it seems that the National Association of the Deaf (NAD) did not even permit Black Deaf people to join until the 1960s.

Since then, however, there has been a significant 'catching up' process. The National Black Deaf Advocates, formed in 1981, regularly draws thousands to its annual conventions, including large numbers of Black Deaf professionals. The Chairman of the Board at Gallaudet, for so many years a white hearing male, is now under Black Deaf stewardship. Nonetheless, these developments may well follow the wider patterns in the post Civil Rights era – a growing Black professional class, and a growing underclass. It remains to be seen how both white and Black Deaf America address what have now also become class issues.

In the 1990s, other ethnic minorities have started their own national bodies, notably Native American, Hispanic and Asian.

It is impossible to give a more detailed picture in this introduction. But in the course of this study, much material has been collected around the fascinating interpenetrations of class, race, gender and sexual preference in the USA and UK, and these will be featured in the next volume.

Deaf Gay and Lesbian groups

In the last decade, Deaf Gay and Lesbian groups have emerged, and begun to gain acceptance from the wider Deaf community. Clubs, organisations and networks have been established and in the UK, relationships with organisations like the BDA were finally formalised in 1985. There is also a strong international Deaf Gay and Lesbian network. One difference between the UK and the USA is that in the discourse of those aged under 28 it is commonly said that there appears to be a much large percentage of Gay and Lesbian Deaf than in the majority society, especially within Deaf families. However, there is almost no research into these subject and speculation would be unhelpful.

Disabled Deaf people

Although there are considerable numbers of hearing-impaired disabled people, the Deaf community (and indeed research itself) knows little about them because professional discourses have determined that they should be educated within other disability categories. Nevertheless there are a number of traditional establishments in which, for example, learning-disabled Deaf people live, and these are beginning to accept Deaf staff, and thus the potential bridge to Deaf communities.

A singular exception is Deafblind people. Many of these are Deaf people who have lost their sight in what is known as Usher's Syndrome. Although there has always been some level of provision made for them within welfare organisations and Deaf clubs, many Deafblind people feel alienated from their former Deaf schoolfriends and colleagues (Taylor & Meherati 1991). This situation may be beginning to change as DeafBlind activists have started to band together.

Mental health services for Deaf people began to take off in the 1980s, after many pioneering years of work by John Denmark, and this field is beginning to employ significant numbers of Deaf people. An interesting observation was made to me recently by one of the prominent (hearing) specialists in the field – he felt that the Deaf community was 'more accepting of mental health issues than the hearing community'. Why that should be, and what it means requires further study – Deaf-based research is very thin on the ground in this field, as indeed is the case generally, of course.

Young Deaf people

Although what I describe here is the UK situation, there are many similarities elsewhere, and the differences would make for fascinating reading.
Whilst 20th century oralist policies resulted in Deaf school-leavers being
unable to communicate easily with Deaf club members (National Union of
the Deaf, 1976, 1982, *inter alia*), most young people made the effort to
develop their signing skills and learn the clubs' traditions, values, and behavioural norms. Utilising the sporting and leisure network described
earlier, once they married and had families, most became regular club
members. As we have seen, the last two decades of mainstreaming has
begun to severely impact the Deaf community, producing young Deaf
people who either do not know about their local Deaf clubs or who have
been encouraged by their teachers to avoid them.

For many, however, the desire to socialise with other young Deaf people
seems not to have diminished and in the larger cities within the last ten
years, they have become very visible – if one attends the right pubs, parties
and sporting events. There is now an informal national network which regularly meets, and weekend journeys across the country are remarkably
common. All this activity culminates in an annual rally at Blackpool attended by around 2000 Deaf young people – a singularly impressive
statistic, and a powerful affirmation that, despite all the odds, Deaf people
are powerfully attracted to being with each other.

Nevertheless, the estrangement of these young people from traditional
Deaf social structures is giving increasing cause for concern, as there is less
optimism that they will join the club community once married than in previous decades. It is therefore unclear how they will learn to be socialised in
the community's values, develop their BSL skills or understand the traditions and history on whose knowledge they could otherwise draw.
Similarly, given the crucial role of new generations of young people in
taking responsibility or intiative in demanding change, concern has often
been expressed about whether and/or how this will happen for the Deaf
communities.

Deaf Organisations and Political Activities

As Schein (1989) has remarked, the 'Deaf community is highly organised', with the numbers of Deaf organisations, local, regional and national
running into the hundreds. The social organisations were described earlier;
this section concentrates on political organisations, that is, organisations
either run by Deaf people themselves or claiming to be. Once again it
would impossible to give sufficient detail about national differences and so
this account will focus on the UK and the USA.

The international perspective

Several national Deaf organisations were inaugurated in response to Milan; for example the American NAD in 1880 and the British Deaf and Dumb Association (BDDA, later BDA) in 1890. Many are Deaf-run; some like the NAD from the beginning, but most, like the BDA only during the last 20 years. In some countries, it has proved necessary to establish new and separate Deaf-run organisations in very recent times – notably the Irish Deaf Society in 1982 and the Australian AAD in 1976. Most countries of the world now have such a national body and most are affiliated to the World Federation of the Deaf (WFD), which was established in 1951. The WFD reverted to Deaf control in 1987, since when its headquarters have mainly been situated in Scandinavia, and it has had two General Secretaries in that time, both women. At the same time regional bodies were established, for example the European Union of the Deaf in Europe (EUD) (which largely operates within EU countries because of funding restrictions placed on it by the EU itself).

These initiatives have led to a much stronger Deaf presence around the United Nations than before but, as with the disabled equivalent, the Disabled Peoples' International, the WFD is disgracefully (given the vast wealth of the UN) poorly funded, grants being available to pay only two full-time staff. This seriously limits the work which can be undertaken, and the WFD is mainly known for its four-yearly congresses. There has, nevertheless, been an encouraging shift towards prioritising radical positions on bilingualism, anti-cochlear implantation and Third World Deaf issues.

The EUD is similarly financially discriminated against, but has made some headway within the EU in respect of recognition for sign languages across all member states. At the time of writing this issue is coming to the boil and will be discussed further in Chapter 11.

National perspectives

The British Deaf Association

Traditionally the largest and most significant Deaf organisation in the UK, the (then) BDDA was founded in 1890 like so many other national Deaf bodies partly as a response to Oralism. The minutes of the inaugural meeting indicate that two groups shared the leadership: one being Deaf people themselves; and the other the hearing missioners to the Deaf (Grant 1990). The role and number of Deaf missioners in its development are as yet unclear.

The BDA's strength lay in its democratic structure, with a nationwide system of local branches and regional councils; by the early 1980s there were over 200 branches and 16,000 members. It sought for a blend of social and political activities, in the form of national and regional rallies, holiday homes, and youth projects, creating a skeleton framework that held the national community together at a time when it was under sustained attack. So successful was it on this social level that one can truly say *that the Deaf community's health is dependent upon the health of the BDA.*

Despite campaigning against Oralism, by the early 20th century, the BDA found itself unable to influence the mainstream political system, so it concentrated instead on working for the welfare of its members, lobbying for limited areas of change like discrimination in insurance policies and driving licensing. It continued to make occasional forays into the political arena in respect of Deaf education; by the early 1970s it was able to employ full-time staff, after which the forays became campaigns that met with an increased degree of success.

In 1980, Arthur Verney became the first non-missioner to be appointed General Secretary, and this combined with the euphoria of the first recognition of BSL and the threat posed by the NUD (see later) saw rapid changes within the organisation. Following an attempt by the 'Old Guard' to remove Verney, a wave of organised resistance not only reinstated him but appointed the first ever Deaf chairman. Growing political activity saw the BDA reaching its peak in the late 1980s with a succession of mass lobbies of the Conservative Government and important interventions in the European Parliament.

However, its political activity tailed off under successive leaders and although it made the transition to being all-Deaf-run with its first Deaf Chief Executive in 1995, it has entered a period of declining importance. It is something of an embarrassment to Deaf people that this decline should have continued despite gaining control of their own internal political discourse: appeared to pose critical questions about Deaf managerial competence and innovative flair, both of which contain their own cultural issues.

The BDA occupies a unique position in Deaf discourses. On the one hand, its large Deaf membership and range of Deaf activities offered very special access to subaltern Deaf discourses, whilst, on the other, the domination of the missioners restricted the expression of those discourses and superimposed their own social welfare discourses on them. Although presenting itself (correctly) as the official representatives of Deaf people, Grant's history of the BDA suggests that this was problematic – that the missioner's ethos may well have dominated policies and strategies from the outset (unlike the American NAD, which was always Deaf-run).

Because of this blurring of discourse boundaries, the BDA has been simultaneously 'of Deaf people' and yet 'not of Deaf people'. This has confused and compromised national Deaf discourses for many years. Now that Deaf people have control of the BDA, solutions to its current crises must arguably be found by recognising and unpicking the strands of these different discourses in order to develop its future directions. If it cannot do this, there will be serious repercussions for the entire Deaf community.

There are many parallels in the above with other post-colonial situations; the fact that one major aspect of the crisis is financial is also relevant. Fundraising strategies require an in-depth knowledge of majority cultures. Those cultures having traditionally oppressed subaltern groups, access to funds and fundraising skills to compensate for the years of oppression are not only not forthcoming in the independence period, but actively withheld. Furthermore, any attempts to assert equality and independence are also pulled back by the noose of the charity system and its discourses, where financial income is dependent on projecting helplessness and where governments abdicate their reponsibilities to that system.

Radical or subaltern Deaf activities

At different points during the 20th century, some Deaf people became frustrated at the BDA's political paralysis, and various short-lived pressure groups were formed. Some based their organisation around their magazines and broadsheets, whilst others focused more on face-to-face activities. No research has been carried out on these groups, but among those known to have existed are the Society for Higher Education of the Deaf (SHED) in the early 1950s, *The Argonaut* (1960) and *ABC Deaf Sports* (early 1970s).

The National Union of the Deaf

It was the founding of the National Union of the Deaf (NUD) in 1976 by disaffected Deaf radicals which provided the springboard for important aspects of the Deaf resurgence. Deaf-led, and self-financed, but working with hearing allies, it made the case for Deaf political leadership and began to take the initiative in campaigning for educational change. Perhaps its greatest achievement was its campaigning for Deaf television programming – its pilot broadcast took place in the BBC's Community Programmes slot in 1979, *Open Door*, while its most audacious move was to attempt to persuade the United Nations to examine and activate its own Charters of Rights, and in doing so to recognise Oralism as genocidal (NUD, 1982).

Despite appearing to oppose the BDA, several times it worked in conjunction with radical sectors of the BDA to good effect, notably in establishing the Deaf Broadcasting Campaign, and in its creation of an Alternative Education Conference in Manchester 1985, when the Milan Congress' successors arrived there. In 1987, NUD mounted the first ever picket of the (then) Department of Education and Science, gaining substantial coverage, but in the year-long negotiations which followed became disillusioned by the department's intransigence, and at the lack of support from the BDA in a situation which needed a long-term, properly funded and prioritised campaign. Disillusionment thus led its most active members to focus their energies on establishing the British Deaf History Society (BDHS). This was a deliberate shift in direction, and based on their beliefs in the importance to Deaf political development of a strong and well understood Deaf history.

Later subaltern groups

Before the birth of the FDP, there are two other groups worth mentioning. The Deaf Tribune Group developed a wide ranging political and cultural programme in the North West, was instrumental in leading the rebellion to reinstate Verney at the BDA in 1983 and joined forces with the NUD to produce the major attack on Oralism in Manchester in 1985. Their work will be examined in more detail in Chapter 9. Less successful was the Deaf Education Action Forum (DEAF) of the mid 1980s, which was born of frustration at the lack of action by the BDA in the educational field. DEAF also attended the DES meetings with the NUD but, like them, became disillusioned at the lack of progress and BDA support and disbanded soon afterwards.

Such subaltern activities were the more notable for the extent of the obstacles they faced – lack of resources, low Deaf self-esteem and fear of retribution from the missioners – whilst lack of access to the telephone and limited English literacy posed huge difficulties for anything other than face-to-face organisation. For these reasons, such activities were necessarily sporadic, and the dissenting Deaf discourses continued as an undercurrent without easy means of expression.

Federation of Deaf People

The FDP is the latest response to perceived BDA inactivity (Alker, 2000) and in the two years since it was established, it has made an impact out of all proportion to its funds. Its main objective is to act as a resource for local community actions and to support and develop a national network of Deaf activists. However, this quickly developed into a national campaign for official government recognition of BSL, and the first ever national Deaf marches took place, as related at the beginning of the chapter, the first attracting 4000 people and the second 9000 (a significant percentage of the community, equivalent to a 'hearing' UK march of 8 million people) and notable also for the large numbers of young Deaf, both as attendees and as organisers. Indeed, in the 2½ years of its existence, there have been 10 marches and three actions – more than the whole of the last century combined. (Even as I write the tempo is quickening – distressed by the absence of media publicity for the marches, younger Deaf people have started to take matters into their own hands, organising non-violent direct action activities like road-blocking. One such action has resulted in the first-ever arrests of Deaf people for Deaf political activity and the 'Wolverhampton Six' have earned a place in Deaf history.)

Since these developments have a significant bearing on bilingual education issues, they will be discussed in more depth in Chapter 10. As noted earlier, one important characteristic of the FDP has been the number of young Deaf activists it has attracted, especially the high percentage of women and also Lesbian and Gay Deaf people.

International radicalism

The British picture is both similar and dissimilar to what has happened elsewhere. In several European countries, other subaltern or radical groups have emerged for a decade or so and then closed, like 2LPE in France. 2LPE stands for 'Two Languages for an Education' and it is interesting to note that it is around this theme of bilingual education and sign language recognition that most of the activity has occurred. In the USA, for example, there is very little serious challenge to the NAD, despite quite widespread criticism of its perceived ineffectiveness. Almost the only group which did put forward consistent radical policies was TBC – 'The Bicultural Centre'. In other countries, from Spain to South Africa, marches are organised at quite regular intervals without the groups themselves sustaining an ongoing organisational structure. There have also been actions such as sit-ins and hunger strikes around these issues, and also around cochlear implant issues.

It can be argued that it is the Scandinavian Deaf Associations which have achieved the most. Because of the strength of these societies' social-democrat philosophies, it has been easier to achieve direct dialogue between Deaf associations and governments. The determination of Scandinavian Deaf communities to pursue their Deaf agendas in these dialogues has resulted in impressive gains across the board, from education to the media to foreign Deaf-aid, all based on the culturo-linguistic model.

Deaf Communities and Governmental Relationships

This introduction to Deaf communities would not be complete if we did not acknowledge the role and relationships of other organisations with which they come into contact in the course of making social policy. Because Governmental administration of Deaf communities varies so widely between countries, the UK situation is again used as a comparative 'prototype' for readers to situate their own similarities and differences.

Readers new to the 'deafness' field might be forgiven for thinking that in matters of social policy, there exists a straightforward 'two-tier' relationship between Deaf community organisations and the relevant government departments. As described earlier, this is indeed the case in some progressive countries such as Sweden (and indeed elsewhere in Scandinavia) where their Deaf organisation, the SDR, receives funding from the government which is then allocated for the adminstration of Deaf community activities and services. It is not yet clear whether this funding is comprehensive, but it is known that Scandinavian funding can range from schools to video services to interpreting services.

Elsewhere, the waters are muddied because each government organises and places Deaf community responsibilities across a range of departments, all of which then need to be lobbied, and all of which perceive Deaf issues as only a small part of their remit. Thus developing a comprehensive programme for community regeneration and language planning is extremely difficult, and the result is piecemeal provision which is 'guided' by short-term and exigency thinking and the strength of competing lobbies.

The additional difficulty here is that none of those charged with responsibility towards Deaf communities has any qualifications in Deaf matters. Their immediate reaction therefore is to 'seek advice', and in so doing, to enshrine certain organisations and professions – in effect even individuals with these unofficial, almost hidden, and unaccountable advisory powers. Were this to be the only barrier, the situation would still not be insurmountable.[9]

However, this is only the beginning of the problem. In the early part of this chapter we saw how confusion around the differences between medical deafness and cultural community have made it harder to identify Deaf educational issues. The inevitable oralist bias built into the medical profession, together with the size and power of that profession itself, means that it is not only able to commandeer the majority of funding around deafness, but then continues to treat the born-Deaf community as if it is simply a matter of an extra 70,000 hearing-impaired people. In so doing, it represents an advisory source which can obtain government attention whenever it might choose to do so – namely, whenever threatened by Deaf community advocacy.

The situation increases in complexity in countries where governmental power is devolved to regional, state or local authority levels. This brings into play many hundreds of officials, again with virtually no knowledge of the difference between deafness and the Deaf community. In turn (at best, and not always), each seeks to be advised by 'experts' and, in many cases, will have constructed over time some formal channels. For example, in the UK, local education authorities have designated 'Special Education' sectors. Their remit includes all disabilities, which immediately places Deaf communities at a disadvantage, as they are then confined to a medical, non-linguistic and individualistic ideology. Furthermore, the 'Deaf' posts within this domain are almost all controlled by oralist-trained professionals. Thus to overturn this system, piece by piece, and replace it by nationwide language planning policies is a huge task, even were there to be a single Deaf community voice that governments would officially recognise.

As if that were not enough, in some countries, like Ireland and the UK, the problem is rendered even more severe. Instead of accepting a two-tier relationship, a tertiary strata has been created by the institution of a national body which inserts itself between Deaf people and governments and advances its own agendas. In Ireland this body is the National Association for the Deaf (Crean, 1997) and in the UK, the Royal National Institute for the Deaf or, as it is known by Deaf people, the 'Really Not Interested in the Deaf' (Alker, 2000).

The existence of these types of bodies seems to be predicated on the existence of the charity system. As we will learn in the next chapter, this dynamics of this system can be simply summarised. Originating in the absence of government provision, fundraising for charities inevitably developes a pattern where funds are sought from the wealthy. In the process, some of these people become involved with the charity – usually those who have deaf relatives or Deaf children. Their involvement over time then increases to either running the charity or manipulating policy from behind the scenes, and the organisation becomes the advisory body to which the government turns. For 'taking care of the unfortunates', they are then rewarded with titles and honours. When their views conflict with those of Deaf communities, the latter are then marginalised. Because of the tremendous amount of power which they can wield as a class, a class often shared with government members and civil servants themselves, the income generated by these charities vastly outweighs that which Deaf community organisations can raise, and over the decades this process snowballs. To give an idea of the scale, the RNID's annual turnover exceeds £40,000,000 per annum. The BDA's is around £2 million, and the FDP's a few thousand.

Thus the existence of this unnecessary tertiary layer actively works against Deaf interests in itself. When one then examines the traditional background of the RNID policymakers, one finds – members of the medical and teaching professions – oralists all, together with wealthy oralist parents and the occasional token hearing-impaired person and the occasional oralist child-become-adult. These are the people installed as governmental representatives of the sign-language-using community.

If one were therefore to conclude that the task facing the Deaf community was an impossible one, that would be quite understandable.[10]

Summary

Political oppression – Deaf communities as colonies

As we know, one of the primary aims of this book is to enable those involved in multilingual issues to not only recognise the Deaf community situation but to accept that a place should be found within its theory and praxis for these rarely recognised linguistic minorities. In order to accomplish this, it is my responsibility to draw the most appropriate cultural and political parallels possible and to construct a framework which encompasses them. If this is achieved, we then have the basis for refusing the mask of benevolence and situating the Deaf struggles within one's own larger understanding of political process and action.

It is from that impulse, then, together with the evidence here, that I have concluded that the experience of Deaf communities most clearly resembles the _colonialist_ situation. In the 1990s, such a reading began to appear, as in Lane (1993a), Mirzoeff (1995) and Wrigley (1996). So far these readings have tended to be (perceptive) observations, rather than a systematic exploration of the colonialist process both outside and inside Deaf communities. The next chapter explores the appropriateness of such a definition. If we are to begin to dismantle the colonialist system we must understand the extent to which its patterns have penetrated and disarmed those communities, so that we can turn them back on themselves. Equally importantly, since what we are proposing is a political alliance or coalition, we cannot carry this out without an informed knowledge of the existing cultural dynamics within Deaf life, and how they might affect us were we to approach those communities.

It is theoretically possible for the reader to put down the book at this point, declare themselves convinced by the _political_ arguments they have read and to begin to act on what they have learned. Should anyone wish to do so, I am sure that the politically aware sectors of the Deaf community would not turn them away!

However, there are other readers who are mindful of the struggles they would themselves face were they to turn to their own professions and disciplines and attempt to make the Deaf case. They will know that they still have to overcome any disbelief about the existence of Deaf communities, their essential differentness from hearing-impairment, and the Deaf self-perception as organic and linguistically whole beings who have not only no interest in 'cures', but actively oppose them, and moreover are happy at the thought of more Deaf children being born. They will thus be aware that in order to convince, they will have to advance academic arguments which tackle the traditional misconceptions on their own terms, and to frame refutations which actually incorporate these misconceptions into an overall pattern of (wilful or unwitting) mistreatment of Deaf communities.

In so doing, they will require new analytical terms which help unpick the locks on the academic doors. These, as it will be seen, are centred around two concepts – Deaf Culture and Deafhood.

We begin, therefore, by taking the widest view possible – scrutinising academic praxis itself, and examining perceptions of Deaf people throughout the history of Western civilisation.

Notes

1. The very fact that so few radicals have experience of Deaf issues has meant that the difficulty in substantiating what I have said here virtually represents a self-fulfilling prophecy. However I am gratified to note that Davis (1997: xi), speaking as a CODA (hearing Child of Deaf Adults), has this to say:

   > People with disabilities, Deaf people ... have been relegated to the margins by the very people who have celebrated and championed the emergence of multiculturalism, class consciousness, feminism, and queer studies ... if I include the the term 'disability' in the title of my talk ... the numbers [attending] drop radically. (p. xi)

   He goes on give other examples before describing how at the end of his talks, members of the audience drift up to talk about their own family experiences and so on. As he concludes: 'There is always an eagerness in their approach, because disability is the bodily state that "dare not speak its name" in radical or academic circles.'

2. I write this shortly after the third anniversary of Holocaust Day, and the first officially recognised by Britain. It has taken Jewish people 50 years to reach this point. One wonders whether this will mark a turning point in our self-recognition as a race? Will we now begin to mark other occasions of similar magnitude, instead of Columbus Day, Australia Day, Commonwealth (now *there's* a bold-faced irony) Day? Or will we, anxious to limit any feelings of guilt or complicity, decide that one such event is quite sufficient?

3. Sir George Downing, after whom the street was named, was a sign language user and Deaf ally of the 1660s who plays a rather important part in Deaf history, as we shall see in the next chapter. Perhaps it is time for mainstream historians to explore this aspect of his life in more depth?

4. Oliver Sacks, that chronicler of unusual human states, has written his own excellent book on Deaf communities, *Seeing Voices* (1989). Significantly, it is the least known of all his works.

5. Raymond Lee (2001 pers. comm.) suggests that it is possible that the capitalised 'D' may have been used by some Deaf people prior to Milan, noting an example from the British *Deaf Times* in February 1880, and goes on to speculate that it may have been hearing magazine editors who insisted on de-capitalising it.

6. To make a personal interjection – I was born deaf (and probably conceived that way too, if we might briefly allude to the ontological realms featured on the cover). Along with friendships with hearing people, the feature of your society

that I most cherished was music, though the quality of what I perceived would have sent those of you who can hear screaming for the earplugs. When in later life I lost the little that I had, I was able to make comparisons between being a Deaf child and a deafened adult. Despite all the oppression in my oralist upbringing, when it comes to psychic pain, the loss of music is in a different league. Believe me in this. The operative word, as Lane (1993b) suggests, is *loss*. And for most born-Deaf people, it is safe to say, one does not miss what one never knew in the first place.

7. The whole terrain of HMFD cultural experience and status is not only absolutely fascinating, but extremely important. As this introductory chapter is not the appropriate place for such a discussion, the reader is referred to Preston (1994) for the best current initiation into the mysteries.

8. In an ideal Deafworld, one which has succeeded in defeating oppression and attaining bicultural status, Deaf cultural membership by such hearing people would become not only become unproblematic, but serve as a positive and powerful bridge for further Deaf–hearing cultural exchange. Given that Deaf communities have been forced on the defensive for so many generations, their suspicions of the recent positive new waves of hearing people are understandable. Likewise, their removal and banning from the natural human roles of nurturing the children of one's own culture, has led (amongst much else) to an unawareness of the extent to which their native abilities can help hearing parents. It is no coincidence that in Scandinavian countries where sign bilingualism is most successful, Deaf–parent relationships are in the positive, 'post-revolutionary' stage.

9. This is a problem faced by other language minorities. Katznelson (1981) describes how the holistic worldview of Black nationalism radically differed from traditional urban politics. School, welfare, police and housing issues were seen as aspects of a total or colonial condition. The authorities, however, were constructed in such a way that only piecemeal solutions or management were possible. Thus, as Henry (1990: 106) summarises, 'black demands for community control challenged the prevailing political economy because they could not be met at the urban level alone'.

10. By way of illustration of the size of the task: some Deaf people devoted their time in the 1980s and 1990s to bringing the Deaf cultural view into the RNID. A campaign to appoint a 'Deaf Chief Now' in 1994 resulted in the appointment of Doug Alker, who had been at the organisation for a decade, as the first ever Deaf CEO. His representation of Deaf issues on cochlear implants and education proved a major threat to the RNID and, after 2 years he was forced to resign, although his management record was unblemished. Recognising that they could not go 'back' to a hearing CEO, the RNID installed an oralist hard-of-hearing person (unknown in the Deaf community) to succeed him. The campaign to reinstate Alker could not gain media attention – indeed in the light of what transpired in the Smithsonian example, their response was very interesting, for they represented the issue as being a squabble between different groups of 'deaf' people, rather than the continuation of an anti-Deaf oralist supremacy. The second half of Alker (2000) is gripping and essential reading for anyone who is interested in how far oralists will go to retain power. As for the new CEO – he was swiftly elevated to membership of the government's Disability Resource Commission. Further honours are expected to follow . . .

Chapter 2

Deafness and Deafhood in Western Civilisation – Towards the Development of a New Conceptual Framework

Colonised man [*sic*] must first recollect himself and critically analyse the results of the influences to which he was subject by the invader, which are reflected in his behaviour, his way of thinking and acting, his conception of the world and society, and his way of assessing the values created by his own people.

Sekou Toure (1974: 63)

In the final analysis, perhaps the most important principle of colonial education was that of capitalist individualism . . . in Africa, both the formal school system and the informal value system of colonialism destroyed social solidarity and promoted the worst form of alienated individualism without social responsibility.

Walter Rodney (1982: xvii)

Introduction

This chapter begins by introducing the central analytical concepts which are applied to the rest of the book, before exploring and establishing the nature of the structural relationships between majority societies and the various groups of Others which they label and administer. Such an analysis enables us to situate and scrutinise the roles of the academy in those processes, thus enabling the creation of a space for Deaf counter-narratives to enter the discourse. These various positions having been rendered visible, Chapters 2 and 3 can then explore how Deaf communities have been conceived and acted upon during the timespan of Western civilisation. Because this history is such a lengthy and complex one, two chapters are required, and this one closes at 1900 at the point when oralist hegemony was achieved.

Theories and Terminology

Before oppressed groups can be understood on their own terms, it is necessary to comprehend the perceptions and constructions of them developed by majority societies. Such a review is particularly important for members of those majorities reading this study, since the process of 'unlearning' and deconstructing one's own culturally inherited perceptions is the precursor to an engaged understanding.

Therefore, in order to appreciate why the concept of Deaf culture is of such critical importance for the present century, it is necessary to understand the historical processes that have contributed to its present status at the cutting edge of thinking about Deaf peoples. Thus we begin a historical review that offers a reading of both Deaf and 'Hearing' perspectives, treating these formally as _discourses_ for the first time.

Discourse analysis

Various domains can be identified within the communication channels and cultural patterns of a society, and it is the sets of dialogues taking place in these domains which we then identify as discourses. As Ashcroft _et al._ (1998: 71) put it:

> The key feature of [this process] is that the world is not simply 'there' to be talked about, rather, it is through discourse itself that the world is brought into being . . . speakers and hearers, writers and readers come to an understanding about themselves, their relationship to each other, and their place in the world.

Each discourse contains its own unspoken rules as to what can or cannot be said and how, when and where. Each, therefore, constructs canons of 'truth' around whatever its participants decide is 'admissable evidence', a process that in the case of certain prestigious discourses, such as those found in universities, medical establishments and communication medias, can be seen as particularly dangerous when unexamined, for these then come to determine what counts as knowledge itself. This is of particular concern when we realise that the convergence of those discourses constitutes a vast, controlling _discursive system._

Lack of awareness of these relationships between power and knowledge can be damaging for the majority society. Foucault (1972, 1979, 1980) is the leading discourse theorist, and his work examines how cultural features such as madness and sexuality have been enshrined in modernist practice, with damaging effect on all members of a society, whether or not they are themselves labelled 'deviant'. Ashcroft _et al._ (1996) contrast the differences between Western and Chinese medical discourses to illustrate how the former, by limiting their discourse to positivism, have excluded many medical avenues which could have benefited Western health.

The beauty of discourse theory is not only that it renders power relationships visible and identifies cultural patterns behind supposed social 'givens', but that in itself it is an egalitarian term. All sets of dialogue, whether taking place in a pub or at a medical conference, are of equal intrinsic merit. Some readers will experience an emotional reaction at this statement – this constitutes an important moment which you can use to begin to unpick your own learned culture and its values. Indeed one can argue that discourse analysis and cultural analysis are inextricably linked; that the former is the key to the latter

The discursive system's control of both power and knowledge is especially threatening to minority groups which embody different value systems. One can make a telling argument for the extent to which control over working-class people has been achieved, not merely by economic constraints, but by the devaluation of their own *discourses*. In devaluing those discourses, routes are then opened up to devalue and then destroy their own *cultures*. Similar arguments can be made in respect of women's traditional discourses (the male establishment of the domain of gynaecology and the relegation of midwives to peripheral importance is just one example) and the treatment of the formerly existing white subaltern peasantry and their own Earth-centred traditions (with their knowledge of herbalism for example).

However far-reaching the effects of these discourses on the quality of life in Western society, their effect is even more intense on groups with specifically different cultures and languages who come into contact with them. Indeed, as we will see, these discourses become the cultural tools by which colonisation is implemented.

Discursive systems are daunting in their overarching reach, but it is important to understand that they are not completely monolithic in their influence. There are always interstices through which (limited) information can be passed to provide tools or weapons for change.

Hegemony

Through such discourse theories, as presented by Foucault (1972) and Bourdieu (1993) for example, we can appreciate that ruling groups maintain power and control, not simply through economic coercion, but also through the development of compelling *ideologies*, that is, belief systems. In developing such theories, the concept of *hegemony*, as initially presented by Gramsci (1985), is important for the development of a more dynamic reading of patterns of social control, since it emphasises that ideologies perpetually compete for acceptance and domination.

Hegemony, therefore, enables us to look beyond simple theories of economic coercion and assign a more active role to disempowered groups and individuals within a society, who must be *persuaded* of the validity of the ruling ideologies. Once ideologies gain hegemony (control), those who command the economic 'superstructure' of a society maximise their persuasive power through their control of crucial sets of discourses. Over time, therefore, many of those who once dissented can come to adopt such ideologies, and even believe that they have always embraced them.

By formalising this dynamic dialectical process, we are able to identify and examine those discourses, their implicit competing ideologies and the relationship of both to the economic superstructure. By rendering these discourses visible we can then begin to develop the tools for deconstructing both the broad patterns and the minute details which lie behind the attitudes, beliefs and policies that have governed Deaf communities worldwide. In so doing, we can create the crucial political and cultural space needed to examine and ratify Deaf communities' own discourses. Having accomplished this, we are then able to return to those dominating discourses and challenge every aspect of their ideologies – not simply their intellectual content but the cultural patterns which lie beneath their forms.

Colonialism

The following reading is also guided by another important set of theories. Having spent a decade studying Deaf and other minority communities in order to formally conceive the treatment visited upon them, I have concluded that the model which offers maximum generative power is that which conceives of Deaf communities as having undergone *colonisation.*

Serious study of colonialism is recent and the discipline of Post-Colonial Studies even more so; thus theorisation is at an early stage. Its central focus is of course those countries and cultures, whose interactions and consequent growth or 'decline' is centred upon Western invasions which were initiated for the purpose of advancing the goals of capitalism. Being a new discipline centred around the traditionally powerless, it is understandably sensitive to maintain the integrity of the terrain it has marked out for itself, and thus it is important to respect Ashcroft *et al.*'s (1995: 2) assertion that:

> The diffusion of the term is now so extreme that it is used to refer to not only vastly different, but even opposed activities. In particular, the tendency to employ the term 'post-colonial' to refer to any kind of

marginality at all runs the risk of denying its basis in the historical process of colonialism.

However, it is also undeniable that in certain instances, domination of one language-using community by another can come to result in a process closely resembling colonialism. The key is in the extent to which we focus on the economic imperative. Lane (1993a) begins the process of examining parallels between colonialism and what he terms 'audism' and locates economic motive in the profits to be made in hearing-aid technology (and now, of course, in cochlear implantation and genetic engineering).[1]

He also begins the process of linking colonialist parallels with the practices of rejecting native sign language use in schools, of which Oralism is but one example. Once initiated, these arguments are most compelling but not developed further. Wrigley (1996) extends one aspect of this analysis by examining the different domains and tropes through which majority society ideologies and discourses about deafness and Deaf communities can be made visible.[2] These groundbreaking works have enabled us to begin not only to examine Deaf communities and their cultures but also to shine a light into the murky cultural beliefs and practices of majority societies themselves. Moreover, as the work of writers like Skliar (1997) indicate, it may be the case that other non-English-speaking societies have begun to make correlations between deafness control systems and colonialism. We might expect to find such literature in countries where Western colonialism's impact has been more profound or radicalism has a higher profile in education (cf. Freire, 1986).

My own starting point, and the point at which the domains of deafness and Deafhood interact with Post-Colonialism,[3] can be summarised by Merry's (1991: 894) assertion that colonialism describes a relationship between two or more groups in an unequal power relationship where

One not only controls and rules the other, but also endeavours to *impose its cultural order* on the subordinate group.

The more closely I examined Deaf cultures, the more obvious it became that these cultures were not only directly affected by majority cultures, but that their own cultural patterns had become shaped by both acquiescence to and resistance against, that cultural domination. Moreover, both sets of discourses, indeed the entire process had been mediated through two sets of languages, and the attempts by one to eradicate the other.

Thus it became clear that my responsibility as one of the few Deaf people who had made it through to academic status lay, first of all, in making these colonial patterns visible. This would then enable a new discourse space to be created in which Deaf people themselves without written language skills could bring their views to the table and at last expect them to be heeded.

But there is also another important set of relationships within colonialism which have so far rarely been examined. These are the relationships between 'lay people' in colonising societies and the power structures which operated colonialism 'on their behalf'. If we are to appreciate the full extent to which colonisation operates on Deaf communities, we need to find an analytical framework which will recognise and situate such lay people, and this is approached in the next headed section.

Even though colonialism is traditionally seen as economically driven, those who have been colonised affirm that culture is often the battleground upon which the colonial hegemony is established, and that colonial liberation or independence cannot be successful without the 'de-colonisation of the mind' (Wa Thiong'O 1986). Thus, even though Deaf communities do not appear to constitute colonies in the traditional sense, there is in my opinion a compelling case for presenting such a reading in order to see what it might teach us.

Being mindful of my status as a Deaf person, and my experience of Deaf and hearing cultures worldwide, I note that the time is also right to offer a Deaf historical reading, a *counter-narrative* which disrupts what many Deaf people would call the 'Hearing' hegemony. There have been very few Deaf attempts to sustain such a reading across the timespan of Western civilisation, yet unless we attempt it, it will be all too easy to continue with an unthinking acceptance of the reductionist readings, the language and the terminology which is used in those discourses. In order to counter these, we stand in need of a 'larger' vision of what Deaf people and their communities are, have been and can become. Such a vision has to be centred within the 'Deaf experience' and to draw on it in order to find a framework for that new reading.

In these post-modernist times, I am mindful of the dangers of falling into *essentialism*, that is, to proceed too far in the direction of assuming a cultural 'essence', whether that be Black, White, Female, Male – or 'Deaf' and 'Hearing'. However, I am also aware of the ironic timing of post-modernism – that is, at the very moment when the discourse of oppressed groups at last becomes visible and they are finally able to position themselves as a counter-narrative to White or Hearing supremacy, that their discourses risk being dismissed along with the Grand Narratives themselves! As Hawksworth (1989) puts it, 'in a world of radical inequality, relativist resignation supports the status quo'.

I contend, therefore, that although at a later stage it is absolutely necessary to examine and qualify minority group narratives, an academic space must, in the first instance, be established which recognises the existence of 'counter-narratives' in themselves, a pole around which resistance thinking can even be organised. Thus in the liberation struggles of some groups, a strong case can be made for what Spivak (1990) calls 'strategic essentialism'. This then creates a countervailing social, cultural and intellectual force which can then create new spaces for more sophisticated liberatory discourses to flourish. I hope, then, that in succeeding years, others may be able to develop readings which refine and 'de-essentialise' this one, as far as that is necessary.

The Deafhood concept

It is from within this new space that I offer the terminological construction that is central to this whole book. Present-day ideologies concerning Deaf people are characterised by the term 'deafness'. Recently there has been dissatisfaction in some quarters of the Deaf community with this term (Bienvenu, 1991; Moore & Levitan, 1992), since the term is medically oriented.

In order to create a space within which Deaf people's own self-conceptions can be situated and examined, another term is needed, and this I have designated as *Deafhood*. It is important to understand that this is *not* a monolithic concept. Indeed, the rest of the book explores different readings of Deafhood by varying sectors within Deaf communities. But, just as Deaf history is framed and penetrated from without by discourses on deafness, so the internal frame of Deafhood, looking outwards, can render visible those unwritten Deaf discourses, and thus both encompass and for the first time, go beyond those framings. In so doing, one is essentially in search of a *Deaf epistemology*, that is, Deaf ways of being in the world, of conceiving that world and their own place within it (both in actuality and in potentiality). It will emerge that a crucial aspect of that epistemology is that it is not simply oppositional, but that it examines and presents the nature and significance of Deaf people's relationships to each other.

The subaltern

It is crucial to any analysis, whether of Deaf or hearing communities, that we do not assume them to form a monolithic, undifferentiate 'block' of experience. Yet conventional definitions of class are a Western construction which we cannot assume applies automatically to the Deaf experience. Thus I have adopted the term 'subaltern', derived from Gramsci, which refers to any group of people denied meaningful access to 'hegemonic' power.

The term itself was later taken up by post-colonial studies in South Asian society, and a series of five 'Subaltern Studies' volumes was produced by Guha (1982). This work is important for its insistence on correcting the imbalance of focus in academic work towards the version of history written by élite groups within post-colonial India; their concern was to show that subaltern groups had played an important role in resisting the British, but had effectively been 'written out' of history by the élite groups who controlled access to academic domains.

It is vital, then, when constructing a Deaf counter-narrative, to ensure that the thoughts and actions of those subaltern Deaf people (that is those whose lack of English-literacy skills rendered them effectively monolingual) are not only captured, but set in relationship to the actions of any (comparatively élite) bilingual Deaf people. In this respect also, the data chapters 7–9 expressly focus on Deaf subalterns who wished me to set in writing their views concerming a wide range of issues. As the book progresses, it will be seen that I propose refinements to the whole area of subaltern theory based on what can be understood of Deaf communities' social structures.

I also begin to construct another kind of reading for subaltern, one which represents the hearing 'lay person' when faced either with the power blocs within their own society which cannot simply be read in class terms, or when they are confronted by the various specialisms which do not allow them access to Deaf communities and their knowledge.

The role of lay people

The counter-narrative also highlights two key features of colonialism of Deaf peoples – the ideologies of specialism and paternalism. As will be seen, both are predicated on the idea of an unthinking or uncaring public from whom Deaf people need to be protected in the name of various skills claimed by those colonialists. It is my experience, and the experience of numerous other Deaf people, both now and through the ages, that this belief is at least partially founded on self-interest, and that what I term 'lay people' (i.e. those who do not work in Deaf-related fields) have often reacted far more positively to Deaf people than has been admitted, and can be drawn into the Deaf struggle as allies – provided that access to Deaf people's experiences and beliefs can be created. I have spent much of the past 25 years, in conjunction with Deaf and hearing colleagues, attempting to create such access, such spaces, in various domains and communication media. This book attempts to formalise a space in which such lay / specialist distinctions can be made, and thus hopefully encourage, empower and refine lay involvement with Deaf communities.

It is important for the lay reader to understand that virtually all discourses about Deaf people have been conceived, controlled and written by people who were not themselves Deaf. Consequently, as with other minority groups, the majority of legislation constructed from these discourses has maintained an ethnocentric bias. In reading those external perceptions of Deaf individual and collective life which have affected Western Deaf communities, it must be emphasised that to account for all the relevant discourses over 5,000 years and across several continents is impractical at this stage and inevitably speculative. This reading, therefore, summarises some of the main patterns in those discourses which are of greatest relevance to the Deaf communities of the present day. Before doing so, however, it is necessary to identify some general principles governing the wider situation in which Deaf people find themselves.

Majority Societies and the 'Other'

Western majority societies, in dealing with people whom they wished to govern but with whom they have no personal interaction, (referred to here as 'the Others'), delegated that responsibility to specific sectors of their societies, which then developed their own discourses to rationalise and justify their actions. These Others include colonised groups (as the term is traditionally used), working-class and peasant groups, language and religious minorities, women, gays and lesbians, prisoners, mental health patients and Deaf and disabled people.

I have identified the following domains within the Western discursive system in order to generalise across different groups of Others throughout historical time and place. Treating them as individual and autonomous is a methodological convenience that I hope others will refine, so that these highly complex and interrelated processes can be further deconstructed.

- *Political and administrative discourses.* These carry executive managerial responsibilities for the Others, being occupied with deciding which aspects of the following competing discourses should be selected to justify their administrative positions, roles, duties and priorities.
- *Academic discourses.* These attempt either to comprehend the Others or, consciously or unconsciously, to rationalise perceptions and treatment of them by other sectors of society. Only recently have they begun to deconstruct the cultural assumptions and political forces by which they come to construct those rationalisations.
- *Specialist discourses.* These have a similar rationale to the previous ones, but are located within professions designated specifically to analyse and 'treat' individual groups of Others. The prestige and power they come to wield in such domains enables them to either bypass the academy or maintain at best a tangential relationship with it, placing an emphasis on practical 'solutions' rather than broader theoretical speculation. As will be seen, where such speculation

exists, it either appears to show little concern for actual outcomes or develops its own quasi-academic methodologies to prove its own theories.

- *Medical discourses*. Although medical discourses apply themselves to all sectors of a population, some of their domains are focused on biological characteristics of the Others. They are identified here as a sub-category of specialist discourse because of their particular influence on certain groups of Others, including Deaf people.
- *Scientific discourses*. Scientific discourses, originating both within the academy and in wider society, are also applied to all sectors of a population, but in the case of Western societies contain discourses of special relevance to Deaf people and certain groups of Others.
- *Media discourses*. The media can be defined as channels through which all other discourses flow and are disseminated to the wider public. They are also impelled by their own particular ideologies and economic forces, and thus contain their own agendas for comprehending the Others. During these processes they of course decide which aspects of the Others' own beliefs and actions should be permitted to be disseminated and in what forms.

The Discursive System, Lay People and Deaf/Disabled People

Each of the discourses described here carries varying degrees of status and power and are constructed differently for each group of Others, although patterns of similarity can be identified. Taken collectively they represent what Lane terms a 'bio-power' discursive system as it applies to Deaf and disabled people, an extension of Foucault's concept of 'bio-power' as representing the nexus of medical, legal and political authority. The system forms a web of dialogues and practices which valorise the most powerful sections of societies, other discourses often go unrecognised simply because they are assigned little or no place in this web.

I will briefly summarise the historical development of these discourses as they apply to Deaf and disabled people so that the positioning of lay discourses can be better understood.

Building on Oliver (1990), we can identify four simplified stages. The first, of which we know little, is characterised by varying degrees of acceptance or otherwise of Deaf and disabled people by lay people in villages and town societies; the desire for custodial care is rarely mentioned.

The second, the initially *ad hoc* development of asylums and institutions beginning in the 17th century, is characterised by voluntary contribution or religious commitment. These were often sited within a discourse of philanthropism, with only the most basic beginnings made for a theoretical discourse of specialism.

The third, emerging with the nation-state and the tremendous centralisation of state powers, created new professional classes given authority on behalf of the nation to analyse and categorise those deemed in need of 'help' and to propose strategies for administering and financing that assistance. In theory these were advisory proposals to be subjected to stages within the democratic process which, by definition, therefore included *feedback from lay people*. In actuality these did not take place, and discourse was virtually confined to professionals, wealthy philanthropists and politicians, mostly from the same social classes.

This closed circle of feedback resulted in a petrified fourth stage during the 20th century in which there was no longer the expectation of a lay role in what had become an institionalised discursive system. Specialism and professionalism thus developed a mystique of its own, creating a free hand to exponentially increase the numbers required to manage the Others and develop training systems which inculcated lay applicants into their ideologies. Any lay knowledge or experience was deemed inadmissable evidence as it were; moreover *by delegating responsibility to the professionals, they were deemed as having given consent to the discursive system* and thus surrendering any responsibilities that they might have had.

The removal of lay people by the fourth stage had severe consequences for the Others. If they disagreed with the policies and structures imposed upon them, they faced four significant obstacles in making their views known to those 'on the outside'.

The first were the barriers surrounding physical and communication access to lay people, which were manned by the professionals and wealthy patrons. Second, the latter controlled access to the media, which was consequently disinclined to disseminate the views of the Others or of their lay allies. This, in turn, led to numbers of lay people becoming a third obstacle, once they became accustomed to believing what was disseminated. The fourth obstacle then became many of the Others themselves, who were inculcated into a system of 'learned helplessness'. When, at a later and more recent stage, it became politically expedient to obtain representatives from the Others, these were selected according to their willingness to cooperate with the system in exchange for small measures of power or prestige.

In many respects then, these developments parallel classic colonialist patterns and can therefore be described within that paradigm.

In drawing Deaf and disabled people into the same analysis, I do not intend to make a case for the latter as a colonised entity. That is for those more qualified than me to explore. As Chapter 3 explains, there are crucial differences between Deaf communities and people with disabilities. In grouping them together in this section, I merely wish to sketch some basic parallels in how they are perceived and administered by external forces.

Lay discourses and the Others

It is the contention of this study that lay discourses are not only historically important, but have relevance for the future development of more democratic strategies which both lay people and the Others can utilise. Moreover, it is indicative of the lack of recognition of these discourses that they have no name of their own. Terms such as 'consumers', 'members of the public', 'the workers' and 'ordinary people' are either theoretically inappropriate or have themselves been conceived in an *ad hoc* manner outside academic paradigms. Later in the book I will suggest that Gramsci's (1985) term 'subaltern' might well be usefully applied within the Deaf domain, but it would be too simplistic to use it here to encompass all the varying types of Others. Thus, I use the term 'lay people' virtually by default, until such theoretical terminology is developed.

It is necessary for studies aspiring to standards of academic objectivity to deconstruct the complex series of relations by which lay people have embraced, lived with or tolerated the Others. A similar process is necessary where they have chosen to avoid the Others, or been encouraged to do so, sometimes against their will or better judgement, by the discursive systems. In reviewing the historical discourses relating to Deaf people therefore, reference will be made throughout to the relationship of lay people to those discourses.

Academic study and the Others

The production of knowledge, its ties to power relations and the expansion of academic institutions alongside the development of the discursive system of the fourth stage, has resulted in research on the Others (where they were deemed worthy of it at all) as being framed almost entirely within existing discursive systems. In a book such as this, therefore, attempts to present data from lay or subaltern discourses must also deconstruct the academic production of knowledge itself as well as the theories which they contain.

In theory there is nothing intrinsically 'wrong' in having one sector of society speak for another if the policies carried out reflect the views and wishes of both lay and 'consumer' sectors. However, since the 1960s, fringe sections of the academic establishment have begun the process of evaluating specialist views of the 'Other' in society, and found them wanting, even within the terms proposed by the specialists themselves.

Even though many of these evaluations have been based on Marxist and other socialist paradigms, and although they represent an advance on classical Marxism, they have unfortunately reproduced the fundamental imbalance of an academia as a Subject which studies the Other as Object. Because their discourse is compromised in this way and because they are influenced by the wider discursive system, they have not recognised the importance of the views either of lay people or the Others. For that reason I refer to them here as 'liberal ideologies'.[4]

During these past 30 years, ruling hegemonies have been challenged by the Others themselves, beginning with the decolonisation struggles of ethnic groups and minorities, and extending to others such as feminism and gay / lesbian struggles. These 'liberation ideologies' have recently been partially adopted by academia and majority communities. However, as yet they have not been extended to recognition of Deaf liberation ideologies, who thus continue to be vulnerable to both conservative and liberal academic discourses.

Since policy change is guided by academic research, the concept of research itself – how it is defined, the frameworks within which it is conducted, and who it should be conducted by – has come in for closer examination by liberation ideologies. This study is therefore framed as an example of that process.

Two processes can be identified. Where such research is undertaken by the specialist or the Others, the requirement is that it should be *Other-centred*; that is, they should seek to understand these perspectives *in their own terms* and to set it down in forms appropriate to those terms. From this perspective, both liberal ideologies and specialist hegemonies are then required to make explicit the values, beliefs and assumptions upon which their work is based, so that they can be measured against those terms in open debate.

Once these two processes have been established within academia, there is finally an opportunity for genuine academic dialogue to take place, out of which Other-centred policies can be proposed and developed. During this dialogue it is also necessary to re-evaluate and re-establish the place of lay discourses in these processes. Once this is underway, attention can be turned to the role of the lay public and its involvement in these dialogues and policies. This latter point is, as will be seen later, of crucial importance when considering the particular situation of Deaf people.

The consequences of Otherness for Deaf communities

The preceding sections encompass attitudes towards all people who constitute the Other in Western cultures. With these general principles in mind, we can now examine more closely how these inherited cultural attitudes have influenced views held towards the British Deaf community today by examining those discourses existing throughout Western history which make specific reference to Deaf people. Because of the complexity and sheer historical range of this subject, any categories identified here are not intended to be congruent with those described earlier. Nevertheless, they can be cross-referenced to identify the forces behind the historical routes which have led up to the contemporary situation.

Majority Discourses and Deaf Communities

Tracing links across milennia and continents is problematic at the present time, both because of the paucity of research and the related poverty of resources available to do so. The degrees to which each era influences those which follow is also difficult to establish; I will therefore delineate certain epochs, societies or philosophical categories in historical order, treating each as separate and suggesting linkage where plausible.

In attempting such a reading whilst trying to identify polarised ideologies, this counter-narrative constructs the basic paradigm of positive *versus* negative perceptions of Deaf people or, as Van Gils (1998) amusingly suggests, *surdophiles* and *surdophobes*. It is important to note that these two perspectives are not mutually exclusive – it is in the nature of theories of discourse (and post-Lacanian 'multiple identity' theories) that *contrasting or contradictory beliefs can exist within individuals according to the relevant degrees of influence and history underlying each set of discourses which is acting upon them.*

The reading which follows is proposed as an initial stage in developing a Deafhood-oriented reading of Deaf history. As such, it is placed in opposition to traditional deafness readings. The latter contains two related strands. One focuses on the medical perceptions and treatment of deafness down the ages, with a focus on the organs of hearing and speech, and does not perceive any significant cultural differences between people who have developed hearing impairments, and those who were born deaf. The other consists of a 'Grand Narrative', where Deaf communities are constructed solely as the individual end product of a lineage of distinguished hearing educators, for example Farrah (1923). Although late 19th century Deaf discourse indicates that Deaf people were very much aware of a quite different perception of Deaf history, one rooted in their clubs, schools and organisations (*British Deaf-Mute*, 1892–3, for example), this was not acknowledged by either of the deafness readings. This pattern was not confined to the UK. Truffaut (1993: 114), in surveying the general European situation, confirms that 'the history of Deaf education written by hearing people stood in for true Deaf history'.

The key observation of those who placed themselves within this Grand Narrative is that before the existence of 'their' schools for the Deaf, Deaf people were barely able to attain a semblance of humanity. Examples of this belief (or, as may be plausibly argued, self-justification) are numerous, but I will cite just one example to give an indication of the strength with which this view was manifested:

> Up to this point [the establishment of Deaf education] the deaf person is a mere ambulatory machine whose constitution (as regards his behaviour) is inferior to that of animals. In saying that he is primitive, we are still underestimating his pitifulness, for he is not even the equal of primitive man in morality or in communication. (Sicard, in Lane and Philip, 1984: 85.)

As will be seen, the convergence of these two strands above during the 20th century reinforced this denial in forming a construction of Deaf people as atomised beings with no intrinsic connection to each other. By conveying this belief throughout the education of successive generations of Deaf children, by destroying Deaf art and lierature (Mirzoeff, 1995), and by reinforcing it with the ideology of Oralism, that is, the banning of sign languages and Deaf teachers from Deaf education, they began to convince Deaf people themselves that they did not have any history of their own.

It is only with the Deaf Resurgence of the last 20 years, and the work of Harlan Lane (1984, 1993a, Lane & Philip, 1984 etc), that a renewal of interest in Deaf history has begun to re-create the Deafhood tradition of the last century. This has spawned many valuable works and historical societies. However, the vast majority of these are pragmatic in intent, seeking to identify or rediscover notable Deaf individuals, groups and movements. They have not yet turned their attention to a sustained analysis of the total process, to formally assert an alternative reading. It is in this spirit that the counter-narrative here is offered.

For the post-modernists among us, I would like to emphasise that I am very aware of the extent to which this counter-narrative is centred around a singularity of Deafhood. This is quite deliberate, since the concern of Deaf communities, like other minority communities, is to clearly establish their traditions in the face of the overwhelming assimilatory, even ethnocidal energies which they have been forced to contend with for hundreds of years. Once a clearly positioned 'centre' is established, then refinements can be made. The rapid changes in Deaf communities over the last 20 years have produced numerous such refinements, and these are described in detail in the second volume of the series. Those who are interested in the latter may wish to explore Wrigley's (1996) valuable, if somewhat critical outsider-observations.

A key factor in this counter-narrative is to bring into discourse the types of life situations in which Deaf people found themselves. We may therefore posit the following situations prior to the establishment of Deaf schools:

(1) the isolated Deaf person within a small community, especially rural environments;
(2) small numbers of Deaf people in those environments, such as families with several Deaf children, or higher proportions due to genetic factors relating to closed community marriages. (In some of these environments, the percentage of Deaf members may be such that numbers of the hearing members use forms of sign language as one of the languages of the community);
(3) gatherings of Deaf people in larger, more urban communities (these might include Deaf people from the first two categories who migrated to those communities); and
(4) gatherings of Deaf people within specialised urban groupings, including artistic communities, monasteries and royal courts.

The importance of the latter three types, which I classify as *ur*-Deaf communities for the purpose of this reading, is that once Deaf people are gathered together in any number, they will begin to develop their own sign language communication and to inform or even educate each other. Moreover, in some of these circumstances, it is known that Deaf communities transmitted their skills down the generations (Miles, 2000). We may therefore question the extent to which the raison d'être of the Grand Narrative is actually true or applicable.

With these factors in mind then, we may begin the reading.

Deaf People and Graeco-Roman Discourses

It is probable that Deaf people who communicate by gesture or sign have existed as part of humanity from its inception; in the West, the first written evidence of their existence can be found at the dawn of Western literacy itself, with the rise of the Mediterrean societies of the fifth century BC.

The accounts of Deaf people most often quoted from this era originate with Graeco-Roman philosophers, who found the existence of Deaf people illuminating when considering the wider issues of human thought and behaviour. They philosophised about the nature of Deaf people's existence and their place in society, a process which eventually resulted in the creation of laws and judicial codes relating to them.

Aristotle, according to Farrah (1923: 2), states that 'hearing is the sense of sound, and sound the vehicle of thought; hence the blind are more intelligent than deaf-mutes'. By contrast, Socrates refers to Deaf people more positively:

If we had neither voice nor tongue, and yet wished to manifest things to one another, should we not, like those which are at present mute, endeavour to signify our meaning by the hands, head and other parts of the body? (Hough, 1983: 38)

Of these two perceptions, it appears that it was Aristotle's views which held sway amongst those with power and influence, as Farrah (1923: 1) describes:

The authority of Aristotle . . . was for centuries sovereign, and it was increased when his system was bound up with that of the Christian Church. We therefore find in the early accounts of the deaf that the writers refer to his dicta on the question of their capacity for instruction, and this generally to their prejudice.

Nevertheless, Augustine in the fourth century AD, philosophises positively about Deaf people in Chapter 18 of *De quantitae animae liber unus*:

Imagine, then, one born and brought up in a place where men do not speak, but rather by nods and the movements of their limbs convey to one another the thoughts they wish to expresss; do you not think he will do likewise . . . Have you not seen then at Milan, a youth most fair in form and most courteous in demeanor, who was yet deaf and dumb to such a degree that he could neither understand others, nor communicate what he himself desired, except by means of bodily movements? For this man is very well known. And I myself know a certain peasant who . . . had four or more sons and daughters . . . who were Deaf mutes. For what does it matter, as he grows up, whether he speaks or makes gestures, *since both these pertain to the soul.* (in Van Cleve & Crouch, 1989: 5–6)

Although these two contrasting positions are, by definition, objectifying Deaf people, a closer examination of the texts reveals an interesting distinction and one of great importance for understanding later discourses.

Those who perceived Deaf people positively appear to be aware of their existence *as a group*. In other words, by observing Deaf people's signed communication with each other, these philosophers became aware that Deaf people, once gathered together, were able to express their ideas just like anyone else, and indeed that their visuo-gestural mode of communication might be perceived as offering potential benefit for humanity as a whole. In some respects, then, this can be seen as centring discourse on Deaf people around a culturo-linguistic model.

Those who perceived them negatively seem only to be aware of *isolated Deaf individuals*, who, lacking a peer group with which to communicate, appeared to function in the world in a condition akin to the 'enfant sauvage'. This lack of awareness of the importance of sign language or peer socialisation thus encouraged a discourse of Deaf people as human beings suffering from a lack or impairment, a deficit model.

However, we should also note that it is as yet unclear how these differing discourses played themselves out in respect of the ones which maintained political power. We know that Justinian law from the sixth century AD devises five classes of deafness and prohibits the class of deaf-mute from birth from making a will, manumitting, contracting and being witnesses. In contrast, those who became deaf-mute, if they had acquired a knowledge of letters, were permitted to exercise all these rights – by writing.

Descriptions such as these are the tip of a fascinating, but unexplored iceberg. First of all, we can conclude, as with Socrates' example, that Deaf people must have been sufficiently numerous to be the subject of philosophers and law-makers. It is therefore quite possible that *ur*-Deaf communities also existed.

Second, since literacy was until the 19th century largely confined to members of the ruling and monastic classes, laws such as these found their greatest resonance within those classes. They had particular significance relating to questions of upper-class primogeniture, since obviously there must have been occasions when Deaf literacy was vital to a family's maintenance of their socio-political position. We shall later recognise the importance of this as it relates to both deafness and Deafhood.

Third, because there is so little historical data, one is forced to use one's own imagination or, I propose, one's Deaf subaltern intuition when speculating further. Since we know now that recognition of deafness in children is often delayed, it is possible to conceive of situations where one might attempt to 'hide the evidence' by treating a born-deaf child as one adventitiously deafened. At the very least, one might strive to teach that born-deaf child to write, and then argue proof of their intelligence upon that basis.

Deaf People in Judaic Discourse

The Judaic literature of the pre-Christian era makes 387 references to Deaf people in the Torah and Mishnah, revealing a complex range of attitudes divided into three schools of thought. Diversity of opinion is a strongly valued part of Jewish culture, so whilst negative views are held by some, the general discourse not only protected Deaf people and allowed them to marry using their own language, but allowed them to prove their abilities by their actions:

> Rabbi Yehuda calls to attention a number of well-known personages of his time, who were Deaf Mutes but who neverthless held highly responsible positions which demanded great learning and understanding in the Temple of Jerusalem . . . who were in charge of purification. (Zwiebel, [1993: 407])

Again we encounter the first of our themes; that Deaf people must have been sufficiently numerous for the literature to be so extensive. Furthermore, because of the detail given in rulings concerning Deaf marriages, we may again feel fairly confident about the existence of *ur* Deaf communities. Zwiebel's conclusion is reasonable:

> As time goes by, the reasons given for seeing the Deaf as possessing a cognitive level like the one of hearing people are based also on cases of professionals who proved through their deeds that they possessed high reasoning powers.

Jewish discourses also considers Deaf people's existential state. In *Exodus* 4.11 we find God's reply to Moses:

> Who hast made men's mouth? or who maketh the dumb, or deaf, or the seeing, or the blind? Have not I, the Lord?

As Van Cleve and Crouch (1989: 2) put it: 'The passages state unequivocally, that some people are deaf because the Lord made them that way . . . it is what God has chosen.'

We can note that the Jewish discourse differs from that of the Graeco-Roman by allowing refinements to be made to certain attitudes and aspects of the law according to emerging evidence. Given this, it is no surprise to find that, as Zweibel (1993: 408) asserts, 'the views expressed in Jewish sources always referred to environmental deprivation rather than deafness as such'.

There is thus reasonable ground for concluding that aspects of both Jewish and Graeco-Roman discourses (1) conceived of Deaf people as a group and (2) accepted that communication *within the group by means of a common language* held at least the potential to enable them to attain their full humanity, however that might be variously defined.

Deaf People and Early Christian Discourse

However, when one comes to the New Testament and to Christianity, a negative perspective begins to prevail. In this religion, deafness is portrayed 'as an indication that an individual [significantly, not a group] has been possessed by a demonic, evil being' (Van Cleve & Crouch, 1989: 3). Within Christianity, then, deafness is used as a vehicle to help 'prove' the supernatural powers of Jesus, and is thus closely tied to the raison d'être of the religion itself. Paul's Epistle to the Romans expanded this perspective – 'Faith cometh by hearing, and hearing by the word of God' – thus excluding Deaf people from even the possibility of becoming Christians.

Somehow in the intervening centuries, despite Augustine's positive assessment, the central Christian discourse around Deaf people has been represented by educators of the Deaf as one of isolated individuals requiring either healing – the deficit model – or exorcism, which might be termed a 'demonological model'. As Christianity spread, it nevertheless developed a multiple of perspectives, and some exceptions to these models emerged, as will be seen later. However, the New Testament serves as the reference point against which such perspectives had to be argued. A notable example of this can be found in Bede's account of St John of Beverley in the eighth century, where he supposedly 'cured' a Deaf youth. The resonance of such examples in the discourse of the educators of the Deaf can be seen in the number of Deaf schools and missions which still bear St John's name today, and in the number of magazines whose title is *Ephphatha* – the word Jesus reputedly used to bid the demons leave the Deaf body.

Deaf People and Monastic Discourses

Over the next thousand years, there are very few references to Deaf people currently known to us. This represents a major interruption to discourses, and one might speculate that the subject was deemed of little importance. However, there are significant exceptions. Lane (1984) mentions that in the 12th century, Deaf people were permitted to marry by Papal decree provided that their signing proved that they understood the concepts involved. This suggests that the more positive of the earlier readings still held good 600 years later. But it is when we consider the relationship between monastic orders and Deaf people that the picture becomes particularly interesting.

Evidence of this relationship has recently emerged (de Saint Loup, 1993). In some cases, wealthy people paid for their Deaf children to be looked after by these orders, whilst in others this may have been a voluntary agreement. Williams (in Fischer and Lane, 1993) also notes that in some cases, this arrangement was extended to the mute poor'. Since we know that silence, and consequent visuo-gestural systems, existed in some orders, it is possible to suggest that these might have been cross-fertilised by Deaf people's own sign languages. Miles (1988) and Hough (1983) trace these systems to 529 AD and 910 AD respectively, so there was certainly plenty of time for such relationships to develop.

Certainly, in the thousand-plus years that literacy was entrusted largely to these orders, we might expect to find some educated Deaf people, and Truffaut (1993: 15) identifies one, Etienne de Fay who, in the words of a contemporary,

> besides reading and writing, knew architecture, Euclidean geometry, mechanics, drawing, architecture, holy and profane history, especially of France.

Indeed, de Fay's architectural skills were considerable, as he was entrusted with the responsibility for designing the rebuilding of the abbey, and the work carried out under his supervision. He was also the abbey procurator, whose responsibilities ranged from planning the abbey's supplies to the furnishing of its libraries with thousands of books.

The significance of the latter role is that it suggests he was able to go out into the wider society to view and obtain these items. His lack of speech was therefore not seen as an obstacle to this work, which must have been carried out in sign-mime and writing. This, in turn, suggests that social attitudes may well have been positive enough for the wishes of such a Deaf person to be acceded to.

De Fay's existence is also important because we are told that he was known as a teacher of Deaf children who had been placed at the Abbey, although at this stage we know only of those whose parents paid for such a placement. Nevertheless, it opens up another dimension for us to consider – that certain *ur*-Deaf communities might well have been sufficiently large to embrace inter-generational instruction. At this historical moment of writing, the details we have are insufficient to confirm these connections, but they lie tantalisingly almost within our reach. Certainly, there is sufficient evidence to indicate that monastic discourse may not have accepted either of the two interpretations of the Christian discourses which have been held up to us by the educators of the Deaf. It is not as yet possible to speculate whether these were influenced by any discourses on deafness from Celtic cultures or the 'Old Religion'. Nevertheless, given the vital importance of the monastic network in preserving literacy and culture throughout the centuries of the 'Dark Ages', it is possible that they sustained interdenominational relationships with, and discourse about, Deaf people.

Lay Attitudes to Deaf People up to the Enlightenment

The status of gesture in lay societies

Thus far in history, we have virtually no evidence of lay attitudes and discourses on deafness. However, it is important to note that there are an abundance of references to the importance and status of visuo-gestural communication modes throughout these time periods. Presneau (1993: 413–6) describes the widespread use of secret hand-codes, the importance of gesture in masked balls, and their role in one of the most popular and enduring artforms, the *Commedia dell'arte*. Indeed, Pierre Desloges, writer of the earliest known Deaf book, states that he learned sign language from a hearing Italian member of one such company.

de Saint Loup (1993: 387) bases his own observations on a large number of paintings, sculptures and other forms of visual representation. Included in his findings are the widespread use of hand signs in paintings and illustrations; one showing God and Adam 'signing' to each other. Hand signs were also used in texts to mark numbers and paragraphs rather than Roman numerals. It is thus possible to speculate that respect for these visuo-gestural modes amongst a wide range of lay people may in subsequent research indicate an encouraging climate for the acceptance of Deaf people, who after all were prime exponents of these skills. Mirzoeff (1995) appears to confirm this degree of respect and acceptance, extensively researching and illustrating the importance of gesture both within and without art, and gives several examples of popular plays from as far back as the 16th century which contain Deaf characters.

As we move into the Renaissance era, we find increasing references to Deaf people which give further clues as to their positive acceptance by numbers of lay people. Gannon (1981: xxv) notes the existence of a Deaf poet, Joachin Dubellay (1522–60), including his intriguing *Hymn to Deafness*. Deusing, who described sign language in some depth in a book published in 1656, describes a Deaf man attending public sermons with his wife and servant as interpreters. Van Cleve and Crouch (1993) draw attention to the existence of a servant indicating status and point out that Deusing's manner of description suggests that this event would not have been considered remarkable in its time – that 'it would be readily accepted as within the range of his readers' normal experience' (p. 18). Zwiebel (1993: 409)also describes three Polish merchants of the same century who were considered well educated and used to conducting business in mime and sign.

I have no doubt that as time goes on, we will not only locate more examples of Deaf individuals, communities and their interaction with lay people, but we will gain a more sophisticated reading of the role and importance of gesture in human societies. In turn, it is not unreasonable to speculate that the two sets of example will turn out to have significant links to each other, thus shedding more light on positive Deaf-lay relationships.

Deaf artists and lay attitudes

But there are three other sets of examples which carry especial reso-nance. The first is the existence of several Deaf artists in Spain and Italy. Of these, the most famous is Juan de Navarette, known as El Mudo, the court painter to King Philip of Spain from 1568 until his death 11 years later. Bernard (1993: 79) states that he 'was very knowledgable about mythology and history because he read widely' and it is known that he used to sign with most people, and used interpreters for his business dealings (which made them legally acceptable). During this time, there were other Deaf people in and around this court, including Deaf noblemen (Plann, 1997), which makes it possible to speculate about the existence of a small Deaf community in Madrid.

We can perhaps go further. De Navarette (along with many hearing artists), travelled to other artistic centres of excellence, and spent 20 years working in Rome, Florence and Venice. He even trained a painter, Hererro, who married his daughter. For a long time, he was the only known Deaf painter. But recent evidence is beginning to emerge concerning other Deaf artists of these times. Di Betto Biagi, a fellow student of Raphael (who is himself known for his painting 'The Dumb Woman'), painted frescoes which still exist in the Sistine Chapel, as well as works in the apartments of three popes. Bernard also records the achievements of other Deaf painters, such as Gaspar, Lopez, Pedro and Del Arco in Spain, and Sarti, Como and Christophoro in Italy. The latter was well known in Milan; his father was trained by Leonardo da Vinci, who had this to say as part of his own meth-odology:

> The forms of men must have attitudes appropriate to the activities that they engage in, so that when you see them you will understand what they think or say. This can be done by copying the motions of the dumb, who speak with movements of their hands and eyes and eyebrows and their whole person . . . Do not laugh at me because I propose a teacher without speech to you . . . he will teach you better through facts than will all the other masters through words. (in Mirzoeff, 1995: 13)

Because the evidence of the existence of these Deaf artists, and their rela-tionships with hearing fellow artists, is not only very recent, but quite extensive, we may eventually be able to posit communicative links between them across these two countries at least. Mirzoeff himself posits that da Vinci's views extended to France, where Montaigne can then be found writing constructively about Deaf people in extending these affirmative views to the field of philosophy. This accumulative evidence supports a reading of at least certain sectors of lay people being positively disposed towards Deaf people and their skills. During the 17th to 19th century, the numbers of Deaf artists grew exponentially, and if Mirzoeff's extensive research on French artists is anything to go by, further research in other countries may furnish equally powerful examples. These numbers may not only indicate a latent Deaf facility for visually-oriented skills, but also, in an age of continuing general illiteracy, illustrate one indubitable way for Deaf people to prove their essential humanity in the eyes of any that may have doubted this.

Although this reading of Deaf history cannot linger at any one site, no matter how fascinating it might be, it is important to draw the reader's attention to Mirzoeff's text. Unfortunately at present little known in either deafness or Deafhood discourse, the sheer depth and breadth of his examination of the relationships between Deaf artists, lay people, philosophers and educational institutions illustrates the difficulties in attempting an overall analysis of all the discourses we have so far brought to light. From his research, however, he is able to confidently assert:

> Deaf artists played a central role in the deaf community, which formulated a cultural politics around both sign languages and art. The deaf used the cachet of high art to resist being categorised as 'primitive', and as a means of demonstrating their intellectual capacities. (1995: 3)

Deaf people in Turkish Ottoman society

For the second example, we must shift our gaze to the Turkish Ottoman court. The evidence which has just appeared is in itself a good example of how research is emerging all the time to confirm a greater role for Deaf people in history than has previously been realised. For the past 50 years there have been rumours of Deaf involvement in the Ottoman court, but it is only with Miles' (2000) dispassionate research that this can be confirmed.[5] As he summarises:

> Deaf people, known as 'mutes' worked in the Turkish Ottoman court from the fifteenth to the twentieth century in various roles . . . Their signing system became popular, was used regularly by hearing people including successive Sultans, and was reportedly capable of expresing ideas of whatever complexity. The Ottoman court mutes' early achievements, at a time when deaf education and employment was barely considered feasible in Western Europe, have been obscured through literary critics' reactions against later travellers' stereotyping of Middle Eastern countries. (p. 1)

Although there is some suggestion that Deaf people may have been court members for frivolous reasons, along with dwarves and buffoons, this is far outweighed by evidence which suggests that sign language held high status, especially in periods where spoken language use by the Sultan and the higher nobility was regarded as 'undignified'. Ricaut (1668) states:

This language of the Mutes is so much in fashion in the Ottoman Court, that none almost but can deliver his sense in it, and is of much use to those who attend the Presence of the Grand Signoir, before whom it is not reverent or seemly so much as to whisper. (in Miles, 2000: 10)

As many as 200 Deaf people at any one time were not only employed as servants, but as exponents of the martial arts, as messengers whose contents were delivered in sign, and even as court executioners. Moreover, numerous accounts attest that some of these were the Sultan's most trusted companions, accompanying them in situations when hearing court members were asked to leave.

As might be expected over such a lengthy time period, the presence of these Deaf people was virtually institutionalised. They had their own quarters, and a significant part of their community's duties was to maintain the Court's language 'system' down the generations. As Bobovius (1679) has it: 'They visit and converse with the young and help them to perfect their sign language by telling fables and histories, sayings and scriptures in sign'. These and other references make clear that Deaf education was taken for granted in this setting, in contrast to the Western discourses which constructed education of Deaf people as a unique feat. Moreover these courts contained as many as 11,000 members, so knowledge of signing had potential breadth and depth. Additionally, noblemen not of the court also had Deaf attendants, and there is also record of Deaf people working in the Turkish bathhouses. Given that Deaf people also served as messengers to other parts of the country, it is clear that knowledge of this register of signing must have been fairly widespread.

What is the significance of this phenomenon with regard to lay people's attitudes to Deaf people? First, it indicates a reality other than the classic Western model of Deaf educational discourse – Deaf people are not a race to be pitied, shunned or conceived of primarily as tools for educational miracles. Moreover, it indicates that it is possible to conceive of situations and societies where sign language is highly valued, and at times more highly valued than the spoken language. Now undoubtedly much of this prestige is owed to the high place accorded Deaf people by the Sultans. But it is important to note that this could not have occurred in a vacuum – *it must have arisen initially from the culture of the society itself.* Finally, we should note that this is one of the few sustained accounts of Deaf life in Muslim society, and wonder whether it is in any way indicative of more positive cultural values in respect of Deaf people in Muslim communities generally.

'Everybody here spoke sign language' – the story of Martha's Vineyard

The third example is remarkable for not owing anything to the overt approval of the ruling classes. Groce (1985) revealed the existence of a sizeable Deaf community on the island of Martha's Vineyard following its settlement in the 1640s, where the incidence of deafness in some towns and neighbourhoods was as high as one in 25 and one in four.

Although there are no Deaf people left there today, many of the oldest hearing people on the island have vivid memories of life in those times. Groce describes the shock she experienced when asking one what the lay people had thought about the Deaf people:

> 'Oh', he said, 'they didn't think anything about them; they were just like everybody else. 'But how did people communicate with them – by writing everything down?' ' No', said Gale, surprised that I should ask such an obvious question. 'You see, everybody here spoke sign language'. (p. 2)

Groce goes on to describe life in that community in great detail. But what is significant for this reading of Deaf history is that many of the old people had great difficulty remembering who was Deaf and who was hearing, so all-pervasive was the bilingual atmosphere. On reading this account, Sacks (1989: 35–6) hastened to the island where

> [M]y first sight of this [signing] indeed, was unforgettable. I drove up to the old general store . . . and saw half a dozen old people gossiping together on the porch. They could have been any old folks, old neighbours talking together – until suddenly, very startlingly, they all dropped into Sign. They signed for a minute, laughed, and then dropped back into speech. (pp. 35–6)

That this should occur half a century after the last Deaf person on the island had died is a powerful testimony to the depth of lay people's bilingualism.

However, this is barely the beginning of the story. It emerges that the 'Deaf gene' was not brought to the island by Deaf people, but by hearing people. Groce traces their migration back to the Kentish Weald in the 1630s, and then locates a telling reference in Pepys' 17th century diaries. Talking of his friend Sir George Downing (after whom Downing Street is named), he remarks that he observed him communicating with a young Deaf boy who was telling him about the progress of the Great Fire of London (1665).

There comes in that dumb boy . . . who is mightily acquainted here and with Downing; and he made strange signs of the fire, and how the King was abroad [out and about], and many things they understood but I could not. (Groce, 1985: 30)

(The reader will note from this account the possibility that the boy may have gained his information either from other Deaf Londoners, thus suggesting a Deaf community or from hearing colleagues, suggesting a wider use of sign language.)

When asked for further details of this signing, Downing replies:

Why . . . it is only a little use, and you will understand him and make him understand you, with as much ease as maybe. (Groce, 1985: 30)

Downing's tone is nonchalant, but one should not assume he is referring to a simple use of mime. Miles (1988) and Jackson (1990) examine the exchange further and conclude that the boy's signing was 'of the type developed among Deaf persons in a community'. Rather, Downing is emphasising that hearing people need not be alienated by a signing person – that 'it is only a little use' and the basics of the language can be learned. The crucial point for us here is that Downing grew up in Maidstone – the heart of the Kentish Weald – at the same time as emigration to the Vineyard started. As Groce concludes:

It seems likely that as a boy . . . he learned the local sign language. If that is the case, it indicates not only that a sign language was used in Kent, but also that hearing individuals learned it. The later easy acceptance of sign language on the Vineyard may in fact be rooted in its easy acceptance in such places as Maidstone. (p. 31)

It would seem to be unarguable then that there were other communities in the UK and around the world, who were either bilingual in this way or accepting of the place of that bilingualism. It is likely, though we cannot be sure, that this depended on a certain incidence of deafness in the local population, but the point is that communication was by signs, not by speech, and perhaps even not by writing. There is a further twist to the Kentish story. Contemporary observers in New England (cf. Bahan & Nash, 1996) have noted that the local sign variation still contains examples of what we now know are old BSL signs. It seems highly probable not only that these signs originate from Kent and are therefore over 350 years old, but given that they form a part of modern BSL, they suggest that knowledge of sign language use may have existed across wider areas than is commonly supposed.[6] Before moving on, I would like to draw attention to a comment made by one of Groce's lay respondents, which illustrates a theme which we will return to in Chapter 3 when discussing crucial differences between Deaf and disabled people. Groce's (1985) use of 20th-century terminology is sharply corrected by an old island woman in her eighties:

> I asked about those who were handicapped by deafness when she was a girl. 'Oh', she said emphatically, 'those people weren't handicapped. They were just deaf'. (p. 5)

This is a key point within many Deafhood constructions, where Deaf people assert that linguistic communication is the prime marker of their being. They are not simply handicapped by being unable to speak the language of lay people – that majority is 'also' handicapped by being unable to communicate when amongst signers. Moreover, when both hearing and Deaf are able to sign together, no-one is handicapped at all. Therefore, the construction has posited across several centuries, one of the fundamental priorities of Deaf communities is to persuade that majority to learn to sign.

The Enlightenment Onwards

Moving on from these three specific examples in search of more evidence of positive Deaf–lay relationships, we may note that from the 17th century onwards, the number of Deaf people emerging from historical obscurity grows exponentially. Bulwer wrote two books dealing with sign language in 1644 and 1648, and we learn of two pairs of signing Deaf knights. The first, Sir Edward and William Gostwicke, are described by Hackett (c.1631):

> . . . whose behaviour, gestures, and zealous signs have procured and allowed admittance to sermons, prayers, the Lord's Supper, and to the marriage of ladies of great and prudent families. (Jackson, 1990: 5)

Bulwer describes the sign language of the second pair, Sir John and Framlingham Gaudy, in great depth, as well as giving examples of their (highly literate) letters to friends and families. It is also possible that they all knew each other, and given Bulwer's listing of 25 other Deaf people known to him, that there may well have existed a Deaf network as well as small communities. It is important to note that signing could not have been regarded with serious disfavour if it were so openly used by those with social prestige.

Examples continue to emerge. Benjamin Ferrers' work is still exhibited in the National Portrait Gallery, whilst Richard Crosse was Court Painter to King George III. John Dyott is still known in the town of Lichfield for his part in its defence during the Civil War. John Goodridge was a Fellow of the

Royal Society [of astronomers]. Lord Seaforth was even an MP in the 1780s and Governor of Barbados from 1800 to 1806. As Jackson records:

> He was a very fluent fingerspeller, and many of his associates such as Lord Melville and Lord Guildford acquired fingerspelling skills. (p. 35)

Clearly, being a Deaf-mute must have met with a certain measure of lay acceptance as evidenced also in the novel by Daniel Defoe (*The Life and Adventures of Duncan Campbell*, 1710), and the short story by Charles Dickens (*Doctor Marigold's Prescription*).

Describing all the other examples which we know of prior to the existence of Deaf education would take many pages, and there is also another powerful set of examples in French history which we will consider later. For now, we can conclude that, although all these examples range across great time and distance, they collectively present a compelling case for at least partial acceptance of Deaf people by lay people.

These, then, are examples from the Christian and Muslim heritage. What of the Jewish tradition which had established a positive model of Deaf people so early in time? At this historical moment, we know very little of the next thousand years of their Deaf history and its discourses. The nature of their culture would suggest that there was historical continuity in the codes of practice established by the Mishnah and Torah. Against this we might set the special circumstances of the diasporic diffusion of these peoples, and the anti-Semitic response to them, which might turn out later to influence their cultural responses to Deaf people. Due to that oppression, therefore, it would seem unlikely that its discourses on deafness influenced the European cultures into which they migrated over that milennium.

Deaf people and the beginnings of educational discourse

For reasons that have not yet been explained, the 16th century saw a sudden upsurge in references to Deaf people. These have taken two forms. The first concerns attempts to educate Deaf children of the nobility. This has been rationalised as a response to the demands of the primogeniture which emerged from the Justinian Code, and for the first time it is noted that some of the practitioners focused on teaching speech, whether by use of signs, gestures or other means. The extent to which this idea spread amongst the European intelligentsia means that this period marks the beginnings of a crucial discourse – *that Deaf people's attainment of humanity depended upon education per se*, which I refer to as the 'pedagogical conditional'. Such a discourse was encouraged by the status awarded to its practitioners, whose methodologies were shrouded in hermeticism as a necessary means of sustaining their reputations and livelihoods in an increasingly competitive era. Inevitably then, another central aspect of the educators' discourse is paternalism – education couched in this form pre-supposed *Hearing masters or paterfamilias*, and *Deaf subjects*.

When studying these accounts, the Deaf eye is drawn, not to the existence of the education itself, but to the prominence given to the 'miracle' of speech production and lipreading. This suggests to us the existence of another discourse – that Deaf people may well have already have been regarded as fully human, so that education simply refines the quality of their humanity. In this discourse, then it is not, as the educators would have it, that speech and lipreading served as the proof of intelligence, but rather as an unexpected ancillary skill.

As later events reveal, these characteristics of the newer discourse have great implication for Deaf communities. For almost nowhere in the classic examples of this discourse over the next 400 years is there any suggestion that *hearing people were other than negatively disposed towards Deaf people*. It is this construction which underpins the claims of certain sectors of society to be compelled to take upon themselves the role of 'looking after' the interests of the Deaf. Thus the implications of positive lay discourses in these earlier eras represents an active challenge to those which later gained hegemony.

Discourses from the Enlightenment to the 19th century

'Hearing' discourses

From the 1750s interest in Deaf people, as recorded in print, grew exponentially over the next hundred years. Both Deaf people and their sign languages became a touchstone for increased speculation about the nature of Man and of language by philosophers emerging from the Enlightenment. Some of the theorists came to negative conclusions, like Kant. Others, however, perceived Deaf people positively. In the search for a universal language, Leibniz posited that sign language might provide the answer, whilst Descartes used the example of sign language as the crucial factor in distinguishing Man from animals. Diderot's theorising took him further:

> One could almost substitute the [sign language] gestures with words; I say almost, because there are sublime gestures which all the eloquence of oratory will never convey. (1755, in Mirzoeff, 1995: 31)

Montaigne's speculations brought him to a similar conclusion. Observing Deaf people, he remarks that 'our mutes dispute, argue, and tell stories by signs. I have seen *some* [my italics] so supple and so versed in this, that in truth they lacked nothing of perfection in being able to make themselves understood' (in Mirzoeff, 1995: 16). This observation is the more notable for the author's apparent familiarity with a Deaf community that he can make distinctions as to the quality of an individual's signing skills.

However, it is another of his pronouncements that gives us important information regarding the relationship between lay and Deaf people, as evidenced in the respect for gesture:

What of the hands? We beg, we promise, call, dismiss, threaten, pray, entreat, deny, refuse, question, admire, count, confess, repent, fear, blush, doubt, instruct, command, incite, encourage, swear, testify, accuse, condemn, absolve, insult, despise, defy, vex, flatter, applaud, bless, humiliate, mock, reconcile, commend, exalt, entertain, rejoice, complain, grieve, mope, despair, wonder, exclaim, are silent, and what not with a variation and multiplication that vies with the tongue . . . There is no movement that does not speak both a language intelligible without instruction, and a public language; which means, seeing the variety and particular use of other languages, that this one must be judged the one proper to human nature. ' (in Mirzoeff, 1995: 16–17)

These examples are but the tip of an iceberg. One could continue with a list that included Rousseau, Condillac and so on.

Also during this period, scores of schools for Deaf children were founded across Europe and North America (Lane, 1984), many by Deaf people themselves, who then became teachers and headmasters in significant numbers. In this explosion, sign languages were almost universally the medium of education, whilst public exhibitions by (or of) pupils at certain of those schools were held several times a week, so great was the interest shown in the place of Deaf people and sign languages in the philosophical issues of the day. Numerous European royalty attended these exhibitions, notably at the Parisian school, and indeed were one of the means by which Deaf education was brought to other European states.

Thus far, the pedagogical condition does not seem to have had any negative effects. Indeed, one strand of this discourse, probably pioneered by L'Epee at the Parisian Deaf school, suggests an overturning of the Christian perspective of faith through hearing, replacing it with the idea of faith developing through linguistic channels, that is, through the language of signs (Lane & Philip, 1984).

The relationship between these academic discourses, with their interest in how Deaf people embodied clues regarding humanity's essential nature and development, naturally carried great status, and can be seen as a re-emergence (or continuation) of the Socratic–Augustinian–Judaic discourses. Moreover, it is certainly possible to posit that they they emerged from and were essentially rooted in the beliefs held by some lay people – that is, awareness and acceptance of Deaf people and sign languages.

Paris and the French Revolution was at the epicentre of the Enlightenment, and studies of the Deaf developments of this era reveal significant relationships between Deaf and hearing people in that city. The Paris salons witnessed numerous examples of Deaf artistic talent and tutoring of hearing artists. Mirzoeff identifies over one hundred Deaf artists who made their living from art or exhibited in public during the following century. Nor were these on the periphery of art. As he notes, they 'competed . . . at the élite Ecole des Ceaux-Arts, exhibited at the Salon, and even won the Legion d'Honneur'. The case of Claude Deseine is significant. Among his many (commissioned) busts were Voltaire, Rousseau, Mirabeau, Danton and Robespierre, and accounts indicate a close relationship with many of the prime movers of the Revolution, even at the height of the Terror (Lane, 1984). Danton even had his wife's body exhumed so that Deseine could create her bust!

Deaf people are known to have written popular political pamphlets during this period, and to have fought (and died) in the Revolutionary army, whilst the Revolution itself became the first political body to officially recognise Deaf people as 'children of the nation', in the Rousseauesque term of reference, thereby inaugurating the first publicly funded school for Deaf people in the world. Lane (1984) attributes a central role to Deaf people like Massieu, the first Deaf teacher at the Paris school, in attaining this objective.

In making the proposal to the National Assembly of 1791, Prieur de la Marne used language very similar to that quoted earlier:

> . . . the deaf have a language of signs which can be considered as one of the most fortunate discoveries of the human spirit. It perfectly replaces, and with the greatest rapidity, the organ of speech . . . If one were ever to realize the much desired project of a universal language, this would perhaps be that which would merit preference; at the least it is the most ancient of all. (in Mirzoeff 1995: 47)

This reiteration of two of the core propositions of the philosophers appears to support the suggestion that their thoughts had been constructed upon lay beliefs.

The Deaf–hearing interactions during the French Revolution have particular significance for this study, as they are among the first indications that Deaf people were not only involved with working-class lay people, but that _they were aware of, and participated in, the political organisations of working-class people,_ from this point in history onwards.

Before moving on, it is necessary to reiterate several qualifications. The first is that it should _not_ be assumed that all lay people had positive attitudes towards Deaf people; rather, it is the intent of this chapter to emphasise the existence of discourses expunged from historical record by the oralist discourses when they assumed hegemony. Speech-oriented and deficit (or medical) discourses continued through this time, first as a legacy of the private tutoring of those children of the wealthy from earlier eras and, second as a corollary to the development of colonialism and imperialism, discussed later. Importantly, through all this period, the discourses of the established church maintained the bias built into it by the New Testament, continuing in certain quarters to conceive of the Deaf as automata, that is, living machines which by definition did not have souls. Although these ideas were pushed back by the Revolution and the Enlightenment, once the former had waned, they were able to rise to prominence again.

There is also evidence that in order to gain recognition and finance for the establishment of Deaf education, it was felt necessary in some quarters to establish a discourse which asserted the animalistic or sub-human nature of uneducated Deaf people as an essential ingredient of the pedagogical conditional. The language used by L'Epee's successor, Sicard, such an apparent supporter of the Deaf cause, in the earlier quotation, is a good example of this.

Sicard, however, is considering the isolated Deaf person. In considering Deaf people as a community, he takes a very different line:

> Could there not be in some corner of the world a whole society of deaf people? . . . They would certainly have a sign language, perhaps a language even richer than ours . . . So why would these people be uncivilised? Why wouldn't they in fact have laws, government, police less mistrustful than our own? (in Lane & Philip, 1984: 90)

In making his case for Deaf schools as essential, Sicard emphasises the linguistic factor as the humanising element; a society of Deaf people would be able to educate themselves through their language. It is the isolation from that language, from other Deaf people, which gives rise to the negative reading. Nonetheless, by stressing the pedagogical conditional for conventional societies, together with the development of the institutions themselves, with their characteristics of *discipline* and *surveillance*, as Foucault has it, the groundwork was laid for this strand of discourse to come to dominate perceptions of Deaf people. The historical evidence makes it clear that even some Deaf leaders entered into pedagogical discourse feeling that they had no choice but to grudgingly acquiesce in such constructions as Sicard's. Although Desloges (see later) and others, notably Berthier and Forrestier, disagreed, the imbalances of power held both within and without those institutions eventually told against them. This was unfortunate, for by acquiescing in this construction, Deaf people were positioning themselves as hostages to fortune, as will later be seen.

Deaf discourses

With regard to the development of Deaf people's own discourses, we can look for clues in the work of Pierre Desloges, who composed the first 'Deaf' text in 1779, a work so powerful that much of what it says is not only still useful today, but is in some ways still in advance of the current situation within Deaf education. A bookbinder and paper-hanger, his commitment to the Jacobin cause during the Revolution resulted in the publication of a text *Letter Addressed to the Voters of Paris*, printed the day after the fall of the Bastille, which 'was widely read and talked about' (Bezagu-Deluy, 1993: 39). Further works followed up until 1794, which reinforce the sense of his contribution to Jacobin theory and praxis. After the fall of the Jacobins we hear no more about him, and it may be that he also fell with them.

It is important to this reading that we note that he did not attend L'Epee's school, but was a member of a separate Deaf community within the city of Paris. His first text was, however, written in defence of that school against what must have been one of the first oralist attacks. There are several important discourse strands which run through his work, which can be extrapolated from this extensive quotation:

> As long as I was living apart from other Deaf people, my only resource for self-expression was writing or my poor pronunication. I was for a long time unaware of sign language. I used only scattered, isolated, and unconnected signs . . . But things are quite different for the deaf who live in a great city, in Paris for example . . . In such a theatre our ideas develop, and when the isolated deaf man arrives, he learns to polish and order his signing . . . Dealing with his comrades he quickly learns the art of portraying all his thoughts, even the most abstract . . . No event – in Paris, in France, or in the four corners of the world – lies outside the scope of our discussion. We express ourselves on all subjects with as much order, precision, and rapidity as if we enjoyed the faculty of speech and hearing. (in Lane & Philip, 1984: 34–6)

Among the discourse strands that we can recognise are: the necessity of a Deaf community for regularising sign language to permit consistently intelligent discourse, the fact of Deaf migration to the cities in search of just such communities, and the downplaying of formal education in favour of what might be termed subaltern means of self-education.[7]

The final strand of Deaf discourse is that Desloges also implies that although he and others supported the burgeoning Deaf education system, *because of the fact of their own self-education, they reserved the right to stand outside and criticise whatever paternalistic shortcomings they perceived within it.*

For hearing people then, the education system begins to be identified as the wellspring of the Deaf humanising process. But in Deaf discourses, it would have been (as it is still is today), *the fact of coming together as a community*, which is the all-important humanising quality. Whether that community was in a school, in a town or village or in a family in a village, is less important, though obviously the largest possible community is desired.

Nonetheless, the establishment of Deaf schools was of immense significance for Deaf communities from this time forward to the present day. By gathering Deaf children and adults into such communities, complete with trade training, artistic tuition and land for farming their own resources, a basis was established for the development of a larger collective Deaf identity, and indeed of a network of national and international Deaf communities (Lane, 1984). The educational and professional achievements of Deaf ex-pupils grew exponentially, and by the 1860s in the USA, this was given further impetus by the founding of the National Deaf-Mute College (later Gallaudet University). Deaf people's own discourses therefore greatly expanded for, as successive generations left school, numbers remained in the vicinity to found Deaf clubs and meeting places right across Europe and North America, and to retain an interest or 'professional' involvement in 'their' schools.

By the 1830s, Deaf Parisians were sufficiently established that their leaders, such as Berthier, convened annual banquets which attracted Deaf people on an international scale; confirmation of the sophistication of Deaf networks from that time. These banquets, which continued for most of the century, invited notables such as Victor Hugo and Lamartine to attend, and were intended to formalise both the strength of Deaf society and the power and beauty of sign languages. As Mottez (1993: 143) summarises:

> These banquets became true festivals of mimicry [signing]. Signs were performed and celebrated. There even was a religious quality to these banquets; it was a religion centred on liberation and progress.

Since numbers of the speeches given at the banquets have been transcribed into French, they represent the most extensive clues we can currently locate regarding issues of Deafhood in 19th century discourse form. The only other sources we have to work with, given that sign languages themselves could not be recorded, are the Deaf magazines, several of which began around that time. The speeches have to be considered carefully – given the nature of the events and what they aspired to, we can expect a degree of idealisation. However, compared to the contents of a magazine, they are much more a 'live' event. And ultimately, the idealisation does not greatly matters, because in itself it tells us much about the breadth and heights of those Deaf discourses.

From these accounts, we can construct the following tenets which illustrate the dimensions of these Deafhood perceptions. The first concerns their views about the language itself:

> Deaf mute foreigners, in their toasts, never missed a chance to emphasize the universal nature of signs, claiming that 'it easily wins out over all the separate limiting languages of speaking humanity . . . Our language encompasses all nations, the entire globe'. (Mottez, 1993: 151)

Berthier's (1984) description was equally lofty:

> The language of Deaf-mutes, that sublime universal language given to us by Nature.

Although later generations would substitute 'God' for 'Nature', the essence of the tenet remains the same; Nature, as the expression of the Supreme Being, vindicated the languages, since all that was natural existed because it was *intended* to exist. An earlier example exists from the life of Laurent Clerc. On his visit to London in 1815, and when mixing in high society there, he was asked to compare English and French ladies. His lengthy reply surprised them in its frankness, but his riposte was:

> It is the privilege of a Man of Nature. (in Lane, 1984: 159)

(The sheer dignity inherent in being able to take such a position is hard to imagine these days, after a century of scientism and the equation of Nature with savagery.)

These Deaf people were very well aware that other countries used different sign languages; the key concept here is the 'universal *nature* of signs', that is, that sign languages contain certain qualities not to be found in spoken language, which enabled them to adapt and improvise – in theory at least to communicate across the entire globe. Berthier expressed it thus:

> The richness, flexibility, clarity and energy of our language of mimicry gives it an incontestable pre-eminence over all spoken languages. (Mirzoeff, 1995: 120)

It is their their implicit awareness of what has now been confirmed as the highly similar *grammars* of the world's sign languages which must have formed the basis of this assertion, although we should not overlook the quality of improvisation in an age when there was not yet a nationally standardised sign langauge. This, together with the need for a coming together of acute precision and visual and metaphorical clarity, goes far to explain why Deaf discourses for the rest of the century and beyond saw signing as an *art* rather than a science. (This belief was handed down the centuries by certain Deaf people; it could be found expressed by older leaders within the National Union of the Deaf in the UK as late as 1978.)

One account from the 1849 banquet speaks of a hearing journalist who was invited to attend, who saw himself:

> . . . an 'incomplete'man according to these [Deaf] gentlemen, a 'wretch' deprived of the language of mimicry . . . having to resort to a pencil to converse with the evening's heroes. An expression of ineffable pity could be read on their faces at his approach. (Mottez, 1993: 147)

His account goes on to observe:

> None of the orators we most admire could even remotely compare with Berthier, Forestier or Lenoir for the grace, the dignity, and the correctness of their gestures. In truth, seeing the speeches that these three young men deliver is enough, I think, to make us wish we could unlearn speech. (Mottez, 1993: 149)

These tenets of Deaf discourse can be summarised as follows:

(1) Deaf communities possess the gift of languages so special that they can be used to say things which speech cannot.
(2) These languages are even more special because they can be adapted to cross international boundaries when spoken languages fail.
(3) Consequently, Deaf people model in potentia the ability to become the world's first truly global citizens, and thus serve as a model for the rest of society.
(4) Deaf people were intentionally created on earth to manifest these qualities, and the value of their existence should not be called into question.
(5) Hearing people unable to use them are effectively 'sign-impaired' citizens.
(6) These languages were offered as a gift to hearing people, that if they joined with Deaf people and learned them, the quality of their lives would be improved.[8]
(7) The banqueteers were well aware that the majority of Deaf people had not yet had the opportunity to attend Deaf education and experience sign language socialisation. But they pledged themselves to continue to fight to ensure that all Deaf people had the 'right' to these experiences.

The majority of these tenets were either lost or only expressed covertly after Oralism. But we can appreciate their scope, their belief in what Deafhood once was, and that it could become so again. They imply, and sometimes make explicit, a belief in a *potentially global Deafhood*, of a separate but equal Deaf race with members in every country in the world. Furthermore, were members of this race to be set against one another by national warfare in the majority societies, this would constitute a following of 'hearing' principles rather than manifesting their own Deafhood. The nearest comparisons which can be found are similar concepts within Jewish and Afrocentric discourses.

Berthier and others applied these theories to practical reality. They posited the concept of the 'deaf-mute *nation'*, consisting of 23,000 fellow French citizens, and argued for direct election and representation. Such developments were profound – a case was being made for an *ontological Deaf discourse inextricably linked to political discourse,* since the banquets make repeated references to tenets arising from the French Revolution. They were only partially defeated by the failure of the Revolutions of 1848, for Deaf people can be found defending the Paris Commune of 1870 and agitating sides in the Dreyfus affair of 1894 (Mirzoeff, 1995).

Interestingly, there seems to be little suggestion that education *per se* was a precondition for these discourses, and this despite the fame of the Parisian Deaf school. The banquets were established as a result of Deaf dissatisfaction with what was happening at the school, particularly the emergence of early versions of Oralism. They were thus not conceived of as social activities, but inherently political acts, in part designed to win the support of lay people for their arguments, and indeed have been described as 'the germ of the future emancipation' of Deaf people (Anon, 1842, in Mottez, 1993).

That such discourses were not confined to France can be seen in the USA during this time, with Flournoy's initiation of a Deaf movement to set up a Deaf state in the Mid-West, and other attempts to establish self-governing communities with their own land (Van Cleve & Crouch, 1989: 67ff). These movements were the subject of considerable Deaf discourse and although eventually defeated, their importance lies in the confirmation of Deaf people's view of themselves at that time as a linguistic, social and cultural community.

One should not infer that a single Deaf discourse existed. The Parisian banquets were attended by a male élite; they also dissolved and re-united around arguments couched in Deaf-political terms, such as the political priorities facing the community. Nevertheless, the texts of the banquets reveal not only a high level of Deaf discourse (rarely matched since) but contained statements of certain principles *with which ordinary Deaf people would concur* (though not of course in the same elevated tones). In this way, *there appears to exist a unitary basis for otherwise divergent Deaf discourses.*

The discourses of hearing allies

I have made this distinction in order to facilitate understanding of some of the dynamics in the section which follows. There are two types of allies that can be identified. The first are those who participated in Deaf affairs and deferred to, agreed with, or extended basic Deaf tenets. One such was Bebian, a teacher of the Deaf and close colleague of Berthier, who was active in the struggle to achieve the kind of education system that Deaf people were demanding (Lane & Philip, 1984).

The second, more numerous, were those who fought to establish and run Deaf schools, whose alliance was chiefly based on supporting *the fact of Deaf education rather than the modus operandi*, such as L'Epee and Sicard. These, therefore, were sometimes profound Deaf allies, whilst at other times almost enemies.

The first group participated therefore in both Deaf and hearing discourses, whereas the second confined themselves mostly to the latter. In making these distinctions, I do not wish to imply a simplified categorical duality. As was previously explained, different, even contradictory discourses can operate through the same person at the same time; a notable example being Thomas Gallaudet, the co-founder of Deaf education in the USA and a much-regarded ally (Valentine, 1993).

Nevertheless, the existence both of consistent allies and of those trapped as hearing people between differing discourses (termed 'liberals' earlier in the chapter) has great significance for subsequent events.

Oralist Discourses and Deaf Communities

Although most of the 19th century saw an explosion in the numbers of sign-oriented Deaf schools, Deaf clubs, organisations and publications, the last 20 years of the century saw a total reversal of attitude and policy. It is important for this reading of Deaf history that the discourses which enabled this be clearly understood. Several are summarised here; however, it is important to note the fact of their convergence into a single discursive system, giving the oralist movement the ability to quickly seize power across two continents within those two decades.

The oralist views which follow were foreshadowed by the work of the Dutchman Johann Amman (1669–1724). His account, an attack on L'Epee's school, indicates the three linking prepositions which would come to dominate oralist discourses:

> The voice is a living emanation of that spirit that God breathed into man when he created him a living soul.

What stupidity we find in most of these unfortunate deaf! How little they differ from animals!

How inadequate and defective is the language of gesture and sign which the deaf must use. How little do they comprehend, even superficially, those things that concern the health of the body, the improvement of the mind, or their moral duties. (in Lane, 1984: 100–01)

These three prepositions then are: the reification of the voice, centred in a Christian discourse, the inherent inferiority or inhumanity of Deaf people and the inadequacy of their language. It is sobering to realise that 350 years later, versions of these arguments are still being advanced, and being favoured in the discourses of the media. It is long past time for a formal analysis of why this might be so.

Colonialism and oralist discourses

Although the Enlightenment initially validated lay discourses about Deaf people, once the Revolution had passed, one of its tenets, that nature could be improved by reason, proved to be a Trojan horse by which some could claim that teaching Deaf people to speak represented a necessary stage in their evolution to full human status. Although the impetus came from the wealthy and the powerful, whose children were still being born Deaf, ideological reinforcement came from the development of colonialism and its handmaiden, the discipline of anthropology, from 1800 onwards (Lane, 1993a). Initial positive relationships between Deaf people and theoreticians who were *both* founding members of the Society for the Observation of Man, devolved into a discourse which eventually described the former as 'disgraced beings of nature'.

The crucial moment of transformation was colonialism. In advising the first anthropological expeditions of the Napoleanic age, members of the Society were advised to employ people who knew sign language to act as interpreters. However, this powerful apparent affirmation of Deaf people and their languages was turned on its head – the fact that both Deaf and Native peoples used sign and gesture, and that neither could speak European languages, was used to construct essentialist similarities between them – both were described as 'savages' in a belief system which constructed a 'civilised Man' surrounded by savages and animals (Mirzoeff, 1995: 68).

Fanon (1968), Said (1978) and others have described such ideological discourses as intending to rationalise and justify colonialism, imperialism and slavery. The mercantile era felt no need to diminish the status of the peoples it traded with – indeed the Other was, if anything, regarded as exotic and the source of alternative wisdoms. In order to justify slavery and exploitation, it was necessary to exclude such peoples from the category of humanity. The second phase of this development can then, in Spivak's (1985) words, 'justify the imperialist project by producing the following formula: *make* the heathen into a human so that he can be treated as an end in himself'. Thus as a result of such discourses, Deaf people were set up along with all the other savages as targets for the civilising mission of the emerging imperial nations. It is probable that later research will confirm that the belief systems of the established churches during this time may have underpinned such discourses. In summary, then, by asserting parallels of this kind, the ideological stage was set for an expansion of the oralist discourse.

The emergence of scientism and medical discourses

Physicians in many societies had probed the composition of the ear, and the possible causes of deafness arising from illness, and speculated as to the relationship between congenital deafness and mutism, one of their motives being to mitigate adventitious deafness amongst the wealthy and powerful. By definition, their perception of Deaf people was negative, centring on the medical model. It is important to understand that a true understanding of the mechanics of the ear did not emerge until the 20th century. Nevertheless, attempts to find cures persisted, and accounts of them read quite bizarrely.

As Hodgson (1953) summarises, by the 19th century they 'were no nearer to curing deafness than their predecessors . . . They had something of the prestige, as well as the mentality, of the African witch-doctor' (p. 117). This may be unfair to 'African witchdoctors'. It is doubtful that any ever tried experiments like those which follow.

At the height of the Paris school's fame, with all its Deaf achievements, there nevertheless began within its walls the first known attempts to systematically attempt a cure for deafness, by the school's physician, Itard. After applying electricity to the children's ears, Itard then tried leeching and piercing of eardrums (one child died of the latter). His next move was more drastic still – he inserted a probe into the eustacian tube and attempted to flush out the suspected (and hypothetical) 'lymphatic excrement'. This was applied to

> one hundred and twenty pupils, almost every last one in the school, *save for some two dozen who would not be subdued.* Nothing at all was accomplished. (Lane, 1984 : 133 ; my emphasis)

The reader may have been tempted to try to visualise some of the scenes described during the course of this book. Here is one which positively lends itself to that process. Behind the calm prose of the mention of the 'two dozen who would not be subdued', we can imagine the uproar and division that must have existed in the school, between hearing and Deaf teachers and pupils alike. Itard was still not satisfied; one of his later attempts involved 'fracturing the skull of a few pupils, striking the area just behind the ear with a hammer' (p. 488). Eventually he gave up, and after 16 years came round to accepting Deaf people and their language. In taking so long to accept what was happening in front of him, his medical attitude foreshadows beliefs which continue to the present day.

How did Deaf people respond to such actions? One of the few recorded accounts comes from Englishman John Kitto (1804–54) who became a Doctor of Divinity. His experiences were similar:

> They poured into my tortoured ears various infusions both hot and cold; they bled me, leeched me . . . and at last they gave it up as a bad case. (Batson & Bergmann, 1976)

And his considered response –

> I cannot pretend to any permanent regret in connection with the absence of vocal or other sounds.

As Deaf readers know, but some hearing readers may not, this response regularly occurs in Deaf discourses as a view held by many Deaf people across all societies. Understanding this position is a task which the hearing reader will hopefully complete by the end of this book. It should not be doubted that Deaf people and this new medical profession were at loggerheads. No sooner had Itard and his revised, positive views departed than his successor Meniere began with views that took the discourse right back to square one. At this time, of course, even Meniere could not but be aware of the strength of the Deaf discourses. His conclusion, then, was all the more remarkable:

> The Deaf believe that they are our equals in all respects. We should be generous and not destroy that illusion. But whatever they believe, deafness is an infirmity, and we should repair it _whether the person who has it is disturbed by it or not._ (in Lane, 1984: 134)

I have said this conclusion was remarkable. But perhaps what is more remarkable is that this belief remains intact even today, as later sections will show.

These failures notwithstanding, the colonialist impulse drove them onwards and the gradual discovery of scientific principles in anatomy, biology, acoustics and electricity coalesced into the conceptual nexus of Science itself, tranforming the medical discourse into a quasi-scientific discourse. From this point in history onwards, the two become inseparable.

Furthermore, the Industrial Revolution which underpinned colonialism was itself inescapably a product of science (Hobsbawn, 1962); thus commenced the development of ideologies asserting science as one of the benchmarks by which racial and class superiority and dominance could be justified, a reifying discourse which is still active today. Then as now, a white working-class might be suffering in the dark satanic mills of Northern Europe, but their products could be held up as examples of progress. Railways, cars, planes, tanks, nuclear power, space rockets – all these (the discourse implies) could not have been invented by the other, therefore inferior races.

Bio-power, this imperialist–medicalist–scientist triumvirate, by definition one which was accumulating great national and global wealth, gave further impulse to the traditional oralist priority of teaching Deaf children of the nobility to speak, and extended it outwards to those same children of the mercantile and industrial classes. As the century wore on, therefore, there was greater pressure to subvert the Deaf linguistic model and replace it by a rejuvenated medical one, using that central trope and euphemism of the 19th century, 'Progress', against which 'Nature' was situated as a regressive trope and technology enshrined as the inevitable and even pre-ordained primary philosophy of the future. This theme is of particular importance for Oralism in the 20th century – its continued failure was masked by an assertion *that the next scientific development, always just around the corner, would somehow produce the desired results which escaped the present age.*

Against this background, Darwin's initially explosive ideas on evolution served to reinforce the medical discourse. Deaf people and their languages were confirmed as akin to those of other savages, and an atavistic throwback who, like them, 'may fancifully be called living fossils [and] will aid us in forming a picture of the ancient forms of life' (1859: 448). Even more ominous for them was the emergence of Social Darwinism, the application of the concept of the survival of the fittest to the social and political structure. By the 1880s, these ideas, combined with the exponential expansion of technological development and nation-state competitiveness for the colonial market led to new waves of suppression for many minorities. These took many forms in the different discourses – 'Manifest Destiny' and the 'Jim Crow' laws in the USA, where ideas of Nordic racial superiority were also applied to would-be immigrants, or the intensification of African colonisation (surprising as it may seem, nine-tenths of Africa was only taken over in the last two decades of that century).

One prime dynamic which emerged from these discourses was the eugenics movement, and it was particularly unfortunate for Deaf people that one of the leading lights of the movement was Alexander Graham Bell. Western Deaf schools and communities had continued to expand and develop a sophisticated culture throughout the century, and their very success was to prove their undoing. As Foucault has remarked, 'visibility is a trap' and what was termed a supposedly invisible handicap in medical discourse was of course highly visible in the social model. The eugenics discourse was notable for its advocacy of the removal of debased stock from the human race and, for the first time in history, this course of action became part of the discourse on Deaf people.

Bell is a useful focus for this summary because he encapsulated several of the forces that have, as we have seen, informed the oralist philosophy. He commanded social and political power from his family background, augmented that with wealth derived from his invention of the telephone, whilst that same success in the prestigious domain of science gave him ideological credibility both within and without the medico-scientific domains. 'Science', he averred, 'adding to our knowledge, bringing us closer to God, is *the highest of all things*' (Lane, 1984: 342).

The resultant discourse formed a formidable web. His campaigns for Oralism not only ran side by side with similar eugenic campaigns against immigration and Deaf intermarriage ('the production of a defective race of human beings would be a great calamity to this world', he argued in 1883, producing research which – unscientifically – linked Deaf schools and consequent Deaf marriages with growing numbers of Deaf childen), but formed two sides of the same coin of discourse. Although he drew the line at extermination, as Winefield (1987: 83) points out, his 'chilling words' were not based on positive reasons, but rather on doubt that 'this would not lead to an increase in the quantity or quality of the desirable [races]; it would simply prevent deterioration'.

Nonetheless, Mitchell (1971) illustrates how these beliefs met with some success. His example, from the memoirs of the rector at the Baltimore Deaf mission during that period, indicates to us the extent and power of these new discourses, and the speed at which they could disseminate themselves:

> news of it [the memoir] spread like wildfire amongst parents of the deaf, their family physicians, and *among surgeons generally throughout the world* . . . He [the rector] came to know many deaf couples who were childless and unhappy as a result of having been sterilised in infancy; he laid the blame on Bell. (in Lane, 1984: 358)

The combination of Bell's resources, contacts to power, (not least with the ubiquitous Deaf children of the wealthy) and his ideological credibility led to the success of Oralism both in the USA and its spheres of influence. Shortly after the turn of the century, sign languages and Deaf teachers were almost totally eradicated from the educational system, and legislation to sterilise Deaf people or prevent intermarriage was on the statute books in 30 states (Mirzoeff, 1995).

Social Class and 19th Century Discourses on Welfare and Charity

Although there have long been discourses on the care of the sick and the infirm, and provision for some by legislation such as the 'Poor Law', it is only with the advent of the 19th century that these discourses became institutionalised. Undoubtedly, concerns for the poor and the Others were given impetus as the urban landscape of industrial capitalism revealed the full extent of its squalor and misery. But as Foucault (1979) has described, the establishment of prisons and mental asylums during this time were founded on twin concepts of surveillance and discipline, a philosophy that was extended to schools and hospitals as they became established. Once the Others could be labelled and categorised by such a discourse, they could be more easily distinguished and separated from 'normal people' and then practised on with little fear of discovery.

Moreover, since the welfare state did not yet exist, these institutions had to be funded by the public themselves. Inevitably, the only classes with sufficient wealth were the nobility and the newly rich capitalists, and the latter indeed became the financial backbone of these institutions and 'voluntary organisations' (Oliver, 1990: 113). These new developments produced new discourse themes, including rationalisations about the importance of Christian charity and of the 'necessity' for the existence of the poor as a class. The other side of the discourse was the implied dependency by those recipients of charity, and the submissiveness and gratitude expected of them.[9]

During this same period of time, increasing numbers of Deaf schools and clubs were required or demanded and, in the absence of resources to build them, the only avenues open were to appeal for public subscription (which was moderately successful), for noble or royal patronage (also moderately successful) or by the establishment of these same voluntary organisations of wealthy capitalists. Thus the type of Deaf discourses exemplified by the Parisian banquets had to be suppressed and replaced by discourses stressing Deaf helplessness in order to benefit from the largesse they hoped to accrue from the discourses of charity. *The result of all these factors was to turn the culturo-linguistic model into the beginnings of what might be described as a 'social-control model'.*

Even more ominously, this new combination of the interests of the nobility and a significant mercantile middle-class meant that by acquiescing in these discourses in their desire to see these Deaf clubs built, Deaf people were once again producing hostages to fortune, for this combination meant that these two groups were able to witness at local charitable levels the by-now highly visible Deaf communities. There were now two groups of parents of Deaf children for whom an alternative to joining this essentially working class Deaf community was felt to be an urgent requirement. And of course there was, for the first time, an immense combination of wealth and political power that could be wielded towards this end.

Throughout this period, there are numerous references to oralist developments being funded by the wealthy, culminating in the Royal Commission of 1889, whose legislation 'was to enact the Milan Congress' resolutions in Britain' (Mirzoeff, 1995: 226). Conversely, there are similarly numerous references within and without the Deaf discourse to signed education as an essentially egalitarian philosophy. The younger Gallaudet, no socialist himself, encapsulated this in his summary of the opponents of Oralism as being 'those who are merely teachers and not capitalists' (Lane, 1984 :369). Nevertheless, those who wished to see universal education and welfare support for Deaf people were caught in the double-bind of this bipolar discourse, so that in promoting the necessary growth of these institutions, they ended up giving impetus to Oralism.

Oralism and the Renewed Religious Discourse

The roles of medicine and science, class and race, wealth and capitalism, in the expansion of Oralism have been described in the previous two sections. However, the crucial role of religion in these discourses has not yet been fully understood. We have seen how established Christianity was rooted in both the deficit and demonological models, and how these existed even beyond the Enlightenment. What is less clear, however, is how they came to assume such power within the French and Italian Deaf education systems, and thus produce the conference of Milan.

Explanations cannot simply be attributed to Christianity itself – numerous Christians supported Deaf people's attempts to use their own languages, to congregate and help themselves and ministers of the churches working with the adult Deaf indeed constructed a (paternalistic) profession from this basis, using the charity discourse as the springboard. The answer may lie in the pedagogical conditional – once this was established, the two-tier structure of hearing specialists rescuing Deaf children could be adopted by any group who wished to do so. In cultures where Christianity devolved significant amounts of power to its priests and ministers, nuns and brothers, the basis existed for such employees of the church to assume or continue the roles of specialists within the Deaf education system (Crean, 1997).

Thus an examination of the texts surrounding the Milan conference reveal a remarkable imbalance in the proportion of religious to secular particpants. Of the 164 attendees, 139 were Italian and French clergy, and there was an strong emphasis on a religious discourse for justifying Oralism. Balestra, one of the leaders of the movement declared:

> We are all children of the one Christ who gave us the example . . . The minister of Christ must open the mouth of the deaf . . . I will add that for a Catholic priest, the mutes must speak. (in Lane, 1984: 393)

The language of Tarra, the conference president, was similarly pentacostal in tone:

> Oral speech is the sole power that can rekindle the light God breathed into man when, giving him a soul in a corporeal body, he gave him also a means of understanding, of conceiving, and of expressing himself . . . no shape [sign], no image, no design, can reproduce these ideas. Speech alone, divine itself, is the right way to speak of divine matters. (in Lane, 1984: 393–4)

However, since Tarra knew very well that sign language had proved itself able to express religious concepts for over a century, deconstruction must eventually probe deeper for reasons to explain his assertions.

A second, related, strand of discourse concerns an expressed hatred of the human body and its behaviours. Tarra encapsulated the relationship between this Victorian discourse and Oralism:

> The fantastic language of signs exalts the senses and foments the passions, whereas speech elevates the mind much more naturally, with calm, prudence and truth. (in Lane, 1984: 394).

Mirzoeff (1995) and others have, as we have seen, demonstrated the importance of gesture and the different degrees of gestural acceptability (according to class of origin) which were previously deemed acceptable within social, linguistic and artistic domains over several centuries of discourse in these fields. Undoubtedly these issues were intensified as the numbers of the mercantile gentry grew, but it took this new found evangelism to introduce a fundamentalist dimension to the debate. (As will be seen in later chapters, there is certainly evidence to suggest that such concerns for social propriety, involving suppression of the body in many of its forms, were a central characteristic of the petit bourgeoisie; thus there is much mileage to be gained from further exploration of this theme.)

Tarra also introduced another related strand, that of hostility to artistic and creative work in general (long seen in some religious discourses as the work of the Devil) and linked this also to signs: 'They enhance and glorify fantasy and all the faculties of the sense of imagination' (p. 393).

Finally, the theme of (petit bourgeoisie?) Christian submissiveness, it was suggested, was threatened by sign. As Tarra put it:

> The habit of pure dependence, which the deaf-mute contracts in catching what is said by the lips . . . takes from them that indocile and wild spirit peculiar to those who express themselves by the fantastic and passionate method of gestures, and also renders them more obedient, respectful, affectionate, sincere, and good. (p. 401)

In this context, Lane points out the subversive nature of sign language in an oralist system where 'the educators' desire for total control of their classrooms . . . cannot be had if the pupils sign and the teacher knows none' (p. 395). This simple linguistic fact reinforces a crucial point about the *totalitarian inevitability of Oralism* – it could not succeed whilst Deaf adults were present in the school to undermine it, nor if the children themselves were permitted to sign (i.e. communicate with each other), even outside the classroom. Tarra prefigures this aspect of the discourse, again in Christian terms:

> Like the true mother of the child placed in judgement before Solomon, speech *wishes it all for her own – instruction, school, deaf-mute – without sharing*; otherwise she renounces all. (p. 393, my emphasis)

In the light of the section on the emergence of scientistic discourse, it is also interesting to note that this newer form of Christianity allied itself for the first time with science. As Tarra put it, 'Never perhaps has a scientific victory [Milan] been proclaimed with less opposition' (p. 395). The relationship between these two previously opposed discourses is in need of further research in order to understand how the web was finally completed.

A major factor underpinning all these discourses is belief in the medical model; however, it is interesting that the acceptance of Deaf people and their language by those earlier oralists who applied the medical model to individual wealthy children now comes to an end. Linkage is thus made for the first time between the necessity of speech *versus* the use of sign language. The reasons often cited for this linkage were that the latter was so easy to use, so natural to Deaf children, that they would be unwilling to learn the former. However, behind this, as we have seen earlier, lie other perceptions of Deaf children's essentialist nature, whether as savages in the colonialist sense or in images evoked of undisciplinable children, both in turn linked to the animalistic nature of human beings since the Fall; in other words, a religious construction.

Nevertheless, these arguments when deconstructed indicate a different rationale; there is little evidence that Deaf people were unwilling to learn to speak but there is powerful evidence that they would refuse to communicate *only* in speech. As has already been stated, Oralism was unable to achieve its stated goals; in the case of literacy and speech, this failure was known very early in its development, but suppressed or ignored. Nor was it able to eradicate Deaf communities, which was also quickly realised. We must look elsewhere for the reasons that Oralism was able to sustain itself in the face of all apparent logic and reason.

The Micro-Physics of Power and the Oralist Discursive System

In his studies of discourses on mental health, hospitals, schools and of punishment and discipline over the last 500 years, Foucault (1972) identifies several themes of relevance to this study. The micro-physics of bio-power consist of the dense web of power relations behind the discourses above; exercised within institutions (the term here also being taken to mean the institutions of state power), it develops a life of its own which is reinforced by the other instutions.

He also identifies the late 18th century shift from punishing the insane to seeking control of their minds by developments of classification systems which formed the lens through which such people were perceived and administered. It is also important to note that these systems were used to justfy confinement of apparently sane people whose deeds could be categorised as having transgressed whichever mental health boundaries were convenient to those in power, for example radicals or unmarried mothers. In this context, once the category of 'Deaf-mute' emerged as a necessary prerequisite for the establishment of Deaf education, a beginning was made for a classification system by which to later administer (control) Deaf people.

Foucault (1979) also focuses on the growing ability of the state to use medicine to dissect, categorise and control the human body itself, occurring, perhaps uncoincidentally, at the same time as negative attitudes to the human body and to sexuality were being promulgated.

Another important shift during this period concerns the relationships between power and knowledge. From the Enlightenment onwards, institutionalised systems also co-opted knowledge itself. Seeking to control what could be deemed knowledge, they were able to mask power behind (apparent) reason, thus controlling the terms on which discourse could be conducted, and retaining the ability to suppress or ignore disputing discourses.

The relevance of these four themes to Oralism are clear; by the end of the century, the rise of universal education and state intervention for the first time, the convergence of several branches of state power, the new disciplines and professions which emerged to institutionalise them, the growth of a specific form of religious discourse, the continued reification of the idea of science, the expansion of colonialism, racial theories and eugenicism, together with the increased speed of international communication and the control of the media, facilitated the desire of the wealthy to control the education of all Deaf children, by forming one immensely powerful *discursive system*.

The role of the media within this system is also important in respect of the almost immediate willingness to believe the oralist dogma. *The Times* reported extensively (and daily) on the Milan Congress, printing an editorial stating that 'Deafness is abolished', one week after the conference ended, itself a profound comment on oralists' influence within the communication process by this time. It also asserted that in Deaf education in general, there was 'virtual unanimity of preference for oral teaching', an immense untruth. Nevertheless, these comments and 'facts' were then widely reported across the continents in other media. The particular importance of both statements is their indication of the media's willingness to believe in them; in part due to its need for spectacle, which is of course economically motivated, and in part because of its close ties with the trope of scientific progress which, as we have seen, is also similarly impelled.

Thus the totalitarian nature of Oralism meshes with the totalising mechanism of the discursive system, helping to explain the two aspects of Oralism which some have questioned; one concerning the reasons why Oralism was not simply content to remain an educational tool for children of the nobility and wealthy and the second, as Mirzoeff (1995) summarises, how what was simply one of several schools of thought became transformed into the *only* acceptable system in the 20th century.

Post-Milan Developments in Deaf Discourse

In order to understand the Deaf response to Oralism, it is necessary to understand the contributions of three groups of people to this discourse. One consists of the hearing professional allies described earlier, themselves falling into two groups. Another is what might be termed the Deaf élite. These consisted of Deaf teachers, headmasters and missioners, whose discourse was reflected in the growing numbers of Deaf periodicals. (In order to put this group into perspective, it should be noted that in most countries, fewer than 10% of the nations' Deaf children were even receiving an education.)

These two groups then, formed a partnership in resisting Oralism. The relationships between them are too complex to unpick at this present stage of historical research. Baynton (1996) makes a good beginning in problematising the idea of pre-Milan relationships between Deaf and hearing professionals as a Golden Age; some of these themes will be returned to later.

The third group is the ordinary subaltern Deaf population and their own discourses. The continued growth of Deaf schools and clubs, combined with increasing urbanisation and transportation systems, all reinforced the development of Deaf communities and their own private discourses, which became regional, then national and finally international as the century wore on. These discourses are rarely recorded, as much because of the impossibility of transcribing sign languages as any lack of respect for the subaltern.

It is not yet possible to measure the degree of interaction and overlap between the discourses of the two Deaf groups, which inevitably varies from country to country and from town to town. Notable examples of united effort can be located however. In the USA, the Deaf schools produced their own newspaper network with almost 50 of these 'Little Papers' by the end of the century (Van Cleve & Crouch, 1989: 98).

Another example of united effort concerns the roles played in the UK Deaf community by Deaf non-conformist lay preachers. Several became prominent by linking with subaltern Deaf people to set up missions (and therefore clubs) on a voluntary basis, some even clashing with hearing paternalists whose activities were threatened (Lysons, 1963: O'Neill, 1997).

Some of the themes of their discourse, identified by Van Cleve and Crouch are categorised as 'cultural guidance', 'gossip' and 'controversy' (pp. 100–3). These include concern about Deaf behaviour in majority society settings and the importance of recording individual Deaf achievements to inspire others. Information exchange, both to facilitate cross-country liason and political activity, was also highly valorised. Since by now Oralism was encroaching everywhere, Deaf discourses were forced to defend both sign languages and the existence of Deaf communities themselves. These latter two themes, both unremarkable in themselves, became radical positions and produced radical responses accordingly.

Responses to Oralism

The emergence of Oralism not only challenged the themes established in the Parisian banquets, but threatened to damage, if not destroy, the whole community. In responding to this, Deaf discourse includes one important perspective which _marks it out from all hearing discourses in the field_. This challenges Oralism not only for the individualism on which it it based, but as a threat to the quality of Deaf _collective life_. Simply put, if Deaf schools under Oralism produced illiterate and emotionally crippled children (as was claimed at the time), then within one or two generations Deaf communities would not be able to maintain their organisations – the quality of leadership would have degenerated too far. As Minakov, the director of the Russian Deaf organisation, puts it:

> Our schools are our weak spot. We expect new staff from them, we expect replacements, but in the majority of cases, the child who has spent eight to nine years at school emerges ignorant and unprepared for an independent life, without any qualifications. (Williams, 1993)

This perspective and the philosophies behind it has always informed Deaf discourse, and contained many more subtleties than the previous example indicates; yet to this day it has remained virtually unrecognised. It may always have been doomed to be unsuccessful, outflanked by those discourses promoting individualism, yet it was the wellspring of a massive international effort particularly between 1880 and 1900, to resist Oralism.

The language used by the Deaf discourses was at times very blunt. McGregor, a Deaf principal of the Ohio school, trenchantly summarised the events of Milan:

> The ascendancy of the pure oral method has been attained by methods that the deaf, as honest, law-abiding citizens abhor, detest, despise, abominate . . . Must not that be false which required for its support so much imposture, so much trickery, so much coercion; which belittles, or utterly   ignores, the opinions of its own output? . . . In this war of methods the verdict of the educated deaf the whole world over is this: the oral method benefits the _few_; the combined system benefits _all_ the deaf . . . Anyone who upholds the oral method, as an exclusive method, is their enemy. (in Lane, 1984: 395)

Another prominent Deaf educator, J.S. Long, stated:

> The Chinese women bind their babies' feet to make them small; the Flathead Indians bind their babies' heads to make them flat. And the people who prevent the sign language being used in the education of the deaf . . . are denying the deaf their free mental growth through natural expression of their ideas, and are in the same class of criminals. (in Lane, 1984: 371)

A French Deaf publication of the time defined Oralism as the method of 'violence, oppression, obscurantism, charlanism, which only makes idiots of the poor deaf-mute children'. Sham congresses like Milan were relied upon by the oralist 'in order to retain his shameful post of murderer of the intelligence and soul of deaf children' (Lane, 1984: 404).

Other publications set themselves to investigate what was taking place under Oralism. The *British Deaf-Mute* published an ongoing series of articles, and in December 1892 it described the situation at one German school in a lengthy piece summarised here:

> It transpired that . . . the pupils had their hands tied behind their backs so as to prevent them conversing by signs, and that they were moreover continually flogged with canes and struck with rulers. On one occasion, twelve of them came out of class covered with blood. The teachers, in   endeavouring to induce their pupils to pronounce sibilants, had forced instruments into their mouths which made the tongue bleed, and in order to make the children open their mouths, the masters pinched their noses so hard as to cause blood to flow. (1892: 25)

These forms of Deaf resistance nevertheless achieved many lasting results. All over Europe and the USA, national Deaf organisations came into being; in the USA the NAD was established in 1880 itself, whilst the BDDA was established in the UK in 1890. The first resolution passed by the latter confirms this connection, protesting Earl Granville's imputation that

> [T]he sign and finger language was barbarous. We consider such a mode of exchanging our ideas as most natural and indispensable, and that the Combined System [sign and speech] is by far preferable to the so-called Pure Oral. (Grant, 1990: 28)

Additional achievements of the time included the setting up of Deaf-run insurance companies and an increase in the numbers of Deaf magazines. In examing the British Deaf-Mute, we find that a notable strand of Deaf discourse was a formal recognition of Deaf history itself – the Deaf schools and clubs had now existed long enough to be seen as part of a historical process. NAD even pioneered the use of film in 1913, recording a number of Deaf speeches to ensure that sign language was preserved, and several of these filmed lectures are still available, containing themes which themselves indicate a new depth to self-perception:

> We American Deaf are rapidly approaching some bad times for our schools . . . 'A new race of pharoahs that knew not Joseph' are taking over the land . . . [but] as long as we have Deaf people on earth we will have signs . . . It is my hope that we all will love and guard our beautiful sign language as the noblest gift God has given to Deaf people. (Veditz in Padden & Humphries, 1988: 35–6)

Political activism also took place both on a national scale – in the 1900s, a petition signed by over 1,000 Deaf people was presented to King Edward VII calling for the restoration of signing to Deaf education – and on an international scale. Half a dozen international Deaf congresses were held in the USA and Europe between 1880 and 1900, culminating in the Paris 1900 conference intended by the oralists to ratify Milan. More than 200 Deaf teachers, headmasters and delegates turned up, but since they outnumbered the oralists, they were not permitted even to attend that conference, having to spend the week holding their own conference next door!

These two decades of intense intellectual activity laid the groundwork for the survival of Deaf communities throughout the 20th century; yet Paris 1900 was almost the last throw of the dice as far as turning the discourse tide was concerned. After that, all that was left was to mount a rearguard action which lasted in some places into the first two decades of the next century. The surviving evidence of these discourses in considerable, but still await its chroniclers to outline and refine the themes. One of them, however, is immediately clear – its attempts to expose the chicanery by which Oralism gained its hold (*British Deaf-Mute*, 1893).

Although these Deaf discourses, both those in printed form and those signed in regular subaltern Deaf communties, were maintained, there were to be no such uprisings and outpourings of comparable quality until the 1970s.

The 'Post-Milan' Aftermath – Defeating Deaf Discourses

Perhaps the most remarkable feature of Oralism was the perseverance with it in the face of such dismal results, and exploration of the clashing discourses can help us to understand how its power still persists.

Despite the results which signing Deaf education had already achieved in producing Deaf professionals, artists, publishers and editors of hearing newspapers and so on, it was of course clear that Deaf teachers had to be gotten rid of, lest they prolong the resistance of Deaf children. One such example from the Paris school manifests some underlying themes:

> As a student you revealed that intelligence, energy, and perseverance that allow the deaf to acquire instruction, even with defective methods, and it is with understandable pride that your teachers saw you become a bachelor of science . . . When steam navigation replaced sail, did the young captains, proud of the perfect instrument in their hands, have nothing to learn from the old timers? Of course not . . . thus . . . let us refer to your experience even if we now say Adieu. (in Lane, 1984: 398)

We can note the remarkable contradictions here, as we gaze upon oralists attempting a tortuous logic in order to try and arrive at the desired conclusions. Of importance here is the trope of Nature *versus* Scientific Progress as manifested in the sailing example.

In an era when there were many highly achieving Deaf people, the more honest of the oralists still had to admit the success of sign language. How then to rationalise this? The power of the new scientistic idealism to dismiss evidence has rarely been expressed so succintly since Bell:

I admit the ease with which a deaf child acquires sign language and *its perfect adaptability for the purpose of developing his mind*; but after all, it is not the language of the millions of people among who his lot is cast. (Winefield, 1987: 23)

Bell (1884) also gives utterance to another aspect of oralist discourse which also exists today:

We should try ourselves to forget that they are deaf. We should try to teach *them* to forget that they are deaf. (in De Land, 1922a: 418)

Barely half a century later, the new generations of oralists, so far removed from encountering able Deaf people, would not even believe that signing was a language, so successful had the powers of denial within the discursive system become. Bell's words reveal that he had little interest in, or respect for, the fact that Deaf and hearing people might communicate in writing. He and his colleagues appear to be caught up in a scientistic ideal – that the *very idea of Deaf communal existence must somehow be removed*, even if there is only one logical method which might produce this end, and even if it risked creating a kind of schizophrenia in Deaf people. His eugenic beliefs were ultimately put into practice in Nazi Germany – and were still unsuccessful, unless one counts damaging the quality of Deaf collective life to be a success (Biesold, 1993). This, it would appear, became a major theme hidden within oralist discourse. As Farrah (1923: 155) puts it:

The oral deaf who are really ambitious to make the most of their speech and lipreading, will retain them through life, and this is more easily done if they refrain from associating with other deaf people as a class.

Thus we can see that one result of Oralism would be to divide Deaf people themselves, and the fallout from this is described in later chapters. Buried within this discourse is the assertion that if Deaf people continued to sign, to meet, to organise and to marry, thus disregarding the teachings of their betters, they deserved whatever fate befell them – including the decline in the quality of their collective lives.

What was the Deaf response to this discourse? Forestier, a prominent Deaf school principal, asserted the role of signing in enabling fruitful integration:

> [to remove it] would be to tear it from our very soul, since it is part of our nature, the life of our thoughts. Sign remains the one true means of leading our younger brethren to a knowledge of the national language. (in Lane, 1984: 405)

Chambellan, dean of the Deaf professors at the Paris, school explained it thus:

> Let us spread our sign language among the hearing. Then the deaf man will be torn from his isolation . . . new progress will be made, and a new service done for humanity. (in Lane, 1984: 405)

Both these assertions contain echoes of the discourse of the Parisian banquets – the spiritual dimension and the idea that the extension of signing will benefit humanity. Those who still suppose that the idea of hearing people learning to sign is a utopian one might consider that the case cannot yet be proved because signing has been so heavily stigmatised in key discourses over the last century. If Deaf developments had maintained the momentum they had built up, if Oralism had never happened, society would undoubtedly have continued to witness Deaf people in ever more prominent places, not least through the growth of sign interpreters. Later sections will reveal a more accurate reflection of lay potential.

What of the results of Oralism? What were the prevailing themes in those discourses? One example can be seen in the findings of the French Ministry for the Interior in 1901, where pupils

> after seven or eight years at the institution, were incapable, not only of speaking, but of writing the teacher's name, or even their own. No doubt some of them – not all – could on graduating, earn a few coins in shoe repair or sewing, but this is rather expensive training over eight years in the institution. (in Lane, 1984: 399)

One has to stretch one's imagination very hard in order to credit how pupils would be unable under Oralism to even write their own name; one direction of thought might be that this would reflect how much the education process had been turned into one continual speech lesson

A more detailed example can be found in Farrah's 1923 textbook, which became in Britain an early 'bible' of Oralism and was carried right across the British empire. The data here, and the interpretation put on it, reveal the standards by which Oralism judged itself:

'Out of 100 pupils, 85 are capable, when leaving the school, of convers-
ing with their teacher, family and intimate friends; 62 can do so easily,
while 11 converse readily with strangers on ordinary subjects'. This
leaves 15 % as practical failures and 74% [*sic*] . . . who stand for the
average successes of the oral method.' (Farrah, 1923: 157)

Gallaudet interpreted these statistics quite differently. For him, Oralism
could be counted as successful only if the pupils could learn to converse
with strangers, for he was well aware that sign language, if learned by
family and friends, could be used for conversation much more swiftly (and
on subjects much less 'ordinary'). Additionally, of course, the conversation
with the putative stranger could be conducted in writing – provided the
Deaf youth was able to leave school with that skill. If Bell's criterion was
that Deaf people must use the language of the majority, then it was with
that majority that research must be tested.

For Farrah, such an interpretation was unacceptable:

If Mr Gallaudet's criterion be accepted, his estimation must admittedly
be regarded as not very wide of the mark.

His expectations then amount to 'a standard of proficiency so superla-
tive as to place the deaf on all but an equality with the hearing.' Thus the
mark itself must be re-constructed. Farrar proposes: 'It would be juster and
fairer to take the largest measure of the average success as the criterion, and
to take [those who can converse with strangers] as representing the super-
lative results.'

Having thus established that the criteria by which Oralism should be
measured are the average results of its own teaching, rather than any external yardstick, Farrah and the oralist establishment manage to close the
circle, and shut out any attempts to redefine the discourse. In so doing, of
course, it constructs those Deaf children who do not achieve its own goals
as 'oral failures', when in fact it is the system that has failed. Thus the only
place Oralism can go from here is to emphasise the subnormality of Deaf
children. And so we find the French inspector general writing in the early
part of the century that

[the school] should begin by purging itself of a dead weight of
twentyfive percent composed of the incapable and the semi-
retarded . . . to classify pupils accordingly . . . all the children should
spend two years in the institution, and only after this delay would the
retarded clearly recognised as such be sent to an agricultural institution. The idiots and the semi-idiots should be shipped out
immediately. (in Lane, 1984: 401)

Here we have a prime example of the classification discourse that Foucault describes. Those who do not show signs of profiting from Oralism are stigmatised for that failure. Other strategies mentioned including segregating classes of children from each other, and downgrading the curriculum so that gardening and fieldwork would become the first choice of profession.

An unsurprising consequence was that there seemed to be very few oral successes of any kind. By 1909, even the oralists at their own convention were mildly puzzled:

> It has always seemed to me that there is something terribly wrong with Oralism when it cannot turn out deaf graduates who appreciate the value of the methods by which they were instructed . . . I thought . . . how thrilling it would be to have a deaf man . . . stand up here and defend the Oral method orally . . . We do not see such a deaf man here . . . we have met together to talk about the education of the deaf, and the deaf themselves reject what we are having to say. There must be some very profound reason for this. [!] (Tillinghast in Van Cleve & Crouch, 1989: 132)

This, however, did not appear to result in any significant pause for thought.

Summary

An in-depth summary is not appropriate here, because the narrative has not yet arrived at the present day, concluding as it does in the next chapter.

Nevertheless. although this chapter has ranged widely across space and time, the remarkable differences between Deaf/surdophilic discourses and surdophobic discourses are easy to identify. Likewise, it is possible to identify significant numbers of lay people and communities whose attitudes appear to be very different from those with which we are familiar in contemporary Western societies. We cannot generalise as to the incidence of these surdophilic examples. But what we can say is that most of the accounts from 'deafness experts' which posit an exile that was virtually total are, to some degree, exaggerated and, in some cases, exaggerated for their own ends. Moreover, the examples uncovered of Deaf–Hearing cooperation carry more weight than a simple righting of narrative imbalance. They are, in fact, deeply inspiring, opening up for us dimensions of human existence we were literally unaware of barely a decade ago and may well be the tip of an iceberg or, rather, the mountain-top of a lost valley.

It is also instructive to see the depths to which surdophobic practices were prepared to sink. The extent to which these are inextricably interwoven with political attitudes and practices in general is also intriguing, and it may have come as a surprise to many to find such overt links between Oralism and wealth. It is Lane (1984, 1993a) who has done most to draw our attention to this, and I would take this insight one explicit step further. Oralism as it exists in capitalist societies would seem to be a class-based issue, and if one does not centre future deconstruction of surdophobia from this perspective, we will never be able to analyse its dynamics with any degree of accuracy.

Finally, the powerful discourses of the French Banquets also represent the tip of an iceberg. Would the Deafhood tenets which they have presented to us here survive over the next century, now that the oralist hegemony appeared to have been achieved?

Notes

1. The first known reference to this idea can be found in Markowitz and Woodward (1978) who state, unfortunately without further comment ' In terms of its economic, political and social relations to the hearing society, the Deaf minority can be viewed as a colony.' My thanks to Harlan Lane for drawing my attention to this.

2. Indeed, for those who enjoy the writing styles of post-modernism, Wrigley's analysis of colonialism in the Deaf context goes further than the one contained in this volume, with an amusing and acutely impressionist examination of various symbols and tropes. He also describes aspects of Deaf linguistic colonialism by ASL on Third World sign languages (see also Ladd, 1994). The crucial difference between our approaches is that in true post-modernist style he problematicises the Deaf counter-narrative to a hearing audience before this much-suppressed creature has even had the chance to grow legs and walk away from the dangers which have surrounded it. This is a common concern of other minorities – that in its haste to achieve hipness, post-modernism is happy to walk all over groups which have spent centuries trying to have their suppressed voices heard. In short, to become another arm of neo-colonialism.

   My concern in this first volume is to firm up that Deaf counter-narrative – to help the lay reader understand it on its own terms as a basis from which succeeding volumes can conduct a more sophisticated analysis.

3. My own epiphany with regard to this subject came after the Gallaudet Rebellion, when the new Deaf President, I. King Jordan, referred to what had transpired as a rejection of the 'plantation mentality' and my first tentative steps to develop such theories were embodied in a signed song, 'Charity Colony' (1988). (See Appendix 1.)

4. Although the term 'liberalism' is widely used in political science, it has almost never been used in the deafness domain. Since it is vital to our understanding of colonialism of Deaf communities, it must be summarised here. Kymlicka (1997) emphasises that liberalism is individualistic in conception, and aspires merely to reforming the status quo. Those aiming to achieve profound structural change on behalf of a collective group are more accurately described as 'radicals'. However, I do not wish to suggest that all radicals have theorised or understood the limitations of individualism.

5. My thanks to Philocophus for locating this work.
6. It has recently emerged that even in the present day, there exist communities where the hearing members sign with their Deaf colleagues, as far-flung as Bali, Israel, in Bedouin tribes and in the Yucatan. Research has also confirmed the extent to which other First Nations approached a state of bilingualism in sign and spoken languages; it is claimed that aboriginal Australians have the oldest sign languages – some 80,000 years and these are extensively analysed in Kendon (1988). There is also an impressive collection of field data on Native American sign languages collected by Clark between 1876 and 1884 (republished 1982). Given the Kentish Weald example, it becomes ever harder to believe that this bilingual impulse might not have been more common than we are led to believe.

I have also noticed myself that hearing people in the East Midlands and elsewhere know the British finger-spelling alphabet – without ever having met Deaf people. The twist in this tale is that their alphabets contain one, sometimes two differences. Exploring how this came to be so, I found that the letters they were using had once been part of BSL – 120 years ago – and had somehow been handed down by generations of _hearing_ people ever since.

Another personal example – on visiting the Deaf community on the Pacific island of Maui, I found that they used a sign for 'year' that I had only ever seen before in the Bristol region of the UK. Bristol, of course, was a port whose heyday was in the late 18th century – the same time in which the British assumed possession of Maui . . .

7. In fairness, we should also note that Desloges (1984) speaks negatively of the attitudes of many lay people in the region in which he grew up and in certain other sectors of Parisian life, as does Berthier.
8. For example, hearing people's hangups about their bodies, about using them creatively, of touching and hugging and so on, could be transformed into more 'feminine' qualities. It is notable that sign language classes across the world are constituted mostly of women and Gay men. Straight men as yet are too afraid for their masculinity to take this step in large numbers. If one were to imagine that signing was taught to all schoolchildren, one might fruitfully speculate about the extent to which expression of these physical qualities might reduce traditional male aggression!
9. Baynton (1996) identifies another related theme – that the intensive labour of Oralism was carried out in the main by women. In a valuable chapter (pp. 57–82) he gives several useful explanations for the interconnectedness of Oralism and gender. In the light of Note 8, one might begin to speculate that for straight men prior to Oralism, the use of sign language did not carry the taboos that have subsequently been recognised.

Chapter 3

Twentieth Century Discourses

> The old medical dream of an end to deafness is now an all-but practicable reality. Despite the work being done by contemporary psychologists to affirm that the deaf use as much of the brain as hearing people, and that sign language is acquired in exactly the same manner as other languages, there seems little possibility that the medical community will alter its viewpoint. As in the nineteenth century, the task of winning the support of the hearing for the deaf community falls to culture.
>
> (Mirzoeff, 1995: 256)

Introduction

This chapter continues the historical counter-narrative through the 20th century to the present day, illustrating how the struggle for recognition of the concept of 'Deaf Culture' represents the cutting edge of 21st century discourses about Deaf communities. We re-examine the medical, social and culturo-linguistic models in the light of that narrative, and explain the crucial differences between Deaf and disability discourses. Difficulties in validating the Deaf culture concept are explored and resolved as far as possible, and an analytical framework is established to identify and situate the various discourses in and around Deaf communities; in the process a new concept, the 'Deaf subaltern', is developed.

Oralism's Influence on 20th Century Discourse Developments

Before outlining these influences, it is important to note that Oralism's hegemony did not result in an immediate and total implementation. It controlled Deaf schools in most of Southern England by 1900, but like the earlier Roman invasion, took time to reach the northernmost parts and the Celtic outposts. It was not until 1945 that Donaldson's School in Edinburgh succumbed, and the Catholic schools of the Irish republic taught in Sign until the 1960s. Similar variations in diffusion appear to be the case in the USA and across Europe – more research is required to establish an accurate world perspective. Furthermore, we should not suppose the takeover to have been unproblematic. Rather, we might expect future historical research to uncover numerous examples of continued resistance, as Buchanan (1993) has illustrated. A simple rule of thumb might be to indicate that, in general, the resistance lasted until the last of the old Deaf teachers had died, that is, until the late1920s.

However, we can note that even after then there were 'degrees of Oralism'. Some schools banned sign languages in the classroom only, whilst others pursued the ban into every corner of Deaf childrens' social interaction, whether residential dormitories or their own homes. Some allowed individual teachers degrees of autonomy in how they communicated, whilst others operated a much stricter policy.

We can also note that no matter which policies the schools espoused, the number of professional, born-Deaf teachers was in Europe reduced to virtually zero. In the USA, a few survived and sporadic recruiting continued, although we do not yet know how this came to pass. Subaltern (that is, unwritten) Deaf history usually makes reference to one or two Deaf staff existing somewhere in each school, whether they worked in the grounds, in the kitchens or, at best, in the trade-training classes, and it is generally felt that the latter may have been responsible for maintaining a greater spirit of resistance to the oralist ethos in the schools of the USA.

Notwithstanding these caveats, we can safely say that any beliefs in _Deaf-centred education_ as a pedagogical concept, whether professionally or 'intuitively' rendered, came to an end in 1900. Resistance may have continued, but it was not possible for that resistance to construct itself into a national professional praxis.

Thus, in the century of hegemony for the oralist discursive system, most of the themes outlined earlier have been maintained. Some, like the scientistic discourse, have enlarged their scope, power and influence, whereas others like the religious discourses have declined. The primary theme of these discourses in the 20th century is that of _intensification_ and consolidation of Oralism, and include the following features:

Control of teacher training discourses

Since most of the formalised training courses for teachers of the Deaf were established after 1880, they were constructed on oralist lines. This involved a continuing dimunition in the expectations of Deaf children and a consequent shrinking of the academic and social curricula (Lane, 1984).[1]

Teaching establishment discourses

Since a primary concern of Oralism was to minimise Deaf interaction, discourses were set in motion to justify moves away from residential schooling. At first this movement focused on the creation of day schools, but in the post-war period it intensified to justify placing Deaf children in mainstreamed schooling (National Union of the Deaf, 1992).

Scientism and the creation of new professions

As Science increased its hegemony during the 20th century, so did its equivalent within Oralism. One manifestation of this was the creation of new professions and disciplines, each with their linked discourses. These included increased medicalisation – otology, laryngology and the like – together with educational psychology and speech therapy among others. These intensified the hold on the reins; the web of the discursive system was now much more dense.

Science, technology and Oralism

At the time of Milan and for 60 years thereafter, science was unable to provide any devices which would actually benefit the oralist process. Once the first hearing aids were developed in the 1940s, a watershed was attained. It now became possible for approximately half the Deaf population to be systematically categorised as Partially Hearing (later Hearing Impaired) and removed from the Deaf environment, and a powerful discourse was set in motion to rationalise this. This discourse mutated and intensified in the late 1980s with the development of cochlear implants, whose priority target was the remaining profoundly Deaf children.

Oralist parent discourses

Parents of Deaf children have rarely been recognised as part of the Deaf education system. However, from the mid 1930s onwards, increasing efforts were made to target them, and discourses emerged which stressed the crucial role they could play. After the war this also intensified, with oralist national parent groups being established, and new professions created to inculcate parents in the discourse (Van Cleve 1993). With the advent of mainstreaming, greater emphasis was placed on this discourse, and in the present day the moves towards cochlear implantation have brought further pressure to bear on parents.

Selective education discourses

One of the consistent characteristics of oralist discourse had been to parade a single Deaf 'success' in order to exemplify the miracle made flesh, and to thus claim that all Deaf children were capable of these achievements. That the examples in question were usually drawn from deafened or partially Deaf children was something that was hidden from view (Ladd, 1979). The most common response to this in the discourses of Deaf people and their allies was that limited success was possible for Oralism only at the expense of huge amounts of time being devoted to a single child, and that signed education was swifter, more egalitarian and more cost-effective. This oralist process, aided by a willing media, marked the beginnings of a selective educational discourse within deafness.

One of the most important requirements of Oralism prior to hearing aids was the need to remove children deemed capable of benefit from the system from contact with other Deaf people (McDonnell & Saunders, 1993). This was achieved either within the school itself or through the creation and maintenance of certain selective oralist schools, some being audiologically centred, as in schools for the partially hearing / deafened. In the UK, the apex of this pyramid was set in place by the creation of a national grammar school in southern England, the 'Mary Hare', in the 1940s. Once this network was established, potential leaders of the community could be steered through oralist channels for their entire educational career and taught to reject contact with the community in which they would have otherwise had a leading role. This discourse is of particular importance because of its effect on Deaf discourses themselves, as will later be seen.

Removal of Deaf history from educational discourses

The enshrining of the medical model, constructing Deaf children as atomistic individuals impaired by deafness, inevitably led to the denial of the existence of Deaf histories. At this point in time it is not possible to identify precisely when those histories faded from view in each city and country. Mirzoeff (1995: 5) relates that perhaps the greatest collection of them all, at the Parisian school, was dismantled 'soon after' the Second World War, when 'the works [the musuem] contained were dispersed, destroyed or given away'. Boyce's (1996) important history of the major Deaf figure of the 20th century, the headmaster Edward Kirk, describes how his book was constructed from materials found in a skip in the playground, and this pattern of last-minute retrieval has been repeated several times elsewhere.

Whether these histories were destroyed or simply consigned to dusty attics, the consequences were that beliefs in a collective Deaf mode of being which had been contructed over time were removed from virtually all deafness discourses.

Paucity of academic discourses

Despite the growth of universities and academic discourses in the 20th century, Deaf issues remained for the most part outside them, except for the deafness themes within some medical establishments. We have seen how there was virtually no research into the results of Oralism, and how this discourse was constructed to protect them academically. One crucial consequence of this was the 'lowering' of the terms of reference anyone from the wider academy might encounter should they have wished to examine the Deaf terrain – i.e. that the critieria in use already presupposed an unintelligent Deaf being, so that the absence of oral success could be attributed to this essential state. Moreover, the dominance of behaviourism throughout this period did not in any case lend itself to the recognition of any minorities, let alone Deaf ones.

Welfare discourses

By the 20th century, the network of non-conformist and Deaf-led missions and welfare societies was mostly taken over by the Anglican church (Lysons, 1963). This had immense implications for both Deaf communities and Deaf discourses. New waves of missioners to the Deaf were trained to administer the newly created Deaf colony; finding by then a low standard of Deaf achievement around the country, it was easy for them to create a discourse based on the (supposed) Deaf inability to support themselves or manage their own affairs. The colonialist nature of this project is clear from numerous references. Hodgson (1953) talks of 'deafness as part of the White Man's Burden', whilst Sutcliffe, a deafened missioner and key figure in the establishment of the network, conceives of his colleagues as 'consuls commissioned by a sovereign state to reside in a foreign land and there protect the interests of its subjects'. (The significance of this parallel is that it is intended as a positive idea, not a negative critique.) The missioners took over and extended the national club network, established their own training programmes and journals, and even took control of the BDDA (Grant 1990). Thus what we might call a *social-control* (or *social welfare) model* was set firmly in place.

These discourses were immensely powerful, and almost total in their grip on the community. Deaf people became dependent on their services for assistance with doctors, hospitals, mental institutions, police and courts, for funerals, marriages, births, wills, social security and other legal arrangements and form filling (i.e. literacy issues). Another important role was finding employment for many Deaf people. Any resentment of the missioners was tempered both by Deaf helplessness in the face of their power and by gratitude that somebody was willing to devote time to interceding between them and the supposedly hostile world. The existence of a missioner and his staff (he was always male) in almost every Deaf club in the UK enabled the welfare discourse to penetrate to the heart of the national Deaf discourse. Ironically in the light of the lessening of the power of Christian discourses throughout majority British society, the 20th century saw the Deaf community come increasingly under its thrall. This version of Christianity, in stressing submissiveness to paternalism, also had a profound effect on Deaf discourses.

This is not to say that these developments met only with compliance. Indeed it is probable that the more one researches Deaf history, the more one will uncover subaltern resistance which has been brushed under the carpet and lives on only as distant memory amongst the few surviving older people. Flynn (1999) has produced valuable work on the Australian situation, in both confirming the 'hearing takeover' pattern described here and locating rebellions against this in 1929 and 1931 that were heated enough to result in police intervention. There have also been brief flourishes exemplified by the creation of radical Deaf magazines. In the UK, for example, Dimmock and Spearing formed the *Independent Courier*, which ran from 1945 to 1953, whilst in 1960 the *Argonaut* made a short appearance.

The RNID and the formation of the discursive system

An crucial development in the 20th century was the medicalised pan-deafness movement. Ostensibly seeking to improve the lot of all hearing-impaired people, this impulse culminated in the founding of the National Institute for the Deaf (now RNID) in 1924. This movement, dominated by the medical-oralist establishment and the wealthy and nobility classes, brought Deaf people's own organisations under its aegis, a process whch the BDDA appeared willing to submit to in return for two places on the board (Grant, 1990). Thus Deaf people's access to the political system was thwarted at both ends – representation upwards towards the RNID and representation outwards from there to the seat of power.

By acceding to the pan-deafness movement in this way, even if they reserved the right to conduct their own efforts on behalf of the Deaf community, the BDDA was unfortunately endorsing the medical model which this represented. Now not only would the Deaf community and its priorities be subsumed amongst the huge numbers of elderly hard of hearing people, this move allowed the RNID to represent itself to the government as having the Deaf community's endorsement. Thus, should the BDDA campaign too overtly against Oralism, the RNID could use its upper-class political contacts to ensure these views were not taken too seriously.

However, perhaps the most significant aspect of the RNID discourse was that it created a central focus where both the medical model and the social-control model could be brought together (see Figure 1); thus the previously separate colonisation systems for the Deaf child and the Deaf adult could now be joined in a huge new discursive system. The repression of Deaf communities and other problems caused by this new system have persisted over the last 50 years, continuing to this day (Alker, 2000).

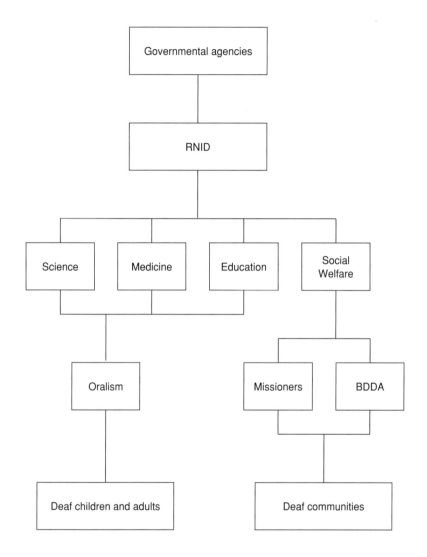

(Linguistic colonialism)   (Welfare colonialism)

Figure 1 The Deafness colonial system

Although this example from the UK may not be typical of the ways and forms in which the discursive system was created around the world, we can note that a similar structure was set in place in Ireland, as Crean (1997) confirms.

Lay discourses

One of the effects of Oralism was to remove Deaf people from the public eye. Whether by ceasing to give art tuition in Deaf schools, as in Paris, so that the numbers of notable Deaf artists dwindled to nothing, or by lowering the educational standards so that Deaf people no longer achieved prominent positions, Oralism reduced the prospects for Deaf individuals to come to society's notice. By cutting short the burgeoning sign language interpreting movement, it also reduced the possibility of Deaf groups being seen in prestigious public places such as the theatre or in the politcal arena.

This, together with the reification of technology and medicine by ever increasing numbers of the general public, and the complicity between Oralism and the media, (manifested in such films as *Mandy* in 1953) would make it easy to theorise that lay people's opinions and discourses about Deaf people were diminishing, not only in number but in quality. To conclude thus would be overhasty – subaltern and working-class discourses have rarely been placed on record; thus there is no sustained evidence that they actually 'bought into' the oralist ideology. One indication of positive lay interest in Deaf people is interest in learning their language. There is some evidence that they wished to do so (Corfmat, 1990). However, one of the primary channels for doing so was controlled by the missioners, and Deuchar (1984) indicates that lay interest in learning BSL was often either directly refused by them, or that very token amounts of sign teaching were given. Their reasons for this are the subject of speculation, but there are strong indications that by teaching BSL to lay people, the missioners' own hold over Deaf people might be diminished. The absence of records of this discourse is one of the themes which emerge in Chapter 8, where the study reveals some evidence in this domain.[2]

Summary

By the 1970s, these intensification processes reached their peak, so that any discourse about Deaf education was couched in terms of differing opinions between groups of *hearing* educationalists – Deaf people's notable earlier opposition had now been completely removed fom the discourse. This totalising discursive system is labelled the 'audist establishment' by Humphries (1977). By this time, these discourses had also removed any trace of the existence of a Deaf community from its records and teachings; the concept of Deaf history could now be deemed to be non-existent, and any lingering beliefs in the linguistic validity of sign language (which even Bell had recognised), were erased. The colonisation of the Deaf community now seemed total, and its eradication imminent.

Deaf Discourses in the 20th Century

Upon the 'defeat' of the Deaf discourses, with the removal of Deaf teachers and trade trainers, and the decline in Deaf literacy and pride, there was a concomitant reduction in the number and quality of professional Deaf discourses. Although a body of literature, chiefly Deaf periodicals exists, no-one has yet made a study of these in the UK. For the USA, Burch (1996) has conducted a valuable study which illustrates how their own Deaf discourses and resistance continued, and the extent to which Deaf teachers continued to find work in Deaf schools. What seems clear, however, is that outside of the USA, such magazines depended on a handful of Deaf writers, and most were founded or taken over by hearing people, mainly the ubiquitous missioners.

Nevertheless, the existence of universal Deaf 'education' and the meshing of networks already established resulted in the development of a set of covert Deaf discourses, whose existence has only recently been threatened by the advent of the mainstreaming policies that physically removed Deaf children from access to them. It is difficult to analyse these discourses, since filmic records are virtually non-existent, and written accounts are almost totally absent.

Thus an important aspect of the framing of this study must be to take note of the increasing distance over the 20th century between what Deaf people as subalterns experienced and expressed and what evidence can be found in the literature. As matters stand at present, past and even present subaltern Deaf discourse has, in effect, been 'struck off the record' by the academic establishment, making the task of establishing subaltern or 'grass-roots' Deaf credibility that much harder. To give an indication of those topics, subjects within the discourse known to the writer but declared traditionally academically inadmissable include the realities of life within Deaf schools, the experiences of Deaf club members encountering mentally damaged young Deaf school-leavers and discourse around the embezzlement of Deaf club funds and the placement of Deaf rebels in mental hospitals by some missioners.[3]

The unrepresentative nature of printed Deaf discourse is given further emphasis by the totalising nature of the colonial system now established. The only profession open to Deaf people was to become missioners themselves, and the selection process was in the hands of those not inclined to encourage rebellious types. For many years also, the Deaf leaders in the

BDDA, later BDA, were also Deaf missioners; thus the professional Deaf discourses are quite unrepresentative of Deaf thinking during this time. This is not to imply that the new Deaf élite were uncaring about the community as a whole, rather that radicalism in any form was thereby eliminated from their discourse.

Any attempts to develop a radical Deaf discourse were also thwarted by the rise to prominence of orally educated hard of hearing Deaf people, usually offspring of the wealthy, several of whom were selected by the RNID whenever token Deaf representation was required. Such co-optation had a significant effect, fragmenting the previous Deaf consensus on language, education and so on.

Among the few areas of Deaf subaltern discourse left in Deaf hands (at least untll the formation of the British Deaf Sports Council by missioners in 1953), was Deaf sport and social club activity, the importance of which is discussed in Chapter 8.

In short, there is no question that Oralism has had a disastrous effect on the quality of Deaf discourses. But there have been very few attempts to bring that information into the academic domain. Recently, however, under the aegis of Deaf history, some Deaf people have begun to set down in print some of the forms which occurred within subaltern Deaf discourse. One strand begins with thoughts and feelings about their oral experiences. This itself is so widespread that it is known to all Deaf adults over the age of 30 right across the world, and to most below that age. Indeed if one is ever at a loss for a conversational subject with a Deaf acquaintance, questions about school experience are virtually guaranteed to get a response.[4]

Examples of this strand include McDonnell and Saunders' (1993: 259) sustained account of the Irish situation. One theme they produce extends the strand into adulthood:

> After school I went to work in a large department store. The principal of the school told the manager that I was not allowed to sign and he circulated a letter to the staff telling them that they should neither sign to me, nor accept signs from me. The following year a second deaf school leaver got a job in the store. The manager told me he would take her on provided she and I would never meet during break times.

It is of course unthinkable that ordinary schools would attempt to influence their ex-pupils in any way, let alone to control every word they attempted to utter. It is not surprising, then, that

> [M]any years after leaving school I behaved as if I was still being supervised. My school experiences affected my relationship with my

children, who are hearing. For example, I was afraid to sign to them . . . It took a long time to overcome this. (p. 258)

A Norwegian account describes three more aspects of the strand:

> Constant apologies made because one does not know enough words . . . sign language should not be used out on the street, in cafes or on the tram . . . Discussions between Deaf people . . . would be interrupted through use of the argument that hearing people have said – so there! (p. 245)

Mally (1993) gives a sustained personal narrative of the German situation, noting how Oralism divided and demoralised the Deaf community, citing Deaf people's unwillingness to pay enough subscriptions to maintain their own organisations (having been brought up to be passive and left feeling helpless), the inability to hold open-minded discussions, and the consequent 'usual dictatorial leadership' (p. 196) that ensued. She describes in detail how those Deaf people who also believed the oralists or who wished to retain the positions of power that better hearing had enabled them to attain, tried to suppress those who wished to take a more 'Deaf' position. These patterns are familiar to Deaf people around the world.

Widell (1993), in describing the Danish situation points out that an inevitable consequence of Oralism is that Deaf children internalise and grow up with 'a feeling that "I cannot, I am no good, to be a hearing person is good, to be deaf is bad"' (p. 464). These two separate but related points lead to another which is equally disturbing:

> Many Deaf people think that the Danish culture is a simply a 'hearing' culture and therefore not suited for them. (p. 470)

This strand of discourse is known right across the world, and has important bearings on the formation of the Deaf cultural concept. The irony in these observations is that *one of Oralism's tenets is that use of sign language alienates one from society and that integration can only occur via speech.* As one can see from the previous comments, this ideology had exactly the opposite effect.

The views in this strand have been known to entire Deaf communities across the globe for a century. Yet in all that time, none of them were able to leap the barriers erected between Deaf and public discourses.

One should not make the mistake of thinking that all subaltern Deaf discourses were negatively oriented. There was much of positive note, including 'simple' everyday issues concerning social life, families, games, pleasures and so on. And beneath all of these was another impulse which would later stand Deaf communities in good stead when the political situation improved:

> Until the 1970s, there was little progress for Deaf people in Germany; there was only their monotonous daily rhythm of [low status] work. The leisure time spent in the Deaf association was the only sense of life for Deaf people. There they could build up and cultivate human relations. National and international sporting events constituted the few highlights in their life. It always struck me that there was such thirst for knowledge among the Deaf. They longed for more information and sat together until late in the night to share information. *This is a typical feature of their own culture.* (Mally, 1993: 178, italics mine)

As will be seen in Chapter 8, Mally seriously underestimates the pleasure, creativity and vivacity of local Deaf life. However, in identifying this ceaseless drive for knowledge, by a people not only cut off from radio, television, film, theatre and public discourses, but also now rendered unable to gain information even from reading, she draws attention to a subaltern determination that continued to operate, albeit covertly, right through the century.

Changes in 'Hearing' Discourses, 1965 to 1980

The profound changes in Western societies which began in the 1960s can be described as primarily cultural rather than political (since the economic and political challenges posed to capitalism during that decade were beaten back throughout the 1980s, whilst certain cultural effects have found their way into societies). Some of these changes have penetrated the Deaf community and its colonial administration in the following domains, among others.

In examining the 'hearing' discourses before turning to the Deaf ones, I do not mean to suggest that positive changes in Deaf people's lives came solely as the result of hearing allies' efforts. Separating and ordering them thus is a narrative device necessary to preserve a certain flow. In reading about the changes, then, one should bear in mind that many of the positive strands therein were also enabled as a result of the Deaf discourse efforts which are detailed in the next section.

To begin with then, it should be noted that there have been two waves of changes between 1965 and 1980. The first is what I have termed the liberal or social democrat discourse, which was an extension of the social control/ medical model. This had a reformist bent, seeking to modify the structures that existed rather than to rebuild them. The second, a resurgence of the linguistic model, was more radical, but because it is comparatively recent, it is beyond the scope of this study to speculate as to the degree of that radical-ism. Certainly there are suggestions that even the most radical advocates, finding that they have had to work with the existing system, have to some extent regressed into a reformist position. This is perhaps a good example of the power which discourses in general hold – in order to engage with them, one must struggle with their terms of reference to subvert them from within – a task which can prove overwhelming and ultimately disheartening, causing one to settle for less than one had dreamed of.

For ease of reference I have noted within some sections some of the Deaf reaction to the liberal developments, whilst retaining the reactions to radicalism for the next section.

Social welfare discourses

Liberal discourses from the generic social work fields, especially that which emerged from the Seebohm Report of 1968, resulted in the gradual removal of Deaf welfare issues from the missioners' control, and the creation of a new profession of Social Workers for the Deaf. This adjustment to the social-welfare model did enable more freedom for Deaf people within their clubs, but there were disadvantages also. Whereas for the missioners, a deep (implicit) knowledge of the language and culture of Deaf people was desirable, the new discourse, orignating from without was unwittingly influenced by the medical model. It categorised all types of deafness together as hearing-impaired, so that finding jobs for Deaf people was handled within the same framework of assisting elderly hearing people to accept and use hearing aids. This combination of models resulted in services for Deaf people often becoming inaccessible to the 'client group', because the professionals knew little sign language and, in any case, the services were oriented towards individual needs rather than the 'community work' approach of the missioners. These changes have led in many areas to a complete breakdown in social work services for Deaf people which is only now being publicly acknowledged.

All this led to a subaltern Deaf discourse which somewhat ironically bemoaned the loss of the missioner. The main strands of this discourse were that the missioners were available at all hours, were present when the Deaf club was open, 'understood Deaf people' and also were accomplished signers. These amount to what we can now see is a culturally-oriented perspective; the missioner was (subconsciously?) aware of the community-oriented nature of Deaf life, the fundamental importance of sign language and the cultural behaviour which linked both community and language. Underneath this discourse was another strand – Deaf people were losing someone with whom they had formed a dependent relationship, as well as an advocate, a role not available to 'neutral' social workers. If we refer back to the list of tasks undertaken by the missioner, it is not difficult to see how many became problematic under the new system.

In recent times, with the development of the linguistic model, some agencies have been able to move back towards a community-based service. Ironically, these have usually occurred in areas where social services had allowed the missions to remain in place, and have often resulting in a more liberal system which has employed more Deaf people as professionals.

Recent awareness of the linguistic model has also resulted in a channelling of resources and posts into a new profession, that of the sign language interpreter. These changes, especially the latter, have resulted in a complex new set of discourses, one within the profession itself and ones within the Deaf community. They have not yet found sustained ways to dialogue with each other, and summarising them adequately is beyond the scope of this study. But we can note that one source of underlying tension relates to perceived power imbalances – on both sides.

Educational discourses

The changes within this domain have been rapid and complex, focusing on the following issues.

The intensification of the oralist web was challenged in the mid-1970s by a liberal discourse inspired in part by the wider social changes. This manifested itself in the advocation of an apparent compromise – stylised forms of sign language, sign systems, were to be used simultaneously with speech. This was known as the Total Communication movement, and was adopted by most schools in the USA and about half of the UK Deaf schools. The results have not been as good as its advocates had hoped. Research has shown that when communicating this way, the full English sentence is seen or heard, but numerous signs which accompany are dropped (Johnson & Erting, 1989), producing what to the Deaf child is visual gibberish. Even when signed in full, the information makes no sense visually, because the signs are of course used in English grammatical structure. No-one could learn French if the only version taught was re-arranged to fit English word order!

Moreover, hearing teachers who know only a sign system do not realise that sign language manifests a 'visual logic' of its own, has its own visual grammar. Unless a teacher is able to use this with children, complex concepts, ideas and explanations cannot easily be transmitted. Even worse, such a teacher is unable to understand much of what the children sign to him/her, or to each other. For Deaf children from the earliest age begin to sign almost instinctively, one might say, by operating from their 'visual grammar' and this communication becomes a sophisticated sign language very quickly indeed.

Indeed, it is a remarakable fact that all the world's sign languages that have so far been researched exhibit the same basic syntactic grammar. Spoken languages, as we know, have a multiplicity of different grammars. But it appears that so great is the visual logic of sign languages, that their grammar might well be a powerful neurological, even biological universal – an exciting concept for humans of the 21st century to engage with. (As we have seen in Chapter 2, of course, numerous lay people and Deaf communities of the past have understood the basics of this idea, been excited by it or attempted to construct philosophies around it.)

Sign systems are thus problematic at many levels of the educative and learning processes, and progress certainly much slower than Deaf people know is possible. It can be argued that this movement is, in effect, an offshoot of Oralism itself. By seeing signing as 'a communication tool' and Deaf staff merely as 'educational tools' or 'role models', the movement has maintained the same power hierarchy as Oralism. Moreover, in retaining the 'us and them' perception, it has been unwilling to stop and ask what it might learn from a shift to a 'Deaf-centred' or 'Deaf child-centred' philosophy, where identifying and enacting 'Deaf ways' of learning might be the way forward.

In these respects, then, we can read the signed systems movement as an example of liberalism, where there was no attempt to reconstruct the power base of the education system or to really replace the medical model. This has meant that Deaf discourses seeking the return of Deaf teachers and Deaf philosophies have faced entrenched opposition.

With the emergence of the linguistic model from the academy, a new discourse attempted to centre Deaf education around that model, and in the 1980s, bilingualism/biculturalism theories began to circulate. However, the proponents of these within the Deaf education system were also of liberal intent and had in any case been trained within the oralist ideology. This movement is still gathering steam, and in the Scandinavian countries, has virtually replaced the oralist system. In the UK, however, since few changes have been made at the teacher training level (and since many of the old oralist trained teachers are still in place), each school has only been able to develop in an *ad hoc* manner. Many more Deaf people work within the schools – but the vast majority are confined to the level of classroom aide, and thus face a double hurdle – their deafness and their work status. At present then, the changes have often been limited and superficial changes ones which have been grafted onto the medical base. In the USA, following the successful 'Deaf President Now' campaign at Gallaudet University in 1988, the number of Deaf heads has risen from two to 18, and this, together with the development of Deaf Studies teaching materials, has begun the process of reinstating role models of the appropriate status who could therefore actually carry out policy changes.

Academic discourses

As described earlier, discourse around Deaf issues (other than scientific ones) was almost non-existent in the academy during the 20th century. This began to change with the emergence of sign language research in linguistic departments during the 1980s.

Stokoe, trained as a structural linguist, made the all important break-through at Gallaudet University in the 1950s (Stokoe *et al.* 1965), and his assertion that sign languages were *bona fide* languages was confirmed by subsequent research. This was of inestimable value to Deaf communities; once their languages were confirmed to be the equal of spoken languages, other important discourses could begin.

Apart from the profound challenge to Oralism described earlier, this development, almost at a stroke, placed many of the philosophical issues of preceding centuries back on the agenda, albeit in modern form. Not the least of these was the idea that once more humanity had something to learn from Deaf people. Sign language linguistics posed central challenges to many aspects of mainstream linguistic theory and via neurolinguistics and psycholinguistics (Klima & Bellugi, 1979; Sacks, 1989), ironically opened up channels by which the medical model itself might be subverted. Similar challenges could also now be made to psychological discourses (Lane, 1993a, Kyle, 1991a).

Once Deaf people were recognised as a linguistic community, it was but a short step to perceive them as cultural communities, thus empowering pioneering works within the traditional disciplines of sociology (Higgins, 1980), history (Lane, 1984), anthropology (Groce, 1985), social work and psychiatry (Denmark, 1981), art (Mirzoeff, 1995), politics (Wrigley, 1996; Jankowski, 1997), linguistics (many examples from Stokoe *et al.* 1965, to Sutton-Spence and Woll, (1998), multilingualism (Skutnabb-Kangas, 2000) and philosophy (Ree, 1999), among others.[5] The newer disciplines, such as cultural studies and disability studies have not yet been the recipients of such groundbreaking work. However, with the exception of linguistics, these texts have at present had only minimal impact on the disciplines in which they operate, although of course they have been influential in chang-ing the discourse tides. Perhaps a primary marker of their value is in their contribution to the development of the discipline of Deaf Studies itself.

These new discourses would appear to pose an immense theoretical challenge to the academic institutions which were the home of medical models. However, the fact that the latter have continued virtually unchanged is particularly instructive for those seeking to deconstruct discourse patterns. The absence of change is not unconnected to the fact that deafness work operates only on the fringes of the academy. On those fringes, they were able to conduct their work relatively unsupervised; their mainstream professional colleagues knew little about Deaf communities and therefore deferred to their 'expertise'. Furthermore, as was described earlier, one central characteristic of Oralism was its inherent refusal to investigate itself academically. Thus the medical–educational nexus was profoundly unacademic in character, and even, given its (unconscious) behavioural positioning, actively anti-intellectual (Montgomery, 1976).

However, once the process of engaging the academy in Deaf issues had begun, 'outsiders' with fresh eyes entered these discourses, effectively for the first time in centuries, so that Oralism stood, *in potentia* at least, at the brink of being revealed for what it was – a class- based power bloc and discursive system which had cloaked itself in quasi-academic language (Lane, 1993a).

Finally, another important development within the academy has been the opening up of universities to Deaf people during the 1990s for the first time in history. The British Sign Language Training Agency, based at Durham University, was of particular importance as a channel for the linguistic model to enter Deaf people's own discourses. One of the original pioneers of sign linguistics, Bristol University, has for the past 20 years developed substantial Deaf Studies research and teaching programmes. In the last few years, other universities such as Central Lancashire and Wolverhampton have also established Deaf Studies programmes.

The importance of Gallaudet University in respect of academic discourses owes much to the publication records of its faculty, the creation of its own publishing house, and the extent to which it supported academic journals such as the *American Annals of the Deaf* (1846 to date). Although the university has existed for 130 years, the flow of knowledge has often been one way – from hearing lecturers to Deaf students. This was also the case at the National Technical Institute for the Deaf, and the Deaf campus at California State University, Northridge. Beginning with the emergence of some Deaf sign linguists, the balance of power has now shifted to some degree, offering the prospect of the development of a Deaf academic perspective, especially in the field of Deaf Studies, and the opportunity to inform wider academic discourse in future. As the prestige of sign languages and therefore Deaf people grows, there is also the prospect of non-Deaf 'new blood' joining this stream.

However, there remains one formidable hurdle within academic discourse – it is almost impossible to acquire funds for research on Deaf-defined social and cultural issues. The funding structure in the UK, USA and much of Europe is heavily weighted towards both social control and medical models, and thus a future in which Deaf people are able to develop and control their own academic discourse, assess their communities' own pedagogical, community developmental and funding priorities, is at present very distant.[6]

Lay discourses

One result of the Deaf resurgence of the 1980s, has been the increased public visibility of the Deaf community. This has led to large numbers of lay people visiting the Deaf community, directly related to their desire to learn to sign, an impulse which, as has been stated earlier, may well be a confirmation of latent positive lay views about Deaf people. Originating from the spread of sign language across the TV and film media from 1981 onwards, and channelled through the British Sign Language Teaching Association (BSLTA) and other agencies, it is currently estimated that over 100,000 lay people have been taught BSL to at least minimum certification. BSL is now the second most popular subject in 'extra-mural' education, and the waiting lists exceed the supply of trained Deaf teachers.

Undoubtedly, the more liberal post 1960s cultural climate has encouraged acceptance and even reification of multicultural discourses. Nevertheless, given the analysis of this chapter, that such positive atttitudes or discourses were often to some degree either present or latent would suggest that once the oral/social control models' grip was loosened, lay people would finally have the opportunity to express their positive attitudes to Deaf people.

New Deaf Discourses, 1975 To Date

It can be seen from the previous sections that the last 20 years have produced an enormous number of changes, for both better and worse, which have been enacted upon and in turn reacted to by what is a small Deaf community. These various waves have resulted in a tremendous increase in Deaf discourse and cultural ferment, with both positive and negative outcomes.

Because of the intensification of the oralist attack on the community, which has coincided with the sheer number of wider technological and social changes in the last three decades, Deaf communities' energies are being extended in two directions at once. One is externally oriented, either to defend the gains made during the period or to resist being pushed further back by mainstreaming and cochlear implants. The other is internally focused, trying to rebuild the community and its art forms and to strengthen and make explicit its cultural beliefs. At the same time it has to deal with the tension created within the community as different sections have grown or declined in power and influence.

One major example is the rise in importance of Deaf families, which began in the linguistics movement. In seeking examples of the most 'typical' and therefore 'best' users of sign language for their research, they began by employing Deaf people from Deaf families, and these people formed a professional core which expanded as demand for their skills arose from some of the changes detailed later. As they 'rose', so those who had previously 'ruled' the Deaf community, those whom Mally describes as having more hearing or being supporters of Oralism, declined in importance, a prime source of tension during the 1980s.

During this time frame also, there have been two more younger generations and the emergence of several sets of Deaf minorities, all of whom have brought new agendas and discourses to Deaf communities. In countries such as the USA and South Africa, where Deaf children and adults from different races were kept apart, these new agendas have brought both pleasure and tension into national Deaf discourse.

A Deaf subaltern movement

For most of the century, Deaf resistance, as has been noted, has been muted. The first signs of change came with the formation of the first Deaf-run pressure group, the National Union of the Deaf in 1976. The NUD's targets were fairly comprehensive – Oralism was its priority, followed by a critique of the BDDA, now known as the BDA, and the RNID. As Chapter 9 will show, this was fundamentally a subaltern movement informed by some Deaf activists who were familiar with post-colonial and Black consciousness developments of the 1960s. The NUD discourse, which had more direct effect on the colonising discourses than on Deaf ones, brought into question the morality of hearing people's control of Deaf affairs, and the suitability of those traditional Deaf leaders who were content to operate under such systems.

One result of this discourse was a move towards political and cultural activism by the Verney administration at the BDA in 1981, a movement which also began the gradual process leading to Deaf control of the organisation by 1994. Given voice by these developments, the issue of (degrees of) Deaf control of affairs concerning them has continued to escalate, peaking in the (temporarily successful) 'Deaf Chief Executive Now' campaign at the RNID in 1994. Once that campaign was derailed (Alker, 2000), a new pressure group, the Federation of Deaf People, took over the NUD's mantle from 1998 onwards.

The creation of a Deaf media

In 1976, the NUD worked towards Deaf access to television via BBC TV's Community Programmes Unit (itself a creation of left-wing activism from the 1960s), and by 1979 was able to make a prototype Deaf magazine programme. Subsequent lobbying by the NUD and BDA, formally constructed as the Deaf Broadcasting Campaign, resulted in the creation of regular sign language programmes across several channels from 1981 onwards. Some of these were more radical and espoused the Deaf agenda (cf. *Sign On*), whilst others were perceived as hearing-led 'cash-ins', and it is the former which can be seen as initiating or contributing to Deaf community discourses.

Not only did this give a significant boost to Deaf confidence and pride, but also brought long overdue visibility and prestige to the community in the eyes of the public, and boosted the morale of the deafened and hard of hearing sectors of the population. In so doing, it gave impetus to a focus on Deaf issues themselves, encouraging a sense of their importance, and was a major factor in the increase of the numbers of lay people wishing to learn BSL.

The extent to which the television media has embraced Deaf views themselves is an issue too recent to summarise easily here. But Deaf people's struggles to gain influence or control over Deaf programming, together with issues of obtaining training in this field, has certainly produced a new set of discourses, although the early hopes of the NUD, that the programming would be consciously constructed to help rebuild and regenerate Deaf communities, has been thwarted, either by those who ran the programmes or the hierarchy which permitted them to be made – on their own terms.

Broadly similar patterns can be observed across Europe, where it can be argued that the British example led the way. In the USA, a spate of Deaf programming in the late 1970s can be seen to fall into these patterns, but by the 1990s, despite (or because of) the proliferation of channels, such programming had become non-existent, a shocking state of affairs in a country which espoused such Deaf pride.

Linguistic minority discourse

The positive effect of linguistic validation of sign languages cannot be underestimated. Mally's (1993: 189) German example can be found right across the world:

> In 1985 . . . the first congress for sign language took place . . . This was a sensation in the German history of the Deaf. 1000 persons attended and heard for the first time: German Sign Language is an independent, fully developed linguistic system which should stand as an equal next to spoken and written German . . . Pardon me? Unbelievable!

The recognition of sign languages then enabled the radical Deaf sectors and their hearing allies to develop a political construction of Deaf communities as linguistic minorities. This new manifestation of the older Deaf discourses has underpinned a global battle for governmental recognition of sign languages, which has found greatest success in Scandinavia and is currently the hottest topic within the Deaf nations within the European Union. A notable attempt to carry the battle to the UN, and to have Oralism classed as a crime under legislation concerning cultural and linguistic genocide, was conducted by the NUD in 1982. Although it failed to be heard, seeds were sown for changes within UNESCO, and the UN later formally recognised the World Federation of the Deaf as a consultation body.

As described earlier, this construction, as carried into the burgeoing bilingual education movement, enabled the re-entry of Deaf views into the Deaf education system, and its effects have underpinned the developments in all Deaf domains ever since.

Deaf professionals and sign interpreters

In 1976, the number of Deaf professionals could be counted on one hand. Following the positive changes described earlier, the numbers have mushroomed so that they now number several hundred, although how one defines 'professional' is another issue. Linguistic recognition also led to over 200 Deaf people achieving qualifications to teach BSL through Durham University, a development that was the brainchild of the BDA. It was these courses which also brought the formal concept of Deaf culture to the community. The development of traning programmes to create sign language interpreters aided the professionalisation process, by enabling Deaf people to break the 'glass ceiling' which had hitherto excluded them on the grounds of communication difficulty.[7]

The rediscovery of Deaf history

The renewed recognition of the validity of Deaf history was sparked off by the publication of Gannon's *Deaf Heritage* in 1981, and especially by Lane's groundbreaking account of American and French Deaf history in 1984. The latter confirmed for the first time in a century that Deaf communities actually had a history, and in describing the rise of these communities and the sheer scale of the oralist attack on them, a profound linkage was finally established between these two themes. In so doing, Lane framed his work in such a way as to indicate that anger with this oppression was a valid, even healthy, emotional reaction (and one which had rarely been overtly expressed for most of the 20th century (Lane, 1993a). His work also validated Deaf attempts to return to the more successful models of Deaf education of the past, and to renewed respect for the 'ancestors', their pride and their more elevated self-conceptions.

Since that time, Deaf historical work has proceeded apace. National historical organisations such as the British Deaf History Society have emerged, and international conferences together with the Deaf History International have developed. This is arguably the site which contains the most overt Deaf discourses in the present day.

Deaf Studies discourses

One can extrapolate a simplified model of discourse development in the modern Deaf resurgence from the accounts given in this section and the one preceding it, and I offer a UK model here so that readers abroad may assess the degree of fit with their own experiences, and thus contribute to a more sophisticated reading.

I identify eight overlapping and interacting stages of development:

- social welfare reform (which removed the missioners)
- the radical Deaf subaltern movement
- the Total Communication movement
- linguistic recognition movements
- Deaf visibility and the media
- Deaf and interpreting professionals
- the rediscovery of Deaf history.

These seven stages have culminated in the eighth, the development of Deaf Studies departments. These have offered Deaf people access for the first time to a range of information about their recent and distant past, and provided the opportunity for numerous young and middle-aged Deaf people to reflect on and research in their own community. These courses therefore constitute the final rung of the ladder which brings Deafhood discourses within reach of academic study.

Crucially for this reading has been the growing conviction during each stage that a 'Deaf Way' of life existed. This has culminated in the fast-spreading concept of 'Deaf Culture', which therefore stands at the apex of the whole movement.

'Third culture' discourses

This theme will be developed later in the chapter, but it is important to place here the emergence of four new discourse domains which have arisen from the Deaf resurgence. The first is the increased numbers of professional hearing allies who have moved to the fringe of the Deaf community in the last 20 years. These have emerged from the changes in sign language status, and include linguists, teachers and interpreters. The second features hearing parents of Deaf children who actively wish to embrace the values of the Deaf community, and the third large numbers of those hearing people who have taken sign language classes. Each finds their attention to integrate into the community is problematic and, in each case the barriers which they meet are now slowly being recognised as cultural ones – that there appears to be a Deaf culture which must be understood if frustration and conflict is not to get out of hand.

The fourth group had always been part of the Deaf community, but had a very problematic relationship with it – the hearing children of Deaf parents (Preston 1994). It is only recently that they have been able to recognise each other, establishing organisations such as CODA (Children of Deaf Adults) in the USA and HMFD (Hearing, Mother–Father Deaf) in the UK. In the process of recognition and exploration, most have realised that, to a large degree, their internal conflicts have stemmed from being members of two cultures (Deaf and hearing), yet fully accepted by neither. In this recognition, it has been the Deaf cultural dimension which has caused the most surprise – they have come to realise that significant aspects of their behaviour, norms and values are, in fact, very similar to those which motivate Deaf people and many of the problems they have faced have been caused by the lack of awareness of this phenomenon by both hearing and Deaf people.

These four groups constitute what Bienvenu and Columnos (1989) have termed 'the Third Culture'. Not only do they considerably widen the potential size of Deaf or sign-language-using communities (at least a four-fold increase), but each has reached a point in their development where the trope of Deaf Culture is of major importance in guiding their future paths. (One might also apply the speculative example of 'what might Deaf life had been like if Oralism had never succeeded' to the status of these four groups. It is highly probable that they would have become a viable part of a larger Deaf community many decades ago and, as such, had a powerful effect on the wider public recognition and acceptance of Deaf communities.)

The Oralist Response, 1980 To Date

As with other minority gains during the last 20 years, this Deaf resurgence was threatened by a backlash, which has taken three main forms.

Mainstreaming

A complex series of discourses formed a new power nexus around the issue of mainstreaming Deaf children and closing Deaf schools. Such strategies existed before the Warnock Report of 1981, but were given further encouragement by it.

Three strands can be identified. One was the liberal/social-democrat move towards including disabled children in ordinary schools, which was supported by many of the disabled élite, but not of course by the Deaf community (National Union of the Deaf, 1992).[8]

The second strand was conducted outside the community within local government discourses, and was characterised by the financial cutbacks of the early 1980s onwards. Mainstreaming was conceived as a cheaper option than Deaf school placement, although, if sign language interpreters had been mandatory for each child, the cost would have in fact been greater. We can thus detect the hand of oralists in the process, and indeed the overlapping point for the discourses was the Hearing-Impaired Services department within the LEA.

This connects therefore to the third strand, the oralist response to the growing use of sign language in Deaf schools. Numbers of such teachers left the schools in the Total Communication movement, and were promoted 'upstairs' to the Hearing-Impaired Service, where they had control over school placements for all the local Deaf children. Seizing the historical moment, they were then able to advocate the removal of Deaf children from those schools and their placement instead within the mainstream, often with the intent of forcing their closure.[9]

The new ideologies used to justify this were convoluted since, in many cases, they contradicted those developed in earlier versions of Oralism. Nevertheless, the net result has been highly effective in achieving Deaf school closure far higher percentages of Deaf children (95.7%) are mainstreamed than for any other disabled group. Thus the linguistic model has made little headway in these three strands. Deaf opposition has been constructed as 'segregationist' and met with considerable resistance (Branson & Miller, 1993). The effect of all these strategies has been profound. Jones (1995: 4) summarises:

> As a result of the fragmentation caused by Oralism and technology . . . it has created minorities within our minority group, differing cultures, languages and communication systems, attitudes and behaviour, leading to aggression and conflict towards one another.

The ancestors, who achieved such remarkably similar results in India, Africa and other colonies, would have been proud of their modern-day descendents.

Cochlear implants

During the 1980s, cochlear implants (CIs) (a form of invasive surgery which implanted electro-magnetic devices inside the cranium) was developed, initially to give some sense of sound to adults who had lost their hearing. However, long before these experiments had provided conclusive evidence of success, oralists seized the opportunity to assert their benefits for young Deaf children (Lane, 1993a). Utilising their contacts in the scientific establishment and the media, a public climate has been manufactured which once again proclaims the advent of the 'miracle cure' and suggests once more that 'deafness is abolished'.

In so doing, they enabled a revival of Oralism itself, and despite considerable worldwide Deaf opposition to these experiments, in most Western countries, the majority of young Deaf children are being implanted. Perhaps the most horrifying aspect of this development is the well-hidden fact that residual hearing in those Deaf children (who could therefore benefit from hearing aids) is being destroyed to be replaced by the technically inferior sound quality of the CIs.[10]

It is illustrative to trace the patterns by which Deaf opposition to these experiments is constructed in these media discourses (e.g. *60 Minutes*, 1993; *Tomorrow's World*, 1994; *Here and Now*, 1994 among many, many others). Attempts to focus on their experimental nature, their denial of the child's right to make their own decisions are diverted instead into a focus on Deaf people themselves, and how they could possibly wish to deny Deaf children this 'miracle'. In taking this path, Deaf people are forced to assert that 'it is fine to be Deaf', which produces further incredulity. The next step is to conclude that Deaf people have come to love their 'sickness' and from this warped perspective are frightened that their kind will be wiped out. Disrupting this representation is a truly difficult task if one does not have editorial control of any section of any media.

Within Deaf discourse, there was immediate and intense opposition. The *British Deaf News* (1985) went so far as to call CIs 'Oralism's Final Solution', whilst national and international bodies passed policies condemning them. The BDA made a rare foray into political analysis in their own assessment of the CI impulse:

> Manufacturers of new drugs, surgical appliance and instruments are compelled to proclaim the benefits of their products in order to remain in business. This consideration already applies at CI centres in the UK; they are under instructions to carry out a certain number of operations per year in order to justify their funding, and are in competition with each other for potential implantees. (BDA, 1994: 15)

Following the worldwide Deaf dissent and resistance, which quickly used the Deaf Culture trope as a cornerstone of their argument, media discourses moved to assimilate it as a negative trope, as Figure 2 illustrates. Medical experts who were previously unaware that such a thing as Deaf communities even existed, found themselves compelled to redefine their terms in order to conduct their own assimilation. In so doing, some of them were in effect forced to reveal their hand, their true views. Responding to one of the few even-handed reviews of the controversy in the _Atlantic Monthly_, Gerald Loeb (1993: 8) declared that

> the cochlear prosthesis, on which I have worked for years with many other scientists, engineers and clinicians, will lead inevitably to the extinction of the alternative culture of the Deaf, probably within a decade.

In an article published by the American Psychological Association, Dr Merzenich made this position even more explicit:

> The simple fact is that if [American Deaf culture] could be reliably wiped out, it would be a good thing to wipe out. (in Fischer & Lane, 1993)[11]

Such apparent hatred of Deaf communities and sign language may seem shocking to the reader. Some may wonder if such views are atypical or extreme, and indeed there are more ostensibly 'liberal' views amongst these professions. However, in their failure to dissociate themselves publicly from such beliefs, and in practising experimentation whilst refusing to allow objective research to take place, the end results for Deaf children, parents and communities are the same. However, what is of course really shocking is the media silence which surrounds and protects them.[12]

CI experimentation is perhaps the first time that the pure commercial impulse of capitalism has impacted so openly and so negatively on Deaf communities. However, as the next section illustrates, it has been swiftly followed by another.

Genetic engineering

In the 1990s, genetic engineering has initiated the process of trying to identify 'the deaf gene', thus bringing within theoretical reach what might be termed the 'final solution' – that of eradicating Deaf people altogether. This has, in turn, reinforced the atmosphere of scientific reification brought back by the CIs themselves. Deaf opposition in this field has been almost instantaneous and, in one respect, quite unexpected by the media. As _The Washington Post_ reported, somewhat incredulously:

> The [genetic engineering] issue has already surfaced . . . [at] Gallaudet University. 'Many of our [Deaf] families are not interested in fixing or curing deaf genes', explains genetic counsellor Jamie Israel . . . 'Many couples come in and want deaf children'. (_Silent News_ 1995: 24)

This desire to have Deaf offspring has been widely reported within Deaf discourse for the last few decades, but is only now being able to cross the discourse barrier, and only when bracketed or commented upon by disbelieving hearing editors, who construct it as a pathological response. In fact it is expressed partly as a reflection of Deaf pride in the quality of Deaf life, partly as a desire to have the opportunity to transmit one's own culture to one's children, and partly because of the knowledge that the more well educated Deaf children there are, the more the quality of Deaf life will be enhanced.

Genetic cleansing, as Mannion (1997) describes it, has nevertheless proceeded apace. As Lane, *et al.* (1996: 420) summarise:

> Practices of genetic counselling and genetic research are commonly aimed at reducing the numbers of, or eliminating, Deaf people, and this goal has been explicitly championed by some scientists and government research institutes in the United States and elsewhere.

These developments have threatened to turn lay people's attention away from the recent pattern of accepting Deaf people and communities and back towards ideas of curing them. The discourses so strikingly resemble those conducted around Milan 1880 that many are disheartened by the ease of their uncritical acceptance 120 years later. The situation is sufficiently urgent that circumventing the gatekeepers to reach positively disposed lay people has become a priority, and debate within the academy and the various medias is also a crucial forum to gain access to. However, given the continued power imbalances within them, it has proved exceedingly difficult to establish a platform.

It is now clear that from this time forth, the existence of Deaf communities is rendered problematic, as the battles above can only intensify with each passing decade. As Truffaut (1993: 20) concludes:

> Deaf generations march down the centuries . . . to us, their faces serious, reaching towards a future which is never secure, because it is constantly endangered. Such is the History of the Deaf.

Deaf Culture as Contemporary Trope of Resistance

In attempting to develop a conceptual base from which to resist this backlash, Deaf people and their allies have espoused arguments which assert that to be Deaf and have access to such a language and a national and international community is a positive state of being. Furthermore, there are valid 'Deaf-centred' ways of perceiving the world which offer benefits to the wider society and which should be heeded in all matters affecting Deaf

Beware the sick world of 'deaf culture'

THE late T.E. Utley, the blind Conservative philosopher, always used to say that he absolutely hated the blind. He was teasing, of course, at least in part; he liked shocking us sanctimonious young things who came to visit him in Fleet Street for enlightenment.

What he truly loathed, I think, was the naive and sentimental assumption that, just because he was blind himself, he must of necessity get on with anybody and everybody else who was blind, and could perfectly reasonably be cast into some job lot of disability with people with whom he had nothing in common other than their regrettable handicap. Nowadays, of course, this miscellaneous group, brought together only by physical accident, would be called the blind community.

The word "community", has suffered so much abuse that it is hard to know what, if anything, it now means. I believe it has come to sug-

gest nothing much more than wishful thinking. There is something rather generous about the wish that those who are oppressed, or sick, or handicapped should, thereby, belong to a mutually supportive community of the like-minded, which will somehow make things all right. But it is a silly and unrealistic wish and possibly

tainted with guilt on the part of those free from these handicaps. It is also oppressive, it denies the differences between people, and ignores their desire to play their life-cards in any number of different ways.

This wishful thinking seems to have developed into a bizarre kind of wishful denial — a denial that disabilities are problems at all. For instance, a passionate controversy has recently arisen in the deaf "community" about new hi-tech hearing implants for deaf children, which enable them to hear and talk, normally. Impossible though it may be to believe, there is an extremist faction among the deaf who oppose the use of these cochlear implants, on the grounds that there is nothing wrong "with being deaf, and that "deaf culture" has its own equal validity. Deaf children should not be deprived of their "deaf culture", any more than black people should be made white.

"Deafness is not a pathological defect to be cured," according to a spokesman of the British Deaf Association. "We're proud of being deaf," said an activist on Radio 4's *Afternoon Shift* last week. Another man interviewed on the same programme, the loving father of a deaf teenage boy, said firmly, "I hope he marries a deaf girl. I hope

There is an extremist faction among the deaf

I have deaf grandchildren. That would be great."

It is not often that I am shocked by Radio 4, but I was absolutely horrified by this. For a man who can bring himself to wish deafness on his own flesh and blood is astonishing. To call it denial would be putting it too mildly.

This father must know in his heart that deafness is a terrible misfortune. It is said to be the loneliest of handicaps. To be deprived of the nuances of other people's voices, of music, of one's children's babbling, of the delights and warnings everywhere — what possible purpose can it serve to suggest that the loss of all that is no loss at all?

I think there is a perversity in contemporary thinking about such things, and not only among extremists, that is rather frightening. I think people fear that a "negative attitude" to deafness — the ideal that it is a defect — must include a negative attitude to deaf people themselves; contrariwise, respect for them must include respect for their hearing defect. Ergo, it is not a defect, but an alternative mode of perception. There is just enough truth in this to make it onto one; it is

true that handicapped people very often develop their unimpaired senses to an extraordinary degree, like the deaf percussionist Evelyn Glennie.

I suspect, also, that this unfortunate father was trying to say the right thing while on air. I am trying to avoid the phrase "political correctness", but I know from my own experience that there is a subtle pressure in the worlds of handicap to take a certain line. This line changes with fashion, but if one has a hostage to fortune (and to fashion) in one of those worlds, as this man has, one wants to be seen as *bienpensant*, for all kinds of reasons.

All too often this does involve talking nonsense. Since so many fashionable ideas about handicap are largely meaningless. But nonsense and wishful thinking are of little use to the deaf child or the blind man; only truth and scientific knowledge will set them free.

Figure 2 Deaf Culture article from *The Daily Telegraph*, 1996

adults and children (Solomon, 1994). As a result of the historical reading in this chapter we are able to see that this is a restatement of the powerful discourses of the Enlightenment period.

Those under the sway of the medical model find these beliefs hard to credit, and identify the Deaf Culture trope as the epicentre of these unpalatable ideas. They have thus begun to attack the very concept which represents the site of contemporary Deaf resistance (see Figure 2). This is perhaps unsurprising given the implications of recognising Deaf culture – *once Deaf-centred concepts are accepted, the whole basis for colonialism is overthrown.*

For the first time this century, therefore, there are two discursive systems, each with their own power bases (albeit grossly unequal ones), competing for dominance, and the central trope of this struggle has become 'Deaf Culture' itself. Given the speed at which the three 'neo-oralist' tenets are being implemented, establishing the validity of Deaf culture has taken on an increasing sense of urgency.

Because of the power and prestige of academic constructions of knowledge, recognising Deaf culture and Deaf subaltern views *within the academic domain* is an essential step in establishing a platform for interrupting oralist discourse, reaching lay people and winning the support required to overturn the colonialism of Deaf people in all its forms.

Summary of Key Differences in Contemporary Discourses

Because of the length and complexity of this historical reading, it may be useful to summarise the situation as it currently obtains.

The medical model

In the medical model, there are two central constructs in play. One is the notion that each born Deaf person is a helpless isolated hearing-impaired individual, with no intrinsic relationship with any other Deaf person, past or present, no group allegiances or history. The other is that these individuals can be 'restored to society' by the use of technology in conjunction with Oralism, especially if they are denied access to Deaf adults and, sign languages and, where possible, other Deaf children.

These concepts are manifested in public discourses by the following strategies. First, the collective existence of Deaf people and Deaf life at all, including the linguistic validity of their signed languages is denied. Second, by judicious use of their connections in the discursive system and the media, examples are manufactured of Deaf people who have the *appearance* of having been cured of their deafness or who have succeeded in 'overcoming their abnormality'. Any Deaf people who associate with one another are therefore constructed as having failed to lift themselves out of their semi-human state. To describe these people, a variety of blaming techniques are employed, so that if evidence of their collective existence does become visible, it is constructed as merely a gathering of failed individuals.

Third, by utilising the academic and media sectors of the discursive system, and playing on lay assumptions of their benevolence, they have kept not only the results of their policies from public view, but also the anti-Deaf nature on which they have been built.

The culturo-linguistic model

This model, which has been implied in numerous recent accounts is formally named and presented here for the first time. This construction focuses on the essentially collective nature of the Deaf experience. Deaf people see themselves as beings who are already whole. The fact of not being able to hear is rendered secondary to the positive experiences created by their social, cultural and artistic lives together, experiences which are situated within the 250-year-old history of their own clubs, schools and organisations. Thus there is a conviction that their own interaction is rich in both its depth and its extensiveness, and of great value in itself. thus their primary concern is to continue to enhance the quality of the collective life, and to ensure the best possible education for Deaf children who will inherit these creations.

In this model, their frustrations stem from the oppression experienced in a range of guises – from low expectations through denigration to active repression – and a belief that if lay people learned to sign, especially as a compulsory part of their own schooling, that both Deaf and hearing communities would be enhanced.

Since a culturo-linguistic group also tends to be a consciously political group, as witnessed in the rise of the Deaf Nation concept (Ladd, 1996; *Sign On*, 1998), there are other implications to this model (Ladd, 1999). As Bhabha (1995) indicates, a physically colonised or language minority group is placed on the defensive; there are always reactionary developments in the majority culture which must be responded to, and thus these languages and cultures are situated in a 'permanent state of emergency'. It might be instructive to review Deaf history as represented in these two chapters, attempt to imagine one's self as a member of a Deaf community and from there conceive of certain aspects of daily praxis.

Figure 3 indicates a distinction between 'wartime' and 'peacetime' issues and agendas. The central box indicates some of the issues in need of urgent attention within the communities. Some of these moreover, would enable the development of positive, joyous and creative activities. These, however, cannot be satisfactorily addressed; resources and human energies cannot be devoted to them when they are needed to deal with the

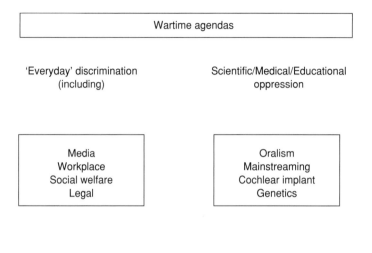

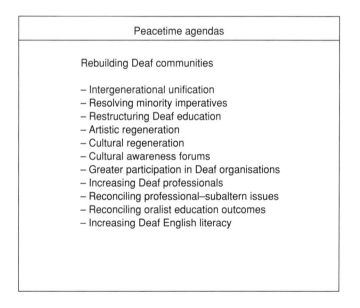

Figure 3 'Wartime' and 'Peacetime' Deaf community agendas

continual external threats. Such pressures can be numbing, especially for the few who have sufficiently survived Oralism and are seen as responsible for tackling them. The recent expression, '24-7-365', aptly summarises the Deaf existential dilemma.

The social model – Deaf and disabled discourses; some important differences

In more enlightened sectors of the academy and society, the medical model has been replaced by the social model, first developed by Oliver (1990). This stresses that the central issue in disability studies is not impairment *per se*, but of societies having constructed themselves to exclude people with disabilities, so that access was something for which they had to beg for. It was theorised that human rights legislation, suitably amended, could lead to societies constructed so that inclusiveness was factored in 'from the beginning' and full citizenship could therefore become a reality for all 'medically different' individuals.

This model therefore constructed d/Deaf issues primarily as access issues. It is true to say that access for deaf people can be improved by government legislation in respect of technological issues (text telephones, TV captioning) and similar improvements can also be made in Deaf access (videophones, sign language on TV, sign interpreters). However, it is also the case that true respect for the existence of a Deaf cultural reality ought then to lead to recognition of those Deaf community issues which lie outside of the social model. The account which follows is the first attempt to make these explicit within an academic framework.

It has long been a central theme of Deaf discourse within certain sectors of Deaf communities that Deaf people are either not part of the disabled movement or a radically different group within it (cf. National Union of the Deaf, 1982). Indeed to give but one example, the World Games for the Deaf (now Deaflympics) have campaigned hard to remain outside the Paralympics, despite the huge differences in financial support and publicity that would accrue from joining forces. These beliefs are centred upon the idea of Deaf people as a linguistic and cultural minority, who should be classed with and 'administered' by political and other agencies concerned with minority languages. Whether or not one accepts this position, it is useful to deconstruct its rationale.

If one understands that sign language is the first or preferred language of Deaf children and adults, and from that basis examines Deaf history, it becomes clear that many Deaf people have always desired to associate with one another, to marry one another, to form local, regional, national and even international communities and to have Deaf children. From that secure basis, they have then sought relationships with majority society, not as individuals desiring to be assimilated into it but as one group seeking recognition and appropriate respect and responses from another. This in sign language discourse right across the world is represented as 'Deaf People' relating to 'Hearing (or 'Speaking') People'.

In the process of associating with each other, they have worked to create schools, clubs, organisations, art forms, culturo-historical societies, libraries and museums of their own. These, traditionally represented in sign as the 'Deaf World', reflect only the external manifestations of their collective life. The internal forms, the values, beliefs, norms and patterns by which they interact with each other, were in some countries signed as the 'Deaf Way' and have only in recent times been given the sign 'Deaf Culture'. Along with this newfound clarity of belief is an awakened recognition that this culture is one impelled by collectivist values, which therefore stand in contrast to Western cultures' essentially individualistic values. For many, the signs 'We' and 'Deaf' are quite inseperable.

The importance of this collectivist cultural value can be seen in its contrast with the individualist values of Western cultures.[13] These augment the medical model by conceptualising the Deaf person as an atomistic individual, so that policies are situated around that belief. In the contemporary manifestation of this belief within the social model and what I term the liberal intelligentsia, this means that the only construction that they can comprehend is that of enabling that individual Deaf person to access majority society. However, as we shall go on to see, this approach not only misses the whole raison d'être of Deaf societies, but has inevitably damaged them as a consequence.

By contrast, Deaf discourses focus on policies which maximise not only the strength of the individual, but also the whole community. Thus, when critiquing the damage created by policies of individualism, their concern is for *how the damage to those individuals negatively impacts on the running of their own communities.* As such, therefore, their concern is for policies which encompass language planning, social, cultural and artistic regeneration and development.

The differences between the discourses of Deaf communities and those within movements of disabled people can be best identified in the field of education. The conventional wisdom of the latter is to push for education within mainstream schools as a prelude to assimilation into society. Indeed, much of this discourse is centred upon an almost violent dislike of their own segregated educational experiences.

By contrast, as we have seen, Deaf communities wish to preserve and redevelop their schools in order to equip Deaf children with the fullest cultural and linguistic confidence possible in order that they may take an active part in Deaf society and, from that basis, have the strength to with-stand the conscious or unwitting oppression that exists in majority society. It is this characteristic which most resembles the agendas of other linguistic and cultural minorities. For these also, education is the background on which the quality, and even the future, of their societies is being fought.

If this is understood, then the sonic dimension can be brought back into play, this time in a more positive light. Deaf education can be seen as a unique site where those who are unable to communicate with the majority, *but also a majority which is unable to communicate with them,* can seek refuge. A member of another linguistic minority, if educated in another language, will suffer psychological, social and cultural confusion, but can become, however unwillingly, part of another culture. A Deaf individual isolated from other Deaf people cannot access any other majority culture in a mean-ingful way, and thus risks not only the confusion described earlier, but actual neurological damage.

People with disabilities, by contrast, appear not to place a high priority on fraternising with each other, other than under the aegis of political or artistic organisation. The disability 'élite' involved with policy lobbies do not seem to socialise with those whose lives are spent in day centres; thus there seems no real cultural core to their interactions (although the last 15 years have seen the beginnings of an exciting artistically-oriented subcul-ture). Another crucial difference can be found in the domain of marriage: 90% of Deaf people who marry choose a Deaf partner. By contrast, most people with disabilities do not see it as a priority or even desirable to marry within the group.[14]

The social model construction has been experienced by Deaf communi-ties as threatening the gains which have been made, but there is sufficient ideological overlap to make it hard for them to refute it. It is for that reason that I have offered in this reading the construction of the 'culturo-linguistic model', as it captured the cultural connectivity and collectivity that marks the Deaf experience and, moreover, renders it much closer to the experi-ence of other oppressed linguistic and cultural minorities.

As if to confirm this reading, it is noticeable that those d/Deaf people who do associate with the disability movement are those who see them-selves primarily as deafened or hard of hearing (or as Deaf people might have it, 'hearing disabled'). It is vital to note that these people share English as a first language with disabled people, and thus there are few communi-cation or cultural barriers. Because these are the people with which the disability movement comes into contact, it is easy for them to mistake the reality of Deaf communities, who face the same linguistic/communication barrier in interaction with disabled people as they do with anyone else. Thus their cultural construction of disabled people as rendered in sign language is 'Disabled Hearing People', and for the hearing-impaired 'Deafened Hearing People' or 'Hard of Hearing People'.

In advancing these readings, I do not wish it to be thought that the issues are as yet this simple. The medical model being an integral part of the discursive system, Deaf and disabled people have been categorised and treated as a single domain. Because of this, and because of the achievements by disabled people in their umbrella movements, Deaf people have been compelled to go along with the political and social changes thus produced.

The prospect of other linguistic minorities admitting Deaf communities to membership of their organisations is still quite remote, and in any case governments are extremely reluctant to ratify linguistic minorities, since they are often political 'hot potatoes'. Thus the effort required for Deaf communities to disengage from disabled legislation is too great – there are more urgent priorities for their energies. The more success Deaf peoples have in gaining government recognition of their sign languages, the more potential there is for the linguistic minority crossover. But it is also possible that once Deaf peoples are satisfied that their different status is respected, they will be happy to participate in the disability movement on a coalition basis. And then, I might add, avail themselves of positive benefit from contact with some of the more impressive activities and creations of disabled people.

Implications of the Counter-Narrative for the Academic Study of Deaf Communities

Figure 4 summarises how the counter-narrative can be seen as embracing a series of ever-widening dimensions or paradigms, which challenges hitherto reductionist academic terminology and indicates the direction in which 21st century conceptualisations might move. Each is now examined in more detail.

For those wishing to conduct research *with* (as opposed to 'on') the Deaf community, the medical model presents several conceptual barriers to be overcome:

Initially, in order to even establish the existence of a Deaf community, one has to work one's way throught a series of ideological strata which attempts to deny its existence. Once that is overcome, the next set of ideologies which appear are those which accept the existence of such a community, but see it as a collection of individuals who are either less than normal or who have failed to achieve normality. It is only at the end of such a process of exploration that one can even begin to attempt an honest academic description of a healthy Deaf community in its own terms. And in turn, it is only after having established and won partial acceptance of *that*,

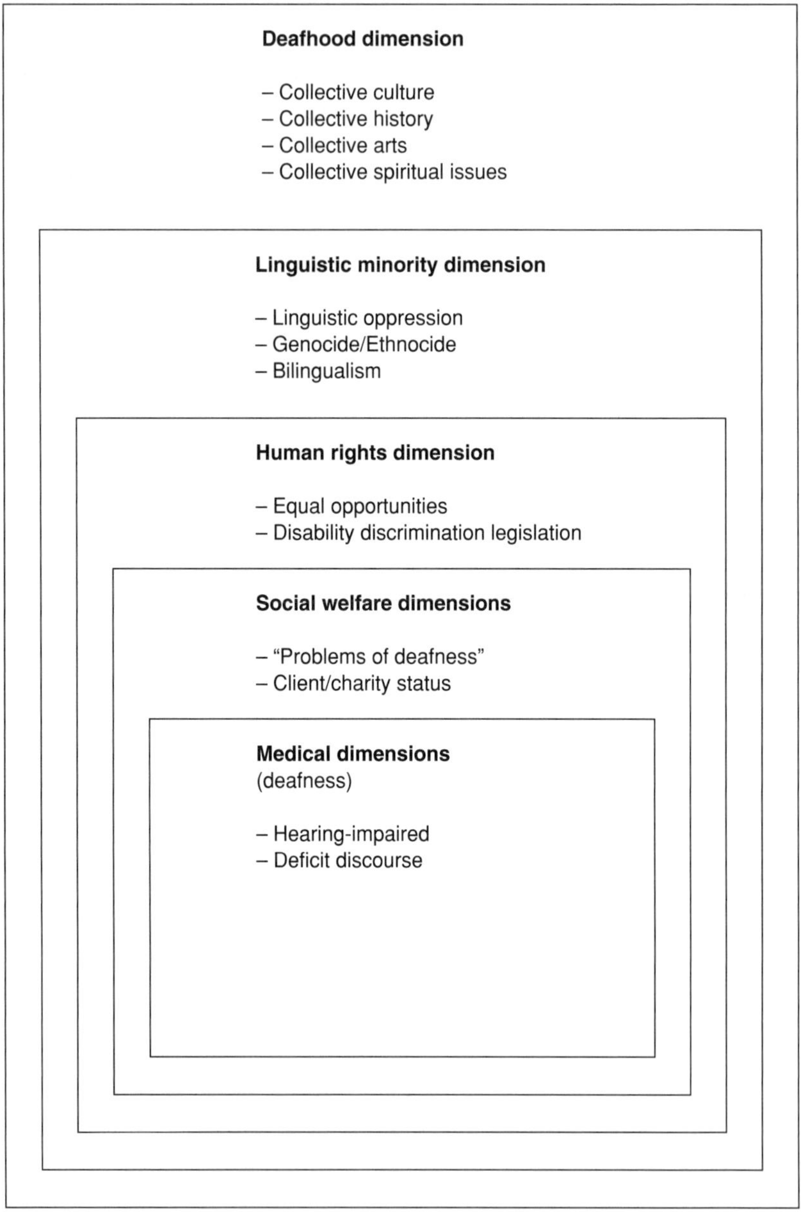

Deafhood dimension

– Collective culture
– Collective history
– Collective arts
– Collective spiritual issues

Linguistic minority dimension

– Linguistic oppression
– Genocide/Ethnocide
– Bilingualism

Human rights dimension

– Equal opportunities
– Disability discrimination legislation

Social welfare dimensions

– "Problems of deafness"
– Client/charity status

Medical dimensions
(deafness)

– Hearing-impaired
– Deficit discourse

Figure 4 Dimensional stages from deafness to Deafhood, together with key terminology for each stage

that one can consider the question of the existence or otherwise of a Deaf culture, let alone build a justification for that perspective, set it into a conceptual framework, and present it to academia and majority society for its consideration.

The necessity of such a lengthy and onerous process goes some way towards explaining *the almost total absence of any academic research into Deaf collective life* on its own terms. Furthermore, these above examples are predicated on the idea of researchers coming fresh into the community from outside. For those already within academia, the process is even more problematic, since they have necessarily absorbed some of the negative views about Deaf people by simply working in their own domains. Definitive accounts therefore, of all the dynamics involving Deaf and hearing people within and without academia have barely begun.

To anyone who is a member or a student of other minority groups, the processes just described will be familiar. Nevertheless, whatever the vicissitudes visited upon these groups, they are at least recognised, both within and without the academy, as possessing a collective life of their own. For Deaf communities to achieve the simple basic fact of that recognition, it is clear that something of a 'long march' lies ahead.

Difficulties in Validating the Deaf Culture Concept

Now that we have an established counter-narrative which not only emphasises the centrality of the Deaf culture concept to a negative critique of colonialism, but describes how this trope is the conceptual battleground for the future, we can begin the process of validating the concept itself. There are, however, a number of issues which render cultural recognition problematic.

Ethnocentrism and hearing impairment

Even amongst the most racist of people, there is now an acceptance that non-white people have their own languages and cultures – the issue in these domains now turns on questions of perceived linguistic and cultural superiority. Yet significant numbers of people find it hard to believe that Deaf communities could have cultures of their own.

There appear to be three main reasons for this. One is the internalisation of the medical model – viewed from that perspective, how can the term culture be linked to a medical disease? In the case of deafness, moreover, a further construction seems to take place. Discourse in the media and elsewhere about blind people or those confined to wheelchairs rarely emphasise the notion of 'cure'. The idea of an education focused on forcing blind children to try and see, for example, is obviously absurd. And yet the equivalent discourse surrounding Deaf communities is heavily laden with ideas about curing or otherwise changing the Deaf state. Despite my years as an activist and analyst, I still find it hard to credit the sheer persistence by which Deaf people are subjected to these notions more than any of the other groups placed in the same administrative category. It would appear that at some deep level of 'folk mythos', that the *pedagogical conditional*, based on the *enfant sauvage* perception still holds good. In one sense we might expect that same folk mythos to credit the cultural perspective – if Deaf people appear like 'savages', then like the so-called savages, they too must have a culture, however primitive. As we have seen, however, this kind of internal discourse has been augmented by the rise of Social Darwinist science-worship leading to oralism's own media-disseminated ideology, that one can 'rise above', 'leave behind' or 'conquer deafness', just as those 'savages' are expected to reject their own culture for the superior one embodied by the White Man.

However, another factor which might help us understand the confusion is the irrefutable evidence that there *is* a continuum of hearing loss. There *are* partially d/Deaf children who become adult and who can function within majority society, or rather, whose speech appears to approximate the social norm and who are assumed therefore to be able to function 'normally'. That many of these might be bluffing or appearing to glide like a swan which beneath the waterline is pedalling furiously escapes notice in the same way as the swan's own hidden efforts. (One difference is that swans will not sink and drown in mid-life because the effort of pedalling has taken its toll on them. But no-one, literally nobody, is researching the mental health realities of partially deaf existence from such perspectives, though Deaf discourses themselves appear very much aware of the downside of the experience that many of their former childhood cohorts conceal from public gaze in attempting to 'pass' (Ladd, 1979, *inter alia*)).

If the reader has absorbed the implications of the Deaf counter-narrative, then they will understand that the Deaf response to partially d/Deaf people is one which stresses biculturality. Why shouldn't those people also be fluent in Sign, be bicultural and move happily between Deaf and hearing societies? Why do they feel ashamed to do so? The answer is that Oralism has made them feel ashamed, but that is only a partial rebuttal. For there is one very visible symbol in play – the 'miracle of science' that is the hearing aid, the white man's own juju which appears to enable its users to transcend their congenital limitations. No magic white stick will enable a blind person to see, no magic 'wheelchair' or implant exists which enables a disabled person to walk. Yet for Deaf people, there apparently exists a little magic box that will turn them into normal people, if they would just quit being so stubborn and use it. It seems to be very hard for some hearing people to give up this example which appears to affirm white people's 'Superiority through Science'. Another reason is that we are all of us in hock emotionally to the medical profession – we cling to deeply held, rarely spoken hopes that medical scientific advancement may stave off all kinds of illnesses and we base our optimism on tangible achievements. *'If 'they', or 'we', can cure or remove smallpox and tuberculosis, surely they/we can find a cure for cancer (and hurry up please before it happens to me)'.*

These forces represent profound cultural obstacles towards the acceptance of Deaf culture, all the more powerful for being unrecognised as majority cultural features, and which are rendered instead as one of the last vestiges of Western 'Manifest Destiny' in our cultures. It is these which blind us to the reality that Granny, who sits alone, isolated from social conversation despite her little magic box, is not experiencing the transformation we have been led to expect. We notice that she can follow some one-on-one engagement, but we are (led to be) at a loss to explain her lack of group participation, and attribute this to age or to a belief that 'she can hear when she wants to'. (In these respects too, we are witnessing the ageism of our society, but that is another cultural feature we do not seem to be ready to confront – not least because it is that same 'Superiority of Social Mobility and Advancement through Science' which leads us to abandon our old people in the first place). If we really understood why Granny cannot cope with group speech, we would be more ready to refute the oralist premises we have absorbed.

Our ability to rationalise in this way can be interpreted as our inability to make connections between some of the various discourses we have internalised, the various selves of which we are made. Our present lack of awareness of this 'psychological philosophy', that we are not simply one indivisible self, but contain and embody multiple identities, thus contributes to the powerful obstacles facing recognition of Deaf culture. In the case of cochlear implants, for example, one would expect the trumpeting of such a 'cure' to represent a contradiction to our absorbed miracle of the Little Magic Box. 'If the box works so well', we might ask, 'then why is such brutally invasive surgery deemed necessary?' There are several speculations we could make as to how this contradiction is rationalised, but the most important one may be that in doffing our caps to science, we are also doing the same to 'The Experts'. 'It is all beyond our comprehension', we seem to say, 'but They must know what They are doing'. Aided and abetted by a powerful media investment in trumpeting abroad these examples of what amounts to a continued but hidden Social Darwinism, we lay our consciences to rest.

It is perhaps unsurprising that, given the extent to which these various discourses have been hammered into our psyche, that one finds so many assertions from the social welfare administrators that 'deafness is an invisible handicap'. To turn this image around, the imposed handicap as we have seen may indeed be invisible, but there is surely no mistaking the striking sight of a group of Deaf people signing to each other whilst participating in public life, a sight which fascinates many for positive reasons as well as negative ones. It is this fascination which leads many Deaf people to believe that lay people have a crucial role to play in achieving social change, for it contains the seeds of a paradigm shift that can hurdle most of the cultural obstacles we have identified. The key lies once again with the media, the only contemporary force powerful enough to expedite paradigm shifts in our secular cultures. Yet these too are controlled by covert beliefs in the individualism of our cultures, and remain hostile to allowing 'airtime' to minority groups which espouse collectivism. Moreover, as we previously saw, explanation of the unique Deaf situation cannot be reduced to soundbites, whereas 'Miracle Cure' may be the shortest soundbite of them all. Deaf communities being small in number, and therefore less able to influence by osmosis (not least because they speak a language few can understand), thus stand in even greater dependence on the media to get their views across than do almost all other groups. The battleground of change, to win the hearts and minds of majority societies, is very much one that must be conducted in the public eye, however disheartening the continued rejection by the media gatekeepers can be;which is a major reason why this book exists in its present form.

Another aspect of ethnocentrism stems from a more benign set of reasoning – hearing people trying to empathise by introspecting about what being Deaf is like take a first simple step by envisaging themselves without hearing. This is a medical construction and one which cannot take into consideration the joie de vivre of the collective Deaf signing experience, but it nevertheless makes the idea of deafness as an impaired physical faculty a difficult image to revise (Lane, 1993b).

Misunderstandings of the concept of culture itself

Unless human beings have studied or intimately experienced cultures in the plural, they struggle to conceive of the world being interpreted in any way other than the forms in which they themselves were raised, a perception which nation-states have encouraged. The very essence of culture is that to its practitioners it is simply 'natural', constituted of a thousand everyday acts and thoughts so intimately assimilated as to be almost impossible to perceive. Thus to be faced with the idea of a separate Deaf culture in one's own land forces people to confront the whole concept of culture itself, and the extent to which our own identities are invested in our own belief systems. The previous section has illustrated just how many cultural features and forces are at play, and how threatening it might be to have to confront them. If we extrapolate these to all the other cultural features that might not bear examination, we will begin to understand why cultural study itself is so subversive, and thus why it has itself only emerged as a subject for examination and deliberation in the last 30 years.

Cross-categorisation of Deaf communities

Thus, the unique status of Deaf communities is itself a problem. No matter which way one tries to categorise Deaf people, there is no clean fit. To define them simply as disabled is to overlook the linguistic foundation of their collective life. To define them as a linguistic group is to overlook the very real sensory characteristics of their existence, both positive (a unique visual apprehension of the world out of which sign languages have been constructed) and negative (communication barriers are not simply linguistic, but sonic also).

Ethnicity, identity and cultural choice

Conventional definitions of cultures also appear to thwart easy recognition of Deaf culture. The characteristic of ethnicity is rendered problematic because only 5–6% of Deaf children at most are born to two Deaf parents (Kyle & Woll, 1985), posing questions in relation to conventional ideas of cultural transmission. Traditional theories also emphasise that cultural development is 'involuntary'; since individuals are socialised into their community from birth, questions are raised concerning the cultural validity of 'choosing' to be 'Deaf'.

It is also difficult to comprehend that children so 'obviously' born and bred as the product of one's own country and indeed of one's own womb can really be so fundamentally different from their apparent compatriots. Furthermore, each generation of Deaf people which (eventually, if at all) succeeds in persuading lay people of Deaf cultural status is then superseded by a new generation of hearing parents, who, naturally unwilling to perceive their offspring as cuckoos in the nest, have their (again natural) fears manipulated by the power blocs of the discursive system who ensure that the more wealthy and vocal of those parents are the ones permitted access to the media to perpetuate the oralist ideology. Thus unlike other cultural groups whose ethnicity situations are unproblematic, Deaf communities must fight the same battles over and over again, set up in apparent opposition to those parents with whom they are carefully denied direct sustained dialogue.

Cultural geography and ontolology

Additionally, Deaf communities do not have their own land nor live (or even choose to live) as geographically intimate communities. There are also very few material productions that are 'Deaf', compared to those of many other cultures. Finally, doubt has been expressed as to whether Deaf cultures have ontological systems which most other cultures possess.

Circularity of definition

The hegemonic construction of a continuum of hearing impairment has resulted in the absence of clear-cut boundaries around the Deaf community. Attempts to define Deaf communities and Deaf culture therefore become circular – 'Deaf communities are those which have Deaf culture/ Deaf culture is a defining characteristic of Deaf communities' (Turner, 1994a). To date, no-one has succeeded in transcending that circularity within English language terminology, although Lane *et al.* (1996) offer a successful reading based on Deaf people's own sign language-based cultural constructions, where reference to the signed concept DEAF-WORLD manages to resolve most of the issues.

Deaf communities and subcultures

Although several of these difficulties can be removed by defining Deaf culture as a subculture, contemporary definitions of subcultures do not fit the reality of Deaf existence.

The proliferation of the 'Deaf Culture' trope

However, none of these definitional problems has stopped Deaf people and many who work with them from rapidly disseminating the term over the last decade. There is clearly an underlying and unexamined need to denote some important aspects of Deaf existence in this way. But the more the term is used unthinkingly, the more confused the situation becomes; thus the longer those who ignore or oppose Deaf people's views can continue to do so. As of the present time, there are very few academic works which focus on Deaf culture, hence the urgent need for studies which attempt to unpick the complex interwoven threads that not only bind Deaf life, but which also link it with the lives of majority societies.

We shall return to these problematics and see which can be resolved, once we have reviewed the literature on cultural study in general, at the end of Chapter 5.

Identifying the Deaf Subaltern

Having established the importance of the Deaf culture concept, it is now necessary to utilise what we have learned in this chapter in order to provide a framework for situating the contemporary Deaf subaltern. This cannot be undertaken without factoring in some of the important effects of both linguistic and welfare colonialism.

Pre-Oralism

Historical evidence suggests that prior to the disappearance of Deaf professionals a two-tier distinction between professionals and subalterns existed, although the Parisian banquets discourse emphasised that important core beliefs were held by both groups.

Post-Oralism

After Oralism, however, the only Deaf people who were *not* subaltern were the handful of Deaf missionaries and welfare workers, together with any oralist children of the wealthy who, where they acknowledged each other at all, formed their own small social groupings. As we have explained, the new 'deafness' trope constructed all forms of hearing impairment as a continuum, so that those previously named were drawn into a hegemonic discourse and thence to denigrate the discourses of the Deaf subalterns. Figure 5 situates the two discourses and their participants:

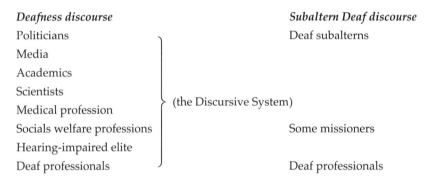

Deafness discourse		*Subaltern Deaf discourse*
Politicians		Deaf subalterns
Media		
Academics		
Scientists		
Medical profession	(the Discursive System)	
Socials welfare professions		Some missioners
Hearing-impaired elite		
Deaf professionals		Deaf professionals

Figure 5 Post-Oralism discourse structures

The two groups omitted from these discourses are lay people and hearing-impaired subalterns. The vast majority of the latter were retired people with a comparatively small degree of hearing loss who have remained relatively uninvolved in deafness discourses (Alker, 1998). This hegemony inevitably rendered subaltern Deaf discourses invisible. Even today, there exists no other term by which to distinguish the 'state of being hearing-impaired' from the state of being 'Deaf', other than the recently capitalised noun. (I have not represented here or elsewhere the existence of what one might call 'children's discourse'. This is not from lack of respect; indeed I believe that present-day bilingual Deaf children, in particular, have much to teach us from observation of their discourse. Our primary purpose here is to delineate the situation within adulthood.)

Fundamental distinctions between Deaf professionals and subalterns

Sociolinguistic studies of British Deaf communities have found that within Deafhood discourse the fundamental distinctions are not degree of hearing loss nor (necessarily) educational achievement or employment status, as would be found in mainstream society (Kyle & Woll, 1985).

However, there is an important unacknowledged distinction which can be made between those who have command of the language of the majority society (whether by being able to partially hear it, speak it, read or write it), and those who do not. Oralism has reinforced this division in that those with a smaller degree of hearing loss have a better chance of attaining English under Oralism (Conrad, 1979). Command of English means that the few d/Deaf élite are able to participate in the deafness discourse as well as other written manifestations of majority society discourse, whereas the others are not. This is identified by the Deaf researcher Philip (1987), who asserts that the Deaf subaltern is *essentially monolingual, and that policies in relation to Deaf communities should be centred around awareness of this.*

This position is unusual; most sociolinguistic models assert a simple demarcation based 'first/native language', and whether that is BSL or English. Although a laudable attempt to accentuate the positive in Deaf life, it is not geared towards a recognition and deconstruction of where power is situated within both deafness and Deafhood domains. Some might feel that moving the demarcation line to apparent 'competence' in the majority language establishes a negative image; but if one has sufficient respect for and confidence in, the myriad forms of subaltern Deaf language and culture, then the overall position remains positive. The monolingualism demarcation also clarifies which discourses are participated in by which Deaf people, and thus liberates academic space for recognition of Deaf subaltern discourses as well as indicating the boundaries within which they find themselves fenced.

Colonialism and 20th Century Deaf Divisions

Linguistic colonialism

Although the earlier missioners appeared to respect BSL, the later ones, perhaps influenced by the growing negative image of Deaf people portrayed by oralists, did not regard it as a *bona fide* language, and promoted the use of a Signed English variant as the only appropriate medium for intelligent communication (Sutcliffe & Sutcliffe, 1976; Kyle & Woll, 1985). This is characterised by constructing one's utterances in English word order, and then reproducing them in sign language, and was considered easier for hearing people to use – signing became a matter of tagging signed items onto speech or English-mouthing. It appears to have been conveniently overlooked that this is virtually no help in comprehending a Deaf adult or child who is signing BSL to you. More than that, it speaks volumes about the conceptualisation of the liberal hearing–Deaf relationship – all that matters is to ensure the Deaf person understands what you desire to tell them. What they might say in response is obviously not important.

Since this variant could only be used effectively by Deaf people who possessed English skills, it was therefore only easily accessible to those deafened after the acquisition of English. Gradually therefore, during the oralist century, a particular kind of relationship developed between the missioners and those Deaf people, who themselves internalised the negative perceptions of BSL, and regarded its users in a similarly negative light. Signed English thereby took over the prestigious formal situations, such as important club meetings and church activities, which were previously characterised by the use of BSL (*British Deaf-Mute*, 1892; Deuchar, 1984), leading to monolingual, subaltern Deaf people becoming alienated from situations which were once accessible to all.

This alienation had a threefold effect. To begin with, it discouraged the subaltern from involvement in formal meetings, including BDA conferences, whilst, those same Deaf people came to internalise the idea that their signing did not constitute a proper language, which helped to lower their self-image further still.

The third effect is more complex and difficult to convey. Llewellyn-Jones *et al.* (1979) describe the results of their matched guise experiments as illustrating a covert pride in BSL by its own users. Holding these two different views simultaneously can be read as a form of linguistic schizophrenia as it were, one in which two sets of cultural values clash internally. Similarly, the converse applies; those BSL users who did attend formal meetings, particularly BDA meetings, reified the Signed English found there whilst not actually being able to understand it. Thus, democracy in Deaf affairs appeared to exist in form, yet not in actuality. This third effect has been exceedingly powerful; it is still widespread even today because it has become a tradition. Attempts to unify the community to become politically active still have to swim against this traditional tide. Similarly, despite the availability of video as a carrier of BSL information, most organisations still print their information in English, even whilst knowing that most Deaf people cannot read it.

It is not difficult, therefore, to establish a distinction between the Signed English-using subaltern and BSL subaltern. We can thus classify the former group as an *élite subaltern*.

Colonialism as loss of history and traditions

Deaf magazines of the late 19th century contained a great deal of historical information about their community, even though it was scarcely a
century old. *The British Deaf-Mute*, for example, featured the history of one
Deaf institution per issue, giving it the whole of the front page. However, as
we have seen, one of the tenets of oralist discourse, that each Deaf child is
merely an impaired hearing child with no relation to other Deaf people
now or before, produced an ahistoricism which resulted in much of Deaf
history becoming neglected and then lost. The tighter the oralist grip on
Deaf schools because, the more the old records, writings and artefacts were
thrown out or destroyed (Boyce 1996; Mirzoeff, 1995).

This discourse was internalised by many Deaf people, creating ignorance of or disinterest in the Deaf life of previous generations. The stories
and traditions embodied in older Deaf people were not drawn upon and
the idea that contemporary Deaf events constituted living history disappeared. In the USA where the existence of Gallaudet University meant that
Oralism could not quite eradicate Deaf pride, Deaf history and traditions
were far better preserved, as their world-renowned collection in their
library indicates (Indeed, more than one major UK book collection was
deeded to them for safety.)

It was not only the loss of historical landmarks and documents that
proved significant. Awareness of the individual as part of a larger group-
self with the ability to make one's mark on history was another casualty of
colonisation. This was particularly tragic given the admirable achievements of Deaf individuals and groups described earlier; the loss of the
knowledge that Deaf communities once achieved great things further reinforced feelings of ontological inferiority and unimportance.

The significance of these developments for our puposes is that, with
Deaf history removed from the picture, those with access to English were
then in a position to reify the only history available to them – majority
society history. Since this resulted in the absorbtion of the cultural traditions of that history, together with what they taught concerning anything
from morality to organisational strategy, this factor widened the gap
between the élite-subaltern and the rest.

Colonialism and mental health

Evidence attesting to the negative psychological effects of colonialism on
subordinated communities is well established (Fanon, 1986).[15] Similar evidence for the Deaf community has been a long time in surfacing, although
Deaf people had complained for the whole century about the damaged
human beings that were emerging from oralist schools. Recent research suggests that the incidence of mental illness (that is, not the 'clinical' conditions

such as schizophrenia, manic depression or clinical depression, but trauma-related conditions) among Deaf community members is twice the national average (Ridgway, 1998). Psychiatrists such as Denmark (1981) point the finger directly towards the oralist system. As yet, there are no figures for the mental health consequences of oral mainstreaming.

Furthermore, it is important to note that, in addition to the more obvious manifestations of mental ill health, there was a general loss of confidence in being able to deal with the majority society, so that many subaltern Deaf people were happy to settle into what became a traditional pattern of 'over-reliance on the hearing missioner' (Kyle & Woll 1985: 11). This dynamic favoured the élite subaltern, since the knowledge which they acquired from English enabled them to dialogue with the missioners, who were then able to utilise them as a group which could enforce their decisions on the rest.

Colonialism and a new élitism

The establishment of the Mary Hare Grammar School (MHGS) in the1940s was a critical move for Oralism. Recruiting its pupils on a national basis, and *by selecting mostly hard of hearing or deafened children*, it became a useful instrument for oralist propaganda. The effect on the children and the community has been profound. By strongly discouraging its pupils from joining the Deaf community, it removed several generations of potential community leaders. The Deaf leader, Clark Denmark, has estimated that of 144 Scottish graduates, only seven were members of the Deaf community. Thus without MHGS the community would have had 137 more leaders in Scotland alone.

Of those who do join the community, many are perceived as holding élitist attitudes, not least towards BSL and its users, so that the community is still alienated from its would-be leaders. The damage done to many ex-pupils themselves is quite significant; unable to fit into either the Deaf community or majority society, numbers are said to have committed suicide (Lawson, 1982, pers. comm.).

This form of colonialism therefore not only removed potential Deaf leadership, but produced generations of English-using leaders who could be relied on to reproduce oralist discourses at critical political moments. Since most did not join the Deaf club community, but either founded their own clubs and organisations, their most important role in our analysis was their involvement with the RNID.

Neo-colonialism

The question of whether the new 'liberal' domains established during the Resurgence can be said to represent potential neo-colonialism has, until now, never been discussed formally. Different ways of phrasing the question produce different answers. If we were to ask 'Are Deaf communities in control of the television output produced in their name?', the answer would be 'no'. If we asked the same question of Deaf academic domains such as Deaf Studies, sign language research or indeed any form of research, the answer would be the same. If we asked this of present Deaf social welfare, bilingualism, and interpreting services, the answer would still be 'no'.[16] These answers alone alert us to the potential dangers that these new liberal developments embody.

There is, however, a further parallel with anti-colonialist developmental patterns. We have become aware that the effects of Oralism are such that there are very few adequately qualified and trained Deaf leaders. If we pursue the colonial model further, we might construct the emergence of the liberal class and its raison d'être as being one of 'preparing the ground for the handover of power', a stage just immediately prior to independence. If this is an accurate representation, then three issues arise.

The first suggests that the degree of neo-colonialism taking place can be directly measured by the time and effort set aside to train and develop the relevant Deaf professionals in proportion to the totality of the work carried out in those domains. The second might be constructed as the amount of time set aside to support the reforms necessary to achieve higher Deaf educational standards in general, and the third, the time allocated for personal interventions to secure a positive, Deaf-centred future for those domains in the face of new waves of oppression.

This is a rather mechanistic way to analyse the situation, yet without such a beginning, we cannot hope to unpick the different strands which operate in daily praxis. All the indications at the moment are that energy is being devoted to the third, rather than to the first two. Only further research can clarify the extent to which this is justified – certainly as we have seen in the examples of the 'backlash' from the RNID, Channel 4 and certain university faculties, there can be little assurance that gains made in the resurgence will continue if they are not consciously defended. Thus those hearing people in charge of Deaf domains at the present time occupy rather unique positions which will come under ever-growing scrutiny with each passing year.

Colonialism and class issues

The previous sections have illustrated the varying degrees to which class issues might be said to have either been created by oralist and welfare colnialism, and the sections which follow will explore other important dimensions. At this point, however, we must stop to consider the issue of colonialism and class in its widest context. Post-colonialist studies make it clear that the class model itself is a Eurocentric one, with varying degrees of applicability outside such societies. It will be immediately apparent that the model is inappropriate for analysing tribal societies, whilst others, such as India with its strong caste formations, reveals obvious countervailing social forces which complicate such a reading.

It was for this reason that Gramsci's concept of the subaltern was brought into post-colonial discourse, so that the social position and discourses of 'ordinary', relatively powerless people could be situated in relation to those of the intelligentsia and comprador groupings. We must be aware of the extent to which the latter two are seen as being culturally compromised by their absorbing of aspects of colonialist culture, especially given the degree to which independence is linked to the 'decolonising the mind' of those cultures in order to find ways to restore the traditional cultures. In this context, the extent to which the subaltern embody those native cultures to a greater degree of cultural 'purity' or monogamy means that restoration of the pre-colonial culture requires finding routes by which the subaltern might obtain a significant degree of power.

All this being the case, then, we might expect that Post-Colonial Studies might prioritise the subaltern issue. However, as Ashcroft *et al.* (1998: 40) point out:

> Since recent post-colonial theory has tended to concentrate on the issues of race, ethnicity, and, to a lesser extent, gender in the colonialist definitions and opposing self-definitions of colonised peoples, the importance of class has been downplayed. Few if any attempts have been made to see how the formation of categories such as race, gender and class, both historically and in modern practice, intersect and co-exist ... An analysis of class has a crucial role to play in emphasising the link between representation and material practice in post-colonial discourse.

Having already come to this conclusion, this counter-narrative has tried to focus on class issues in Deaf communities and to formalise an analysis built on the subaltern concept. This analysis will be therefore be sustained and deepened as this book progresses.

The Deaf Resurgence and Deaf Community Change

The eight stages identified earlier have had profound effects on Deaf social demarcations. In less than 20 years, the 'balance of power' between élite subaltern and the others has swung hugely in the latter's direction.

Emerging prestige of BSL users and Deaf families

During this period the tremendous improvement in Deaf self-image and self-confidence has been particularly noticeable among BSL users. Of the eight stages of change outlined, five have laid specific emphasis on the importance of BSL, and have almost consciously focused on the 'grass roots' section of the community, especially Deaf people from Deaf families. The origins of that emphasis was the universities where BSL research was carried out. In seeking the strongest possible linguistic models, members of traditionally Deaf families were sought out and recruited as research assistants, BSL teachers, trainers of teachers and, very recently, lecturers in Deaf Studies. The BSL teaching agency (BSLTA) played a crucial part in changing the community's image about its language, as it formed the major bridge between the linguistic findings and the Deaf subaltern.

Another major reason for the resurgence of BSL was the prestige gained from its prominence in Deaf television programmes. This was not automatic; the first two series of *See Hear* were delivered in voice and Signed English, and behind the scenes campaigns were required for that to change. Once this was achieved, and BSL added to the BBC's language teaching series, with an accompanying text (Miles 1988) introduced by Princess Diana, the status of the humble BSL user changed radically. This was re-emphasised when the BDA published the first ever *BSL Dictionary* in 1992 – again Diana provided the foreword and signed at its launch. Newspaper photgraphs of her signing with Deaf children and her support for bilingualism also carried inestimable power in the battle to discredit Oralism.[17]

A further boost for BSL users came from changes in the education system. After Oralism was removed from many Deaf schools, the liberal system of combining speech and Signed English, known as 'Total Communication' gained a foothold. Linguistic research indicated that this was only a half measure, and that BSL, as part of a bilingual, bicultural education was crucial for Deaf children. BSL users then began to be employed in Deaf education in numbers for the first time this century, albeit only as classroom assistants, but this nevertheless tipped the balance away from Deaf Signed English users who had previously been held up as the model Deaf person in the liberal educational domain.

The cumulative effect of these changes has been to downgrade the status of Signed English users. Although these people still hold much power within social work and further education establishments, the growth in the numbers of BSL professionals has created several tense discourses within the community on issues arising from this power shift.

Subaltern Deaf professionals

Although a 'Deaf middle class' has existed in the USA for some time, there were barely a dozen Deaf professionals in the UK in 1976. As a result of the resurgence, several hundred Deaf people now occupy professional positions, mostly within 'Deaf work' itself. This has become a two edged sword:

[There are] Those who have moved out of the Deaf clubs or who are still in the clubs but in a smaller role, either giving up or reducing their voluntary work . . . They are now finding it difficult to maintain their old friendships . . . The consequence is that the Deaf clubs have become weakened because of the loss of their leaders and the leaders have lost their support network. (Redfern, 1995: 8)

Moreover, almost all of these held 'blue collar' jobs in their previous working life and very few have been given opportunties for professional training as the term is generally understood; limited job-specific certification is usually the norm. At this present historical moment, this has left numbers ill-equipped them for dealing with issues like management, teamwork and professional codes of behaviour, and this has become one of the central themes of the Signed English users' criticisms.

The Deaf Resurgence and Changes in the Model

Now that several hundred Deaf subalterns have obtained professional and semi-professional posts and training and numbers have thus begun to participate in the deafness discourses, this may problematicise the Deaf subaltern concept. Do these people constitute a new category, and has this really affected the basic dynamics of the hegemonic discourses?

Within recent Deaf discourses there has been much debate along these lines, as evidenced by the emergence of the two BSL signs in Figure 6:

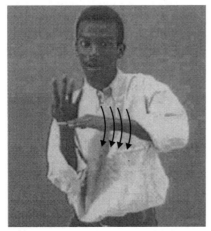 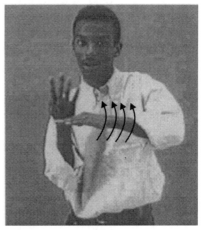

'Grass Roots'   'Grass Roots Out'

Figure 6 The signs for 'GRASS-ROOTS' and 'GRASS-ROOTS-OUT' – the essential difference between the two signs is the reversal of the directional movement of the left hand

These signs are about ten years old. 'GRASS-ROOTS' adapted the English phrase into an iconic form, and was not widely popular for that reason. Nevertheless it was accepted to the extent that a pun was developed which reversed the movement to indicate those who had 'uprooted' themselves from the subaltern community.

Although the community has begun to make such a distinction, there are reasons to believe that the uprooted group are still essentially subalterns:

(1) Both groups still share BSL as their first language and the culture developed from it.
(2) Both still share common cultural backgrounds based around the Deaf school experience.
(3) Both experienced Oralism and internalised its effect on self-worth and so on.
(4) Both share a knowledge of Deaf social organisation and of Deaf history and tradition.
(5) Although the English skills of the 'uprooted' have improved, they are still not comfortable with printed and spoken English discourses, as evidenced by the continuing absence of written papers. In effect very few have moved across to participate in the deafness discourse, though *some have internalised it as part of their training*.
(6) Most 'uprooted' still socialise within the Deaf community, albeit in different forms than before (*Sign On*, 1998).
(7) All are committed to maintaining and developing the Deaf community (Baker & Cokely, 1980), even if they have different roles or strategies for doing so.
(8) Both sectors have embraced the 'D' concept (Redfern 1995), and are still perceived and treated as 'Deaf' by the hegemonic discourses (except where the latter find it politically expedient not to do so).

Items (1)–(8) support the continuing applicability of the term subaltern, whilst only (5) and (6) have resulted in some dissension and confusion within the community. Therefore this study will continue to use the term. However, some demarcation is necessary, so the new Deaf professionals will be referred to as the '*subaltern-élite*'.

These are simplified schemata; the recent development of mainstreaming, for example, has produced young Deaf people who are not easily placed within the subaltern strata, and there are also problematics around the siting of recently emerged Afro-Caribbean and Asian young Deaf people, and young Gay and Lesbian Deaf, among others.

Refining the bipolar framework

All these factors require a refining of the formerly bipolar framework (Figure 7):

Deafness discourse	Deafhood discourses	
	Subaltern elite	*Traditional*
Discursive System Members		
Some Subaltern Deaf Élite		
	Subaltern Deaf Élite	Subaltern Deaf Élite
		Trad. Subaltern
	Self-selected Lay People	
New / Young Professionals	New / Young Professionals	

Figure 7 Bi-polar framework refined

This newly emerged 'intermediate' discourse has also created a space for lay people, chiefly those who have started to learn BSL or Deaf Studies, to finally enter the Deaf world. Likewise it offers space to the other new professions such as interpreters and sign linguists, as well as new and more enlightened entrants to the traditional professions of teaching and welfare work. It is this space that Bienvenu and Colonomos (1989) have labelled 'the third culture'.

Finally, spaces for Deaf minorities are still not easily identified, but can be said to vary between participation in the Deafhood discourses and the creation of private discourses of their own. In the case of Gay Deaf discourse there is actually a sociolinguistic example, manifesting itself as GSV (Gay Sign Variation).

Lay people, Deaf communities and discourse channels

We have seen throughout the last two chapters, a very wide variety of ways and domains in which lay people have interacted with Deaf people over the centuries. In the previous sections we have noted the recent changes since the Deaf resurgence, including the emergence of the 'third culture'. Given the increasing importance of lay people to Deaf community and culture, either through attempted entrance to the culture by new BSL learners, or through the new radical politics demanding support in the language recognition arena, it is important for us to attempt to understand how Deafhood discourses stand in relation to the overall structure of majority society discourses. From this we may begin to understand the difficulties faced by Deaf and hearing people in penetrating the barriers

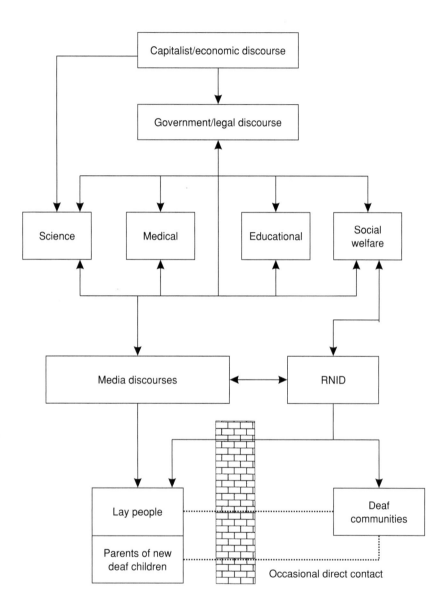

Figure 8 Barriers (shaded area) placed between Deaf communities, lay people and the government

around certain discourses in order to achieve change. Figure 8 gives a simple illustration to initiate the debate; it is hoped that readers may contribute to develop an appropriately sophisticated model.

The diagram represents the situation prior to the Deaf Resurgence. You will note from it that lay people are positioned on the other side of a media 'wall', without sight of the Deaf community, and that there is a path marked for the occasional direct contact. In the post-Resurgence period, this path has reached the point where it has developed a 'box' of its own, that we can ascribe as 'Third Culture' for the time being.

The other notable aspect of the diagram is that parents of new Deaf children are situated with lay people. This is their starting point; however what then happens is that they are removed from that position, and placed in a tiny box, still without sight of the Deaf community, surrounded by the scientific, medical and educational discourses on three sides, and the media on the fourth.

In the post-Resurgence period, what has happened is that they remain in this box, but a 'tunnel' has been dug by the Deaf community and the Third Culture through to their box, and thus a few of the parents are able to travel backwards and forwards betweeen these two. However, each night their resting place is once more within their box.

Clearly this has severe implications for both themselves and Deaf communities, especially in an era of intensifying scientific, medical, educational and media pressure on them in the form of cochlear implantation and genetic engineering. Any gains made by the Resurgence are at risk if future generations of Deaf children are directed away from the communities. A firm discourse 'box' has to be established to provide a firm footing for Deaf–parental dialogue.

In that respect it is useful to look towards a Scandinavian model. Such a model would establish a direct connection to government, bypassing both RNID and Social Welfare boxes. Both the parental and Deaf community boxes would be brought down away from their current positioning to be situated next to each other, establishing as formal a relationship between them as can be achieved.

Finally, the other conclusion that can be drawn from Figure 8 is that there is an extremely urgent need for Deaf communities to gain media prominence, so that their cultural beliefs and actions can be conveyed to both lay people and parents. The increasing power of scientistic discourse shows signs of becoming engraved on the 'public mind'.[18] Television represents the only practical possibility, partly because sign languages can be seen in this medium, and partly because newspapers and periodicals have no regular ideological 'space' allocated within their structures for Deaf issues. The amount of sign language programming will change very little in the foreseeable future; thus the only discourse channels left are the arts, news and current affairs.

The arts have been used as valuable discourse channels by various minority groups. Of these perhaps the most potent, carrying valuable subaltern cultural capital, is the music business, and within these channels we have observed Black music and their communities' concomitant issues come to prominence in the USA and elsewhere, whether through jazz, rhythm and blues, reggae or rap, to give but one set of examples. There is a reasonable case for assuming that, were a Deaf–hearing music group to be formed, presenting signed songs which expressed the Deaf agenda, progress could be made towards gaining the cultural capital embodied in the concept of 'hipness', enabling ongoing lay access to a positive representation of the Deaf medium and message (cf. Ladd, 1991).

In order to gain the attention of the news and current affairs channels, a sustained political campaign involving official recognition of the national sign language, using whatever means are necessary to gain serious public debate, represents one of the few opportunities left. Given the descriptions at the start of Chapter 2 of the current lack of media attention to the BSL marches, *the path logically leads to an escalation of campaigns characterised by non-violent and even violent direct action*. And whichever turns out to be the case will in no little measure depend on how seriously the government addresses the issue.

In summary then, the models offered above represent as contemporary a framework as can be constructed, and will be used for the remainder of this book.

Summary

Chapters 2 and 3 have taken us on a historical journey, presenting us with various new approaches from which to read Deaf communities and culture, and their relationships, both direct and indirect, to the reader. It is hoped that each group of readers can utilise the models offered to assess the degree of fit with their own national Deaf communities, their own minority groups, their colonialised peoples and language minorities (and of course to shed valuable new theoretical light where the fit is problematic).

The counter-narrative has enabled us to perceive that the challenges facing Deaf communities in striving towards the equivalent of colonial independence are situated around language recognition in the first instance. The next requirement, that of ensuring that there are sufficient numbers of Deaf people trained and equipped to run the 'Deaf Nation', is still dependent on winning the educational battleground, and upon the degree of involvement of those in the Third Culture and the 'Neo-colonialist' domains.

The narrative has also stressed the importance of understanding both the situation of the Deaf subaltern and of lay people. Indeed we can establish an important tentative link between the two – one which points out that lay people occupy a subaltern role in respect of those holding power in the domains of medicine, science, law, education and the media. It can be argued that in Western societies, class structures intersect with this reading, so that, for example, a middle-class lay person might be more successful in making interventions into these domains because they share the 'language of power'. However, when it comes to Deaf issues within those domains, it is by no means clear that any interventions they can make therein are of more significance than the extent to which those specialised professions can brush them aside. Thus a tentative case is made for what might become, in Deaf issue terms, a 'subaltern alliance'.

As the counter-narrative has continued, the centrality of the Deaf culture concept as a key tool for change has become clearer. We have learned how its identification, recognition and acceptance will directly challenge and threaten the maintenance of colonialist practices. However, we have also learned that such identification can be seen as problematic. Thus the next task on this journey is to see whether the existence of the Deaf culture concept can be formally confirmed. To do this, we first need to explore what has been discovered within the academic disciplines which have focused their attention on the study of culture. In so doing, we can continue the journey towards achieving a greater understanding of the extent to which we too are governed by cultural forces beyond our awareness.

Notes

1. Those of us who were fortunate enough to get a glimpse of the range of attitudes held by hearing people across societies had long felt that those displayed by professionals working with Deaf communities were more negative and not representative of the positive feelings that were 'out there'. But it took a freak turn of events to confirm this. Musgrove (1974), in examining the culturo-political views of students of that era, happened to include those training to be teachers of the Deaf at Manchester University, the UK centre of Oralism. Of the 20 disciplines studied, this group came in at 19th on his scale – that is, the second most 'reactionary' group of all.

2. Using the term 'discourses' to describe lay views of Deaf people during the 20th century is a methodological convenience. One exception to this might have been in Edinburgh, where hearing children were educated at the Deaf school, Donaldsons, between 1856 and 1939. That city was consequently famous in the UK Deaf community for the amount of Deaf–hearing interaction which occurred.

3. In 1988, a team from the London Deaf Video Project was about to set off to record on film an example of the latter from one of the last survivors of that time. Just as we prepared ourselves to leave, the phone rang. It was his daughter telling us that he had died the previous night. For the record, the story as he had signed it to me was that in a certain West London Deaf club during the 1940s, one Deaf person who had challenged the local missioner's decisions once too often had been 'put away' in the local mental hospital.

    I came across this incident quite independently when working in West London during the 1970s. We came across a Deaf man in the local mental hospital who had been there for 30 years – he was known as the 'Birdman of St Bernards' because of the relationships he had built up with the wild birds in the grounds. Two independent witnesses both told me that they felt that he was not really mentally ill.

    This same Deaf informant had also related to me a story of how two Deaf-blind members of the club had been forbidden to marry by the missioner, and how the man had committed suicide in despair. When the club had sought to hold a memorial service for him, the missioner had refused, saying that suicide was a sin. Outraged by this, several members of the Deaf church choir, including the informant, left the club and built another social life elsewhere.

    How atypical these incidents were is hard to gauge, but Cameron, a prominent Scottish Deaf leader described how the local missioner – a nationally known figure – refused to allow him to marry the woman of his choice. And this incident took place in the 1970s . . .

4. During my time as a Deaf activist, we found that, after giving a talk to Deaf audiences about Deaf rights and then inviting questions, that the first one and indeed the majority of the discussion thereafter, always concerned Deaf education and the need to change the system. This has remained consistent for 25 years (and indeed has probably been the case from 1880 onwards). A recent committee of Deaf people meeting under the short-lived Alker administration at the RNID placed this topic as the highest priority and well ahead of the rest (Ladd, 1996). The average person might imagine that if one asked a Deaf person what they most wanted to happen, that they would plump for a better job, or more personal benefits. Yet overwhelmingly, the Deaf response has been to wish to change things for Deaf children of the future.

5. A full listing here is impossible. My apologies to those omitted, and examples welcomed for future editions.

6. A notable example occurs when trying to obtain funding for researching the social and psychological effects on cochlear implantation. The 'grant-refereeing' discourse is so intimately connected to those committed to the medical model that virtually no application has made it through to the funding stage.

7. The relationship between interpreters and Deaf communities is a fascinating and complex one which has resulted in two sets of heated but separate discourses. Although this is not the place to explore them, it is appropriate to draw attention to the extent to which application of colonialist and cultural theories might provide a bridge to mutual understanding. Mindess (2000) represents a valuable beginning for the latter.

8. A good example of the problems of studying Deaf discourse, and of their impotence in the face of the discursive system, is the fact that this story, told to me by a Deaf professional who gave evidence to the Warnock Committee in 1979 has

not found its way into being published. Throughout the day, various disabled people had given evidence in support of mainstreaming, and my informant and 'her' interpreter (one of the very best in the UK at that time), were the last to give theirs. She signed at length about how the Deaf community cherished its schools, about the history of these schools which dated back some 200 years, and some of the implications for the quality of Deaf people's individual and collective lives if they closed. In the deliberations which followed (which were leaked to her by a sympathetic member of the Committee), it was concluded that, since the Deaf evidence was so very different from the rest, it was not only untrue, but the interpreter must have got it all wrong. Her evidence was therefore dismissed.

9. Although in my role of Deaf activist, I have had many brushes with oralists, one example stands out in this context which illustrates the deliberate nature of their policies. In a meeting with a prominent oralist member of the teacher training establishment, in front of two witnesses, an interpreter and a TV researcher, the individual said: 'You've lost now. With the Warnock Report, we can put Deaf children in as many schools as we choose. And you [plural] will never be able to find them.' He wasn't far wrong.

10. This development is an interesting example of how oralist discourse is prepared to grasp at any straws, even if it means jettisoning some of its own central tenets. For much of the 20th century it was claimed that 'all Deaf children had useful residual hearing' and thus could benefit from hearing aids and Oralism. (This despite numerous Deaf protests about the painfulness of the sounds they were forced to endure.) With the emergence of CIs, we see a sudden flip – this residual hearing is now regarded as functionally useless, thus rendering it morally justifiable to destroy it in the operation. When we link this attitude with the fact that conventional hearing aids have approximately 1000 sonic channels and the CI only 22, the whole discourse appears even more sinister.

11. Thanks to Brice Alden for help with these.

12. Chilling and dispiriting examples of the new dimensions CI experimentation encroaches on occur almost every week. The latest one, at the time of writing is deeply disturbing in its implications.

A couple in the UK, the mother Deaf, the father hearing, split up and their Deaf child was temporarily taken into care. Upon reconciliation they applied to have their child back. The judges' decision was that they could do so – provided that the child was made to have a cochlear implant first. It is hard to know which is more sinister – this effectively illegal encroachment upon human rights of parents and child, or the dark unlighted channels by which parties unknown were able to convince the judge that this should happen.

13. A useful summary of one aspect of this issue can be found is Friedman (1988), who describes individualism as 'the privilege of power. A white man has the luxury of forgetting his skin colour and sex. He can [therefore] think of himself as an 'individual'. (p. 39). However, the development of individualism as a cultural ideology is an American-derived feature of post-scarcity capitalism.

14. It should also be stressed that Deaf people have ease of mobility compared with most other disabilities, which goes a long way towards explaining how they have consolidated their culture nationally. It is also possible that other groups subsumed within the disabled movement may see themselves collectively, yet not have that viewpoint permitted within disability discourse.

I recall in the early days of the NUD our positive liason with the National

League of the Blind owed not a little to their unique construction – they were situated wholly within the blind Sheltered Workshops and acted as a (TUC recognised) union for their people. To this evidence of collectivity it might be added that blindness, being a sensory impairment, might well involve certain psychological patterning which, when reinforced by time spent together, might add up to a phenomenon with some notable cultural features. The existence of organisations of dwarves (who, incidentally, refuse the terminology of 'people of restricted growth'), who socialise and marry each other is also a striking example of how the social model does not adequately cover even its own members, whilst villages of 'mentally handicapped' people have also dissented from the mainstreaming 'ideal'.

15. Duran and Duran (1995), working from within Native American traditions, offer an invaluable analysis of these effects in tandem with strategies for restoring mental health. The analysis they use includes this memorable quotation:

> If the labelling and diagnosing process is to have any historical truth, it should incorporate a diagnostic category that reflects the effects of genocide. Such a diagnosis would be 'acute and chronic reaction to colonialism' (p. 6)

One wonders how many of the Deaf people Ridgway identifies would fit such a diagnosis in respect of Oralism.

16. To give but one academic example, Deaf people who initially welcomed the positive changes brought about by the entry of linguists into Deaf domains in the early 1980s, have come to express an ever-growing dissatisfaction with the extent to which those hearing people have developed an infrastructure on which they have built careers, whilst their Deaf 'informants' have remained in the sâme position as 20 years ago – on short-term contracts as research assistants. This concern came to a head at the international conference on sign linguistics (TISLR) in Amsterdam in 2000, when all 50 Deaf participants walked out in protest at various practices which they felt to be unacceptable (Ladd, 2001). The discipline of anthropology came into crisis from the 1960s onwards when the post-colonial impulse directly challenged both its practices and career structures (cf, Asad, 1973). It is as yet unclear whether sign linguistics or even linguistics itself is aware of its closeness to such a crisis.

17. Those coming from outside the Deaf domain will be unaware of the importance of Princess Diana to the British Deaf community. In becoming Patron of the BDA, and in using BSL in public, she 'proved' herself to the community in much the same way as her public support for AIDS sufferers did to the Gay community. Her visits to the BDA showed its Deaf workers that she had a tight grasp of the issues (and even some of the personalities involved). The Deaf subaltern discourse network quickly spread this information, which confirmed that her interest was not tokenistic. This commitment was confirmed even at her funeral, where Deaf people walked in the front row of mourners behind the Royal family (this was, of course, ignored by the media). Those radicals who find this reverence hard to swallow may like to reflect on how this indicates their present inability to grasp the re-ordering of political priorities within minority cultures. Far from being an example of paternalism, what is highlighted instead is the absolutely central role of language recognition in Deaf cultural and political struggles.

18. An example of the extent to which this has taken hold was related to me by one of our Deaf Studies students, Emma Kelty. Upon informing a friend of her chosen career path as a teacher of Deaf children, she met the response 'Why would you want to do that? There's no future in it. Soon there won't be any more Deaf children.'

Chapter 4

Culture – Definitions and Theories

Sometimes [peoples of colour] are compelled by a hunch that the answers to questions of identity lie in another's culture.

Toni Cade Bambara (in Early, 1993: 314)

Introduction

Before we can embark on verification of the Deaf culture concept we need a basic understanding of what has been discovered and theorised in respect of culture itself. The chapter therefore reviews the wide range of academic disciplines which have involved themselves in this task. It is difficult to present a simple summary which can indicate the depth and breadth traversed by each discipline; what follows is an attempt to strike a balance, to provide a resource from which readers new to any of the disciplines can pursue these various leads at their leisure. I have also attempted to identify concepts and theories from each discipline which appear to have relevance for Deaf cultural study so that these, too, can be followed up in greater depth.

As the review develops, the reader will find that certain criteria can take us most of the way to confirm the existence of the Deaf culture concept. The previous chapter identified eight problematics to be tackled before that confirmation can be granted. However, we must acknowledge that some of these questions can be reversed: Are any of these endemic to *the inadequacy of definitions of culture themselves?* A parallel situation existed within linguistic theory; prior to the validation of sign languages, definitions of 'language' itself contained several criteria which appeared to exclude non-spoken languages from recognition (Deuchar, 1984). We now know that this was founded upon definitional inadequacies. With this precedent in mind, we can now proceed to examine cultural theories.

Traditional Theories of Culture

Wider definitional problems

It is important at the outset to emphasise the magnitude of the task. Keesing (1974: 92), one of the anthropologists most concerned with analysing and assessing different types of cultural theory, has concluded that:

The possibility of analysing a cultural system in any complete sense . . . remains far on the horizon – and may forever remain so.

Likewise, Williams (1976: 76) summarises:

Culture is one of the two or three most complicated words in the English language. This is so partly because of its intricate historical development in several European languages, but mainly because it has come to be used for important concepts in several distinct intellectual disciplines, and in several distinct and incompatible systems of thought.

Such definitional problems are not unique to cultural study, but obtain within other social sciences; consensus even about the meaning of terms such as 'language' and 'sociology' has not yet occurred (Boudon, 1980). These problems are intrinsic to the nature of social science; imposition of standards derived from 'hard science' are fundamentally misleading. Certainly, the fact that Kroeber and Kluckhohn identified a minimum of 164 definitions of culture as long ago as 1952, makes the task of assessing 'culture' a daunting one.

Initial categorisation of cultural definitions

It is possible to make a beginning with Kroeber and Kluckhohn's (1952) creation of six definitional categories (with sub-categories) 'on the basis of principal emphasis' (p. 77).

(1) broad definitions with an emphasis on taxonomical accounts of cultural features;

(2) definitions which emphasise historical, traditional or social heritage features;

(3) emphasises 'normative' features, that is 'rules' or 'ways' (one sub-category is marked as 'ideals or values', where behaviour is assessed in relation to them);

(4) centres on psychological features, including 'adjustment . . . culture as a problem-solving device' (other emphases centre upon learning and habit);

(5) 'structural', emphasising 'the patterning or organisation of culture'; and

(6) 'Genetic'; this takes three primary forms – an 'emphasis on culture as a product or artefact', an emphasis on 'ideas' and on 'symbols'.

Thus cultural analyses have been centred upon author's individual orientation or priorities, and because these vary so widely, attempts to locate a consensus are marked by discussions often at cross-puposes with each other. For further enlightenment, therefore, it is necessary to examine some of the traditional sites of cultural study to see what bearing they have on the present research.

Sociological Traditions

The lay reader might imagine the discipline of sociology to be the primary site within which cultural theories might be formed. Indeed, during the 150 years in which the tradition has existed, there have been many historical moments during which ideas about culture have emerged into discourse. However, the main thrust of the discipline has been impelled by, and oriented towards, a different set of agendas, so that cultural theories *per se* have formed but one aspect of a concern with what we might call social theorising in general. For sociology itself is the core discipline of what has come to be known as the social sciences and its initial impulse was to

> build scientific theories of society through observation and experimentation thus demonstrating the laws of social development. (Osborne & Van Loon, 1996: 25)

This scientific impulse led to theorising across a wide range of social patterns. De Comte (1822, 1838) theorised about the evolution of human society in general, whilst writers as politically diverse as Adam Smith, Marx and Engels posited laws which they claimed expressed or directed human economic behaviour. The latter also extended their analysis across a huge range of social domains, including politics, religion, philosophy and latterly (mostly published long after their death) arts, media and culture (Marx, 1970). They stand apart from many academic traditions in their insistence upon social action – that is, that science should not be content simply to interpret the world but to change it. Their influence will be felt throughout the whole of this chapter across a wide range of disciplines.

In contrast to the 'conflict models' offered by Marx, a major strand of 19th century sociology concerned what is termed 'positivism', that is, the confinement of theories to that which can be directly known and observed. The thrust of this movement was towards understanding Western societies – initially to counterbalance the radical social changes of the Industrial Revolution which resulted in the rise of capitalism. During this upheaval, large numbers of agrarian workers and peasants began to form the new industrial working class, but in the process, numbers were falling through the social net, as it were. However, positivism's later emphasis shifted to a concern with identifying patterns in order to expedite social control.

These dynamics, social stability versus social change, have informed work carried out within the discipline ever since, each gaining hegemony in different epochs (Gouldner, 1971). The first two decades of the 20th century, known as the period of 'classical sociology' were notable for attempts to accomodate both positivism and Marxism (cf. Durkheim and Weber). These were followed by the development of the 'Chicago School' who were particularly interested in small social groups now emerging in urban societies and a later turn towards positivism, reinscribed as functionalism.

During the social and political upheavals of the 1960s, neo-marxist perspectives and theories emerged, the most important of which originated from the Frankfurt School (cf. Adorno, Habermas, Marcuse, Benjamin). These encountered that decade's bohemian explosion which produced the hippies and their own 'counter-culture' (Roszak, 1971), as well as the huge expansion of mass communications (McLuhan, 1964). Consequently, a cross-fertilisation of social and cultural theories began to take shape.

All these developments would seem to indicate much fertile ground for cultural theorising. Indeed the emphasis on deciphering social systems, forms and functions has led to useful basic research within the Deaf Studies domain, such as Higgins (1980) and Kyle and Allsop's (1982) examinations of Deaf clubs. Yet anyone approaching sociology hoping to find questions concerning the systematic formation and manifestation of cultural patterns and impulses which motivate or thread together the various features would be disappointed – what we might term a 'sociology of culture' itself (Meyersohn, 1969) did not appear to exist up until that time.

One reason for this is that the general definition of culture as the entire way of life of a people in effect covers everything that sociology might attempt. Another is that Western industrial societies are so large and so complex that the idea of being able to hold any one of them squarely within a single gaze is effectively impossible. Thus it seems that sociologists decided that any interest they might have in a total cultural theorising should be left to their colleagues in anthropology (see later), who, by studying small-scale societies, could carry out that project more easily. Nevertheless, from the 1960s onwards its legacy, chiefly that of the Frankfurt School above, had an important part to play in the development of disciplines such as Cultural Studies, and we shall therefore consider its implications for Deaf cultural theorising within that section later in the chapter.

Anthropological Traditions

In exploring these traditions and their origins, I focus on the work of Keesing (1974, 1981) because of his concern at that period in history to embrace and situate all of the theories and themes developed within the discipline.

Culture as totality

Anthropology appears to have been the first formal discipline to emerge from the interest in studying the ways of life in societies other than its 'own', although investigations had been underway for several decades in several other domains before the culture concept was formalised. Tylor (1871: 1) is thought to have proposed the first (English-speaking) definitions, considering culture as

[T]hat complex whole which includes knowledge, belief, art, morals, law, customs, and any capabilities and habits acquired by man [sic] as a member of society.[1]

The many subsequent definitions differ chiefly in their emphasis on one or other aspect of his taxonomy. All appear to agree that it is an essential part of any conception of culture that it embrace that whole. Mair (1965: 6) uses this idea to distinguish anthropology from sociology:

We consider it our business to observe the *totality* of relationships operating between the people in a social unit that we study, not only those directly relevant to a particular problem.'

Even when anthropologists have studied 'a particular problem', the terms of reference are almost always framed within those same 'totality of relationships'.

This is because the human species is the only one which encompasses such tremendous diversity in behaviour, lifestyles, beliefs and communication systems (Spradley, 1979). When studying the underlying factors behind such diversity, one comes to the conclusion that this is most efficiently explained by humans' unique ability to *create* ways of life, cultures, for themselves. To be human, then, is to create culture, albeit not under conditions of our own choosing, to paraphrase Marx. Thus, anthropology's aim is, in the first instance, to study each collective totality of human creativity, towards an ultimate goal that can be summarised as 'to describe and explain the regularities and variations in [human] social behaviour' (p. 10). As such, then, 'cultural description . . . is the first step in understanding the human species' (p. 10).

The relationship between 'culture' and 'society'

Within the English-speaking discipline, two traditions developed. 'Social Anthropology' was essentially British, and focused on the organization and integration of societies in what has been called the 'functionalist tradition'. In this tradition the concept of culture was subsumed within terminology like 'social structure' and 'society'. An example of such a definition is Fortes' (1953):

Social structure is not an aspect of culture but the entire culture of a given people handled in a special frame of theory. (pp. 17–41)

The second, 'Cultural Anthropology', is primarily American. In this tradition, the relationship between culture and society is inverted. Culture constituted all the learned and socially transmitted ways of a people, subsuming their modes of social organisation into models of value systems and belief systems. An example of this type of definition is Kroeber and Kluckhohn's:

Patterns, explicit and implicit, of and for behaviour acquired and transmitted by symbols, constituting the distinctive achievement of human groups, including their embodiment in artifacts. (Kroeber & Kluckhohn, 1963)

As a result, as Keesing (1981: 349) puts it, that 'until the late 1950s, there was a tendency for scholars working in these traditions with different theoretical perspectives to talk past one another'.

Since that time there has been a growing rapprochement between these two traditions, as summarised by Geertz (1973), in Keesing's (1981: 349) words:

The integration of a social system is 'structural-functional' – the fitting together of institutions and modes of defining social relationships; the integration of a cultural system is 'logico-aesthetic' – the coherence and logic of a system of symbols.

Such a perspective enables us to hold concepts of culture and of society within the single gaze. It is too early to assess the relative value of each tradition for investigating Deaf culture. Given the difficulties of establishing the structures of Deaf communities because of the 'deafness' confusions, it is certainly easier to pursue themes from cultural anthropology in the manner of Padden and Humphries (1988) groundbreaking work on Deaf culture.

One major difficulty in taking such an all-embracing position is that, as Keesing (1974: 73) notes, such positions are so all-inclusive that they are in danger of saying nothing at all. Importantly for a study of Deaf culture, they do not easily accommodate the phenomenon of cultural change, or the important relationship between the individual cultural agent and his/her culture/society. In order to frame such questions, other possibilities must be explored.

Cultures as adaptive systems

One possibility is the perception of cultures as adaptive systems, 'which serve to relate human communities to their ecological setting' (Keesing,

1974: 74). Proponents of these theories, perceive 'economies and their social correlates as in some sense primary' (p. 75). An example of such a definition is Meggers (1971: 4):

> Man is an animal and, like all other animals, must maintain an adaptive relationship with his surroundings in order to survive . . . he achieves this adaptation principally through the medium of culture.

Adaptational theories are useful when considering how Deaf culture might be reactive to the majority culture and its actions. Likewise, if one considers that the 'Deaf environment' is the 'hearing' world by which they are surrounded, adaptational strategies may form an important part of individual and collective Deaf life. However, they do not address how such strategies might be assessed, thus requiring us to examine the potential of ideational theories.

Cultures as ideational constructs

Keesing (1974) identifies several types of 'ideational theories of culture'. One perceives cultures as cognitive systems, typified by this definition from Goodenough (1957: 167):

> A society's culture consists of whatever it is one has to know or believe in order to operate in a manner acceptable to its members. Culture is not a material phenomenon; it does not consist of things, people, behaviour, or emotions. It is rather an organization of those things. It is the form of things that people have in mind, their models for perceiving, relating, and otherwise interpreting them.

Unfortunately, theories of this kind have 'not progressed very far beyond a mapping of limited and neatly bounded semantic domains' (Keesing, 1974: 78). A related approach treats cultures as systems of shared symbols and meanings, existing not in people's minds *per se*, but between them, being shared by social actors, and thus public, not private. This places the emphasis not on deciphering a cultural system, but interpreting it. Geertz (1973: 44)suggests that:

> Culture is best seen as . . . a set of control mechanisms – plans, recipes, rules, instructions . . . for the governing of behaviour.

Ideational models would appear to be of use for Deaf culture, where there is less frequent social interaction (and thus proportionately more time spent existing in a 'mentalist' mode), and fewer material constructions; however, as traditionally expressed, these leave little space for cultural variation between individuals or changes over time.

Cultural competence and performance

One suggestion for incorporating individual cultural strategies is to posit an idealised individual actor (Goodenough, 1971), much as Chomsky has done in linguistics. However, life in contemporary Western society is too complex for such a representative individual to be selected (or indeed, one might argue, in any society). It is much easier, though still limiting, to use this concept in the linguistic domain, where rules of grammar and language learning can at least be posited as finite.

Keesing attempts to resolve the dilemma by utilising the linguistic terms of 'competence' and 'performance' to draw the two sets of theories together:

> Culture, conceived as a system of competence . . . is then not all of what an individual knows, thinks and feels about his [sic] world. It is his theory of what his fellows know, believe and mean; his theory of the code being followed, the game being played, in the society into which he was born. (Keesing, 1974: 89)

To paraphrase Keesing, this construction proposes culture, not only as a matrix of symbols, but as a 'system of knowledge' which allows for each (Deaf) individual *not* to know about all sectors of their culture, but to perform from their theories of what they perceive. The rules of the game can, in turn, be altered or changed by their actions; thus this dialectic might provide a mechanism by which to understand (Deaf) cultural change.

Culture, power relations and authenticity

Keesing's proposal is useful, but assumes a 'level playing field' in which each aspect of a culture carries equal social and political weight, equal 'authenticity'. This is a weakness within traditional anthropology as Asad (1979: 609) summarises:

> [the] basic social object which is presented in the discourse of such anthropologists, whether rationalists or empiricists, [has been] constructed out of an *a priori* system of essential human meanings – an 'authentic culture'.

Traditional emphases on authenticity mask power relationships between the investigating majority cultures and the 'objectified' minority cultures, and has been challenged in recent times by members of those cultures, such as Asad (1979) and Deloria (1988). Indeed, re-assessment of the origins of the discipline has located its emergence within colonialism itself, that its raison d'être was used to justify the whole imperialist project (Mirzoeff, 1995). Appreciation of its own history thus led to what has been described as 'the crisis of anthropology' during the 1980s. Strategies for resolving these problems had therefore to begin by accepting, as Street (1993: 27) puts it, that

> [T]he reification and naturalisation of 'culture' hides the kind of questions about power and social change that are currently at the forefront of anthropological enquiry.

Once traditional anthropological ahistoricism is questioned, as Thornton (1988: 26) puts it:

> An understanding of culture, then, [becomes] not simply a knowledge of differences, but rather an understanding of how and why differences . . . have come about.

Such discussions are important for Deaf culture because they offer a means of re-interpreting the dynamics of minority or oppressed cultures in general. However, within anthropology these are in their infancy; we must look elsewhere, for example, to Cultural Studies for assistance. Cowan (1990) gives one example from this discipline which might be of use – Gramsci's concept of hegemony, explained at the start of Chapter 2. As she puts it:

> The analytic usefulness of the concept of hegemony is that rather than presupposing a moral consensus, it makes it problematical. The concept thus opens up the question of how members of different social groups – variously positioned – accept, manipulate, use or contest hegemonic (that is dominant) ideas. (Cowan, 1990: 12)

A further usefulness of hegemony is that it opens up an issue which anthropology traditionally elides, namely the idea that all cultures are equally 'good' and healthy systems. Although this kind of 'cultural relativity', like linguistic relativity, was a noble one, intended to counterbalance colonialist ideas of 'superior' cultures, it is now possible to move beyond those positions.

For once we admit that cultures are shaped by hegemonic principles it is possible to admit that *majority cultures may be ruled by groups whose interests are inimical to the health of the culture as a whole, so that these majority cultures themselves may be conceived of as 'damaged' in some way.* Such a perspective can be found in the work of Marcuse (1968), which 'brought together the arguments of the 'Frankfurt School' that capitalism generated false needs, false consciousness and a mass culture that enslaved the working classes' (Osborne & Van Loon, 1996: 112). This approach was central to the New Left movement of the 1960s onwards, in psychiatry (Laing, 1965), psychology (Cooper, 1968), sociology (Reich, 1972) and what was known as the 'counter-culture' or 'hippie' movement (Roszak, 1971; Neville, 1970). Since that time, numerous newer disciplines (cf. Women's Studies, Black Studies) have pursued critiques of Western (and Eastern Bloc) societies and their Grand Narratives, reinforcing the importance of challenging positivist assumptions about cultural 'health'.

This perspective is crucial for our study of Deaf cultures because it creates a fissure in the positivist position underpinning both the medical and social models of deafness, and creates a space from which Deafhood proponents can critique majority society itself, as seen in the tenets of the French Banquets. It also creates a space in which it is possible to admit that minority and Deaf cultures might also be damaged by these oppressive processes. Furthermore, there may actually be a correlation between the nature of the damage caused to the minority culture and the nature of the endemic damage within the majority cultures, as Churchill (1994), examining Native American cultures, and feminists (Daly, 1979) have illustrated. Indeed, Churchill's explication is one that can give us all pause for thought:

> We [Native Americans] understand that the colonisation we experience finds its origins in the matrix of European culture. But, apparently unlike you, we also understand that in order for Europe to do what it has done to us . . . it first had to do the same thing to all of you. In other words, to become a colonizing culture, Europe had first to colonise *itself.* ' (Churchill, 1994: 234)

Churchill goes on to explain this process in some detail; here it will be sufficient to sketch its outline. Over time, European cultures became unaware of the loss of their traditional 'shamanic' cultures in the Christianisation process, and projected its Christianised fears of the body and of Earth-centred behaviour onto other cultures. In the present age, dimly aware of this loss, it has sought either to replace it by absorption of aspects such as the spiritual beliefs of the colonised cultures or to dissociate itself from the majority culture which produced such oppression, leaving its members 'with neither an established point-of-departure from which to launch [their] own struggle for liberation, nor any set of goals and objectives to guide that struggle other than abstractions' (p. 235).

This is a profound analysis, versions of which can also be found in the gaze of other non-Europeans upon Western social, cultural and academic philosophies (Nandy, 1983) and are examined later in Post-Colonial, Black, and Women's Studies. The implications for the Deaf cultural project are multiple – this kind of framing enables one not only to unpack the cultural patterns enacted upon Deaf communities, but also to identify its own versions of these patterns which operate within them.

Power relations and cultural change

Debates emerging from these concerns are still new. How might the mechanics of such processes be theorised? Bohannan (1995) reaches into Cultural Studies to adapt Hall (1966): all life events can be conceived of as 'action chains'. He proposes patterns of cultural trajectories and cycles, and develops a theory of 'recontexting', where 'meanings are transferred from one range within a particular cultural tradition to another within the same cultural tradition' (p. 69). This, if extended to theorise across cultures, forms the basis for a dynamic theory of Deaf culture where majority culture features are absorbed by Deaf communities, but adapted into forms and patterns to which they give their own meanings. This enables us not only to resist assertions that Deaf cultures simply 'copy' majority cultures, but also provides a tool with which to explore the types of situations in which re-contexting takes place.

Bohannan is essentially concerned with creating a perspective from which to explore cultural change itself, particularly with respect to historical time. In doing so he posits concepts of cultural 'equilibrium' and 'turbulence', that is, patterns in evolutionary time when such changes occur. These are also characterised by terms such as cultural 'cusps' and 'new cultural paradigms' (p. 115).

Once cultural change can be dissected and framed, it then becomes possible to identify other features, such as 'cultural lock-ins' (p. 173) and 'cultural traps', defined thus:

> A [cultural] virtue turns into a cultural trap if people slavishly follow some specific formulation of it . . . As conditions change, any religious explanations or political convictions that stifle thought and preclude questioning become deadly. When that happens, the very culture that had helped its people solve whatever problems they in fact solved, can become a trap that destroys everything their ancestors worked for. (Bohannan, 1995: 125).

The strength of Bohannan's work lies in his application of his ideas to both Western and tribal societies. In dealing with the meeting of two cultures, or of rapid changes within a single culture, he develops concepts of 'cultural dissonance' (p. 135) which are also applied to both cultures.

All of this is of particular relevance to the situation in which Deaf cultures have found themselves. Re-contexting describes one mechanism by which Deaf and other minority groups adapt majority cultural forms in order to sustain their own distinct identities and values, as Levine (1977) brilliantly illustrates for African-American culture.[2] Cultural traps are also particularly apposite for an analysis of pre- and post-independence colonial cultures, as Fanon's (1968, 1986) analysis of the Algerian situation shows. For example, in Deaf societies, cultural values absorbed unconsciously from majority cultures may come to be thought of as Deaf cultural features, and held onto to rather than submitting to self-examination as a necessary prerequisite for political change. (This is examined in detail in Chapters 8 and 9.) Likewise, cultural dissonance is useful for analysing the recent rapid changes within Deaf cultures, as well as partially accounting for the dissonance caused by the conflict of social-medical and culturo-linguistic models in and around Deaf life.

However, there is still a need both to formulate the role of the individual agent, the role of different 'fields' within a culture and the imbalances of power within those fields.

Situating the individual agent

Once the crisis in anthropology resulted in a (partial) acceptance of the necessity of including 'native' perspectives and accounts of their own cultures, questions regarding the representative nature of those perspectives, measurement of accuracy of subjective reflections, and the dynamics of moving from orality to written texts and styles, all came into play. Reed-Danahay (1997) is one example of the examination of such themes currently circulating in the discipline, and which are currently termed theories of auto/ethnography. Such work is important for Deaf cultural research, for if we are to move from Hearing examinations of Deaf peoples to a Deaf-centred perspective, all the problematics described above immediately come into play. These, being crucial to this study, will be examined in depth in Chapter 5.

Cultural change and futurology

Once cultural analysis embraces historical change, a further dimension is opened up. Post-colonial studies have begun to raise the question of how to reclaim/rebuild their cultures, whilst Bohannan includes the future as an essential feature, not just of cultural process, but of cultures at any given time. Indeed, as he asserts:

As long as ethnographers fail to look at the ideas people hold about the future, they are not doing their jobs adequately. (Bohannan, 1995: 192).

He then proceeds to delineate types of 'futurography'. Although this theory is very new, it has striking relevance for minority cultures. It appears to be a characteristic of majority cultures that conceiving of, thinking about or planning for their cultural future has a very low priority. However, dissident cultural groups, oppressed in the present may give high priority to imagining and realising alternative futures (Roszak, 1971).

This prioritising of strategies resonates even more strongly within minority cultures, for the future not only of their culture, but their entire community may be threatened, as is currently manifested in medical-model attacks on the Deaf community (genetics and cochlear implants), and in the 'education'-based assimilation of aboriginal and other 'First Nation' cultures (Davidson, 1992; Ihimaera, 1998; Beresford & Omaji, 1998). Alternative conceptions of the future are thus a necessity rather than a luxury.

Thus two major axis exist in the futurology of minority cultures – the (external) oppression which threatens their ability to conceive of a future; and the (internal) alternative vision of a cultural future which they must put forward in order to _even maintain an existential equilibrium_.

As Chapter 2 showed, each stage of Deaf advancement has been met by a wave of reaction. The global spread of Deaf-oriented schools and communities was halted by Oralism. The sign language resurgence a century later was countered by mainstreaming and the closing of those schools. And now the general Deaf resurgence and public prominence has been challenged by cochlear implants and genetics. It is impossible therefore, to develop a satisfactory analysis of Deaf culture without incorporating the very real effect on a community where each attempt to achieve equilibrium has been defeated, and where fear of the future is an important dynamic.

Summary

We can see that anthropology is an appropriate site for the investigation of Deaf culture, providing us with many concepts and theories of value for that investigation. The criticisms it poses of its own shortcomings are particularly useful to us, since we face the difficult task of analysing a minority culture imbedded within a Western (post) industrial majority culture. Because the Deaf situation does not fall within any of the social categories found in this discipline, it is not possible to adopt any one model, so I will draw on concepts and theories where appropriate.

Cultural Studies

Origins of the discipline

Cultural Studies is a comparatively youthful discipline, whose existence has been synonymous with controversy from the very beginning. This introduction presents what is arguably the dominant version of its origins and history (and I should add the caveat that, as so often, such an accounting tends to reduce it to a 'Great Men' narrative). The seminal texts, by Richard Hoggart and Raymond Williams, both published in 1958, began a process which culminated in the former inaugurating the discipline in the late 1960s at the Centre for Contemporary Cultural Studies (CCCS) in the University of Birmingham. Since then it has spread across the world, in the process mutating and developing different emphases according to the academic traditions and imperatives within which it finds itself.

As will be seen, it was conceived as an inter-disciplinary field of enquiry – indeed some of its founders intended it as a non- or anti- discipline, although its work has been marked by its engagement with two main disciplines, sociology and English literature. Importantly, it was also conceived as a form of political intervention both within and, crucially, outside the academy. Indeed, it conceived its own praxis as a collective undertaking, where post-graduate research culture had a central role to play. This commitment to egalitarianism enabled Cultural Studies to become a fruitful site for some of the first feminist challenges to male academic hegemony. All these qualities were perceived as threatening by the traditional academy and much of the subsequent work has been informed by the passion with which its initial struggles were conducted and by the political beliefs which fuelled its enquiries.

Cultural Studies was originally committed to re-discover or re-present the voice of the working class and agrarian subaltern; this commitment widened to pluralise the notion of a single (ruling-class) cultural voice into disparate voices, so that class relationships could be analysed in their intersection with factors of gender, sexuality and ethnicity.

Initial theorising of culture within cultural studies

Williams traced the historical development of the English term 'culture' from the 15th century, where it was used in two contexts – one concerning honour and worship, and the other in 'husbandry, the tending of natural growth' (Williams, 1976, 77). From here he charted a path towards two further usages, still commonly utilised today. The first is one in which a ruling section of society perceives itself and its social forms to be 'cultured' (as in 'cultivated'). These are used as a contrast with the lifestyles of other sections of society perceived as lacking in those qualities.

The second usage, initially linked with the term 'folk' to produce 'folk culture', constructed 'an alternative idea of human development . . . to the ideas not centered on "civilisation" and "progress"' (p. 77). It wished to support the values of the agrarian era, particularly the values found in the lives of the 'common people', perceived as intimately connected to 'Nature', and whose societies were perceived as being organised according to more 'collective' values. This concept was 'used to attack . . . the 'mechanical' character of the new civilisation then emerging: both for its abstract rationalism and for the 'inhumanity' of current industrial development' (p. 79).

Once the agrarian class had been moved en masse to populate new industrial towns, a new class emerged and took form. The social and political organisation and the cultural behaviour of this 'working class', the speed of its proliferation and the increased power gained for itself, all combined to alarm the 'cultured' classes.

Arnold's *Culture and Anarchy* (1869) warned of the consequences of the spread of this 'philistine culture', which would be hastened by the extension of literacy and democracy. In order to lessen the effects of that culture, and replace them by the more 'civilising' values of the ruling class, the discipline of English Literature was established in schools and universities in 1918.

Nevertheless, despite the élitist ideas behind the discipline's establishment, its humanist values broke with the previous traditions of the 'dismal drills and exercises of a Latin-based grammar in the classroom' (Inglis, 1993: 32), replacing the notion of received values of artistic worth with a vigorous injunction to students to form and assert their own opinions and ideas. This liberal humanism was epitomised by the life work of F.R. Leavis.

Leavis 'led a vanguard of English petit-bourgeois students . . . [who] pitted against the ruling class . . . their own vigorously independent, hardworking and sternly conscientious set of values' (Inglis, 1993: 38). These values were seen as originating with the ancestors of those students, the agrarian classes, progressing through the Romantic revolution and its assertion of individual responsibility and potential, into the folk-cultural tradition, epitomised in the work of D.H. Lawrence, whom Leavis was the first to champion.

Thus, from that first usage of the term 'culture' emerged a discipline which, in the hands of its most able practitioners, evolved into the second usage of the term, a discipline which Inglis identifies as having three 'master values'. These are: a close study of the text, the development of a methodology and tone of 'judicious detachment', and a surrendering to the elevating and enlightening pleasures within a text 'until a very different standing-outside-of-oneself is attainable' (p. 15), one which nevertheless has to be integrated into that same judicious detachment.

The third, implicit in the desire to follow one's personal beliefs and to confront authority when necessary, asserted both 'the inevitable creativeness of everyday life' (Leavis in Inglis, 1993: 42) *and* the belief in the concept of 'community', as opposed to the capitalist ideology of individualism.

It should not be supposed that Leavis found it easy to come to terms with the cultural developments and forms within working-class communities themselves. Nevertheless, once the children of that class were permitted in the post-war years to enter universities and study this 'Great Tradition', they were able to apply those three master values to their experiences within the cultures in which they grew up. Hoggart and Williams were two such 'scholarship boys', and in 1958 they published *The Uses of Literacy* and *Culture and Society* respectively.

Hoggart applied Leavis' principles to the study of everyday working-class community and culture, whilst Williams also attempted to construct Leavis' 'organic, common culture' into a more explicitly socialist analysis of culture within society. These two approaches then converged to form the new discipline of Cultural Studies at the CCCS. Under Hall, the themes of working-class resistance and cultural conflict were foregrounded and examined (Hall & Jefferson, 1976) and these themes have since been extended to the cultural resistance found in other minorities.

Relevance of the tradition for this study

Cultural Studies' commitment to the re-discovering and re-presenting of oppressed 'voices' immediately confirms its relevance for Deaf cultural study. Likewise, since the discipline is ostensibly an *activist* discipline, validating subaltern culture goes hand in hand with creating political change by revealing the hidden dimensions of capitalist forces and cultural politics. These theories enable us to move on from the anthropological positions and enable a reading of Deaf cultures as *cultures of resistance* and even oppositional cultures. It is just such a reading which has informed Chapters 2 and 3.

The master-value concerning close textual study is of relevance to our examination of Deaf cultural activities once we extend the concept beyond 'text-as-book' to 'text-as-cultural event/artefact'. For this to be effective, the Deaf cultural events we go on to observe and record must then be read 'across the grain' in order to extract as many levels and dimensions of meaning as possible.

The value of 'surrendering to the text' is particularly important. Reductionist readings of Deaf community life are the norm in medical and social control models. Instead, by seeking to allow the Deaf text, whether as cultural event or ethnographic interview, to convey its *emotional* importance, resonance and range without trying to reduce it to previously developed academic categories is crucial if we are to credit the true breadth and depth of Deaf subaltern culture. Validating such emotional resonance allows the 'poetry' of that perspective to come through. It also enables deeper and more vital levels of connection to be made across different sets of cultural features, fields and domains within the Deaf experience. This is in essence what Williams (1975) refers to as the *structure of feeling* of a culture and, for this study, this appears highly compatible both with Geertz' 'thick description' concept (situated near the end of Chapter 5) and the importance placed on 'subjectivity' within Women's Studies (MacKinnon, 1982).

Furthermore, the value of willingness to confront existing majority cultural norms and assert the 'creativeness of everyday community life' enables the study to valorise everyday Deaf subaltern activity, recognising symbolic importance particularly in the minutiae of examples, which academia and colonialists find insignificant. Finally, Cultural Studies validates the concept of subaltern researcher; it implies that insights into working-class culture could not be so easily supplied by researchers external to those communities.

Later developments in Cultural Studies

Casting widely for theories to refine and expand cultural analysis, Cultural Studies found compatible analytical tools in continental structuralism, in the neo-marxist sociology of the Frankfurt school and in semiotics, emerging with what, in Turner's (1990) opinion, are five basic theoretical approaches to culture, of which the following are of most use for this study.

Addressing the questions of how cultural, economic and political divisions and hierarchies are reflected in daily life, and seeking to replace notions of passive absorptions of culture, Cultural Studies sought to examine how those lives were reproduced, resisted or transformed, and in so doing, Althusser's (1984) crucial concept of 'ideology' was expanded. Earlier versions of Marxism had constructed ideology as a kind of cultural filter imposed on the working class, disguising its 'real' relations to the society around them, a filter which was at all times subject to economic and political determinism. The work of Althusser and colleagues asserted that a third force, namely culture, had a vital role in a *network* of determinations, and was thus able to assert that ideology 'not only produces our culture, it also produces our consciousness of ourselves' (p. 27). Thus for Hall (1983), ideology becomes *the actual site of struggles within a culture*, the battleground which different social groups contest for the control of their cultural 'reality'.

Third, Althusser's implications were refined by reference to the ideas of Lacan. Since ideology is an implicit cultural force, our unconscious is also formed by it and the notion of a single individual self dissolves into a series of selves, 'subjectivities', which can be contradictory and changeable; when deconstructed they can enlighten us both as to the origins and impetus behind these subjectivities and to the different discursive weight and prestige that they carry. This essentially post-modernist concept has proved useful in Women's Studies and Black Studies.

Cultural Studies also explored a structuralist approach. Barthes (1975) applied Saussure's linguistic principles to social and cultural features of contemporary urban societies, isolating each sign ('the smallest unit of communication within a language system' – Turner [1990: 17]), into its denotations and connotations, creating a 'chain of signification of ascending complexity and cultural specificity' (p. 18). These principles were brought to bear on a wide range of cultural manifestations ('texts') within contemporary capitalist society – advertising, television programming, print media and so on – to reveal the impulses which lay behind the 'natural', 'innocent' or 'common sense' cultural imagery used by ruling classes as part of their ideological approach to domains they controlled or influenced.

Broadly speaking, then, there has since developed what might be termed two 'wings' within Cultural Studies, which are more a set of tensions than formalised positions. One seems more interested in the forms and structures which produced cultural meanings, whilst the other perceives this to be too deterministic and sought approaches which could reflect the individual agent within a culture.

In attempting to reconcile these, Hall *et al.* (1977) re-presented some of the ideas of the Italian neo-marxist, Gramsci, whose *Prison Notes* from the 1920s had only recently been translated into English. In particular he highlighted his concept of hegemony. Gramsci (1971) believed that in the process of state control, the production of consent was as important as the threat of coercion, and thus that the struggles between classes could be more fruitfully analysed as a constant and ongoing struggle for hegemony – that is, for moral, cultural, intellectual and thereby political leadership of a society. Crucially, hegemony is not maintained by simply suppressing the opposition, but by selective absorption of opposing cultural interests into its own ideologies, attempting to secure *the cultural consent of those governed*. Cultural forms and manifestations thus form the battleground for the control of society.

This concept helped to open up the way in which a society's hierarchies find ideological justification at the level of 'common sense', that is, beliefs which many of its members appear to accept as 'normal', 'rational' or 'reasonable'. In stressing the dynamic interplay between such beliefs and those held by dissenting sectors of society which sought to contest them (as far as they themselves were aware of what they had assimilated), a means of theorising and assessing cultural change could be accommodated within the theoretical framework of the discipline.

The cultural politics of deconstructing 'common sense' as it informed the making and consumption of media 'texts' benefited in turn by its embrace of Foucault's notions of 'discourse'. This was due not least to the notion of discourse enabling analyses of texts to include how they were produced, circulated and negotiated. Foucault's re-introduction of the historical dimension to this textual analysis also enabled further conceptual development, notably the concept of 'social construction', applicable to a wide range of studies, from Dyer's (1986) study of Marilyn Monroe _vis à vis_ discourses of constructions of sexuality in the 1950s, to Showalter's (1987) account of the 19th century's construction and treatment of, madness. It is from the convergence of these very different approaches that 'post-structuralism' has since emerged.

Attempts to situate the individual agent within this construct are still very recent. Gramsci suggests an approach which unites this with an introduction of psychological and even spiritual dimensions, defining culture thus:

> It is organisation, discipline of one's inner self, a coming to terms with one's personality; it is the attainment of a higher awareness, with the aid of which one succeeds in understanding one's own historical value, one's own function in life, and one's own rights and obligations. (in Bennett _et al._ 1981: 194)

Although this definition is useful on a wider scale, it is particularly appropriate for oppressed members of cultures, where the struggle to tran-scend imposed models is seen as a priority. As yet there seem to have been few attempts to develop this position.

Summary – relevance for Deaf cultural study

The approaches outlined here are important for Deaf cultural study; they validate the perception that in cultures which are striving to maintain their own values in the face of oppression, many apparently ordinary everyday acts and beliefs _become_ fundamentally political/oppositional. Recognising this enables us to penetrate beneath surface readings of Deaf culture and glean a deeper reading of a 'collective resistance', which is not necessarily conventional resistance, but simply carrying out one's every-day cultural values in a hostile world.

Ideology as the site of cultural struggle is important on two levels. The first concerns 'external' struggles, in the domains where the Deaf commu-nity contests cultural meanings with majority society. The second is 'internal' and is crucial for this study. Oppression results in a perception of minority cultures as homogeneous entities; yet the reality is that divisions within these cultures _may have even greater significance than in majority cul-tures_. The extent to which different sectors of minority communities support or reject the values and beliefs imposed on them leads to intense in-ternal ideological struggles; both this intense cultural pressure and the positions themselves must be identified and explored for an accurate reading of Deaf culture.

In this respect the concept of self as a series of subjectivities is even more important. Some aspects and domains of the self may overtly reject oppressive ideologies, whilst others may covertly and subconsciously absorb them. The classic example is the petit bourgeoisie, (the upwardly-aspiring working-class), and is an issue with growing relevance for African-Americans (Landry, 1987). Another example is concerned with how the latter absorb ideas about American superiority which affect their attempts to develop solidarity with the rest of the African diaspora (Gilroy, 1993b). One cannot rule out the possibility that such ideas may also have permeated American Deaf culture. Similarly, some Deaf subalterns may aspire to certain 'hearing' ideals, or 'rebels' absorb notions of the superiority of English.

Understanding hegemony is helpful to us on four levels. The first has already enabled us in the previous two chapters to develop an understanding of the ways in which majority cultures have assigned responsibility and power to certain sectors of society (the 'specialists') for all matters concerning Deaf people and their communities. Once theories of ideology enable us to deconstruct attitudes towards those with hearing impairment in general, and Deaf people in particular, hegemonic theories enable us to deconstruct the ways in which members of the majority culture are manipulated into giving their consent for whichever actions the specialists deem necessary.

The second concerns the ways which members of the Deaf community itself are manipulated or pressured into consenting with the received ideologies. This, in turn, leads to a third dimension, where different Deaf élites have developed their own ideologies towards their colleagues; this enables us to analyse how different subjectivities and ideologies coalesce and 'enforce' that hegemony, whilst the fourth dimension is concerned with how the Deaf subalterns gave 'consent' to those ideologies.

Finally, Gramsci's definition of culture focuses attention on questions of Deaf attempts to transcend the limits placed by Oralism on their individual and collective value and the importance of historical awareness in attaining that transcendence.

All these enable us to revise 'monolithic' models of Deaf culture as a 'noun', and to construct it instead as a pluralistic site wherein its members *contest* Deaf cultural meanings. Thus it is clear from all these examples that there is immense value in utilising theories from Cultural Studies to explicate important aspects of Deaf cultures.

Post-Modernist, Post-Colonialist and Other Recent Theories

The political and cultural upheavals of the 1960s resulted in the formation of several important new disciplines which can be conveniently termed 'minority studies' (where 'minority' refers to the amount of power held by members of those groups in relation to the Western discursive systems rather than to the numbers in those groups per se). These include Women's Studies, Post-Colonial Studies and Black Studies. Theories which have emerged from these disciplines are considered here with post-modernist theories, since they have, in many instances, informed each other.

Post-modernism, emerging in the 1980s, has been concerned that mod-ernist theories, such as those found within the earliest work within Cultural Studies, do not account for the realities of post-industrial societies, where the effects of consumerism and the mass media carry their own unique weightings. It identifies the present age as one which has attained sufficient history in order to have become self-conscious and has therefore begun to draw together cultural forms from different periods of that history into new syntheses. This belief has led to a retroactive suspicion of the effectiveness of any of the 'Grand Narratives' like socialism, capitalism or patriarchy, and questioned the extent to which they could ever offer a comprehensive explanation; indeed whether any single explication is pos-sible, thus positively valuing multiplicity, uncertainty and creativity.

Resistance and pleasure

One concern for post-modernism is how the concept of ideology fails to acknowledge and thus account for, ways in which individuals and groups construct their own realities and responses to political and cultural domi-nation. De Certeau (1984), in examining the ways in which the 'practices of everyday life' are carried out, in the workplace, in schools, in structuring one's own home, in one's selection and re-arrangement of consumer goods, illustrates how people, whilst 'making do' with the forms presented to them, 'make them over' to their own ends. This resistance is perceived by de Certeau as 'pleasure' oriented, aesthetically governed and, thus to some degree, operating separately from ideology. This has relevance for ways in which Deaf communities approach their own lives which are so embedded in, and interpenetrated by, majority society cultural structures. Without the 'pleasure' perspective, we might be in danger of creating a reading of Deaf culture that was overtly 'ideological', one which ignored the beauty, power and fun that can be generated through the physical uniqueness of sign languages themselves. A similar reading can be developed to emphasise the joys inherent in creating Deaf spaces and folkloric forms.

Hybrid identities and subjectivities

The notions of the created self from multiple cultural selves have been extended by post-modernist and other theoreticians to deal with multiple identities which have been created _across_ cultural boundaries, by Gilroy (1993a) in Black Studies, Hall (1993) in Cultural Studies and Bhabha (1994) in Post-Colonial Studies. All share the belief that cultural identities are not inherent, bounded or static, but are dynamic, fluid and constructed situationally in particular places and times. Some writers are beginning to propose that this is 'not just an urban phenomenon of the 1990s' (Wright, 1998), but a concept which may always have existed in some, if not all, earlier societies.

It is highly relevant for individuals in the Deaf community who were not socialised into Deaf culture, but had to create their own identities, moving from 'hearing-impaired/deaf' to 'Deaf'. Likewise the limited everyday contact between Deaf people also leaves more 'space' for self-construction in the absence of social and cultural support. Similarly, the co-existence of two polarised identities, 'Deaf' and 'Hearing' operating both within individuals and with collective life, has numerous cultural ramifications, as Chapter 8 and 9 will show in detail.

Essentialism and Anti-essentialism

A major issue for all minority cultures is the extent to which essentialism plays a role in their collective self-conception. Initially essentialism was a product of a colonial gaze which saw each native group as a homogeneous entity holding the same views and thus reduced them to racist caricature. The understandable post-colonialist reaction against this has been reinforced by many theorists within Black Studies and Women's Studies; augmented by post-modernist refutations of Grand Narratives, essentialism has become almost a pariah in contemporary cultural discourse.

This is unfortunate for groups like Deaf communities who are still struggling to conceptualise their post-colonial identity in the first place, and who have traditionally ascribed assertive meanings to the idea of 'Deaf', as well as to the obvious biological factors inherent in being 'Deaf-Mute' people. However, there are those who feel that it is impossible to completely discard the concept (Walby, 1990), especially in Women's Studies where there has been a significant assertion of woman's basic biological realities as an eradicable marker of difference (Daly, 1979), whilst in Post-Colonial Studies, Spivak (1996) argues for the necessity of a 'strategic essentialism' as a means of breaking the contemporary theroretical deadlock. These latter discourses are in their infancy, but reinforce my belief that essentialist concepts such as Deafhood are at the least strategically viable for the foreseeable future, and thus work in this field may be able to make a contribution across the several disciplines concerned with essentialism.

Diasporic theories

Although this concept originated within Jewish Studies, it has been taken up by some post-colonialists as an important central concept (Gilroy,

1993b). A culture is said to contain diasporic features if it has migrated out from a central point of origin and is now found in different countries and continents in culturally mutated forms (though see Clifford [1997] for a more detailed reading). Its importance for future cultural theory lies in bringing into dialogue both the essentialist (shared cultural features) and the hybridity (variation within cultural identities) discourses, offering an academic space in which further exploration may be conducted. However, diasporic theories are very new and in need of further culturally-specific studies in order to enable useful cultural parallels to be made.

Diasporic theory is important to Deaf culture, not because Deaf people share a common geographical origin, but because they are unique in being *the only linguistic group to have a community in every country in the world.* Awareness of this, together with an awareness of sign language as a language with uniquely global connotations, is central to many Deaf subalterns' self-concept and pride. However, since diasporic theory is so new, the Deaf contribution requires more space than is available to this study.

Other Minority Studies theories

Minority Studies disciplines are not only new but on the ascendant, meaning that valuable new texts are emerging all the time. In Women's Studies, this means that particularly profound challenges are being mounted to the traditional beliefs and methodologies of the academy (Tannen, 1986, 1990;Wolff, 1990), and have begun the development of what might be termed 'feminist epistemologies'; and some of these will be drawn on later in the study. Black Studies has developed a wide range of texts analysing the negative relationships between white and Black peoples. In so doing it has begun the process of and delineating the effects of Eurocentric cultural theories on Black peoples (Fanon, 1968; Campbell, 1985; Pityana *et al.*, 1991) and of developing Black epistemologies (Karenga, 1993, Gordon, 2000) . Post-Colonial Studies has built on the work of Said (1978) to begin a similar critique (Ashcroft *et al.*, 1995); (Duran & Duran, 1995) and has developed a cross-over point with later Cultural Studies in the work of Nandy (1983).

One other important feature of these disciplines is the extent to which they problematise and challenge each other. Thus, Black Studies has been critiqued for being too male-oriented (hooks, 1989), whilst Women's Studies has had to embrace similar critiques of being too Eurocentric (Sardar & Van Loon, 1997). Also, the newness of these disciplines means that they have not yet developed theoretical positions which span Minority Studies *per se.* These factors, together with the huge range of cultures that require consideration within Post-Colonial Studies, has resulted in bodies of work of such complexity that drawing on them as deeply as they deserve is beyond the scope of this book, and will form the basis of subsequent volumes. However, research and theories from these disciplines are of such importance for exploring Deaf culture that they are drawn on where appropriate, especially in the concluding chapters.

Summary

Post-modernist and minority group theories offer great scope for analysing aspects of Deaf culture. Since they are new, utilising them as a primary tool to unpack Deaf culture is difficult. However, in addition to those already mentioned, the following clues can also be offered:

- Certain strands of post-modernism and post-colonialism are helpful to subalterns who do not fit into the classical modernist traditions built around class theories. For example, these help us to situate Deaf subalterns themselves, to examine the ways in which they have refused the majority cultures' constructions of them and how they have decoded mainstream cultural values to create their own cultural realities.

- Given the fact that Deaf communities, unlike many minority groups do not live and work in close contact with each other, some of the earlier theories may assist us in comprehending the ways in which both individuals and communities collectively construct themselves in the absence or reduced nature of everyday contact. Here, work such as Anderson (1983) on 'imagined communities' is particularly useful.

- We have seen how Deaf linguistic minorities differ from others in the reduced role of ethnicity in cultural transmission. For the individual deaf person, becoming Deaf is, to some degree, a matter of personal choice, a pattern that has become more pronounced with the advent of mainstreaming. In having to deconstruct one's Hearing-Impaired (deaf) self and reconstruct it as a Deaf self, much can be learned from post-modernist theories of selfhood (a process that later may well be able to draw on parallels within Queer Studies).

Post-modernist approaches have also begun to inform Deaf Studies in the works of Mirzoeff (1995) and Wrigley (1996) and, whilst these have been introduced from without, offer great potential for cross-fertilisation when Deaf accounts emerge. However, a common criticism of some versions of post-modernism is that they do not take sufficient account of the different political weighting carried by the various cultural features they examine, nor of the disparity in power bases between researcher and researched Object. To accommodate such features, we might look to Bourdieu.

Bourdieu and Epistemology

Bourdieu (1990, 1992) shares with the post-modernists a concern for epistemologies which emphasise indeterminacy and flexibility, and which also conceive of a place for the individual actor within a culture. However, he parts company with them in his belief that an overarching theory can in fact be worked towards and developed. There are many aspects of his work which are of relevance for this study; some are highlighted here.

One of his primary concerns is to reconcile or to straddle the antinomies which are so prevalent in social science, whether between the 'individual' and 'society', synchronic and diachronic theories, between subjectivist and objectivist epistemologies, between symbolism and materialism, or between theory and research. To do this he takes an initially structuralist position – that social phenomena and culture are grounded primarily within relationships – but then moves beyond the discreteness of manifested forms to assert that they interpenetrate each other (Bourdieu, 1992).

This interpenetration informs another major conceptual theory; society consists of relationships between 'fields', 'agents' and their 'habitus'. Fields are conceived of as relatively autonomous spheres of play with their own values, rules and centres of gravity, where each contains _social and cultural capital_ which reflects and is reflected by the social power and prestige of each field.

Each field, however, is a contested terrain where boundaries are not easily identifiable because they are always at stake in the contestations within the field, and it is these contestations which support his assertion of the fundamental _indeterminacy_ of cultural life. He resists the idea of a homogeneous state system or apparatus except as a 'terminal' form of field development in totalitarian societies and situations, seeing the ruling class as an ensemble of fields and groups rather than a monolithic entity.

Individuals are conceived of as agents rather than passive recipients of a cultural system – although they are socialised to a degree, they are able to develop strategies of their own, which are reflected to some extent in the amount of cultural capital each possesses (Bourdieu & Passeron, 1977).

However, this by itself cannot explain individual tendencies and strategies nor the patterning mechanisms which each field imposes on the individual. To this end the concept of habitus acts as a 'Janus-face', where the individual's habitus, on the one hand, constrains and shapes them to some degree but, on the other, manifests itself in _a range of dispositions_. One is disposed towards certain beliefs and behaviour but there are numerous possibilities within that disposition.

These three concepts are conceptually inseperable, bound up in dialectical relationships, and allow for generative theories of multiple beliefs and actions which are therefore historically situated. By extrapolation, Bourdieu is also able to develop analyses of the socio-political construction of academia, the 'false' conceptual authority of disciplinary boundaries and the spurious roles played by the intellectual classes in general, all of which are grounded in another important concept – *reflexivity*.

Although this has much in common with the theories of critical ethnography described in Chapter 6, Bourdieu's 'structuralist' approach sees the latter as essentially individualistic and in danger of reifying those individuals who utilise it. By grounding the individual's reflexivity in their habitus, so that one is forced to examine one's own social background and the dispositions which form part of it, the academic/intellectual/ researcher's status and behaviour is demystified (Bourdieu, 1993). Such demystification is presented, not only as an important political tool, but as a necessary prerequisite for a truly disinterested and objective science, and forms the basis of my self-analysis as subaltern-researcher in Chapter 6.

Summary - Bourdieu's relevance for Deaf cultural study

Most of the cultural theories examined in this chapter, despite their usefulness, do not cover the particular situation of a Deaf culture completely surrounded and permeated by a majority culture and its materiality, where cultural transmission through ethnicity is problematic and where individual Deaf identity processes are disrupted by a particularly intense form of educational oppression. Many Deaf social and cultural forms resemble those of majority culture – however, *their expressions are different*, in ways which we have not yet examined. Bourdieu's conceptual framework offers a means by which to explore all these issues, suggesting that the range of Deaf individual and collective dispositions may offer an important explanatory mechanism, as will later be seen. It comes close to being a conceptual framework for this book.

However, because it is an initial study, it is not possible to generate a model which is congruent with the full range of Bourdieu's theories, nor necessarily advisable to impose an external model as we have seen from Black critiques of the Eurocentric academy. It is more appropriate, therefore, to draw on his theories at relevant points.

Sub-cultural Theories

Having explored theories situated around macro-cosmic cultures, it is now necessary to examine those which specifically examine minority and bicultural groupings.

Sub-cultural theories rose to contemporary prominence under Cultural Studies; however, the concept was first developed within sociology (Lee, 1945; Gordon, 1947), and used in the broadest terms as 'a subdivision of a national culture' (Brake, 1985: 7). Downes (1966) was among the first to argue that a distinction had to be made between different types of sub-divisions, between those sub-groups which emerge as a result of the demands of majority society structures, and those which developed in response to what Brake characterises a as follows.

> Meaning systems, modes of expression or life styles developed by groups in subordinate structural positions . . . which reflect their attempt to solve structural contradictions arising from the wider societal context. (Brake, 1985: 8)

The thread which links subcultures to Cultural Studies has been described by Hall and Jefferson (1976: 5) thus:

> Our starting point, as for so many others, was Howard Becker's 'Outsiders' – the text which, at least for us, best signalled the 'break' [with] mainstream sociology.

In this context, this 'break' can be described as a movement away from the reading of subcultures according to a deviance model to one which utilises the three master values described earlier.

The social groups defined as subcultures and studied as such were initially youth cultures. The term has now been extended to cover 'criminal' sub-groups and others such as gay and lesbian sub-groups. The significance for this study in that *all have grown up with a shared national culture* which the sub-group then rebels against for a variety of reasons, proceeding to create sets of cultural meanings of its own to serve a variety of purposes.

Sub-cultural theories are particularly useful for examining the collective responses of Deaf communities to the attitudes and actions of majority societies. They are also useful in enabling us to consider the ways in which Deaf communities are both similar and – crucially – dissimilar to subcultures.

The most important issue is whether Deaf and other minority cultures should be perceived as subcultures, or some other entity. In this context, Downes (1966) has argued that

> [S]ubcultures originating from within a society can be differentiated from those that originate from without, such as with immigrant groups or traditions. This particularly holds true for ethnic or minority cultures. (paraphrased by Brake, 1985: 7)

Unfortunately this analysis is not developed further, but consideration of the differences ensuing from two different sites of cultural origin reveal three strands worthy of further evaluation.

In the first strand, taking Asian communities in the UK as an example, it is clear that their cultural life is based on origins and traditions developed outside the UK. Deaf communities do not originate from outside the majority society in this sense. However, what is described as 'traditions originating from without' can be reworded as 'separate origins and development'. Under this refinement, there is sufficient theoretical space to initiate the argument that traditional Deaf communities have to a degree developed separately from majority cultures via Deaf residential schools.

The second strand is that of language. If a community uses a radically different language to the majority, it can be argued that their worldview is consequently radically different. Turner (1990: 13) paraphrasing Saussure asserts that

> Language does not name an already organised and coherent reality ... The function of language is to organize, to construct, indeed to provide us with our only access to reality.

Although it can be argued that this is overdeterministic, the idea that meaning is culturally grounded and mediated leads nevertheless to the conclusion that

> Different cultures may not only use different language systems, but they also, in a definitive sense, *inhabit different worlds*. (Turner, 1990: 14–15; original emphasis)

In the case of Deaf communities, there are two aspects to this linguistic strand which are especially pertinent. The first is that prior to residential school life, and outside the Deaf environment, Deaf people are unable to access the majority language through which an understanding of majority culture is mediated. This reinforces the argument for 'separate origins and development'. Second, once they have learned sign languages as their first language, their primary worldview is then shaped by this lens. Thus even whilst co-existing with majority society, they have always *'inhabited a different world'*. This is reflected in the central sign language trope of 'Deafworld' (Lane *et al.*, 1996). Furthermore, the source of that language is either the older Deaf children in the school (Reilly, 1995), or the Deaf children of Deaf parents, who bring the language into the school from home (Johnson & Erting, 1989); one can argue, therefore, that the language originates, *for the most part*, from outside the majority culture.

This, in turn, leads to a crucial historical moment in this study, given that the existence of 'Deaf culture' is doubted by so many, both inside and outside the community. Since the culture of a group is mediated by its language, it follows that *those groups with different languages from the majority also have different cultures from the majority.* Furthermore, those Deaf children of Deaf parents accept the responsibility to pass on and explain to the other children, information about the world of Deaf clubs, local and national social activities and other features that, when taken together, amount to Downes' 'outside traditions'.

The significance for Deaf communities is that these theories can be drawn together to infer that *if a group of people have a language of their own, then they clearly possess their own culture.* Furthermore, they suggest that Deaf cultures *are therefore not subcultures of the majority society, but cultures in their own right.* This distinction marks an epistemological turning point for a study such as this which attempts to validate the existence of Deaf cultures.

However, we can go even further. To term them cultures is insufficient to mark their particular status and characteristics. In this respect it is more meaningful to begin a process of hypothesising outwards, by beginning to describe them within a larger epistemology, which I theorise as *minority cultures.* This development is expanded in the concluding chapters, but marks another turning point, one which finds the study of Deaf culture not only to be of value for itself, *but as a bridgehead for illustrating how it has value for work currently being carried out in other disciplines.* It may be too early to claim that Deaf cultural study can affect 'mainstream' disciplines to the same extent as sign linguistics impacts upon mainstream linguistics. But it seems that the very fact of Deaf culture falling outside of most other models of culture and ethnicity can *paradoxically be of great use in assisting them to reframe their own work.*

In this respect it is useful to refer to other minority cultures where at times similar patterns to those described earlier exist, notably the example of African-Americans. Although a case can be made for a history of separate development under 'Jim Crow' laws, it is the question of whether Black English is a separate language from American English or simply one of its dialects, that is crucial in confirming whether their lives are best regarded as sub-cultural or minority-cultural. On this subject, one of the leading voices of Black Studies, Henry Gates, remarks:

> We have been deconstructing white people's language since that dreadful day in 1619 when we were marched off the boat in Virginia. Derrida did not invent deconstruction, we did! (During, 1993: 127, emphasis in original,)

Systematic descriptions are given of such 'deconstruction' by Herskovits (1958) and Levine (1977). The former highlights the use of Africanisms within Black English and the latter the adaptation of American English to manifest Black realities. The evidence collected here and elsewhere leads almost to the position that Black Americans are minority-cultural and that Black English, although containing considerable amounts of English, is actually linguistically impelled by *both* its origins from without and their separate development within the USA.

Another useful parallel is the case of Native Americans and other First Nation peoples, who unquestionably originated from within the country, yet whose evolution took place very separately from the latterly developed white majority cultures. In this case also, possession of their own languages and cultures marked the existence of worldviews that owed nothing to the consensual majority cultural reality (Churchill, 1994).

In summary then, certain aspects of sub-cultural theory are of relevance to the study, but its most useful contribution may be to help us distinguish ways in which Deaf cultures differ from majority subcultures so that they can then be classified as minority-cultural.

Bicultural Theories

Bicultural theories are the least developed of all the theories in this chapter; this is unfortunate since they are importance to a conceptualisation of Deaf culture in that, if Deaf communities have developed *bona fide* cultures, their existence inside majority cultures, together with the large numbers of Deaf people being brought up within hearing families, therefore suggests some degree of biculturalism. One might therefore expect bicultural theories to offer a means by which to assess the actual impact of one culture upon another in this way. However, Webster's dictionary definition of biculture is ' The existence of two distinct cultures in one nation'. (in Paulston, 1992: 116).

This definition is a useful starting point, but soon breaks down, begging the question not only of what might constitute 'distinct' but also by its assertion that bilingual situations occur only in countries with a total of two cultures. In countries where a plurality of cultures exist, should this be regarded as a collectivity of bilingual situations, or a multicultural entity? These definitional difficulties render the already complex questions around biculturality and multiculturality even more problematic.

Unfortunately, Paulston finds that 'There is virtually nothing written on biculturalism' (p. 116), and goes on to describe the use of the term in recent academic work as

almost invariably in the sense of the almost slogan-like 'bilingual/ bicultural education programmes', where such dissertations *typically ignore the bicultural element* and rather examine language proficiency or self-concept. (Paulston, 116 ; emphasis added).

Proceeding to examine definitions of culture as they impinge on biculturalism, she concludes that 'the emphasis is always on the patterned behaviour of the group – not on the behaviour of individuals who cross the boundaries of ethnic groups ' (p. 117). Given the immense complexity of cultural theories, as evidenced in this chapter, the lack of attention to this further complication is not really surprising.

However, it may well prove to be the case that more extensive studies of biculturalism will assist those struggling to define culture, by approaching the phenomenon from the opposite direction, as it were. If resources are invested in the exploration of biculturalism it may be possible to locate patterns which help us to see in which domains individuals within any one culture construct their identification with that culture and in which they intentionally deviate from it.

Keesing's competence and performance approach described earlier allows one, in Paulston's words, 'to deal with the difference between a collective ideational system and the psychodynamics of the individual' (p. 119). Nevertheless, utilising this approach raises the question of whether bicultural individuals have only one set of cultural competence, but two (or more) sets of performances. Although this issue is in the earliest stages of development, Kleinjams' (1975) model appears to be helpful.

He suggests that a model for learning a second culture delineates three categories of what is learned – cognition, affection and action. Cognition is concerned with knowing the what and why about another culture, and can be partially learned from outside the culture. Affection concerns the process which begins with 'coming to know and like another culture'. Action moves through three stages: changing one's values; changing the direction of one's life as a result of adopting some of those values; and finally in some cases to 'becoming one with the people of the other culture'. This would appear to offer the beginnings of an analytical framework.

Nevertheless, with regard to cultural competence, the task of analysis is made harder by Keesing's insistence that competence does not have to involve a complete understanding of everything which occurs in any one culture. As Paulston comments:

> An obvious difference between bilingualism and biculturalism is that when you speak Swedish or English, it is perfectly obvious which set of rules you are drawing on. But with behaviour, it is not necessarily clear just which cultural system your performance rules belong to. (Paulston, 1992: 125)

Furthermore, it appears that bicultural theory has not examined the different types of situations in which the phenomenon ocuurs. Such situations range from Paulston's more 'voluntary' biculturalism (that is, from freedom of movement between two Western nations), through varying degrees of imposed biculturalism (as evidenced by traditional colonialism), through biculturalism imposed by a majority culture on its own minority cultures, (as evidenced by Spanish–Catalan struggles or spoken language-signed language struggles), to biculturalism arising from enslavement or 'involuntary migration' (African-American and Irish experiences). Biculturality in these contexts is a qualitatively different experience than one created from two relatively equal Western cultures like English and Swedish.

In the case of the Deaf experience, there is a further significant difference. Almost all bicultural theory, especially as it relates to educational issues, is based around the concept that there is one language at home (the mother tongue) and another at school (the dominant language). Yet the Deaf child brought up in the UK, or indeed almost anywhere in the known world, has for the best part of a century had no access at all to the home language, in theory its dominant language. In fact, for Deaf children the situation is reversed. When attending a Deaf school, they begin to learn their real mother tongue and, as linguistic research has shown, decode the basic grammatical rules very quickly.

All told, although bicultural theory and practice is the most appropriate for the investigation of Deaf culture, the virtual absence of research means that it is of limited assistance to the present study. Nevertheless, if one draws on the cultural theories from earlier sections, it is possible to begin to examine Deaf biculturalism in respect of those other theories and thus bring this investigation into a sharper focus.

Other Multicultural Studies

The developments within bilingualism have been augmented by four other movements which are beginning to have a growing relevance for those seeking to identify and situate Deaf culture.

The multilingual/multi-cultural movement

In the past 30 years the increased contact with and travel between, nation-states, together with increased immigration to Europe from former colonies has resulted in a renewal of certain forms of racism. In response, both liberal and radical sectors of societies have been concerned to offer resistance and to attempt to assist or support the incomers and their offspring. The impulse has tended to play itself out at the level of social policy, particularly with regard to education. In so doing a burgeoning multilingualism/multiculturalism movement has emerged, developing its own theories and practices to account for the social and cultural implications of these 'new' multiracial societies.

This work has extended conceptual thinking within several mainstream disciplines, such as linguistics (Edwards, 1979), and politics (Crawford, 2000). They have also impelled the beginnings of such extensive discourse within the discipline of education that, inextricably linked with bilingualism (e.g. Baker & Jones, 1997), they are almost ready to constitute their own discipline. There now exist so many strands to this work in the UK and the USA alone that examining the complexities of the various discourses is beyond an initial study such as this. However, it is possible to say that examining policies and practices towards minority languages and cultures may assist us in redrawing and refining the 'minority culture' concept described earlier.

One example can be briefly given. The next chapter explores academic perceptions of Deaf people that question the validity of their claim to actively 'own' their own languages. In this respect, Magnet (1990: 293), when examining language rights, finds himself able to assert that

> Language rights are collective rights. They are exercised by individuals only as part of a collectivity or group. Legal protection of language rights, therefore, means protection of that linguistic community . . . *vis-à-vis* the larger community which would impinge upon it or restrict its right as a group to exist.

For a typical majority-society member, the idea that he or she might 'own' English is something of an alien concept (though as Crawford [2000] illustrates, there are situations in which such a claim emerges). For some minority-language users, it seems, personal identity is much more closely linked to language identification. Such a belief in linguistic collectivity is linked therefore to questions of cultural collectivity. One set of questions which arises concerns the degree to which these minority cultures are inherently collective in their country of origin. Another is poised to ask whether migrant status itself is a factor in any increased cultural collectivity. At some point in the future, a further set will arise which will theorise any emerging links between these two forms of enquiry.

Of all the disciplines currently engaged in cultural study, it is this movement which stands the closest to the Deaf discourses. This is partly because of the cross-fertilisation which has begun within socio-linguistics, partly because of the beginnings of inclusion of sign language within its discourse (cf. Allardina & Edwards, 1991, Skutnabb-Kangas, 2000) and partly because of the Deaf political movement within the European Union which has brought sign languages into minority-language discourses.

Thus, answers to these sets of questions will have increasing relevance for Deaf linguistic and cultural study. Indeed it is one of the aims of this book to reach across and draw in practitioners from such discourses. At present, it is those working in the Deaf bilingual and multicultural fields who 'travel outwards'. But I anticipate that those drawn in from without will also come to find examples in the Deaf situation which will inform their own spheres of interest, so that Deaf cultural issues will have relevance for their own cultural theories. In this respect, examples such as the one given here form the barest beginnings of the light which multilingual studies might be able to shed on conceptions of Deaf culture.

Ethnicity studies

A similar though smaller movement is also developing towards ethnicity studies *per se*. Although these have not yet developed the kind of cross-fertilisation described earlier, the writings found in texts like Guibernau and Rex (1997) indicate that this field will have growing relevance for certain considerations of Deaf culture. One set of examples may suffice. In exploring the relationships between constructs of race, biology, ethnicity and nation-states, they draw on Weber's recognition that some forms of ethnic self-conception can be theorised by a concept of *ethnie*, that is, where the characteristics of an ethnic group as manifested (or constructed) in myths and symbols 'are used to stand in for the presence of actual kin' (p. 3). This bears some relationship to Anderson's (1983) 'imagined communities', which as we have seen has implications for a Deaf community which is not built on geographical proximity, but appears to go beyond this in offering a conceptual term which can be refined and developed.

The field of intercultural communication

The USA's dominance in world affairs during the post-war period has led to an increase in relationships with various national cultures, and four strands of discourse have emerged in respect to the linguistic and cultural conflicts which have ensued. One is primarily capitalist in impulse, being concerned with the extent to which cultural barriers have negatively affected trade (cf. Trompenaars, 1993), whilst another originates from the cultural and political dissonance that has characterised foreign aid programmes such as the Peace Corps (Hall, 1959). A third concerns the sets of cultural problems experienced by foreign students and workers who moved to the USA (cited by Mindess, 2000), whilst the fourth might be termed the American equivalent of the multilingual discourses (Seelye, 1992). These have come together to form the new discipline of Intercultural Communication. Hall (not to be confused with the Stuart Hall of Cultural Studies fame) has become regarded as the 'founding father' of this discipline and an examination of his works reveals much that is useful for Deaf cultural study.

Hall applied his anthropologist training to the first three strands, and his work, from *The Silent Language* (1959) to *Beyond Culture* (1981) has attempted to theorise across these cultural clashes and misunderstandings. In so doing, he has developed what might best be described as clusters of cultural characteristics which can be tentatively attributed to a variety of national cultures. Five examples include concepts involving cultural space (proxemics), cultural time (seen as polychronic or monochronic), value orientation in relation to Nature, collective *versus* individualistic and high context *versus* low context.

Some of these examples appear to have considerable resonance within Deaf cultural study and will be discussed in the next chapter. The extent to which these examples form the beginnings of an overarching cultural framework is not yet clear – for example, whether cultures which are collective in philosophy are also characterised by any of the other four qualities. Although this development is highly promising, the discipline itself is highly pragmatic in intent; that is, it exists to serve the practical needs of workers engaged in intercultural communication. Thus the questions which have been asked of anthropology concerning the role of the individual cultural agent, cultural change over time, gender and age factors, and 'cultural authenticity' remain to be tackled by this new discipline.

Summary and Conclusions

This chapter, in reviewing the most prominent disciplines from which theories of culture have been generated, has encountered tremendous epistemological variation. This, together with the unique social status of Deaf communities which fall between medical, social, linguistic and cultural definitions, results in the absence of a single theoretical base from which to link Deaf culture and culture in general.

Nevertheless, as indicated in the text, several aspects of cultural theory within each of the disciplines cited have relevance in initiating a model of Deaf culture. The relative usefulness of each can only be fully assessed after an examination of the work so far carried out on Deaf culture, as described in the next chapter. However, we should re-emphasise the vital conclusions of the section on sub-cultural theories, where the linguistic arguments put forward appear to make a very strong case for validating the Deaf culture concept – that if a group of people have their own language, then they will also have their own culture.

Finally, if we are searching to understand the various ways in which our own cultural reponses have shaped both our perceptions of Deaf communities and our own societies in general, we can do worse than to begin with the insights on page 213 regarding Gramsci's concept of hegemony. I have used this to posit that many cultures can be viewed as 'damaged' in the sense that their cutural values and traditions may not result in a satisfactory life of equal rights to self-fulfilment for all their members. This construction then 'allows' the reader to pursue whichever disciplines and texts cited that would assist with their own cultural awakening.

Notes

1. Interestingly, this 'first textbook of anthropology' also contains a very detailed account of 'the Deaf and Dumb'. Whether Tylor's interest emerged from the more enlightened pre-oralist lay discourse, or whether this was a continuation of the discourse established with the *Societi des Observateurs de l'Homme* described in the last chapter is not yet clear. It is perhaps uncoincidental that once Oralism had emerged, many decades would pass before anthropologists took Deaf communities as seriously as Tylor does here.
2. Although note Franklin's (1984, p. 145) criticism that Levine ignores a flourishing secular folk culture which reinforced the values of resistance against unjust oppression.

Chapter 5

Deaf Culture: Discourses and Definitions

It is not the truth that varies with social, psychological, and cultural contexts, but the symbols we construct in our unequally effective attempts to grasp it.

Clifford Geertz (1973)

Introduction

In reviewing the history of discourses around terms denoting Deaf Culture, this chapter will also identify some of their more significant characteristics and controversies. The key cultural issues which emerge are then summarised and compared with what we have learned from the general cultural theories of Chapter 4. The resulting assessments weigh up what is practicable and possible for this initial study and culminate in the identification of theories and paths along which we can proceed.

There are essentially four discourse strands around the trope of 'Deaf culture', two of which are conducted in English and two in sign languages. (I have confined the review in the main to English-using countries; due to the paucity of translated materials – it is hard enough to obtain finance for Deaf studies, let alone translate them – it is difficult to assess the extent to which this analysis applies in other languages, and feedback on this topic is very much welcomed.) These are:

- the English print media, in academic texts and journals;
- the wider Deaf media of newspapers, magazines, teletext pages and professional magazines;
- in sign languages, chiefly in workshops one conducted by Deaf professionals and rarely translated into English; and
- subaltern Deaf discourse (the existence of this has barely been registered).

Terminological Overview

The term 'Deaf Culture' emerged very recently from (mostly hearing) academic circles during the late 1970s, although there is also a limited literature on cultural features which stems from sociological writers, under such headings as 'subcultures' (Lunde, 1956), 'Deaf community life' (Higgins, 1980) or 'social aspects of deafness' (Christiansen & Meisegeier, 1986).

The BSL term 'DEAF CULTURE' appeared in BSLTA courses around 1985. Its origins seem to stem from the signed equivalent in ASL, and carried very much the same set of meanings. The sign itself was inspired by the need to translate the spoken English term (as used in the USA at that time) for teaching purposes. Very little of this discourse has been printed – a small amount is available on 'official' videos and the rest on 'private' videos used for university teaching purposes. These being inaccessible, I refer to translated teaching materials, handouts and notes from these sources.

There are also subaltern-generated signs for concepts which bear some similarity to the term 'Deaf Culture' and these are discussed later. There is virtually no printed or video discourse around these terms. Some of these, like 'DEAF WORLD', 'DEAF COMMUNITY' and 'DEAF WAY', can be found, translated back into English as it were, in Deaf periodicals and literature from the 19th century onwards, but these are presented simply as givens, so that there is little real debate about what they might mean or signify.

English-Generated Definitions

The first mention in the UK of 'Deaf Culture' actually appears outside the mainstream deafness discourses of the time, in the subaltern Deaf literature of the NUD in 1977. Two examples are given:

> To encourage Deaf theatre groups to perform for hearing people, but also to act from the heritage of our Deaf culture, not only from the hearing one. (NUD, 1977:10)

The other simply states: 'To get sign language and Deaf culture onto a University course and downwards [*sic*], as in the USA' (p. 11). There is no attempt to explain what the term might involve, but we can see that evidently there was a belief in a social phenomenon which was rooted in history and tradition, which was distinct from the one known to majority society. We can see that it also had some kind of relationship with sign language itself, since it would have been in this language that the heritage would be channelled into theatrical performance.

As this quote suggests, it is in the USA that the majority of Deaf cultural discourses began and were carried forward. 'Culture' in relation to descriptions of Deaf collective life occurs first in Stokoe *et al.* (1965) where an appendix makes passing reference to the 'social and cultural characteristics of deaf people', no distinction being made between the two terms. (The 1976 edition makes a similar reference, again without elaboration, on p. 300.)

In 1971 Schlesinger and Meadow stated (without further explanation) that 'profound deafness is much more than a medical diagnosis; it is a cultural phenomenon'. The following year, Meadow takes the first step towards locating a definition. She uses the term 'Deaf Subculture' interchangably with the term 'community', but situates identification of the group around endogamous marital patterns and sign language use. (It may seem remarkable to people reading about these events 30 years later, but at that time, the idea that Deaf people even constituted a community was a controversial one, so deeply had Oralism and its conception of atomistic deafness taken hold.)

Kannapell (1974: 14) takes the debate a step further, by making an assertion similar to the one proposed by the NUD:

> Neglect of the language of deaf persons is accompanied by a neglect of their history and culture. There is no course of study on the history of [*sic*] culture of deaf people in schools for the deaf except at the American School for the Deaf in Connecticut where an optional course is offered.

I have not been able to find out what was taught in this rather far-sighted course (nor whether it was the source of the NUD position). Her account was published in the *Deaf American*, which, at that time, would not generally be circulated in the UK. However, those concerned to import the 'Total Communication' philosophy were actively looking to the USA for clues which might advance their case.

By 1976 Padden and Markowitz were defining community as 'a group of persons who share a common culture' and applying this to Deaf communities. A related development can be found in Erting (1978), where she refers to the Deaf collectivity as the 'deaf ethnolinguistic group' and the 'deaf ethnic group'.

Erting's background was in anthropology; in 1980 two accounts of Deaf communities also sharing that approach were published. Becker's (1983) study of an elderly Deaf community listed several sets of cultural features, framing them by reference to two historical 'traditions' – Deaf from Deaf families and residential schooling, whilst Benderly makes reference to 'deaf culture as a minority culture'.

In 1978 there was another significant development when Rutherford, another writer with an anthropological background, developed a course in

'History and Culture of the Deaf Community' ('the first of its kind nationally' – Rutherford [1993: vii]). Although the contents of this course are not known, we can assume that it was based on the various features identified by sign linguistics studies, possibly developing material from Rutherford's interest in folklore.

Baker and Cokely (1980), working in the sign linguistics field, seem to have been the first attempt to develop a model of the Deaf community, in establishing a contrast between definitions of Deaf people from 'clinical-pathological' and 'cultural' perspectives. Although they do not use the latter term again, they do construct a Venn diagram based on four factors – 'linguistic, political, audiological and, social', with the last doing duty for what might now be thought of as cultural, and which as a result identified a core community which encompasses all four at the heart of the diagram. Their approach is perhaps the most influential of perspectives; Kyle and Woll (1985: 8) summarise that '[this seems] to be the most consistent of the theroretical views of the community'.

It is not until Padden (1980) that a specific definition is attempted, headed 'the culture of American Deaf people'. Having taken culture to mean 'a set of learned behaviours of a group of people who have their own language, values, rules for behaviour, and traditions' (in Baker and Battison, 1980: 92), she then states:

> Members of the Deaf culture behave as Deaf people do, use the language of Deaf people, and share the beliefs of Deaf people towards themselves and other people who are not Deaf. (p. 93)

She concludes that 'the most striking characteristics of the culture of Deaf people is their cultural values – these values shape how Deaf people behave and what they believe in' (p. 95).

From this point on, increasing reference was made to Deaf culture, most citing either Padden (1980), Baker and Cokely (1980), or Kannapell, although most of these accounts did not go beyond stating the existence of the concept. Where reasons were given, they were usually expressed by reference to ASL (as in 'if a community has a language, then they must have a culture') or by reference to 'cultural norms and values' (cf. Deninger, 1983).

During the 1980s, there was an increase in accounts of Deaf community life, beginning with Higgins' (1980) thesis on the white Deaf Chicago community. His study originates within sociology, taking his lead from Becker's (1963) concept of 'outsiders', describing features like membership issues and attitudes of different groups of Deaf people to each other, all situated as aspects of 'deaf community life' (p. 38). Together with Carmel (1997), whose thesis appears to cover the same city, this constitutes the most detailed description of a Deaf community, although Schein and Delk

(1974), Neisser (1983) and Schein (1989) all contain much significant information. (We might also make reference here to Gannon's [1981] text on the 'Deaf Heritage', which contains a huge amount of material that can now be isolated as cultural features.)

In the UK, Kyle and Allsop (1982) and Jackson (1986), began the examination of the Deaf community, work which unfortunately has not been built upon since. All these descriptions of Deaf community life cover much that would now be understood as Deaf culture, but only Carmel and Schein explicitly refer to the concept.

In 1981 the Canadian educationalists, Freeman, Carbin and Boese, devoted a chapter of their handbook for parents of Deaf children to the subject of 'Deaf culture'. Their definition is founded on Tylor's definition but is not systematically explored, although, as Kyle and Woll (1985: 9) note:

[i]n their usage, culture is distinct from community in that it includes the knowledge, belief, art, morals, and law as well as the practices of members of the community.

The first British article explicitly referring to Deaf culture was Brien's in 1981, who applied Baker and Cokely's analysis to the UK Deaf community. In all these countries during the 1980s, use of the term spread widely, although most described aspects of Deaf culture – notably Myhre's (1983) 12-page bibliography – rather than attempting to measure or comprehend its totality. Bienvenu and Columnos (1986), Kannapell (1989), Ladd (1994), Schein (1989) and Kyle (1991b) began to use the term as an all-encompassing framework and give taxonomic descriptions, some of which are rather unsystematically constructed. The focus of these perspectives can be described under three headings – pedagogical, linguistic and political:

- Pedagogical accounts inform Deaf people of the existence of the concept, relating it to what they already understand of their own lives (Bienvenu & Columnos, 1986; Kannapell, 1992) or explain it to mixed groups of Deaf and hearing people (Rutherford, 1985; Ladd, 1995; Kyle 1991b).
- Many linguistic accounts explain its importance in efficient learning of sign language (Stokoe *et al.* 1965, Baker & Cokely, 1980; Philip, 1987), whilst others approach from sociolinguistic perspectives. These either attempt to bring wider bicultural theory to the Deaf domain (Grosjean, 1992), or to demonstrate the relationship between language, culture and Deaf identity (Kannapell, 1992).
- Political accounts explain to those involved with Deaf education the need to shift from a medical model to a linguistic-cultural one (Freeman *et al.*, 1981; Brien, 1991; Lane, 1993a) or bring to the attention of

outsiders the importance of perceiving Deaf issues in cultural terms, such as Erting (1985) in anthropological discourse.

Finally, throughout this period there have been references to, or debates about, 'Deaf Culture' in Deaf and professional magazines, in which polarised positions have been taken. Examples will be examined later in the chapter but, in general, this discourse does not enlighten us greatly, since both sets of positions are contested without supporting evidence and reveal numerous misconceptions. The discourse would, however, be of interest for those wishing to study it in and for itself – that is, for what it reveals about the Deaf and hearing communities of the time.

Sign-Language-Generated Definitions

The signed term 'DEAF CULTURE' being both recent and inspired from without, it is necessary to examine the history of equivalent signs in BSL and ASL.

The absence of research into 19th century Deaf publications makes it unclear whether terms like 'Deaf World or 'Silent World' were sign language or English-generated. However, 'DEAF WORLD' has probably been in use for over a century in the USA and UK, although different signs are used in ASL and BSL. Bahan (1994) appears to be the first to discuss such (American) subaltern signs in print when he brings to the table not only this term, but also 'DEAF CROWD', 'DEAF THEREABOUTS', 'DEAF CLUB' and 'DEAF^WORLD KNOWLEDGE' ('^' in original text).

The latter four terms mark internal Deaf relationships, whilst 'DEAF^ WORLD' is used to contrast with an 'opposite' term 'HEARING^ WORLD', which is used both as noun and adjective. Interestingly, Bahan does not mention two other signs in use in the USA, 'DEAF-HIS' and 'DEAF-WAY'.

In 1989 a particularly historic international Deaf conference was held in Washington DC. Intended to draw together and celebrate all the intellectual and political developments of the Deaf Resurgence, the conference was also notable for selecting its title from ASL and translating that into English, instead of, as is so often the case, the other way around. In the introduction to the collected papers of this conference Erting *et al.* (1994) make reference to two other ASL signs. One, 'DEAF-TEND (THEIRS)' is also used by Barwiolek and McKinney (1993) in the title of their Deaf comedy revue, 'Deaf-Pa-What?', where 'PA' is in this context another gloss for the sign 'tend', based on the mouth movement which accompanies it. The other, 'DEAF (THEIRS)', is close in meaning to 'DEAF-HIS'.

Several of these signs can also be found in the UK, where 'DEAF-HIS' appears to pre-date 'DEAF-WAY'. It is difficult to ascribe dates, but the former may be up to a century old, and the latter perhaps 40 years old. Kyle and Woll (1985: 9) are almost the only people to have mentioned these signs in print:

> We have frequently had the experience that deaf people questioned about such and such a happening will simply shake their heads and say 'it's the deaf way.' They are very clear in the division between what deaf people accept and what hearing people will understand.

The signs in BSL for 'DEAFWORLD', 'DEAF-ALL-THEM', 'DEAF-ALL-OF-US' and 'DEAF CLUB' have also not been discussed in print.

There is controversy within the community around the spread of the sign 'DEAF CULTURE', some arguing that the original Deaf terms such as 'DEAF-HIS' and 'DEAF-WAY' are good enough. Nevertheless, Bahan (1994: 245) describes how DEAF^CULTURE has not only begun to be accepted, but has started to develop an extra level of meaning:

> There are Deaf people who go out and say to others, 'YOU NOT DEAF CULTURE.

Asserting that there was never a time when any Deaf person would go up to another and say 'YOU NOT DEAF WORLD', he concludes:

> What the [first comment above] is making them do is to assess different things that they have internalized while growing up. It becomes an avenue for checking into the values and patterns that one has internalized in the hearing world. It is not that those hearing values are bad, but rather, it is a reminder that this is now our world you are in. (Bahan, 1994: 245)

Bahan's conclusions lead one to ask whether past Deaf communities did not attempt to exclude or criticise other Deaf people or whether it is simply the recent emergence of Deaf pride that has led to such distinctions. They also suggest that one can be in the Deaf World but not have or always manifest 'Deaf Culture'. This is important as the data chapters will show. It is unfortunate, though of course quite symbolic, that this discourse strand has been given so little attention.

Academic Perspectives on Deaf Culture

Since the pioneering texts described earlier, there have been innumerable references to the Deaf culture concept in articles and journals. Rather than continuing to ennumerate them, I have attempted a schemata which enables recognition of the different backgrounds and thrusts of those texts. Feedback to refine this would be particularly welcomed.

Membership perspectives

Once studies of Deaf community and culture made a serious beginning, it became necessary for researchers to formalise what might constitute membership of such a culture. Padden and Humphries (1988: 2) proposed a refinement of Woodward's (1972) definition:

> We use the lowercase *deaf* when referring to the audiological condition of not hearing, and the uppercase *Deaf* when referring to a particular group of deaf people who share a language . . . and a culture.

This is a step forward from the earliest definitions, which were still influenced by the medical model, as typified here by Higgins (1980: 34)

> Members of the deaf community predominantly come from the 'prevocationally deaf', and perhaps even more so from those who lost [*sic*] their hearing before adolescence.

Distinguishing between audiological and cultural issues created the space for Deaf internal life to be examined. Without this, even sociological accounts tend to focus on audiological ways in which Deaf people are outsiders, rather than giving full focus to what they have developed in their collective lives, as his mentor Becker (1963) does with other outsider groups. A Deaf person reading such accounts finds it difficult not to feel as though one is in a cage in a zoo.

Baker and Cokely's (1980) model, as we have seen, distinguishes four membership criteria: audiological (having a hearing loss), linguistic (using sign language), social (participation in Deaf social life) and political (influence in community organisation). They are represented by four partially overlapping circles; the central area is deemed to be the 'core' culturally Deaf community.

One of the most problematic issues is framing 'degrees of membership' to situate those deaf from birth but brought up outside the community, those deafened later in childhood and those who lost hearing later in life. This is particularly important when attempting a historical overview, since all three 'types' were present in the community in the pre-Milan era and even past this time.[1]

Membership issues are also important when attempting to place 'fringe' membres of the community. Hearing children of Deaf parents who have internalised many Deaf cultural values, can be said to be more 'Deaf' than many mainstreamed Deaf people. Yet their acceptance is ambivalent, and further research in this area would be valuable. Undoubtedly the fact that at times some of these 'CODAs' express views which place them on the 'wrong' side of Deaf political issues contributes to this and in the UK, the fact that a high percentage of missioners and social workers were CODAs is certainly one factor in resistance.

Hearing parents of Deaf children who have adopted the bilingual model are also moving to the fringe of the community, although they have also met with some resistance. By contrast, in Scandinavia, acceptance is much further along, and indeed the success of the campaigns for sign language recognition owe much to the coalition formed between parents and Deaf organisations. Discourse around this theme elsewhere is just beginning, and Lentz (1995) has a moving sign poem putting the case for acceptance.

Finally there is the question of the status of the growing numbers of hearing people who have begun to learn sign language and now work or socialise within the community.

In each of these examples, the resistance met has been framed in terms relating to 'Deaf culture'. Certainly the distress caused to those people is in no little part due to the absence of sufficient information about Deaf culture to help explain to them how that resistance is constructed.

Bienvenu and Colomnos' (1989) workshops proposed a model to sche-matise these differences, constructing three circles where the inner circle constitutes cultural membership the second circle social membership, and the outer circle 'political membership'. They refer to the latter as constitut-ing a 'Third Culture' – that is, a meeting point between the two cultures. This argument represents a start towards exploring these issues further.

Normative perspectives

I use this term to describe approaches which have built on Baker and Cokely's (1980) distinctions. These have been developed by American Deaf writers who have taken the 'social' category, renamed it 'cultural' and focused on examples of 'norms', 'values' and traditions'. Kannapell (1992: 2) builds the first two into her definition of Deaf culture:

A set of learned behaviours and perceptions that shape the values and norms of Deaf people based on their shared or common experiences.

Bienvenu and Colomnos (1989) extend these categories to include 'rules for behaviour' and 'identity', whilst Philip (1993) adds 'attitudinal deaf-ness' to these.

Philip (1987: 55) elsewhere also developes a slightly different set of cate-gories:

There are three important aspects, or dimensions, to any culture. The first is called the material dimension, and addresses the observable phenomenona in a culture. The normative dimension looks at the rules for behaviour. Finally the cognitive aspect deals with the attitudes, values, and world view.

These perspectives have had great influence on the current understanding of Deaf culture, being responsible for a modus operandi stressing comparisons between cultures as the way to maximise identification of Deaf cultural characteristics.

Symbolist perspectives

The only published book-length text on Deaf culture, Padden and Humphries (1988), develops an excellent and inspiring anthropological perspective of what it means to operate from within one's Deaf identity, with themes such as 'learning to be Deaf', 'images of being', 'the meaning of sound' and 'historically created lives'. Their approach is explicitly influenced by Geertz (1973, 1983):

> In Geertz's terms, the special condition of human beings is that their behaviors are guided by, indeed are dependent on, the presence of significant arrangements of symbols, which he calls 'culture'. (Padden & Humphries, 1988: 24)

Their text is significant for utilising ethnography to collect and classify examples of symbolic arrangements, of which, as they rightly say, 'we rarely saw anything about these . . . in print' (p. 9).

It is a pity that this work has not subsequently been developed by others, although Carmel (1987) and Rutherford (1993), in their focus on Deaf identity issues, also work from anthropological perspectives to bring to the surface 'deeper' examples as manifested in symbolic relationships, focusing particularly on Deaf folklore. Carmel, in particular, has built up an impressive filmed collection of such folklore, which must be a goldmine for anyone wishing to develop symbolist (and other) approaches further.

Linguistic perspectives

Each of the previous perspectives acknowledge the centrality of sign language to culture. This does not, however, constitute the main thrust of their analysis. Other accounts, such as Kyle and Woll (1985), Kannapell (1989), Wilcox (1989b) and Kyle (1991a), operate specifically from linguistic and psycholinguistic perspectives, seeing sign language as the one clearly unique cultural characteristic of the Deaf community. As Kannapell (1982: 21–27) eloquently puts it:

> ASL is the creation which grows out of the Deaf community. It is our language in every sense of the word. We create it, we keep it alive, and it keeps us and our traditions alive.

A similar perspective underlies Bahan's (1994) arguments outlined previously.

Structuralist perspectives

Stokoe (1989) is among the few to attempt this perspective, applying Trager and Hall's grid system to what he calls the 'ASL and English-based cultures' (p. 49) and attempting to map onto this 100-cell matrix some basic differences between 'Deaf American culture' and 'Mainstream American culture'. As yet, there have been few attempts by others to fill in these cells.

Ethnicity perspectives

Johnson and Erting (1989) and Terstiep (1993) appear to be the only proponents of this perspective so far. This perspective emerged from Erting's research (1982) which was centred in social anthropological and the sociology of language, and lays out the argument for taking a processual view of the Deaf ethnic group. In this the role of personal, interactional and structural variables and their interplay is considered crucial in the production of social forms. This posits, therefore, that cultural content can be distinguished from social process.

Johnson and Erting (1989: 44) are concerned that all the treatments reviewed here are taxonomic: 'basically labeling theories which place people in groups on the basis of interpretations made by those who are doing the labeling'. As they go on to say:

> Sets of traits that define the behaviours and attitudes of the members of a Deaf group are identified, and individuals are labeled as Deaf or not depending on the extent to which they exhibit those traits.

As a result they are concerned that

> [S]uch labels can correspond to salient behaviors and values of a cultural group but they are unlikely to provide substantial insight into the processes that account for the emergence and maintenance of those values and behaviours as identifying features . . . For this reason we align ourselves with anthropologists who study phenomena similar to the Deaf sociocultural experience under the title of ethnicity.

Although both they and Terstiep find mainstream definitions of ethnicity limited by lack of knowledge about the Deaf experience, they still find the concept able to explain more about that experience than traditional ideas of culture, particularly in respect of boundary relations. However, few writers have risen to their challenge.

Biological perspectives

Although biology is almost always accompanied by a pathological perspective, Hall (1994) attempts to relate biological factors to a cultural reading. Although emphasising the symbolist perspective, he focuses on cultural differences marked as 'manifest-prescriptive' and 'personal-tacit'. The former constitutes:

> [W]hat people talk about and use in the course of the politics of everyday life, their 'designs for living', including myths, beliefs, values, dogmas, ideologies, religious beliefs and any other criteria for getting others to conform. (Hall, 1994 : 4)

The latter is seen as its antithesis, not only shared by group members but also unique to each person. It includes the 'programming of the perceptual systems, including the senses', and includes three classes of 'body communication' and eight markers. Hall believes that these are generally 'out of awareness' of cultural members in a qualitatively different way than manifest-prescriptive features which result in actions or manifestations more easily studied.

This perspective is valuable but does not clarify ways in which such features are specific to Deaf people. Further research may well prove this approach to be valuable, not least because Hall believes that 'tacit culture' is deeply personal, which enables us to approach the thorny problem of individual agency which we saw in the last chapter..

Political perspectives

Harris (1995) is the only example I have found so far which tackles cultural issues from principles developed in the discipline of politics. Although she interviews and quotes Deaf subalterns more extensively than anyone except Higgins and Carmel, the absence of Deaf input at either the planning or analytical stages contributes to a number of contentious extrapolations and conclusions. Her assessment, that deafness is 'a socio-political experience with a cultural meaning' (p. 174) is hampered by inconsistencies in defining both culture and Deaf culture, and thus only confirms her starting perspective that socio-political categorisations have primacy.

'Anthropological' perspectives

I use this lable to distinguish Carmel's work (1980,1987a), from the previous perspectives. His accounts draw on linguistic, membership, ethnicity and structuralist perspectives, but are notable chiefly both for the amount of anthropological data given and for an emphasis on examining diversity within the Deaf community. He concludes that 'this diversity is truly one of the most important cultural phenomena in Deaf culture as it is in all cultures' (Carmel, 1987a: 336). It is somewhat puzzling that there is virtually no reference to his work in the subsequent literature – his perspectives have neither been adopted nor even challenged.

Recently there has also been a valuable contribution from Mindess (2000). Working from the intercultural communication field, with the aim of reducing tension between Deaf people and interpreters, she has taken several of Hall's cultural clusters and applied them to the Deaf community. Ones she finds of value include:

- individualist or collectivist cultures,
- low context or high context cultures and
- cultures manifesting time as monochromatic or polychromatic.

In her estimation, Deaf culture in each case fits the latter category and she draws up an impressive collection of examples to make her case. Some are drawn from the informal discourse around Deaf culture but have rarely been committed to print, whilst others bring qualities presented by other writes (e.g. Philip on 'Deaf reciprocity') within reach of a framework. What is exciting about her account is that it provides a 'home' for many cultural features which have either been consigned to taxonomic lists or to some extent buried by an insistence on normative perspectives. This is partly achieved by making much wider cultural comparisons than is usually attempted (a benefit of being in a discipline whose concern is precisely that).

Most of these accounts of the culture have not really enabled the predictive element to come into play, that is, where one can begin to generate one's own examples based on the analytical principles used. Mindess' is the first I have read that brings me close to being able to 'predict' other qualities of Deaf culture, the generative framework which we are seeking. Tantalisingly, her account does not say whether her three clusters have a relationship with each other that we are not yet able to identify. Hopefully this beginning will prove promising enough for such questions to be explored by others.

Summary

These nine perspectives have in common their very recently development, so that there have been few attempts to cross-reference them, apart from Turner's laudable attempts (1994a, b). The process of finding a workable consensus has only just begun. Crucially, since most have not produced a sustained subaltern-oriented ethnography, there is little 'hard data' for others to re-interpret.

Thus most of these perspectives remain taxonomic, focusing on differences between Deaf and 'hearing' cultures rather than exploring Deaf culture in and of itself. Consequently they fall victim to what Wright (1998: 8) has summarised in another context as 'the old idea of culture':

- bounded, small-scale entity
- defined characteristics (checklist)
- unchanging, in balanced equilibrium or self-reproducing
- underlying system of shared meanings: 'authentic culture'
- identical, homogenous individuals.

We will return to these issues after the next section.

Deaf Culture Contested

The swift dissemination of the unexamined Deaf culture trope has resulted in considerable resistance from some quarters. Contestation falls into three discourse categories. The first, non-academic/'semi-academic' discourses are found mainly in Deaf/professional periodicals, and the second primarily in the only printed academic debate so far (see Turner above). The third, that of subaltern resistance, has not yet been recorded in print.

Semi-academic discourse

One of the most intriguing characteristics of Deaf cultural debate is the extent of the attack by colonialists and older Deaf élite sectors, who resist the idea of Deaf people having a culture of their own. Erickson (1992: 48), for instance, states:

> Accurately defining deaf culture is as elusive as finding the source of the term . . . nowhere is there an outline or a profile of what constitutes deaf culture, except the presence of sign language . . . None [of the authors] display more than an intuitive contention of its existence, much less a description of how we might recognise it.

In making this assertion, however, he appears to overlook the views of the range of writers already cited. Stewart (1992: 130) concurs that 'the term has yet to be satisfactorily defined', but fails to demonstrate how this is the case. In a similar vein, Hurst (1992: 1) asserts:

> In strict anthropological terms, 'Deaf Culture' is not a culture. It cannot marry people, it cannot bury people, and you cannot guarantee that your children will be members of it. It has no independent value system or religious system that answers the deeper questions of the meanings of life or death. It does not stand alone, complete, independ-

ent of other cultures. (Here it stands in parallel to 'women's culture', which is not a culture in the strictest sense either.)

Hurst's critique raises useful ontological questions, but disregarding all other aspects of culture suggests a covert agenda, which can be seen if one is aware that her remarks occur in the context of debating whether the establishment of Deaf Studies courses is a desirable goal. She states:

> My objection to the term 'Deaf Culture' in this way is that it is isolationist. It rejects the hearing world completely . . . Deaf people live and work as part of a larger world outside the deaf community. In sociological terms this is a subculture . . . I simply do not want to see academic validity given to a definition of the deaf community that serves a political or polemical purpose of rejecting the hearing world and hearing people and of rejecting any deaf people who do not agree with this isolated position. (p. 2)

Since none of the texts cited earlier can be construed as rejecting the hearing world, her concerns (as a hearing person) indicate an agenda akin to the fears white people originally held regarding the establishing of Black Studies or men towards Women's Studies, namely the fear of a minority group establishing its own identity in ways that might develop hostility to the majority.

A closer examination of Erikson (also hearing) reveals a similar fearfulness:

> The emergence of a deaf cultural élite [sic] has brought with it a rejection of all that is not deaf, or not deaf enough . . . The result is that deaf people are sometimes encouraged to reflexively reject the very support they need because the program is not for deaf only, or the provider is not deaf . . . A glaring example is the dogma that hearing people cannot understand deaf people because of the cultural differences; therefore hearing people cannot perform as therapists, teachers, leaders or models for the deaf. (Erikson, 1992: 49)

The last phrase is key – the fear that colonialist attitudes such as these will no longer be acceptable to Deaf people. Stewart's position is more explicitly stated. His article is essentially a polemic:

> Arcane linguistic and cultural theories are being promoted concerning 'the language of the deaf', 'the culture of the deaf', and 'the failure of deaf education', presented not as the pure speculations that they are, but as absolute facts. (Stewart, 1992: 129)

He criticises political correctness, and ideas that 'only black people know what is best for black people' (p. 135), summarising as follows.

All in all, considering everything this country is doing for deaf people, anyone who says deaf people here are being oppressed . . . needs serious attitude adjustment. Such an adjustment would occur instantly through a week's stay in some country like Iran or Cuba, where they would learn a new definition of 'oppression'. (p. 136)

It is crucial for this study to note the wider political stance, normally implicit, but here made quite explicit, in resisting the Deaf cultural concept. Extrapolating from his argument, it is possible to argue that those who oppose Deaf culture do not think that Deaf people are oppressed, nor that Deaf education has failed, nor that Deaf people know what is best for their community. Many of those arguing against Deaf culture link this with a similar opposition to the emergence of the concept of ASL. Parsons, another opponent of ASL (1992, 1993), describes the linkage thus:

First it was Ameslan, then ASL, then bilingual, and then bicultural until something more like a cult emerged . . . The movement accumulated strength and power as school after school and college after university classroom succumbed to ASL. (Parsons, 1992: 106)

At the time of publication there were only two Deaf schools in the USA which pursued bilingual/bicultural policies!

Parsons and Stewart were Gallaudet d/Deaf academics; thus if one is to understand the full parameters of this discourse, it is important to deconstruct their perspective. Stewart (1993: 142), deafened at 8 (therefore after acquiring English), asserts that it is 'our responsibility and our duty, to maintain as our first culture the American culture, and as our first language, the English language'. Parsons (1992: 103), partially deaf from birth, reminisces about her childhood thus:

The word 'culture' was unheard of. We never considered ourselves minorities with our own cultures but instead as simply proud Americans.

This perspective is linked with a distaste for 'the uneducated or low-verbal deaf who are content at not having to learn any more than the limited gestures they already have' (1993: 126). She views with alarm the 'proponents [who] glorified the ASL of [such] grassroots deaf people' (1992: 106), contrasting it with her approval of an earlier era:

Back then in 1915, Gallaudet students were predominently deafened adults or adventitiously deaf. They looked happy. They used classical American signs in English word order . . . (p. 104)

Her advocacy of this elitist position is challenged by these recent developments:

In a recent lecture on Deaf power, Barbara Kannapell, Gallaudet's 'consultant on Deaf culture', showed a chart illustrating that hereditary [ASL-using] deaf people are moving up to the top through English skills and leadership, with the adventitiously deaf moving down to the second level. (Parsons, 1993: 131)

It might therefore be argued that the covert agenda is fear of displacement and loss of power to the subaltern movement, a position similar to minority élites who identify primarily with the majority culture (Carter, 1991). However, where such 'Black conservatives' argue primarily against affirmative action and other political strategies originating _outside_ the Black community, in the Deaf discourses, the arguments here would seem to be aimed at its core, against their own subaltern language and culture itself. The English orientation of such writers appears to confirm Chapter 2's description of this language as a crucial demarcation of Deaf cultural values.

A similar attack is found in Bertling's _A Child Sacrificed to the Deaf Culture_ (1994). Deafened in childhood, Bertling's stated resentment at being placed in a Deaf school (by his Deaf mother) is constructed as an 'exposure' of Deaf culture; his account also expresses the negative attitudes to ASL found in Parsons and Stewart, and despite being virtually the only book-length account of Deaf–Deaf interaction, is expressed in unremittingly negative terms.

These critiques are important in that in the current medical–cultural battleground, these dissenting views are given a prominent platform by those seeking to continue the oppression of Deaf people, a pattern parallelled with Black conservative co-option. Bertling became the first Deaf person to be invited to speak at an American Cochlear Implant conferences – as a 'representative' of the Deaf community!

Thus it can be seen that for minority groups as a whole and Deaf culture in particular, community dissension is a volatile issue _because it can be used by oppressors to maintain their practices_. This is not the case for majority cultures, where dissension rarely threatens the cultural continuity of their societies. And as we have seen earlier, the relationships between the factors of oralist dominance, age of onset of deafness and reification of English is one set of issues. The fact that membership of the Deaf community is still possible for those espousing such views means that cultural analysis has some way to go before resolving such problematics.

Both these two points carry immense importance, as will be seen in later chapters.

In the UK, a similarly critical discourse exists in the UK, although the main objections come from those who are deafened, but not members of the Deaf community. James (1994: 9) states:

> I also refute entirely the cultural aspect of deafness. It is a disability and a very severe and traumatic one at that – ask anyone who has lost their hearing.

The inability to distinguish between Deaf and deafened people appears to be a consequence of internalising the medical model. Likewise, Craw (1993: 19) asserts:

> BSL has been portrayed as a cultural phenomenon. A disability in no manner can ever be considered a culture.

Beneath these assertions appears to lies a similar fear; that BSL subalterns will supplant the English-oriented hard of hearing and deafened élite, as Craw makes explicit:

> BSL operates through a hierarchy which takes to personalized BSL mode [*sic*] at the expense of deaf people and other organisations. (p. 18)

It is unfortunate that these are the only examples in print, for there is a growing trend of subaltern Deaf people justifying all manner of trival examples of negative behaviour towards hearing people by claiming 'it's Deaf culture' (Turner, 1994a). To speak out against these examples is to be seen as anti-Deaf; there is at present no middle ground. This is mirrored in other minorities; the O J Simpson and Hill–Thomas issues similarly polarised Black debate (Chrisman & Allen, 1992; Morrison, 1992).

In summary, the dominant English discourse is led by those attempting to problematicise the concept of Deaf culture in order to resist the pro-subaltern changes of the last 15 years. Such highly charged debate makes it all the more important that definitions and frameworks for understanding Deaf culture be carefully developed.

Academic Critiques of Deaf Culture

Urion (1991: 13), a Native-Canadian professor of anthropology coming to the texts as a partial outsider, remarks:

> What I find in the literature about deaf culture is a restatement, and then a restatement, followed by a restatement, that there is a deaf culture.

His main concern is that using culture as a conceptual base for liberation is dangerous because

- culture can never be described adequately,
- by so relying, group social activity can be constructed as static and boundary-oriented,
- it implies 'that deaf culture exists only as reactive to majority hearing culture' (p. 12) and

- 'the most dangerous aspect is that it becomes almost impossible to describe the relationship between the cultures we are comparing except in terms of dependency and conflict'.

He describes the dangers thus:

> The concept of culture, as it has been used for research and policy dis-
> cussion [about First Nation cultures] . . . has proved to be divisive, to
> trivialise and to discredit our culture, and to provide a license for
> sterotyping. (p. 5.)

These are timely warnings. However, these arguments appear to confuse the need for academic precision and the political implications of rendering oneself visible by espousing a cultural politics. It is possible for cultural self-examination to have even a central role in building confidence for the political battles ahead, as Biko's Black Consciousness movement in-dicates (Pityana *et al.* 1991). Nevertheless, Urion's concern that Deaf cultural work has not yet taken on board the political dimension is an im-portant one. This concern is central to the those addressed by Bourdieu in Chapter 4, and are thus important for this study.

Related concerns are presented in the only printed academic discussion on Deaf culture. Turner (1994a: 105) begins with a comparable critique:

> We have a self-referential definition, therefore, which gets us nowhere, except into more vicious spiralling into infinity.

His concern echoes those presented by Paulston (1992: 10) in the bilin-gual section of the last chapter:

> From Padden's summary, one can again infer that her aim is largely political – to get the notion of Deaf people as constituting a human group, rather than as a bunch of tragic pathological cases, onto the agenda . . . (Turner, 1994a: 107)

As with other minority-culture struggles, it is notable that only the sub-altern activity is labelled as political – any politics residing within the hegemonic discourses appear to be read here as the social norm and remain unanalysed.

Turner (1994a: 110) also considers traditional definitions of culture to be inadequate:

We get little snippets of nothing-very-substantial because the model encourages us to see a simple checklist of criteria rather than any kind of inter-related network of elements. The model points to a concern with particular aspects or items of culture, with what are often called cultural traits, rather than with the analysis of cultures or societies as systematic wholes.

These concerns are valid and mirrored in the post-structuralist critiques in Chapter 4. However, the interpretive model of culture (as exemplified by Geertz in that chapter) is dismissed for its suggestion of the impossibility of describing cultures via participant observation:

As soon as you reach in, any claim to objectivity is endangered, and so you're caught between a rock and a hard place. (Turner, 1994a: 109)

This over-concern with classical objectivity stymies progress towards definition via ethnographic research and would particularly hinder subaltern reseachers, who are already members of the Deaf community.

Nevertheless, Turner offers two useful alternative perspectives: the first positing that culture is 'not about states at all, but about processes' (p. 112), citing Street's (1993) idea of culture as a verb; and Frake's (1980) conception of culture as a dynamic creation of readings by the individual – 'culture does not provide a cognitive map, but rather a set of principles for map making and navigation'.

The second is the application of Gramsci's concept of hegemony to current definitions of Deaf culture. Were it applied, he argues, a series of questions would emerge:

By what process did [people] come to [their] conclusions? What information was made available . . . ? What information was not made available? . . . Who set the terms for the debate . . . ? How were they able to do this? (p. 115)

In summarising, he cites Cowan's (1990) conclusions on the inadequacy of existing models of culture:

The concept of hegemony explicitly makes problematical the links between consciousness, sensory experience, and power in a way that the concepts of culture as a set of collectively shared symbols and meanings, does not. (Turner, 1994a: 116)

These points are valid and extremely important. although the absence of Deaf cultural data from his critique means that it is not easy to see how his alternative approach might be constructed. The irony of a hearing academic operating within a hearing-controlled academic discourse establishing the debate in hegemonic terms – without the self-referentiality required by those terms – is also unfortunately inescapable. It is to be regretted that more Deaf researchers did not participate in it, since it is only by entering into these discourses that progress can be made. This is a particularly sharp example of how few Deaf people feel able to participate in academic discourse, even when the results might be crucial to the community's development. In this respect, Bourdieu's strictures about the partially masked power and role of the academic/intellectual become particularly useful.

Another concept that I wish to draw attention to here which will recur in later chapters is what I have termed the 'double-bind'. In the situation we have before us, a well-meaning hearing person may wish to advance a matter of importance to the community, but because of their status as a hearing person, is caught in a double-bind. That is, in so doing, they leave themselves open to criticisms from a community not ready to hear their case. There is no doubt that in these 'politically correct' times, this dynamic results in an unfortunate self-censorship. It is to be hoped that Deaf cultural awareness will evolve to the point where inter-cultural discourses like the one Turner has tried to initiate will manifest themselves in the form of more conferences and workshops.

Stokoe (1994c: 99) responds to Turner's dissatisfaction with circular definitions of community and culture:

> The concept 'community' implies to a sociologist or demographer a countable population and a clear criteria for who is included and who is not, but knowledge does not come in integral packages and people behave in ways best described by fuzzy logic. An individual can be Deaf, American, Hispanic, an Elk, a Baptist etc all at the same time . . . Some aspect of culture is required to delimit a community, and to describe a culture requires finding a community whose culture it is [no matter how circular that might appear].

Stokoe's use here of the idea of subjectivities is especially helpful. He also replies to Turner's concern to 'fit culture into some systems of knowledge', by pointing out that cultures are themselves an all-embracing system:

> The familiar Western cultures contain science as one subsystem; science in turn contains such different subsystems as the physical and social sciences. It is too much to ask that a subsystem of a subsystem of a culture be able to explain culture itself, a super-system of which it is entirely unaware of being a part. (p. 100)

He also points up a key anthropological principle – the emic principle – that one must seek to represent the group studied in the terms of self-definitional which they themselves use. Thus if Deaf people say they have a culture, they are referring to a belief system which they hold, which is itself sufficient evidence for the existence of such a concept, no matter what the definitional limitations are. Speaking of the so-called 'Gallaudet Revolution' of 1988, and the statement made by one of its leaders to the TV cameras that 'the protestors would not be satisfied until they had a new president of the university who "knew and respected their language and culture"', Stokoe (1994b: 267) says:

> She was not reifying the terms . . . but expressing the eminently reasonable demands that one who wields power in a community be fluent in that community's language and consequently aware of at least the general outlines of what members of that community express and think in that language – especially *its* values. (Original emphasis)

Summary

These two discourses contain either unacknowledged agendas or do not appear to follow their concepts through. However, it is necessary to devise a framework capable of refuting or accomodating the critiques offered. Certainly Turner's suggestions indicate that it is becoming increasingly clear that the post-modernist concepts in Chapter 4 are especially relevant.

Furthermore, when it comes to explicating what Deaf culture might be, it is also clear that it is the responsibility of academia to elicit views about Deaf culture from Deaf people themselves. As Terstiep (1993: 233) remarks: 'Since Deaf people have applied the term Deaf culture to themselves . . . this term should be respected'. However, it is clear that much work needs to be undertaken before we can reconcile subaltern definitions with the élite/academic discourses on Deaf culture. *The extensiveness of this work therefore imposes its own limits on what can be achieved by this study.*

Re-evaluating Problematic Aspects of Deaf Culture

Having now examined the discourses around culture and Deaf culture, we return to the problematic aspects of defining that culture given near the end of Chapter 3 to see what can be said about each.

Ethnicity issues

Although the Deaf community did not appear to satisfy ethnicity conditions, there are other relevant characteristics. As Johnson and Erting (1989: 47) point out: 'Many of the . . . deaf children who are born to two deaf parents are born into a family with a history of deafness through several generations'. These lineages extend to as many as nine generations, that is, to the 1820s (which is usually the extent of written documentation). Furthermore, through a complex series of cross-marriages, a number of Deaf families have extended their kinship network to constitute wide-ranging and complex structures of consanguinity mirroring the kind of kinship structures associated with conventional ethnic groups. There is also the beginnings of documentation of the importance of these Deaf families in enculturating the other Deaf children (Johnson & Erting, 1989; Mason, 1991).

Although it would appear strange to claim that those growing up in hearing families do not 'belong' to their culture, there are additional characteristics which counterbalance this. One is the high rate of endogamous marriage: 90% of Deaf people who marry, marry another Deaf person. As Montgomery (1994: 260) puts it:

> Deaf people have one of the highest intermarriage rates of all social groupings. Economic, racial, religious, class, political, and national boundaries are much more frequently crossed by intermarriage than the deaf/hearing divide.

Linguistic criteria also offer a counterbalance. Since the child's first language is sign language, and since very few parents master it, the child clearly has a different set of semantic structures and neurolinguistic patterning (Klima & Bellugi, 1979) from its parents. We also noted the tremendous cultural vacuum between a Deaf person and majority society in terms of access to the information and culture of that society. It is within that vacuum that Deaf people experience their collective similarities and shape their collective responses. As Johnson and Erting (1989: 50) put it: 'Proficiency in spoken English, or lack thereof, is the major factor defining an externally constituted boundary around deaf people as a socioeconomic group'. In these post-oralist times, there are also boundaries which relate to written English. The fact of English literacy both pre-Milan and post Resurgence both informs and complicates this issue – a fertile ground for further discourse research.

Issues such as these are reinforced by Bahan and Nash's (1996) assessment of those societies where most members used sign language in everyday life, even when there were no Deaf people present. There is little suggestion that Deaf people in those societies gather separately from the hearing people and produce their own culture. Thus a Deaf culture appears to require the presence of a *linguistic vacuum* in order to exist, and where it exists, appears to take precedence over traditional definitions of ethnicity.

Cultural geography

As we have seen, Deaf communities do not generally choose to live in proximity. However, this is also true for other groups, including Jewish-Americans, and other former immigrant communities who initially lived together (as did Deaf children in Deaf schools). They have subsequently dispersed, yet continue to claim a common cultural identity. It is therefore unclear whether this criteria is a significant problematic in defining a culture. Indeed this may actually be a cultural *feature;* privacy in Deaf culture may simply be differently defined, weighted and manifested.

Material constructions

The apparent lack of uniquely Deaf material constructions may actually lend credence to a different set of cultural theories. As Hall (1994: 35) points out:

While the Deaf share practically all non-language components of the dominant culture, *they have put their own stamp on everything.* Differences are a matter of shifting emphasis. (My emphasis)

This draws Deaf culture nearer to Bourdieu's emphasis on culture as disposition., and offers the beginnings of a basis from which to investigate that cultural 'strategy'. Furthermore, similar critiques can be proferred for Jewish-Americans, Scottish and Welsh people etc., where distinctly different material constructions constitute a very small part of their total way of life, yet this does not threaten their cultural identity. It is difficult not to feel that cultural identity may be based more on the *idea of a shared past.* This, in turn, opens another window for frameworking Deaf culture.

Ontological systems

Many cultural descriptions suggest that societies develop beliefs about their origins, their place in the larger scheme of things and the cultural importance of birth and death. It appears to most observers that if Deaf cultures have developed such beliefs and rituals, they are either extremely well hidden or so rudimentary as to cast doubts on the community's abilitiy to innovate in this way.

However, with regard to Deaf culture, this question can be re-formulated. Geertz (1973) suggests that culture consists of 'stories we tell to ourselves' about ourselves, our place in the world, the reasons we hold such a place and the attitudes and behaviours that we should adopt which are commensurate with these stories. Quoting Jewish informants, Myerhoff (1980) suggests that alongside the Grand Narratives of Western thought, there are 'Little Traditions'; in essence folk renderings of the experiences of living, covertly held and transmitted. It cannot be ruled out that this may be the case for Deaf communities.

Padden and Humphries (1988) in particular, but also Gannon (1981), Carmel (1987) and Rutherford (1993), all give examples of Deaf stories and folklore which could well be classified in this way, while Moore and Levitan (1992: 160) are more explicit:

> In the negative interpretation [of Deaf existence], a soul is born as a deaf person as a punishment – i.e. bad karma. But according to the positive interpretation, a soul chooses to be born as a deaf person as a challenge or learning experience. The Deaf soul experiences the restrictions, prejudices, and hostility of the hearing world so that it may progress to a higher level of spiritual understanding.

This is not necessarily typical of Deaf people's spiritual beliefs, but the example has significance for being presented as part of a textbook ('For Hearing People Only'), seeking to explain all things Deaf to the curious in mainstream society. It is perhaps significant that it is only in having to explain ourselves to others that we are forced to make overt cultural features and beliefs that we have taken for granted.

Ontologies are not only 'stories we tell to ourselves', but stories which we desire to pass on to our children (which itself is a similar impulse of 'explaining ourselves to others'). It is the children who then embellish them as part of the folk process, similar to the pidgin-to-creole linguistic process. Conversely, a culture impeded from passing on its beliefs, as in First Nation cultures, 'dies' or, more precisely, becomes something else, usually a version of the majority culture. True genocide being extremely rare, it is usually cultural ethnocide, via enforced schooling in majority-culture language and values, which achieves this end. This is a strategy strikingly similar to Oralism.

If a culture is not permitted responsibility for the education of its children, then it is not able to actualise its spiritual impulses on its own terms. Therefore, given Deaf ethnicity issues, one would have to look to the Deaf schools pre-Milan as the source for actualising any Deaf ontologies. If this is correct, then one would expect, in the present era where Deaf people are regaining some responsibility for 'their' children, re-emergence of this actualisation.

Indeed, this is what seems to be happening. For the last 15 years, as soon as they were allowed back into the school systems, Deaf people have been creating and videotaping stories for Deaf children. The significance of this is that it has not resulted from conscious policy-making, but from some other impulse. Examples of such work, which go beyond simple storytelling to develop Deaf-centred folktales and mythologies, are numerous and include Bahan (1992), Supalla (1992) and Katz (1993) in the USA, Miles (1983), Daunt and Hanafin (1995) in the UK.

If Deaf communities had developed ontologies pre-Milan, one might expect to find examples in early 19th century France, where the best evidence of a strong Deafhood exists. This is indeed the case, as the Chapter 2 has indicated. Mottez (1993: 151) notes:

> The bust of the abbe de *l'Epee* . . . sat like an altar at the centre of the U-shaped table . . . The Deaf Mutes called him *our spiritual father, our messiah, our saviour, our redeemer* . . . It meant the begetter *(geniteur)*, the original parent: 'He who led us from night once and for all. Now it is up to us!' (Emphasis in original)

Padden and Humphries (1988) also note this religious construction of the 'Deaf beginning', and go on to give special attention to the concept of moving from darkness to light, that is, from being lost in the world to finding one's people and one's home in the Deaf community. Images of darkness and light are of especial resonance to those who use visual languages (cf. the 'lamp-post' trope, Daunt, 1995). There are numerous other examples from both historical and contemporary sources which are couched in similar imagery, suggesting a possible belief system. Of especial interest is the absence of overt discussion of these beliefs; they seem rather to be manifestations of deeply held feelings which surface in some rituals and in some Deaf art.

Other tropes, such as 'home' and 'family', are widely used (Kyle & Woll, 1985; Lane *et al.*, 1996) and might well be drawn into a coherent symbolist system.

One would therefore expect that as Deaf people gain more influence over the upbringing of Deaf children, these beliefs will become more conscious and later ritualized. Unfortunately, this process is too recently begun for this study to be able to draw on them.

At the time of writing, however, there has been a significant development towards making explicit Deaf spirituality in the form of what is termed the 'Blue Ribbon' Ceremony. This has taken the colour blue from French Deaf activists' assertion that this colour was the one attributed to Deaf and disabled people by the Nazis. It has merged this with the looped ribbon originating in Aids campaigns (which symbolises governmental ignorance and repression, not the medical fact of Aids itself – this misunderstanding has already caused confusion).

The symbol has an autonomous political function, being used chiefly by the radical Deaf organisation of the UK, the Federation of Deaf People, in their recent marches for BSL recognition. But it has also been used as the basis for a ritual enacted in community gatherings, the first at the FDP conference in 1998, the second at the World Federation of the Deaf Congress in Australia in 1999, and then at subsequent events. If we examine the text of the latter ritual, we can see how it inextricably links themes of Deaf identity and oralist repression with a set of spiritual beliefs. Beginning with a candlelight procession, the text is then signed by a number of different representatives of different countries, as well as a CODA and a hearing parent of a Deaf child. (For the full text see Appendix 2).

Christianity may be another ontological source. Much of the Deaf spiritual impulse may have been sublimated, with their membership of Christian churches, into Christian constructions, but Levine's (1977) account of African-American adaptation of these to their own covert agendas suggest that Deaf dispositions might follow this pattern. One such thread is expressed by Baillie (1998):

> When I see Deaf people from different regions all signing together, or Deaf from different countries all making themselves understood, I say 'Thank God for the gift of hands, the gift of our sign language'. (My translation.)

Given Baillie's age (80), and her membership of a Deaf Christian group in a traditionally strong 'Deaf town' (Edinburgh), it may be that her formulation formed a central part of the Deaf Christian belief in earlier Deaf societies. The way it assigns a relationship to the two ideas, one of the global Deaf signing/community and the other of approval of Deaf existence by a higher spiritual power, is certainly uncannily reminiscent of the language, not just of the Paris Banquets, but of the immediate post-Milan era of Deaf resistance. The resemblance is probably close to conclusive evidence of the centrality of these tropes (as indeed can be seen in the cover of this book) which has been created by a Russian Deaf artist.[2]

Identity as cultural choice

The extent to which the adoption of a Deaf identity can be a conscious choice is represented in the rapid growth of literature describing isolated mainstreamed Deaf adolescents' journey towards the Deaf community (Ladd, 1979; Lawson, 1981; Robinson, 1995 and Dodds, 1998, _inter alia_). These examples make it clear that even when brought up outside the Deaf community or in oral schools which suppressed all things Deaf, there is a major impulse towards redefining and reshaping one's self by moving from a 'hearing-impaired' identity towards actualising a Deaf one.

Cultural boundaries and biculturalism

Chapter 4 indicated the current analytical difficulties in developing a framework which can handle either biculturality or the relationship between minority cultures and the surrounding majority cultures. It is therefore unsurprising that within the Deaf cultural discourse that only two writers have attempted an initial examination of those dynamics.

Bienvenu and Colomnos (1989) list six features of American culture as shared values between Deaf and hearing peoples. These are 'freedom', patriotism, materialism, the importance of the family (for Deaf of Deaf parents – they consider that Deaf of hearing parents value Deaf community life above family life), the English language and the importance of education.

Kannapell (1989) constructs a similar list. Under 'shared values', she cites 'democracy', 'holidays', materialism, food and clothes. However, she takes the analysis further by developing a category of 'shared but different values', which include 'children', 'education', employment, language and 'communication', where her intention is to highlight cultural 'meta-categories' which Deaf culture adapts to its own purposes. Under a further heading, 'different values', she contrasts some Deaf and majority-culture values. These include (ordered respectively) 'community *versus* individualism', 'visual beauty *versus* music', Deaf schools *versus* public schools and 'eyes and hands *versus* ears'.

She also develops an interesting technique for analysing different degrees of cultural influences: 11 statements to be graded on a ten-point scale in two stages. The first is the respondents' own personal values and the second their assessment of the values of 'Americans in general'. Unfortunately the data does not include any statistical detail, being intended primarily as a workshop exercise; it does, however represent a potential direction for unpacking and asserting Deaf biculturality.

Summary

All these characteristics pose problems for definitions either of Deaf culture or for culture in general. The account here suggests that in most of the instances, *the problems lie with the latter* and thus highlight a need to re-think present academic definitions.

Summarising the Review

This section summarises the strands emerging from the discourses reviewed in Chapters 2 and 3, and re-assesses them to indicate the direction this study should take, together with some methodological criteria which will be put forward in the next chapter. We might accept that any community which has a language must also have a culture, and that a high endogamous rate in a community of language users would appear to reinforce this. However, it is possible for particularly relentless critics of Deaf communities to point to the strong 'peer transmission' of sign languages and suggest that deafness might simply produce generational 'layers' of people who at best would form a subculture. *It thus falls to analyses of Deaf cultures to establish a convincing case that there exist historically transmitted cultural patterns which in effect 'bind' the generations and irrefutably confirm a multi-generational community and culture.*

Weaknesses in current Deaf cultural analysis

As Turner has indicated, analyses of Deaf culture suffer from an imposed homogeneity, which has created the following difficulties, among others:

- There is an assumption that Deaf culture is a universal concept; the idea of different national Deaf cultures appears not to have occurred to most writers. One of the first tasks before us must therefore be to illustrate and clarify differences between such cultures as a starting point for deeper analysis.
- Virtually all the analyses are synchronic – there is little mention of the historical dimension which could indicte how cultures have changed over time. This is especially relevant in an age when the traditional cultural paths, that is, moving from Deaf residential schools to Deaf clubs, has partially disintegrated through oppression and what we might term 'post-industrialism' with its new freedom of movement. Identifying historical continuities and disruptions, (particularly patterns of disruption of they exist), therefore represents one of the first tasks at the next level of analysis.
- Little or no mention is made of the *cultural* significance of different groups within Deaf communities – they are all constructed as sharing the same culture in equal measure. Furthermore, although limited mention is made of Deaf families, hard of hearing and mainstreamed Deaf young people and the like, there is almost no mention of the distinctions of class, race, gender, age and sexual orientation. It is therefore vital to investigate what roles these might play within Deaf cultures at the next level of analysis.
- The use of taxonomic models is understandable in the light of historical development and socio-political exigency. But as Turner indicates, it is indeed time to move forwards. Non-processual and prescriptivist models cannot assist us to site the individual Deaf agent's creative and strategic responses to their culture; that is, their *dispositions*. This must be seen as the next level of analysis and indeed, where possible, built into the first three.

It is precisely these four challenges which the rest of the book intends to address.

Academic cultural discourses and their relevance for Deaf cultural study

Although the review assessed the relevance of each set of disciplinary theories to the Deaf situation, I summarise them here to illustrate the strategies which might be implied for Deaf cultural study.

Within anthropology, both adaptational and ideational frameworks have relevance to Deaf culture. Similarly, theories of cultural competence and performance are extremely useful, as is Bohannen's conceptualisation of cultural change, traps and dissonance, as well as the importance of futurology.

Within Cultural Studies, the necessity of 'surrendering to the text', the importance of the researcher's role in creating political change by giving voice to the subaltern, and the assertion of the creativeness of everyday subaltern life are important principles for the study. Theories of ideology, hegemony and discourse are also relevant for situating Deaf communities as oppositional cultures, as well as enabling us to examine the communities' own practices.

From cross-disciplinary and post-modernist studies, theories of multiple subjectivities are useful, as are ideas formed around essentialism and diasporic concepts. Bourdieu's explications of social and cultural capital, of indeterminacy and dispositions, of fields, agents and habitus, and of structured reflexivity are of particular importance. To these can be added various other strands which emerge from minority studies, post-colonial studies, ethnicity and bicultural studies.

Review conclusions

This array of epistemologies, theories and insights can appear bewildering. However, from the perspective of this initiatory study of Deaf culture, several conclusions can be reached:

- Since we know so little about Deaf culture, it would be highly premature to impose any overarching theories.
- These theories being conceived outside the culture, to impose any of them would continue the epistemic violence already visited upon it.
- Culture remaining among the most contentious of academic issues, it would be extremely unwise to attempt a resolution of cultural theory within a rarely explored field.
- Since the special nature of the subaltern-researcher is from being far from understood or even conceptualised, adopting any one of the theories described would be premature.

These being the case, there is no evidence that any one cultural theory has an *a priori* basis for validity. We must, therefore, return to some of these theories to decide which might best serve as working principles for the first examination of UK Deaf culture.

Theoretical Grounding for Deaf Cultural Study

The restrictions imposed on Deaf cultural study by the very newness of the disciplines, epistemologies and methodologies which are of most relevance for it, means that an eclectic mixture of tools ('bricolage') must be utilised. However, such studies cannot proceed without a theoretical grounding. Our initial starting point must be a definition of culture itself. Influenced by the work undertaken by Cultural Studies, Quantz (1992: 483) in reviewing critical ethnography provides one which is especially appropriate for minority cultures:

> Culture is an ongoing political struggle around the meanings given to actions of people located within unbounded assymetric power relations.

The emphasis here is external perceptions of a cultural group. This should be complemented by a definition which is situated within the group experience itself, viz:

> [C]ulture is better understood as a contested terrain than as a set of shared patterns. (p. 483)

From here we require a perspective on the attempt to locate cultural grammars themselves. The one I have selected takes as its starting point Keesing's assertion that they are:

> impossible to achieve in the face of the vast intricacy of what humans know about their world – the subtle shadings of understanding and mood and meaning that defy representation in formal algorithms.

I have therefore turned to the theoretical position suggested by Geertz (1981: 92):

> So far as social sciences are concerned, any attempt to define them in some essence-and-accidents, natural-kind way, and locate them at some definite latitude and longitude in scholarly space is bound to fail as soon as one looks from labels to case.

In respect of the Deaf culture discourse itself, Stokoe's (1994c: 100) prioritisation of 'description' is also useful:

Cultures can be defined and explained only after they have been described with some semblance of accuracy and completeness. Description of Deaf culture is far from complete, and confusion of logical types will not improve its accuracy.

Although in his own work Stokoe appears not to rule out the development of Deaf 'latitude and longitude', historical contingency brings his position close to Geertz' own. Geertz himself also goes on to note the changing nature of social science research, where academics:

> trying to understand insurrections, hospitals, or why it is that jokes are prized, have turned to linguistics, aesthetics, cultural history, law, or literary criticism for illumination rather than, as they used to do, to mechanics or physiology. (Geertz, 1983: 8)

Similarly, feminists have focused on a re-centring of fieldwork, where reflexivity and emotionality are perceived as valuable and admissable sources of data (Hochschild, 1976; Coates, 1996).

Mention of literary criticism also brings into play the second of Inglis' 'master values from Cultural Studies. Williams (1975, p. 64) suggests that the researcher should attempt to locate the 'structure of feeling', whether of a text, a group or a cultural process. This can be explicated as emphasising the task of identifying thought and feeling from introspection, and searching for a language in which to describe both the 'object' under study and the researcher's response to them. Such a language, it is suggested, strives both to capture the 'essence' of the object and to simultaneously represent it to others.

Although this can be subjected to criticisms of essentialism, Geertz (who seems not to be familiar with Williams' work or indeed *vice versa*) asserts two ideas which can be used to reinforce this perspective. The first concerns the basic nature of anthropology, and indeed of ethnography:

> That [which] we call our data are really our own constructions of other people's constructions of what [the group under study] and their compatriots are really up to. (Geertz, 1973: 9)

Geertz argues that therefore all such work can aspire to is an interpretation of cultures, which can only be 'measured' against each other by non-scientific criteria, although, not wishing to submit to complete relativism, he gives suggestions for assessing the value of different texts.

This perspective is extended into his later concept of 'local knowledge' (Geertz, 1983), which asserts both the singularity of the culture under study and the extent to which the language used to describe that culture is compelled to become culture-specific in order to render the fullest description of the event, ritual or custom studied, a description which has to take in 'whatever is insinuated as background information before the thing itself is directly examined' (1973: 9). This can be construed as the historical perspective of the group under study, as rendered by them, and as perceived and interpreted by the subaltern-researcher. He summarises:

> To an ethnographer, sorting through the machinery of distant ideas, the shapes of knowledge are almost ineluctably local, indivisible from their instruments and their encasements. One may veil this fact with ecumenical rhetoric, or blur it with strenuous theory, but one cannot really make it go away. (Geertz, 1983: 4)

His approach has been termed 'thick description' and is thought to highlight the following qualities:

> What generality it contrives to achieve grows out of the delicacy of its distinctions, not the sweep of its abstractions. (Geertz, 1973: 25)

Therefore, a primary goal of this theoretical approach is described thus:

> The essential vocation of interpretative anthropology is not to answer our deepest questions, but to make available to us answers that others, guarding other sheep in other valleys, have given, and thus to include them in the consultable record that man [sic] has said. (Geertz, 1973: 30)

In the case of oppressed minority cultures then, giving voice to the subaltern shepherds becomes even more crucial.

Geertz (1983 : 21) sees the development of such approaches as ones which are steadily growing within the social sciences:

> It has thus dawned on social scientists that they did not need to be mimic physicists or closet humanists or to invent some new realm of being to serve as the object of their investigations. Instead, they could proceed with their vocation, trying to discover order in collective life, and _decide how what they were doing was connected to related enterprises when they managed to get some of it done._ (My emphasis)

Although Geertz' practices have been criticised from several perspectives, including issues concerning the accessibility to the subaltern of the language used to represent such 'local knowledge' (Clifford & Marcus, 1996), this theoretical approach appears the most realistic one for Deaf cultural study to adopt.

Summary

What are the implications of all these perspectives for the study of Deaf culture which follows? To the theoretical grounding outlined here, we can add several key epistemological and methodological principles and strategies which can be utilised from the various disciplines which have placed culture under study. These can be summarised as follows.

• The maximally useful way to research Deaf culture at this point in time is to utilise bricolage, including methodologies which affirm introspection as a member of that culture to intuit the direction which the research should take, what should be observed, who should be questioned and what they should be questioned about. It could be argued that this results in similar methodologies which 'outside' ethnographers generally adopt (Spradley, 1980), but such questions can only be resolved by examining the resulting 'insider' texts and comparing them with the existing outsider texts (cf. Lincoln & Gabba, 1985).

• It is important to focus on capturing and articulating aspects of Deaf culture which can give the reader a sense of the 'smell, taste, and feel' (Geertz, 1973) of that culture, utilising 'thick description' to achieve a sense of its local knowledge'.

• This is not to suggest, however, that the research must be asystematic. A further aim must be to proceed with full awareness of the academic constraints summarised by Geertz' 'interpretation of interpretations'. *Thus all the stages and factors involved with one's intuitions and interpretations stages must be rendered as transparent as possible.* In so doing, mindful of the importance of understanding and incorporating theories of hegemony, and Bourdieu's (1992) strictures regarding the influences of individual fields, the research must attempt to stand back from the work far enough to incorporate the processes of history and the structures of academic power to render both the micro- and macro-picture similarly transparent.

• In examining, drawing out, selecting and describing aspects of Deaf 'local knowledge', the concept of the 'structure of feeling' must not only be utilised, but in a dialectical relationship. Thus observations on Deaf cultural manifestations or statements made by interviewees have to be situated alongside this (subaltern-élite) researcher's own introspected interpretation of what is meant by such manifestations or statements and for that interpretation process also to be rendered as transparently as possible. This must be carried out using language which attempts to capture the flavour of what is understood within the examples given.

Although it must be noted that despite the reservations concerning the success, or even desirability at establishing a conceptual framework at this point in time, these strategies do contain the possibility of developing concluding hypotheses which may contain or suggest maximal generalisability power in the Chomskian sense.

With these principles in mind, we can now proceed to establish the methodology used to explicate aspects of Deaf culture as gleaned from informants and participant observation.

Notes

1. Subsequent accounts in exploring these themes will find it useful to analyse how I. King Jordan, who was deafened in an accident and came to join the community as an adult, accrued sufficient 'cultural capital' so as to become the subject of the successful campaign to elect the first Deaf president for Gallaudet University. Such a situation could never have occurred in the UK, not least because no deafened person would have considered even joining the Deaf community once Oralism gained its stride.

2. Recently, December 2000, at the local (bilingual) Deaf school in Bristol, UK, a school play enacted by a group of 9- and 10-year-old Deaf children, featured an innovative use of the Blue Ribbon. This was apparently generated by the children themselves, and might be traced to their exposure to (and indeed performance at) the FDP marches of 1999 and 2000; thus we can see in minature how the transmission of powerful Deaf cultural beliefs can take on its own life once oralist barriers to Deaf-centred thinking are removed.

Above '*Adoration of the Shepherds*' (c. 1570) by Deaf artist Juan de Navarette (El Mudo), court painter to Philip II of Spain. Art played a significant role in convincing lay people of Deaf intelligence prior to formalised education, as Leonardo da Vinci attested. Evidence inceasingly suggests that a Deaf community existed in Madrid during this period, with links to other Mediterranean Deaf communities. (© Patrimonio Nacional, Madrid)

Left Illustration from Bulwer's *Chirologia and Chironomia* (1644). There is growing evidence that British Sign Language vocabulary can be traced back to at least the 1630s, and that in certain parts of the UK, numbers of non-Deaf people were able to use it.

Above Recent remarkable evidence indicates that from the 15th to the 20th centuries, Deaf people played prominent roles in the Ottoman Court, where sign language was of greater prestige than speech. (Pictures © The Royal Library, Sweden)

Below Native Americans, aborigines and other First Nation people have used sophisticated sign languages in many roles, including storytelling and religious ceremonies, for thousands of years.

WHITE MAN	WITH US	FRIENDS	FOUR	WINTER	FINISHED
Chief Lean Wolf draws his thumb across his head, meaning "man who wears a hat."	*He brings his hand close to his chest.*	*He holds out his open hand.*	*He holds up four fingers.*	*He crosses his arms and shivers.*	*He holds his clenched fists together, then pulls them apart as if breaking a stick.*

The Parisian Deaf banquets from 1840 onwards have bequeathed to us indications of a more powerful vision of Deafhood, Deaf spirituality and Deaf Nation politics, existing before the rise of Oralism. (From Fischer & Lane, 1993)

Left The Parisian Deaf community appears to have been highly visible around the French Revolution. Clause Deseine's access to its leaders in order to sculpt their busts is one of the more notable features, as his *Bust of Robespierre* indicates. (From Mirzoeff, 1995)

Below In the initial post-Milan period, sign languages were still widely respected. Queen Victoria is shown fingerspelling with a Deaf servant. (© RNID)

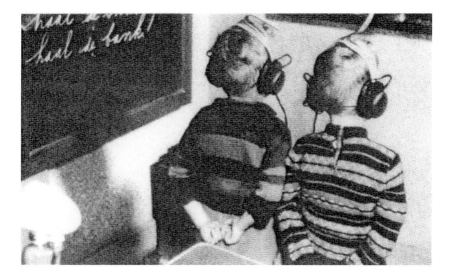

Above The numerous strategies used to enforce Oralism included hands being tied behind backs, taped to desks, beaten or simply sat upon. These were among the less severe deterrents practised right through from the 1880s to the present day. (From Fischer & Lane, 1993)

Below *Education for the Deaf*, by Betty Miller (1971). The Deaf Resurgence of the 1970s utilised art as another medium by which to try to draw public attention to what more and more people are acknowledging as Oralist child abuse. (© National Association of the Deaf)

Left The Deaf Resurgence saw renewed campaigns for the return of sign languages and Deaf teachers. Of the pressure groups which sprang up worldwide, the most radical and successful was probably the UK's National Union of the Deaf. (Photo © *The Times*)

Below The Gallaudet University 1988 campaign for their first Deaf President in its 130 year history was one of the most significant moments of the Deaf Resurgence. (From Gannon, 1989)

Above The Federation of Deaf People's marches for BSL recognition marked a new stage in Deaf activism from 1999 onwards. (Photos © Paddy Ladd)

Below As a result, even the British Deaf Association was emboldened to issue a challenge to the Labour government. Note that this sign means 'idle' in BSL! (© BDA)

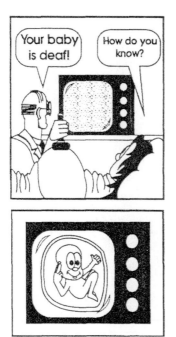

Left The encroaching threat of genetic engineering has forced Deaf communities to make explicit their belief in the importance of Deaf people's existence, as bearers and custodians of sign languages denoting positive examples of human diversity. (© Colin White)

Below Frustrated by the lack of media interest in the BSL marches, younger Deaf people of the Deaf Liberation Front began to embark on direct action in 2001. Note that the theme of education remains a constant – one getting ever nearer to Parliament. (Photo © Mike Theobald)

Chapter 6

Researching Deaf Communities – Subaltern Researcher Methodologies

> We argue that there is a distinct black politics based on a unique style and combination of worldviews that informs black political behaviour. This black politics contains the possibility of a synthesis between selfish individualism and group responsibility that could provide an instructive moral vision for the entire society.
>
> Charles P. Henry (1990: 11)

Introduction

The first half of this book has traced a path through the foothills, forests and ravines that have characterised the complexities of Deaf community history and of cultural investigation. Now that we have emerged into the open landscape of the tundra and can see before us the mountain ranges of Deaf culture, it might prove useful to cast our gaze back along the path we have carved out, in order to locate the markers we have left behind to keep us from losing our way. Having accomplished this, we can then select the equipment we will need for the final ascent.

The route we have taken thus far was constructed in order to deal with the following issues.

Broadly speaking, the traditional structures and discourses of academia are characterised by a privileged subject investigating an underprivileged object. This is closely linked to traditional beliefs about objectivity in social science research, which express concern about the 'accuracy' of results presented by members of minority groups investigating their own communities. There exist, therefore, very few theories or methodologies which either support such research or dispassionately confront the difficulties which this research must encounter.

Cultural study is one of the most problematic research domains, which is in part due to the complexity of the culture concept itself. Cultural research is primarily conducted by several disparate disciplines whose discourses rarely 'speak' to each other. Additionally it has also been undertaken as a 'fringe' activity by many other disciplines, ranging from psychology through education, linguistics and history to the numerous minority studies, and these discourses also rarely formally confer. We are thus confronted with the absence of a unified cultural research discipline through which we can assess any theories and methodologies we wish to employ.

When it comes to research in the Deaf domain, we find that because of the dominance of the medical model of deafness, only the barest minimum of resources have been made available to examine Deaf communities as communities (and this without even making comparison with the vast sums expended on research into medical aspects of deafness). Indeed it is only in very recent times that they have even been granted the status of communities. The idea of Deaf cultural research, then, is anathema to the majority who hold power and practise in those domains.

The social model of disability also presents us with obstacles to research. It has failed to realise the extent to which it is still medically constructed. Even though it places an emphasis on commonality of experience of social oppression, all the groups within its aegis are undeniably those who are characterised by having a physical impairment. It is also conceived around the tenets of individualism – that is, the social and political barriers facing individual disabled people in their attempts to gain full access to society. Thus it has been unable to cope with the collectivist life experience that characterises Deaf communities (and those communities' consequent very different priorities). However, since disability constructions have been given political and economic primacy, the dissenting Deaf voice has been pushed aside and there is almost no discourse space in which to establish that dissenting view, with its insistence on the crucial nature of the Deaf cultural concept.

We have seen that Deaf communities should instead be constructed around a culturo-linguistic model. Its patterns of experience and oppression are therefore similar to and should be classified with other linguistic minorities. However, these minorities are themselves caught up in the medical model and reluctant to admit sign language cultures to their domains and discourses. Moreover, there is almost no formal academic focus on linguistic minorities *per se*; thus bringing compelling Deaf linguistic and cultural evidence to their attention is extremely difficult.

All these issues stand between the Deaf researcher and the attainment of satisfactory academic outcomes. However, there are also 'internal' problems. Because of the devastation caused by the dominance of Oralism, few Deaf people have left the system with the type of educational qualifications which permit the initiation of academic research into their own community. Of those few who are qualified to do so, most either have other priorities (establishing a career in a mainstream field where genuine opportunities for advancement exist) or do not consider Deaf community research to be an urgent need.

When we gaze back over these markers along the trail, we can appreciate why the climb has been so ardous and tricky. But we may also recall that the view along the way has been not only interesting but at time quite inspiring:

First, we have learned that despite all the oppression Deaf people and their communities have faced through recorded time, there have also been times characterised by great clarity of observation and exhilarating actions from both Deaf people and their allies. These have suggested that the existence of Deaf peoples constitutes an affirmation of the diversity of human life and one that can be found, not in some exotic land, but right under our feet, as it were. They have also suggested that, rather than viewing Deaf people as individuals to be 'helped', we might actually find that their collective life and language embodies principles and patterns that can assist us in tackling deficiencies in our own social beliefs, theories and policies.

Second, we have observed that through this recorded time, Deaf communities have maintained their own discourses, with their own covert belief systems and agendas. These have been the bedrock of their stubborn refusal to be eradicated. We have obtained glimpses of what these beliefs stand for and amount to, but await confirmation of any systematically passed down tradition of cultural beliefs.

Third, we have also learned that in the last 25 years there has been a worldwide Deaf Resurgence, and that it is this essentially political development which has rendered them visible to us, and enabled the beginnings of dialogue. These developments have culminated in the emergence of the Deaf culture concept. However, we have also seen how attempts to improve the quality of Deaf education and services have brought new groups of people into contact with Deaf communities, and that this contact has often been characterised by conflicts which have soured some of the initial enthusiasm. We have been able to see that these conflicts are often caused by a lack of awareness that it is Deaf cultural principles which they are encountering, and that hearing–Deaf exchanges should be more properly viewed as cross-cultural encounters. It has become clear, too, that the rapid growth of this contact, combined with the equally rapid growth in unexamined use of the Deaf culture concept, has created a situation in which Deaf cultural research is needed as a matter of maximum urgency. This urgency is increased by the resurgence of Oralism through the cochlear implant ideology, and by the advent of genetics which is viewed by some as the 'Final Solution'. The emergence of the latter threatens to compel Deaf communities to justify their continued existence, and it can only be through a clear understanding of the benefits of Deaf culture to the wider society that such a justification can be framed.

Fourth, we have noted the extent to which Deaf cultures do not easily fit with established models, rendering it more difficult to 'prove' its existence. However, we have identified a linguistic process by which that existence can be validated, and are ready to begin to reinforce this by a search for coherent, historically transmitted cultural qualities. We have also identified several consistent weaknesses within most cultural research and set ourselves to conduct studies which tackle these head on.

Fifth, to assist us in our investigation of so many trails along the complex path of Western history, we have focused on the discourse concept as a tool for identifying both intra-group beliefs and actions, and inter-group disparancies in political and economic power.

Sixth, in so doing, we have become aware that all Deaf discourses have been subsumed within discourses labelled 'deafness'. One of the first requirements therefore has been to name and, therefore, to create a conceptual space for Deaf discourse and this has been given the appelation of *Deafhood*.

In this sense, then, our entire journey has been one undertaken in search of Deafhood. However, simply naming it has not deproblematised it. It has therefore been necessary to emphasise that Deafhood is not a state, but an ongoing process containing different readings of what it might consist.

We have followed an analysis that suggests the existence of different Deaf discourses and noted that they can be initially identified as 'professional' and 'subaltern'. Because of the possibility that professional discourses have been penetrated by the medical model, we have identified the investigation of subaltern discourses as a priority for examining and identifying Deafhood. Thus my responsibility on the journey ahead is to 'let the subaltern speak' for themselves.

In addition, given the fact of my membership of a Deaf community and culture which espouses collectivism, I am also bound by values which require the empowerment of Deaf informants through the research process itself. In so doing, I am required at times to come into conflict with the traditional values of the academy.

These, then are the landmarks of our journey so far. This conflict threatens to make our trip a circular one, one where we end up right back at the start. This makes it all the more important, therefore, that we look for radical developments within the academy which might house other theories which we can utilise for our methodology. These tools will then form our crampons, ropes, pitons and harness for the final ascent.

This chapter begins by outlining the philosophies of ethnography and critical ethnography. The latter requires the researcher to situate themselves in relation to the research project, and so my own detailed 'autoethnography' follows. At this point we are then ready to trace the path of the actual research project itself.

Ethnography

Arguably the primary methodology for investigating social groups is ethnography, a research method which was first developed within anthropology (Spindler & Spindler, 1992) but has since been utilised right across the social sciences. It falls under the rubric of what is referred to as *qualitative research*, as opposed to the 'questionnaire and statistics' approach that can be said to characterise quantitative research, and is characterised by immersion in the culture under investigation, and by the development of particular strategies for obtaining data – 'participant observation' and 'ethnographic interviewing'. It has also set itself, when recording that data, to represent the beliefs and values of the groups under study within their own (emic) terms of reference.

Although quantitative research methods can be used in conjunction with the ethnographic project, the primary thrust is towards qualitative methods. These two methodologies have a history of heated conflict between each set of adherents and have only fairly recently been reconciled.

Qualitative research has been faced with the necessity of justifying itself according to 'traditional' scientific principles. One response it has made is to question scientific objectivity itself, holding that this is an inappropriate principle for research with live and active human beings operating in groups. This response has been augmented by studies of the history of the hard sciences which indicate that its own principles of objectivity have been misconceived (Kuhn, 1962), and these beliefs have been reinforced by the emergence of both quantum physics and chaos theory (Capra, 1976; Gleick, 1997).

Nevertheless, since all research must (in theory) satisfy validity requirements, it has been necessary for ethnography to attempt to develop standards by which its results can be assessed. Traditionally this has been a weakness within ethnography (Hammersley & Atkinson, 1983) and many ethnographic studies have been fundamentally descriptive, with little theorising across the various accounts.

However, another significant weakness has been identified. In emphasising the importance of representing groups within their own terms, ethnographers hoped to achieve increased social and political respect for those groups, with consequent changes in social policy. In some respects this can be characterised as the liberal-humanist impulse. But in recent years, some ethnographers, more radical in intent, have drawn attention to the extent to which these aims have not been achieved. In particular, they have been concerned with what they consider the 'failure' of the ethnographic project within the academic system. They argue that the groups under study have still remained the objects rather than the subjects of research and that consequently they have remained disempowered. In order to rectify this situation, these ethnographers have searched for different methodological principles. Various ideas have been tried in different disciplines (such as 'action research', 'applied' and 'action anthropology'), but a consensus seems to be appearing around principles of *critical ethnography*. This argues its case by raising the stakes, as it were, so that it directly questions the whole mission of the academy, and carries its answers to its own logical conclusion – if the academy conceives of itself as existing for the betterment of society, then it has an obligation to examine the extent to which its own methodological shortcomings contribute to the failure to achieve that aim (Quantz, 1992).

For a study such as this, focused on a minority oppressed community and its culture, one whose existence is perceived as problematic by certain sectors of the academic establishment, it thus becomes clear that critical ethnography offers an opportunity to reconceive theory and praxis as it is enacted upon Deaf communities.

Critical Ethnography

Simon and Dippo (1986) define critical ethnography as being founded upon three essential tenets:

(1) The work must employ an organising method which defines one's data and analytical procedures in a way consistent with its project.
(2) It must be situated in part within a public sphere that allows it to become the starting point for the critique and transformation of the conditions of oppressive and inequitable moral and social regulation.
(3) It must address the limits of its own claims by a consideration of how, as a form of social practice, it too is constituted and regulated through historical relations of power and existing material conditions (Simon & Dippo, 1986: 197).

Partly because of its focus on social inequity, critical ethnography has been accused of bias. Its response is to critique the ways in which traditional social sciences have not only been mistaken in assuming an objective, value-free hermeneutic tradition, but points out that this tradition, in fact, contains its own hidden biases which reflect cultural power structures. To transcend issues surrounding bias, it is necessary to make transparent all aspects of the research project, including the wider historical and power-structural factors which lie beneath or behind the project itself. In respect of this book, this process began with the historical review in Chapter 2, has continued through to this point and will be maintained until the end.

Because of the need to combat accusations of bias, as well as needing to meet the higher standards which it proposes, critical ethnography is also strongly concerned with verification processes and theories. Six strategies feature prominently (Lather, 1986). Of these, triangulation, respondent validation and judgement sampling emanate from traditional ethnography, whilst reflexive subjectivity, catalytic validity, and typicality are particular to critical ethnography. These are now described; reflections on their use in this study are presented at the end of the chapter.

Respondent validation

Some ethnographers argue that a crucial aspect of verification, is, as Hammersley and Atkinson (1983: 195)put it: '... whether the actors whose beliefs and behaviour they purport to describe recognize the validity of those accounts'. Although assessing such recognition is complex and problematic, it is nonetheless important as a guiding principle.

Triangulation

Respondent validation represents one form of triangulation, which can be described as the principle of checking inferences from one set of data against data collected from other domains (Hammersley & Atkinson, 1983). Two primary manifestations of this are methodological triangulation, in which data are cross-checked after being collected through a variety of methods, and data triangulation, where the cross-checking process takes place after data have been collected from different actors within the arena of study.

Reflexive subjectivity and transparency

Simon and Dippo (1986: 200) summarise the principle of reflexive subjectivity thus:

> We need to recognise our own implication in the production of data and must thus begin to include ourselves (our own practices and their social and historic basis) in our analyses of the situations we study.

However, Bourdieu (1992) asserts that it would be optimistic to imagine that a researcher would be able to identify and account for all the external forces and internal impulses acting upon them, and that there is thus a danger of producing 'individualist' texts. He insists that particular attention must thus be given to the underlying limitations imposed by the various fields and domains of power, especially with reference to academic or intellectual bias. Such a target is highly challenging and still rarely achieved. Nevertheless, pursuing maximum transparency within reflexivity enables me to expose my intellectual and emotional motivations and analyses, so that others can identify factors, connections and issues overlooked by this self-accounting.

Typicality

Although it is a central tenet of social sciences that data sampling must aspire to minimise bias, the particular nature of critical ethnography is such that additional caution must be employed. Since such work is concerned with 'assisting' marginalised groups to express their perspectives and beliefs, one must always seek to check the degree of typicality of such beliefs among group members, and thus avoid homogenising or over-determining the responses. As Hannerz (1992: 12–13) expresses it:

> When anthropologists claim to 'take the native's point of view', we have not been in the habit of asking 'Which native?' For what the anthropologist saw must depend upon the view of the person over whose shoulder he was glancing.

This issue is also central to judgement sampling.

Judgement sampling

Sampling procedures are also a tenet of social science in general. However, insufficient attention is sometimes paid to the larger social picture within which the sampling takes place. Sometimes participant observation has reflected insufficiently on the partially subconscious processes by which such information is collected; it has not always examined the social status and relationships of the informants within their own society, and the effect that this has on the data. Judgement sampling seeks to render this process more transparent by illustrating the basis on which those observed or interviewed were selected. It also seeks to balance 'introspective' and 'intuitive' aspects of ethnography by drawing such subconscious assumptions to the surface for reflection.

Catalytic validity

This requires that the praxis and results of the research study should have positive effects for the group studied. These range from a greater awareness among group members, through increased self-confidence and greater involvement in their society, to the ideal described by Simon and

Dippo (1986: 199) as a group who are 'in a position to use ethnographic work as a resource . . . for [its] ability to clarify the basis of everyday life and the possibilities for its transformation'.

Each of these principles was adopted for this study, and are discussed later where appropriate.

Subaltern-Researcher Status and Implications

Despite the laudable intentions of critical ethnography, it has not yet really begun to theorise about the status of members of minority communities who intend to study their own community. Although all the previous principles still apply, something more is needed which addresses the 'validity' or representative nature of the minority researcher. To assume that a white middle-class female's status as a woman is sufficient commonality for studying white working-class women's collective lives is to overlook certain crucial differences which might have great bearing on the quality of the research. Similarly, as Caulfield (1973) points out, a subaltern who has been trained in the traditional colonialist academy might be compromised by the origins of the tools they are using, so that a search for tools appropriate to the culture should be instigated.

Thus it is too with Deaf research. However, for this initial study it would be asking too much to be able to identify and operate such tools in a political vacuum – Deaf people have barely begun to even practice, let alone initiate it, in terms which they have not yet made explicit. But it is clear that this must be the eventual aim, so that this study must end by pointing us towards the beginnings of such a Deaf epistemology.

Nevertheless, these problems must be faced and formally incorporated into the research. The absence of conceptual tools is clear when we simply consider the absence of terms to describe those who are the recipients of policies and services. The only English term we can find is 'consumer researcher', which has obviously limited applicability since it is already two-tier in emphasis – providers and recipients. Fortunately, within post-colonialism, the concept of *subaltern* groups as represented by the work of Guha *et al.* (1982) and Spivak (1996) is especially useful to us.

Taking its cue from Gramsci's definition of the subaltern as a collective description of dominated groups which lack explicit class-consciousness, the Subaltern Studies movement (1982–87) theorises a distinction between the resisting discourses and actions developed by intellectual élites and those taken by 'grass roots' or subaltern movements, which are largely discounted by such élites. Since only the former discourses have been recorded, the result is a partial and therefore inaccurate representation of the resisting culture. This has particular relevance for post-independence where that élite gains the power to control its own society according to its own ideologies, which may continue to exclude the subaltern experience.

'Enabling the subaltern to speak', therefore, is a priority for studies of such cultures which are concerned to challenge definitions of academic validity constructed around traditional discourses. This is particularly apposite for Deaf communities and others with a marked divide between the viewpoints of those few members literate in the language of the majority culture and the majority who are not.

But the subaltern concept also offers another possibility for correcting academic bias. Because it enables us to demarcate social distinctions in groups which do not fall into conventional Western class divisions, we can make use of it here as a starting tool.

However, we should also note that from the outset we are in comparatively uncharted waters. Spivak (1990) and others have suggested that once the subaltern can 'speak', they are no longer subaltern. Such a bipolar perspective can only carry us so far, and it would also appear too simplistic to assume that there is no interplay or interpenetration between subaltern and élite (Miller, 1993). Furthermore, as yet not even Subaltern Studies posits the subaltern-as-researcher.

But if we marshall this term carefully, and apply to it Bourdieu's theories regarding habitus, field and agent, it is possible for us to use it to bring to the surface social and cultural features, aspects and categories which might come into play in deciding whether the researcher in question is a subaltern or a member of the elite; or indeed, as a starting point for investigating the cultural valences of all those features. In the process we would learn much that would point us towards, and reveal the nature of, those Deaf epistemologies.

That, however is a mid to long-term aim for Deaf Studies. For the moment we can make a beginning by creating the classification of _subaltern-researcher_. To be a subaltern-researcher therefore means to come to an area of study with an experiential knowledge of one's own minority community. Subaltern study could, in theory, also be predicated outwards – that subaltern-researcher status still obtains if one studies the practices of the group directly oppressing them. But that is a refinement too far for our immediate purposes.

How does this apply to the Deaf community? At this point the reader might find it helpful to return to the end of Chapter 3, where we identified the different groups participating in Deafhood discourses and, in particular, the changes which have taken place in the last 20 years. There we note the distinctions made between 'Deaf professionals' and 'Deaf grass-roots' and also attempt to formalise a more helpful distinction, that of 'subaltern élite', which reflects more accurately the status of the former. In so doing, we listed eight features that assist us in making that distinction.

The very first step that I must take then, in the research itself, is to apply the analysis to myself, to reflect and make explicit my own status. However, if we are mindful of Bourdieu's strictures about the dangers of producing individualistic texts, it is therefore necessary for me to build into that analysis an accounting of all the fields that make up my own habitus.

Situating Myself within the Study

I was born partially deaf into a hearing upper-working-class family in the 'Home Counties' of Southern England during the intensified stage of post-war Oralism, and placed in mainstreamed education from the age of four through to the end of my first university degree. Isolated from contact with other Deaf people, the experience resulted in 'academic success' but was traumatic both socially and emotionally (Ladd, 1979). Upon leaving college, I found that my applications to become a teacher of the Deaf were rejected on the grounds of my deafness, although the same people had stressed throughout my education the oralist doctrine that I 'was not deaf, but a hearing person who could not hear' (Ladd, 1979). The realisation that I had been deceived was an epiphany in realising how Oralism had manipulated me.

During the following 3 years of social work with Deaf children and their families, it became clear that this manipulation was part of a national pattern which had existed for almost 100 years and was continuing to damage the educational, social and emotional health of those I encountered in my work. I was fortunate in entering this profession at a time when Oralism was beginning to be questioned, and began to seek out other d/Deaf people who wished to challenge this status quo. This resulted in the formation of the Deaf-run pressure group, the National Union of the Deaf, in which I was active for the next 10 years.

Having grown up in isolation from other Deaf people, I found it an immense personal challenge to confront and shed aspects of my personal oralist conditioning, even as I intellectually rejected its raison d'être. However, by perseverance and proven commitment, I gradually came to be accepted by Deaf people, and simultaneously begin to accept their very different worldview and history, thus moving from 'deaf' (i.e. the condition of situating my worldview around audiological perspectives) to 'Deaf' (situating it around cultural and linguistic perspectives) during that process. During the later years, my audiological condition also changed, and I became profoundly deaf. However, it should not be assumed that I (or anyone else) can completely expunge all traces of oralist thinking, and it is best accepted that a lifetime's vigilance is required to continue to identify those traces as part of the process of coming into full self-awareness.[1]

A crucial personal breakthrough (which has subsequently informed all my life actions) occurred earlier when I attended university during the tail-end of the 'hippie' movement of the late 1960s. In contrast to my mainly negative experience of hearing people as represented by grammar schoolboys, I found the hippie-oriented students to be open-minded and interested in human differences rather than contemptuous of them. Entering college at such a time was serendipitious, and is one that very few other Deaf people in the UK have had the opportunity to experience.

Of equal importance were the intellectual, political and spiritual philosophies of that era; my exposure to them made it possible almost overnight to question and reject the entire conservative base on which my self-image had been founded, and to embrace a worldview that can be summed up in four essential tenets. One was the realisation of the existence of 'invisible' ruling-class discourses which represented themselves as 'reality'; another was the realisation of the damage these caused to a wide range of oppressed minorities who did not fit into that reality, together with the more subtle damage caused to those who acquiesced in it. The third was the desire to conceive of alternative realities which might serve society better, and the fourth was to work to achieve those realities.

My subsequent work over the following 20 years within Deaf communities locally, nationally and internationally has been focused around those four tenets. This process has combined more conventional political and social activism with attempts to innovate processes rooted in the conception of alternative realities, and has been underpinned by further academic degrees in the fields of linguistics and Cultural Studies, the latter stimulating my interest in theorising Deaf culture. It also proved important in understanding the role of class in society and in reclaiming my own working-class experience, which was temporarily suppressed or ignored during the hippie era. As a result of this, I was able to see my wider situation in society as parallelling what has been termed a 'working-class scholarship boy', a group who turned out to be particular active in initiating change in the post 1960s period. (Indeed both Richard Hoggart and Raymond Williams of Cultural Studies were two such boys.)

Thus my habitus has been formed not only by three sets of subaltern experiences: Deaf, working class and hippie, but also by many of the 'opposing' middle-class values embodied in the fields of grammar school and university education. (Being white and male also carry within them their own sets of implications.) This conflict also occurs at the heart of my own family. Like D.H. Lawrence, and, I suspect, many other scholarship boys, my father remained working-class for the whole of his life, whilst my mother aspired to membership of the middle-class, and where that was not possible for herself, desired it for her children. Although she died when I was small, this aspiration remained alive within the family and was the site of numerous conflicts and tensions as I grew up. This inclination towards membership of what is best described as the *petit-bourgoisie* was reinforced by the Home Counties English environment – working-class values are much more ambivalent there due to their proximity to the seats of power and Royal prestige.

We can take this analysis further. Some of the experiences and values within each subaltern setting are congruent with each other – for instance, a dislike or resentment of oppression. Others are in explicit conflict, such as hippie and working-class beliefs about the family or numerous cultural institutions. Deaf and hippie values may share a belief in the 'tribe'. But the latter's belief in freedom of movement conflicts with Deaf values of lifelong commitments to localised social circles.

The number of different fields of input bring with them their own advantages, not only in the number of life experiences available, but also the opportunity to see more easily 'across fences' as it were. However, it must also be pointed out that such experiences could also lead to confusion and distress, and certainly in later life pose problems for locating a 'home' which can fulfil all of these subjectivities. It is beyond the scope of this study to speculate whether these have had any effect on the research, but in the interests of transparency they must be noted, so that others who choose to follow this methodological path can be aware of and critique them in later research. It remains only to say that one can never fully see oneself as others do; for this reason alone therefore, feedback as to the deficiencies of this critique are welcomed, in order that the model may be better presented the next time around.

How then do all these factors affect my status within the Deaf community? We must assess this in terms of the nine subaltern qualities identified in Chapter 3.

(1) *Use of BSL as a first language and the culture developed within it.* Being orally mainstreamed to a secondary school level of English literacy, I am situated outside this experience. English remains my first language. Twenty-six years of BSL use has brought me 'inside' to some degree, but mastering every nuance is a lifetime's process since it can never be the same experience as that of native users.

(2) *Common cultural background arising from the Deaf school experience.* The same reservations as for (i) above apply here, but even more so, because one is exposed to BSL 100% of the Deaf interaction time. The amount of time spent discussing and thus learning about the Deaf school experience is minimal – 1% at most – although certain of its cultural significances can certainly be acquired.

(3) *Experience of Oralism and its effects on self-worth.* These experiences are shared by both myself and Deaf subalterns. However, inasmuch as I was able to succeed despite Oralism, that angles the effects slightly differently, leaving me more open to subconsciously maintaining some of its tenets (in relation to English) in a way that a monolingual Deaf subaltern-élite might not do.

(4) *Experience of being audiologically Deaf in a Hearing world.* These experiences are also shared. Again, however, my original partially-deaf status, and my consequent ability to speak English reasonable clearly and competently, marks my everyday experience out as different from those whose voices could not be understood by hearing people. This reinforces the 'risks' identified earlier. However, it is also interesting to note that those espousing Deaf cultural concepts do not see audiological hearing levels as a defining aspect of cultural membership – thus possession of other cultural values may come to outweigh this one in gaining community acceptance.

(5) *Knowledge of Deaf social organisation and informal Deaf history and tradition.* Despite not being a native speaker, my active participation in the Deaf community for the last 25 years situates me firmly within these discourses.

(6) *Monolingualism.* Being bilingual in this context is a telling obstacle to overcome – for example, understanding the degree of helplessness felt by a Deaf subaltern has not been an easy task and, in a real sense, I stand outside this crucial experiential space.

(7) *Socialising within the Deaf community.* My socialisation patterns place me firmly inside the community. However, my membership is distributed over a national scale – I could not say that I was a fully-fledged member of any one local community.

(8) *Commitment to maintaining and developing the Deaf community.* This has been very visible over the last 26 years and, it would seem to me, contributes greatly to my acceptance, thus outweighing some of the 'minuses' in respect of cultural acceptance.

(9) *Embracing the 'D' position and being perceived to do so by agents of the hegemonic discourses.* The nature of my political commitment to the 'D' quality of the Deaf community has resulted in those agents perceiving me as an opponent of their discourses, and thus certainly identified me

as operating within it. This has also assisted with cultural acceptance. I am thus placed in a position most akin to a subaltern-élite advocate of subaltern values.

Now, how one weighs those factors in terms of my own cultural membership is open to question, since we do not yet have adequate subaltern documentation of the process of social and cultural acceptance. Nevertheless, it would be safe to conclude that my status is akin to that of the subaltern-élite, and thus we can proceed with the appelation of 'subaltern-élite researcher' for the purposes of this study. This is only possible, however, with the application of the greatest vigilance in being aware of the extent to which (1), (2) and (6) might handicap or distort the research task, and thus it is my duty to draw attention to examples of these as and when they affect this study.

The conclusion for the purposes of this methodology is this – that it is the acceptance of my cultural membership on the terms above which enabled me to gain meaningful access to the UK Deaf community, and thus carry out the work described below.

Subaltern-Élite Researcher Status and the Origins of the Study

The Deaf subaltern-researcher therefore brings to the area of study an experiential knowledge of the Deaf community, and it is this experience which can then be entered officially into the academic records as a valid basis from which to introspect and prioritise each stage of the research process, provided that this introspection is rendered as transparently as possible.

Having adopted the principle of catalytic validity, I had also to use this introspection in conjunction with discussions with Deaf subaltern in order to prioritise the political needs of the Deaf community, and how my research could best serve those ends. These two strategies thus resulted in an interpretation of those needs which then influenced how the first stage of the study should be carried out.

There are two major implications here. The first was that over the previous four years I had become known in the community as someone studying and writing about Deaf culture. As a result, I was asked by some Deaf people if I would either 'write a book' or 'come and research' the subject. The reasons given indicated an awareness of the importance of Deaf culture both as a political tool in the struggle against 'Oralism' and for reinforcing changes towards Deaf-centred policies in workplaces like schools and colleges. Considerable anxiety and urgency was expressed either about the need to 'prove we have a culture' or whether this was 'another Hearing idea imposed on us'. Others asked me to do this within a doctoral study both to 'prove Deaf people can do it' and so that 'you can get a job where you can teach what you've learned'. Most who made these requests were concerned that 'you tell them [those deemed to hold power relevant to Deaf communities] what the real Deaf people have been trying to say'. The signed term 'REAL-DEAF' here implies grass-roots views.

All these factors, plus my own temperament (which space does not permit analysis of, although the reader might attempt to reconstruct that following the details of my habitus), led me to adopt these suggestions and to attempt both 'proof' of that culture and to speed up the process of its acceptance by concluding with a workable framework.

I had completed a preliminary study in the preceding year, during which I was based at Gallaudet University in Washington DC – the world's only Deaf university. From the data generated there (which will appear in the next volume), I built working hypotheses for approaching the present study. I was also able to draw conclusions from the methodologies used in that research.

However, researching my own British community presented particular potential difficulties as, like any other Deaf community member, I occupied a position with a history in the British Deaf community, which could affect the data collected. Many subalterns also see my position as one with status. The positive effects are considered later. Potentially negative ones included various types of reactions by informants to that status.

First Stage of the Study

Introspection based on experience and the working hypotheses described earlier formed one set of inputs into how to theorise Deaf culture. However, in order to orient myself towards theories with maximum generalisability, I had to study the literature which existed, both on Deaf culture and on cultural theory in general. This has been completed in the reviews in Chapters 2–5.

After drawing on all these inputs, there were four primary objectives for the first study:

- to understand the cultural relevance of social groupings within British Deaf culture;
- to ascertain what differences historical change might make in conceptualising that culture;
- to understand the role of individual dispositions and strategies within the culture; and
- to remain aware of any significant variables which might require pursuing.

Initial strategies

I adopted a participant-observer approach in four sets of domains. The first was my immediate working environment, a Deaf Studies department with a high percentage of Deaf staff and about 20 Deaf students, all interacting with hearing staff and students in many different ways, both inside and outside the university. Of especial importance was the fact that such a department was very new for the UK; there were thus many new perspectives for both Deaf and hearing people, resulting in visible cultural conflicts and misunderstandings on a daily basis, as well as a sense of cultural exploration.

The second was my involvement in the local Deaf club, I regularly visited the old people's Wednesday afternoon club, and the all-age open evening that night. Here my approach differed from many anthropologists, for I was not totally immersed in one single community. The reasons for this are of interest. One is that the time limitations imposed on the study did not allow the same intensity of immersion. The second concerns my place in the wider Deaf community, where there were heavy demands made upon my time as one among very few national activists, which negatively affected the energy available for local involvement.

The third area was that national community. Although the demands made upon my time were heavy, there were advantages in that I was able to experience and informally test some of the cultural issues more widely and deeply.

For triangulation I utilised the written, video-recorded and televised Deaf media, as well as in historical texts and papers.

My starting point was to meet with and interview subaltern-élite Deaf people whom I knew from experience to have strong views on some of the issues around Deaf culture. The four I interviewed came from Deaf families; they would, I hoped, be able to shed light on what it meant to grow up in a family environment where to be Deaf was considered normal. In particular, they would be able to discuss multi-generational Deaf experience, which I intuitively felt was central to understanding Deaf culture.

One of the four had Deaf parents only. Three had an extensive network of Deaf grandparents, aunts, uncles and cousins. One was fifth generation Deaf, whilst another was sixth generation with Deaf children and grandchildren constituting an eight generation span.

All were white women, aged between 35 and 50, and one was Jewish, working at the time in the same organisation. Each had only obtained professional posts in the previous ten years; three had spent their formative years as housewives, on factory assembly lines, or in other manual work. Three had only recently undertaken a degree of professional training; all therefore thought of themselves as 'ordinary Deaf people', though whether that opinion was shared by their community now that they had 'risen' in occupation is another matter. Two lived in their city of birth, whilst two came from London. All knew each other, though they socialised mainly according to their place of origin.

Initial interviews

All those interviewed were known to me previously and were comfortable both talking with me and with the use of video cameras from their own work. They welcomed the opportunity to discuss the issues raised with another Deaf person; as Lorna Allsop put it: 'I'm always having to ask other Deaf people questions for my work; but no-one ever asks me for my views'. All wanted to explore what Deaf culture might mean and on several occasions expressed their pleasure at having the chance to think things through; they were particularly pleased when spontaneously expressing views which they had not realised they had held.

They were also keen to further Deaf people's self-knowledge and development, and saw the research as an opportunity for them to participate actively in that process, thus bringing two aspects of catalytic validity simultaneously into play. All were highly aware and critical of the usual patterns of 'Hearing' research on Deaf people which saw them purely as subjects, and who 'never' made their resulting knowledge available to the Deaf community. They also trusted me in this regard.

Thus they were happy to be interviewed on subsequent occasions; the length of time for each person ranged from two to eight hours. Despite this, not all the question areas were covered.

The interviews were open-ended, but designed around a set of core question areas (see Appendix 3). All were recorded on videotape and transcribed. In each situation I did not lead in with the questions of the list, but let the first topic arise spontaneously from our knowledge of each other and our past interaction, so that the atmosphere was more like a natural 'Deaf' conversation. (This approach has been noted in Jones and Pullen (1992) as characteristic of Deaf culture.) Once the first topic had run its course, I selected a question from the list which most closely related to that topic; this 'flow' approach was repeated throughout the interview.

There were three basic question areas. One was to see what they thought about certain of the ideas commonly assumed by previous researchers to constitute Deaf culture. The second was to focus on the socio-cultural patterns and structures thrown up by the preliminary study. The third was to remain open to new areas thrown up by my ongoing observations and any that might emerge from these interviews. Throughout the remainder of the study, I had to reflect on my own knowledge and experience of Deaf life (and from discussions with other Deaf and hearing people), as to how these three sets of questions might link with each other, and at which levels, allowing this to guide my strategies.

These areas yielded four themes and 22 questions on the core list, some of which were added following the initial interviews. These can be categorised as follows:

- six were questions about what the informants understood and felt about particular cultural terminology;
- three were questions arising from the problematic areas of conceptualising Deaf culture;
- four were questions about certain signs used in BSL which suggested cultural attitudes towards one's self or other Deaf people; and
- nine were questions about certain aspects of Deaf behaviour which I had noticed from my experience.

Discussion forum

In order to further the spirit of collective enquiry described here, which served well in getting relaxed responses from the four individuals, I invited seven other Deaf people working in the Deaf Studies department to form a forum in order to examine typicality. All were in the professional class; three were new to that class, while the other four had always held white-collar posts. Two had Deaf parents and relatives whilst the other five came from hearing families.

Two initial meetings were held, and the group were eager to continue this process. Indeed I noticed on several occasions that members of the forum were having further informal discussions about material which had come up in the meetings, during which further topics were discussed which they had never considered hitherto. It seemed clear that this form of research continued the process of catalytic validity, and had effects on its participants in ways that most research on Deaf people does not touch on.

Each meeting lasted an hour (a lunchtime session) and the topics were presented by Dorothy, one of the original four interviewed. They focused on material produced in those interviews which none of us had seen or considered before. I remained silent during the sessions, partly to make notes more easily and partly to see how the material would flow without my influence.

Filming this group proved difficult, because the number of Deaf signers that can be easily 'read' and transcribed from videotape is two; three is difficult, and four upwards is nearly impossible. Thus the number of cameras involved and the synching up of tapes on different machines for the transcription process was particularly time-consuming. Indeed, the unwieldiness of this exercise served as a deterrent to organising further sessions, even though those involved wanted more.

This deterrent to future sessions was unfortunate in respect of my silence mentioned earlier, as I came to feel that if I had 'guided' the sessions by interjecting questions at specific points, the discussions could have been more focused.

Implications for the second stage

The interviews and forums generated data of so much richness, breadth and depth that it proved difficult to establish boundaries and limits for the rest of the study. Themes completely new to me emerged; several appeared never to have been touched on in any Deaf-related literature, whether focused on culture or not. Some of these became so important that the rest of the study had either to incorporate them or, in some cases, shaped the rest of the study in their own right.

Of the two which were of greatest significance, one concerned the opening up of historical dimensions within Deaf culture. The other revealed the emergence of that dynamic within the culture which I termed the 'deafness–Deafhood' dynamic – the internal tensions that inform and help shape Deaf behaviours and philosophies, which chiefly concern whether to orient one's self towards Deaf or 'Hearing' ways of being. Both were intertwined in their own complex set of dynamics.

Given the difficulties of defining Deaf culture at a time when all cultures are undergoing transformation, I decided to focus on the historical dimension and the two 'traditional' sites in which Deaf culture evolved – the eras when all Deaf people attended Deaf schools and then moved onto the clubs; and the manifestations of the dynamic described earlier found therein.

Second Stage Strategies

The implications for the methodology were that I had to adopt a judgement sample strategy, and this was conducted as follows:

Initially I had to seek out Deaf people whom I knew from experience could contribute to the historical dimension or who could lead me to others who could make such a contribution. This led me to interview some older Deaf people, including those with whom I made contact at the local old people's club. I also had to locate middle-aged Deaf people who were particularly historically oriented. I also found it necessary to interview one hearing child of Deaf parents. Some of the respondents were chosen for their potential to speak in an articulate way to the subject, while for others it was a matter of painfully trying to draw them out about past Deaf life.

(Chapter 8, as will be seen, contains considerable evidence of past social divisions. It was particularly difficult to draw information from the old people to support or refute these. Initially I assumed that the failure was mine, but even after I had enlisted the help of one of the middle-aged club members that they most trusted, the difficulty remained. Other ethnographers have drawn attention to the difficulty in eliciting certain kinds of information from elderly people, especially on subjects which reminded them of past negative feelings. This, then, is the best explanation I can presently offer for my lack of success in that domain.) It also became very important to read as much Deaf historical material as could be found in order to triangulate some of the data that were being generated.

At the same time, I had to seek out Deaf people who could contribute to the Deafhood/deafness dynamic using similar strategies. Four main routes presented themselves from the data. The first necessitated locating Deaf people with 'strong Deaf' views. Most were middle-aged, but one or two younger Deaf people with Deaf parents were also able to 'dig deep' and articulate some of their deeply held perspectives. The second required me to investigate several sites where such Deaf people were in the rare position of working with young Deaf children, to study how the process of transmitting their 'Deaf' ideas was shaped and developed by their self-reflections on such themes, and how this related to who and what shaped their own lives.

Aware of the extent to which cultural rules and traditions only emerged when such rules were broken (cf. Garfinkel, 1967), led me to interview Deaf people already known to challenge these rules and traditions. The fourth, which emerged from the American data, concerned the signs of cultural fragmentation which began with the growth of a Deaf professional class. I decided to focus on the views of this class rather than the views of others towards them, partly because this introduced more complexity than the study could handle, and partly because, by selecting these from among the 'strong Deaf', aspects of self-division could be observed and discussed with those informants. In all of this, I drew on my Deaf experience to pursue judgement sampling in locating the appropriate informants.

Additional Strategies

At this point, one aspect of research with subaltern Deaf people became clear; that what are known as 'Strong Deaf' views had never been recorded in any depth nor, apparently, any attempt to let such people speak on their own terms. I attempted to encourage them to articulate the deeper cultural beliefs that gave them that strength and guided, shaped and motivated their daily actions.

I came more and more to feel that if I could locate forms and forums that simply allowed them to express themselves and reveal the underlying beliefs, that the study could achieve catalytic validity in its own right. This was because (to give one example) Deaf education stood in great need of understanding the children from a Deaf-centred point of view. It became clear that revealing these 'Strong Deaf' insights could speed up this process.

Having pursued 'Strong Deaf' themes and individuals, I was then confronted with methodological issues surrounding typicality and variation. On the one hand, there was more than enough data to focus solely on expressing their insights. On the other, I felt an obligation to attempt a certain amount of typicality. Deciding on the latter course, I interviewed a number of Deaf people, mostly young, who were completing a Deaf Studies course, intending to glean a dual set of perspectives, loosely described as 'before and after'. Although a number of these interviews did not reveal much, others proved extremely rich, whilst others opened up further areas which had to be set aside in order to focus the study.

In considering typicality further, I felt that since I had examined the 'centre' of the Deaf community, it was also necessary to observe marginality and its relationships with this centre. Consequently, I met with and interviewed younger 'hard-of-hearing' people on the fringe of the community to see how their perspectives on Deaf cultural life related to some of the realities that had been documented. At this point, I felt that the study was also risking becoming too 'thin', and decided to put aside other 'marginal' examples, although if they emerged in interviews, I allowed them to develop. It was with regret I had to set Black Deaf issues to one side, deciding that these were more easily investigated and contrasted when 'traditional' British Deaf culture was better documented, although the Black Deaf dimension of the preliminary study had proved valuable in suggesting leads to be followed.

Thus, by the end of the study, I had formally videotaped interviews with 31 Deaf and hard of hearing people, ages ranging from 18 to 85, mostly coming from different parts of England. I had informal discussions with over 90 more, most of which were not filmed, and therefore notes were made after the event.

Third Stage Strategies

Finally, I intended to test out some of the emerging data by bringing it back to the forum for discussion, and by giving lectures or facilitating some discussions based on the data, the results of which were, in turn, fed back into the study. Time did not permit the former, but the latter proved valuable.

Once the study reached its penultimate draft, I intended to satisfy the conditions of respondent validation by sending those who could read English the quotations I had taken from their interviews, and inviting comment. For those who were not comfortable with English, I intended to meet each again and either go through my translation of what they had said or ask them to watch the video and comment further. The latter course proved difficult to achieve, as some had moved away and many lived a long way from my home base; thus time and money intervened to limit our contact. Additionally, since the penultimate draft was still being written and revised near to the closing date for submission, it was not always possible to seek out comment when the text could not easily be changed.

Another qualification concerns the use of video cameras. It was not practicable to use a second camera focused on myself, which meant that, unlike audiotaped interviews, it was not possible to study and analyse the way I framed my questions, and how that might have influenced the responses. It has been suggested that I could have included myself in the single camera shot, but I felt that this was seriously detrimental to an accurate analysis and rendition of the informants' *affect*, which I deemed as important as what was actually said.

Questions surrounding the feasibility or otherwise of developing an overarching framework were considered throughout but allowed centre place only in the last months, when all the data had been collected and final assimilation of the accumulated knowledge and experience occurred.

Additional Issues

This being the first study of its kind, a tremendous amount of data was generated which could not be included in the final text without rendering the data too 'thin' to sustain the concepts presented. This included material which illustrated Deaf culture's national, international and diasporic dimensions, dynamics of present-day Deaf club life and the different new social groupings in the community which illustrated important changes. Presentation of these data will therefore be deferred to the next book in this series. However, these themes tended to amplify the concepts presented in the data chapters rather than alter them qualitatively.

Nevertheless, the special nature of researching the cultural features of a visuo-gestural language community produced some additional methodological issues.

Translation and transcription issues

Translation brought its own methodological considerations. One concerned the length of time necessary to transcribe the data. The implications of filming, translating and transcribing group data applied, in a lesser degree, to the single subject interviews. Each minute of sign communication required on average 10 minutes to initially translate and transcribe; this figure was at least double for a response considered for inclusion in the final drafts. The length of this process tended to act as a deterrent for conducting further interviews.

Similarly complex issues surrounded the nature of the translations themselves. Although transcription orthographies have now been conventionalised in sign language linguistics, there has been little printed discussion about translation (though in regard to other languages, see Hymes, 1974, 1981; Gee *et al.*, 1992).

This posed difficulties whenever the responses from Deaf participants required more than a 'flat' English rendering of what was signed. Since the data I had collected were often passionately expressed and sometimes metaphorically and poetically rendered, I faced the possibility of actual mistranslation if the effect was not properly captured in English. Yet without any conventionally agreed strategies for so doing, or even suggestions and guidance, it proved difficult to move beyond subjectivity.

In many cases, I was satisfied with my renderings. But in others I was less sure that it was possible to capture the passion and beauty or the poetical and metaphorical depths of the responses in English without having to quote at considerable length. This then negatively affected the amount of data which could be quoted, and thus *the number of themes that the reporting chapters could handle, and the depth of the coverage.* This, in turn, posed difficulties for rendering the total 'picture' in sufficient depth or for capturing each stage requiring explication which built up to the final picture. Because deafness is such an unknown field, and the subject under investigation radically new, the limitations imposed on the explication were particularly frustrating and challenging. This particularly affected the aim of rendering the 'structure of feeling' of Deaf cultural life.

I identified five characteristics of the data which contributed to these methodological problems:

(1) Deaf culture and BSL is particularly strong in descriptive detail, storytelling being a major way of making points. (Some commentators including Foley [1988] have drawn attention to the prominence of storytelling in informal social settings, and the parallels with other 'oral' cultures.) Some of this detail proved difficult to shorten without failing to do justice to the full depths of what was said.

(2) A related theme, the detail involved in what are almost literally 'theatrical' re-enactments of key moments, proved especially difficult to render in full without absorbing large chunks of the available wordspace. Direct speech dialogue 're-enactments' were particularly common.

(3) Repetition is also a feature of sign languages, and many oral cultures (Gee, 1989c; Edwards & Sienkewicz, 1991). Removing them 'hurts' the underlying sense of the texts.

(4) One feature of sign languages rarely remarked upon is the ability to create new lexical items and metaphors on the spot, many of them extremely 'clever', which may or may not be used again in the future. To merely translate the sense of these does a disservice to the text and, as with the other points described here, ultimately produces translations that are affectively, and thus ultimately, inaccurate.

(5) Lengthy poetical responses, which to the native-researcher are extremely beautiful, are not necessarily seen in this way by outsiders (cf. Blauner, 1987). To explicate the importance of such beauty also ate into the word-count.

Some of these issues occur in anthropological accounts of societies which couch their reponses in story, metaphor and symbol. However, there appears to be little systematic discussion of translation issues as a methodological problem. And of course, these are all spoken languages which differ in fundamental ways from signed languages and their use of the visual domain and neurolinguistic processing channels.

In summary, the linguistic richness of the responses is a major part of Deaf culture, *representing part of its joie de vivre in the face of oppression*, and counterbalances the apparent negativity of some of the data. Capturing this adequately required much more space than is available.

Strategies of submitting the study partially in video form posed severe problems of confidentiality. Because of the wide variation in BSL dialects and idiolects, it is not easy for another native-speaker to 'imitate' the excerpts, and this too still requires a breach of confidentiality. Presenting the study in this form is extremely rare, raising questions of assessment in the absence of a formal academic tradition (though see Myerhoff [1980] and Rollwagen [1988]).

One other translation issue was of particular importance. Each respondent had their own idiolect, partly attributable to class and gender factors. Some also used more BSL than others, who used a BSL/ Signed English mixture. The boundaries between these two concepts are themselves still a hotly debated issue. Thus the question also arose of how to locate different English styles which might not be equivalent.

For some, it was tempting to use a particular kind of 'semi-English' which also reflected some BSL structures. However, it must be remembered that the study deals with an oppressed group, and to render excerpts in 'pidgin-English' is risky and also not necessarily supported by the respondents. Consistency was crucial; thus if half the respondents were happy with such a rendering and half not, the whole idea would have had to be abandoned and some other translation methodology devised. Often, those 'deep BSL' users that this was most relevant for did not have a confident enough grasp of English to check my translations, other than for basic meaning. Faced with this 'Catch–22' situation, I compromised by discussing some of the more 'extreme' examples with those involved, and gaining their approval for their final versions.

Finally it should be noted that these issues added considerably to the amount of time required to process the data into its final form. I estimate that this brought the translation time up to one hour per one minute of data used.

Confidentiality issues

These were unusually important. Since the Deaf community is a small and closely knit, it was all too easy to reveal the speaker by even the slightest piece of background information. Additionally, the majority of people likely to read the final text would be hearing people in Deaf work, some of whom might be in a position to oppress the Deaf persons they identified. Consequently, in circumstances where two sets of information could be pieced together to identify the person concerned, the only strategy I could devise was to divide responses from one person to create a second individual. Fortunately this was only necessary in one case.

Respondent validation issues

Respondent validation could have been handled differently if the scope of the study had been less wide, and this also affected the interviewing strategy. Spradley (1979) considers it ideal to conduct 'cross-interviews' to tease out contradictions, ceasing to interview when the data are 'saturated' – i.e. generates nothing new. This was not possible with such a wide sample of respondents and range of subject matter nor with the translation issues mentioned earlier.

When transcribing the data, I also noticed some informants had a negative attitude to subaltern Deaf people and to BSL, which came through in their signing *affect*. This made respondent validation difficult – where I had commented in the text on these attitudes, I had to decide whether to show them to the informants and risk their anger and withdrawal of cooperation/printing (Rubin, 1976) or whether to not do so and have them read them in the text later, constituting an act of betrayal. The ideal solution, to use my comments as a springboard for further discussion, was not possible due to time constraints.

I attempted to remedy this by interviewing central respondents again in the final year, consciously seeking out apparent contradictions or discontinuities. This was a partial solution at best, since this process continued to generate new data which, although it enabled further depths to be explored, could not always be accomodated in the final text. This methodological problem is not really dealt with in critical ethnography literature, where little consideration is given to word limits as a factor affecting the research.

Finally, I wished to allow each person to select their own pseudonym or even use their own name where desired. Although this is traditionally seen as undesirable, Myerhoff (1980) and others attest to many informants' desire not to be 'depersonalised' and a few did, in fact, wish to be identified by their own name.

Loss of main informant

The methodologies and strategies discussed here were greatly influenced by the loss of my main Deaf informant at a very early stage in the study. Dorothy Miles was unique in that she had lived in both the UK and the USA for over 20 years, had consciously studied both languages and cultures, created signed-art in both languages and, unusually for Deaf people, had studied both majority cultures. I would never have devised my particular strategies for researching Deaf culture if I had known she would not play a major role in it, as I had hoped to utilise her skills to help decide each round of strategies. Without her presence, the sophistication and subtlety of my methodology was greatly diminished.

Just before the third stage, another major informant, a uniquely talented Deaf cultural theorist, died suddenly. This also had an impact on shaping the data. The further loss of three more people had less effect, but the cumulative stress of this affected the study. Clearly, although being a member of a collective community offers numerous joys, it also increases the number of friends and acquaintances whose death one must experience. Although such setbacks might occur to ethnographers who are not members of the groups they study, events such as these confirm the special nature of the methodological issues surrounding the subaltern-researcher.

Subaltern-researcher issues

The subaltern-élite dynamic is classically found within other minority discourses – the First Nation or Black person placed within majority education who becomes alienated and thus radicalised (Fanon, 1986) or the working-class 'scholarship boys' who became the founders of Cultural Studies (Hoggart, 1958; Williams, 1958).

We have already discussed the cautionary notes expressed by Hannerz (1992) and Caulfield (1973) which suggest that a native trained in the colonialist academy might be compromised by that training. Similar reservations can been posed within critical ethnography, where much of the work is still felt to be 'constrained by the language games of the academy' (Quantz, 1992: 469), whilst Corrigan (1989) questions whether breaking through such constraints will meet with academic recognition and advancement, and posits that awareness of this might act on the individual researcher. Although advancement is a temptation for everyone, no matter what their class, it is certainly true that the subaltern researcher will experience conflicting pulls in this respect which might lead them to hide from themselves certain aspects of that conflict in order to pursue the opposite course.

Nonetheless, it can still be posited that the data in Chapters 7, 8 and 9 could not have been obtained by non-community members. Similarly, at this point in history, very few Deaf people would have been able to do so, partly because of lack of access to higher education, and partly because of the truism that those fully inside a culture often take its basic tenets for granted, and think them not worth remarking upon. It seemed that my coming late to the community gave me a bicultural perspective which assisted the data collection.

Nevertheless, some methodological problems arose from my own status. The research process itself was profoundly personally challenging. Although I thought I had overcome the prejudices implanted by an oralist education, conducting the study showed me otherwise. I found that my own unrealised prescriptivism prevented me for some time from seeing what was happening before my eyes; having based my community membership around commiment and activism, the 'Deaf should' syndrome had become a veil between me and some aspects of Deaf reality. This is examined more closely in Chapter 10.

Another set of problems concerned cultural over-familiarity, which has only received minimal discussed within ethnography (Spindler & Spindler, 1992). It took a long time to sit back from Deaf social interaction and 'make the familiar strange', and this was only partially achieved. This was also complicated by my particular status in the Deaf community; it was very difficult to go into clubs and groups without conversation and discussions being converted into topics centred around the issues for which I was known.

Thus my status was a two-edged sword; on the one hand, it allowed me deep access to respondents who felt they were part of a shared project ('doing it for all Deaf people') whilst, on the other, it limited my participant-observation opportunities. It was at times like this that I acutely felt the absence of anthropological or ethnographic guidance. It is also possible that some of the younger respondents were intimidated by my status and would have opened up more deeply to younger Deaf interviewers.

Whilst transcribing the data, I was struck by the number of times the informants questioned me in turn. My initial analysis of this phenomenon was that this indicated the co-operative spirit of the research; I then realised that it also indicated some Deaf cultural discourse strategies. There was not sufficient time and space to analyse this or organise these responses into categories.

All these issues and several more besides, have implications for the development of subaltern-researcher theory and thus for wider ethnographic and academic theory (see Chapter 10).

Summary – Implications for Research Chapters

The reader has already experienced some of these implications – the experiences and interactions with both community and informants made it possible to offer a much more sophisticated reading of both the Deaf historical review in Chapters 2 and 3 and the review of the Deaf cultural literature in Chapter 5. Indeed, the community's own epistemological processes and discourses resulted in data and theories previously excluded from academic recognition being incorporated into those chapters.

This being the first study of UK Deaf culture, it is concerned to seek hypotheses with the capability of maximal generalisability. Thus Chapters 7–9 prioritise the identification of a series of dimensions within the culture which can form the basis for those hypotheses. These are gleaned from the two major domains within which Deaf culture has developed – the residential schools (Chapter 7) and the Deaf clubs (Chapter 8).

The two major dimensions manifested in these chapters are historical time and social class. From these emerges a third, the dialectical relationship between the colonialist concept of 'deafness' and Deaf people's own self-concept, which I have already termed 'Deafhood'. Chapter 9 describes how this dialectic has continued to manifest itself in more recent and contemporary Deaf cultural life, and thus enables us to confirm the existence of long-standing Deaf cultural patterns. This, in turn, enables us to confirm fairly confidently the existence of the Deaf cultural concept.

The approaches thus developed in this methodology are then followed through to produce conclusions and implications for a wide range of domains, both within the academy and without, both within the deafness disourse and with implications for other academic discourses. Chapter 10 therefore assesses these dimensions against the academic literature relating to culture and community in general and Deaf culture in particular, identifying implications for those criteria. It also assesses the extent to which the study has satisfied critical ethnographic and transparency criteria, and suggests implications for the academy from the subaltern-researcher perspective gained. Finally, it identifies key conceptual and policy implications for both Deaf communities and external agencies.

Having utilised these new tools to make the final ascent, therefore, we can now to begin to look around the vistas of the Deaf landscape thus revealed. We begin by descending into the valley of childhood.

Notes

1. This principle also applies of course to other aspects of one's habitus – one can be a 'recovering oralist' in the same sense as one might refer to being a recovering Catholic or a recovering alcoholic. And of course this forms part of the similar work of eradicating sexist and racist traces from one's life.

Chapter 7

The Roots of Deaf Culture: Residential Schools

My mother, bless her . . . three years before she died we had a hell of a row . . . She said, 'They told me I must never sign to you and they were right' . . . Oh God! 'You think I got a good education simply by you not signing to me?! *If I hadn't signed with the Deaf, I wouldn't have got an education at all!*

(Raymond Lee)

Introduction

As we have seen, apart from the Deaf networks that existed prior to formal Deaf education, the first Deaf cultural site which represents the tradition we know today is the Deaf residential school experience. This chapter identifies two fundamental dynamics – the negative effects of oralist colonialism on the culture and the positive *collective* responses of Deaf children to that oppression. The interplay between these dynamics informs and expands our understanding of the 'deafness–Deafhood' axis within the culture.

The Significance of Deaf Residential Schools

Chapter 2 described the importance of Deaf schools – the domain where the community language was learned, overtly at first, and covertly after Oralism; where manifold aspects of socialisation into Deaf experience occurred; and (again prior to Oralism), where instruction in how to conduct one's self in an alien majority society was provided by the Deaf teachers and adults who worked in the schools.

Most of the data here are given by people recalling the period from 1945 to 1960. The negative experiences were triangulated with other accounts of the Deaf school experience under Oralism, and found to be congruent. Many of the dynamics may well apply also to the period 1880–1945. The data revealing positive and collective Deaf experiences and actions have rarely been described in the literature – this chapter brings aspects of these to the forefront, many for the first time.

Community and identity

Peggy, from the North-West and in her early fifties, left the Deaf community for 20 years and then returned. She was thus in a good position to summarise the importance of the school experience to Deaf identity and culture:

> When you're out of Deaf life, no matter how much you deny it, there's something missing inside of you. The same for those I see who've come from hearing [mainstreamed] schools, when they watch us talk about residential days. It feels like a private club membership – 'Been Deaf school? Here's a badge. Been Deaf school? That's it, finish, in'. Very difficult for others to get in; can do but not straightaway . . . When out of community for a long time, then back, it's really hit me that I have that identity and community deep inside, and know who I am. Deaf, that's fine.

Other informants also indicated the importance of identity and community formed and developed in the schools.

Resistance to hearing influence

Emma, from a London Deaf family, summarised the difference between those who attended residential schools and others, when talking of her parents, who both completed their schooling before the war:

> Both my parents are from hearing families – father stayed at home and grew up very oral, Mother went to Deaf school at 4 and stayed there almost all the year. I used to watch their arguments when I was little. She's more like 'Don't hearing tell me what to do!', and he's like 'Respect the hearing'.

This example is interesting because there are many others (cf. Widell and Mally in Chapter 2) which suggest that post-Oralism, Deaf people grew up with a profound inferiority complex towards hearing people. I take this example to be relative – being in close contact with one's parents (whether or not one could communicate with them) meant that one was more likely to develop a deferential relationship with hearing people generally, whilst if one's Deaf peers formed the primary relationship in life, then one might be more able to stand up for one's Deaf rights in later life.

School as primary family

Deaf primary relationships were akin to, or even replaced, the birth family relationship. Several informants used the image of 'family' to describe their school situation, mostly memorably, 'a family of brothers and sisters moving onwards and upwards', and several referred to the reluctance of Deaf children to go 'home' at weekends and holidays. As Raymond Lee, in his late forties and from the North-East, put it:

> The pupils . . . who travelled home everyday really wanted to stay at the school like those who were boarders. They were happy just signing away with the others for the rest of the night, but were made to get on off home. Where their oral parents would be wagging their fingers at them and going 'Buh, buh, buh' [Deaf way of mocking people speaking at them]. And inside they were really resentful. When they came back next morning, they were frantically signing away to make up for lost time!

(He talked of others who were happy to go home, but 'for one simple reason . . . they could stay up later and watch the old-fashioned black and white TV. And better food at home too!')

Peggy concurred:

> Home was all right, but boring. I was excited to get back to school. And as for holiday times, it was like, 'Oh nooo, holiday time's coming', and we would all become very sad.

This sadness or even fear of school holidays marks a significant difference between Deaf and hearing childhood experience. A further difference is that Deaf children only experienced the place in which they were 'normal' as a 'working' time – having holidays and relaxing time out of school together occurred so rarely as to be almost non-existent. If we were to calculate the number of hours of actual, direct communication in one's own language with one's peers, it is only in the residential school that this number would even begin to approximate the number of hours experienced and taken for granted as socially necessary for every hearing child. In this respect, communication for many Deaf children was literally, as Raymond says, a matter of 'lost time'. To make matters worse, of course, this domain of normality was also marked by the everyday experience of 'failure' in the standards set by Oralism, and the effect that this feeling had on the levels of discourse possible. All these differences have therefore also left their imprints on the culture of the community they grow up to join.

Several informants emphasised that in past times Deaf children went home much less often, and for shorter periods of time than nowadays, so there was much more time to build on their own group experiences. Others gave descriptions of all the activities, the hobbies and sports which took place after lessons finished, none of which they could have such easy access to if they had been at home.

'A normal community life'

Several informants were at pains to stress that the residential school experience not only established Deaf identity and community, but also built one's character as an individual, and helped one become independent and self-reliant. Raymond gave a moving in-depth description of one aspect of that experience:

> It's especially important for the stages of life, up through your childhood. For the very youngest children, at such a young age, when they might be psychologically nervous/uncertain about being Deaf, to see other children like themselves helps them to feel good about themselves. They start to *realise that they are kin,* start to jostle and play. Safety in numbers, you might say. That's the start of communication, the start of friendships. That's the first re-assurance.

He then identified the next stages:

> Then you can look up towards the next oldest group. 'Ooh, they play football, they play tennis, oh, me will same when older. They talk together differently', (maybe psychologically a bit higher up), 'I will same too' . . . Then the next stage, intermediate, there's the bigger boys, strong and sturdy, who protect us. We'll be like them . . . Then up again, there's the senior boys. 'Oooh! Men!' 'And there's no end to it. You don't die at 16.'

Interestingly, this account is told from the perspective of the smallest children, giving a visual emphasis that is part of the power of sign languages, creating a picture of one's future identities manifesting themselves before their young eyes. (The reference to not dying at 16 has an importance that becomes clear shortly.) He continued:

> When they themselves move up, the older boys they saw before – they've gone. Where? Then sports day, in the old boys' football match, ahhh, there they are! Life outside! 'You been where?' 'Me work.' 'Work – oh, what's that? Where?' and so on.

Finally he gives an eloquent summary of the entire process, which carries even more power when seen in BSL:

> And so round and round it goes, in an ever-ascending spiral of knowledge and development; you grow in confidence and you know where you will be going. It's important! On this journey, you have to accept language development, community development, and cultural inheritance. They develop themselves, yes, but they inherit it too. And they become part of the larger Deaf whole as the cycle moves on. So,

through this, *Deaf people have the knowledge that everything IS normal – to them!* [peaceful contented smile].

Of course, this is also the last place where they are able to feel 'normal', before leaving for a life of 'permanent exile' in another world. This assertion of normality is crucial. The experience which Raymond describes resembles that of a 'normal' hearing childhood. That such a 'normal' life experience *cannot be found outside the residential environment* informs Deaf perceptions of the Deaf school experience, no matter how awful we might think the oralist experience was. Consequently it informs their present views about day schools and mainstreaming.

'First contact'

The delight described here was felt by several informants when they entered school, once their first traumas of leaving home were overcome. As Olivia, a North-West Deaf woman in her mid-twenties, put it:

When me small, me believed I was the only Deaf person in the world. Then I went to Deaf school, and found I could gesture to them and be understood, and that was *it* right away – I loved it!

Another in her mid-twenties from the South, Ursula said:

I started to sign outside in the playground – 'shh! be careful' – it was sooo easy to take in – I went round with my mouth wide open! I loved to sign so much, me and the others, we were the same, so I would copy, copy, copy, and improve my signing.

This thirst for one's own language was widely reported. Raymond's experience was slightly different:

I saw all these hands waving around; I was awestruck and froze to the spot. I remember that – I was four and a half, five, and a kid came up and signed to me, and I shrank back . . . Yet I identified myself with him like that < snaps fingers >. Yep, that moment *opened me to the world, really.*

Once again, there is nothing ostensibly abnormal about these experiences. But of course, many of these Deaf children had waited for at least 5 years before being able to begin a 'normal' interaction and relationships with other human beings. It is hard for a lay person to grasp the enormity of the situation obtaining under Oralism which has resulted in a linguistic (and to an as-yet unresearched degree, emotional) orphaning of the Deaf child. However, this can also happen in situations where the parents do sign, since to understand this Deaf need for one's own peer group is to begin to understand the importance of the residential school in Deaf culture.

There is, however, another kind of first contact, however, as Barry, in his fifties from the North-West, describes:

> Me 3 when first arrived at school – remember, wow, vividly the nuns' huge headpieces [acts this all out with great detail and power] . . . couldn't sign or talk . . . when they strapped these huge hearing aids on me, and me trying to figure out what was happening, what they were for . . . slowly worked it out – mean I can't talk, still can't hear with this thing, *means I'm deaf!*

This is a difficult passage to transcribe as it was rendered so intensely. In essence it contrasts with the peer group experiences described earlier. Those contacts resembled normality, Deafhood, whereas the classroom experience saw one absorb the deafness label representing abnormality. The battles which took place between these two readings informs not only the rest of the chapter, but the rest of the book.

A national identity

The residential school was also important because of the regional and national catchment system which many used. These suggest a cultural awareness of a Deaf nationhood. Ken, in his fifties from the North West, explained:

> We would get out a map of the UK, and work out where everybody came from. At the end of it, you'd have dots for Deaf kids from Land's End to John O'Groats! We used to say 'We cover the whole country, mate – *we have a Deaf country of our own!*'

Raymond had the same experience, and added:

> We began to know the geography of Britain based on that. 'You from there [points to map], 'me here, him there.' They think of their community as an island – the Deaf British Isles. Not some little tiny dot's worth of nothing. Their community *is* the whole island to them . . . Whereas with mainstreaming, where are you? Just a tiny dot within another tiny dot of a local town or village? No thanks. Me – my community is from Liverpool to Aberdeen down to Brighton to Torquay!

These accounts might surprise the outsider given the negative experiences of oral schooling; however, the number of positive Deaf responses on the subjects confirms what the informants say. Indeed, the extent to which the experience of being together outweighed such negativity indicates the importance of more research into this core of Deaf life, especially since it is a major problem for Deaf communities that these perspectives are literally incredible to those in power and to parents.

Many day pupils or those from day schools may have had somewhat different experiences. They too loved to be with their fellow Deaf, but not having the opportunity to participate in the intense post-school activities, meant that they had many hours less, and cumulatively many years less socialisation, less world and Deafworld-knowledge, and less chance to develop their full identity. In effect, they experienced the negatives of this chapter with fewer of the positives.

Life under Oralism

Almost all the informants talked extensively of their experiences under Oralism – the 10–15 years of ritualised humiliation which constituted their education (which, if the outside world had been informed, would long ago have led to prosecutions for widespread child abuse). These experiences, described also in McDonnell and Saunders (1993), and other Deaf accounts, seem to have obtained for most of this century. Since these have already been recorded, only the bare minimum of examples are given here in order to establish the background against which to understand the significance of the Deaf cultural responses.

Barry gave another vivid description, this time of the nuns in full flight:

> They would come striding towards you, walking right at us, forcing us to stumble backwards, mouthing out words, spitting as they did so – afterwards you could be full wet, but never knew what they said! Poking you, twisting your ear, sometimes you didn't even know what you supposed to have done.

The images of yawning mouths and wagging fingers were widely used. In working out what infringements had been committed, one was of course very clear – signing. Gefilte, a Jewish woman from the South-West, in her mid-twenties with a Deaf mother, described her first moments in the oral classroom:

> Teacher said, 'name? where from?' all in speech. Came to me, I fingerspelt my name ... oh oh – Boom! Teacher picked me right up off the ground, held me dangling in front of the class and said 'What's that? That's a monkey!' I just stood there wondering what was happening. Teacher said 'Out' ... The rest of the class just sat there trembling.

A similar experience was related by Gloria Pullen in one of the very rare TV documentaries that was actually about the lives of Deaf people (*A Certain Pride*, BBC TV, 1983). We will see later what effect equating those who signed with animals had on those who internalised such imagery. Punishment for signing was usually more ritualised, and several informants described a kaleidoscope of such rituals. Peggy mentioned having to go without meals, whilst Ursula talked of a speech marks system, where those with the least marks (i.e. the most Deaf) were also punished at the end of the week. At Ken's school, the children were encouraged to inform on each other if they saw anyone signing. Barry's summary of punishments was the most concise:

> Cane on hand, buttocks, flick-of-wrist smack on legs – the nuns were really skilled at that one! – hams . . . sent to 'prison', dunce cap, not allowed out, loss of privileges like evening parties – that meant a lot because of the food there! Girls had some different types of punishments. Lots more really.

As if these were not enough, he went on:

> But you should ask the older folks; it was even worse for them, even crueller.

For Martha, from the Midlands in her mid-fifties, the 'prison' was the coal cellar, which we will hear more of shortly. Accounts such as these could fill a whole book in themselves (and indeed should do). Peggy's account of mealtimes was particularly poignant:

> In dining room, caught signing, told to leave the room or to sit facing the wall – no food. But it was so hard *not* to sign in there! Imagine eating a meal going 'Fessaba, Fessaba' [a Deaf sign for imitating speaking] – with all that food visible, rolling around in their mouths. Everybody would bring their hands up and down, signing tiny little bits, using bits of body language, of face expressions, then stop suddenly, look round and make sure you hadn't been seen, then more little bits. Impossible situation.

Several others also gave vivid accounts of the difficulties of trying to 'sign whilst not signing', which were likewise simultaneously amusing and sad.

Other accounts were simply sad – each person described other children who were too Deaf to begin to comprehend what they were supposed to do, and the extent to which they were consequently victimised by teachers. Peggy's was perhaps the most concise:

> I remember one boy, 'Um Deaf' [completely Deaf], absolutely no lip patterns at all, and in class we'd have to be reading to ourselves from a book going 'Fessaba, Fessaba' – everyday if you over 12, and teacher check we reading by watching us mouth those words. And of course that boy had nothing to produce of course. I remember thinking 'Why

make him? Why make him go through this?' And all our faces like stone, would only come alive for our own signed stories. Every day. Like we all just knew, we all accepted that there'd be these meaningless mouth movements and we'd just go with it.

This experience, like all the others, has almost never been captured on film. The only example I know of is the equivalent scenes in Channel 4's *Pictures in the Mind* (1987), a rare Deaf-centred drama-documentary on their education. So complacent about the whole Deaf education situation were the teachers, that in allowing their oral work to be filmed, they had not even given any thought to what the film might 'give away'. More appropriate settings for Foucault's concepts of *discipline* and *surveillance* than these, where almost every act of communication was forbidden, could scarcely be imagined.

The actual 'educational' experience was described in similar terms by many; they spoke of the intense efforts of spending many hours being forced to make sounds at the expense of actually learning, of trying to lipread or make sense of what was happening, of trying to bluff, of giving up and 'letting it all sail past them' (still a common sign-trope in BSL and ASL), and of copying from the board. Barry described the latter:

They'd write on the board, and we would copy it. Then they would give you good marks and you would swagger about. But what did those words mean? Ha! Nothing! It all went past us . . . Yet those two-faced people would give us good marks and pat us on the head.

Even those deemed successful at school described the process as an intense struggle. A number found their speech praised, yet on reaching the outside world endured the humiliation of finding their teachers had been lying to them. This realisation shattered the self-image they had built up to protect them through their school years – suddenly they were not who they thought they were.

Life under Oralism varied, of course. Some schools would turn a blind eye to signing outside the classroom, whilst some pursued it relentlessly. However, the accounts given here can safely be taken as the norm from which variations can be measured.

Creating a Positive Deaf Experience

What follows has rarely been recorded, yet is fundamental to an understanding of how such intense oppression can be regarded as a domain of equally intense pleasure and cultural development for so many. This section focuses on the collectivity and unity which stands at its core.

The joy of signing

Almost all the informants described situations and strategies that they devised so that they could communicate with each other. Barry summarised their experiences:

> We'd get together in the playground, stand in a circle or an oval, so the teachers couldn't see in, and sign away to each other. To tell stories, we'd hide, round corners, in the toilets, wherever. Or go downstairs, and one would keep their foot by the door so when somebody came by, they would feel that person's vibrations, and tell us, so we'd all put our hands down sharpish.

(One unfortunate consequence of this was that for many, BSL came to associated with the smell of toilets [see also Mally, 1993 for the case in Germany] – hardly conducive to feelings of respect for one's own language.)

Another famous signing domain was the dormitories. Ralph, in his thirties from the South, described how they got round the problem of lighting:

> I liked playing with electrical things, so I rigged up this device; when the dorm door was closed, the lights came on, and when it opened, they went off. And it worked fine for a long time, but one night, the teacher left and the door went shut and then opened slightly, so of course the lights went on and then off again! They took a closer look, and then of course that was the end of that!

From the outside, such escapades conjur up the image of prison camps, yet none of the Deaf informants expressed that connection, so normal did it all seem to them; if the parallel seems exaggerated, many other examples confirm it in the extreme degree to which the farce was sometimes carried. Barry explained:

> Even when the lights were out, we'd be lying in bed trying to sign to each other. But we knew the teachers would be watching us through a sliding panel. So we'd try and sign without moving! [gives demonstration] But next morning, some of us would be in trouble for signing in the dorm. And we'd say 'How can you tell? You didn't see anyone signing – it was dark'. And they'd say 'I saw your toes moving, boy'. Yes, really! Deaf would be given away through their feet were moving!

Many accounts were told so animatedly that it was clear that no little amount of pleasure was gained from these fights against the odds, gambles which existed for every minute of every waking day for 10–15 years. Such a dynamic creates its own essential characteristics, which could certainly be explored in more depth. Certainly it is undeniable that the joy of communication must have been the greater for never being taken for granted.

It can also be argued that a '1001 Victories' concept, described more fully in the next chapter, originated in the Deaf school under Oralism, since, as these accounts suggest, each getting together and communicating was a significant 'little' victory. The remainder of the chapter should be read with that concept in mind.

Storytelling

Storytelling was the most common positive theme. Stefan, from London and in his fifties, even linked this to Nature:

> My bed was next to the window, so that gave me authority over the curtains. Now my [Deaf] sis always signed me bedtime stories. So when people wanted stories, I'd open the curtains and sign some. But of course there wasn't always enough moonlight. So what it came to was that when the moon was full, we could have plenty of stories, that one period of the month... Then someone had a brilliant idea – if moon was there but cloudy, then we'd add a torch!

His roommates used a voluntary rotation system for storytelling, as did Martha, Peggy and Barry. (An example of this experience can actually be seen in Francois Truffaut's film set in the Paris school in 1775 – *L'Enfant Sauvage*.) The topics of the stories varied widely and were drawn from book-based accounts (ghost stories, fairy stories adventure stories) or film and TV based accounts, freely adapted. Raymond described how he would use famous names, and then make up stories for them. Another important aspect of the Deaf experience was passing down tales of pupils long since departed, a subject to which we shall return later. Raymond gave an amusing account of one who had developed a particularly skilful way of stealing bikes from shops. Barry's account was the most instructive, as befits his 'master storyteller' status in the community:

> My influence, [Jack D] . . . when I was small, I'd see a group of Deaf, about 13/14 years old, signing, and him signing beautifully with them. Stories about the war, a pilot parachuting down to earth [gives more details]. Well, I crawled my way between all the legs to the front. They told me to go away – it wasn't suitable for small children. But I wouldn't give up.

He went on to describe how he set himself to learn from the best signing models around him:

Some of those boys would pass the same stories onto me. In the playground, we'd hide, to tell stories, round any corners, *all learning so much
from each other.*

This learning was, of course, not only in how to sign well, but in the information exchange – each piece of information wrung by ingenuity from
the world by one of the 1001 Victories, and without a second thought then
shared with each other – a cooperative and collective experience to a degree
not found in hearing schoolchildren.

When I was at school, I was never thought of as a major signer; we all
thought we were the same, took it in turns . . . what I have now, I got
from all of the others I watched. I was surprised when people recognised my skills – I can't see myself.

When asked to explain what he has that is special, Barry's replies are very
halting and touching. He makes it clear that certain of the others, including
that rare post-Milan beast, a Deaf teacher, were 'streets ahead'. Although
some might perceive this as contradicting the previous statements, this
account in fact operates on two levels – one is that they were able to make aesthetic judgements about BSL quality and the other is that everybody's
contribution was equally valued. 'Didn't matter if you were rich or poor –
you shared what you knew – all were equal.' In fact, there was one situation
in which those from wealthy families could make their own special mark:

Those kids who were rich would go home to families, go to see movies.
We nothing home – from poor families – so when they came back they
all had stories for us. We'd beg them to go to the pictures so that they
could get some more stories!

This is another one of the '1001' strategies. One of the additional creative
factors in this experience was that the children, obviously unable to hear
the film dialogue, superimposed their own plot theories onto the original.
This seemed well understood and added to the pleasure obtained from
such stories. A similar pattern obtained in the USA, where Gil Eastman's
own dramatised accounts of *Deaf Stories from the Movies* reveals different
layers of styles between different types of Deaf children.
    The extent to which a good signer-storyteller was given higher status
was implied in several accounts. Peggy presented one example:

We'd get in a circle for storytelling; one or two we didn't want in, slow
learners, would refuse. But one girl . . . she was brilliant. We'd all lap it
up, mouths wide open in sheer rapture; you could believe these stories,
the way they were told . . . If people saw her in conversation with some-

one else, *they would just gravitate towards her* . . . knowing the story wouldn't be planned, it would just happen.

The suggestion from several informants was that although the groups would accept stories from anyone, no matter what their signing style, the best storytellers used 'beautiful' BSL. To be capable of that meant one inevitably experienced more clashes with the teachers. Thus those more compliant and academically successful (mostly with more hearing) were set in opposition to those who were popular counter-leaders of a different ethos.

Teaching each other

The importance of storytelling in Deaf culture should not be understood as simply a form of escapism. The thirst for information is a major theme in a culture not only denied access to broadcast media and public communication through ignorance, but, because of the additional oralist restrictions, exclusion from parental and educational information. To complete the almost total isolation from majority culture, because of Oralism, access to written information was also thus seriously curtailed.

Therefore, given the Deaf cultural tendency to render almost everything in story form, the children's storytelling would also include whatever practical information they could pick up from 'outside', by their reading of adult actions or from the Deafworld outside.

Within the classroom it was almost universally reported that each assisted the others to try to understand both what the teachers said, and what they meant by what was said. This was undoubtedly a core of what became a culture of collectivism, especially in view of the dangers involved in slipping signed explanations in when the teachers' backs were turned. (Mindess [2000] also draws attention to this selflessness, noting that in so doing, of course, those passing on the information would often then miss the next piece – and so on.) Raymond summarised the totality of this information exchange thus:

My mother, bless her . . . three years before she died we had a helluva row . . . She said 'They told me I must never sign to you, and they were right'. 'Whaat! They were right?! How?' 'Yes, look at you – you got a good education'. Oh God! < buries head in hands > 'You think I got a good education simply by you not signing to me?! If I hadn't signed with the Deaf, I wouldn't have got an education at all!!

Others agreed; thus all these themes are fruitful sites for further research.

The importance of humour

Perhaps unsurprisingly in such adverse situations, humour also came to play a major part in surviving the oralist experience. Peggy gave the most eloquent example:

> One boy, his skill was humour..one look at him and you were finished. If anything came up, he'd always have a quick witty remark for it. If people were sad or depressed, or something had gone wrong at school, or got broken, or if we were all being punished for something, or if the head had to be called in, he'd have something to lift us. Ah, we really needed that, that was sooo good. Gave us strength to carry on, you see. That was our strength, having that humour. Something that could keep us together, block out those trying to squash us; they weren't allowed into that place that we had. And it [confirmed] yes, *we really had something of worth ourselves* . . . It wasn't planned – it was just like Deaf joining ranks really [goes on to sign this beautifully in more depth].

Most other examples of humour given were either incidental, or implicit in the accounts given, but reinforced Peggy's description. We might also note of course that in the storytelling humour played a vital role. Indeed, it is one of my regrets, that in confining this account to structured headings, and rendering it in English, so much humour has to be left out. It may be the case, therefore, that the high degree of teasing and humour that has frequently been remarked on by visitors to Deaf culture, originated at school.

Mentoring

Only one person, Albert, made reference to the existence of a mentoring system, but this seems to be the tip of another important feature. Perhaps significantly, his example dates back to the 1930s:

> [S]'s father [R], he was a Deaf missioner up in Scotland. His wife was at the same school as my father. She was younger and father was given the job of looking after her. Mother's school also had this. Mother was saying it was very much the same. Maybe not formalised, but mother said those kind of relationships existed there too.

Unfortunately, his parents passed on during the lifetime of this study, so it was not possible to obtain more details of what is obviously a significant clue for us.

Resistance and leadership

Most informants brought up this subject; the examples given appeared to fall into several categories. One is the mode of continual rebellion which occurred every time someone raised their hands to sign. Another, given by Martha, cogently illustrates one set of dynamics:

We didn't have any leaders as such. The kids followed the naughty ones. That was all based round storytelling too. They'd be put in the coal cellar for one or two hours . . . Kids would gather round, feeling for them, Deaf stuck there in the dark. When out, 'Oh I'm alright'. 'What happened in there?' They'd make up stories about what happened. The story was the key – it'd be like 'Oh I burrowed through the coal and saw this secret world ', or ' I found some matches and saw..', or 'saw a mouse', or whatever. They'd become heroines to us . . . So they'd become leader for 2/3 days, till we got fed up, or found another leader when someone else did something naughty.

Martha goes on to say that most punishments were for signing. What is interesting about this account is that it stresses the egalitarian nature of their society; anyone could become a leader – *provided that they endured the punishment that went with it*. This process was taken a step further:

Sometimes a topic would become 'talk of the week'. How did it become that? Kids would ask that person questions over and over, and they would keep building and exaggerating the story to keep attention. So if they became good at storytelling, they could prolong their leadership. Didn't matter if it was all exaggerated, or even made up – that was part of the rituals. Then of course if the teachers saw us around them, we would all get punished, and so it would keep going, round and round.

Albert, a hearing child of Deaf parents from the Midlands in his fifties, recounted how this ritual of exaggeration was very much part of the Deaf club culture he grew up in as a child:

When they'd meet [at the club], if something funny happened in the week, they'd tell people, and then you'd get additions to the story, [by other people] and additions, and additions.

It struck me that this seemed be a manifestation of Deaf culture that had begun with school life, and Albert agreed:

They shared tears, laughter, *everything* they would have shared. You can't, you can't just ignore that. That's one of the biggest families in the *whole world* < laughs >. I mean, it really is.

Another form of rebellion was to run away, as Stefan recounted. Others included a process of continual rebellion, couched in skirting the borders of insolence. Bonnie, a Jewish Deaf woman in her forties from London, stressed that 'they couldn't keep us down – in any class there'd be ten or more of us and only one of them, and they probably knew deep down what we thought of them'. Another set of responses can be paralleled with the small sabotages carried out by assembly line workers or plantation slaves – playing dumb at carrying out instructions. Raymond gave one example:

> Those trainee teachers on Ewing's course – in their second year they sent them out to Deaf schools . . . One took a shine to me, maybe because she thought she could sail through her qualification with me . . . So when the exam day came, and the hierarchy of Manchester came to test her . . . she asked me, 'Raymond, what is an intransitive verb?' 'I don't know', I said. She went bright red. 'I've told you only last week'. [turns to his classmates] 'She didn't, did she?' 'Yes she did'. 'Nooo, she couldn't have.' 'Yes she did'. 'Funny I can't recall it'.

As the story goes on, he is sent to the head, and told to go back and apologise:

> Mr Green told me that I had to apologise to you', meaning 'I don't apologise, understand?' . . . Mr Green told me to tell you that I have been taught about intransitive verbs' . . . As we were leaving the class, I said to the examiner, 'I never understood half of what she said . . . That's the kind of teacher you are dumping on the valuable education of Deaf children'. I got whapped six of the best for that!

This example points up once again the significant difference between rebellions of these kinds in Deaf and hearing schools. It is difficult to imagine a situation in the latter which could carry the in-depth cultural resonances exemplified here. It can be argued that these were typical 'schoolboy pranks'. Nevertheless, because resisting Oralism overshadowed all that happened, such actions undoubtedly fed into the general pool of rebellion.

Hearing aids were a prime symbol of Oralism around which to rebel. Damage to or loss of hearing aids, and switching them off until caught out by the teacher (they were made to wear them with the controls externally visible) were primary strategies. Dorothy, from the South West and in her fifties, described her school's equivalent:

> We would throw them into this huge thorn bush, and then pretend we'd lost them. Of course after a while, they caught on, and every so often a teacher would cut their way into the bush and pull a few out. But we were smaller, so we got to be able to put them beyond their

reach. God knows how many rusty aids will be in there when they finally cut it down!

Such rebellion climaxes in Raymond's highly symbolic example. It is the final day of school, and the pupils and some of the teachers have walked to the station to take their final train journey of school life:

> 'Right, I'm leaving now. I've got everything, but I must leave behind my bitter enemy', and I took off the hearing aid . . . tied it up with its own wire, dropped down to the railway line and taped it tightly to the track . . . the teacher started blowing his top and saying 'It's Government property, bring that back!' . . . And then the train went over it and it just splintered into tiny fragments. 'Hooray, it's died!' . . . 'I'll report you to the headmaster', he fumed. 'Go ahead', I said. 'Because I am going in *this* direction, and you are going *that* way!'

The story continues as the teacher splutters that he will refuse Raymond a reference, as the pupils mount the train, and most of the rest of the group (8 or 9), tie up their aids and fling them out of the window as the train pulls out, people ducking hastily as the aids flew around them:

> And we never wore hearing aids again! There was a voice screaming in my mind – Freeeeeedommmm! Phew! All those years of noise pounding away at the side of my brain . . . !

This account goes on to talk about the distress caused by having such loud amplified noise pumped into one's head throughout one's childhood, and ventures a suggestion that this created bad tempered Deaf children. Of course, such gestures could only be made at the end of one's school life, but the intensity expressed in this last example gives an indication of the levels of stress behind this physical imposition.

The 'Deaf mentality'

Raymond summarised the basis of resistance in his account of the 'Deaf Mentality', which demands an in-depth rendering:

> The 'Deaf Mentality' is linked with language . . . If education is oral, I, the Deaf person watch them and develop my own opinion of what that [oral] person really is. I start to say 'What For?' signed right down here in my guts about them and their whole way of doing things, the whole way this hearing world seems to be run.

It is very difficult to translate this passage, but one interpretation of the placing of the sign 'WHATFOR' deep down by the navel (instead of at its usual site) indicates the beginnings of the Deaf mentality, born *directly* from a questioning of the oralist/'hearing' way of doing things. To translate it as 'What the hell is all this charade for?' captures this refined sense better. Raymond is also suggesting that the idea of 'Deaf' as a concept is actually born within the semantics of this sign, perhaps *the* root sign which marks the departure from accepting the Hearing norm. He goes on:

> That whole process [described here] is interlinked. My language is communicated from my guts to my mind and back; that's the directionality of Deaf language – not anything coming from the out-side, because nothing is coming in from there. Hearing way is from outside to the head and ear, then down to the guts. Deaf, because noth-ing coming in from outside, *develops their own language from their guts to their minds back and forth in a two-way relationship.* When Deaf eventually master hearing people's language like English, they can adapt to that hearing directionality system. But the mentality – that's uniquely their own. You can't remove that.

This unique construction, even if the meaning were better rendered in English, is not necessarily one which can be defended against the findings of cognitive psychology. However, if one examines this piece for its deeper meanings, one finds that both the 'WHATFOR' sign and the site of lan-guage origin are placed in the guts as a starting point for a continually developing interior monologue which reinforces one's Deaf identity in direct relationship to oralist absurdities daily visited upon it.

Therefore this alternative identity is arguably born from the oralist era. Prior to that time, the Deaf identity might not have been so heavily predi-cated on oppression. Nevertheless, because of the century-long maintainance of Oralism, identity appears inseparable from that oppression. As Raymond summarised:

> There is a wall between them and us. Because of that Deaf get nothing from them – have to fend for themselves, think for themselves, make judgements for themselves.

Mindess (2000) draws attention to the extent to which adult Deaf deci-sions are based on just these judgements and shared knowledge, whether about buying a house or a car, or solving medical problems. They are a col-lective resource on which anyone can draw. Raymond insisted that the only place it could truly flourish was the residential school, where there was enough 'Deaf time' for it to grow. There it became, in his words, 'I know that I am different, that I am Deaf. I accept my identity, and I'm not going to change myself'. Thus Deafhood was born and grew in a thousand little ways into a collective selfhood nurtured by a thousand little acts of rebellion, by a thousand and one little victories.

Summary

These examples illustrate some of the domains of positive Deaf experience, and the range and extent of rebellion. The important theme of collectivity runs through most; rather than being disparate acts by individuals or small groups, as in hearing schools, these 1001 small victories cohere into a internally coherent cultural system of Deafhood values and norms. Furthermore, they indicate that Deafhood is a learned process of actualisation in which develops from an empty 'deaf' vessel, in part defined by 1001 acts of resistance to the trope of deafness. It is too early in research into these subjects to assess the extent to which positive Deafhood experiences and identity development can be separated from an identity inextricably related to reactions against oppression.

Access to Deaf Traditions and a 'Historical Self'

Those interviewed also revealed other sources for positive Deaf identities.

External Deaf influences

Olivia gave an example all too common amongst Deaf children:

> When me about 6, friend said 'When we 16 or 18, *will die, cos no Deaf people older than that*. When me 11, at next school, Deaf adults would visit [for school reunions etc]. We'd run up to them 'Hello, how old you?' '25', or '30', or whatever. Ahhh, thank God, mean me not die young after all.

In her case, then, she spent five or more formative years believing that she would die soon after leaving school. Others essayed another interpretation with equally damaging implications. Ursula said:

> I know a lot of Deaf who thought that when they grew up, they would become hearing.

Thus the appearance of Deaf adults were literally life-confirming experiences for many Deaf children. It seems probable that these two negative constructions held more power in day schools, where there were fewer old pupil reunions or visits for sports days and so on.

Ursula went on to describe an experience often noticed by Deaf adults who visited schools during that time:

When Deaf people visited the school, we would all just run over to them and drown them in questions . . . we were like puppies, we were so enthusiastic.

Martha concurred:

When they gone, they would be talk of the week, about that person, everyday, till it wore off. We never had lead storytellers – only the adults had that status.

The importance of these Deaf visitors was not simply identity affirmation. The information gleaned and disseminated by the children about life was the primary focus; unsurprisingly, since it was almost their only source of information about the world. Confirming this, others noted that in schools which had more recently accepted sign language and Deaf adults, Deaf visitors no longer held the same desperate attraction for the children. It must not be forgotten that such adult visits were intermittent – further research is necessary to establish whether this intermittent nature was simply seen as exceptional or whether they carried resonances throughout the times of their absence.

For some luckier children, access to the adult Deaf world was obtained through early attendance at Deaf clubs. Interestingly, the four informants from hearing families who did so are all known as having strong Deaf identities; similarly a fifth had a Deaf handyman living in her otherwise hearing family. Barry summarised:

I was adopted by this Deaf couple when my parents disappeared, and they would bring me to the club every week, and I would just stand there in amazement and delight, drinking it all in, all that BSL, and that sheer information, whole range of informations about life, I just absorbed it all, just learning, learning all the time right up to this very minute now. Deaf think me hot signing means mother–father Deaf. No, from community, taking it all in from there.

His emphasis on information, lifelong learning and equality (that each had things to teach the others) echoes Dorothy's points in the next chapter. Similarly, this early attendance at Deaf clubs offered these four a potential awakening of their 'historical selves'; for the children would witness as many as three older generations of Deaf people. How much actual use was made of this awakening potential is discussed later.

For all these children who came into contact with Deaf adults, both the information collected and the positive valuation of Deafhood helped themselves and their peers not only to resist the deafness construct, but to begin to actualise themselves and their Deafhood.

Importance of Deaf families

Although Barry's example stresses the importance of the whole community over the single Deaf family, without this family he would not have had that access to Deaf life. Ursula's account explains why she never thought she would become hearing:

> My class, out of nine, three had Deaf parents, one had a Deaf sister and they strongly influenced us . . . I knew my destiny was to be Deaf [beautifully signed as 'aim high and far'], because I saw those parents; it was obvious really.

She and others described their experiences of staying with Deaf families:

> I was about 13, and it < struggles for words > was, just amazing. To be there and watch adults talk; it was the first time I had ever experienced that. It was so strange. Before that there was always a wall between me and adults.

This poignant example illustrates a gulf between Deaf and hearing culture; having to wait til 13 to have even a simple taste of adult conversation or, in many cases, never to get that at all until leaving school and joining the club. Raymond's description of a similar visit captures another important dimension of Deaf family experience; 'They have a closeness, *a spiritual closeness* . . . those children are confident and sign away to their parents, debating with them and everything ' .

The confidence that comes of a Deaf-focused identity, the ability to debate and the information about both Deaf life and majority-society life are the cornerstones of the influence brought into Deaf school life from Deaf families. Likewise, their visits to Raymond's school were also summarised in similarly powerful language; 'It influenced me to respect Deaf as a community, *a way of life, a culture,* before I knew those words'.

In Stefan's case his Deaf sister, 12 years older than he, 'was everything to me, my mother, my sister, my friend, my girlfriend, oh so much'. By contrast, he noted the limitations placed on Deaf families, 'We had a car; they never did', which illustrates their comparative poverty; he also noted their difficulties in getting their homework done at weekends because of the intensity of Deaf weekend life. He, like the others, also learned from their fluency in BSL and their wider vocabulary range.

Deaf families, then, were the conduit by which the wider construct of Deafhood could be brought into the schools, and those external influences absorbed into their own alternative traditions. This was especially true where Deaf families had built up those traditions within the schools over successive generations. There is not room here to detail the experiences of those from Deaf families themselves, but several explained at length the burden of responsibility most either felt or were given by their parents and the Deaf club community to instil ideas about Deafhood in the others. These subjects will be explored in the next book.

The Deaf alternative identity

There is some evidence that a number of children did not accept the negative valuation even prior to adult contact. Stefan told the story of his birth, as seen through his sister's eyes:

> Sis often told me the story of how I was born. She spent 3 years hammering away at my parents for another child, so that she could have a Deaf brother – I don't know how she could be so confident, but she was . . . When my mother was pregnant, she started to tell all her schoolmates that her Deaf brother was coming . . . Finally, when I was born, she proudly told them 'My baby brother Deaf – can sign'. And so she got revenge on any of her schoolmates who had been cruel to her!

This (possibly idealised) story illustrates the positive valuation the children placed on being Deaf; Stefan's sister's was able to 'get revenge' for the behaviour of her schoolmates simply by having something to which they aspired – a Deaf sibling.

A Deaf alternative

In the North-East and Scotland, Oralism did not gain full control until the 1930s or so which is fortunate for this study, since it enabled Raymond to describe processes that stopped at least two or more generations earlier in other parts of the UK. The difference between Raymond and most other Deaf is that, with his strong belief in his Deafhood, he went on to actively explore its roots, initially through his regular meetings with Jim Mackenzie, 50 years his senior, who became one of his two 'mentors':

> I met him twice a week for years. He taught me so much about Braidwood's pupils. I'd say, 'which book was that from?' He said, 'No, it was passed down to us' . . . Where from? Fitzsimmons, Deaf before him . . . Then, back to Atkinson . . . He was around in the 1840s [gives details] . . . Atkinson went to Edinburgh School under Kinneburgh . . . Kinneburgh was trained by the Braidwood Academy. The old Thomas Braidwood – his pupils would come down to Newcastle School to talk to them. Wow! Signed   history, down the generations to me . . . My biggest regret – *if I knew of the importance of Deaf history at that time, I would have had*

screeds! It fascinates me, how the Deaf passed things down like that back then – a sort of chain.

Braidwood set up the first UK Deaf school in Edinburgh in the 1760s. The stories Jim told came from the 1780s, taking four steps to reach Raymond. My italics here indicate the extent and effect of the loss of this alternative Deaf history which, as he pointed out, was transmitted not in print but in sign. It seems all that is left to us now (which is nevertheless so crucial to record in this text) is the distant memory of its existence and the ability to confirm a few names. And conversely, of course, without Milan such lore would have continued to be recorded, probably even in print.

One of the most remarkable part of Raymond's data was confirming evidence of what he recalled from Jim of just such a 'Deaf chain'. He went on to give detailed accounts of his own research to locate those pupils based on Jim's information and of his success in corroborating several of his stories:

Jim told me 'One pupil from Shrewsbury, a woman. Name forgot. W something, three women in that area, names me don't know now'. And about a year ago, I did some research in the records of that area and I found – Ann Wilcot, in a tiny village, Biterley, near Shrewsbury. And then, Jane Poole, and Metcalfe. Now these were all Braidwood's pupils! So him saying Shrewsbury was spot on!

One result of the emergence of this chain is that Braidwood was not the oralist that many history books claim him to be. As Raymond put it, 'When I read them, I thought the old man's [Jim] gone potty [in saying Braidwood taught by signs]'. His subsequent research uncovered no evidence of Braidwood being an oralist and, at this time of writing, it seems that the Deaf history chain may actually be right and the textbooks wrong.

Barry also gave detailed accounts which confirmed that this chain was maintained by Deaf teachers themselves, being fortunate that one of the last such teachers was then still active in his school. In so doing, he also gives a sense of how a Deaf pedagogy might have opererated:

He could sign the Bible beautifully, really attracted you to it . . . He was a chain smoker, then stopped. When I was 16, he called me in one day, and reached into a drawer and got out a white hankerchief, breathed into it and showed it to me – wow – there was a big black mark. I never smoked after seeing that. See he knew Deaf Way – *visual proof.*

Several important conclusions can be drawn from all this. One is the confirmation that prior to Oralism, Deaf schools passed down considerable information about their own communities and individuals in their own line of 'oral' history. Secondly, their knowledge of that Deaf history played an important part in supporting their self-concept, their Deafhood. Third, this history survived in places up until the 1960s, but has not made it past that time, except in very partial form to those who had a strong sense of Deafhood and wished to develop it by finding their place in this alternative history. This in itself offers important clues for further research. Fourth, the demise of this history can be directly attributed to Oralism, which diminished Deaf pride in their own tradition. Fifth, any Deaf 're-actualisation' consequently requires a re-instatement of Deaf history as an essential core of the Deaf experience.

I have not so far referred directly to the 'historical self'. The term itself was brought to my attention by Jim Kyle, but it does not seem to have been directly explored, and I have preferred to use it informally, as it were, to indicate my intuitive feelings that *something* within an individual's identity needs to be isolated and framed within this kind of diachronic perspective.

When considering a typical individual from a majority culture, we might note that such a diachronic perspective is developed in two particular domains. One is the extent to which the individual absorbs the way majority society constructs and disseminates versions of its collective history. These are formally manifested in education, 'semi-formally' manifested in the media and informally digested and re-presented by those with whom one socialises. The other domain is within the family itself, where earlier generations re-present their own personalised versions of that larger history and also manifest their own family history together with examples which lead outwards to that larger history. In each case, factors like class background affect the weighting given to these forms of socialisation. For those from the upper classes, these two domains can be constructed so as to present an intentionally congruent fit – that is, that the family and national history reinforce the ideology of being 'born to rule', to give a simple example.

This is one way in which we can conceive the historical self within individual identity. Another form it might take is that if the family conveys a sense of pastness, of a 'world' in which different values operated, this can reinforce an individual's ability to resist the ethos peculiar to some capitalist societies (such as the United States) which seek to focus on the present in order that such resistance is minimalised (Zinn 1980, Schultz & Schultz, 1989). The greater the distance from the present that such information is drawn on, the greater the contrast, which is where the grandparental role can assume such importance.

For most minority cultures, then, retaining and maintaining a strong historical self is crucial to their pride and to their ability to resist majority-culture constructs of what they should be (hooks 1995). Given the apparent collectivist values of many minority cultures, and therefore the extent to which individual identity is informed by and interpenetrated by the identities of other members of the culture, as Jade describes on the next page, we can perceive the existence of another dimension of the historical self at work.

In Deaf minority cultures, because 90% of parent–child relations are 'cross-cultural', the role of Deaf history as transmitted through the education system is of particularly crucial import. Its removal or denial can arguably have especial significance for the mental health of the individual, and thus the Deaf historical self would seem to be a vital concept for developing strategies of 'Deaf Wellness' in the future. (Deaf Wellness is a valuable concept developed by Griggs [1998] to counterbalance the pathological emphasis of the medical model when considering Deaf mental health provision.)

Other Deafness/Deafhood Contestations

These accounts of resistance and unity are only the first step in such research. Interactions around normal childhood fun and games, socialisation patterns, cliques, bullying and abuse all remain to be unpicked. However, I was not able to locate overt divisions around the basic deafness/Deafhood contestation – all Deaf children were equally low in status and apparently relatively untouched by any systems of honour or patronage, as Martha described:

> Even though I was head girl, it didn't carry any prestige for the other pupils. Wasn't like hearing school where it means something. It was just like I had a lot of extra responsibilities. It wasn't like I had power either.

It was only with the advent of the two oralist grammar schools that such overt deafness/Deafhood divisions can be found. Several informants gave extensive accounts of these divisions at those schools, whilst Dorothy and Frances were among those who described its first manifestations in their club in the 1950s. This aspect of social division forms part of a series of deeper levels of Deaf cultural experience, and will be explored in the next book.

Martha described how, since being head girl conveyed no special status amongst her peers:

I had to develop ways of persuading Deaf to do things; it didn't work to tell them. So that's where I learned how to tune into each person and find what worked with them.

This passage is uncannily similar to Dorothy's descriptions of working class/subaltern Deaf organisation in the next chapter, suggesting that this trait may have actually developed within the schools, and is important when later considering Deaf organisational strategies. However, apart from Barry's description earlier, there was almost no mention of class. In his example, the benefits of having middle-class parents was explicitly turned to collective advantage by the children. Martha was the only other one who commented on class at school:

> Because we were equal at school, *then in Deaf community became same too* . . . You mean, if your parents had more money, you'd become a leader? No, nobody knew about things like that.

Wealth seems only to have meant that one could go home some weekends (which, apart from going to films and staying up later, was a very mixed blessing as we have already heard). It does not appear to mean having more or better possessions (except food parcels, as Dorothy noted) or rather that such possessions counted for anything in the Deaf value system.

In summary then, it appears, as Dorothy suggests in the next chapter, that it was only on leaving this everyday Deaf environment that sufficient Hearing influence could act to fragment such Deafhood unity.

Other Positive Effects of Oralism

When a ceiling is imposed on a minority group, their experience contains less diversity and thus more collective similarity as Fowler has explained (*Sign On*, 1998). Raymond explicated:

> When Deaf leave school and meet other Deaf, they realise they are the same. Not just language, and ways of communicating, but we had the same experiences in Oral schools, and *exactly the same thoughts*, the same examples.

Such a common national and international experience undoubtedly strengthens or underpins the already existing global Deaf bond described in Chapter 2. However there is also a deeper level. When discussing the realities of the pain above with Jade, a hearing parent of a Deaf child, she remarked:

I used to think that Deaf people just happened to support one another because it was 'the right thing to do', if you like. But something else is going on that doesn't really happen much in the hearing world. It's like you are inside that person, experiencing their pain, and their pain is actually *inside you as well*.

This was a breathtaking observation which exactly captured the Deaf reality. It may well be that other minority cultures have an equivalent characteristic – certainly it is one which is foreign to majority cultures.

Negative Effects of Oralism on Deaf Culture

The earlier sections indicate an essentially collective attempt to construct an alternative, positive sense of Deafhood. However, informants gave many examples of how Oralism negatively affected Deaf culture.

Fear and submission

An all-pervading sense of fear was implanted early and easily re-evoked by those who wished to utilise it. When I asked Raymond about the 'WHATFOR' sign at the stomach and asked why more Deaf did not now appear to manifest this, he replied:

Remember, oralists would put their big mouths right in front of the children, wag their fingers; the child would shrink back in terror, not understanding. They were really frightened. If they raised their hands to sign, they were slapped. 'Ow' < copies look of bemusement and distress > *They didn't know what it was they were supposed to do, and they had no ways of finding out in those situations.* So fear was their living reality when they were very small and alone. Oralism's power was simply Fear . . . Like those old-time religions; 'Give me a child for the first seven years and he is mine for life' . . . Oralism is a control system, aimed to control. If you let them [Deaf] have sign language, they collapse – they're finished.

He then signed the WHATFOR sign at the stomach, the single vibrating finger, with a claw hand hovering above it, ready to swallow, twist or tear, and went on to explain that 'The Fear' never really left Deaf people; that it was augmented by the sense of being in a small community outnumbered in a 1000 to 1 ratio, and reinforced by the lack of access to information that might explain how society worked. 'The Fear' thus informed all encounters with anything outside of a simple Deaf club life, intimidating many from taking political actions on their own behalf.

'Stupidity', self-confidence and fatalism

Peggy described how the children knew that they were Deaf but that, to her peers, Deaf meant 'stupid' and that all things Deaf were inferior, and were not worthy of regard, of saving for posterity, or of passing on to future generations.[1] Inevitably this led to lack of confidence. Ken summarised:

> You and I know how seriously Deaf lack confidence . . . Oralism alone did that; it concentrated on what they couldn't do well and ignored all their other skills.

Although this had changed during the Resurgence, he went on: 'They've got some of it back. But they still feel deep down they can't do anything significant.' Frances, from the South West in her fifities, described her attempts to develop others' confidence:

> Sometimes try change them. They say like from school, 'They said I was bad, rubbish.' You say 'Don't worry, not your fault, education at school, you learned what? Zero! Well done; you still trying'. 'Oh thank you, thank you'. 'You have skill like storytelling', or whatever, 'Well done! All of us not the same. Me, storytelling, hate it, can't do it, leave you to do it'. 'Oh I see . . . right, right'. You know, have to encourage, encourage all the time.

With loss of confidence came a sense of fatalism. Renata, in her forties from the Midlands, describing the lack of response from the community to the loss of its only BSL TV programme, explained:

> It all goes back to school; people have said to me, 'We not surprised. Anything we get, we know hearing will take it away from us again one day'. That belief is very deep rooted.[2]

This feeling that 'we can never be safe' is very important. Barry confirmed it, but dealt with it positively. Giving examples of why Deaf history was crucial for Deaf children, and why therefore resources indicating Deaf achievement must be collected and saved, he added, without any self consciousness:

> Like Doug Alker getting the RNID top job, keep all these resources for the future, long-term, so when we're all dead we have proof that Deaf did once get that top job . . . there'll be all those photos of him, and the Deaf Comedians material [Alker formed this troup] . . . Imagine future it will all see Deaf crash to the bottom again, another Milan, then we can bring out our hidden resources . . . It's like the cycle of a wheel that always crushes the Deaf again and again . . . so we must keep proof that Deaf-and-Dumb really could once do these things like we are now.[2]

We have seen in Chapter 2 how such a belief was also shared across Europe (Schroder 1993, Truffaut 1993).

Neurological damage

Raymond asserted something which has been widely reported:

Many Deaf have poor attention span. Teacher at my school would write on the board and they don't seem to take it in; same when I've tried to explain stuff to them, hard to keep their attention.

It is this kind of imposed 'attention deficit disorder' which has caused Deaf activists to become frustrated in their attempts to explain the need for changes and action, and which has therefore required, different kinds of strategies.

Retardation of opinion development

All these factors combined to produce another aspect of Deaf culture frequently remarked on – the fear of giving one's own opinion or even developing one. Stefan illustrated:

When I put forward a motion at BDA conference . . . I watched how people decided which way to vote – by looking around and seeing what others were doing! Followed their friends or someone they feel has a strong mind. Means they understand issues? No. Means some of it goes past, so they look to others, 'You understand? Me not. OK, you do, me follow you'. *This is an exact copy of what happened in the classroom.* Many had no hope of understanding, so they let the others help them.

Although it can be said that parallels exist in the hearing world, the difference in degree is so tremendous that it essentially constitutes a different cultural situation.

Horizontal violence

One cultural characteristic commonly spoken of among Deaf people both in the United States and elsewhere is the swiftness to criticise and reluctance to praise. Several informants referred to this; the linkage they made, as for most of this section, was unprompted by me. Stefan summarised:

Why? Because of upbringing, school abuse – Oralism really is abuse you know – years and years of the same pattern, *so negative is what they know*, what sticks in their minds and gets passed on to other Deaf.

His analysis is unusual in emphasising the repetition factor. Most accounts simply take the negativity as a whole. Bonnie added:

A person who was labelled a failure at school can get their own back by being more critical of others.

Since an awful lot of people were so labelled, the potential for critical responses would appear infinite. Indeed, a related consquence is the degree of backstabbing commonly spoken of within the community, which Frances also refers to as jealousy. After the previous example, she added:

If not encourage them, it becomes 'It's always him/her that gets the attention, what about me?' Jealousy. That goes back to school, 'They can do it, me can't'.

In the oralist school, of course, those who had some hearing, or had become Deaf, were the ones who could make some limited progress. Because, as Chapter 2 described, these were singled out by Oralism for exhibition whilst, at the same time, their deafness status was hidden, it was unclear to the children why some were progressing and the majority not. Hence the bewildered sense of fatalism which underpins Frances' description. Her analysis emphasises that if others felt they had more worth, and also recognised what they could do, they would be less jealous of jobs and credits going to the emerging Deaf leaders of the Resurgence. Although there are parallels with small hearing communities, the difference in degree, i.e. that 99% of Deaf people left school with no recognised qualifications, results in a qualitatively different cultural situation.

A related and highly important set of ideas were described by Bonnie:

A child may sign a lot of information and get it right, but get criticised for signing it. Yet for just pronouncing two words correctly, they get praised. _That leads to an obsession with 'getting it right', but only with regard to very small things._ Or big things will be picked apart for very small reasons, or there is an obsession with small details of procedure, not the wider picture.

Certainly, one can imagine Deaf culture continuing to have difficulty in articulating the 'wider picture' whilst Deaf adults cannot determine the path of 'their' children's education.

Damage to BSL expressiveness

Mark, a Midland hard-of-hearing ex-mainstreamed man in his early thirties, summarised:

From 3–8 I was in the local Deaf school … from 8–11 I was moved to the local PHU. I remember trying to sign there and the hearing kids just stared at me … That was a totally oral place too – _that was what messed up my sign language skills._

Although in this example it is the extra dimension of mainstreaming which reinforced this damage, it does appear that the absence of creative play in sign, and the lack of much signed theatre and poetry, can be attributed to the limits placed on sign language development by Oralism. Martha and Barry also laid great stress on the importance of teaching Deaf children 'good, strong, visual BSL, same as hearing have to polish their English' and other forms of creative sign play.

Both Barry and Jim, a Deaf man from Newcastle in his eighties, contrasted modern Deaf sign aesthetics with that of earlier eras. Jim referred to an old missioner, Rev Gilbey, whose signing was so attractive that Deaf people in London would choose to belong to his church for that reason alone. Whilst researching old Deaf magazines, I found in the 1893 *British Deaf-Mute* what can best be described as a review of sermon performances. This account praised a young minister for his promise, whilst critiquing his BSL – a remarkable indication of the extent to which good BSL was then publicly appreciated. The young man in question? Reverend Gilbey.

Barry's example was of a Deaf missioner, Hayward:

> He would sign Deaf way – would point out people in the audience, refer to them, and draw them into what he was saying . . . Never used much mouth pattern, just clear, strong, smooth signing. We would just sit there mesmerised, our tongues hanging out! He would travel the country giving talks, Bristol, Sheffield, invitations from other missioners. Train, bus – never had cars then . . . No it wasn't like formal church signing – that style made us bored, fall asleep – 'false from the situation'.

These examples indicate what has been lost, but also give two other fascinating hints. One is the existence of 'preaching styles' *per se*, which is something which African-American literature and culture makes much reference to, especially in relation to the apartheid period there, when Black culture had freedom to develop, and when the role of the preacher was to lift Black morale. The other is once again a suggestion of the 'Deaf way' of pedagogy and organisation which we have encountered earlier.

Enforced impotence

Another response, obvious perhaps in itself but with less obvious consequences, was the amount of pain felt by Deaf people who, once they had left school, could not help but be aware that generations more were having to go through the same experience whilst they were helpless to intervene. Barry captured this feeling in this poetic description:

Deaf like a pearl buried in the shell; all Deaf have skills in their pearls. And Deaf children have theirs too; they waiting in their shells at the bottom of the sea, waiting for Deaf adults to come down. Why? Because they have so many skills to offer, if they'd only open their own shells and leap gracefully out and present them to Deaf kids. Give the children a chance to take them in and pass them on themselves to others. All this time they've been sitting at the bottom of the ocean, just vegetating sadly. Why?!

It is hard for the translation to capture anything like the visual power of this example. Lorna Allsop, from the South West and in her forties, expressed related thoughts:

You ever notice how few Deaf families work in Deaf schools even now they've changed a bit? I think that's because Deaf of hearing families, they're used to low expectations, and so the awful things there don't bother them so much, or they just used to it being so bad. But Deaf families, we are used to expecting things to be normal and equal . . . And so, going into a Deaf school, it just causes us too much pain and stress to see what could be, what should be.

The response from Deaf of hearing families to this was along the lines of 'We know it's bad, but we have to try'. Nevertheless there was also a strong sense that Lorna was 'right', in that they were more easily able to adjust to negative school environments. It is not easy to immediately pinpoint how carrying this deep pain and the concomitant feelings of impotence affects specific areas of Deaf culture; it is safer to conclude that further research is needed to draw out examples, and that these feelings probably inform many aspects of the culture at a deeper level.[3]

Self-division

The conflict between one's positive Deaf image and the imposed 'deafness' model must have inevitably resulted in inner conflict, knowing which one to trust or follow in particular circumstances. Raymond gave an overall assessment of this process and produced a perspective of great significance for the study:

[lists Deaf people he considers to now have the 'Hearing Mentality'] . . . But don't forget; they all had the Deaf mentality once . . . What happens is that either they don't have the courage *to believe in it, to trust it, to go with it*, because of the Fear I mentioned earlier, or some of them decide to try and adopt the Hearing mentality . . . they try to suppress their Deaf mentality, but in the heat of argument, they explode, and – voila! – out it comes!

He went on to liken such people's vain attempt to 'cling to the coat tails of the Hearing Mentality' as that of 'a man trying to chase his cough'. This account exactly mirrors Dorothy's descriptions in the next chapter, except that her group expressed it more compassionately.

Chapter Summary and Implications

Undoubtedly, there are many other ways in which Oralism has directly affected Deaf culture; these, however, were the most common themes the informants raised. Similarly, there are many more aspects of positive Deaf cultural life at school than this study has identified. But both of these are for future researchers to build on, hopefully with this as a valid structural basis. We can, however, draw together some themes to carry through the rest of the book.

Deafhood as actualisation

The key points of these complex passages is the collective Deaf Mentality and the struggle to trust in it; an internalised site of the battle played out between deafness and Deafhood, and the struggle to actualise this in everyday praxis. We can perceive it also in terms of actualisation – the process of growth from the 'little d' into the 'big D', and then the effort to maintain it.

Deafhood as essentially covert

The data show that little space was available to the children to overtly express their Deafhood (and indeed until Deaf schools are Deaf-centred, this cannot really happen). The covert nature of this expression is reinforced by the experiences under missioner colonialism in the next chapter. Confirmation of this came from Cameron and others who attended Gallaudet University. Although being immensely impressed by the Deaf confidence, pride and achievements there, they found the less oppressive Deaf experience of the USA resulted in difficulties in forming an immediate bond with those American Deaf people who had not experienced the same degree of struggle towards emergence. Their reaction, as they told it, was to find and develop friendships with African and other more orally-oppressed Deaf. Interestingly enough, I found myself experiencing that same reaction, 20 years later. In Black literature and in white critiques of white suburban society, we find a similar dynamic, where the absence of this struggle is characterised by the trope of 'soul', its presence or its absence.

We can therefore carry forward a working hypothesis that UK Deaf cultural unity is predicated of necessity on a 'lower' and more covert level of social praxis and political activity, the '1001 Victories', rather than the overt 'Deaf Pride' concepts and actions.

The historical self

Although we have glimpsed the importance of this throughout the chapter, it appears that it too is covert since strategies for passing on one's own history have been quashed by Oralism. The historical self then appears to be a characteristic of a higher, overt level of Deafhood, one which presently is still being nurtured back into existence. The next chapters show that the simple fact of a maintained socio-historic continuity at club and national level has left the community with a reasonably solid (if not necessarily strong) preserved a basis for that redevelopment. In part this is dependent upon historical research to locate, describe and explicate whatever can be unearthed of the earlier eras of Deaf society.

One dimension that has been mentioned for exploration is the extent to which children of majority society have access to versions of 'their' history through the media and, crucially, through their grandparents and others of that generation. It seems to be the intimate contact with a generation two steps removed from their own which is important in signalling the *idea* of history. Most Deaf informants from hearing families reported that they had no access to, and therefore no sense of, this dimension in either Deaf or majority cultures. Further study must explore the extent to which children from Deaf families could access this through by contact with their Deaf grandparents or other older Deaf.

The battle with passivity

The chapter illustrates many positive aspects of Deaf collectivity. However, one other unifying aspect is built on the knowledge of shared 'weaknesses' which may come to be rationalised as a virtue. When one examines the children's move from oralist colonialism to missioner colonialism, this battle with the 'virtues' of passivity and paralysis becomes a major cultural theme.

Raymond's argument summarises these processes. Chapter 9 will show how he and others were dissatisfied with the limited ways in which Deafhood actualisation was manifested. Able to perceive that the Deaf self was larger than the imposed 'blinkers' suggested, they then attempted to create a progressive movement to further the deafness/Deafhood discourse.

Deafhood as inherently collective

One theme running through these accounts is a sense of the extent of collectivity. The signs 'we', 'Deaf' and 'all' seem inextricably bound up with each other. The extent to which this phenomenon, uncharacteristic of majority societies, occurs in other minority groups is worth researching, as well as the extent to which they are either synonymous with oppression or represent some more existential Deaf reality.

Deaf *joie de vivre*

Because these accounts above focus on the deafness/Deafhood dynamic, they do not capture anything like the full range of strategies for creativity, pleasure and self-development experienced by those Deaf children, although some examples have been given. Further research is required to bring these to the surface.

How do all the characteristics and dynamics exhibited in this chapter manifest themselves in adult Deaf life? The next chapter examines these in relation to the second traditional site of Deaf culture – Deaf club life in the era of missioner-colonialism.

Notes

1. This was painfully summarised for me following the screening of the first-ever captioned film in the UK in 1978 at Acton Deaf club. A common response to this first-time access to hearing discourse was 'Wow! I never realised hearing people talk rubbish too!' Imagine going through one's life convinced that only your own kind talked 'rubbish', and that those who used their mouths to communicate conducted lofty discourses even in the smallest everyday acts of life . . . If anything illustrated the comprehensiveness with which Oralism cut off communication with one's own family, this must be it.
2. This example has, alas, proved all too prescient, since two years later Alker was indeed ousted in the oralist coup of 1997.
3. Since these interviews, more from Deaf families have taken the plunge and are working in Deaf schools. Their experiences there and the dynamics involved deserve more attention in a later study. Young *et al.* (1998) offer a useful beginning in unpicking those dynamics.

Chapter 8

The Roots of Deaf Culture: Deaf Clubs and Deaf Subalterns

> Tell someone a fact and you reach their minds; give them a story and you touch their souls.
>
> (Hasidic proverb)

Introduction

On leaving residential schools and the oralist colonial system, Deaf young people then entered the second of the two traditional Deaf cultural sites – the Deaf clubs. However, in these sites another different stage of colonialism obtained, with its own implications for Deaf culture.

The data collected here suggested that one crucial cultural marker could be described as distinguishing between those who either actively supported or went along with that colonialism, and those who resisted them. This distinction is broadly made in the first instance – more subtle dynamics would be expected to emerge from further research. The data also suggest that resistance was shaped both covertly and overtly by beliefs in the existence of a subaltern 'Deaf Way' consisting of a different set of 'Deafhood' values. However, one should not let these distinctions obscure the absolutely essential role of cultural unity; the data illustrate cultural strategies used to develop and maintain that unity.

Once we have understood some of the dimensions of traditional club and school life, it is then possible for later research on contemporary Deaf culture to identify the ways in which that culture has changed, and how this has affected the Deafhood concept.

The Missionary Tradition

Chapter 2 described how numerous Deaf clubs were created by Deaf people before being taken over by the 'Mission for the Deaf', whilst others were established by the Missions themselves. The resulting two-tier administrative structure consisted of a board of management consisting of hearing people and a Deaf club social committee mainly consisting of Deaf people – this is the essential colonialist structure. The sole intermediary between the two was the Missioner to the Deaf. The accounts given here are intended to present a broad picture of the dynamics which ensued, and the relationships they manifest which help us to examine Deaf culture itself. More research is needed to unpack the dynamics between the ruling groups themselves – for example, the extent to which the missioners decided the general policies and the extent to which they had to find compromises between the board's policies and what they themselves felt to be in the best interests of their Deaf 'flocks'.

By 1980 most missioners had disappeared from the scene, but the structure itself is still in place today in almost every Deaf club in the UK. It is for a further study to examine their present-day 'liberal' regimes and the extent to which these have moved towards 'independence'.

During this period the titles of the Missioner changed. Deaf respondents used the same sign throughout but indicated those titles in lip patterns, which included 'Welfare Officer' (WOD), 'Social Worker' and 'Vicar'/ 'Chaplain' depending on the time period referred to and the religious denomination in question. I have used either 'Missioner' or 'WOD' for the earlier period and 'social worker' for the post-1970 years. Most of the data here are drawn from the period 1900–60, particularly the 1920s and 1930s. Almost all of it is new to the literature.

Dorothy, a sixth-generation Deaf working-class woman in her fifties from the South-West, drew on her own experience, plus the stories passed down to her by her Deaf ancestors, to describe life between 1900 and 1970. Her memories of the linking role played by the Missioner were vivid:

> Old club, football chairman who? Missioner. Cricket chairman who? Him. Cycle club, snooker, everything you can think of, chairman him. Deaf would put up with it. Why? Because of 'Please can you phone for me?' That! 'Phone help you, I'd better be chair then.' 'Oh, alright then'. (Thinks to themselves, 'Damn!').

Dorothy also placed especial emphasis on his ability to raise money for the club. Albert, a child of Deaf parents (HMFD) in his early sixties with extensive experience in the voluntary sector, confirmed this pattern from his own life and work in the Midlands and the North West, and gave a comprehensive explanation of why such control was tolerated:

> If you wanted a job, you went to him, if you wanted to buy a house, unless you maybe had family that would help . . . if you wanted a council house, if you wanted to go to the hospital, you had to go to him. Oh the list just goes on and on.

The missioners not only facilitated and controlled Deaf people's access to the society which surrounded them, but was the gatekeeper for that society's representatives. When I gave examples, which had been related to me of particular severe cases (e.g. page 192, note 3), Albert concurred:

> Their word was powerful . . . he alone could claim to understand Deaf people in the eyes of the law . . . It's undeniable that some missioners might have had Deaf people put away [into mental institutions] because they were a nuisance or challenged them too much.

In respect of the club as a whole, 'in some areas, not all of them, the missioner would make the decisions [without consulting] the Deaf committee members' so that 'there was a lot of tension'.

This apparent control over every aspect of Deaf people's collective lives was manifested in many small examples. Ken described the situation he found in many clubs in the North of England:

> Deaf . . . made the tea and biscuits . . . made a small charge, and at the end of the evening they'd add it all up . . . and give it all to the missioner to put in his office. They had no idea of any ongoing totals . . . they'd say 'Must, must, missioner look after money.' I'd say 'why don't you look after it yourselves; it's your money. You could buy cakes, or save up for trips out'. 'Oh no, missioner – his. Very good. Helps us'.

Albert described how these examples extended to the administrative structure of the Mission:

> The decisions made by the hearing committee were never brought down to Deaf people – they were never informed. Never received annual reports, never knew how much money was being collected or spent, never knew what power the committee had, *and the relationship of it all to their lives they never really understood*. They were totally disenfranchised. Totally! No voting rights about the building, about the employment of staff, about finance or any of that. Now if you think about that, that is total and full oppression!

It is not yet possible to give precise dates when missioner control began. Some Deaf people suggested that it began after Oralism, when those Deaf able to read, write and debate died out. Others, sceptical of such a 'Golden Age' reading, suspected that this pattern existed from the very beginning, as soon as money was raised to purchase a building. Lysons (1963) appears to support the former theory.

However, Ken felt:

Most missioners of a pure church background were well meaning, and the Deaf needed their pastoral care, especially the older ones. But . . . those with a 'welfare officer' type background, they were the worst.

He was referring to the 'WOD' trained by the Deaf Welfare Examination Board, where the religious aspect of the work was a smaller part of the qualification. Albert described them:

It was a truism that these were people who decided they wanted to work with the Deaf, and kind of 'had' to do the religious training. They weren't exactly 'men of God' by a long way, many of them.

Nevertheless, as Lysons' (1963) figures showed, all put in long hours at the Deaf club; many lived above it or nearby. In a world hostile to Deaf people, this dedication was cited as a positive quality and cited whenever some Deaf people dared to criticise them. Ken gave an example:

I know 3, maybe 4 areas where . . . it was eventually revealed that the missioner had been fiddling the money and got fired for it . . . some Deaf would say 'missioner fiddle, bad, fiddle, should out'. These were the same people who had attacked you when you criticised him, 'Shame on you attack missioner, whatfor? He *heart-for-Deaf*, him!'

In a significant percentage of cases, the missioner was a child of Deaf parents, especially in the earlier part of the century (Lysons, 1963) and thus even more intimately tied to Deaf cultural life. The ambivalence of the current cultural status of such 'HMFD' may owe something to this tradition but this cannot be explored here.

'Class' Differences in Deaf Society

Chapter 3 explained how Deaf people from these eras were all subalterns. Virtually all worked in manual trades; the exception being the occasional Deaf missioner or a few high-ranking members of the BDDA. Nevertheless some respondents identified class dimensions, and patterns of resistance which they related to class; I follow this distinction and draw conclusions about that terminology in the summary.

Dorothy was the first to bring these to my attention. This was a very significant insight; in all the literature on deafness, there is virtually nothing about differences between social groups. In fact, she herself was surprised by her memories, 'I never thought about any of this before. You asked and it came out of my hands.' She gave several lengthy accounts, so rich in minute detail that only the broadest themes can be covered here. The two groups she identified had their own areas within the clubroom:

Old club, long hall, all one area. Curtained off part for old black and
white TV – Deaf not have their own TVs. The first group you see when
you walk in? The working class group, arguing – [Town] *versus*
[United]. They'd all bring the [sports] paper – Pink 'Un, Green 'Un . . .
The women sat near them, but separately. 'Look at your man, arguing
again!' 'Ah, I'm fed up with him', and so on. Women would be talking
about children. The middle class would sit separate, leave them to it . . .
the other group who were separate was the old people. But – important
thing – *they were all in that one hall together.*

The significance of being 'all together' is explored later. When describing these two groups, Dorothy's terminology varied. Sometimes she
referred to them as the 'upper' and 'lower' groups, and sometimes in the
terms used here. I have chosen to narrate this chapter in class terminology
for comparisons with other societies to be considered. In numerical terms,
she felt that the upper group consisted of about 25% of the club, and the
lower group, 75%.

Albert also noticed the cultural geography:

The seating situation was very much related to where the tables were
set up . . . groups focused on where you could see the door, hierarchies
related to being near to the canteen and so on.

Because the information was so new to the literature, it was important to
verify it. Some material was presented to the discussion group, but the presentation focused on 'class'. The only people in the group who were
consciously aware of such differences were in their fifties; even those in
their forties were not aware of it. Afterwards however, I presented the information in a different form, referring to the 'middle-class' Deaf group as
those who were 'in' with the missioner. Each person immediately understood and were aware of such patterns in their own clubs. Their own
terminology for the two groups varied and will be used within their own
quotations. Frances recalled the difference after this re-presentation:

There was your workingman's group over here, all laughing and signing all over the place . . . and then over here was the other group, acting
rather dignified, wanting to be left alone a bit, not to be bothered.

Ken described the 'middle-class' group by focusing on a 'typical' couple:

I have a picture in my head of an old couple similar to the black Andy
and Amos characters . . . they were nice, respectable, and they'd come
to the Deaf club well dressed . . . they had their own little world, their
own church, their own code of conduct, very respectable . . . outside

their little world they mean absolutely nothing at all < snaps fingers > but within it they had some social standing and importance.

Albert also gave a vivid description of that group, albeit a much more sympathetic portraiture, explaining why they behaved as they did. He noted:

> Their body language was much more formal . . . so their signing was much more restricted in space, instead of the full body use, it would be reduced to a small area in front of their chest. And their facial expression maybe wasn't as open, and also the way that they walked and greeted each other.

His accounts were essentially compassionate – he understood the tremendous daily oppression they experienced, and the need to find ways to carry themselves with pride, in how they dressed, how they ran their lives and so on.

Dorothy explicitly linked the middle-class group with their (hearing) parental background:

> Did the upper group have better jobs? Some. Was their education better? No, sorry, some weren't very clever! Their families had money- they left it to them in their will.

We will shortly see how this financial issue came to affect the clubs and culture. These social groupings are similar to those within majority society, but with certain significant differences. Apart from the fact that there appears to be no Deaf 'upper-class', those in the 'middle class' group were different from their hearing peers, as Albert was aware:

> I met some of their brothers and sisters, and they were much more, how to put it, relaxed and confident middle-class people. But their Deaf siblings were much more tensed up and cautious, more restricted in their views and their beliefs. Similar really to what they call the petit bourgoisie, you know, the working class trying to climb. *Very obsessed with what was 'right' and 'proper' in ways that their hearing siblings weren't.*

This suggestion of the absence of a 'comfortable' middle-class is consistent with the concept of all Deaf people as subalterns – the upper group seemed to be striving to re-create their 'birthright' as manifested in their family. Because they were Deaf, they were not able to attain membership of the social class to which their parents and siblings belonged – they had to conduct their lives within the limited strategies and socio-cultural space available to them in the Deaf clubs. Hence the emphasis here on the 'striving' dynamic itself. These differences are important, as will later be seen, and consistent with information given by Dorothy, Ken, Raymond and Frances, the four giving the most detailed accounts of the past. So, although the term 'petit-bourgeoisie' seems to me a description which most accurately reflects their behaviour and attitudes, I will stay with the phrase which indicates their actual class origins.

Significant also is that, unlike the majority society, the Deaf club and community felt compelled to maintain a unified community, and had therefore to devise strategies for co-existence. As Albert put it:

> Everybody knew everybody else's business, or not all of it, but an awful lot of it. We had people who didn't like each other, but to survive, had to be together, and find a way of working and living together.

The cultural consequences of these two dynamics – class difference and the need for unity – inform the rest of the study.

Another difference from majority society concerned Deaf concepts of a good job. As Dorothy put it:

> Deaf women working as typists. Call that working-class? Deaf community didn't. Typing is a posh job! Working-class jobs? Dressmaking, laundry, sewing. 'Wow you've got a job typing! Hey everyone! Congratulations! Mine, [job] poor, me. Or if you worked in [famous name factory] – got lot of praise – firm's name important. I don't see that as middle-class [but they did]. Even if you only a packer there! That's all part of why it's hard to describe Deaf class from the 1970s onwards.

There were also some Deaf people who did not fit into either group, although only Albert and Ken talked about them. Among these were members who had married across 'class lines', whilst Dorothy also identified this process happening in certain types of recreational domains – for example, a member of the upper group with a passion for sport (and therefore for socialising with the others). One 'type' of these Albert called 'isolates', who were content to sit quietly and watch. Another was the disabled Deaf, or those with a mental handicap, of whom he said:

> We had an acceptance of mental handicap, for example . . . There was one chap, Brian, he had quite a number of problems, mental health problems, and mental handicap, but he was accepted, particularly in the old folk's club.

We should, however, be cautious about accepting this kind of evidence without interviewing these people for their own perspectives – certainly in modern times, Deafblind members feel far less accepted than the accounts by Deaf members would have one believe. No class distinctions were mentioned with reference to the clubs' youth groups. Amongst the old people, only Dorothy remembered a distinction:

> The old people sat in two separate groups too, but next to each other. They dressed differently too – one was more formal than the other. And the way they were with each other – when someone came to their own area [of the club], they would shake hands or hug the people on their table, but be very cool with the other table. In fact they were much more standoffish with each other than the younger groups were – there were some who wouldn't even speak to each other.

Since Dorothy is talking about the 1940s when the old people were in their seventies and eighties, *it would appear that such class differences have existed from at least the turn of the century onwards.* It was impossible for an initial study such as this to explore the dynamics described in this paragraph any further.

The cultural significances of these class differences, and how they combine to suggest the 'deafness/Deafhood' polarities will now be explicated.

Inter-Group Characteristics

Language and class attitudes in the early 20th century

Growing up in a time when hearing aids were rare, it appeared that the distinctions made in modern day Deaf culture between 'Deaf', 'hearing' and 'hard-of-hearing' people, between 'BSL users' and 'Signed English users', were configured quite differently; Dorothy illustrated this:

> This sign for hearing [shows sign with its root in 'speaking'] – that used to be the old sign. Then it changed through missioners' influence to this [uses sign that indicates 'good ears, good speech']. It's only recently we've been able to get back to our true, Deaf's own sign. Deaf not know meaning of what it is to 'hear'. But know what 'speaking' means - when hearing speak, you will see things start to happen!

(Note the observation almost 'thrown away' in the last lines here. There is an apparently profound set of parameters operating in the idea that 'Deaf not know meaning of what it is to hear'. The 'deafness' construction that operates in majority society often expresses itself in the 'birdsong' trope – 'poor Deaf people, they miss the beauty of the singing of birds'. Once Dorothy makes this point, however, it becomes more a case of 'Of course; how can you miss what you never had?'

Likewise the idea that 'when hearing speak, you will see things start to happen' – one must place ourselves in Deaf shoes, and imagine watching a situation where one person's mouth moves, and another then goes and does something as a consequence. To the young Deaf child, this strangeness must also seem somewhat 'magical'. In the film *A Certain Pride* (BBC TV, 1983), Gloria Pullen recalls watching hearing people go into tall, narrow red boxes for long periods of time before emerging, and wondering what on earth was going on, before her uncle enlightened her as to the mystery of the telephone. These perspectives undoubtedly underlie the traditional perception by both Deaf and hearing people which saw Deaf people described as 'Mutes'. The inability to speak the majority language is viewed in the Deaf tradition, as a far more distinctive marker than not being able to hear.)

She then recalled a significant example of how the earliest generation here referred to those with speech:

> This the old sign for what we call HOH now – 'Deaf and dumb, hearing (speaking) skilled'. See, everybody was 'Deaf and dumb'. Just some happen to be able to speak, that's all.

Albert confirmed this reading:

> They were all 'proudly Deaf and Dumb' – speech was just an added bonus; the others were Deaf and part of the community, but they could speak, that's all.

This inclusiveness is significant for examination of Deaf unity, especially since more partially Deaf and deafened members were members of the community in those times. Similarly, it is important to note that speech was seen as merely an individual attribute, a skill which could be used as part of a *'Deafgelt'*, that is, a talent, ability or behavioural quality which could be *used to benefit the whole community*. Dorothy extended this example from spoken to written English skills:

> There was so little attitude around English in those times. People would say 'So and so clever at writing English – best ask them' when they needed to [acts it out]. No big deal at all. None of this stuff like now about 'What, you've never heard of that?' or 'Oh, can't you spell that?!'

She gave an extended example of how those with good English would be called round of an evening to assist:

> First you had to invite them to tea. After the meal then they would sit down with father and mother and work on whatever the problem was – a letter to the council and so on. Must give the meal first though –

means 'respect'. Now, those people (unlike today) never said 'what, you can't read? Tch tch.' Never, never never.

Despite these more unified attitudes around English, there were class-markers within different styles of BSL. As Frances described it:

They had like refined behaviour in their signs [mimics] 'leave us alone now please', polite signing, yes, they signed different, yes [laughs]. Not like the others, signing all big and all over the place, rough and tumble 'ah it's alright mate, it doesn't matter, let's get on with it'.

Albert also discussed the two signing styles, but attributed their use situationally, according to whether it was Saturday night downstairs at the club or Sundays upstairs after church.

It is part of received Deaf tradition that the older generations fingerspelt far more than today. Raymond discusses this at length in the next chapter, but Dorothy distinguished between types of fingerspelling:

Working class use more flourish, some letters almost like a sign them-selves. Also use larger area of space. Look [demonstrates both styles, with 'sacked' and 'shocked'].

On my visits to the old people's club I was able to observe this, particu-larly on certain letters like 'k'. Indeed, the renditions of some (whose dress and manner marked them out as working-class) were so exactly like Doro-thy's, inflections, mannerisms and all, that this lent all of her accounts a greater validity.

Class patterns in social activities

Most informants felt that both groups attended church. This owed not a little to the Deafworld truism 'Not at church Sunday, missioner won't find you a job Monday'. Dorothy pointed out that their motives differed some-what:

The upper group, they went to please the missioner, or because they believed in all that stuff. The others, they went for social reasons. What else was there to do?!

She subsequently fleshed out the differences, noting particularly how much was really understood of what the missioner signed, how much was just pretending to understand and both groups' attitude to this pretence. One especially telling (and amusing) example of the working-class attitude to the proceedings was this:

Our missioner love himself, not God. Old Deaf would sign 'God-His' to describe that! His signing style showed that attitude too.

It is difficult for this joke to come across in translation, but the sense of it is that God belonged to the missioner rather than vice versa. Certainly many were perceived to act as if their views were a direct extension of His.

Sport was an extremely important part of Deaf community life; class differences were apparent there too and are discussed in more depth later. Club outings, holidays and visits to and from other clubs likewise manifested class distinctions. In some clubs workshops for learning trades and repairing items produced similar patterns and are discussed later.

The next three sections examine further manifestations of the values and attitudes of the different classes.

'Middle-Class' Attitudes

Towards the missioner

Given the missioner's dominance, one of the most important sites for Deaf social expression was through the social club committee. Dorothy attributed the origins of class differences to the manner in which this committee was selected:

> Committee mostly upper-class. Hard to get onto it. Maybe related to their [upper group] parents' funds supporting the club? My father always said 'If you rich, easy involve Deaf club; if you poor, difficult'.

Albert elaborated on the effects of the missioner's selection of committe members thus:

> One of the biggest problems facing the community was that when people became committee members, sometimes they became a bit too arrogant.

Unsurprisingly, different attitudes between the classes towards the missioner could be distinguished. Dorothy explained how she felt this operated:

> The working-class, if they don't like a committee decision, some would get a group together to go to the missioner. The middle-class would just keep quiet . . . They want the missioner to like them. Perhaps they were afraid to rebel in case their families got to hear. When the two groups would argue, working-class would say, 'We help you, but you bow down to missioner, what for? Stupid, you'. Oh they didn't like that!

Thus, what emerged over time was a 'middle-class' or petit-bourgeois group selected and approved by the missioner, and used to carry out many aspects of his policies and beliefs in his absence. The strategies varied from club to club, as did the types of situations in which they were employed, but this basic pattern, as reported by a number of the informants, appears to have obtained over much of the UK for most of the century. When one considers the central issue of funding the missions, it becomes clear that, under the UK charity system, one stood a greater chance of success if the Board of Management incorporated members of the 'good and the great'. Thus those wealthy people who had Deaf offspring were more likely to join if their children were given committee positions. Thus one of the essential features of the wider capitalist system creates a route by which it can penetrate the Deaf community.

Albert's portrayal of this group was more sympathetic. He described how, in a world which so intensely looked down on Deaf people, their primary opportunities for gaining self-respect lay in how they dressed and carried themselves in public, with a necessary dignity. Likewise, their prominent roles on the Deaf club committee were vital to support that dignity. His illustration of the fragility of that self-image was moving:

> So you had a position [at the club], and you were smartly turned out. But you might be a manual labourer or a carpenter, and maybe the missioner would visit you at work to talk about club issues. So he'd come in, in his suit, and you're there as a labourer, in your overalls, with your collar open and maybe dirty hands and face, and your position would drop – wham – right down low compared to his. And you felt it, I think, very much. It must have inside, you know, kind of *given the lie to the reality you wanted so badly to portray* . . . Take [G] for example – people think of him as a very important Deaf man of his time, and yet . . . he worked on the docks as a labourer, waiting to be picked for the privilege of unloading ships. And the missioner could play on that.

These internal contradictions are not only a marker of the difference between Deaf and hearing class structures, but seem vitally important in informing the petit-bourgeois angst that informed many of their actions and beliefs.

Towards the 'working-class' Deaf

Dorothy described how the middle-class group regarded the others:

> The upper Deaf will say 'Deaf-his-shame'; they're referring to the lower class Deaf and talking about their way of signing. Also they'd say, 'Deaf, lamp-post-his, meaning they would look down on those

who stood around the lamp-post talking after the club closed . . . They could afford the bus fare; the others couldn't!

It should be noted here that the lamp-post, a source of light at night for Deaf people, is a significant symbol within Deaf culture, one that carried even more weight in the era before homes were lit with electricity. It also rendered Deaf people and their signing highly visible to the public. Since most Deaf gatherings took place after work, willingness to be seen signing in public was symbolised by the lamp-post. By looking down on those Deaf prepared to expose their Deafhood thus, the middle-class revealed attitudes which go beyond class to the core of their self-identity, as explored later.

It is also crucial to note the way in which the group refer to the others as *'Deaf'* to denote the differences between them. Since they are not denying their own deafness, 'Deaf' in this context appears to connote 'behaving Deaf' as opposed to 'rising above one's deafness'. But what did the term 'Deaf' connote for them? Ken offered a common description:

> The 'Favoured Group' saw themselves as the clever ones, and the others, who were strong BSL, were seen as the 'stupid Deaf – shamc'.

This phrase was extremely widespread and still exists. Lorna remarked:

> Yes, that was it, 'the Deaf', or the 'stupid Deaf'. Eventually I turned round to one of them who was sounding off and said, 'Yes, the stupid Deaf – you're talking about me – I'm one of them!' He didn't know what to do, because no-one ever challenged them that directly.

This particular challenge was not mounted until after the Deaf Resurgence, however, when Lorna was herself engaged in professional life. 'Shame', the other part of the phrase, is significant to the study. Dorothy caricatured and encapsulated the full meaning of that response:

> 'Oooh look! Isn't that naughty?! Shh, say nothing..look at the Deaf signing awayhow . . . stupid they are . . . how shameful . . . they're embarrassing us'.

Another phrase Dorothy demonstrated, one which is hard to translate, was also significant – 'SHAME, NOT BAD/CAN'T HELP IT'. Although this particular phrase is dense in cultural information because it was used in many different ways, it was also used in a context similar to the previous one, as Albert recalled:

> Yeah, 'Shame, can't help it'. It would be used if a person was disabled or very poor < struggles to express exact meaning > It means 'their situ-

ation was not of their own making', and they wouldn't pull themselves up by their bootstraps, the situation had been forced on them.

There are actually two sets of meanings here. One is the 'middle-class' attitude described earlier. But the other – 'the situation was not of their own making' – is vitally important in respect of Deaf unity, and we will return to it in the next section. Ken gave a similar example, also discussed later. He drew attention to how the middle-class values interrelated with both the working-class and the missioner:

> Anyone who challenged them . . . oh dear oh dear! 'Shame on you, you should behave like us'. Of course they would tell the missioner and the others what you had said . . . And if any Deaf came along to suggest Deaf people should have more power, then he would get you ostracised or thrown out by using his Deaf lackies to spread the word that you were a no-good so and so.

This interrelatedness was observed by Dorothy even on occasions when the middle-class were trying to be helpful:

> The upper group when they reported back [from meetings] *were* honest. They *did* try to give good information. But they would, like, stand at the front, flash the lights, and make everyone watch. The Deaf would look at each other and make faces . . . [The others] want a nice orderly formal meeting – all must sit down quietly, like in church, with themselves as missioner! The information would go past us; we only saw their attitude, that's all.

In this example, Dorothy also refers to her 'own' group as 'the Deaf', again quite unconsciously; although it is not clear which group initiated the label, its emergence here suggested that the working-class Deaf were quite happy to accept the label. Another situation gave a telling example of middle-class attitudes:

> Middle-class Deaf would give money to the others [for their sporting activities]. 'Oh, thank you very much.' 'Now [join your] committee, me?' So the others couldn't refuse them! Also it was part of how they oppressed them without their realising it. 'Wow, they gave us 10 shillings! Hope they'll do that every year'.

This example is contrasted in the working-class examples later. Both groups would give to each other, but only one *asked for something back in return*. Thus, in contrast to the emphasis on practical Deafgelt, covered in the next section, this form implied a purchase disguised as reciprocity.

Towards lay people

Four primary situations and attitudes emerged from the data. The first relates to behaviour in public. Dorothy contrasted this group's attitude towards hearing people with that of her own. We have seen earlier that signing in public was disapproved of. She continued:

> The Deaf upper group, they would try to be oral with hearing people, not want them to see their signs . . . They wouldn't sign much in public. If they did, and they got mocked, like we did on the bus, they would sign small to each other, 'Best ignore them'.

Indeed, signing on the bus emerged as a significant theme among the respondents. As Frances, whose family's social status tended towards the middle-class group, remarked:

> When mum went out on the bus, she always told us 'don't sign' or 'keep it low, down there – hearing will call us monkeys, or go for us'.

Albert produced this same story almost word for word, except that he added that his father was less bothered than his mother, going on to say:

> And yet, if they were together on the street, they would be signing away to each other and not be bothered [laughs].

Frances told of the same pattern and laughed in exactly the same place, adding 'Why? What's the difference anyway?', although of course such difference is not only a marker of cultural importance, but indicates the degree to which culture is precisely that which is 'taken for granted' about social life. Further study would be able to bring deeper features such as this to the surface and explore them.

The second situation was the workplace. Dorothy gave examples of confrontations that would occur between Deaf and hearing working-class people, and described the middle-class's reaction when they told stories of oppression at their workplaces:

> If they got into a hassle at work similar to us, they'd say 'Best me patience with it, have good job [that I don't want to lose]. I'd say, 'No, go on, tell your boss what happened'. But they'd go 'Ooh, no, no.'

Dorothy's inference here was that reporting incidents of harrassment would not really result in them losing their jobs. Nor were their jobs necessarily better than the other Deaf group. Rather, it was the general attitude of fearful respectability that was key.

The third public situation involves obtaining information from hearing people. Dorothy described the contrast with the working-classes' *modus operandi*, as described in the next section:

When my parents told that story about the tram at the club, the upper group said 'Oh, I couldn't do that'. Or 'Ooh, that was rude'.

The significance of the sign 'rude' is also examined later.

The fourth public situation involved generalised attitudes towards, and confrontations with, hearing people. The examples given in the next section of such clashes were contrasted again by Dorothy:

> Would the middle class tell a hearing person that they were stupid because they couldn't sign? No! They'd say 'Hearing right. Have speech, talk can. Wrong you argue, pleeeease don't.'

In summary, then, it was their general unwillingness to confront hearing people that was in her view ultimately damaging to Deaf people, as will be seen.

'Working-Class' Attitudes

Towards the missioner

Albert described one significant aspect of the missioner culture:

> The missioner could come to your house at any time of the day or night! I've been home when they've arrived at 11 o'clock at night! Oh there was no appointment – he'd just arrive on your doorstep! And expect to be welcomed, to sit down and have a cup of tea.

Dorothy confirmed this, adding:

> It's always the working-class who didn't want the missioner around. 'Get lost! Not going to look into my affairs, my rent how much etc. Get lost'. The middle-class would ask him for help with forms. Working-class, most ask their family, keep it within themselves. Or my father would ask someone at work for help with forms. In return, he'd buy them a cup of tea.

As we have seen, those Deaf with good English would also come round to help in similar situations. Another story has particular resonance here, especially given the pathos of Albert's equivalent example:

> One day, foreman came to father and said 'Go to office'. Arrived, found the missioner there. Asked boss why – he said 'I can't sign, so I called him in'. Father said '*You can fingerspell – I taught you,*' so he slowly did. Then father turned to missioner and said 'I don't want you coming here in future'.

Dorothy described how the working-class group would on occasion band together to challenge the missioner. Albert observed what happened on such occasions:

> If the group really didn't like the decisions, then yes, one or two in the group, not the whole group would go up and meet the missioner and say 'we don't agree' and explain. But so often the missioner would just patronisingly dismiss them . . . They didn't stand a chance.

Hemmed in on all sides by attitudes and decisions they did not agree with, the working-class Deaf nevertheless continued to resist in whatever small ways they could. Dorothy told a long story about being in church when very small, becoming bored and kicking the pew in front. The missioner being the only who could hear it, there was soon a confrontation:

> When the missioner told me off, Deaf working-class straightaway said to him 'She's not bad / can't help it', and they explained why to him. Father would encourage me to say my piece – he'd only defend me if I couldn't cope. He asked me 'Why kick?' 'Bored.' 'Well tell him then!' Oooh dear, that was something. The missioner was shocked. The middle-class just sat and looked down their noses at me.

Another example concerned the sacking of a junior missioner who the Deaf loved 'because he respected Deaf people'. When the missioner put up a notice announcing his departure, one of the working-class group wrote 'Sacked' across it. This was reported to the missioner, who came and interrogated the group:

> We played dumb, each denied it, and when he finally pinned someone down, we all said 'We told him what to write', so he couldn't punish anyone.

The example may appear somewhat child-like but, in fact, illustrates a cultural differences between hearing and Deaf communities. It is not that the example is necessarily child-like or that Dorothy is obsessed by minutiae, but that the power wielded by the missioner and his loyal Deaf group was so all-encompassing that such 'victories' were of necessity very small. This example, and the others in this section reinforce the Deaf cultural concept of '1001 [small] Victories' which, as Chapter 7 mentions, may have been developed in the oral school. The other significance of this example is the display of working-class group solidarity and willingness to share the consequences; this *collectivity* is a resonant cultural feature, as will be seen.

Towards the 'middle-class'

The respondents identified four areas of responses to the middle-class's attitudes to them. One was to argue about principles. The most common examples given by Dorothy concerned money and the principle of contributing to the community:

The working-class would help the club in their own ways. They'd repair shoes at the club workshop and charge tuppence or threepence less than you would pay outside. Or they'd clean the church on Sunday, or polish the brass or repair the building.

Albert described similar situations:

If there was a silversmith or goldsmith and you had a chain that was broken, you might bring that into the club and ask them if they might repair it for you. And always at the end you would say, 'I'll pay you'. Meaning I don't want you to do it for free for me. But knowing there would be a reduction in price, based on friendship or whatever.

This reciprocity, as we have seen in Dorothy's example of English skills, required that self-respect be maintained by payment or the giving of something in return. This pattern in confirmed for the traditional clubs in the United States by Philip (1993).

When asked by the middle-class for contributions towards the club, there would be tension and refusal: 'They can afford to pay – let them! Me, I do it by working for the club'.

The second type of response was to assert their own achievements:

If there was a sporting event on and another club visited us, we have to cook dinner for them of course. The working-class wives would do the shopping, and the middle-class wives would cook it . . . At the Fayres, the working-class would make the food for it, but this time the middle-class would be in charge of laying it all out nicely on a stall, do the serving, and run the raffles. So the working-class wives would go round pointing out to everybody that it was them who had made the cakes and stuff.

When this situation was presented to Albert, he responded:

[laughs] That's right. Oh they were so proud, yes! And rightly so. There was tremendous pride at sales of work . . . seamstressing particularly, and some of the stuff was really beautiful . . . So they would say 'I made this' or 'I made that'.

This refusal to be cowed, even at such a public event (among the very few times hearing people came into the club), was indeed one type of response that those without power could make.

The third type of response was a strategy for keeping the middle-class in their place. At a time when cars were rare in the Deaf community, the first people to get one (after the missioner) were invariably middle-class members:

> The Deaf would go over to that person by their car, look it over and say 'Nice. Lucky that your mother died and left you the money. This nice way to remember her'. You see the working-class have ways *to put him in his place without being mean*. It was said nicely . . . so that they would stay friends.[1]

The last words are also crucial. Given the pressures on a community which has to actively maintain the co-existence of a wide range of people, such cultural strategies were essential. In this example there are two underlying principles: the need to put an individual or group in their place but to do it in ways that do not result in community division. This is an absolutely central point which arguably informs all Deaf dynamics, and will be enlarged upon in the next book.

The fourth type of response actually underpins all of the previous ones:

> The working-class would sign 'His way, shame, not bad / can't help it'. See that sign I've used? It means they can't help it, poor things. It means they understand *that it's not their fault*. Why? Go back to school days; both signed the BSL way . . . When they grew up, they changed. *See, the middle class were proper Deaf before.* When they got out in the hearing world, they felt they had to change, but the working-class kept their own Deaf pride; know the others lost something, so they sign 'not bad / can't help it'.

Albert, as we have seen, despite growing up 120 miles away (a long way in those times of course), also recalled the same sign and the same set of meanings. This sign and its connotations has all but disappeared now. It is too early to note if it has been replaced by something else, but the fact that no other current sign comes to mind tells its own story.

This example confirms the assertions of informants in Chapter 7 that class differences were not noticed at school. Its significance also lies in its *understanding and fundamental compassion*, marking a crucial difference between hearing and Deaf class-cultures. It is virtually impossible to imagine such compassion being expressed towards the middle-class by working-class hearing people, and illustrates the depth of (covert) Deaf pride felt by working-class Deaf people and the importance attached to values centred around being a 'proper Deaf' person. Again, this pride is made visible in (necessarily) small ways; the '1001 Victories' are exemplified in each situation in this section.

Towards lay people

As with the Deaf middle-class, responses indicated four basic situations and attitudes. The first, general public interaction, reveals a striking contrast. As Dorothy tells it:

> If hearing people mocked us, we were used to standing up to them. One time all our family were on the bus going to [V] . . . and two people behind were mocking our signs. So we'd turn round and go [gestures] 'Yes – What?' That would shut them up, then at the end of the journey they would come up and say 'sorry'. Father would tell them not to do it again, and that would be it, shake-hands.

There are numerous examples of this type of confrontation, some intending to achieve a positive end, and some, like the stories Frances, Albert, Raymond and Ken recounted, where the object was simply to put the others to flight.

The second arena of interaction was the workplace. Dorothy describes the working-class's raison d'être thus:

> They always carried ABC [fingerspelling] cards and forced them on hearing when they started a new job. I remember going to the works' Christmas party and being amazed that everyone there could fingerspell to me.

Colin, a Deaf Welfare Officer to the Deaf (WOD) in his sixties, gave a similar and very detailed example, noting the degrees of expertise in the various sections of the factory. It would be naive to assume this approach was universal, but set in the wider context of this section, does seem to contain a significant degree of truth. Albert's response to this question was interesting:

> If the other workers approached Dad, he would give them a card, but he wasn't going to force them to do it. But they did tend to approach him anyway. And if the managing directors were coming round, he'd always make sure he gave *them* cards! [Laughs heartily.]

By illustrating the Deaf refusal to be daunted by their 'superiors', Albert's version is in tune with the spirit that Dorothy is describing. However, it was not always so harmonious, as Raymond described:

Stan Woodhouse said when he worked on the shipyard as a welder, they would say 'you do this or that, pick that up', things that were not his job, so he wrote down 'I'm a welder, not a cleaner.' So they hit him. And there were a number of them gathered round looking down at him – 'Pick that up'. There he was, one Deaf person alone. No Deaf community at work . . . it was from incidents like that that he came to describe us as 'The Little People'. He said he felt like a beetle looking up at the Empire State Building . . . and Deaf life, what is it but dodging feet coming down around you all the time. Feet look big to a beetle that has to spend its life weaving in and out of them!

In situations like this, it was impossible to successfully assert one's Deafhood. But others did so wherever possible. Raymond went on:

Dearey – he was a Deaf bugger! A master craftsman with his own business too. Employed Deaf and hearing apprentices . . . One time a hearing man borrowed £5 from him, spent it on drink and he and his hearing gang laughed him out when he went to get his money. So he went to the man's house, took all the slates off his roof! Police were called, D wrote 'yes I have his slates and will give them back when he repays me.' So the gang had to go and have a whipround and just scraped up the money. So then C. said 'Those slates - they're in your garden shed!' You see, he was crafty enough not to actually steal them. Oh he was a tough bugger!

Dearey also insisted on the hearing learning to fingerspell:

He was like Hitler! 'Respect time! I pay you'. 'Finesse, finesse, that's what you need. Know what it means? Well go and look it up then.' They had to learn English with him around! But in the end they thanked him – 'My hands brilliant now'.

This is quite a dense passage to unpack. The next chapter will draw our attention to the significance of Deaf people's English abilities in the early 20th century. The other theme is captured in the BSL itself – that the employees' hands were 'brilliant' both at their craft and in their signing skills – Raymond's performance of this brings out a sensuality almost impossible to render in English.

Dorothy told a story where one Deaf man who was being harrassed went to his foreman and said 'I quit because of this'. The man panicked, told the manager and the next day the parties involved shook hands and changed their behaviour. (Shaking hands as an important reconciliation trope was also a cultural marker which frequently came up, though space does not permit its exploration here.)

Another example of the 1001 Victories I observed concerned a Deaf man who had got himself the unlikely job of driving a radio cab. When asked how he knew what his next job would be, he replied 'Oh I make the passenger call my base and get that address. Some won't do it, of course, so then I'd have to drive back to base to find out. But most did. No problem really!' His nonchalance was impressive.

Several stories were recounted by respondents relating to the frustrations of being excluded from union activities, since the men's fingerspelling would be lost in the heat of meetings. Nevertheless they made attempts to get the information. Albert gave one example:

> Father stopped a meeting once . . . he was asked to vote and he said 'I don't know – you tell me what it's about so I can vote'. And they stopped the meeting. And he changed the vote! . . . Because he had the information he was able to persuade them to change their position < looks proud >.

Not all examples were of conflict, and respondents cited instances of co-operation and mutual help, told with a similar pride in each small victory.

The third situation, that of obtaining information in public, produced several stories. Dorothy told two such:

> We had a lot of interaction with those we knew on a sort of 'all right mate?' level. But also . . . I remember one time in the town centre when a tram knocked somebody down. Mother went up to hearing and got out of them what had happened so she could give all the other Deaf the information.

The trope of 'Information' is beginning to emerge here as a highly significant Deaf cultural value. Obtaining it for the collective pool of 'Deafworld Knowledge' is an important part of the 1001 Victories, and deserves a whole chapter in itself. The contrasting middle-class response to this example was described earlier. Another story illustrates Deaf ingenuity in respect of neighbourliness:

> One time when I was small, the ambulance came to my street; my parents sent me out to find out what had happened . . . I got the information and brought it home. The next day father was able to go up to the woman whose husband was the victim, and use that information to get the woman 'talking', and she told him the full story. So he was able to show sympathy, *and* he could bring the full story home to us < indicates father's signing it with much smiling and pride at his achievement >.

The fourth area of response concerned general attitudes. Raymond and Dorothy both gave examples of situations where if the hearing person did not sign, the working-class Deaf, far from being cowed by their own minority situation would call the others 'stupid'. This is very important indeed. For many lay people, the idea that Deaf people might view them as deficient because they could not use sign language appears extraordinary. But, as we saw in Chapter 2, this deep Deafhood belief in the importance of sign language to the whole world is clearly maintained here. This belief in essence constructs that hearing people are, as the Parisian banquet quotation states, 'incomplete beings' to the extent that one is only a full human being if one can communicate with any member of any society. In this construction, it is not that Deaf people feel less human because they 'cannot' do this. ('Two people can't communicate in speech, like foreign? Then use sign. Simple!') It is that the others have imposed their lesser humanity upon Deaf people.

This position represents what is known in sign as a 'Strong Deaf' perspective. Maintaining it in the face of a world where everything that existed appeared to be invented by hearing people, whether buildings, transport, government, media or whatever, could not have been easy. Indeed we have seen the very different middle-class responses to such situations. The Stan Woodhouse example above also illustrates this idea of something lacking. Even when on the ground looking up at the group of faces of the bullies:

> He noticed that they were physically quite soft, that their only power was in their face, threatening and gesticulating. He thought that like barking dogs, they won't bite.

This reading of something lacking can be found in other minority groups who make direct links between the oppression experienced and the cultural 'weaknesses' which enabled the oppression to take place. Usually they then go on to suggest, as the Deaf do here, that they themselves possess certain cultural attributes which position their culture as equal and even superior in how they manifest a more caring and inclusive society of their own. Deloria (1988) and Churchill (1994) make such an analysis for Native American culture, as do Pityana _et al._ (1991) for African culture and Van Deburg (1992) for African-American culture.[2] It is important to emphasise that the means of communication used by the working-class in these interactions was mostly pen and paper, with only a limited vocalisation. We shall learn more about the dynamics of written communication in the next chapter.

Significance of 'working-class' interaction

The picture which emerges from the previous two sections is one of middle-class Deaf avoiding conflict and working-class Deaf meeting it. One dimension remains to be noted – the implication that working-class hearing people are the ones who 'attack' Deaf people. However, the situation contains a more profound reading. Corfmat, a hearing child of Deaf parents, gives an account of differing class attitudes to sign language:

> Our friendly [Air Raid] volunteers were not from the factories; they were mainly clerks . . . but I have found that factory hands were usually more extrovert and less inhibited, and they would wave their hands and create efficient communication. (Corfmat, 1990: 104)

In this context we might also note the 'hidden histories' of the use of gesture or sign in certain British factories. Deaf tradition seems to have it that this was particularly notable in the North West, and in the cotton mills.

In recounting his father's life story, Corfmat verifies much of what our informants have said, including a moving account of his father's (1001 Victories) ingenuity in becoming the First Aid officer of his large factory. In consequence:

> He had taught many . . . the rudiments of the Sign Language, and . . . his friends grew to a sizeable number. The number was unbelievable at times, for when we were out together he would often wave his walking stick to a distant 'friend' across the road.

Albert summarised the essential class differences:

> I feel that working-class hearing people may have been more accepting of Deaf people than the middle-classes, funnily enough, because the latter would say one thing and do another, or think another. Or . . . go all the way round to say something, not be direct. Whereas the working-classes might clash with Deaf people, be rude to them, but in the hurly burly, the Deaf would respond to that, and the two groups would find some level of respect for each other. They both got their hands dirty, so to speak.

There remains one more significant example of working-class Deaf and hearing interaction, namely the relationship between Deaf working-class rebels and pub life. This is examined in the next chapter.

Class differences and organising strategies

Dorothy's accounts here revealed extremely important differences between the 'Deaf way' and the missioner-influenced ways. She described the latter as standing at the front, calling for people's attention and delivering what was felt by the working-class to be a self-regarding monologue. This way of organising was referred to as 'Flash-Lights', which was the signal for such announcements to be made. The others had a different approach:

Working-class very clever – know how to unify and engage people's interest. Would use their particular hobby or passion, or their knowledge of that individual, to pull them in.

This is strikingly similar to Martha's account as head girl in the last chapter. Dorothy used a sign to describe this process:

> You need to use 'TAP-TAP', tell one or two people what you wanted to achieve, and then each would go out from there, tap-tapping the others, drawing them in based on knowing their individual ways, and that would do it. We'd get a large turnout, whereas 'flash-lights' would get a poor turnout.

Albert, however, felt that this strategy was also used by the other group, but from my own observations and the data from other respondents, the 'word of hand' method continues to achieve a greater degree of collective activity without the disadvantage of a few people being identified as leaders and thus vulnerable to personality clashes.

Dorothy also identified other strategies. Years later she herself gained a position of authority as an Executive Councillor at the BDA. This brought with it a crucial responsibility – bringing information from 'HQ' to face-to-face interaction with the local and regional community – a task made especially important by Deaf illiteracy. I asked her how she dealt with the 'Flash-Lights' mode of working she was expected to continue:

> Well I didn't get up and flash lights, for a start! I'd slowly tell everyone on individual level. Would feed them information-way first, so that Deaf said 'Oh, never knew that' etc. Then they would report that to the local branch. That's how Ann and Frances got interested in the BDA . . . Branch would say 'Please come to meeting and explain; someone said you told them XYZ and I don't know about it'. Oops! I guess I missed out one person. Because they thirsty for information.
>
> You have to be there in club most of the time with them – it proves you are committed. You can't just go one night and try and just talk BDA stuff – if I always hit them with BDA stuff it would become same as 'flash lights'. They would think you snob, and not listen. < gives more examples > Best to give half the information, not all, then next time they want the rest. Then you've got them coming to you! _That's_ the crucial breakthrough point.
>
> Also sell them idea of coming to regional council [political] meetings by having a dance afterwards, but tell them they have to be there early, so they don't realise there's a meeting first! But by end of dance they've enjoyed whole thing. Means you've brought together the two halves of Deaf life.

... I learned all this from when I was small, and how working class talk about 'Town' and 'United'.

This section has particular importance for those Deaf organisations who have been wondering for years why they cannot attract people to their work. It is the middle class who have largely constituted the membership of these committees in organisations like BDA, as the next chapter shows. And it would seem that it is, unsurprisingly, subaltern cultural strategies which will attract subaltern participation. Indeed, put thus, it is perhaps more remarkable that the BDA went for decades without noticing it. Such, apparently, was the strength of the 'deafness' ethos of those times.

Class differences, Deafness and Deafhood

As noted earlier, the term 'Deaf' was used by both groups to designate the working-class Deaf group. When I pointed it out to Dorothy, she was surprised; it was so habitual as to have escaped her notice. I asked her to tell me more, and she replied:

> I feel they are truly Deaf because they are strong in saying 'I do things my own way'. Sign strongly, in public sign openly, gather at the lamp-post, challenge hearing on the buses and other places. If the police can't sign, they will say to them 'You don't sign? Stupid, you'. All these positives accumulate to make up a strong Deaf pride.

Thus, the 1001 victories/strategies working-class Deaf group used to negotiate their environment reflect a belief that 'Deaf' people are those who hold fast to their Deafhood, their own cultural values in their dealings with the majority culture of the 'hearing world'. This standing firm in situations is the more impressive when one considers how at times this would create even more conflict and open themselves to more scorn, in a world in which plenty of ridicule and discrimination was already directed their way.

This links to a deeper cultural value within Deafhood. Dorothy's bus journey example, when she pointed out that the middle-class Deaf would avoid such conflict, holds what she feels is the key to it all:

> And so [because they didn't challenge the hearing], by the end of the journey, *hearing would have learned nothing. Still wouldn't have learned to respect Deaf.*

Thus an individual event of this kind becomes *an act that is carried out, in part, on behalf of the whole group.* One can thus glimpse a world in which a whole group of people, standing firm within their 'Deaf self', asserting their rights at work and in other places, entering into conflict with hearing people in public, are actually engaged in the task of day-by-day, person by person, drop by drop, *attempting to make their world a better place for Deaf people to inhabit.* Some of the benefits will rub off on the individual involved in each of those situations. But many of these activities must by definition be 'cast to the winds', in the hope or belief that the gain will not be their own, but other Deaf people's, including the middle-class Deaf.

This collectivist philosophy contrasts with the middle-class concern which was based on a more individualistic philosophy, where the prime concern was their own comfort or welfare, and where taking chances on behalf of the Deaf collectivity appears to have been avoided. Dorothy took the analysis deeper:

> The hearing [i.e. the middle class Deaf!] . . . yes they Deaf, but we can tell they have Hearing attitudes; can't call them 'Deaf' because they're already swaying back and forth, trying to balance on a tightrope between two worlds. They won't jump on the Deaf side; they always trying desperately to pull themselves towards falling on the Hearing side.

This BSL passage is rich in metaphor, and difficult to do justice to in translation, but includes an acknowledgment that, despite the struggle to pull one's self away from falling on the Deaf side, it is impossible to fall on the Hearing side – they will always be Deaf in the sense of being unable to hear and participate in the hearing world. Consequently their lives involve a psychological condition of perpetual tension and internal struggle. It is this *self-division* which may go some way to explaining the petit-bourgeois difference Albert noted between their hearing siblings and themselves.

Dorothy confirmed the analysis above by making an explicit link with culture:

> The middle-class got nothing to say, nothing to look back on, because they always value hearing things, bow down to them . . . so *got nothing inside of themselves.* Working-class don't care what hearing think of them, so in the end got rich culture.

This working-class appreciation of their Deafhood could not have come easy. 'Not caring' what hearing people thought may well have come at a price, involving strategies which helped them to deal with any pain from being so universally looked down upon.

Likewise, the sign 'NOT BAD/ CAN'T HELP IT" tells us several crucial things about Deaf culture in earlier times. As used by Deaf people in the study, it contains a wide range of linguistic 'affect', from mockery, anger and contempt through neutrality to sympathy and sorrow. The working-class Deaf's compassion for the others' loss of their former 'Deaf' state was understood only too well; the temptations to give in to the constant pressures of the majority culture to define one's self within its cultural expectations, when Deaf people's own self-definition was so scorned, and (even now) so misunderstood. As Dorothy put it earlier, '[that sign] means they [working-class] understand that it's not their [middle-classes] fault . . . back at school they were "proper Deaf before" . . . working class know . . . that the others lost something'.

The use of this sign contains both an analysis of how things came to be the way they were, and a route by which the 'underdog' group could rise above their frustrations with the others to maintain community unity. As Dorothy summarised:

> You see, the point is that in those days, unlike today, there was no envy or craving like 'Oh they lucky, they rich'. It was more like 'Me have job, family, Deaf club, what-for complain? We happy. Are they *really* happy?'

Deaf missioners

Given these fascinating dynamics, one becomes interested in those Deaf people who were themselves missioners. How did they fit into the overall picture? Lysons (1963) research indicates that, like the HMFD, their numbers declined as the Church of England hegemony increased. But much more research is needed to paint a full picture. We do know, however, that some were deafened and thus did not attend Deaf schools. But the extent to which they came to internalise aspects of Deaf culture and situate their actions from within that space or the degree to which they went along with the general missionary ideology is as yet unknown.

The data did produce some interesting clues. Barry gave lengthy descriptions of his club's Deaf missioner. We have heard how his sermon styles already attracted Deaf subalterns, but there was another feature:

> In the club, people would be standing around drinking, and he would come in, and they'd make an oval of chairs around him and he would sit in the middle and put his fag down, and sign about anything, like the newspapers. Deaf would say 'This bit here, don't understand what it means', and he would explain so good, and so we would all learn from one another.

The last phrase may appear to be surprising given the context. But insomuch as no explanation would come forth unless each Deaf person manifested their curiosity, their contribution indeed was to come up with a question that would release more information to the pool. Rev Hayward also read/translated stories from newspapers of his own choosing. Albert's experience brought him into contact with several Deaf missioners.

He was not able to come to a conclusion regarding how the other missioners saw the Deaf ones – whether they were seen as equal (and thus in some
essential way unlike other Deaf people) or whether they were looked down
upon. But he was able to draw upon one fairly common characteristic:

> Your Frank Goodridges and your Benny Morgans, I think they were
> the ones who realised that the Deaf were desparate for information, be-
> cause they were experiencing it themselves, so they gave out a lot of
> information. Stories, stories particularly. Old Tom Sutcliffe was full of
> stories, and Benny was too, and Frank. See, the Deaf missioner, well,
> clerics mostly, they seemed to see their role as giving a lot more infor-
> mation compared to the hearing ones.

As he was telling this story, he recalled another example, which will be
crucial for our analysis as the next chapter will show:

> [M], he became deaf when he was seven or eight. He always talks about
> Mark Frame – Deaf again, see. And a missioner again! M always says
> that Mark gave him information, stories and knowledge < triumphant
> smile > .

It seems clear then that at least three aspects of Deaf culture, the information trope, the reciprocity principle of skill-sharing and the rolee of
storytelling, had been internalised. This is as far as we can go for now.

Cultural Unity

We have noted that although there are similarities with class patterns
found in UK majority culture, a crucial difference is that Deaf people have
to find ways to live with each other and make their culture cohere, and the
previous accounts indicate some strategies. Albert waxed eloquent on the
extent to which cultural unity was achieved:

> ... at that time, the joy was that people actually worked *together*. Very
> much like a village ... We had people that didn't like each other, but to
> survive, had to be together and find ways of living and working
> together ... it was very much an extended family ... And I still feel very
> warm when I think about what happened when I was a child. I don't
> think I've felt anywhere else so fully and totally accepted as a person as
> there. It was safe, supportive, can be critical, but it was always there for
> me. Total, total acceptance. Unconditional love I would call it. That
> only families can give < grins > ... and I think that's what we're possi-
> bly losing now [with the advent of mainstreaming and the closure of
> Deaf schools].

We shall return to the 'village' theme later. Elsewhere Albert refers to the fact that any adult could discipline any child, and that he called several of the other adults his 'aunts and uncles'. The 'family' trope is also very characteristic of Deaf club culture, as Frances commented:

> I think of the Deaf club as my home – it's where I grew up. And the people there are my family. But recently some of them have died – it's really broken my heart, because *they are part of me, you know.*

It was impossible to miss the extent to which Frances felt the italicised phrase to be literally true – the Deaf collective 'we' noted throughout the study implies an inter-connectedness of great depth, as Jade observed in the last chapter. Clara, a young Deaf woman from the North East, noted that these Deaf club traditions were still alive in some places in the present, and used the same image:

> They're a really tight group; if any one of them's ill, the others always come round and help them get better. If someone dies, absolutely all the Deaf go to the funeral . . . [M] club is like one big family.

Unity as a superseding cultural value is thus manifested by this imagery. But there were other strategies by which this unity was maintained.

Sport as unifying activity

Dorothy earlier described how both sets of wives shared their work when hosting a visiting club. She became more explicit:

> With sport, both groups joined in well. The middle-class wives did what? Made the sandwiches. Working-class wives made the cakes. The middle class would then dress the cakes up, make them look beautiful. The Deaf [i.e. the working-class] were satisfied.

In giving the earlier example relating to preparing meals for the visiting club, she concluded:

> To me, what is important is that they worked together. That's why they were never in serious conflict, because there was that kind of co-operation there.

In respect of the men's own strategies, she gave several examples, including this:

> Cricket was the best mixed sport..the middle-class were good at it; the working-class – some would play if they were good at it . . . the rest of the working-class would go to cricket because they wanted to support their club. So then the middle-class would do the same at

football, *once they saw the others make the first move* . . . This would keep us all together.

Albert added:

Actually, sport overcame some of the age barriers as well . . . You would find the older men particularly would talk to the younger men on an equal level about sport. The younger ones played football, the older ones remembered when they played football!

Frances explained how this became true across genders as well:

We set up a women's team – football – and slowly the men began to support us. We'd go training with them, and then when we travelled to other matches, they would all come, and then then they saw us drinking after the match – hee hee, they never saw us drink at the club, only cups of tea! . . . We were champions five years in a row. That helped change their attitudes too.

The reciprocity that sporting activities fostered was cited in much more detail. An example which arose out of sporting activities, as we have seen earlier, is the varying roles in relation to cooking and the canteen. As Albert put it:

And again, that was an interesting point – who managed the canteen. It was quite a powerful position for women in those times . . . so to manage and serve at it, was you know, indicative.

Frances also discussed aspects of the canteen dynamics, which will be examined in the next book.

Club outings as unifying activity

Albert gave a detailed account of how this process operated:

Then you had your trips. Mother–father and I and the rest would go off to Blackpool, or Chester, or wherever, and those were special times too because rather than just having four or five hours in the club, for a whole day you would be talking to people and you got to know each other much better. And sometimes those who were isolated in the club, nobody was isolated on the bus, because you would be sat next to someone and talking away to them, and so on. And they would join the group when they walked around the place.

Frances cited another type of bonding situation:

We'd all go on holidays together. BDDA . . . every year, on the coach. HMFD, they would go too, so we all grew up the same way.

As with sporting activities, these offered single Deaf men and women the opportunity to meet others in different towns, and form friendships, relationships or marriages. This manifestation is also presented in the Pullen documentary *A Certain Pride* (BBC TV, 1983).

National Deaf consciousness as local unifier

A cultural trait particular to Deaf community life is the national orientation of its consciousness. The trips to other clubs and participation in regional or national social and sporting events created a sense of Deaf nationhood which helped to create a larger Deaf identity which, in turn, reinforced unity at the local level. Albert talked about the amount of national experience he had at a young age as outstripping that of his hearing peers:

> My father took me all the round the country, and he would meet friends that perhaps he went to school with . . . and we'd be there for hours talking about the old days . . . If it was a friend he'd met through sport, then you would watch the bond strengthening each time; it was really lovely to watch.

An important point to note here is that schools formed a first 'band' of friendships, which were then augmented by those formed at the club when people left school and went back to their native towns. Later for a variety of different reasons, they moved to different parts of the country, and formed further bands. Thus the basic framework for nationwide contact was set in place. Albert explained this with precision, although the translation does not do justice to the richness of the description:

> [S]'s mother went to the same school as my mother, so if she went to [L] and they met up, they'd be talking about the school, and then they'd be introduced to somebody else who would in turn introduce them to somebody and so on in ever widening circles, until over time that process would bring them all close together, bring them all in/back home [this is a beautiful and touching sign that translation cannot render] . . . You must remember as well that the schools' numbers in those days were enormous; so the chances of meeting someone from your school were very high.

The previous chapter illustrated how this national Deaf consciousness originated to some extent in the wide school catchment systems.

Another important national cultural site was the monthly 'Around the Country' section of the national Deaf publications, often cited as the most popular section because almost everybody had an interest in other clubs and knew the names which cropped up in each section. Even today the *BDNews* contains those sections as well as birth, death and marriage announcements – a 'village'- type cultural manifestation in a national magazine.[3]

Reciprocity and 'Deaf-Gelt'

Another crucial unifying strategy was the cultural belief that all skills possessed by individuals had to be shared. Dorothy and Albert have already described the ways that these skills were used to maintain the club building, and how spoken and written English skills were also shared. It seems, though more research is needed, that both classes appeared to concur with this cultural norm, although Dorothy has suggested some subtle differences as we have seen.

Language and humour as unifiers

A crucial aspect of Deaf culture difficult to explicate briefly is the power inherent within sign language itself. Albert gave three examples:

If you think of a group of people who've known each other for years, that have had their rows, and still stayed together, and there's still warmth and affection there; when they meet, if something funny has happened during the week, they'd tell people, *and then you'd get additions to the stories, and additions, and additions.*

By this he means that different people would embellish the story with a signed flourish, so that by the end it became a group-created story. I have found this to be true from my own experience, and it tends to suggest that Deaf humour is collective rather than competitive. If one stops for a moment to compare this with spoken languages, this makes a great deal of sense. It is difficult to verbally embroider another's funny remark; however, with visual languages it is easier to visually extend or refine a signed metaphor. Albert also explicitly drew a comparison with spoken language equivalents:

If somebody saw something happening at work, now on the face of it [in speech] it doesn't look funny; but *when they sign it, it actually becomes funny.*

Clara gave a similar example:

So much Deaf humour is in the signs, like [signs 'the dog lifted its leg against the wall']..but hearing, if you said that in English it wouldn't be funny..If you try to interpret the joke to hearing people, they would just give you a funny look, whilst Deaf would be crying with laughter.

There were a tremendous number of assertions of this example, including the United States informants. Maria, a middle-aged woman from a Deaf family, also explicity rejected the idea that Deaf people's passion for interaction was solely due to the isolation that would be felt after going from the club back into an alien society:

> There's a positive aspect to our culture that's being missed, and it has to do with language. There's something primally powerful about it, the way it engages all of our bodies and faces, its scope for storytelling, jokes and fun. I think anyone would be hooked if they had access to such intense communication experience.

Sally, a middle-aged American, extended this physical/biological dimension:

> People go on about how deafness is a visual experience. But there's more ... We're also tactile – we feel vibrations, don't we? We stamp on the floor, bang tables for attention, hug each other more than hearing, and so on. And we feel vibrations of things happening around, people's movements and lots more. We are rooted to the earth! We draw it up from the ground into our bodies and out through our arms and faces and hands. It's all part of one thing, a sense of physical wholeness that links to our minds and hearts and is expressed in our language. It's about aliveness, feeling really alive, and all parts of us being engaged in that aliveness.

Albert also remarked on the extent to which this total physical immersion (remember also that to be involved in signed discourse, one must permanently engage one's eyes) affected the sense of the passing of time; this coming from his membership of both cultures should be given some consideration:

> Have you ever noticed how clock time loses its dimension when Deaf are signing? Something happens to time somewhere in there – it's just conceived of, it just happens in a different way than at other [hearing] times.

Whilst several others drew attention to the importance of humour as a unifier, Albert's summary was the most concise:

> There's an awful lot of teasing in Deaf culture, but it's warm, always warm ... A person's characteristics are well known to all of those people ... my mother was a little bit snobby, so they called her Lady [W] ... People would tease her about it, about wearing her pearls and so on ... And she *loved* it, loved to be teased. She would laugh and laugh about it with them for hours and hours.

He told similar stories about his father and others, but the significance of this story is that it indicates how it was possible to use teasing across group/class boundaries to deflate in a nice way the very characteristics that caused friction in other situations. Moreover, as the story recounts, such teasing was actively welcomed as a sign of being included. Similar stories are widespread today – it remains one of the characteristics that impressed the hearing people new to Deaf life most forcefully.

One should not underestimate the importance of the sum total of these various descriptions and dimensions to sign languages. Clearly they differ in certain fundamental ways from spoken languages, and investigation of what that might be has barely begun (not least because of the focus on the extent to which they *do* resemble spoken languages, an impulse born from the desire to defend the Deaf experience). It is certainly not inconceivable that they offer a multi-dimensional communication experience which carries sufficient power of its own to attract and bind users, and thus the habitual focus on 'lonely, emotionally starved Deaf people' might prove to be another example of reductionist thinking.

Summary

These are but some of the previously unrecorded features which enable class differences to be transcended and unity to be established. Others which were taken as read between the informants and myself include the 'obvious' ones of the kinship felt from shared Deaf identity, the necessity for unity in the face of a hostile world, and the bonds formed by shared cultural activity over time. Finally, these socio-cultural patterns described here were considered to have broken down by 1970; Dorothy and others had difficulty in analysing them after that time.

Chapter Summary and Key Points

Space does not allow for in-depth comparison with the modern day community, so conclusions in that respect are premature. Nevertheless, we are able to sense the importance of a diachronic perspective in defining Deaf culture.

These responses brought to the surface for the first time the role of class differences within Deaf culture, though it is too early to conclude whether 'class' is the most appropriate framework for this experience. Although the petit-bourgeois concept seems in some ways more useful, there remains the important difference that the equivalent hearing group does not experience anywhere like the same degree of oppression and control from above.

A similar dynamic means that we need to consider how the middle-class group fit into the subaltern concept we have been using. There does not seem to be an English term which encapsulates it – 'élite subaltern' suggests something with more wider social prestige than obtained here, for any privileges gained by this group were slight compared to the extent that they were still viewed as lowly people by both missioners and lay people. 'Upper subaltern' comes closer but still does not 'feel right'. We also require a term to mark the distinction between local middle-class and those few who were part of a national élite, involved with the BDDA or its sporting equivalent, the BDSC. Perhaps 'deafness subalterns' might capture something of this, although even this does not leave us much room to mark a further distinction – those very few Deaf people who were social workers, or involved with the RNID, who could very much be described as within the 'deafness' mindset, yet were certainly not subaltern.

Even more significantly, there appear to be strong connections between class attitudes and Deafhood. This also indicates that Deafhood is something that has to be *actualised* for the majority with hearing parents via numerous strategies, including how they conduct themselves both in and out of Deaf social groups. In Deaf families that actualisation is produced partly in the *acculturation* process of 'normal' family life.

Nevertheless, the existence of this élite subaltern group indicates that this whole complex set of relationships within the Deaf discourse system needs to be accomodated within a model of Deaf culture.

Having established some of the fundamental dynamics within the two traditional sites of Deaf culture, we can now look at how these have been manifested in later eras.

Notes

1. The quote above continues:

   > 'Ah, it doesn't matter – life keeps going'. Notice that sign I've just used? Important.

   I grin with amusement looking back at this moment. From not having thought consciously about any of these issues, Dorothy has moved to a point where she is so actively involved in the re-construction that she has become conscious of the various philosophical and cultural tropes which emerge, and has taken over the interview in a motherly way, to direct me as a Deaf person from a hearing family through the mysteries of past Deaf subaltern life. It is examples such as the sign used here which if explored further would probably reveal clearer examples of Deaf ontology, whether a straightfoward stoicism or a variant of existentialism.

2. This is a timely moment to illustrate the extent to which the basic construction which Raymond puts forward is perceived as applying across society. We have seen how Bourdieu emphasises the need for academics to reflect and analyse their own position in the production of knowledge. The Stan Woodhouse example in the Newcastle shipyards leads immediately into the following:

If you look at the universities and all their power; the 'seat of learning', great intellect, impressive writings, and the many years of tradition that all add up to great power, and then see a Deaf person go up to them, and write something down for them to read, that is about Deaf people and their feelings, they would tear it up and throw it away in contempt.

This example is signed using the same conceptual handshapes and positions as for the Newcastle shipbuilders. One could hardly obtain a more concise encapsulation of why this book is needed, and what its acceptance means to Deaf people.

3. Since this text was written, the magazine has been taken over by younger people who have dropped this section, a significant example of how young Deaf people have become unaware of and unappreciative of, the importance of their community's traditions and values. The American Deaf activist M.J. Bienvenu noticed the same development in US Deaf magazines some 10–15 years earlier, with the same sense of dismay that older 'grass-roots' Deaf people were being disenfranchised by the turn towards individualism.

Chapter 9

Subaltern Rebels and Deafhood – National Dimensions

> The intellectual and spiritual health of any group is secured only to the extent that its members are permitted to be themselves and still be accepted as part of the group.
>
> Julius Lester (1991)

Introduction

Chapters 7 and 8 have illustrated the magnitude of the task faced by those who might wish to see a larger sense of self and Deafhood develop, to move beyond the patterns characterised by covert resistance and '1001 Victories' to ones which could encompass more overt forms of expression or rebellion. This chapter traces some attempts to achieve this from the late-missioner era to the present day, and illustrates how the cultural patterns of the earlier eras still inform the contemporary situation in its first 'post-independence' phase. In doing so, it examines club-level cultural patterns, then illustrates how these were extended to the national level.

Although the data collected by the study ranged widely across other themes of importance to Deafhood, some of which were more purely 'internal' cultural features, such as differences of opinion between groups of Deaf people over how one should conduct one's self in relation to Deafhood or the pressures on Deaf families to take responsibility for a entire community, these would require considerable space to do justice to them all. I have chosen, therefore, to focus on the more 'oppositional' aspects of the culture. In doing so, I run the risk of implying that Deaf culture has developed in reaction to 'hearing' culture rather than being a 'pure' culture in its own right.

However, it is altogether too early to draw conclusions in either direction. Clearly, as we have seen, Deaf children and adults have developed a strong sense of 'us', which is necessarily predicated on a very real awareness of 'them'. Both the review and the data hint at a less oppositional past prior to Oralism, but that history being largely lost, it is understandable that there is little awareness that perhaps the colonialists were not typical of hearing people as a whole, so that throughout the period of study, all my observations and data were steeped in an intense climate of 'them _versus_ us'.

As the chapter proceeds, it becomes clear that those in overt rebellion could only clear a space for cultural development by confronting the 'hearingness' of what they faced; having done so, it remained for that space or void to be filled by the development of new cultural forms. A major factor in developing confidence for confrontation, as will be shown, was contact with lay people in specific domains which enabled some Deaf sub-alterns to see beyond the boundaries imposed by their colonialist upbringing.

Deafhood and Learning from Elders

Although Oralism did much damage to Deaf school-leavers, they still retained the potential for Deafhood development. As Raymond put it:

> Deaf people in their young days . . . were controlled, meaning that the Hearing Mentality was imposed on them . . . but because Oralism could not get through to them fully, since fundamentally they couldn't communicate with them! . . . there was a grey area between what was Deaf and what was Hearing.

Within this grey area, young Deaf people's first sustained contact with Deaf adults were of great importance in shaping their future path. Raymond's accounts of those Deaf elders who inspired him were the most extensive accounts collected, but his experiences parallelled some of the other Deaf respondents. Here he talked of Jim Mackenzie, whom we met in Chapter 8:

> I went into the Deaf club; he was the first person to meet me. My mind was blown! No mouthing, just fingerspelling! It was like running into a brick wall! . . . Well I knew the ABC of course, but _that_?! So I went home and practiced in front of a mirror . . . in the bedroom where nobody was watching! Passages from my works of Shakespeare, for a full week. Then I met him again . . . Fascinating. Truly dumb, but his English, brilliant!

The 'culture shock' manifested in the fingerspelling skill of the older Deaf people who were educated prior to the complete oralist takeover is typical of the experiences of many Deaf school-leavers. One thing immediately struck him:

Those old Deaf people are living evidence that . . . Oralism is wrong *on its own terms*. Many that I met would write things down in public – that fluent English there, where has it come from, then?!!

He went on to give examples of how the old regarded the younger ones brought up on Oralism:

> They'd say that one of the greatest books ever written was, what? The English dictionary! They'd say 'these younger Deaf, they need pictures, like a rabbit bouncing along across the page, whatfor?! All I could say was 'Oh' . . . I thought that was an amazing thing to say![1]

The dictionary, of course, is a marker of the intense study the older Deaf undertook in order to unravel the mysteries of the English language. In other places it has been described as their Bible, and it constitutes a manifestation of the 1001 Victories principle in a tangible physical form. Ray added: 'Me, I thought I went to a better school. But I tell you, I never saw Deaf people write like that there'. In other words, the 'average' Deaf school before Oralism achieved better English than the supposed cream of the oralist crop. Whether true or not, this view is widely held. He gave examples of the kind of interaction between the generations amongst a similar group in Edinburgh:

> The old Deaf there, fascinating. Writing is great, their fingerspelling is spot on. They would keep trying to put the young Deaf right. They'd say things like 'Him sent off, whatfor?' 'Kicking'. The old would intervene and say 'No . . . for tripping; they're different things'. 'Kick, same'. 'Ah, no, no', and they'd explain.

Another example was more remarkable:

> One old Deaf, blind too, an old lady at the RC club in Newcastle < does beautiful description of her hand being fingerspelt on > . . . fascinating. I felt really ignorant next to her. She loved Daphne du Maurier books. And they were all fingerspelt to her. I never read those books. I asked her how she could do all this. She said her mother fingerspelt to her all the time when she was growing up . . . then she got braille. She didn't like it – she missed the warmth and sensuality of the human touch.

Sean, a young Irishman in his twenties described how the example of elders extended into dealings with lay people. His epiphany came in a shop queue:

> . . . There was me, trying to use my voice, and all the time the queue behind me was getting longer [because the shokeeper could not understand his voice], and I felt so ashamed. But this old Deaf man, he

just stepped in and wrote down what I wanted, and the shop wrote down the price, and that was it – done in a flash. I'll never forget what that taught me about *true* Deaf dignity and pride.

He realised that using his voice to make unintelligible noises was grotesque by comparison with the simple dignity of writing; the old Deaf even carried special notebooks for that purpose. It is indicative of the degree of brainwashing that prevented him and others working this out for themselves, although lack of confidence in English undoubtedly played its part. His choice of words also indicate a knowledge deeply buried inside him that there actually *was* a 'true Deaf way', despite all he had been taught.

It should not be assumed that the old people's sense of Deafhood gave them total self-confidence. Raymond gave a moving example from watching an old Deaf man conduct an interchange with the railway ticket office, writing 'Please may I have the correct fare to London, King's Cross'. He noted:

> That word 'may'. It's a permission word . . . It gave me the realisation that inside there was inferiority, that he was still one of the Little People [see last chapter]. But the English was still really smooth, and his example inspired me.

He continued with a remarkable point:

> Now those Little People are brave. They are aware that a lot of hearing people can't read. *But they don't know which ones!!* They have to stick their neck out, take a chance, every day of their lives < acts out example with Chaplinesque overtones > .

This example is of course especially significant in eras when hearing illiteracy was comparatively high, for the old man's writing shows his English register to be quite formal. One has to project oneself into the old Deaf shoes, and imagine how they had to assess each person they dealt with, the kind of risks that they took, since some of these people would not take at all kindly to the idea that supposedly ignorant Deaf and dumb people could do something they could not – and their self-image would already be sensitive in this precise domain.

It must have been a bitter blow to young Deaf self-confidence to realise the system they had endured not only had not always been the norm, but that something better had actually once existed. Furthermore, since their educational day had now come and gone, there was little prospect of achieving the literacy their elders possessed.

Some more determined souls did make their own efforts. James, in his fifties from the North-West, had a good command of written English, and explained how he patiently taught himself to read and write after leaving school:

> I would use *The Daily Express* and the dictionary, and slowly build it up from there, until I could read all those political type books. It took 12 years to get to the basic level, then I could build on that. I would also meet hearing people in pubs and political meetings, and we would write back and forth, and so I slowly managed to make sense of it all; how there was *another* hearing world under the surface of the one we were made to focus on!

James was of course in a minority, but the sense he gives of a lifetime's struggle informs our picture of what other Deaf people had to do. Michael, an Irishman in his forties, gave a similar example of a self-taught Deaf man:

> He taught himself English, not only from books, but from these written conversations with hearing people. It was dealing with hearing people, mostly in pubs, that actually improved his English, and built his strong Deaf identity, and now he has his own business with hearing actually under him!

We shall return to the significance of 'hearing people and pubs' later, but one other theme is significant:

> Interesting – the older Deaf still left alive say they don't need interpreters! They say 'Me fine with writing with hearing – not need anybody's help!'

Raymond summarised the sense of history implied in these cross-generational accounts in a resonant metaphor:

> Sign languages are far better than Deaf people themselves; they live on after individuals die. When those old people signed, whew! Ghosts danced on their hands!

This example echoes the pre-oralist sense of sign language being the ultimate gift to posterity, since Deaf generations come and go, but a trope, or as I will explain later, a meta-concept, 'Sign' remains. This dimension was encapsulated by Maisie Baillie, a Scottish Deaf woman in her eighties:

> When I watch Deaf from around the country all signing together with their different dialects, or Deaf people from around the world doing the same, I say to myself, 'Thank God for this gift He has given us – our beautiful language, our hands'. (*Sign On*, 1998)[2]

She also indicated that this was a theme within Deaf church in past eras. It is worth noting that her joy was founded on two themes – the multiplicity of signs for the same concept, and the unity that Deaf people could create by communicating across those linguistic boundaries – *e pluribus unum*. It was clear that this meta-concept was either part of a Deaf spirituality or a manifestation of the human spiritual impulse – it is too early to conclude.

The data also indicated a beginning to the process of understanding the transmission of other beliefs, morals and attitudes. Jim Mackenzie taught Raymond other lessons:

> He gave me some good advice. Never trust anyone, even me. You – I don't trust you. Never. We are friends, but trust me never. Why? I could go mental one day and then . . . He said it as a joke, but basically it was – 'Decide for yourself. If you think something is right, don't let others influence you. You can listen, but the decision lies with you. You're the one that has got to live your life' . . . *You could say a part of him lives on in me.*

This takes on greater significance in the context of all the pressures on Deaf people to follow majority society beliefs. The italicised phrase echoes what we have heard in earlier chapters about a 'primal' interconnectedness between Deaf people. Here Raymond consciously embodies that experience; carrying forward the much-repressed values of one's ancestors is imbued with greater weight than in majority society.

Michael also recalled other contexts in which the old Deaf set examples:

> One Deaf friend, brought up orally and his English no good, went for a job, but he and the boss couldn't communicate. So the boss called in an old Deaf man who worked there and he became like an interpreter, but all done in writing, and my friend got the job!

Other situations of importance included old Deaf from Deaf families forming a linguistic bridge in clubs and meetings, between the old and the young who could not fingerspell fluently. Likewise:

> Remember, back then, Deaf had no information. No TV then; no access to radios. So it all had to be got from writing, whether newspapers or written conversations, and then passed on to others. Knowledge was like gold dust!

However, Michael identified how the importance of written media led to a reification of English, causing conflict:

> The old Deaf, they talked of becoming smart through English. Deaf my age trying to develop signs for new ideas – old didn't agree. They said 'You don't become smart through sign language. Focus on writing!'

This observation is crucial. Although the old Deaf had not experienced Oralism, and did not reify English or denigrate sign in the way that oralists did, they nonetheless reified English (perhaps unconsciously) as a *practical* and 'Deaf-traditional' means of expression. Indeed, one of the most difficult areas to clarify is the extent to which all the old Deaf fingerspelt and the domains and styles in which BSL might have been used. The reification had consequences for the younger Deaf who sought to emulate them as will later be seen.

Raymond met Jim twice a week 'for years' to develop his awareness. His other mentor was [Dodds], a Deaf tramp; he gave a long account of the man and how his mind worked:

When I first met him in the pub, he gestured me to sit. Asked my name. 'My name is Ray'. 'Sounds a common sort of name'. I raised my eyebrows. 'I have a lot to tell you. Get me a drink'.

He told me about the Deaf club missioner and asked why I went to that club. I said, I guess because Deaf go there, to meet there and then from there go somewhere else. He said 'All the donkeys go there; the missioner sits back proud as punch to have captured them all'. I said 'You got a problem with him then?' He said 'Oh yes, I hit one of them long time ago'. 'Did you?' 'Yes' and he leans forward and says 'Who says I can't hit a priest?' 'Well I never asked that question'. 'WELL I AM ASKING YOU THAT QUESTION!' 'Errr, nobody?' 'EXACTLY!'

The account continues in this vivid vein:

He would encircle you, tying you up with questions ... He was capable of making you believe that the Eiffel Tower was an optical illusion ... that the Queen Mary was a rowing boat. He could show you that this was that, and therefore that was the other, and therefore the other was this, round and round ... If he came back now I'd be prepared to buy him clothes and he could live upstairs! I had a good 6 years experience with him.

He was a master conversationalist, at the arts of debating, of pulling you in, point by point. And *that's how I developed my way of talking to Deaf*, to put something out and wait for the reply, step by step, question by question ... He influenced me on how to keep their attention throughout. He died on the streets; no home.

Indeed, Raymond is still known for his 'Socratic' style of conversation. In his interactions with Dodds, two of these themes recur – the meetings took place in pubs all around the town and Dodds mixed freely with hearing people there by written communication. A third theme was developed – Dodds rebelled against the missioner control and this cost him club friendships. The convergence of these themes is developed later.

Rebels and Reprisals

The new wave of young Deaf people, including those graduating from the selective private schools, entered the clubs in the early 1960s with positive expectations. However, those seeking to use their ideas to develop the clubs met with a shock. The first example here commences when 19-year-old Ken is confronted by the missioner in an attempt to diminish his credibility with those he might influence. After some months of argument on a wide range of issues, he was challenged to come to the after-church social to debate the existence of God, Ken being an atheist himself. He went away and developed his most sophisticated arguments ready for the night. However:

> [Missioner] starts and says 'How do we know we've had a war? 1939–45? How do we know?' Deaf hands go up (like teacher and pupils!). 'From books'. 'Yes that's right' . . . and he went through several examples . . . 'Yes, that's right; it's recorded history. The Bible [pause for effect] the same . . . That. It's fact'.

Ken had not reckoned on the missioner's cultural tactics of playing to the gallery:

> I thought, 'Oh God!' Because the Deaf were sitting there with their mouths wide open on the edge of their seats, tongues hanging out . . . I thought 'You crafty bugger!' . . . I was geared up for a Bertrand Russell type debate, or Thomas Paine . . .

He had no choice but to attempt to match those tactics:

> Well I picked this book out of a box that was lying there. An Enid Blyton book. I said, 'Five children, one dog. This book true!' Deaf, – 'No, no, rubbish, rubbish, story. Made up'. 'No, true, look, History!' . . . [Dramatic pause, points to Bible] 'This one same. Made up!'

Despite Ken's gallant attempts to match the missioner's use of cultural patterns, the struggle was unequal, with both missioner and the audience taking recourse in comments such as 'shame on you', 'blasphemy', and so on, at each turn. Translation does not do justice to the gallery-playing aspects, which were crucial if the threat of Ken to the missioner was to be quashed (although his image was enhanced with a small younger group, as will be seen). The example also indicates, as Ken put it, 'their determination to prevent Deaf people from even learning how to think and debate'. Even more significantly, 'this missioner was more advanced than most of the others. He wasn't popular with them – 'Whoah, you're going too far! Slow down!' '

If strategies like this didn't work, there were others, as Raymond explained:

> Someone'd say 'let's have a bar here at the club. He'd foam at the mouth. 'Drink is Sin!' 'Say who?' 'Bible'. 'OK, I will ask Ray; he loves to read the Bible, to come.' So I went, and said 'OK, what book, chapter, verse?' 'You trying to be clever?'. 'I am clever'. He couldn't show me anywhere! 'You're winding yourself up.' 'Right, you're banned!

Battles to obtain a club bar seem to have been a major site for subaltern challenges to the missioner ethos; one informant told me that not until 1967 did the first club, in Coventry, succeed. Another tactic was to keep records on the 'troublemakers' to ensure later missioners continued the strategies. Dorothy explained:

> One new Principal Officer [ie the new breed of social worker] found in the files a secret blacklist. Slowly he met all the people on it, and realised we were rebels, and then called a meeting of those on it, and explained about the list. All my family's names were on there. Then he tore it up in front of us and threw it away. Why were we on there? Because we always argued with the missioner. The idea of the list was to warn the new missioner! Interesting; the one before him was horrible to me for no reason. I set up Girl Guides and everything, but he'd give me lots of problems with the minibus and so on. Now it's clear . . . It hurt so much 'cos father good in club . . . my mother said he should be buried outside the club. He'd work for all the events, nick materials from work, make prayer stools for the bazaar. Missioner not interested in his good side. I never told my mother about this – it would destroy her.

Given the vital importance of the club to Deaf people, the ability to ban someone for disagreeing with the missioner carried immense resonance, which served to keep other less bold souls quiescent. However, for our purposes, the most significant aspect is that the missioner would use his (middle-class) committee to carry out some of his decisions. Importantly also, they would sometimes do this without being aware that this was the case – a clear demonstration of the process of hegemony. As Raymond put it:

> If you disagreed with one of his boys, you disagreed with 75. If I told one of them he was wrong, the next Saturday night, the other 74 would come and argue with me. That's how it works.

Several informants gave in-depth examples of how this group enforced these decisions. Ken's example was typical:

The Favoured Group had the power, because they were carrying out the missioners' instructions, to throw you out of the club, your only lifeline to a social life. So what with Oralism and the big hearing world, they had little confidence and self-belief to challenge that.

One of the things the lackies loved to do was run the doors at events with their little badges on. It made them feel big and important that they could exclude you from things. You used to get another version of that at every Deaf club too – you always had the little bloke who would sit at the door all night and when you came in, he would say 'You member? You paid up? Oh all right you can come in.' He'd spend all night there – he'd even have his back to the club so he missed all the fun anyway. Yes the whole ethos was of these Deaf lackies loving to say 'No' – to things or to people. They never said 'Yes' to anything in life really!

I have had numerous experiences of this syndrome in the past, certainly up to 1986 which was the last time I deigned to expose myself to that kind of power. On that occasion, I turned up for a national conference and enquired about the week's evening event tickets, only to be told by one of these individuals ' It's sold out'. Disbelieving him, I arrived in the evening with a nationally known interpreter. Again he told me it was sold out, whereupon my companion passed me her ticket and walked in, as did I, handing over her ticket as I did so. The next day I went to the person who actually stored the tickets, found out they were available for each night, and bought the rest of the set. That such a degree of apparently petty exclusionary behaviour could be visited on me in 1986, when I was already nationally famous, speaks volumes for the kind of thing that was visited on lesser-known and powerless club rebels.

A similar pattern may well have existed in the USA, since a comparable character occurs in Bergmann and Bragg's (1981) _Tales from a Clubroom_, which was written with capturing typicality in mind. Importantly, one can find countless examples of a similar dynamic within the Native American experience, on reservations controlled by BIA (Bureau of Indian Affairs) lackeys (Churchill, 1994). In these cases, the consequences were far more violent and even life-threatening. Other accounts suggest that this was a standard tactic of colonialism – to set up a structure whereby a small group would be given power – so long as they wielded it as and when directed by the colonialists (Davidson, 1992).

Another strategy was for that committee to keep their power at all costs. As Albert explained:

You look at the old committees; it's the same people on them again and again. Once they got there, they held onto it. They needed it, they really did. They had something, but what about all the others who had nothing? All the others who did their manual work, their carpentry, their sewing, they had no real power. And they were extremely bright people who couldn't give of it.

Raymond gave detailed accounts of how attempts to develop the Deaf club were continually thwarted by such committees:

They accused me of trying to disrupt the traditions of the club. Like Wednesday nights, church service. No one do anything except church. I organized snooker games that night – furious clashes. Snooker upstairs, church downstairs – no harm. Tradition! Noise of the balls! But they're all Deaf!! No, it was 'Vicar can't concentrate'. Committee voted it out. 'OK, Thursday then?' 'Nope, traditionally closed Thursdays'!!

It seemed that any activity which did not originate with the missioner or his group was prevented simply because it might enlarge the possibilities of what Deaf people might aspire to or give them sufficient confidence to 'rock the boat':

Likewise trying to join the hearing darts league. Or to have a quiz night. Or a variety night, where Deaf could get up on stage and perform. *It would get put down as a hearing influence,* or vicar would say no. You couldn't get anywhere. That's why we gave up.

This negative ascription of the 'hearing equals not proper Deaf person' dualism is here clearly used as a cultural weapon to maintain a tradition which the 20th century missioners may have shaped. Ken illustrated the way the missioner/Deaf network joined forces not only to bar club membership, but also to have them barred from as much Deaf life as they could influence:

I got banned from a couple of clubs actually . . . at some dance or other. The missioner, in front of a fair few people, actually, said 'Don't come back again – we don't want people like you here' – and he'd never met me before!

Raymond told several lengthy stories with great gusto about being banned from similar events.

The importance of these examples is not to show 'Deaf versus hearing', but how classic colonialism meant setting Deaf against Deaf, especially where the newcomers wished to enlarge ideas of what being Deaf meant.

Subaltern Rebels and 'Deaf Pub Culture'

For those who wished to create lives unrestricted by what could be done, said or even thought, the alternatives were few. Jim, an old Deaf rebel in his eighties, summarised the dynamic:

> The missioners were surrounded by their group of Deaf syncophants, who would not challenge them . . . The few who were clever said 'Fuck 'em' and would go and meet and drink in the pub, and then get banned from the club because they drank!

Ken gave a similar example:

> We showed people we had the ideas and enthusiasm, but the Favoured Group didn't want to know and they would close ranks . . . oh God, they were so powerful . . . So we ended up in the pub and were better off there too – you could mix with hearing people and do all sorts of things you wouldn't have been able to do in the club.

Several informants talked about the importance of the pub scene as not merely a social place, but as an alternative site for shaping and developing Deaf identities not defined by the cultural values of the missioner and his adherents. This information has never been printed before; indeed it is barely known, and is therefore of crucial importance in understanding the multi-sidedness of Deaf culture. It also begins to illustrate the extent to which *the idea of what constitutes 'being Deaf' is itself a contested domain* extending beyond the dualistic 'deafness *versus* hearingness' construct people have used hitherto. I would formalise this as 'differing ideologies of Deafhood'.

It is also important to bear in mind the last chapter's emphasis on the risky enterprise of entering into 'hearing' territory. None of the informants went into 'middle-class' pubs – their terrain in some cases seemed to be among the roughest of pubs. Raymond gave the North-Eastern example:

> The pub we went to was frequented by prostitutes, pimps, Irish navvies, the lowest of the low in [M]. Deaf loved that pub! They'd go in white shirt and tie and suit [laughs]. We'd have a laugh and mix with them all.

His detailed examples illustrated the degree of Deaf pride developed in holding one's own and being accepted as uncompromisingly Deaf people in such situations. Stefan, a Jewish Deaf man in his late forties, was sceptical about the level of interaction in the pubs:

Those who are satisfied with all that 'thumbs-up' stuff, being bought a drink out of sympathy, fine, but . . . Maybe they do have some written communication, but Deaf pride in that situation? I don't see how.

However, Raymond and others gave detailed accounts of how the relationships with hearing people were formed and what they entailed:

Stefan is talking rubbish – what does he know? We would communicate at length in writing, as well as gestures, and of course some of them learned to fingerspell too. As well as all the rude crude talk, both sides would ask each other for advice. Like, good places to try for jobs, or health problems, or how to get a council house, or where to get the car repaired – why that garage and so on. Hearing respected us and asked us for advice too.

Such information-obtaining sessions were of great importance for those not wishing to have the missioner intervene in their own lives. Conversations went deeper too. Jim gave several examples from his lengthy repertoire of topics like politics, religion and general 'saloon bar philosophising'.

The matter of respect in pubs was very important – winning over hearing people without trying to be anything other than Deaf was a matter of great pride, and numbers with the other 1001 Victories. One example of the rough and tumble of the discourse of winning over an intransigent individual was narrated by Raymond:

There was one guy who held out against us longer than his mates, big [Tom]. He would always mock our signing with the flap-flap sign. One day he came in a bit quiet, came up to us and wrote a note, 'My baby born Deaf, what do I do?' We wrote 'Throw it in the Tyne'. 'No, what would you advise?' 'Bugger off'. So he went and talked with his gang, then he came back again. 'How educate you?' 'How educate *you* – we always wondered!' Anyway we took pity on him and wrote the address of our local Deaf school, and he bought us all drinks, and we never had problems with him again.

This is not to say that there were no fights. Raymond described several which arose from the Deaf being mocked, and Albert also gave examples. It appears that many were resolved with greater respect for the Deaf thereafter (a similar pattern to the confrontations in the last chapter). Indeed, one of Raymond's stories involved the missioner turning up at the pub to harangue the Deaf and being not so gently ejected by these hearing acquaintances.

Around this alternative axis, Deaf ideas began to coalesce. As Ken put it:

The Deaf pub culture was thriving, thriving all over the country. If you wanted to meet Deaf people with real ideas or enthusiasm, go to the pub! There was always one in every town . . . It's interesting to speculate what might have happened to the Deaf community if that Favoured Group/missioner attitude had been different.

Some Deaf activities actually began to be organised from the pub scene. Ken gave an extended example of a Deaf football team which were forced to site themselves at the pub, organise their own fundraising, and so on. This example had significance because not only did the club in question have a bar (so alcohol was not the issue), but they were the most successful local Deaf team for some time, winning Deaf national trophies, yet were still banned from the club. A further dimension of this tension is revealed in this comment:

> The missioner influenced the Deaf management committee to have a go at us; and this worried a few of the players because they still depended on him [for interpreting, employment assistance etc.]. Those players from outside [town] weren't worried. But those inside actually had their social work service threatened.

That such services should be threatened with withdrawal because of disputes ostensibly over sporting matters indicates the extent to which professionalism could be disregarded. However, the example also illustrates the interplay between the middle-class and the missioner; it would be too professionally risky for the latter to make this threat, and it would be carried out by the Deaf on his behalf. Crucially, in order to achieve this, he had to convince the significant few that this was necessary.

Other more significant Deaf political developments from this axis will be examined later. Before moving on, we should note Dorothy's response to the pub scene:

> No, we didn't go off to the pub like that in our club. We stayed at the club and fought it out there.

There are a number of reasons why this might be. One includes Dorothy's own sixth-generation Deafhood, which rooted her more strongly in the club, which was 'my home'. This contrasts with Ken and Raymond, who both had hearing parents. Another is that both felt that the missioner/middle-class hold was, if anything, even stronger in the North of England, and that almost none of the working-class Deaf would seriously confront the system in the ways that they wanted them to, as they appear to have done in Dorothy's club. Moreover, at their young age, they were not yet ready to settle for a lifetime of 1001 Victories inside the club, and at this moment in historical time were finding enough younger Deaf who felt similarly, even if they were not willing to express it so overtly. Finally, coming from outside they may have been able to identify the 'structure of feeling' of the culture in a way that those inside it were too close to do.

However, as Jim pointed out, groups of rebels existed during the first half of the century too. Some contented themselves with meeting in pubs and developing lives outside the missioner paradigm. Others later broke away and actually set up alternative clubs. Two examples were cited by the informants – one, in Liverpool, based itself within a hearing bowling club. (Albert and Raymond's reactions to this were very different.) Another was set up in Gateshead, under the aegis of the Social Services, with 'between 150–200 members'. Jim Mackenzie was chairman; Raymond described his philosophy:

> [I] welcomed everyone. He didn't drink. But he didn't object to those who drink. He was non-authoritarian – he was kind and human . . . He could have gone to the other two clubs [in the area, and mission-controlled], . . . but he didn't follow the line, he followed what he felt and who he was comfortable with.

However, breakaway clubs were the exception. Indeed, in London, four such clubs were actually formed by upwardly aspiring / oral Deaf people who did not want to mix with subaltern Deaf people.

Deaf pub culture and Deafness/Deafhood

Barry was often in conflict with the rebels of his club:

> [John Glancy] and me – always oppose each other, argue over the priests and nuns. I would try and defend them . . . but afterwards always shook hands.

He perceived the conflicts very much in Deaf-hearing terms:

> Some Deaf, if [John] showed up they would make faces . . . he'd start saying 'Priest wrong'. He would spoil the community, confuse them. If he had information, *he got it from a hearing pub somewhere*. We'd say, 'stop all this confusing stuff' and eventually he would go.

Once again 'hearing influence' is cited as a justification for refuting his arguments, and indeed John was more 'hard of hearing' than most. Nevertheless his idea of Deafhood included making further public demonstration of his Deaf status and allegiance. Raymond remembered him:

> Oh, a lovely man! . . . I remember him at the Manchester oralist conference in 1985. He went off on his own to the airport and stood there with

a placard saying 'Van Uden [noted oralist] Go Home'! And of course when they went to argue with him, he just went 'Deaf me', and of course they couldn't sign anyway. Imagine going into the heart of Hearing territory and doing that!

He responded to Barry's point about 'hearing' information:

We Deaf who went to the pub, had conversations with hearing people, whether we developed our own ideas or adopted some of theirs, if we tried to bring those back to the Deaf club, they would *all* get labelled as 'hearing ideas' and dismissed. *To me, they were the ones who had the hearing mentality!* It was implanted with Oralism, obeying the hearing teachers, the hearing system, and then they left school and came under the hearing missioner and followed *his* hearing system! . . . If you think about it, they [missioners] would let Deaf do this or that, kind of give them the 'lease' of things. But the 'freehold', ah, they would keep that to themselves!

This passage is extremely important. Clearly there are two polarised views on what constituted Deafhood, suggesting that after Milan (and maybe even before it), Deaf culture absorbed colonialist values *which then became internalised as Deaf cultural values.* By going out into the hearing world and still retaining their Deaf identity, Jim, John, Raymond, Ken and others contested this definition of 'Deaf'. Their own definitions were constructed similarly to Dorothy's, around the Deaf working-class / subaltern and their uncompromising interactions with the hearing world. However, they were carried one step further, actually constructing meaningful ongoing dialogues with that world, taking the '1001 Victories' to another level, by *converting those 'Hearing' ideas into potential Deaf cultural ways of the future,* and expanding the idea of what 'Deaf' could mean.

Before changes could be achieved, the hegemony willingly adopted by the 'Favoured Group' had to be transformed; Raymond developed another set of imagery to emphasise this:

The Deaf are like . . . a man says to them, 'here, you're in this room at the moment. But if you go outside that door, you'll find there's a wonderful life; you'll be the richer for it'. And they say, 'But I'm happy with this room; it took me years to build this environment to suit myself. I'm frightened to go outside that door – what might be there?' So what do you find? A dead skeleton in that room! . . . or they bang on the door, so the guard gives them some paint to do the room up with, or a TV [plays with images further] . . . But they're still within that cell of Hearing Mentality. And you can't release them because [dramatic pause] . . . they locked *themselves* in!

Ken's own images were similar, using phrases like 'mental prison'; it is interesting to note that both located culture and change primarily within a mentalist construct. It is also notable that the contestation of what Deafhood/Deaf Mentality was or 'should be' about originates from a similar mentalist place, and is important because the issue is still very central today.

(It is important also to point out the existence of another dimension to Deaf club members' resistance to what the rebels were trying to tell them. There was a perception that some of the rebels had good written English skills and were perhaps just a little too proud of the fact. It may well have been the air of superiority in some cases which caused what they were saying to be dismissed. My own interviews contain clear examples of similar attitudes, usually focused around a certain derision expressed towards the BSL used by club Deaf members.)

'Middle-Class' Deaf, Deafness and Deafhood – National Dimensions

These readings of Deaf club cultural and political life take on greater importance when it is realised that they also applied to regional and national life.

Deaf national sporting culture

Although Dorothy described the missioner as chairing all Deaf sporting committees, often the sport groups were able to run their affairs the way they wanted to. Unlike social committee activities, which affected everything which went on on a day-to-day basis in the club, sports were more 'externally' conducted. Consequently who they played against, when and where they played, who they mixed with and the values that were used to operate, facilitate and develop these activities was left more in Deaf hands. In some clubs, as Albert described, the missioner would operate even more of a hands-off policy, whilst in others, the Deaf would fight for as much autonomy as they could get, which, unless it had an obvious effect on the club power structure, could more easily be granted.

Thus the working-class Deaf had more control of the local and regional Deaf sporting activities and organisations which grew up in the early 20th century. Dorothy gave an in depth account, including this summary of her own regional body:

> The SDASA brought the two classes together more because it covered a range of sports . . . Before that each group went more 'alone' to their own sports. For SDASA, the middle-class 'forced themselves to go' [to our events]. So their [regional] committee was more mixed. And our

club started to have officers there, rather than just reps – that was a big step . . . and these officers were our club's working-class.

However, in the early 1950s, the British Deaf Sports Council (BDSC) was set up. Albert explained the significance of this:

> See, really missioners . . . wouldn't *manage* sport. So there was a whole *huge* shift when the BDSC was formed . . . Ooh, I can remember father coming back from . . . the first meeting – he'd gone as a delegate. He was furious; absolutely furious! . . . Because these two [names missioners] were running it and manipulating it and making decisions and so on.

Thus by establishing the BDSC, Deaf sporting events previously run by working-class Deaf people came under the control of the missioners and thus their Favoured Groups, as Ken confirmed:

> The interesting thing was that at regional and national level, the whole set up was very similar to clubs . . . the only people who stood any chance then were the Favoured Group . . . it was remarkable how many good people there were . . . with so much to contribute, but of course they disagreed with the views of the top people, so they couldn't get in . . . Some went off and set up alternative competitions, but a lot just gave up and quit. It was so stupid, such a waste.

Once some of those middle-class/petit bourgeois individuals, who we have previously identified as still being subalterns, went on to regional and national power, they arguably formed an élite subaltern group along with those who gained similar power in the BDDA. This élite is a different one from that of the present day, and comparisons between them would be a very productive direction for future research.

Within Ken's observations is the tacit awareness that Deaf sport was one of the very few avenues for self-expression, organisational skills and creativity in a colonised community. Dorothy recounted her local experience:

> Only one of our club was in the BDSC . . . Middle-class but heart-for-sport. He tried to involve Deaf in BDSC, but they'd go 'No way'. Didn't like him; he liked attention. His way of telling all about BDSC meetings was like 'I went all the way to London, then I went to this tube station, then that famous landmark, looking for the meeting place. Deaf would go 'Bo-oring. Get to the point.

This example is interesting considering the strength of storytelling as a Deaf cultural feature – clearly there are boundaries in this domain where a perceived 'attitude' or focus on oneself breached working-class Deaf cultural norms. She went on to describe how he tried again to gain their support:

> [G, a national BDSC Deaf figure then], strutted in, and was announced by his friend. Deaf went 'What for [this interruption via 'flash lights']? Then he spoke with an affected Signed English. So people turned away, and he got cross. 'Pay attention! Watch please.' 'The cheek of it', the Deaf said to each other. 'Bad'. I remember it all very clearly . . . You know Deaf, they mostly see one person from a group, they judge all the same, in terms of 'bad attitude' . . . So when this one came in, everybody realised 'Aha, BDSC are like *that* one'.

Apart from anything else, an imperious manner was not appropriate when speaking outside one's own club, and we have already seen how 'FLASH-LIGHTS' was identified as a non-subaltern strategy and thus counter-productive. Consequently:

> We'd travel far for SDDASA events, even the old people, raise money for them, but BDSC? No thank you. Even the tournament winners wouldn't go on to the BDSC finals. One group who did go, came back and said 'urgh, BDSC attitude problem'.

The concept of [bad] attitude is a very powerful and widespread trope in British Deaf culture, as befits a culture positioned to habitually receive the consequences of it. Another cultural feature which is important in sporting dynamics was the question of the way in which dissenting behaviour was actually conceived. Dorothy summed this up: 'Their AGMs – all docile . . . *criticism is seen as 'rude'*.' 'Rude' was the sign used in the last chapter to describe the middle-class reactions to the other group's information-getting strategies. (I was also informed by a Deaf Australian that the same dynamic, right down to the same signed term, operated in his club in Melbourne.) It is clearly an important sign used in the hope of controlling behaviour which strayed from an unusually rigidly defined 'Deaf' model.

Ken's experience of the BDSC was very similar although he was determined to persevere. Beginning with managing the local Deaf football team and taking them to national success, he also managed a local hearing team – no mean feat for a totally Deaf person. The next step was to set up a regional Deaf league, which appears to have been the only one in the country at that time. None of this was well received by the Favoured hierarchy:

> Obviously that wasn't very helpful for them . . . a man with 'undesirable' stamped on his forehead across the whole network, running a winning team . . . 'Can't have that, Deaf people doing well, tch tch'!

Clearly in this example, the middle-class group appeared to prefer the status gained from colonisation rather than be part of an egalitarian Deaf future, *even when it was successful.* The tension grew when his group went training at Lilleshall, and had the national cup final moved to a Football League ground. Their motives were clearly defined, and again reflected two different concepts of what 'Deaf' meant:

> The BDSC focus, money, and grants went on the international team. They should have gone on the rest of the Deaf in the country, encouraging them to develop.

Their definition of 'Deaf' was similar to Dorothy's, and centred around the value of collectivity and of raising the confidence and self-belief of the whole community. The other definition took a [hearing] nationalistic focus which supported an élite and chosen few. Ken's account contained much more detail, but ultimately, his efforts came to naught:

> It was the proverbial brick wall. Plus any fighting back we did affected our region's players' chances of being picked for the national team. Plus, I had a family to support and the hearing team were even paying me. So in the end I left the Deaf world for 15 years . . . Then when I came back, blow me, that same lot were still there! And the Deaf were still doffing their caps to them, 'Yes sir, No sir'. 15 years and no change! Imagine that!

Thus subaltern Deaf control of their national and regional sporting activities was usurped by the missioners of the BDSC and their lackeys in the early 1950s. The situation is still very similar today.

Deaf national political culture

The BDDA was established in 1890 partly to protect Deaf adults and children's rights against advancing Oralism. From the beginning, the missioners and the Deaf (usually Deaf missioners or teachers) shared the key posts, but as the 20th century advanced and Deaf confidence and literacy declined, the hearing missioners gained control of the organisation. The colonial paradigm of the Deaf clubs began to expand to embrace national Deaf political culture. As Ken put it:

> [names people] were running the BDDA, and it was like a *glorified Deaf club*, with the chief focus on old folks' trips and holidays, and bingo and so on!

We heard earlier from Frances of the positive consequences of the BDDA's work in maintaining structures which promoted a national Deaf social life. The rebels' objections were not to that *per se*; rather to this being deemed all that was permissable. Raymond also extended his 'Hearing Mentality' metaphor to the national scene:

> Like I said, it started in the schools, then on to the clubs. Then when they got to the BDDA level, they joined the other generations of Deaf with the same mentality . . . BDDA was really run by hearing – the Deaf were only like the nodding dogs you see in the back of the car. Every congress you'd see the sea of heads nodding in time with each other!

Albert had considerable experience of the BDA, and he described one of the strategies used to manipulate Deaf people which in turn set them up to manipulate others:

> See, if you want to stop people thinking in depth, you give them small things that they can make decisions on. And you keep them focused on the procedures, so that your real in-depth decisions are kept away from them . . . Say you were organising a BDA Congress . . . you would ask the Exec to make decisions about festivities in the evening, to decide if they wanted a magician or a dance . . . Very easy to get them feeling like they've made important decisions . . . whilst you go ahead and make the big decisions without them.

The example confirms the cultural parallel; 'a magician or a dance' could apply as easily to the Deaf club party as easily as to the BDA Congress – and the Favoured Group understood this very well. As Ken put it, 'They knew exactly which buttons to press'. This focus on 'getting little things right' was already, as Bonnie explained in Chapter 7, a characteristic born of Oralism.

Dorothy's experience was interesting, as she moved from being anti-BDDA to a prominent member of it. The stages she describes are of great cultural relevance:

> The upper group . . . want nice orderly formal meeting – all must sit down quietly, like in church with themselves as vicar! They don't know how to engage the Deaf. That's why we all laughed at BDDA – I was one too . . . Later father start go BDDA – said 'not bad'. See that sign again, 'not bad'? 'Cos father not like being suppressed! For example he'd say BDDA holidays 'not bad'. I knew what that meant, so I would-n't go!

In fact she did not join until after the mini revolution inside the BDA in the early 1980s:

> When I realised BDA has politics now, I got interested. I wanted to see the doors flung wide open so Deaf can have own rights, own say.

Once she joined the local, then regional committee, she began to experience the typical cultural reactions of the middle-class group:

> They [regional council] didn't welcome me . . . they kept telling me, 'If you're busy, you don't have to bother to come!!' . . . Then they wouldn't send me the minutes . . . at the next election there were three of us, so we could fight back. But it was same kind of shutting out in BDA as we found in BDSC.

On the National Executive, by then almost all Deaf, but still from the Favoured Group, she experienced how culture clash could also be engineered for political ends:

> We had a Deaf Chair now, but he'd learned all the missioner's tricks. I would jump in and say what I wanted, but he and others insisted that we had to put our hands up as it was the Hearing, proper way to run Important Meetings at this level. So that made it hard to challenge things because there were many more of them than us and they [took the heat out of any challenge by all speaking in reply], even if they just repeated what the last person said.

She imitated their sense of self-importance, adding 'Ooh I didn't like how they talked about Deaf in the meetings'. Notable also was the Chair's cultural tone – expressed as reproof for using 'low Deaf' ways, a tactic which usually succeeded in daunting most rebels, at least for a time. Nevertheless, she felt she remained undaunted. Undoubtedly, this was due in part to the new era and the changes that were being wrought generally – the tide was turning. But when I asked her what sustained her, she said:

> This is important question. When I'm there, I think of grass roots – what would they think of this or that issue. I felt strong to stand up to the others because I knew Deaf had voted me there to do the things they believed in.

The importance of the BDA is that it is not just an abstract political entity, but the one organisation with the most power and potential for transforming Deaf culture, not least because its branches extended into virtually every club in the UK and also facilitated a strong socialising network via its rallies and holidays. Were subaltern Deaf to gain control of it, they could initiate reforms intended to alter cultural patterns and perceptions.

Thus Dorothy's account represents a reformist strategy for re-asserting Deaf subaltern control of their colony. She continued to persevere, notably by using the TAP-TAP and other strategies described in Chapter 7 – and was gradually joined by other Deaf rebels as a result of the different strategies they used and events they described in the next sections.

Deafhood and Deaf Political Culture – Subaltern Rebellions

Earlier rebellions

There were limits to what subaltern rebellions within Deaf pub culture could achieve, partly because of the logistics of communicating with other like-minded groups. The telephone was inaccessible, travelling was difficult in eras before motorways (and even more so before subaltern access to cars). Use of the printed media was also problematic, as Jim explained:

> The only Deaf protest group between Milan and S.H.E.D [in the 1950s] was a French one protesting to the Germans over the dismantling of the Epee statue in Versailles . . . The old clubs like Glasgow, Newcastle, Oldham etc kept nice records back then; the English was good and the handwriting was smart. This was 1880–1900. Then it started to decline because of Milan of course. By the 1930s and 40s it just wasn't the same – and after Ewing [major British oralist] came along, things got much much worse! We had the *British Deaf Times,* but we couldn't find Deaf people who could still write. It was left to the older people, David Edwards and George Donaldson and others to keep it going; but in the end there was only me left. These were the Dark Ages of the Deaf in Britain.

He went on to describe the genesis of SHED, Society for Higher Education of the Deaf (a mixture of 'pub' Deaf, Deaf missioners and hearing people) and their battle for higher educational standards, saying: 'It was thought that SHED's pressure gained recognition of grammar school status now held by the MHGS'. This story is long and complex, and if researched would shed some interesting light on how a rebel movement ended up having their efforts diverted into supporting a major oral school. When I asked him to comment on the pub rebels in general, he added an important dimension to the picture:

> Most of them would just mouth off and complain, and do nothing. They had good ideas, but no confidence or courage to put them into action. At least the missioners did actually go out there and help Deaf people, for all their faults.

This gives a background against which to assess eventual subaltern action. Notable also is that, once English-literate Deaf people diminished and died off, control of Deaf magazines fell more easily into the missioners' hands; even the Favoured Group were unable to write well enough to control this outlet. Frank, a Deaf man from the North-West in his mid-fifties, described the outcome and its implications:

I felt we needed a magazine for Deaf by Deaf. The others were hearing-written really, about the old people's trip, the church service and the nice harvest festival – they'd probably give that 4 pages!! . . . No debates on issues that affected everyone – nothing. I mean, hearing have things like the *New Statesman* . . . Look at people's situation – where could they turn to? And how could they contact others like them in different parts of the country? You didn't have motorways at that time. No telephone access either. And Deaf couldn't write English much any more.

He described the magazine he set up in 1959, how its name was significant, and how six copies were sent to each Deaf club secretary:

> I should have known better because of course, the missioner opened all mail addressed to the Deaf club secretary . . . Some missioners sent all six back to me, 'We won't offer that kind of thing to the Deaf club'! . . . Canon Mackenzie [a famous BDDA missioner and an HMFD whose father was the first Deaf man known to get a degree at Cambridge, ironically] was one who sent them back, so in the next issue I wrote 'Shades of fascism – . . . let Deaf people decide if they want to read it or not!' and I sent him six more of the next issue. And I got a letter from someone saying 'How dare you criticise such a good man, has a heart-for-Deaf people'. I thought that said it all! . . . I got a few Deaf responses, but it just sank really.

Frank's efforts, as with the SHED group, illustrate the impossibility of the task facing subaltern Deaf rebel culture. (There may well have been other similarly short-lived attempts that we do not know about; Jim and Raymond recalled a rebel Deaf sports magazine, ABC Deaf Sports from the 1970s that also failed to take off.)

The emergence of the NUD

As described in Chapter 2, the Deaf resurgence began with the emergence of the NUD in 1976. Raymond and Jim both described how the organisation emerged. As Raymond put it:

> By the mid 1970s, some of us had had enough of the domination of the missioner and his blue-eyed boys, and we were also dying to put a stop to the oralists. So the NUD was born – in a pub, of course! If you look at who was involved with the NUD, they *nearly all came out of the Deaf pub culture!* And the Deaf people they attracted as members from around the country, many were outsiders in their own areas, like John Glancy.

He described what led the NUD to recruit Jim:

Before I met him in 1975, I met some of the old guard who knew him. They said 'Oh him; he's a really *rude* man'. 'Why is he rude'. 'Well he calls us stupid.' Well, instantly I thought he must be an intelligent man! After that, I heard stories about him walking out of two or three BDDA meetings . . . and as you know that was about the most radical gesture you could make in those days . . . So I knew he had all the ingredients the NUD needed, a strong Deaf Mentality, and the respect he commanded from those the NUD needed to recruit, those with fire in their bellies.

Some of the achievements of the NUD were described in Chapter 3; Raymond gave some insights into the Deaf cultural dynamics that informed the organisation:

I realised that picking strong individuals meant that they would clash with each other . . . but I felt it would be dishonest of me not to, because each, even if I didn't like them, have a contribution to make. Did it work? In a funny kind of way, yes. Because although we lost potential members because of them, and even lost some of them because they were too hot-headed to agree on some things, without strong personalities, the NUD couldn't have survived all that pressure that was thrown at them.

He also described one of the major sources of cultural tension within the organisation:

We on the committee wanted a direct action approach . . . but [X] wanted committees and discussions. That's the Hearing mentality. We wanted to do it the Deaf way . . . and to me, NUD was designed to have a short life – 10 or 15 years, get in there, change things, and then let the changes carry on the work.

These two examples give us the beginnings of deeper insights into subaltern rebel Deaf culture. The first is the desire to do things the Deaf Way, however that might be construed. In the second there was dissonance and conflict between the cultural values of Deaf collectivity, and the strong-minded individualism which developed in the NUD as a necessary trait to resist colonial dominance. Exploration of these deeper levels is, however, beyond the scope of this study.

During my research, I was intrigued to note that many of the NUD's major figures placed great importance upon Deaf history. (Many of them are now active in the new British Deaf History Society.) Indeed as one person put it:

They knew what they were doing when they chose Jim. He represents the last link to the strong Deaf going back to the last century who fought Milan, because he knew some of those people. So the younger Deaf rebels were attracted to him because something called them to seek out Deaf history and thus find the Golden Age when Deaf were strong and literate. He *helped them get in touch with that stronger, older Deaf self.*

This historical dimension gives us a new insight into Deafhood and the Deaf 'historical self'. As well as the debate about what constituted 'hearing ideas', it seems there is confirmation of the historical existence of that other set of 'Deaf ideas' about a larger Deaf self before the one designated for them by the Favoured Group. These 'Deaf ideas' have to do with reference to a period of historical time when literacy and pride in all things Deaf enabled rebellion to (theoretically) take place. It is too early to tell whether such a 'Golden Age' was illusory or a needed construction, but the scale of the Deaf response to Oralism described in Chapter 2 could not have taken place without considerable talent and effort being devoted to it.

Thus the idea of a 'Deaf' history in itself enlarged the vision of those who were touched by it, and strengthened their resolve to maintain the tradition in their own ways. In this respect, this tradition is the equivalent of Dorothy's six-generation Deaf heritage. One significant difference is that it appears none of the NUD had Deaf parents; as was earlier explained, Deaf families were reluctant to join the pub scene because their sense of cultural responsibilities and lifelong friendships within the Deaf club may have made it very difficult to turn their backs on their less courageous friends, whereas those from hearing families could more easily walk out and join the pub rebels or the NUD.

Effects of the NUD – subaltern responses

Frank described the next significant developments:

> Once the NUD turned things upside down, the BDA *had* to act, had to change. So when Verney [new hearing Chief Executive] came in ... and started to make it more of a campaigning organisation, that gave ordinary Deaf people their first big confidence boost. And the word got out so you had all these Deaf coming out of the (pub) woodwork, like Ken and [names others].

These changes were, of course, contested by the Favoured Group, who now became known as the 'Old Guard'. Ken noted how, on his return 15 years later, he was spotted coming up the path towards a BDSC meeting:

One of those in the meeting told me afterwards that [notorious mis-sioner] saw him coming, and turned to the meeting's [Deaf] chair and said 'Let me chair this meeting and deal with him. We mustn't give him a platform'.

He gave lengthy accounts of the struggles which were then renewed, and how the missioners and their Deaf 'stooges', as he called them, were outwitted by a sustained group effort in the North-West to set up their own BDA region and thus gain the freedom to develop their own cultural activi-ties and politics. The details given reveal much about Deaf cultural practice, but an in-depth description is beyond the scope of this study. These examples indicate the wide range of strategies employed:

First thing we did was set up training courses for Deaf – how to run a bar, how to fundraise, how to campaign . . . we expanded the regional social rallies from 1–200 to 2000 . . . we had open debates, including oralist speakers for the Deaf to learn how to challenge them . . . we de-veloped regional sporting leagues and proper training . . . we set up festivals of Deaf drama and comedy, so Deaf could finally start to think about *what being Deaf meant*, and did plays that took the piss out of the traditional Favoured Group idea of what Deaf plays should be like.

These examples all have in common the idea of empowering Deaf people to develop their larger, latent Deafhood selves, although space is in-sufficient to describe how Ken illustrated each example.

Frank described at length how the Old Guard removed Verney from his post, and how a momentous response from Deaf rebels and young hearing social workers culminated in what amounted to the first ever nationally or-ganised Deaf rebellion to be successful, which defeated them at the BDA Congress in Torquay in 1983.

A whole range of cultural strategies were employed to pass this initial information around the country, to draw together groups of Deaf people in various areas who wanted to fight back, and to manipulate the AGM vote itself. There were no public meetings or 'FLASH-LIGHTS' strategies; instead the TAP-TAP method Dorothy described in the last chapter was used. In the immediate buildup to the AGM, certain patterns of cultural awareness were utilised – for example putting carefully placed rumours around that the rebels had a majority among the delegates, designed to get reported back to the Old Guard. At the AGM itself, the order of speakers from the floor was carefully selected and planned, not all for their rhetori-cal powers *per se*, but so that they would be 'slapped down' by the Chair and executive, and thus win the sympathy of the uncommitted voters.

What becomes clear from the accounts is that the success was due to the convergence of the three social factors we have already explored. The first of these is the involvement of the young subaltern Deaf radicals from hearing families, with their own enlarged concept of Deafhood. The second is the involvement of the Deaf families whose own vision, previously limited to Deaf club resistance, had begun to step out onto the larger stage following their involvement with BSL research and the confidence that had given them. The third was the active involvement of 'social work liberals' and those hearing people who had begun to form the 'third culture' itself. None of these, of course, would have taken up the cause had not Verney's policies already lent themselves to the heady atmosphere of radical change so tangible at that time. (It is hard to believe it now, but the BDA was well on the way to supplanting the RNID as a Deaf voice in the first line of contact with the government, as Alker (2000) confirms.) The next volume will explore these themes in detail.

This still remains the only actual known example of a UK national Deaf rebellion, that is, a tangible, even successful insurrection, although the remarkable marches for BSL recognition, organised by the new subaltern rebel group, the Federation of Deaf People (FDP) in 1999 and 2000 deserve their own lengthy analysis. After this, the last missioners resigned as chair and committee members, the first ever Deaf chair was elected, Verney was re-instated, and Deaf people were theoretically in charge of their own organisation.

In effect this meant that the Favoured Group were finally in charge but for the first time without any backup, whilst a handful of 'young Turks' (in their thirties themselves by then) snapped at their heels. Furthermore, since most of the senior paid staff were hearing liberals from social work (as opposed to missioner background) and effectively of Verney's choosing, they represented a challenge to the Favoured Group because they were seen both as hearing radicals and as people who did not fully understand traditional Deaf cultural life. Likewise their liberalism was a challenge to members of the younger group who either thought that, as hearing people they should not be there, or that they would still not push Deaf demands with the urgency or into sufficiently high political domains to effect a difference.

This closely parallels classic colonialism at the moment of handover. The cultural threads from those three different sources – missioners, pub rebels and social work liberals – have then proceeded to weave in and out, against and across, each other over the intervening 16 years. Although there is ample data to illustrate each, space does not permit. We thus jump forward to the present day to see how each of these threads has developed.

The Contemporary BDA and Deafhood Issues

Despite the resurgence described here, there were repeated comments that the missioner pattern still dominated culturally. Frank, observing recent BDA political activities, remarked:

Even now, after all the changes we fought for and won, even though we have an all Deaf Executive Council, *the mentality* is still the same. They still run it the same way that they run their Deaf clubs – a national equivalent of bingo and whist drives!

Raymond saw the old cultural paradigm as still very much alive:

Those who were pub rebels before, now have become just like the old ones' 'Ohh, that's right, that's proper, leave it alone, be careful, BDA right, Executive know'. Back to the old ways – suppression of other Deaf people.

He analysed how this came to be by linking it with the mentality planted back in oral school:

When they reach a high or unaccustomed position, the Fear comes and their legs collapse under them. That 'leave it alone' attitude shows through and they turn it into fake outward pride and confidence. Because deep inside there's still the roots of Oralism that took away their real Deaf confidence, and when that's been taken away, they'll never get it back.

Frank found the external cultural manifestations to be very visible:

You can still see the Favoured Group mentality now . . . they are full of it, like they have All This Information they can't tell you about! That smug air . . . you can actually pick them out just like that < snaps fingers >.

It is perhaps uncoincidental that the trope of Information surfaces again, this time wielded to keep subalterns at bay and preserve their position. Ken gave the key explanation:

You have to remember the BDA isn't like the RNID or something that is just another Welfare body. It's a cultural entity, made up of Deaf people and their attitudes, from generation to generation. And so it can only change slowly, as cultures change. The Deaf people who are now at the top of the BDA – they are the last wave of those who grew up with the missioners' attitudes planted inside them.

Albert concurred, adding:

Take [BDA high official] for example. He grew up under the missioners – [one Deaf missioner] was his mentor when he was young. And this is true for all of them over 50 or so – the missioners' way must still be there inside them.

Ken described the effects of such cultural continuity:

You could see it at the last AGM [he was referring to the Glasgow conference of 1995] – their disdain and distrust of their own membership. They are just reproducing the missioners' ethos and attitude. For example, they decided to have a new logo. Now that was a great opportunity to get the members involved and feel part of the BDA. But no, they were saying, 'Deaf can't do it. We must have a hearing professional to do it'. A simple thing like that! Let alone all the policies and major issues that need mass enthusiasm to carry off . . . they want to be *accepted* by hearing people and the hearing establishment rather than fight for what Deaf people want . . . it's very sad because it's very clear that at last Deaf people are ready to go . . . but there's no leader . . . ready to step up on that platform and inspire them, call them to arms.

The 'absence' of Deaf leaders is too complex a topic for this study, although plenty of useful data was generated around these themes.

One of Frank's explanations for the rebels' change in values is also significant in this context:

Maybe they were OK when they joined, but then they changed to *fit in with the atmosphere* of the BDA.

This colloquial phrase hides deeper meanings which, when extricated, indicates that the cultural mores, values, norms and behaviour of the 'deafness Years' absorbed or transmuted attempts to write subaltern Deafhood onto the pages of cultural history and into the community at large.

Unwillingness to confront hearing people, 'petit bourgeois' anxiety to be seen to be doing the right, respectable thing, and other Favoured Group patterns that were described in the last chapter, all continued to dominate the cultural climate of national Deaf expression in two domains – outwardly towards the hearing power structure and inwardly to gain a hegemonic consensus for suppressing subaltern Deaf aspirations towards the larger image of Deafhood that history had indicated existed.

Indeed Dorothy, although devoting her energies over the next ten years to trying to change the BDA, concluded:

My long fight to make sure BDA focuses on Deaf comes down to this. Remember father saying 'Not bad/can't help it'? Well, they *still* 'not bad/can't help it!

Summary and Key Points of Data Chapters

These accounts of the dynamics of cultural formation, maintenance and change, of subaltern and class differences, and of deafness / Deafhood conflict, are of crucial importance in understanding British Deaf culture in the present day. Far from being a nostalgic account of Deaf life at the turn of the century, the cultural patterns and ramifications are shown to be still in effect at the present time. It is my contention that these patterns are sufficiently consistent over historical time, and display sufficient variation within those patterns, to confirm that they are indeed cultural features and therefore that the concept of Deaf culture is a valid one.

Chapter 7 outlined the extent to which the cultural value of Deaf collectivity was formed in the residential schools; that, to some degree, it was forged by resistance to oppression, but above all it was centred on the positive and celebratory social interactions mediated through sign language. There is also significant evidence of the existence of a Deaf 'oral tradition', which survived through two centuries, but which, in the end, died out by the 1960s. It is clear that Deafhood itself was essentially covert during the last century, but remained a cultural feature which had to be actualised and maintained in the face of oppression. In this chapter we also learned of positive and negative cultural traits developed by exposure to Oralism.

Chapter 8 illustrated these same traits writ large in adult life, and showed how certain class-oriented features intervened to divide those once-united children along the Deaf community's own equivalent lines. As a result of this, and of the pressures of having to interact with majority society for the first time, those who wished to maintain their Deafhood values faced a daily struggle which they overcame by honing their beliefs. In doing so, they adopted a stance intended to benefit all Deaf people, whereas those who had succumbed to petit-bourgeois values ducked such public and private conflict. An important aspect of these accounts is the positive interaction with lay people, chiefly working-class lay people, which arose from engaging in conflict. Finally, despite all their differences, the cultural value of collectivity and unity was set into operation to ensure that the club held together.

Chapter 9 has focused on those who would neither accept the missioner's rule, nor remain in the club and confine their life battles to that domain. By gathering in hearing pubs and interacting with lay people, significantly, lower-working-class lay people, they passed through a similar engagement in conflict to positive interaction. From that interaction they developed their own (larger) reading of what Deafhood might come to mean and attempted unsuccessfully to persuade club members of that interpretation. As the century moved on, these rebels made national contact with each other and together with those who emerged from the clubs, insti-gated changes which altered the entire face of Deaf community life. However, despite this, within the BDA itself, the petit-bourgeois mentality persisted and the larger readings of Deafhood still seemed to be excluded from consideration.

In conclusion, then, Chapter 2 described Deaf education as a conceptual battleground within which maintaining and enlarging the numbers of Deafschool children, their English literacy and a larger sense of their Deafhood affects the quality of the entire community's future Deaf cultural life. The internalisation of colonialisms, rooted in the deafness model of linguistic colonialism and the petit-bourgeois mentality of welfare colo-nialism, both in the BDA and outside, hinders the chances of new generations of Deaf children finding that enlarged Deafhood identity and even their place in the Deaf world. Thus, in an era requiring urgent re-sponses to cochlear implants, mainstreaming and genetics, a continuation of 'The Fear' threatens the community's very existence.

Notes

1. This does not refer to an actual picture of a rabbit – rather it is a satirical meta-phor used to describe young people's dependence on cartoon-strip stories!
2. My editor, a hearing man with some experience of Deaf people, commented at this point 'It is even better than this. Deaf people who sign use "NVC" (non-verbal communication) e.g. facial expressions, head movements, proximal dis-tance etc., and many seem superb at this'.

   Even after centuries of interest in the visuo-gestural arts we have barely begun to explore these sorts of implications. After watching a recent perfor-mance by the Australian Deaf artiste Rob Roy Farmer, my colleague the linguist Adam Schembri contributed a further perspective. He related how he had taken skilled hearing mime artistes to watch Farmer, thinking that the latter's use of mime would render him easy to follow. In actuality, Farmer, took mime to an-other dimension of rapidity and complexity 'simply' by incorporating standard Deaf (NVC) linguistic practices, practices which had seemed visually obvious to us, but evidently were not.

   Ironically it is as much these NVC features, especially those marked on the face, that have evoked fear or dismissal in certain hearing people down the cen-turies, as anything to do with what is done with the hands. The observations above, one lay and one professional, are useful in augmenting the Deafhood tenets which emerged from the French Banquets – namely their contention that hearing people are less than the full selves they could be if they do not know sign language. Such an idea is easier for some hearing people to grasp if we think of these NVC features as being part of the 'general' gestural language of the body which, for example, Anglo-Saxons, especially straight males, have great emotional difficulty in coming to terms with.

   One wonders how many more years it will take for these kind of Deaf contri-butions to the human race to be re-recognised.

Chapter 10

Conclusions and Implications

> In America, the color of my skin had stood between myself and me; in Europe that barrier was down. Nothing is more desirable than to be relieved from an affliction, but nothing is more frightening than to be divested of a crutch. It turned out that the question of who I was was not solved because I had removed myself from the social forces which menaced me – anyway, these forces had become interior, and I had dragged them across the ocean with me.
>
> James Baldwin (cited in Gates, 1993: 151)

Introduction

This summarising chapter returns to the seven key concepts outlined in the introduction, and examines what we have learned during the course of this journey. We examine the recognition of the Deaf culture concept itself, and the implications of this recognition, both for work in Deaf domains and for cultural and multilingual theory in general. We also examine the importance of the concepts of subaltern researcher and lay people, and their implications both for qualitative research and for the academy as a whole, before concluding with future directions for research which will inform the next volumes.

Validation of Deaf Culture Concept

The Deaf informants' perspectives and attitudes combine to give a sense of a socially complex community with its own beliefs, norms and values which can be traced through historical time. Internal contestations within the culture also appear to form coherent patterns and continually evolving dynamics. These features, together with cultural characteristics such as endogamy, and the indication that any group with its own language must also 'possess' its own culture, confirms that 'Deaf Culture' is a valid concept.

On this basis also, it is reasonable to conclude that each Deaf community around the world which has its own distinct sign language and its own history of Deaf collective activity, also has its own Deaf Culture. We cannot, as yet, identify the extent or importance of similarities and differences between these cultures. In respect of similarities, we might cite the globally shared commonalities of experience and the linguistically remarkable fact of the major grammatical similarities of the world's 200-plus sign languages. However, as Chapters 8 and 9 have shown, the extent to which UK Deaf culture is interpenetrated by UK majority culture suggests that culture-specific differences have significant effect, both on daily lives and strategies, and on the historical development of Deaf communities. Much more research from around the world is required before we can hypothesise the extent to which there is a global 'core' or 'home' to the Deaf experience.

Implications of Validation

Once we confirm the Deaf culture concept, we are able, once and for all, to establish that Deaf communities have world-views of their own which are both internally coherent and valid. The medical and socio-control models' disregard for these world-views was initially predicated on a denial that Deaf people actually had a language with which to think. Once linguistic status was conceded, this ideology had to be replaced by a denial that this world-view was collectively generated, coherent or worthy of respect.

Linguistic recognition cannot *per se* demolish this argument. But once the existence of Deaf culture is confirmed, then cultural relativity can be brought into play, so that the idea that Deaf worldviews are of at least equal value to those of their colonisers can be sustained. Indeed, in Deaf or Deaf-related domains, as many Deaf people would argue, these worldviews may be of greater importance because they are based on cultural experience.

Acknowledging Deaf culture implies two further concepts: the pathological 'deafness' model centred on *individualism*, with each Deaf person within it treated as an atomistic being; and the 'Deafhood' model, which acknowledges the *collectivity* of Deaf self-perception, as exemplified throughout Chapters 7–9.

This collectivity results in a concept of the Deaf individual as an *organic* being – an individual engaged in a dialectical relationship with a community and culture, who is influenced by that culture and who in turn, has a desire to influence it. This organic being contains individual dispositions and strategies shaped by his/her habitus and by the range of possibilities within that culture. However, despite these differing dispositions, most of the individuals in the group have a concern for and a commitment to the present and future health of that community and culture. This organic, collective concern therefore forms a core belief which should be heeded by those involved in the social and political policies which are enacted on Deaf communities. This has implications for the following domains.

Deaf education

The partial changes made within this domain in the last decade can bring only partial improvement in Deaf children's educational achievements and psycho-social development. Significant advances can only be made when the schools themselves become 'Deaf-centred'; that is, acknowledging that Deaf children and adults have their own epistemologies, their own ways of thinking about and constructing the world. Full success in reaching those children's minds can only be attained according to the following conditions:

(1) Acceptance that those minds 'work differently' to their own.
(2) Acceptance that these workings may be more valid a basis for Deaf education.
(3) Recognition that education is the primary site of Deaf concerns for the health and quality of their community's future. Thus concern for the individual Deaf child has a dual focus – as an individual in their his/her right; and as someone who can function well enough to enrich and maintain that community.
(4) Acceptance therefore of the Deaf community's primary responsibility for devising strategies for reaching into and drawing out Deaf children, and for shaping their Deafhood towards maximal participation in both Deaf and hearing communities.

In summary – official recognition of the existence of Deaf culture implies the taking of an irrevocable step forward – decolonisation of the education system by transferring control to the Deaf community.[1]

Other colonised domains

Acceptance of the validity of the collective Deaf way of life also implies that the entire range of social and political policies enacted on Deaf communities, from social work to mental hospitals to court and legal practices, cannot function efficiently without operating from a Deaf-centred worldview and stipulations similar to (1)–(4). This also applies to Deaf televisual media, to lay people learning BSL, to parents of Deaf children, to Deaf Studies departments and to Deaf organisations themselves.

Moreover, linguistic and cultural recognition poses a direct challenge to the domains from which the colonising discourses originate – central and local government, legal, scientific, medical and academic – demanding of them that they completely rethink and restructure the terms of reference from which their praxis towards Deaf communities are derived.

Political implications

Recognition also requires that the domains concerning linguistic minorities, lesser-used languages and bilingual and multilingual issues rethink their own terms of reference so that sign language communities are fully included and involved in their own programmes.

It is not for this initial study to detail how the governments might best restructure their relationship to Deaf communities. We can learn much by studying the various Scandinavian initiatives. However, it seems a useful exercise to propose certain basic possibilities for discussion with the readers of this book.

In a genuinely democratic society, linguistic or ethnic minorities might be expected to have their own departments aand ministers within central government, staffed by their own members, to which all matters concerning their communities would be referred and to whom medical, scientific, social welfare and media domains would be answerable. If necessary, they would need to create specific 'sub-departments' within those domains to ensure day-to-day continuity of practice. These government departments would have the powers to centralise and regulate existing piecemeal services situated around local governments and charities, so that, in the Deaf case, Deaf education would be nationally planned and executed.

Accountability of those departments to their communities is a crucial issue. The healthiest solution might be the creation of an overseeing and policy-determining parliament of each language group whose members were elected by vote. It might be feasible also for the executive governmental minister to be elected in this way, and to even be the 'leader' of that House.

Experienced political scientists would point out the extent to which capitalism controls existing governments. Nevertheless, it is perfectly possible for governments to regulate the scientific and medical sectors for example, and to determine their boundaries of what is permissable, for example in genetic engineering or cochlear implantation. Perhaps more pertinently, some radicals would identify the dangers of entering into any kind of parliamentarian structure with its well-worn co-optative risks, and indeed might be wary of any kind of formalised relationship. Yet Deaf communities feel sufficiently pessimistic about suggestions that they should remain unprotected against the oralist impulses endemic to capitalism. Given all that has been said so far, it would be a positive sign if radicals would condescend to engage in discourse with these differing perspectives.

In some respects it is depressing to think that this political model is not so very far from that proposed by Berthier for his French 'Deaf Nation' in the 1840s. However, if one looks towards Scandinavia, their belief in strong centralised social democracy, and the major role accorded the official organisations of sign-language users in each of those countries, it is clear that a significant proportion of what is suggested here can actually be implemented. It is the task of future volumes to explore such themes in detail, but one point is immediately obvious – colonial control over sign-language-using communities cannot be said to have ended until all these requirements are satisfied, in one form or another.

Finally, it should be noted that the political enshrinement of Deaf language minority status is inextricably intertwined with the destiny of language minorities in general. It would be optimistic to assume that the Scandinavian model would be adopted across the world without the need to become involved in language minority politics and, in any case, there is much to be gained and learned from forging such alliances. Thus it is partly because of the intention to achieve such alliances, that the following sections on the relevance of Deaf cultural recognition for other academic domains are given considerable explanatory space.

Deaf community domains

Despite the Deaf Resurgence, the revelation of the intellectual complexities of their languages has only partly carried over to Deaf respect for the intellectual quality of their own opinions and beliefs expressed in those languages. Full acceptance of the fact that they possess their own culture offers the tools for beginning the process of decolonising their own minds from the medical and social-welfare models.

This process necessitates Deaf self-examination of their own organisations and social structures in order to ascertain which are cultural features are internally generated, which imposed from without and those, which originating from without, have come to be seen, erroneously, as Deafhood traditions. The group forums described in Chapter 6 suggested that such self-examination is not only feasible, but very much welcomed. Thought must be given therefore to establishing Deaf cultural forums so that the community can move confidently towards an assertive Deaf entrance into the domains where linguistic and welfarist colonisation is institutionalised. This idea is considered later.

However, before that can take place, the externally derived concept of 'Deaf Culture' has to be reconciled with the community's own equivalent terms and semantic codes, as Bahan (1994) pointed out. If these are not the starting point for self-examination, so that the 'Deaf Culture' term is not explained by reference to those concepts, then it remains an external imposition, no matter how well meaning, and only limited success may be possible.

The sections so far represent dramatic and far-reaching sets of implications, some of which are expanded on in the next chapter. What follows here are the implications for a wide range of academic theory, all of which can assist in the 'long march' towards recognition and achievement of these political implications.

Implications for Deaf Cultural Theory

The five weaknesses in present Deaf cultural analysis described in Chapter 5 have been addressed as follows:

Plurality of Deaf cultures

The Deaf views presented in Chapters 2, 3, 7, 8 and 9 suggest that at some levels, Deaf communities share characteristics which indicate a profound cultural commonality. However, given the extent of majority cultural influence on them, each Deaf culture is almost certainly nation-specific. Thus much more research into other Deaf cultures is required before one can assess the advisability of attempting cross-national generalisations about the term 'Deaf culture'. It may be that when the new field of diasporic theory is developed, it may be possible to utilise some of these tools to identify commonalities which could inform the development of a central 'core' of cultural identity, similar to those being attempted for the 'Black Atlantic' and for Jewish culture (the dangers of essentialism notwithstanding).

In this respect, I should append some comments in the light of Mindess' (2000) recent analysis. A very high proportion of the examples she gives of USA Deaf cultural features are also found in the UK, notably those described under 'collectivist' and 'high context' cultures. This confirmation offers us exciting directions for future research if factored in with the conclusions in this volume; to what extent do these harmonise with the minority-culture concept, and what can we learn from thinking about features which do not align? It may well be that such future research will offer up invaluable theoretical possibilities, not only for minority-cultural studies but for sociology and anthropology as well.

There is one other feature to which I should draw attention, and that is the profound grammatical similarities between all sign languages so far researched. There is a very real sense in which this fact is linked in Deaf peoples' self-conceptualisation with the idea of a central 'core' of Deaf similarity. One image which has recently emerged to express this is of Deaf people as seeds planted in each society in the world; that they all produce the same flower, but its size, shape, fertility and so forth vary according to the majority culture climate, soil and attitude to horticulture.[2]

In this theory, Deafhood comes from maintaining a clear focus on the seed itself. Certainly when one attends international gatherings, it is infinitely easier to communicate across the languages if one sets aside as many majority cultural-specific features as one can. An obvious example would be fingerspelling alphabets.

However, one does not approach these communication events from 'negative' intention of deleting the various linguistic ethnocentrisms. Rather, there is a positive focus in attempting to render ideas in as 'pure' a visual form as can be conceived, something which carries a tremendous emotional power of its own, akin to a feeling of returning to 'the source' – the seed, perhaps.[3]

Deaf cultures as diachronic

However, the chapters above also indicate the central importance of a diachronic approach to Deaf culture – present-day manifestations cannot be understood without being grounded in an explication of traditional social patterns traced forward through historical time. As Chapter 9 indicates, the present attitudes of the hierarchy of the BDA are seen by some subaltern Deaf as conditioned by the social patterns formed in oralist schools and missioner-run clubs. Further research along such lines would enable the development of more sophisticated theories concerning the process of cultural change itself.

Cultural homogenity

The weakness of homogenised accounts has been partly addressed by the identification of class-like features within British Deaf culture in Chapter 8; some of the data also stresses the importance of age as an important socio-cultural marker. This suggests that other variables such as race, gender and sexual orientation should also be factored into Deaf cultural theory. Future Deaf educational and social-welfare research which does not factor in such variables may fail validity criteria.

Taxonomic accounting

Chapters 8 and 9 also suggest that taxonomic approaches are limited – British Deaf life is clearly permeated by the culture of the majority society. Many of the forms within and around which Deaf cultural action moves in these chapters are either modelled on or resemble wider British culture. What marks the culture as distinct are the different expressions, dispositions and strategies, and the different cultural weighting each carries. In order to produce useful data, it is therefore necessary to frame Deaf cultural theory within an exploration of the epistemological processes of Deaf communities themselves.

Adopting a commitment to a rigorous ethnography and to transparency and subjective reflexivity also avoids the dangers of prescriptivism. By illustrating the varying responses of Deaf subalterns to oppression in the domains of school and club, the data confirm the relevance of Bourdeiu's assessment of culture as containing 'fields' which generate their own influence on the 'habitus' of Deaf people, whose cultural responses are therefore 'dispositional'.

This contrasts with analyses which perceive Deaf culture as determined by a simple 'base-superstructure' framing, and with accounts which seek to reify a simple essentialist approach, as adopted by the cultural nationalists criticised by Parsons in Chapter 5. However, one should note that *these approaches are in themselves cultural manifestations*, and could be studied as such, thus bringing them within a Deaf cultural framework.

Deafhood and Deaf Cultural Theory

Throughout Chapters 2, 3, 7, 8 and 9, Deaf subalterns have indicated a desire not to be restricted by the parameters of the 'deafness' trope. However, as we have seen, there has been little conceptual 'space' available to them to create terms for their own alternative self-concept. The development of the Deafhood term, however, offers a space within which Deaf cultural beliefs and values can be articulated, collected and examined. Not only is this important in its own right, but it also represents a counterbalancing *positivity* to the negative atmosphere existing within pathological and social-welfare domains. This harmonises well with emerging work such as Griggs (1998), which explores 'Deaf wellness' as an alternative to the traditional focus on 'Deaf mental health problems'.

Perhaps the most significant aspect of the data chapters is the extent to which individuals and groups have been reaching towards realising what might be termed 'Full-Deaf' (or in BSL, 'BIG D') positions in both their individual and collective lives. Some of the themes which manifest 'strivings towards Deafhood' are examined later, but I must signpost certain aspects here.

One is that I have no intention of suggesting that Deafhood is a finite state of being. Rather, it is a process; one moves towards it, to actualise it. Second, contestations of what Deafhood might mean within and to different sectors of the community is a valid cultural process in itself – indeed it is these contestations which can help reveal deeper levels of Deaf cultural meaning than we at present understand. Third, it is inevitable that some will wish to understand where Deafhood stands in relation to Deaf culture.

The simplest answer I can suggest at this historical moment is the setting up a contrasting relationship which, if explored, might reveal deeper layers of meaning.

Deaf culture in many respects is centred around Deaf traditions. Indeed, Mindess (2000) raises the question of whether it might be more 'past-oriented' than some other cultures. What Deafhood offers is the chance for a community to find out what it might *become* once the weight of oppression is lifted. A simple example is that of racial discrimination within Deaf communities – this is clearly part of inherited cultural traditions. Deafhood, however, by drawing attention to the global Deaf self, is able to reject one aspect of Deaf culture by appealing to another, which it can argue is a 'deeper' one. Such a construction, therefore, not only 'permits' a belief in cultural change but actually suggests directions towards which that change might orientate itself. So, although in the end this is a false dichotomy, it does seem to provide a tool by which the community can 'draw a line' under old colonialist patterns, and enable a release of energy for taking the initiative in rebuilding itself. And of course, what is most striking about this is that the same process can be found in other post-colonial and minority cultures.

Deafhood, Deaf Culture and the Study of Deaf Communities

To some extent, the account given in this book has taken a defensive stance. For example, instead of assuming the existence of Deaf culture and proceeding from there to a swifter examination of Deaf community life, much time and effort has been devoted to validating the concept. This decision was taken partly because of the political implications described earlier – since they are so profound, considerable opposition can be expected, and thus the advocating case needed to be as solid as possible.

However there is also a very real sense in which these conclusions lead us into an pro-active mode. The culturo-linguistic case, together with the other academic dimensions – historical, psychological, sociological and so on – seems to me to be so strong that we can propose that any future d/Deaf research which does not centre itself in this model *can be said to fail academic validity criteria automatically*, and thus the majority of their findings can not only be discarded but read across the grain as further examples of colonialist thinking.

The reader should not underestimate the importance of these implications – that the vast majority of work at presently being conducted on deafness in the medical, scientific, educational, psychological and social welfare domains is *academically invalid*. This, in turn, means that the whole superstructure of funding and refereeing deafness issues is also invalid and in need of immediate deconstruction and reconstitution.

Implications for Wider Cultural Theory

The roles of lay people and subalterns

Throughout this study we have seen examples of lay people who have been regarded by Deaf communities as actual or potential allies, yet we have noted that their inability to become so has been rooted in two factors – the development of specialist professionalism; and lay people's consenting to the surrendering of their democratic rights to participate in Deaf-related discourse. These factors have thus allowed the two forms of colonialism to develop, to disseminate themselves through the media and become enshrined in practice. Nevertheless, Deaf communities' renewed optimism that lay people could become a force for change through coalition, provided that the Deaf view can gain media access, gives us pause for thought in respect of cultural theory in general.

Minority Studies, Cultural Studies and Post-Colonial Studies have understandably made their initial focus one of analysing the cultural and political attitudes which led to the oppression of the various groups with which their work is concerned. However, there is a danger that in over-emphasising the theory that 'all white people / males are inherently and unavoidably racist / sexist', that an opportunity is missed to establish the more subtle dynamics by which racism and sexism are maintained.

In historical terms, this leads to a blurring of distinctions between what were in fact contending forces – for example the tension between piratical pre- and post-colonialism activities and the attempts by churches to ameliorate or prevent those actions (cf also the anti-slavery movements of the 1830s). It is perfectly understandable that colonised peoples might consider these to be two sides of the same totalising coin. Yet to continue such a one-dimensional analysis leaves no place at which the individual 'lay' agent (or any organisations they might form) may insert themselves into the discourse.[4]

This issue assumes greater importance, both for theory and praxis, when we consider the present-day situations in respect of racism, sexism and colonialism. If we wish to see these conditions ameliorated and removed, we are required to find ways in which individual lay people can locate the power to act, either in their daily praxis or by combining to form organisations. Blanket assignation of white or male guilt without regard to the cultural processes by which the ideologies were developed, disseminated and unconsciously absorbed (that is, the manufacturing of lay consent), leads in the end to paralysis, as could be seen in the case of the various men's movements which formed and then died away in the 1980s. Such paralysis then creates an ideological vacuum into which reactionary forces can, and have, inserted a backlash.

Furthermore, the more we learn about post-modernist thinking about subjectivities, the more we are able to identify subjectivities which involve varying degrees of racism/sexism. Perhaps the most notable example is the class differences in racial interaction. It has often been noted that working-class people make racist remarks in front of minority people, yet claim friendship with the ones they know ('You're different from them'). Yet it has been argued that there are more friendships between white and black at this level in the UK than between white middle-class people and black people, whose response more closely resembles what has come to be known as 'white flight'. Blanket statements about racism or sexism, therefore, prevent useful examination of subjectivities which might provide an impetus for lay involvement, action and change. The example is especially interesting because it closely resembles what we have learned in Chapter 8 about Deaf and hearing working-class interaction.

These problems can also be identified in the failure of the Left to understand the relationships between political and cultural struggles. Indeed, given the length of historical time over which Western Marxist political analysis has existed, this analytical failure may be said to pre-date the issues raised by minority studies. In downplaying the importance of working-class culture and art forms, much valuable ground was ceded to those hegemonic forces which controlled, among others, the education system (leading to embourgeoisement), and media (leading to the mis-representation of working-class people in images reflected back for their consumption). Thus over time the only issue left on the class agenda was employment. Although the New Left tried to reinstate a wider cultural critique of Western societies during the 1960s, it was too late to halt the process by which Thatcherism could drive a wedge into the working-class vote by seizing control of crucial aspects and subjectivities relating to the (media-manipulated) working-class agenda. And, albeit over a longer period of time, we have seen the takeover of the party of Labour by the middle-class, leaving us with two middle-class parties, akin to the situation found in the USA.[5]

Thus the insistence in this book of both problematicising the classification categories which have been created around Deaf and lay relations, and encouraging the lay reader to begin a genuine cultural self-examination, represents implications for cultural theory which reach far beyond deafness/Deafhood domains.

Discipline-specific theories

One major criticism (see Hammersley, 1992) of both anthropology and critical ethnography is that the many descriptive accounts are rarely drawn together to create cultural theories. This chapter attempts to redress that weakness by suggesting directions which might be pursued.

Although it is too soon to assess the implications of Deaf cultural theory for cultural theory in general, the data do offer some useful indications, as we have seen earlier. Concerning anthropology, the importance of disposition and strategy in Deaf culture indicates support for processual models of culture, but more research is needed before it is possible to confirm the prioritisation of either adaptational or ideational frameworks – at present a case can be offered for both.

With regard to the former, Bhabha's (1995) assertion of the importance of subversive mimicry as a form of resistance practiced by the colonised, and Bohannan's similar concept of 're-contextualising', resonate for a Deaf community greatly outnumbered and penetrated by a majority culture. In this respect, Brydon (1995) notes that one of the strongest forms of resistance to colonialism has been the development of ideas by the colonised of their own nationhood (the 'Lakota Nation, the 'Black Nation' etc.); the concept of the 'Deaf Nation' has been presented by Ladd (1996a) and used as the theme for two conferences at Central Lancashire University and a TV series (_Sign On_, 1998). Thus, Anderson's (1983) concept of nations as 'imagined communities' indicates that 'mentalist' theories of culture may be especially relevant for minority groups.

Bohannan's (1995) theories of cultural change, traps and dissonance do appear to be relevant for Deaf culture. Indeed it may be that they are more suitable for examination of minority cultures in general, where cultural issues are more pressing and thus more visible on the 'surface' than in the huge dispersed nation-state cultures.

In respect of Cultural Studies, the data would appear merely to confirm the importance of theories of ideology and hegemony rather than to add to them. When considered in conjunction with Post-Colonial theories, however, an important and relatively new dimension emerges. Various dispositions and strategies within the data indicate patterns which can be hypothesised as _marking a distinction in cultural theory_ between 'majority cultures' and 'minority cultures'. These are now explored.

The 'Structure of Feeling' of Deaf and Minority Cultures

It seems plausible that Deaf cultures express aspects of Williams' 'structures of feeling', which may be parallelled within other minority cultures.

Some of these may also be relevant for majority cultures but appear to find much less resonance there.

Minority cultures as bipolar and oppositional

It can be argued that the characteristic which distinguishes minority cultures from others is precisely that minority positioning. Minority cultures exist within a bipolar framework, where their own cultural 'core' is subsumed by an opposing cultural force. The daily lives of minority individuals are therefore characterised by forces and impulses which pull them towards one or other of these poles; these then affect the groups' cultural strategies, which Wrigley (1996: 11) has described as the 'tension between resistance and compliance'. We have seen these manifested in the Deaf 'class' issues of Chapter 8 and in the dynamics described by Raymond and Ken in Chapter 9, whilst within Black discourse, Du Bois (1903) has characterised this as 'double consciousness':

> One ever feels his [*sic*] two-ness – an American, a Negro; two souls, two thoughts, two unreconciled strivings; two warring ideas in one dark body whose dogged strength alone keeps it from being torn asunder. The history of the American Negro is the history of this strife – this longing to attain self-conscious manhood, to merge his double self into a better and truer self. (cited in Early, 1993: xviii)

From this perspective, therefore, the 'existential' reality of minority cultures is inevitably characterised by degrees of *oppositionality*.

Although this description can be sensed when 'reading' various minority cultures, there seem to be no formal theories which make this explicit; this study therefore takes the initial step towards formalising such concepts.

Discourses and representations within bipolar structures

Deaf and other minority cultures can be deconstructed to reveal polarised discourses and others which consequently develop from those tensions, as outlined in Chapter 2. The initial colonial impulse was represented as two sets of discourses – majority colonialist discourses and those of the colonised subaltern.

Once it becomes expedient for colonialist discourses to co-opt selected members of the colonised, a third intermediate discourse develops. This is the site within which discourses about the treatment and administration of the colonised takes place. However, only certain élite subaltern are permitted access to these sites and, by definition, on terms laid down by the colonialists, as Dorothy and Ken illustrated in Chapter 7.

The data chapters reveal a further development of this model. Once the decolonisation process begins, whether impelled by subaltern forces or by changes in the majority culture, that intermediate discourse is then challenged by subaltern forces and their allies. Growing professionalisation, whether among Deaf and other minority subaltern, then sees a fourth discourse develop among that 'class'. This is characterised, in part, by discussion about how to transform the intermediate discourse and by attempts, for example, to consciously determine what 'Deaf' might mean as a tool to be utilised in that transformation. We have seen in Chapters 8 and 9 how Ray's and Ken's thinking exemplified that process.

It is these developments, together with the changes produced by the first waves of the Deaf resurgence, the re-emergence of BSL, together with the bilingual movement, from which 'young liberal' hearing professionals and lay people have emerged, that have produced a fifth set of discourses which Bienvenu and Columnos (1989) called the 'third culture'. We can see parallels here with the American Civil Rights movements of the 1960s, and the anti-apartheid discourses in South Africa in the 1970s. In both cases there was a struggle for 'control' of these discourses resulting in the assertion by some of the need for an all-Black leadership setting out its own agenda. In the end this led to breakaways and the formations of the SDS (Students for a Democratic Society) and the Black Consciousness Movement respectively.

If this analysis holds good, we should expect a similar movement within Deaf communities and, certainly in the UK, the formation of the FDP appears to confirm it.

A further set of discourses then open up within the 'traditional' subaltern Deaf/minority discourse as this new group of subaltern-élite then attempts to discuss these issues with the other subaltern Deaf. Within this space discourses begin to emerge concerning wider Deaf/minority priorities (including newly emerging Deaf-minority issues themselves), all of which ask which factors might be involved in redefining themselves and their community. Dorothy's and Ken's attempts to work within the modern BDA is just one example of this development. The equivalent within African-American discourse might be the work of hooks (1995), although her own works are focused more on drawing attention to the need for such discourses to be recognised and respected.

The extent to which the subaltern-élite can still be considered subaltern is under contention within post-colonial theory. Spivak (1996) as we have seen, suggests that the moment that the subaltern can speak, they are no longer subaltern. The data in this study suggests that the situation is much more complex and that theories concerning 'subalternhood' would benefit from being actively applied to specific minority-cultural or post-colonial situations.

Minority cultures and collective selfhood

Virtually all the informants cited reveal a profound sense in which Deaf people conceive of themselves in the plural – it seemed that the words 'we' and 'Deaf' were felt to be almost inseparable. This collective selfhood may be a product of oppression in modern society (it is too early to generalise to tribal societies), and thus an important feature of other minority cultures. If this were so, then one might expect to find this collectivity breaking down as oppression lessens. This seems to be the case in the USA, where the rise of the new Black middle-classes has taken place at the same time as a sector of the working-class has been displaced downwards to a position similar to that held by the old 'lumpen-proletariat' (Marable, 1992). My own research at Gallaudet University in 1992–3 found some evidence for a similar detachment developing between the new Deaf professionals there and their former cohorts. Further research might confirm this hypothesis and also shed light on these types of minority cultural processes.

Colonialism and internal cultural dissension

Colonialist strategies such as the creation of compliant status groups and the drawing of discourse boundaries according to their own priorities appears to result in the development of highly charged internal cultural dissension among the colonised, as seen in Chapter 8. Externally imposed structures of 'deafness' thus established a legacy which has resulted in increased tension between the colonised the closer they come to independence and the ensuing responsibility and power which that implies. As Ken's observations in Chapter 9 implied, the BDA's leaders' reproduction of old cultural patterns in the post-Deaf resurgence era is the more fraught because the stakes are now higher – patterns which served to run Deaf sporting events and trips for old people have to be re-thought for the running of a national socio-political organisation. They are higher also because of the threat to the community posed by cochlear implants and genetic modification – for the first time the 'Final Solution' is actually on the horizon.

Fanon (1986), Pityana *et al.* (1991), hooks (1989) and Gilroy (1993a, b) indicate that similar patterns can be found in Black communities on several continents, whilst Deloria (1988) and Churchill (1994) describe the equivalent within Native American communities. Geertz's (1973: 243) summary of the Indonesian situation may be the most concise:

> The move towards national unity intensified group tensions within the society *by raising settled forms out of their particular contexts, expanding them into general allegiances and politicising them* . . . Marxists looked mainly to the folk melange of peasant life for the essence of the national

heritage; the technicians, clerks and administrators of the 'classe dirigeante' to the Indic aestheticism of the Javanese aristocracy, and the more substantial merchants and landowners to Islam. (My emphasis)

Thus all the patterns described in this section may be a characteristic of minority cultures in general.

Oralism, colonialism and totalitarianism

In this respect it should be noted that, although there has been considerable focus on Oralism in the study, it appears that the more pertinent theoretical framework is actually that of colonialism. The situation which obtained when the first Deaf schools were established were akin to pre-colonial conditions between the West and the rest of the world – that is to say, there was a trading of skills. The first teachers of the Deaf had to 'trade' their knowledge of majority languages for Deaf peoples' knowledge of sign languages.

Once the forces of capitalism and the powers of the nation-state were brought to bear on Deaf education, the balance of power came down heavily on the side of the majority language. Thus, even prior to Oralism, hearing people took control of Deaf education, becoming the gatekeepers with whom governments consulted, whilst the lay population accepted that such work was for specialists acting on their behalf. In the case of French Deaf education, an artificial signed system based on the majority language was set in place.

In this respect, then, it is possible to adopt a Foucauldian reading and suggest that colonialist patterns predated Oralism itself. The numbers of prominent Deaf teachers during the 18th and 19th century, together with the numbers of schools founded and run by Deaf heads, suggest that the slide into colonialism was not a straightfoward path. But the same is true for the development of colonialism in general. It is only when the administrative apparatus is firmly in place that colonialism can then move into a period of exponential development.

These arguments are crucial because it is then possible for Deaf schools to teach using either signed systems or sign language, yet be as repressive of Deaf cultural development as 'missionary schools' in other continents (Churchill, 1994). If we seek confirmation of this position, we are able to find it in an unlikely source. In Ireland, where Oralism was not introduced until the 1960s, literacy levels seemed quite impressive but the (strongly Christianised) school regimes do not appear to have encouraged Deaf culture or art forms, or the development of independence of thought and action, so that on leaving school, pupils were very much 'passed on to' missionary welfare colonialism.[6] This being so, even schools which have adopted bilingual policies in the present day nevertheless remain firmly within the colonialist framework.

Oralism is thus best read as an especially totalitarian form of colonialism, perhaps akin to schools for First Nation children wherein eradication of the native culture has often been an explicit goal (Beresford & Omaji, 1988). Both Oralism and the Deaf response to it in Chapters 2, 3 and 7, therefore, offer useful data for the development of cultural theory in respect of minority education.

Minority cultures, pressures and self-definition

One effect of experiencing the opposing cultural force of a majority is summarised by Bhabha's adaptation of Benjamin (1994) – 'the state of emergency in which [minority cultures] live is not the exception, but the rule'. It is necessary to develop cultural theory founded on this insight.

One aspect of this phenomenon, both within the data and among some other minority cultures is the concept of *pressure*. Among its manifestations are the pressure from both cultural poles to define one's self to their satisfaction, and to choose allegiances. Demands to make such choices are exacerbated by the amount of external pressure implicit in definitions of colonial oppression, since there is *insufficient relief from that pressure* to create the space required to make choices in one's own time and according to one's own agendas. Pryce (1979) illustrates this well in his study of Afro-Caribbean culture; the title itself *Endless Pressure* demonstrates the importance of the concept.

The pressure from both poles also exacerbates the condition of self-division and self-doubt, and the energy required to suppress these also takes its toll on both the group and individual; in turn the pressure to create one's own self-definitions that may relieve that pressure also increases. As Chapter 9 illustrated, the negative cultural influences of Oralism create greater pressure in the Deaf resurgence period where Deaf actions now carry more weight and responsibility. Although there is still room for a range of individual dispositions and strategies to exist, these are nevertheless caught within the bipolar dynamics which operate on their habitus. This may explain why so many of the accounts of Deaf culture in Chapter 5 have focused on issues around membership and self-definition. As Fanon (1968) puts it 'colonialism forces the people it dominates to ask themselves the question constantly: "In reality, who am I?"'.

The pressures of unity

These pressures manifest themselves in another form – the limited cultural space available for dissent. Unity in the face of opposition is a commonly expressed imperative in minority cultures, operating even at the expense of resistance or action. As Gilroy (1993: 3) puts it:

> The position of black cultural critics is rendered still more uncomfortable because . . . the space in which serious public discussion of the politics of black cultural productions can take place has dwindled . . . In this climate, to be critical or analytical is often perceived to be an act of betrayal.

This dynamic operates on Deaf culture also, as evidenced in Chapters 8 and 9.

Furthermore, since a minority community is necessarily made up of an extremely heterogenous population which would not normally be forced into proximity; the *pressure to create unity is therefore increased whilst simultaneously being rendered more difficult to achieve.*

The pressures of prescriptivism and essentialism

One characteristic of minority cultures is the extent to which they have to resist majority-cultural prescriptions of who or what they should be; without that resistance, cultural change will occur in one direction only – towards the majority culture by osmosis. Consequently there is cultural pressure to reject all aspects of majority culture in order to maintain one's own, even to the detriment of one's own cultural development, as evidenced by some Black nationalism (Fanon, 1968). Similarly, as Raymond's and Barry's disagreement illustrates, some of the Deaf constructions develop cultural forms which are rationalised as 'Deaf', yet perpetuate the oppression. These are examples of 'cultural double-binds', and along with presecriptivism are explored in more depth later.

The pressure identified here also impels the search for minority identity which is often cast in essentialist terms. Non-Deaf minorities appear to be passing through this stage (Walby, 1990; Gilroy, 1993b; etc.), whereas Deaf communities are still either caught up in it or just embarking on resolving it. Thus it may well be that Spivak's 'strategic essentialism' represents a useful concept for 'cooling' the Deaf debate .

Multiple identities, selfhood and hybridity

The post-modernist development of the concept of multiple subjectivities has begun to inform the thinking of some minority-cultural groups, and the concept of hybrid identities is developing as a potentially positive self-image for groups living with majority-cultural permeation (Bhabha, 1994). This is also beginning to manifest itself within the British Deaf community (*Sign On*, 1998).

However, compared to majority cultures, the bipolar construction of necessity implies a much larger 'cultural distance' between core subjectivities. In white male society, for example, the distance between one's identity within the tropes of white, male and British is much less than the distance between white and Black, male and female, or Hearing and Deaf. This distance means that the connectivity of identities, and of 'in-between' identities is difficult for many to accept. Pressure to repress certain of one's multiple subjectivities is thus much greater, so that exploration of this subject within minority studies is charged with a greater resonance and tension (hooks, 1989). Given the experiences described in Chapters 7 and 8, very few of the Deaf informants were comfortable with the idea that they might, in any way, have what they saw as a 'Hearing' identity. Further exploration of the subject, if given a higher priority, might serve to reduce that tension and also serve as a comparison point for other minority cultures.

Self-actualisation

One characteristic noticeable throughout the data was the importance given to the process of 'becoming Deaf'. The small percentage of Deaf people who receive Deaf enculturation through family life has parallels with 'sexual preference' minorities whose identity is also actualised in the face of a differently oriented upbringing. Members of other minorities, especially those whose parents have attempted to assimilate into majority culture, may also experience similar desires or peer group challenges to 'become more Black/Native American' etc. (e.g. Gates. 1997: 18). Furthermore, as Dorothy and others indicated, maintaining one's subaltern identity in the face of the different external pressures manifesting in different eras, together with the pressures of aging, etc. means that the actualisation process is a lifelong one.

There is another dimension, as Raymond and Ken illustrated in Chapters 8 and 9, where questions are posed about actually developing and extending what 'becoming Deaf' might mean, especially after experiencing the two colonising domains which sought to suppress or limit any understanding of what this might entail.

In this context also, 'Deafhood' is a useful concept to encompass all forms of actualisation aspirations, whether maintenance or development, and study of its equivalents in minority cultures might well prove fruitful.

The '1001 victories' hypothesis

The research reveals substantial numbers of examples to support this hypothesis, especially within the Deaf subaltern groups in Chapter 8 who found themselves with little room for maneouvre. It may well be that this concept has resonance within other minority cultures, where scope for self-expression and collective action is similarly limited. Gilroy's (1993a) concept of 'small acts' would appear to confirm this; thus further research might be illuminating.

The 'Double Bind' hypothesis

During the course of this study, numerous situations were observed which appeared to place minority cultural members and their allies in strategy dilemmas resembling 'no-win' situations. The data reflect the range of situations involved – Deaf children wishing to better their education facing rejection by their peers, Deaf rebels protesting missioner actions facing ostracism by their community or élite-subaltern desiring to object facing withdrawal of privileges or status by the hearing people holding power over them.

These dynamics may be unique to minority cultures, since the underlying characteristic seems to be one of being trapped in positions where one can find it difficult to support some of the actions taken by one's own people, yet feel unable to criticise them without appearing to reinforce majority-cultural dominance. Cultural forms thus developed may simultaneously enable people to cope with social conditions and limit their ability to change them, as is classically illustrated in Willis' (1977) study of working-class schoolboys or in the Hill–Thomas dilemma faced by Black Americans (e.g. Morrison, 1992). In the Deaf case, these might be summarised as being trapped between 'deafness' and 'Deafhood' impulses. The result seems to be an increase of confusion and pressure in and around minority cultures, resulting in damage to cultural unity.

These appear to refine Bohannan's (1995) theory of 'cultural traps'. This refinement I suggest, can be represented for minority cultures as the 'Double-Bind Theory' and also appears to offer a fruitful direction for further research.

The historical dimension and the historical self

The data from this study illustrate the importance of understanding the past before present-day culture can make sense. However, although this historical dimension is important, even central to any culture, there seem to be few formal explorations or hypotheses concerning the operation of this dynamic.

Nevertheless, when examining minority cultures in particular it is noticeable that, at a certain point in their resurgence, history becomes uniquely important and takes on a much more conscious and explicit role. Of course, reclaiming a suppressed history is an inevitable part of cultural rebuilding and self-liberation; however, what is still not yet clear is the precise role of this 'historical self' in forming such positive self-images. The data suggest that colonialism has destroyed most of the historical continuity of the Deaf community, so that it is harder to actually place oneself within that framework unless one has experienced not only Deaf parents, but Deaf grandparents. Attempts to (re)construct the historical self must therefore inevitably involve conscious strategising, such as those suggested by Martha and Barry; one might imagine that introducing Deaf 'grandparents' to young Deaf children might constitute one such strategy.

Additionally, the role of cultural forums, described earlier, begin to illustrate cultural redevelopment; looking at who one is and what has shaped this inevitably calls upon history and brings it into everyday consciousness. Further research into this dimension would appear to be particularly important.

Summary – minority-culture implications for cultural theory

Many of these examples suggest that an altogether different definition of culture might be proposed. Rather than seeing it as an entity constructed by the acts of bounded groups, it may be better understood, as Quantz (1992) suggests, as 'a contested terrain rather than as a set of shared patterns', where culture is not so much 'the area of social life where people share understandings as that area where people struggle over understandings' (p. 487). Although this may inform majority-cultural experience, it seems to be particularly visible in minority cultures, as illustrated by the 'class'-oriented data in Chapter 8, or the disagreements between Ray, Barry and Stefan. Research exploring such dynamics in minority cultures, where the 'struggle over understandings' is exacerbated by majority-cultural impositions of their versions of 'understanding', might well prove to have significant implications for cultural theory in general.

We cannot leave the subject of minority-culture parallels without noting one aspect of post-colonial theory. Ashcroft *et al.* (1995) locate binarism as one of the discipline's key concepts. They identify the 'binary logic of imperialism' as a tendency of Western thought to see the world in terms of binary oppositions which lends itself to what they term a 'violent hierarchy'. These can extend beyond the colonising project to other relationships – doctor *versus* patient, teacher *versus* pupil. Once established, energy is devoted to confirming one or the other side of the binarism, e.g. Anglo-centrism or nationalism.

Post-colonial theory is therefore concerned to identify 'existential' states or strategies which enable us to disrupt these hierarchical patterns. As they put it:

It may be argued that the very domain of post-colonial theory is the region of 'taboo' – the domain of overlap between these imperial binary oppositions, the area in which ambivalence, hybridity and complexity continually disrupt the certainties of imperial logic. Apart from illuminating the interstitial spaces, post-colonial theory also disrupts the structural relations of the binary system itself, revealing the fundamental contradictions of a system . . . In this way it uncovers the deep ambivalence of a structure of economic, cultural and political relations that can both debase and idealize, demonize and eroticize its subjects. (Ashcroft *et al.*, 1995: 26)

This represents an impressive aim. However, one of the difficulties that newly recognised minority cultures face in dealing with this kind of post-structuralist analysis is that it takes for granted the existence of a significant recorded tradition of both Grand Narrative and counter-narrative. For groups such as Deaf communities which have not yet established the academic 'validity' of their own counter-reality, as Gates (1997) terms it, the critique of post-structuralism represents yet another oppressive devaluation of their existence by 'hearing people'.

It is only once a considerable body of published Deaf discourse is established that there exists a counterweight of sufficient power to actually create a safe space for examining the interstitial zones. Until that time, for many Deaf people, post-structuralism is a 'luxury' in which middle-class theorists can indulge.

The irony of this, of course, is that radical Deaf thinking must privately conduct its own discourse aimed at preventing the continuation of both the old petit-bourgeois nationalism and the newer 'BSL nationalism'. It is thus a marker of precisely that binarial existential dilemma which Deaf and other minority communities face, that they cannot make this discourse public without playing into the hands of those colonialists who wish to maintain their power.[7]

Thus the admirable post-colonialist aim to identify transculturalism, so that 'the engagement with the colonies [becomes] an increasingly important factor in the imperial society's . . . understanding of itself' (Gates, 1997: 27), is by no means as unproblematic as its theorists would like to believe.

These reservations notwithstanding, post-colonial theory represents an exciting direction for development, not only of Deaf Studies, but the whole colonialist 'deafness' administration.

Methodological Conclusions and Implications

'Studying up' and futurology

It would appear that the study validates the necessity for subaltern and other researchers to adopt the technique of 'studying up' and the usefulness of turning the colonial gaze back towards the colonisers' own actions and rationalisations. In so doing, the data yield is effectively doubled as two strata of information are revealed . The first concerns views of one's own situation, and the second the attitudes of those in higher positions, as experienced and interpreted by the subaltern group. As the data in Chapter 9 reveal, the Deaf subalterns have a good grasp of the behaviour and values of the 'middle-class' Deaf and also how to transcend them. By contrast, the 'middle-class' group seems unaware of how their behaviour affects the subaltern group and how they are regarded by that group.

This dynamic seems to apply to other minorities – women, ethnic minorities and so on. As Du Bois (1989) and others indicate, minority groups have to know how the majority culture works in order to survive and sidestep its worst effects; there is no comparable need or impulse in the case of white and male majorities.

The two-tier structure of studying up also offers potential for further studies based either on Bohannan's futurology concept or a more neo-Marxist reading of the discrepancies between potentiality and actuality (cf. Adorno, in Quantz, 1992). These would indicate how oppression leads minorities, especially their elite-subalterns, to impose limitations on their own self-definitions and thus their potential, as illustrated by the clashes in Chapter 9 between Raymond and his Deaf club.

Subaltern-researcher implications

It would appear that taking a subaltern-researcher approach to the study may have justified itself in terms of the quantity and quality of data unearthed which is new to Deaf Studies. However, to generalise further would be risky; it would be glib to suppose that any subaltern could simply produce such work. Perhaps the most useful conclusion is that many subalterns could be ethnographically trained in participant-observation techniques, but to augment these by a carefully developed use of their own introspections and interpretations. From there they can utilise two other essential characteristics of subaltern research – the trust of their informants and, consequently, their access to deeper levels of information.

Nevertheless, this study revealed some potential dangers for subaltern-researchers. One concerned catalytic validity. I found myself constantly desiring not only to identify the problems and issues around Deaf culture, but wishing to 'solve' them as well. This affected my ability simply to observe. Likewise, although this impulse helped inform a study focused on powerful culturo-political data, this did not permit study of simple 'positive' intra-Deaf cultural behaviour. I cannot therefore stress too highly that to limit one's understanding of Deaf culture to the types of data presented here will result in an unbalanced picture of Deaf communities.

I must also add that in the interests of critiquing my own work as thoroughly as possible, and thus to achieve transparency, that it is possible to set my self-description in Chapter 6 alongside the whole thrust of the data chapters, and to locate a correspondence. Does this invalid the data? It is my judgement that it does not – that the evidence given by Dorothy, Albert, Frances and others is too detailed and too consistent to be 'wrong'. Gates (1997: xxvi–ii) addresses this issue of representation rather eloquently:

> Woven through this book are issues I've thought about for most of my life, and so there may be distorting effects of the partiality and perspective I bring. Always I hope that the sympathetic intimations I think I hear aren't echoes of my own rumblings. There's a strong temptation simply to elicit a meaning you know in advance . . . Avoiding that pitfall is the thing I struggle for the hardest . . . [However] if the saints and sinners of this book have nothing to teach me, then I am a poor student.

Indeed, perhaps we should note the irony that at present within the academic and other domains, it is only (precisely?) those who are disempowered who are required to render their self-justifications transparent (and thus giving those holding power a further potential weapon to use). It is only those who are disempowered who are forced to engage in defensive actions regarding issues of who is or might be the 'true representatives' of such groups. Nevertheless, if critical ethnography persists, it may one day create a climate where all research or publicly published work cannot sustain its own validity without incorporating transparency. This is one reason why I persist.

The other is that the ultimate implications of critical ethnography is that its published works should actively invite dialogue in order not to perpetuate the reification process of academia, and indeed to help overthrow it. I therefore invite responses on this issue as well, of course, as any others that may occur to the reader.

I also presented an evaluation of my own status as subaltern-élite Deaf researcher in Chapter 6. To what extent has this study proved it to be an accurate assessment? Again, that cannot be made without the kind of feedback from other Deaf people that a later section describes. It certainly became clear during the study, especially when dealing with the residential school experience, and the intensity of the impotence experienced by monolinguals throughout life, that someone like me whose first language is English and who did not grow up socialised into the culture, faces severe restrictions when it comes to considering the research domains which can be investigated under that label. There are undoubtedly aspects of Deaf culture which, if I were to study them, I would have to do so from a position which in numerous ways would be similar to that of a hearing outsider.

Given the miniscule resources allocated to Deaf studies, and the scarcity of Deaf academics, there is still a strong case for continuing – it is possible for the other aspects of my Deaf status to gain me a good degree of access to subaltern conversations and reflections. Yet that status cannot enable an intuitive understanding, and thus accurate analysis of certain Deaf mono-lingual experiences. If I proceed in this project, therefore, it is on the understanding that more definitive accounts await the arrival of subaltern Deaf researchers themselves. Inevitably this in itself begs the Spivackian question – in order for them to attain this status, they must be by definition competent in English – and thus bilingual. This is an example of the classic double-binds which encircle minority culture research.

However, it is possible to utilise one aspect of my Deaf status as a bridge to another – the ease of Deaf relationship enables (if carefully constructed) research which brings on board 'native-informants' in a meaningful way. Of course, the colonialist administration in its academic funding strategies does not encourage this more democratic research – funds are almost never available to pay such informants in a consistent way and, of course, there is not even a funding structure in place which acknowledges this.

The language of interpretation
The study has reinforced a belief held by some practitioners that a major part of the problem inherited from the pathological discursive system is that not only has it disguised the fact that its work is merely interpretative, but in so doing has created a reductionist linguistic register with which to write about Deaf people. I have attempted to use language and dimensions in this study which write Deaf people 'larger' – i.e. nearer to the emotional 'size' of a community with such unique national, international and histori-cal dimensions. Indeed, I strongly suggest that future accounts of Deaf communities must address the question of interpretative language as a matter of urgency. This applies particularly to colonialist research, both re-actionary and liberal. It is also relevant for subaltern-researchers; without a firm grasp of a wider political picture, their own work may simply mirror the reductionist registers of the medical and social-control models.

Indeed, it is noticeable that from the beginnings of the Deaf resurgence, activists have attempted to borrow salient contemporary tropes in order to draw the attention of majority society to Oralism and other abuses; 'com-munity', 'linguistic minority', 'genocide', 'child abuse', 'nation' and 'colony' and now 'culture'. However, only the first two have gained consis-tent acceptance and use either by academics or Deaf organisations – the others are still expressed in reductionist vocabulary like 'increased Deaf awareness'.

These themes are of particular importance for the future shaping of Deaf Studies, where it can be argued that the discipline should not be focused on teaching 'facts', but on transforming students' own constructions and interpretations to embrace the widest possible dimensions. In order to achieve this, the discipline has to focus on what these might be, and how their present interpretations still contain the colonialist 'seeds', in order to best equip both Deaf and hearing people to work in and around a post-colonial Deaf society, rather than just fulfilling academic quotas.

Prescriptivism and cultural relativism

A related academic legacy of colonialism is prescriptivism. Although it may apply to some other minorities, it seems particularly prevalent in the deafness domain, and may be a legacy of the pedagogical conditional. Two examples may suffice – the attitude of oralists and others that 'the history of the Deaf is the history of the education of the Deaf' (Hodgson, 1953), and the way in which Deaf television programming on both BBC and Channel 4 is subsumed under their Education Departments (not the case for disability programming, which is consequently more overtly political). Such deployment may see itself as a step forwards from categorisation under 'health' (Britain)/'defectology' (Russia)/'communication disorders' (United States); however, it remains inherently liberal and, as we have seen, equally misguided.

A similar liberalism is manifested by those recoiling from the idea that Deaf oppression should be clearly framed. Responses such as 'it's too negative – it makes Deaf people look helpless' indicates an inability to see the positivity or 'heroism' inherent in rebellion and survival which Chapters 7 and 8 demonstrate. By contrast it would be inconceivable for other minority studies not to centralise slavery, the 'Indian Wars' or witchburning. Rejection of these as 'political not cultural' risks cultural descriptions being not only incomplete but fundamentally erroneous. Given the extent to which this is realised within other disciplines, as the work of Bourdieu, Foucault, Hall and others has demonstrated, the incorporation of such thinking would appear to be overdue for the academic domains of Deaf education, Deaf social work and the medical disciplines.

In a similar vein, Chapter 5 illustrated how attempts to ratify the Deaf cultural concept have met with attempts to refute parallels between Deaf and other minority communities by locating and highlighting differences. It would appear more useful to see differences between Deaf, Black, Gay and female minorities as marking important clues which can _refine_ each's distinctive qualities rather than invalidate them.

Another form of prescriptivism illustrated in the chapter concerned responses that can be summarised as 'that feature can't be Deaf culture because other cultures also have this' or 'Deaf cultural features are merely built on physical restrictions'. This failure to recognise that claims are not being made for the uniqueness of the feature in question but for its cultural weighting not only reflects the failure to understand culture as a structure of relationships, as Bohannan and Bourdieu have illustrated, but, as with all the examples in this section, suggest a (possibly subconscious) attempt to suppress Deaf subaltern emergence.

Prescriptivism also informs the apparently laudable desire to see Deaf culture purely in and of itself, and not just as 'reacting to Hearing culture'. However, the fear that Deaf culture may be seen as reactional fails to recognise the possibility that to be oppositional is not simply to react *per se*; rather oppositionality colours, informs, deepens and even enriches many cultural features. Levine (1977) has illustrated that the spiritual practices within Black churches may carry greater resonance primarily because of their inspirational transmuting of Christian texts in order to endure or transcend oppression, a dimension lacking in most white religious worship. This extra dimension might be rendered for minority cultures as 'majority culture – *plus*'.

Thus the search for models, prescriptive or otherwise, may be recognised as a majority-cultural dynamic in itself. This also applies within Deaf minority culture; images and terms such as 'family', 'village' and 'home' should be perceived as tropes to be deconstructed in future studies.

Nevertheless, whilst linguistic relativity is more or less accepted, cultural relativity remains problematic. Oppressed cultures can also be read as damaged cultures, especially if it can be shown that individuals and groups have been forced to inhabit limited normative realms. This is one reason why some minority cultures have resisted exposure of cultural 'weaknesses' (in so doing unfortunately limiting the amount of data available for cross-minority study). Such fears may also underlie the views expressed by liberals (see earlier). However, some minority theorists, especially feminists, have constructed arguments to illustrate the extent to which majority cultures are actually damaged by the dualistic and self-alienated perspectives which motivate their oppression of minorities. Such theories may assist in resisting liberal fears and in constructing a model of Deaf culture which asserts cultural relativity positively.

In the interests of transparency it is also important to repeat that I found myself to have absorbed this same prescriptivism. My desire to 'solve', described earlier, interfered with simply observing Deaf behaviour. It was, however, also informed by prescriptive tendencies and attitudes exemplified in the BSL trope of 'DEAF-SHOULD'. This also had to be overcome – how successfully is for the reader to judge.

Typicality and academic validity

Judgement sampling raises questions around typicality and validity and requires that, for this study, we satisfactorily locate and account for the perspectives expressed by subaltern rebels like Raymond, Dorothy and Ken. This is best addressed by acknowledging that cultural members have their own theories about what they perceive and what they are doing, and to see the data not as statements about reality but *as part of the reality being studied*. Thus it is not necessary to 'believe' them, so much as to register their existence as cultural or personal rationale, and to present them as a series of hypotheses for further research. Viewed collectively, they may also be hypothesised as contributing to an overarching set of perspectives; one such concept being Bourdieu's (1991) 'folk theories'. This issue can only be resolved if the outside observer has access to the full texts of those interview conversations so that they can decide for themselves. It is for this methodological reason among others, that these are intended for publication as *Conversations in Deafhood*.

Mention must also be made of the academic validity of the reading given in Chapters 2 and 3, particularly the issue of whether lay people were as positively disposed towards the average Deaf person as I have posited. There are numerous quotations which can be offered which appear to refute this, not all of which can be explained away by self-interest on behalf of those making the claim for public hostility and indifference.

However, the vast majority of examples that we presently know were of statements committed to print during the process of establishing this or that organisation. We still do not know anything like enough about Deaf–lay relationships in informal domains. The evidence presented in Chapter 9 of positive relationships between Deaf and hearing lay people in the pub domain suggests that there a case for maintaining the counter-narrative until such time as we have more evidence.

Deaf cultural forums

Both the methodology employed here and the type of data revealed strongly suggest that a next step for research and catalytic validity might be the construction of 'cultural consciousness forums', in which subalterns might examine their Deaf experiences in order to understand and validate them and thus to extend their Deafhood.

During such a process, developing an understanding of how colonialism has shaped their own responses also enables the beginnings of a deconstruction of Deaf cultural features to reveal the extent to which certain traditional 'Deaf ways' are but internalisations of colonial features. Experiencing this process would thus open a cultural 'space', offering a sense of liberation and confidence that might lead to action and conscious cultural renewal.

Possible Deafhood exercises might include envisioning Deaf (and hearing) worlds where Oralism had never happened and exploring differences between these and the contemporary situation. Likewise, exploration of which Deaf people are selected for co-option into colonialist structures might enable a greater awareness of the patterns and dynamics found there and how they might be resisted.

Such cultural consciousness forums might also circumvent the problem found in other post-colonial movements and 'cultural nationalists', where a simplistic notion of 'Deaf Pride' leaves underlying patterns intact and thus at risk of replacing Hearing oppression by a Deaf one. This is of especial importance in an era of mainstreaming, since Deaf culture may not survive in a historically transmitted and coherent form without some degree of focus on a 'cultural core'. Re-directing respect for this core and its traditions, and teaching it to new generations without developing an overemphasis on cultural nationalism is of particular urgency.

The forums also offer a potential site to draw out the positive aspects of Deaf cultural experience, to counterbalance the 'negative' features which, for reasons of space, have dominated this study, as well as to explore the extent to which present-day attitudes to potential hearing allies, such as parents of Deaf children have been shaped by their own experience of Oralism.

Catalytic validity and Deaf access to this study

Creating access for lay people to the final ethnographic text, is one of the challenges of catalytic validity. In the case of the Deaf community, the combination of low English literacy and the suitability of video as a medium for sign language transmission suggests that serious thought must be given to translation of the text to DVD as an inextricable requirement of Deaf research and funding resources.

I would go further. Because of factors such as time and resources, it has not been possible to undertake the process of consulting with the informants. Simple presentation of the excerpts used in this book would be tokenistic if the whole context in which they were set were not to be explained. The necessity of context-setting, which might entail signing most of the book to each person in turn, is an issue that confronts most critical ethnographers. How many will take the time and trouble needed to do so, *especially when grant-driven research permits at best only the most token of funds for doing so?*

Thus I consider this study to be incomplete, indeed to have failed unless this process is somehow undertaken, and that before too much time has passed and the contents of this book become enshrined with their own status and power. This is why the project, as described in the Introduction, involves three phases, of which this is only the first. The second must therefore consist of a feedback process which is developed through workshopping to culminate in the making of a BSL DVD, and the *Conversations in Deafhood* book mentioned earlier. This then will be the nearest we can come to ensuring that they have control over how they are represented and respected.

In turn, the data gained from the informants' reflections on the project open the doors to the third phase, where their suggestions form the direction of future research.

Summary – Additional Directions for Further Research

The situation which confronts Deaf Studies is that external funding is very rarely made available for Deaf-centred research (as opposed to deafness research, or research on BSL etc. where hearing people are the intended beneficiaries). Furthermore, there is no consideration given to the translation of this material into BSL texts – i.e. video – so that Deaf access is limited to face-to-face tuition. Where there is some Deaf input into research priorities, Bhabha's 'state of emergency' described earlier means that Deaf cultural research is considered something of a luxury best reserved for 'peacetime'. However, the need to clarify the concept and its implications is also urgent, given the rapid dissemination of the term in advance of studies which explore its meanings.

In this situation, acceptance of the existence of Deaf culture opens a 'Pandora's Box' – a new field of study in which it is arguable that a multitude of research projects are necessary. However, five guiding principles can be identified:

(1) The urgency of identifying Deafhood approaches in domains where there has been some limited Deaf entrance, especially regarding 'Deaf ways' of teaching Deaf children.

(2) One unfortunate side-effect of the urgency of clarifying 'Deaf culture' is that it encourages research to be constructed in dualistic form – 'Deaf Ways' *versus* 'Hearing Ways'. This needs to be counterbalanced by research which can identify multiplicity and range of viewpoints and dispositions within Deaf culture. In this respect, priority should also be given to studies with catalytic validity, possibily through Deaf Cultural 'Consciousness' Forums, with specific reference to empowering Deaf people to conduct their own research, and with training opportunities provided.

(3) Research should also bear in mind the importance of perceiving Deaf community and culture as a collective entity. Strategies devised must therefore seek to draw on those collective resources in an active manner, attempting to encourage and create a national cultural climate based on the spirit of enquiry.

(4) Recognising the importance of collective Deafhood unity to the cultural health of the community is also necessary; research which explores the cultural dynamics within Deaf club life and within Deaf organisations is important to maintaining that unity in an era where communities in general are becoming fragmented. As Chapter 3 illustrated, this fragmentation is exacerbated by the increasing numbers of subaltern-élites and consequent increased misunderstanding and ill-feeling as exemplified in the sign 'GRASS-ROOTS-OUT'. Urgent research is required to assist each section of the community to understand the process and attempt re-unification strategies. A similar case can be made for understanding the different cultural needs of Deaf young people and ethnic Deaf people, and for devising strategies which enable those 'lost' in mainstreamed education to find their way 'back' into the Deaf community.

(5) Finally, the recent ascendancy of pathological models also requires a prioritised response. Given the rapid dissemination of cochlear implants, there is an urgent need to assess these from a Deafhood perspective. Similarly the intense interest within genetic engineering in locating and eradicating 'Deaf genes' confronts Deaf communities with the need to penetrate existing discourses with a public justification for their continued existence. There is a need, therefore, for cultural research which can highlight such features in order to underpin the Deaf case.

In a textbook on BSL in 1988, I wrote 'for the first time, the hearing public on a wide scale are active participants in the struggle for final recognition or obliteration of the deaf community and British Sign Language' (Miles, 1988: 43). In the decade since, the pathological model has sharpened its tools. Validation of Deaf culture now, in turn, provides a sharpened tool for the linguistic model as the struggle intensifies.

However, the huge disparency in the 'size' of the tools and the resources which drive them is something which the academy must now recognise in order to accept its moral responsibility to establish the level playing field which supposedly underpins ideas of a genuinely democratic research and education system. In this context, a critical examination of the (very largely hidden) system which underpins grant awards and the allocation of resources is long overdue.

Ultimately, in order to inspire research in these directions, one might do well to reflect on the remarkably positive example set by Deaf communities in the data. The re-emerging pride in the survival and resurgence of their unique languages and art forms from a century-long oppression that might have decimated other cultures is augmented by their similarly unique national and international dimensions, and by their sense of what they can contribute to the colour and diversity of human life. The search for Deafhood, then, may enrich us all.

Notes

1. A recent meeting made it clear to me that the analytical steps described here are indeed at least subconciously perceived by numbers of teachers and heads involved in the bilingualism movement in Deaf education.

    The past 25 years have been characterised for Deaf activists by a two-stage process of initial encouragement, followed by disillusionment. The relief felt at the relative 'success' of the liberal Total Communication movement had much to do with the knowledge that, whatever happened educationally, Deaf children were at least free to communicate in Sign with their parents and with each other, and thus to teach or support one another. When this philosophy became a system for trying to imposed a English-based syntactic form on signing, and when there was little movement towards creating policies for training and employing Deaf teachers, disillusionment set in.

    This was replaced by a hope that bilingualism would, by recognising the centrality of BSL itself, lead to a demand for Deaf BSL users to assume important roles in Deaf education. This has not yet manifested itself. The number of Deaf classroom aides has mushroomed, but only a few schools have any Deaf teachers, only one has a Deaf head, and there is virtually no involvement of Deaf people at teacher training or other higher levels. (I should make mention of a notable exception – one school has an astonishing five Deaf teachers; perhaps significantly it seems to be at pains not to draw attention to that fact.) Bilingualism has so far proved to be another liberal movement and the colonialist framework remains intact.

    It is generally understood that bilingualism implies biculturalism. The participants at the meeting I attended seemed reluctant to include biculturalism in their planning, and I came to realise that, deep down, they understood that to take this step in any serious manner would be to begin the process of having to defer to Deaf views, and would ultimately lead to the loss of their power. Although the final process of decolonisation cannot take place for another decade, when there are reasonable numbers of experienced Deaf teachers (and, moreover, 'strong Deaf' teachers), the intermediate stage will be characterised by potential tension and stress for all the staff involved. The gradual loss of authority, or of one's whole raison d'être as a 'qualified teacher of the Deaf, and the gradual loss of prestige, all pose their own problems even before one comes to the loss of power.

2. My thanks to Jim Kyle, Jordan Eickman and Clark Denmark for their ideas here.
3. Readers should also be aware that there is also a growing tendency towards the use of ASL as a *lingua franca* in certain domains. The complexity of the interaction between these two 'discourses' will be examined in the next volume.
4. Such one-dimensional readings can also falsify history closer to home, for example, the British nation-state's ideological reading of all Germans as being complicit in the process of Nazi rule conveniently ignores the hundreds of thousands of deaths of Germans who opposed the regime. It is, of course, probably uncoincidental for such a reading that most of these were socialists and trade unionists who died in the camps wearing the Red star. This type of racist read-

ing allows British people to see fascism as something which 'could not happen here' and obscures the extent to which the British government condoned the existence of the camps. The importance of such a reading is that British culture is then shaped in such a way as to prevent its people from asking the question 'where would I stand if it happened here?' By contrast, people in the occupied countries were confronted with just such questions, and the answers to the dilemma of 'resistance or compliance' were written in blood.

5. These failures continue; one example can be seen in the Left's incomprehension of the working-class love of soaps, daytime chat shows and competition programmes. As a working-class person myself, it is quite obvious that the vast majority of television dramas are created for middle-class viewers, and working-class people represented as deficient in a variety of ways, whether cast as criminals, 'bits of rough' or whatever, and I have no doubt that working-class people are turned off by this. Thus what we witness in the popularity of these types of programmes is in no little part fuelled by a sense of relief and enthusiasm at seeing 'ordinary people like themselves' represented on television.

6. This position reveals further interesting complexities which require more investigation. Numerous hearing people in Ireland (cf. Joyce [1916, later 1960], and Geldof [1986]) and elsewhere have reported on similar experiences which might be interpreted as Christian colonialisation of their own people.

7. The best example of this dilemma can be seen in the current colonialist strategy of tokenism. The RNID's selection of gullible Deaf people to be their 'house niggers', holding them up to government bodies as 'true representatives' of the Deaf community, (FDP *The Voice* 2000), and contrasting them with 'Deaf extremists', leaves those radicals who know that it is necessary to critique the extremes of 'BSL nationalism' with a dilemma – to do so is to place on record statements that can then be twisted to legitimise colonialist ends. In other words, a further Double-Bind.

Chapter 11

Afterword

> Those of us who are always anti-racist long for a world in which everyone can form a *beloved community* where borders can be crossed and cultural hybridity celebrated . . . If that longing guides our visions and actions, the new culture will be born and anti-racist communities of resistance will emerge everywhere.
>
> bell hooks (1995: 272)

Imagined Futures

Cross-cultural participation in the Deafhood project

And so we reach that always-welcome point in a book where the arduous climb reaches camp, where we can take time to pause and acknowledge the tremendous energy we expended to ensure that the details of each footfall rang true, whilst at the same time keeping the destination clearly in sight. We can begin to allow ourselves the luxury of speculating on the next stage of the journey, discussing the directions that might be taken and what we might find, based upon the knowledge we have gained. Phase 1 is complete. What might the second hold in store?

The second phase, of course, is one in which you, the reader, can play a part. For the first task is to corroborate or amend any aspect of what has been written, and build that into the decisions which I must take regarding which aspects of Deaf culture should be explored next. For Deaf communities, the issue of dissemination is still outstanding, for a bitter irony is that you now know more about these questions than our own people do. Hence the urgent need for financing the DVD translation, the creation of workshops and Deaf Cultural Forums to discuss all these issues and to explore how useful the concept of Deaf culture and Deafhood are to us. For if we are to hold true to the principles of critical ethnography, exploration of a minority-group culture should indeed be a national project involving as many members of that culture who wish to participate.

434

For those working with Deaf communities, similar questions arise. How useful is Deafhood and Deaf-centred thinking, a Deaf epistemology, to our work? Are we willing to surrender our privileges and power when the time is right? And how do we know when that is the case?

For those involved with wider multilingual and minority-culture issues, questions of strategy also arise. What resistance is there to sign-language recognition in government domains, in minority language domains, in United Nations domains and how that can best be challenged?

For those involved with disability issues, different strategy questions appear. Can the Disability Movement adopt genuine coalition principles, which can factor in the culturo-linguistic model of Deafhood with the social model of deafness and disability? Are there other disability groups for whom some of these subaltern-oriented data speaks; and what lies beneath the surface in need of similar resolution once such issues are raised?

One thing is clear. Deaf communities must be enabled to operate on the same principles and political plane as other linguistic minorities. The concept of language planning, its social and cultural implications and agendas must be as foregrounded and as clear as those which have been and are being constructed for Welsh people, for Catalan and Basque people, and so on.

This volume has sought to make the case for Deaf evidence finally to be rendered academically (and politically) admissable. But compared to all that we need to know of Deaf subaltern views, it is a slim volume; all the discourses I have listed here would be well served by more examples. And the same is true – perhaps even more so, for the development of the discipline of Deaf Studies itself, which is handicapped by the tiny amounts of money that governments are willing to expend on Deaf social and cultural research, so that instead of being able to produce substantive evidence for course units, it has to fight the charges that what it knows about Deaf people is 'merely anecdotal'. To make matters worse, the inability to finance the collection of subaltern data pulls departmental attention away towards whatever 'They' will fund of deafness, be it technology or the processing patterns of the brain, or whatever 'Their' current obsessions might be.

Furthermore, if such research should be a Deaf-national project, who am I as the privileged professional to confine subaltern observations and opinions to the limited extracts I have lifted from their conversational context and dropped into a framework of my own devising, however much validity it might manifest? Everyone, both Deaf and hearing, deserves to have access to those observations. And thus, for all these reasons, Phase 2 must include publication of *Conversations in Deafhood.*

Of all the many battles Deaf communities have been obliged to fight, perhaps the most all-pervasive is reductionist thinking and its consequent reductionist language. Given our commitment here to enable those communities to represent themselves on a scale which they find appropriate, we have much to gain by removing the blinkers from our imagination. For no goal can be reached if it cannot be visualised first.

Which terms might be most useful? I have mentioned language planning, but this needs to be put in context. We know that independence from colonialism is the goal, but we also know that much work must be undertaken to ensure that sufficient numbers of Deaf people can become qualified to fill the posts occupied by the gatekeepers. Let us then term this intermediate stage 'Reconstruction of the Deaf Nation'. My account is focused mainly on the UK, but it should serve as a useful comparative guide for other countries, since comparison will help reveal the extent to which the book's overall analysis can be refined in future via your feedback. I am sure we would all especially welcome Scandinavian responses because of the groundbreaking achievements each has accomplished in persuading their central governments to undertake forms of national Deaf reconstruction.[1]

Political Reconstruction

We should begin by noting the shocking fact that it is estimated by the WFD (World Federation of the Deaf) that 80% of the world's Deaf children do not receive any education at all. From what we have learned in this journey so far, we will realise that although hearing children suffer from not being educated, for Deaf children lack of education also denies them the chance to be brought together and to begin to form their communities, to take the first steps along the road to global citizenship that many of their Northern Hemisphere compatriots enjoy. It also condemns many to a life of isolation and denigration.

Perceiving matters from such a global dimension emphasises the need for the United Nations to allocate some of its financial and other resources to the WFD, so that the organisation can function, not only to enable enfranchisement and human citizenship to other Deaf peoples, but to be able to liase with the UN and all the other international agencies charged with political and other responsibilities. The present contrast between a WFD limping along on two full-time staff at the mercy of whichever national Deaf association can persuade its government to pay for them, and the ostentatious wealth of the UN's resources is a disgrace. As much as one might hope that national Deaf associations might be able to fund the WFD, the fact that most exist on poverty resources themselves renders this impossible.

The same appalling contrast can be found between the European Union and the European Union of the Deaf. Political action cannot be seriously developed without the availability of equivalent resources.

Chapter 10 began the debate around modes of political reconstruction at the national level, which contain their own financial implications. However, language minorities seeking independence and / or the removal of colonialism vary considerably in strength, wealth and self-belief. In order for us to position the Deaf situation, I propose here three basic 'types':

- Language minorities which have a proportion of able or professional members similar to the language majorities in which they are embedded, and which are equipped with sufficient material resouces to carry out the changes they desire. The chief hurdle they face is political opposition. These are exemplified by Catalan- and Basque-speaking peoples.
- Next there comes the language minorities with a smaller number of professionals and resources and a large 'underclass' legacy from colonialism, such as Black South African groupings and African-Americans.
- Finally there are the language minorities with absolutely minimal professional classes and resources such as Native Americans, Australian Aborigines and other First Nation societies.

The reconstruction involved in achieving liberation or independence for each of these types clearly requires very different forms and approaches. In the first type, the language and culture are relatively strong and do not experience much residual psychological inferiority. In the second, that inferiority has been deeply implanted, so that the professional class is caught between attempting change based on the Western model in which they were trained, and any desire to reclaim whatever exists of their traditional cultures in order to integrate these into the political structures they have been forced to utilise.

In the third type, the traditional culture has been virtually destroyed, requiring a huge effort to preserve it. These peoples have also been almost completely marginalised by the majority society. These two factors taken together means that for them, enclaves of self-government are a priority requirement in order for them to have the time and space to rebuild.

For the second and third types, the financing of political reconstruction includes repairing the damage enacted upon those cultures, and is considered to be a matter of *reparations*. Unsurprisingly, reparations as a political concept is still highly contested by those deemed responsible for making such payments. A few minorities, such as the Maori in New Zealand, have been relatively successful in making progress along these lines, and the international conference on reparations in 2001 has raised the profile of this discourse.

In attempting to situate Deaf communities, we find that they exhibit characteristics of both the second and third types, so that reparative efforts are required in engendering separate redevelopment and also in redeveloping a professional class.

Finally, in order to enable authentic self-representation and reconstruction, there is a need to physically dismantle various colonialist structures. We might thus conceive of an end to charity organisations, to the RNID in the UK and the NAD in Ireland and so on, as part of their replacement by nationally conceived and funded Deaf-centred policies for Deaf education, Deaf welfare services and so on. In order to solve the question of creating a genuine relationship between deaf and Deaf people, we might imagine the construction of a coalition of each d/Deaf consumer group, to which all professional bodies in deafness and Deafhood are politically answerable.

Reconstruction and 'Hearing Bilingualism'

Perhaps the most intriguing aspect of the FDP's current campaign for BSL recognition is one of the supporting propositions they are using. Entitled 'Sign For All', it can be summarised thus:

> We are seeking the recognition of BSL, not simply for Deaf Britons alone, but so that what is one of the four indigenous languages of the UK can be seen as a genuinely British cultural resource which should be made available to all British citizens.

This emphasis on sign languages as a medium for improving the quality of lives for non-Deaf people represents a very different tone from the usual pleading and supplication that forms so much a part of Deaf–governmental discourse. In Finland there are also indications that a similar concept is being mooted. Following this new emphasis, then, we can imagine the day when sign languages are placed on the National Curriculum, so that every child has the opportunity to claim their birthright, to be able to express themselves with their bodies as they already are encouraged to do with their mouths.

Educational Reconstruction

Oralism, child abuse and reparations

We might also imagine a day when Oralism is recognised for what it is – an institutionalised form of child abuse which, like any other, should be outlawed and subjected to prosecution and punishment. In very recent times there have been suggestions that the staff of formerly oralist schools in both Ireland and the Netherlands have issued an Apologia for their past activities. Yet one can be sure that until Oralism is banned, the deafness discursive system will do everything in its power to prevent the news of such apologies from reaching the ears of parents with new Deaf babies. Accumulation of evidence to substantiate such charges should be collected, not only from contemporary parents of Deaf children and Deaf people, but from the latter's own hearing parents, who can attest to the ways in which they were deliberately misled.[2]

The colonialist mind may be impervious to most forms of logic. But the one that it can comprehend is economic logic. Thus this scenario will not come into play until another imagined scenario, long overdue, occurs. That is, individuals, be they Deaf people or their parents, suing local authorities, medical bodies and governments for the damage caused by Oralism. Were such cases to succeed, it would not be too hard, on the basis of the arguments assembled in this volume, to imagine the colonialist parallel being taken to its logical extent – and a formal demand issued for reparations.[3] At the time of writing, the Irish Deaf Society appears to have taken the international lead on this issue, by trying to build a case to be considered within the present Government enquiry into all forms of child abuse in the Irish education system.

It has long been clear to me that if properly guided and framed research existed into Deaf mental health issues, it should then be relatively easy to demonstrate that much of this has been caused by oralist teachers, doctors and so on. From this position, such information, forming a central part of a Deaf campaign, can then be used to underpin the reparations case, to assist with the 'Oralism as child abuse' cases, and the 'Cochlear Implants/ Genetic Engineering as knowing child abuse' cases of the immediate future. The absolutely shocking 'initial' statistics – of 45–50% emotional problems, double that of hearing people – have laid the groundwork. Continuing failure of will and nerve by Deaf organisations, mental health professionals and educationalists in this respect is completely unacceptable.

We have seen how an individualist culture constructs human rights and discrimination issues in a similarly individualistic way – that the minority-culture person has a claim based on the extent to which they are denied

majority-cultural participation. However, from a minority-cultural perspective, as we have also seen, the burning issue is the quality of their
collective social and cultural life which has also suffered from colonialism.
It is for that reason that they see the financing of their own agenda as being a
matter of reparations. And it is the application of this principle to Deaf
Nations which can then supply the basis for community regeneration. This
may be a theoretical stance and derided by some as idealistic – after all
African-Americans have yet to receive the promised 'forty acres and a
mule'. Yet Native-Americans and the Maori of New Zealand to name but
two have achieved some success precisely because of their determined
pursuit of the collectivist 'Nation' principle. Certainly one can imagine that
if a government found that they had to pay out for damage caused by
Oralism, they would swiftly amend their cosmetic 'hands-off' policy
towards its pursuance.

Supporting parents

We might imagine a day also when parents of newly recognised (note:
not 'newly diagnosed')[4] Deaf children would be granted all appropriate
forms of support in a structured language-planning approach. This would
encompass access to properly trained Deaf people, genuine access to the
local Deaf community ('Deaf Godparents' and 'Deaf Grandparents'), two
years or more free tuition in sign language and Deaf culture, even given
paid leave to do so. Various aspects of these ideas are already in operation
in Scandinavian countries.

We could look forward to quality research which can identify for us the
tremendous burdens they bear as a result of present-day piecemeal service
provision, for 100 years of Oralism has reduced discussion about parenting
Deaf children to such a facile level that it would be fair to conclude that intelligent debate has barely begun. From that research we will learn the
national policies that genuinely support parents which need to be put into
place and funded.

Deaf model schools

We might imagine the day when model bilingual secondary schools are
established, so that all the children who have come through the primary bilingual stages have the right to continue to receive quality education in this
form. Where Deaf Studies is a central part of the curriculum, aimed at
giving the Deaf child the confidence and security of knowledge in where
they have come from and where they might then be able to go, whilst ensuring that they guard against élitism and do not forget their cohorts and
community. Where, if you like, Hearing Studies also exist, to enable them
to understand how majority culture works, what might be expected of one,

both reasonably and unreasonably, how to tell the difference and how best to negotiate paths between the two.

A crucial part of such studies would be to ensure that Deaf children learn to understand basic moral issues in a systematic way, for example learning to respect and obey parents whilst understanding why this should be. We might also imagine genuine nationally planned coordination between parents and Deaf communities, each attempting to understand the realities and pressures the other faces and to support them.

Control of Deaf education

When conceiving the way in which school systems should be run, we have to realise that they should be consumer-controlled, and that there are two groups of consumers involved. There is the Deaf Nation, which will either wither or blossom according to the quality of the education provided; and there are the parents, who represent the interests of their own children, and know the kinds of situations that happen outside the school which need to be understand and then incorporated into the school's philosophies. Ideally, these two groups should be able to govern and run the education system, so that the teachers, having come to agree on the aims and methods, and having brought all their professional knowledge and skills to the table, can then apply them in the classroom.

It must be acknowledged, however, that such a model for educational praxis involves a degree of risk.We know from what we have learned in this book that there will always be Deaf children born to wealthy families, who will resist strenuously any policies that group 'their' children with the common herd. There will always be other parents, already 'got at' first by the medical people waiting virtually at the door of the maternity ward, who will reject a Deaf alliance and attempt to subvert it by setting up their own links to government.

Thus in the end, we might conclude that we might travel the long way around, and campaign instead for a comprehensive national bilingual Deaf education system to be set in place and funded to the same degree as the oralist system. In doing so, we would be placing our trust in that Deaf Model School to produce results which themselves show the success of bilingualism. With that genuine choice finally in place for the first time ever, we could feel confident that the results could speak for themselves to persuade other parents to change systems or act as a catalyst to remove Oralism forever.[5]

Reform of mainstreaming

At the same time we might also imagine a total reform of the present mainstreaming policies which are bleeding Deaf schools to death. Since

95.7% of all deaf children are currently mainstreamed in the UK, it is easy to conceive of the scale of the potential damage being caused. If we have made the case for Deaf culture convincingly, it will be clear that this development has to be rolled back. So long as Deaf children are considered as disabled, they will continue to be conceived of as atomistic individual 'special needs' children, rather than children who need to be with their linguistic peers for healthy social and emotional development, as well as for education. If we are to make the language minority case convincingly, we need to draw on whatever models we can find which might be appropriate. One such can be found in Gross (1973):

> Where blacks have been forcibly *excluded* (segregated) from white society by law, Indians . . . have been forcibly *included* (integrated) into that society by law. That is what [is] meant by coercive assimilation – the practice of compelling, through submersion, an ethnic, cultural and linguistic minority to shed its uniqueness.
>
> (cited by Kymlicka, 1997: 238)

If for 'blacks' we read 'disabled', and for 'Indians', read 'Deaf', the Deaf community position is more easily comprehended. It is just this kind of understanding of Deaf issues which underpinned the NUD's 1982 appeal to the UN to classify oralist mainstreaming as genocidal by the UN's own criteria for minority languages and their users. Were such policies to be reversed, a genuine flexibility could be introduced, so that Deaf children in any one area could have the opportunity of moving back and forth between types of educational placement depending on their needs or desires at any particular time in their lives. Similarly, reparations should be used to help ex-mainstreamed deaf young adults gain belated access to their Deaf communities and culture.

(Is it not interesting, dear reader, that, given the time and space to look up at the stars, that Deaf attention constantly turns to the education of future Deaf children, rather than, as one might suppose, to better jobs or better TV programmes for themselves? If anything hallmarks Deaf communities as collectives and as language minorities, it is this . . .)

Psychiatric reconstruction

Minority groups have often been disinclined to draw attention to the extent to which their community members have been damaged by oppression, usually because description of their mental states can be used as ammunition for the more extreme of their opponents. Since Fanon's work, however, there has been a growing acceptance of the need to address these issues, as the work of Duran and Duran (1995) with Native Americans has shown. As hooks (1995: 138) summarises:

The wounded African-American psyche must be attended to within the framework of programs for mental health care that links psychological recovery with progressive political awareness of the way in which institutionalised systems of domination assault, damage and maim.

Given the disturbing statistics mentioned earlier of induced (as opposed to innate) mental ill-health amongst Deaf people, it would seem reasonable for Deaf Nations to demand a complete paradigm shift for all matters psychological, centring on this kind of diagnosis by Duran and Duran (1995: 6):

The past five hundred years have been devastating to our communities; the effects of this systematic genocide are currently being felt by our people. The effects of the genocide are quickly personalized and pathologized by our profession via the diagnosing and labelling tools designed for this purpose. If the labelling and diagnosing process is to have any historical truth, it should incorporate a diagnostic category that reflects the effects of genocide. Such a diagnosis would be 'acute and/or chronic reactions to colonialism'.

The effects of such a paradigm shift would be to require a national restructuring of facilities and support, much greater research, and Deaf-wellness-centred medicine and leadership. Given the earlier quotations, it is easy to perceive the financing of these coming under the rubric of reparations.

Although our first concerns here are for the minority communities themselves, there is a growing sense that one day these can move out of the 'defensive' role of reconstruction, and be able to activate the process of turning the mirror onto those contemporary forces which continue to maintain colonialism. Duran and Duran (1995: 7) summarise this succinctly:

It is no longer acceptable for psychology to continue to be the enforcement branch of the secularised Judeo-Christian myth. Through the worshipping of logical positivism, our discipline has been a coconspirator in the devastation and control of those peoples who are not subsumed under a white, male, heterosexual, Christian subjectivity ... A post-colonial [psychological] diagnosis for such objective scientists would perhaps be 'chronic or acute Cartesian anxiety disorder.

It is hard not to smile at such apparent audacity, especially when they go on to remark that 'fortunately this is a disorder that has a good prognosis when treated with some of the new postcolonial therapeutic interventions'. But if we have learned anything from Women's Studies, Black Studies and the rest throughout this book, we will be aware that the emphasis is slowly shifting away from simply righting wrongs towards finding out what we can learn from the Others to heal our own split-consciousness, to becoming truly whole people.[6] Practitioners like those cited above are merely rendering visible the next steps which this implies.

Cultural Reconstruction

There is an urgent need for National Sign Language Centres, with Deaf History archives and cultural museums, a resource to benefit both Deaf and hearing Nations wishing to learn about their languages and cultures. A site where any of the thousands of videos of artistic and cultural performances and narrations from around the world can be viewed, copied and circulated. For which linguistic minority has neither created nor dreamed of creating such a building, such a resource?

Cultural reconstruction must also address artistic and aesthetic issues. The quality of young Deaf people's sign language, in the UK at least, which uses English mouth movements as a crutch to replace the more traditional visual skills, leaves much to be desired, if compared with the USA, where there is a stronger emphasis on creative visuality and gesturality. Similarly, whilst the Deaf visual arts are in a reasonably healthy state, Deaf theatre and poetry stands in great need of Deaf culture-centred training and performance, which needs to be funded and structured on a national level, as has occurred in the USA and Australia for example.

Community Reconstruction

Reconstruction of Deaf communities themselves naturally encompasses many dimensions, and some of these are presented here. If we begin by positing the question 'What if Oralism had never happened', we will gain many clues. One overarching feature would be that external Deaf–hearing relationships would be substantially different. Inside the communities themselves we would not find separation and suspicion between Deaf people, parents of Deaf children and CODAs – instead we might expect to see dual cultural membership clearly felt, expressed and enjoyed. Such a 'triple alliance' of sign-language users, together with lay people who have learned to sign, constitutes a powerful 'Third Cultural' space containing much knowledge and expertise about both sets of cultures. Real utilisation of this space could produce a long-awaited force for change.

Deaf professionals

In working towards independence there are other burning issues, such as the regeneration of cultural pride and assertiveness at all levels of the Deaf Nations. One reason is defensive – so as not to create a thin professional class which is then prey to being 'bought off' in the manner of African-American and other post-colonial societies. The other is positive – that a truly healthy nation requires creative social and artistic input from all its members. Hence the need for Deaf Cultural Forums and workshops, since self-reflection is important for the social health and maturity of any community.

Neverthless, independence also requires that sufficiently qualified or experienced Deaf professionals be set in place, which means that the reality of the lost Deaf generations of the last century needs to be confronted. Again, programmes devoted to 'fast-tracking' Deaf expertise into qualifications, via Deaf epistemological training methods could be seen as part of reparation funding.

Deaf clubs

Reconstruction is urgently necessary at the local level, in reforming the paternalistic structures under which Deaf clubs are still forced to operate. This, too, requires many more trained Deaf professionals than currently exist. Deaf clubs themselves are declining around the Western world, and it will not be possible to attract young people to them unless they can become a more exciting resource. Internet facilities are essential, but perhaps even more valuable is the idea of adapting the video-conferencing technology. Thus Deaf club members could on any given night meet at the club to participate in 'phone-ins' with another club across the country. Because of the sophisticated Deaf networking which already exists on a national scale, there would be a high demand for group contact between clubs.

Deaf ethnic minorities

There is also a pressing need to adequately recognise and support the many ethnic minority members of Deaf communities, so as to ensure that they can play their full part in the Deaf Nation. This requires a range of strategies applied to different levels and domains. Perhaps the overriding point to be borne in mind is that these, too, need to be perceived and developed from a consistent national perspective, rather than continuing the current piecemeal strategies.

Young deaf people

It is clear that a major part of Deaf community reconstruction will involve strategies for bringing the young generations of Deaf people into meaningful relationship with their Deaf Nations. In countries such as the USA and the UK where the majority are now hidden away in mainstreamed education, this is a huge task. However, foreign readers might like to consider how far the following example applies to their own communities and what that might have to tell us.

In the UK, the Deaf Resurgence was led by Deaf people who are now, on average, in their late forties. The leadership of this new generation and the extent of the changes produced masked the fact that comparatively few Deaf people were coming through behind them. It was only when the FDP was established and the marches took off that it was possible to notice a new generation of young Deaf people coming onto the scene, and willing to take on the responsibilities necessary to move the Deaf Resurgence forward. People were then able to reflect that there was, in effect, a 20 year age gap between the two, representing the loss of at least one generation who would normally have been expected to shoulder the burden – a serious indication of the success of Oralism in weakening the community (and an indirect tribute to those who were forced to labour far longer at the wearying task of reconstruction than they would have wished).

The emergence of confident young Deaf people is heartening, but there are still many more who are caught in a no-mans-land, where they mix only with their peers and are unaware of the Deaf history, tradition and culture described in this book. On the positive side, their identities seem to be less constrained by that tradition's 'Deaf–Hearing' divide, less insular and therefore able to negotiate some new paths and inroads into majority society. These identities have become multiple, in line with post-modernist expectations.

However, what the post-modernists are unable to appreciate is that minorities require a strong and clear tradition of their own history and culture in order to resist all the assimilating forces of majority societies. In denigrating the search to identify and maintain Deaf 'essences' and epistemologies, which the young Deaf people urgently need to anchor their new multiple identities, they are in effect complicit in any future deterioration or destruction of Deaf communities as a whole. This particular tension between 'core' traditions and multiple-identity innovations will be a particular feature of the next volume in the series.

Hearing children of Deaf parents

A similar bicultural, multiple-identity approach must be taken for hearing children and adults with Deaf parents. If a Deaf Nation agenda is clearly worked through, their place within Deaf communities can be more properly understood, and the valuable contributions which these people can make to both Deaf and hearing communities can then become more focused. In so doing, research is necessary in order to identify and rectify some of the negative patterns of experience which they have suffered through centuries of falling between two cultures.

Sign language interpreters

The recent growth in sign interpreters is both welcome and necessary. However, the limited epistemological awareness surrounding deafness issues at the time of their initial training has meant that numerous, more hidden issues have yet to be directly confronted. Whilst these continue to be disregarded, the psychological effects continue to take their toll on both Deaf people and the interpreters themselves.

These issues include administrative power – whether interpreting agencies should be run or overseen by the Deaf Nation; and cultural factors such as the extent to which these problems are cultural clashes caused by a limited understanding of the nature of culture itself. Similarly, given the huge imbalance of power between Deaf and hearing communities, an interpreter attempting a fully neutral stance will end up reinforcing the energies emanating from the more powerful group.

These issues are beginning now to be addressed. But there is an even more fundamental issue at stake. If you, dear non-signing reader, should wish to meet and communicate with a Deaf person, who would you conside responsible for organising and paying for the interpreter – you or s/he? If you nominate the Deaf person, that would be an understandable swallowing of the basic colonialist principle – that s/he, being the deviant, should be the one to close the communication gap.

However, in reality, you are the one who cannot sign to communicate. Thus, given that the same is true in reverse, the situation is then one of two people *equally* unable to bridge the gap, and thus responsibility and payment should be shared. Of course, it would be impossible for Deaf people to spend their daily lives paying this 50%, whereas you yourself might do so for a one-off situation. Thus we are taken to a wider perspective which asserts that, until hearing people have learned to sign as part of the future bilingual vision, that governmental and other bodies are responsible for making good the negligence they have enabled and should foot the bills.

Of course there are still some group situations such as conferences, in which it would be unreasonable to assume or force people to express themselves in a non-native language. Financial responsibility for these types of situation could be dealt with by factoring interpreter costs into the conference fees and overall budgets – linguistic inclusion rather than assimilation, since a genuine multilingual society would provide interpreters as and where needed as a matter of collective responsibility. What is absolutely *not* required is a provision of interpreters based on any outdated ideas of 'helping Deaf people'. Since all these issues are in the early stages of recognition, more refined arguments will obviously emerge.

Spiritual issues and reconstruction

There is also a case to be made for the regeneration of spiritual issues as a force not only for healing, but for asking advanced questions which can pull a community forward – parallels can be found in many other post-colonial societies (cf. Duran & Duran, 1995). As hooks (1995: 259) summarises:

> To be truly effective, contemporary black liberation struggle must envision a place for spirituality. This does not mean continued allegiance to patriarchal capitalist religions, or the institionalized traditional black church . . . [but] to create new structures for the expression of spiritual and religious life and develop progressive strategies for transforming existing structures.

It is from these perspectives then, that I offer one other set of criteria which may be useful – defining Deafhood in relation to Deaf culture. As we have seen, Deaf communities have become caught up in the whirlwind of changes that have taken place in the last 20 years; externally, in changes within majority societies and their effects on the communities and, internally with respect to the changes Deaf people and their allies have initiated. These, on the one hand, represent movements towards independence yet contain, on the other, as with any culture, an inevitable cultural lag in respect of some other members of the communities. Traditional Deaf cultures, it is fair to say, have not yet adjusted to deal with the realities of that coming independence.

Thus we have found definitions of Deaf culture which enshrine beliefs and practices which may be outdated and unhelpful – the 'cultural traps' of which Bohannan speaks. Given that we cannot deny that these are Deaf cultural features, how might we re-formalise them? One suggestion is to see Deaf culture as it is presently constituted as 'Deaf traditions' and Deaf culture as it might become as *a movement towards Deafhood*. Although it is important that we see Deafhood, if one likes, as a verb rather than a noun, and do not attempt to enshrine it in any one set of beliefs or practices, it is this movement towards deeper, further and 'larger' collective self-actualisation embodied in the Deafhood concept which can mark the distinction between what Deaf culture presently is and what it can become. In so doing, we can finally create a conceptual space for cultural action.

As we have seen in earlier chapters, the largest visions of that state of Deafhood have been couched in spiritual terms. Berthier's concept of the Deaf Nation in the 1840s was intrinsically linked with spiritual beliefs, that Deaf peoples existed on Earth for a reason and were deliberately created, whether by God, Allah or Gaia as an integral part of the whole of Creation. Likewise the Blue Ribbon Ceremony in Appendix 2 stands as a manifestation of what can only be described as a political–spiritual nexus. It remains to be seen how swiftly Deaf communities are able to shed the limitations of their colonialist conditioning and raise their vision to encompass these dimensions.

Media Reconstruction

'Minority television' in general has found the carpet being rolled back throughout the 1990s, so that British TV, for example, no longer features Black and Asian programming in any serious way. Assimilation into white programming seems to be the name of the game. Reform of Deaf TV would no doubt meet the same opposition. This should not prevent us from envisioning how things should be.

The priority must be to have one programme per week for each age group on each channel, to be run by Deaf people from a Deaf Nation perspective – that is, one which is aware of the overall state of the nation and what forms of reconstruction are needed at any one time. From that position, the programmes then serve as a means for Deaf communities to dialogue with each other, speeding up the reconstruction process.

At the same time, structured entry points into the wider TV and newspaper media must be established to ensure that reporting and representation are not only non-discriminatory in the narrow sense, but encompass the Deaf Nation agenda in the widest sense.

Academic Reconstruction

Reform of the piecemeal academic system which administers 'deafness' is long overdue. In the first instance, this requires a centralised structure where the total of the financial resources available is rendered visible. All proposals into any aspect of deafness can then be submitted and assessed according to Deaf Nation priorities by bodies which contains a majority of Deaf and hearing-impaired people. And if we are to ensure the collection of the type of information so badly needed from Deaf communities, research priorities themselves need to be completely rethought.

In respect of academia itself, although those already working within it should be encouraged either to qualify as researchers, or have their experience incorporated into carefully planned research programme structures, we have to face the fact that we also have to focus on those young Deaf people beginning to emerge with degrees and to work to ensure that there is a viable career in Deaf Studies for them. We will still need and welcome hearing researchers working under the directions that have been established by responsible Deaf academics. And in the field of Deaf culture, certainly, we cannot yet plan these directions with complete confidence until we have broken camp, continued our journeying across the terrain, and reported back in the next volume of our findings, Phase 3.

However, attention should be drawn to the fundamental imbalance within Deaf Studies. Unlike other minority studies, Deaf Studies has (inevitably, because of Deaf English literacy rates) been instigated and run by hearing people. Although well meaning and indeed most valuable, the historical weight of research which is hearing-led has resulted in a critical imbalance of praxis which must be highlighted here. The main subjects within most Deaf Studies are sign languages, linguistics, psychology and education. Subjects found within other minority studies but which are virtually non-existent in Deaf Studies include communities and cultures, politics, critical analysis of the mechanics of oppressive discourses, the arts, history and philosophy. In their absence, the cumulative effect is that we, as Deaf people, feel that we are still objects of lingustic or psychological analysis. Instead we should be empowered subjects embarked on the task of drawing together in a holistic way the central themes necessary to guide Deaf communities and their cultural and political reconstruction.

Other minority studies have focused on this academic role in creating a space and a climate for reflection upon and a shaping of the re-emergence of their own communities. In such academic projects, the need to explore and commit to print the unheard voices which together create such a holistic balance has long been a guiding principle, one which gives much greater emphasis to qualitative research, to ethnography and so on. Giving legitimacy to those unheard voices is absolutely fundamental to all the questions posed both earlier and later regarding both Deaf Nation reconstruction and mounting a successful opposition to the continuing medical hegemony.

It may be helpful here to make visible some of the domains which those voices either occupy or need to occupy. Data already collected for the next volume but in need of augmentation and refinement include the following topics:

- Deaf people's own signs and definitions for concepts similar to the Deaf culture trope. The one fundamental marker of cultural attitude – the construction of the 'Hearing' trope, what that consists of, and what space does that demarcate for the groups of signs?
- Deaf families; their experiences, their role in the transmission of Deaf culture, and their relationships with Deaf from hearing families.
- Deaf clubs between the departure of the missioner and the rapid changes of the 1990s, what other cultural dynamics operate apart from class issues?
- Deaf humour, both in and for itself and for some of its cultural characteristics – the power of sign language and the importance of features like sign-metaphor, 'Deaf anthropomorphism' and so on.
- The experiences of the new subaltern-élite; how becoming professional affects cultural dynamics and the strategies involved.

- The experiences of this sector when trying to implement Deaf-centred policies in schools or other organisations.
- The cultural effects of the oralist Deaf grammar schools on the community, and whether these are leading towards resolution or further dissension.
- Young Deaf people and the process of actualising Deafhood. To what extent, in breaking away from Deaf cultural traditions to take a more positive view of hearing people, will they unwittingly jettison transmission of those traditions and render themselves a group of people without a history? What does that then teach us about the role of history within culture? What does it mean to say that if one can make history come alive, one can perceive and walk through a door to a larger Self?
- Similarly, what can we learn from the multiple subjectivites which are emerging in young Deaf discourse, and how can we use that information to teach us more about the subjectivities which already exist, largely unrecognised?
- How do Deaf ethnic minorities experience their lives within the national Deaf communities? What needs to change, and how might that be effected in cultual terms?
- What more can be said about the contestations of Deafhood, and the different ways in which sectors of the community conceive of Deafhood? It is already apparent that some conceive of it in 'cultural' terms – that is, that the road to deepening the Deaf self lies through sign language wordplay and creativity, and through intensifying social contact – whilst other construct it 'politically', that is by conceiving the route as being primarily activist, of asserting oneself in the majority culture and taking action to enforce, if you like, a deeper awareness of the issues of the tribe. What do these two patterns have to teach us of dynamics faced by all minority and post-colonial cultures?
- To what extent is British Deaf culture similar or dissimilar to that of other countries, particularly the USA? What does investigation reveal of the extent to which imbibing the majority culture creates international tensions and to what extent is international harmony achieved by a resolute focus on shared Deafhood? To what extent does that same imbibing contribute to class and race issues, and how do Black Deaf people conceive themselves and their situation as a double minority?

An underlying theme linking all these is that of 'class' or race distinctions within Deaf culture. At first sight these would appear to continue the weighting of this first volume towards the examination of cultural divisions. But, just as one can best learn about one's own culture and oneself by coming into meaningful contact with another culture, so too can this process operate on other boundaries and margins. Research on such boundaries produces, to a certain extent, 'double evidence', that is, observations on the 'other' can also be interpreted back towards the initial conceptualisations. And the dynamics of difference and dissension, as we have seen, exist in a dialectical relationship with the striving for cultural unity in minority cultures, so we also learn how these two tensions play themselves out. After all, as the study has showed, there are very few Western cultures where the whole range of different classes are compelled to interact, not only on a daily basis but also to strive to agree a collective set of aims for their peoples.

As we have already seen, much of this has indirect benefit for majority-cultural study. But there are also domains in which the Deaf–hearing interface needs to be researched through cultural-study-centred tools. Some examples:

- When a school becomes bilingual, how does the tension between Deaf-centredness and Hearing-centredness play itself out, and how might such cultural conflict be resolved? Deninger (1983), Erting (1985) and Young _et al._ (1998) have begun to open doors of vital importance to the very success or failure to the bilingual project.

- Similar dynamics exist in other workplaces such as Deaf television, Deaf organisations and in the tensions between Deaf people and the new sign interpreters (a matter of great concern since this is a new profession created supposedly to help remove Deaf–hearing barriers, yet it is caught up in a hierarchical relationship with cultural implications that neither side fully understands).

- Hearing children of Deaf parents, how do they experience the tensions and benefits of biliguality and biculturality; and the changes they might wish to suggest.

- The Deaf ex-mainstreamed and their struggle to find their way across the cultural boundaries which are, at present, preventing so many from 'coming home'.

- Deaf–hearing marriages, growing in number, yet still appearing to fail in numbers. Which cultural issues are informing that pattern and to what extent are they responsible for it?

- New hearing parents with Deaf children who wish their children to grow up bilingually, but are all too often meeting with resistance in certain sectors of the Deaf community. How can both they and Deaf people learn to share 'their' children and take appropriate responsibility at each stage of the children's development?

All these research areas and delineations of difference are also important with respect to a burning theme within multilingual societies – the issue of representation. Who speaks for the minority culture, who 'should' speak, and why.

In exploring these features, we may well learn some interesting information about our own majority culture and its own interactions from comparing and contrasting these findings with those of mainstream sociology. Who knows but from all this Deaf research there may one day emerge researchers to 'study up' and reveal majority culture to itself, and from thence to actually participate in these 'hearing' discourses? Now *that* would be real inclusion rather than assimilation!

The Wider Academic Project

Although all of us, Deaf or hearing, have a role to play in achieving change, it can be argued that those in positions carrying some degree of power or influence have more cultural capital to wield. This is especially true in academic domains. Duran and Duran (1995: 7) summarise this best:

> As we move into the next milliennium, we should not be tolerant of the neo-colonialism that runs unchecked through our knowledge-generating systems. We must ensure that dissemination of thought through journals, media and other avenues have 'gatekeepers' who understand the effects of colonialism and are committed to fighting any perceived act of hegemony on our communities. Postcolonial thinkers should be placed in the positions that act as gatekeepers of knowledge in order to ensure that western European thought be kept in its appropriate place.

An important dimension to factor into academic praxis is comparison across minority cultures. To what extent are these Deaf minority-cultural features reflected in others? Which features, in both directions, are not 'universals'? Can these be grouped and what does that process tell us in turn? Although this book is unable for reasons of length to reflect it, so much of its underlying thinking has already come from studying minority cultures – chiefly African-American, but also Afro-Caribbean, First Nation and Jewish text sources and people. They are the unseen shoulders upon which the Deaf cultural project stands and the next volume will examine their own work more deeply so that the minority-cultural model can advance to the next level.

Medical Reconstruction

Many of these visions cannot be accomplished without a forcible scaling back of the powers of medical domains and discourses. Even in Scandinavia, with enlightened language policies in place, medical neo-colonialism is making inroads. What follows represents some possibilities for resisting and turning these tides.

Cochlear implant experimentation on Deaf children

Although Deaf Nations would be radically different were all the previous visions of change to be implemented, much of the good work would be undone if the present cochlear implantation (CI) experiments were allowed to continue. It appears that as many as 80% of newly recognised Deaf children are being implanted, with their parents denied access to information regarding alternative options, such as the Deaf cultural choice. The few parents who have fought their way through to access and heeded the Deaf message are being put under increasing pressure to submit to operations, with little or no support from Deaf organisations. This pressure, it is reported, comes not only from the medical–educational nexus, but from a new peer pressure of other parents. 'How can you say that you love your Deaf children,' they ask, 'if you will not let them have this miracle operation? Surely any improvement in hearing is better than none at all?' Resisting such emotional blackmail is an intense, heart-rending struggle for those parents who have accepted the Deaf message, but who have not received any support from the senders of those messages.

A similarly uphill struggle is experienced on the few occasions when Deaf communities gain some media access to debate these issues, framed as they are within terms of reference laid down by the discursive system. Figure 2 gives a good idea of what transpires, and the issue is often framed in terms of Deaf communities simply being selfish and fearing for their survival.

How might such patterns be reversed? Clearly there is a need to apply 'reverse spin' and focus attention on the experimental nature of CI. Thus, instead of being honed on consenting deafened adults, these are being foisted upon non-consenting children whose nearest peers are Deaf community members who, knowing what it is really like to live as Deaf people in the wider world, state that if they had the choice, they would refuse such operations. This argument can be used in tandem with a focus on the extent to which CIs are a new experience in Deaf communities, a strategy driven by a profit motive, so that one is able to present a soundbite equation – 'Experimentation for Profit'. Such a focus would enable the issue to be brought into line with the child abuse issues described earlier.

Ideally, this focus on non-consenting experimentation would be supplemented by data which revealed the actuality of the post-implantation experience, its lack of success on its own terms and the social and psychological damage which is being caused. Unfortunately, such research is all but impossible as the funding and refereeing resources lie in the hands of those experimenters themselves. Perhaps the only hope (apart from having to wait a whole generation to sue for damages) is that governments can be forced to intervene and establish similar criteria to those being established for breast implants, namely a specific age of informed consent such as voting age. This is also the only way to tackle the fact that new devices will continue to appear, so that by the time we have shown the uselessness of the old, the oralists will, as they always do, be saying 'Ah that's out of date now. These new ones really do work', whilst offering no apologies to those damaged by the old.

One other important ideological dimension of implantation should be considered. At best, all an implant can do is provided limited noise input which can be reinterpreted as meaningful sound. As such, the net result would be to turn a profoundly Deaf child into a partially deaf child. The current ideology (where it is even compelled to articulate itself at all) assumes that this is a gain. And to some extent this represents the assumptions of societies, that if deafness is an illness then a lesser degree of deafness will be more healthy.

In fact, it may well be that the opposite is the case. The key issue again is language, and it turns upon the following argument. Deaf people often define a young person with partial hearing in two ways. If they can hear and lipread sufficiently to be able to communicate unproblematically in groups of hearing humans, then they are 'hard-of-hearing'. If they cannot, managing to simply scrape by with one-on-one communication, then they are 'deaf'.

The crucial issue is group communication for that is where cultures are learned and enacted. If a person can communicate in such a group in, say, English, then they are essentially English speakers. If a person cannot use that language in such groups, then their primary language, whether they realise it or not, is sign language. A young person struggling to access spoken language and group behaviours and cultures in such a way is a person condemned to a life as an outsider from that culture, to experience psychological distress and identity confusion. As the saying goes: 'The edge of a conversation is the loneliest place on Earth'.

Thus to take from a child their (actual or in potentia) strong Deaf cultural identity, and subject them to a life without an identity is an abusive and ultimately criminal act. Enacted on wide scale, it amounts to the same cultural ethnocide that the NUD presented to the UN back in 1982.

This is all the more criminal when one asks a simple question: 'What is actually wrong with the idea of a child being secure in one identity, but having two languages, and being able to move back and forth between different communities to their best of their ability in a confident manner?'

But then, if the world had demanded such a answer a century ago, we would have been spared generations of Oralism, never mind cochlear implants. Deaf communities still await their diligent, high calibre reporters of the John Pilger/Michael Moore ilk....

Genetic engineering

The previous paragraphs have even greater resonance when we consider the developments in the genetics field – the emergence of genetic modification (GM) and the Human Genome Initiative, which move the issues rightwards into wholly new dimensions. With CIs, the theoretical powers of consent remain with the parents, although we cannot be sure for how much longer even this will be the case. Genetic manipulation however, as Blume (2001) suggests, may lead to (capitalist-oriented) state assumption of those powers of consent.

Oralists everywhere have been given new hope by the thought of being able to locate and remove the so-called 'Deaf Gene' and Deaf people have begun to realise that soon the only path left open to them will be to make the case that Deaf communities and their 200-plus sign languages are a valid and valuable part of creation [insert your own deity if required] and to demonstrate reasons why they should continue to exist.

Hence, in response to this realisation, the beginnings of the development of a conscious spiritual dimension in Deaf life, such as the Blue Ribbon ceremony. Deaf people have also started to realise that their beliefs in themselves as 'beings of Nature' intersects with the newly emerging ecological thinking about bio-diversity, and are pondering how to obtain the support of Green movements. Still others are already trying to locate discourses with those engaged in other multilingual forums in order to widen their own terms of debate. There are also indications that the Deaf movement could actually spearhead the growing opposition to genetic engineering, partly because in sign languages they have a very visible and beautiful creation that should arguably not be lost to the world, and partly because they have had 120 years of experience in contesting attempts to eliminate them (cf. Ladd 2001).

Positive developments – yet it becomes clear once again that Deaf communities, instead of being able to concentrate on the 'peacetime' redevelopment of their communities and arts, are being forced into a wartime engagement. Bhabha's (1994) identification of a major criterion of minority cultures as one of 'permanent emergency' ('24/7/365') is proving to be a concept with increasing relevance.

Thus the theories and examples set forth in this book reveal themselves to have a central part to play in helping to resolve an extremely live GM issue. More than that, the publication in Phase 2 of the interviews in full will bring emotional colour to dry text, and deepen any appreciation of Deaf peoples and their sign languages which Phase 1 has established. It is now possible to conceive that when these two are combined, a new channel of discourse can be inaugurated between Deaf communities and the wider academia. Deaf culture and Deaf people, instead of being seen as an exception or anomaly standing outside of the rule of academic theory, might instead one day be seen as – the exception which illuminates and enables many of those theories . . .

If we can take this positions one step further, it becomes easier to see that what is required is a kind of academic 'Rainbow Alliance'. McDonnell (2001) describes the symbiotic relationship which exists between governments, clinicians and technocratic experts and to this we must add the controllers of media and many of their practitioners. The GM issue now impinges on a wide variety of academic domains. For the first time in recent history, in seeking to re-enact the eugenic policies of the Nazis, the scientific establishment has over-reached itself and revealed its hand, its true face behind the mask of benevolence. It has thus created a historical moment in which a broadly based academic coalition could intervene, not merely to turn the spotlight onto those aforesaid symbiotic relationships and to collectively demystify them, but also to seek once and for all to remove their unquestioned powers.

Current Affairs

It is my hope that the basic analytical structure of this book has given the reader a lens through which they can deconstruct and re-interpret any subsequent activities they observe, whether in Deaf communities or in the world which presently administers them. In closing this book where it began, then, I present an updating from which the reader is invited to assess the accuracy of the total analysis.

No doubt some readers are wondering about the official status of the world's sign languages at the present moment. Krausnecker's (2001) attempt to locate patterns in their overall international status identifies constitutional recognition in Finland, Portugal, South Africa and Uganda, and governmental law in Sweden, the Czech Republic, the Slovak Republic and Columbia. Unspecified official recognition is cited for Byelorussia, Ukraine, Lithuania, Uruguay, Thailand and several American States, and Special Education recognition for Denmark and Greece.

It should be realised that such recognition is not the be-and-end-all of the matter, but merely the beginning. Recognition that does not factor in all we have mentioned here is but a hollow statute, and it should be apparent by now that it is the Deaf cultural and Deafhood dimensions which flesh out the bare bones of any recognition laws.

We may close by returning to what has transpired since the first march for BSL recognition described at the very outset of this book. That march and 12 others since, both national and local, have indeed begun to build up attention. However, their success has impinged on the consciousness of the RNID as well. Thus, instead of Deaf organisations conducting the primary dialogues with government, it appears that the RNID has inserted itself into the process and attempted to marginalise the wider implications of recognition. It also appears that New Labour, far from demonstrating a desire to listen to Deaf communities, has decided to maintain conservative colonialist attitudes and thus its primary, if somewhat covert, relationship with the RNID.

Instead of the recognition movement being established as the core of a national bilingual educational programme for Deaf education, for example, the (oralist) RNID appears to have altered and downgraded its priorities. In this new form the movement currently reads as a programme merely for training BSL interpreters (to 'help the deaf', of course), and in this context in 2000 the first substantial grant was handed over by the Minister for the Disabled (!) to the RNID to train 20 interpreters – possibly for their own use . . .

Furthermore, instead of the expertise and manpower of university Deaf Studies disciplines being engaged by the government in developing the BSL recognition proposals put forward in the 40-page FDP document, it appears that someone behind the scenes not unconnected to the RNID has declared that they must be excluded – 'because they are biased towards BSL' (a bizarre statement in itself).

Mention of the FDP's document enables us to take the analysis of the 'deafness discursive system' one step further. The analysis which follows may be of use for those wishing to investigate the situation in their own countries.

In recent years a supposedly 'official' body has been created as the representatives of Deaf community and deafness discourses. Known as UKCOD (the United Kingdom Council on Deafness), it consists of 33 member organisations, (listed in Appendix 4). If we analyse this list and analyse them according to the models found in Chapter 3 (deafness / Deafhood, medical, social and linguistic, etc.), we find:

- that 18 are not only 'deafness' oriented but also that most are actively oral, medical or even anti-Deafhood;
- that 10 have the Deaf community as their focus but are situated within the social welfare model; and
- that two are unknown to me.

This leaves three out of 33 which are actively Deaf-consumer-led. One of these is concerned only with Deaf television. Another has as its focus 'Deaf–Hearing' integration, which itself indicates that its focus is outward, not inwardly focused. And the third, the BDA, has already been discussed in these pages in respect of its own Deafhood weaknesses.

Yet this is the body which is supposed to represent all things Deaf to the government, a body which apparently sees nothing incongruous about its structure and orientation, and seems unaware of the fundamental deaf-ness/Deafhood dichotomy, let alone its imbalance.

One would, therefore, not be surprised to find that, when the FDP's BSL campaign led to the government requiring a submission on which all of these 33 organisations could agree, the resulting document was hopelessly compromised. How could the medical nexus be expected to support a movement in which BSL recognition was but the first step towards render-ing their own practices not only unethical but *in potentia* subject to criminal proceedings? Even the social welfare organisations, as we have seen throughout this book are at this point in time unable to comprehend the wider aims of Deaf cultural recognition, Deafhood and Deaf Nation recon-struction that have been described in this chapter.

Thus these recent culturo-political events serve to illustrate all that this book has put forward concerning the incompatibility of deafness and Deafhood discourses, and the need to separate them from each other as the first step in the reconstruction project.

By way of contrast, the FDP itself has always demanded that their case be put to the Home Office, which has responsibility for other indigenous languages, with special reference to the creation of an Act of Parliament comparable to the Welsh Language Acts of the 1990s. The government, however, re-routed their submission to the Disability Resource Commis-sion (on which no sign-language user is represented, just the Chief Executive of the RNID). In a compromise solution, the Commission appears to have referred the matter back to the government, with a recom-mendation that BSL be put forward for recognition within any relevant legislation of the European Union. Although this seems a positive step, there is widespread suspicion that the thinking behind such a move is simply to play for time. Such a delay might ironically turn out to be helpful to the recognition movement, in order that the Deaf cultural principles involved in reconstruction as described in this chapter can be given a place in the overall analysis and ultimate language-planning processes.

I hope that this narrative, seen in terms of the overall structure of this book, will enable foreign readers to attempt an analysis of their own situa-tions, to see how far they can be applied and to join with the process of feedback so that a more internationalist accounting and deconstruction can be developed in the years ahead.

Fittingly for a chapter on imagined futures, we conclude by returning to the importance of the lay people concept. Hooks (1995: 264–5) describes the importance of black–white relationships in the Civil Rights struggle:

> The process of decolonization (unlearning white supremacy by divesting of white privilege if we were white or vestiges of internalized racism if we were black) transformed our minds and our habits of being . . . Understanding that love was the antithesis of the will to dominate and subjugate, we allowed that longing to know love, to love one another, to radicalize us politically . . . *beloved community* is formed, not by the eradication of difference but by its affirmation, by each of us claiming the identities and cultural legacies that shape who we are and how we live in the world.

The examples in the sections immediately before present the lay reader with an opportunity to break out of colonialist conditioning and to offer support, alliance and coalition in forming such a beloved community.

The choice is stark, but sometimes crisis can produce a worthy response. Should the world's 200-plus sign languages, their arts and their cultures be eliminated from the Earth? Or can lay people, recognising that their minds and bodies might directly benefit from the existence of sign languages, liberate themselves to become able to communicate across language barriers in the fundamental linguistic grammars of the human body and thus to take up their place as true global citizens?

If it is through vision and challenge that the human spirit renews itself with each succeding generation, then what better one might we imagine at the outset of a new millennium? What long strange trip still lies ahead?[6]

Notes

1. Reconstruction almost by definition is a concept in which the major role is played by central governments and their resources. We might go further, whilst noting the positive Deaf situations in Scandinavia, together with the decline in Deaf quality of life in the former USSR since Communism fell, and conclude that 'free-market' capitalism is actually inimical to the building of strong Deaf nations. Even in the USA, we should note that Gallaudet University is that rare thing – a university supported by large federal government grants. It may be that other minorities experience a similar dynamic.

2. It is tremendously important, and also relatively easy, to establish research which collected such evidence from parents whose children are now grown to adulthood and have experienced the realities of Deaf life – for example seeing their children marry other Deaf people. This research would also reveal the numerous hidden ways in which Oralism has damaged families. One example is the divorce rate among couples with Deaf children. It has long dismayed me

that national Deaf associations have failed to collect such evidence, especially since it can be easily gathered – after all, 90% of their members have hearing parents, many still living.

3. There is an interesting semi-precedent already in existence; in recent times the Canadian authorities have paid over $1 million to the Deaf community in Vancouver BC in respect of child abuse suffered during their education. Significantly, this sum has been regarded, not as money for individuals, but as community money, to be invested in a community project. Although this award was for 'conventional' child abuse, it is not difficult to envisage an equivalent scenario – once Oralism has been officially recognised in this way.

4. Thanks for Jo Smith for this concept.

5. I would like to thank Jo Smith and Jeff McWhinney for their insights here.

6. As Jesse Jackson put it in a recent TV interview, 'If the Black community can find the power to heal itself, it will have the power to heal America'.

7. Upon reading my previous draft, my editor requested a more punchy close. In the tradition of modern television comedy, then, I propose a double-punch ending. This one is in English. The one which follows (and perhaps appropriately the last word of this volume) originates in sign language; one of the signed songs of Deaf liberation that awaits its ear-skilled musical collaborator. For this particular imagined future, you are free to visualise whatever images most take your fancy.

LANGUAGE IN YOUR BLOODSTREAM

1. *Did you know?*   *In Rome they killed us in the ancient days*
                 "   *We were the idiots in the village games you played*
                 "   *We were imprisoned in asylums that you made*
                 "   *That even then, our signs they took away*

No you didn't?   *Why is that?*
Did they give you all the facts?
No they didn't, now it's time
For you to hear our sto-o-o-ry

We got this language in our bloodstream
We won't go away
We got this language in our bloodstream
We are here to stay!

2. *Were you told?*   *They tried so hard to make us talk like you*
                 "   *They tied our hands behind our ba-acks too*
                 "   *We gained some pride and tried to cut them loose*
                 "   *Now they're trying hard to close down all our schools*

No you weren't.   *Where our pride?*
Could no longer read or write.
Then you weren't.   *Now you are*
So listen to our sto-o-o-ry

We got the language in our bloodstream
We won't go away.
We got a charter in our bloodstream
We are here to stay!

3. *Did you know?*   *When a baby's born it first begins to sign*
                 "   *If its voice comes through it can put them aside*
So you know   *That your body knows, and's kept it all this time*
Now you know   *If you learn it with us, re-connect your lives.*

Learn it with us   *Realise*
It will open up your eyes
Learn it with us   *Celebrate*
Your half of this sto-o-o-ry.

You got the language in your bloodstream
Never went away
You got a charter in your bloodstream
Bring it out to stayyyyyyyyyyyyy!

                                                           (Ladd 1988).

Further Reading

The list which follows is intended to ensure that there is at least one reading given for each of the areas covered in this book. Lack of space prevents fuller listing for some subject areas. The full references are given in the bibliography. Websites are worthy of investigation are also included.

Deaf History

For anyone desiring to read one single book which captures the oppression, pride and passion of the Deaf experience over historical time, **Harlan Lane's** *When the Mind Hears* (Random House, New York, 1984) which we might term a 'docu-novel', is written from the viewpoint of Laurent Clerc, the Deaf teacher from the Paris School who moved to the USA with Thomas Gallaudet to found the American Deaf education system.

Jack Gannon's *Deaf Heritage* (National Association of the Deaf, Silver Spring, MD, 1981) is a powerful collection of data and artworks spanning American Deaf history.

Fischer and Lane's *Looking Back* (Signum Press, Hamburg, 1993) is an excellent edited collection of historical articles spanning a large number of countries, and serves as a useful 'primer'.

Mirzoeff's *Silent Poetry* (Princeton University Press, NJ – 1995) is a marvellous analytical account of Deaf art and artists, focusing on 19th century pre-oralist France.

Groce's *Everyone Here Spoke Sign Language* (Harvard University Press, Cambridge MA, 1985) is an impressive account of the native bilingualism in Martha's Vineyard between 1580 and the present day.

Boyce's *The Leeds Beacon* (British Deaf History Society, Feltham, 1996) is a good account of the last pre-Resurgence Deaf headmaster in the UK, Edward Kirk.

Alexander Atkinson's _Memoirs of my Youth_ (British Deaf History Society, Feltham, 2001) was originally published in 1865, and gives an extensive account of Atkinson's time at the 'Braidwood' school in Edinburgh between 1814 and 1820. It is a remarkable find – at 200 pages, it may well be the first in-depth Deaf autobiography, containing both useful descriptions of BSL from 200 years ago and particularly clear accounts of the process of learning English.

All of the other historical texts referred to in this book have much to recommend them.

Deaf Studies

The single most useful source of work can be found in the Gallaudet University sponsored _Deaf Studies Conference Proceedings_ (Washington DC, College of Continuing Education). These now extend to eight volumes, and contain a wealth of information and perspectives across many domains.

Lane, Hoffmeister and Bahan's _Journey into the Deafworld_ (Dawn Sign Press, San Diego, 1996) is the only Deaf Studies textbook which currently exists and contains much of interest.

Deaf Culture

Padden and Humphries' _Deaf in America_ (Harvard University Press, Cambridge MA, 1988) is the only other full-length book on Deaf culture which exists. Although easy to read, much of what it contains is profound in its implications.

Mindess' _Reading Between the Signs_, (Intercultural Press, Yarmouth ME, 2000), a cultural guide for sign language interpreters, contains important new insights into Deaf cultural features.

Colonialism of Deaf Communities

Lane's _Mask of Benevolence_ (Random House, New York, 1993) remains the most radical analysis of the oppression visited on Deaf communities.

Wrigley's _Politics of Deafness_ (Gallaudet University Press, Washington DC, 1996) offers a useful analysis with a postmodernist approach.

Deaf Community

Moore and Levitan for Hearing People Only (Deaf Life Press, Rochester NY, 1992) offer a useful guide to Deaf communities and their key issues.

Many of the texts referred to in sections dealing with Deaf communities have much to recommend them.

Deaf Politics

The **National Union of the Deaf's** *Deaf Liberation* (NUD Press. Feltham, 1991) is the most concentrated collection of Deaf political perspectives, developed at the very outset of the Deaf Resurgence.

J. Christiansen and S. Barnartt's *Deaf President Now!* (Gallaudet University Press, Washington DC) is an in-depth analysis of the historical campaign which centred on Gallaudet University in 1988.

Doug Alker's *Really Not Interested in the Deaf?* (Darwen Books, 2000) is the most explicit account anywhere of the machinations involved in resisting Deaf leadership, and the extent to which certain organisations will go to achieve their ends.

Deaf Education

The **National Union of the Deaf's** *Charter of Rights of the Deaf Child* (NUD Press, Feltham 1982) which was addressed to the United Nations, remains the most radical approach to a Deaf educational issue yet. Their *Deaf Liberation* also contains many of the strongest early papers. *When the Mind Hears* (Harlen Lane) is also centred around Deaf education.

Johnson and Erting's *Unlocking the Curriculum* (Gallaudet Research Institute, Washington DC) remains one of the clearest analytical summaries which presents the Deaf bilingualist case.

Mashie's *Educating Deaf Children Bilingually* has useful information about the Scandianvian Deaf educational situation.

Sources

Forest Bookshop is the UK's major supplier for the books and videos given here and many others besides. *www.forestbookshop.com*

Other Websites

The present explosion of activity on the internet means that this list is far from comprehensive, but it may serve as a useful beginning.

www.deafhood.com is the site where the discourse initiated in this book can be pursued, and where your own contributions can be placed.

Some of the more radical Deaf organisation websites include *www.fdp.org*, *www.irishdeafsociety.org.* and *www.deafpowernow.org.*

A useful site through which to obtain links to many groups and organisations is See Hear's *www.bbc.co.uk/see_hear* as is *www.deaflinks.info.*

Hopefully in your feedback you can help us locate valuable websites for black, feminist, post-colonial and Queer Studies discourses.

Appendix 1

Charity Colony

chorus
Oh we don't want to live by your charity
Dont' want to live here on your colony
Don't want to have to beg ya for to give it to us free
Don't want to have to wait upon your sympathy

We wanna make it on our language
This is what we'll give ya if you start but treat us right
We wanna make it on our language
We're tired of looking up at the pity in your eyes .

Ain't asking you to come and look at the zoo
'We really wanna help ya – ah it makes me wanna spew!

1.   We found ourselves in asylums
     All because we live in silence
     Then up we started to fight it
     So then you start to decry it.

     'Why you waving your hands? It ain't good for your glands;
     You hafta learn to speak to reach the Promised Land.'
     Any night we could, we'd sneak off to the woods
     Then we'd sit on our hands all day and be good.
     Still you wouldn't think – now we're on the brink
     Schooldays are over and you give a little wink -

     So badly you tied us
     Couldn't even read or write.

chorus

2.   Free, we work your plantations,
     Run by your missionary Masons
     'Don't get above your station.
     Forget about your Deaf Nation!'

'So you wanna work? You didn't come to church!
Go on, get in the office – where d'you get that shirt?
And that girl you're after – I've heard your laughter
Don't think He can't see you when you're up in the rafters.
And I'm telling you, I ain't a'marrying you,
So never in your lifetime will you say 'I do' '
And that boy went away and he scrounged a rope,
And they found him hanging with his cross on a note.

No funeral for him you decided
All because he'd suicided . . .

chorus

3. So we sit and wait for a flag day
    Trying to get your money in a sad way
    Have you ever seen us on a bad day?
    Have you ever seen us getting mad, eh?
    OK!
    Well here it comes – better reach for your guns
    Our hands'll keep a' waving till the battle is won
    We want equality of opportunity
    We want our proper place in society
    We still want your money – does that seem funny?
    But we want it in taxes, not in bread and honey.
    You thought that when you die, you'd get that heavenly pie,
    So you give a little something to the RNI.
    Well do that if you like, but we'll keep up the fight
    We're gonna keep on pushing for our human rights –

    We call it reparations.
    Healing the damage to our Nation!

chorus to fade

Ladd (1988)

Text of the Blue Ribbon Ceremony, XIII World Congress of the World Federation of the Deaf, Brisbane, Australia 25–31 July 1999

Scene: A large auditorium holding several thousand Deaf and hearing people from more than 80 different Deaf Nations. All sign language interpreters are asked to stand down – what follows, it is explained, will be communicated in International Sign in such a way that everyone present will be able to understand. Lights are then dimmed and seven figures holding lighted candles enter the hall. Video screens above the stage follow their progress and subsequent narration. The side video screens show supporting images throughout.

The seven figures arrange themselves in a semi circle. Each in turn moves into centre stage, and when they have finished their piece, moves back into the shadows.

Each narrator has translated their piece from the original text, which is written in English and appears here.

Narrator 1 (Colin Allen): We are gathered here this week to celebrate our Deaf lives and communities. To bear witness to what is in front of our eyes here – Deaf people from every part of the world, of all ages and all colours – this diversity joined in unity. We celebrate our proud history, our arts and our cultures. And we celebrate our survival. Despite adversity and oppression we are still here, and stronger than before.

But let us remember that we are *meant* to be here, alive as a part of the rainbow diversity of the human race. And today, let us remember that many of us and our ancestors have suffered at the hands of those who believe we should *not* be here. We are here to remember them too.

Narrator 2 (Libby Pollard): We remember those Deaf people who were placed in mental hospitals simply because they were Deaf and then were left neglected without communication at all for their rest of their lives.

And we remember too those Deaf people who were experimented on to try to make us into hearing people – a practice which you all know has reared its head once more, gathering steam by the day, so that somewhere in the world at this very moment, a Deaf child is being experimented on. **Narrator 3 (Hank L. Stack):** We remember those Deaf people who were victims of Oralism in their education, denied their sign languages and Deaf teachers, and forced instead to attempt only to hear and to speak, as indeed has happened to most of us here. And we remember those who were brainwashed into fearing contact with their Deaf communities; who, rejecting them tried to fit into the hearing world as a hearing person, and failing, spent and still spend the rest of their lives in isolation.

We remember the constant attempts either to eliminate us or to prevent us from being born, by not allowing Deaf people to marry each other, or through enforced sterilisation. We are all too aware that this spectre has not vanished with the Nazis, but has gained new life through the immoral glamour of genetic engineering.

Narrator 4 (David and Levi Wallace): We remember those Deaf people who were divided from their families because of Oralism. We remember the suffering of all of our hearing parents, brainwashed and confused, unable to communicate with their own Deaf children.

And we remember our own hearing children, who suffered the daily oppression that comes with being members of a Deaf family. We remember how the responsibility of interpreting for their parents led them into having too grow up too quickly, into a world which does not recognise their own identity.

Narrator 5 (Laurene Gallimore): But we *are* meant to be here! We offer the world the example we set as Deaf citizens of the world. Our sign languages communicate right across the Earth, over the borders of petty nationalisms. We show that all races can unite as equals.

Our beautiful sign languages enrich the entire world with new ways of seeing and being. We inspire those who lose their hearing to know that being deaf need not be the end of the world. We take joy in our Deafhood, and we are strong and positive as Deaf people.

Narrator 6 (Liisa Kaupinnen): These experiences and beliefs have come together in the symbol of the Blue Ribbon. The ribbon itself represents remembrance of those who have suffered oppression. And blue was the colour given to Deaf people by the Nazis. We encourage you all to bear the ribbon home to spread its message around the world, in your own ways, in your own clubs, in your own schools. Take this message to the hearing media that it may spread more rapidly.

To wear the Blue Ribbon is to pledge yourselves not only to the memory of those who have suffered, but to those who are still suffering today. And it is to pledge yourselves to fight to end that oppression now, for all the world's Deaf children and the others still to come.

At the end, the narrators move to the front of the stage in a close semi-circle, with the Deaf child at the centre in front of them. They pause for a moment, look down at him, pause, and then look back to the audience. They hold the pause for a moment and file file offstage.

The video-recording of this ceremony is available from The Australian Association of the Deaf. It has both a voice translation and English subtitles. Students of sign languages will undoubtedly find the variations between the original English text and the signed pieces to be of some interest.

List of Initial Questions and Topic Areas Presented to Deaf Informants

The questions which follow are those which were used to conduct or guide the very first interviews. New directions and themes which emerged from the responses were either pursued at the time or used in later interviews to hone in on those topics.

0. Deaf cultural pre-interview process

Observe Deaf cultural ways when meeting informant – take the required time, however lengthy, to enquire after health and well being and to allow any topics arising to be pursued. If have not met informant before, establish mutual friends or experiences. When the atmosphere feels appropriately relaxed, proceed to interview.

1. Introduction

Explain that this is only a discussion, and that the person can change their mind later about anything they have said; likewise to contact me if any new ideas occur to them. Explain that we Deaf people are just starting to open up the whole area of Deaf culture, to see what is inside, and that we are all learning together, including me, so that it is a joint exploration. And one that is strictly confidential; none of the filming will be shown to anyone else without their permission. (Unsaid at the time but alas, now necessary, without their permission of their heirs either.)

2. Intermediate step

Follow whatever general topic is 'in the air'. This may have emerged in 0. When completed (bring discussion to a close or the interview will never begin!), move to the following questions and topic areas below according to which ones feel right at that moment.

3. Interview topics

(A) Deaf cultural terms

(i)	What are the terms Deaf use to talk about their community?

(ii)	What do you think about Deaf terms like DEAF-WAY, DEAF-HIS etc.? When would you use them and what do they mean to you?

(iii)	What do you think about the sign DEAF-CULTURE? Or the hearing words from which it comes?

(iv)	How do you decide what you think is DEAF-WAY or not?

(B) Deaf cultural features

(i)	If Deaf people don't live close together, can they still be called a culture? Why don't we seem to want to live close together?

(ii)	Some say the Deaf way is never to praise, but only to criticise. What do you think?

(iii)	Some say Deaf people must share skills? Do you agree? Can you think of examples? What happens if you don't do this?

(iv)	In the Deaf community, does the group decide what to do, or do leaders make the decisions? How does one get to be a leader? Is there any particular behaviour or qualities that makes somebody a leader? Is this different between young and older Deaf?

(v)	Terms like PROPER-DEAF, REAL-DEAF. What do you see of these? When and where are they used? How does one decide who has Deaf culture? What about HARD-OF-HEARING? What about those from Deaf families who are 'hard of hearing'? What about if a Deaf person marries a hearing person? What about the status of HEARING-MOTHER-FATHER-DEAF in the Deaf community?

(vi)	Do you think Deaf have special rituals related to birth, death, marriage etc.? Or views about these that are different from hearing views?

(vii)	Some say Deaf Culture is different/no such thing because it's not passed from generation to generation. What's your view? [If person is from a Deaf family, use this to open up the whole topic of life from the Deaf-of-Deaf worldview.]

(viii)	What about English and English skills? What are Deaf attitudes to these? What are your feelings about English?

(ix)	What about Deaf attitudes to hearing people? What are your own feelings? Is Deaf culture based on attitudes to hearing people, or is it more based on what Deaf do together? What examples come to mind?

(x)	Are we too sensitive to what hearing people think of us? How does this affect our lives? Do we want to prove we are equal to hearing people, or is it more like 'DEAF-CAN'?

(xi)   Is it part of Deaf culture not to like to see Deaf thinking they are above others? How and when does this happen, and how does it manifest itself?

(C) Cultural variation

(i)   Are Deaf people the same all over the UK? Are they different in your area? If so, how?

(ii)   Black Deaf people – how do they fit into the Deaf community? [Question adapted if asked of Black Deaf person.] What about this debate at the moment – 'YOU FIRST, WHICH, DEAF OR BLACK?' What do you think about it? What attitudes do you experience from which different sorts of Deaf peoeple?

(iii) Do Deaf have any different groups within the community, maybe with different signs used to label them? Do you know the term 'STUPID-DEAF'? Who are they and who uses it to describe them? What do you think of it yourself?

(iv)   Are Deaf professionals 'less Deaf '? Do they behave differently? What's going on in the community between Deaf and those who are Deaf professionals? What do you think of the signs 'GRASS-ROOTS' and 'GRASS-ROOTS-OUT'?

(v)   Young Deaf – are they learning to fit into Deaf community and culture, or what?

(D) Language issues

(i)   Do you think more Deaf now accept BSL as a language? What's your own view?

(ii)   Has BSL research been important for the Deaf community? If so, in what ways?

The reader will notice that the information presented by the informants in Chapters 7 8 and 9 shows considerable diversion from these topics. This is partly because the information arising from those topics has been held over for the next volume in the series, and partly because the discussions which took place moved into those new areas. Having arrived at those domains and 'struck gold' in the quality of certain themes raised, subsequent interviews pursued those themes with each subsequent informant, including revisiting earlier informants to raise them there also.

United Kingdom Council on Deafness

N deafness-oriented organisation, SW, social-welfare-oriented organisation and D, Deaf community consumer body.

N	Association of Lipspeakers
SW	Association of Sign Language Interpreters
N	Association of Teachers of Lipreading to Adults
D	Breakthrough (Deaf/Hearing Integration)
N	British Association of Audiological Scientists
N	British Association of Community Doctors in Audiology
N	British Association of Teachers of the Deaf
D	British Deaf Association
N	British Society of Hearing Therapists
SW	Catholic Deaf Association
SW	Church of England Committee for Ministry among Deaf People
SW	Council for the Advancement of Communication with Deaf People
N	Cued Speech Association UK
?	Ddeaf Equality Forward
D	Deaf Broadcasting Campaign
N	Deaf Education through Listening and Talking
?	DeafMail
N	Defeating Deafness (Hearing Research Trust)
N	Ewing Foundation
N	Hard of Hearing Christian Fellowship
SW	Hearing Dogs for Deaf People
N	Hearing Concern
SW	Jewish Deaf Association
N	LINK – the British Centre for Deafened People
N	National Association of Deafened People
N	National Cochlear Implant Users Association
N	National Deaf Children's Society
SW	Royal Association for Deaf People
N	Royal National Institute for Deaf People.

SW Scottish Council on Deafness
SW Sense – National Deafblind and Rubella Association
SW SIGN – The National Society for Mental Health and Deafness
N   Telecommunications Action Group

Bibliography

Alker, D. (1992) From over the wall. *Signpost* (Spring). University of Durham: International Sign Linguistics Association (ISLA).

Alker, D. (1998) Are there really ten million of us? *The Voice* 1(1). London: Federation of Deaf People.

Alker, D. (2000) *Really Not Interested in the Deaf?* Darwen: Darwen Press.

Alladina, S. and Edwards, V. (eds) (1991) *Multilingualism in the British Isles – The Older Mother Tongues and Europe*. London: Longmans.

Althusser, L. (1984) *Essays in Ideology*. London: New Left Books/Verso.

Amsterdam Statement (2000) *The Amsterdam Statement – Deaf People, Sign Linguistics and the TISLR*. [email circular]

Anderson, B. (1983) *Imagined Communities*. London: Verso.

Anderson, Y. (1994) Comment on Turner. *Sign Language Studies* 83. Silver Spring, MD: Linstok Press.

Aramburo, A. (1989) *The Black Deaf Community*. In C. Lucas, and C. Valli (eds) *The Sociolinguistics of the Deaf Community*. San Diego, CA: Academic Press.

Arnold, M. (1869) *Culture and Anarchy*. Bristol: Thoemmes Press.

Asad, D. (1973) *Anthropology and the Colonial Encounter*. London: Ithaca Press.

Asad, D. (1979) Equality in nomadic social systems? Notes toward the dissolution of an anthropological category. In *L'Equipe Ecologie et Anthropologie des Societes Pastorale*. Pastoral Production and Society. Cambridge: Cambridge University Press.

Ashcroft, B., Griffiths, G. and Tiffin, H. (eds) (1995) *The Post-Colonial Studies Reader*. London: Routledge.

Ashcroft, B. Griffiths, G. and Tiffin, H. (eds) (1998) *Key Concepts in Post-Colonial Studies*. London: Routledge.

Atkinson, D., Morten, G. and Sue, D. (1983) *Counselling American Minorities*. Dubuque, IA: Brown.

Attwood, B. and Markus, A. (1999) *The Struggle for Aboriginal Rights*. New South Wales: Allen and Unwin.

Bahan, B. (1992) *Bird of a Different Feather* (videotext). San Diego CA: DawnSign Press.

Bahan, B. (1994) Comment on Turner. *Sign Language Studies* 84. Maryland: Linstok Press.

Bahan, B. (1997) Deaf Nation. *Video of talk at Deaf Nation Conference, University of Central Lancashire*. Derby: Chase Video Productions.

Bahan, B and Nash, J. (1996) The formation of signing communities. *Deaf Studies* IV. Washington DC: Gallaudet University College for Continuing Education.

Bahktin, M. (1968) *Rabelais and His World*. Cambridge, MA: MIT Press.

477

Baillie, M. (1998) In _Sign On – Deaf Nation 1_. Newcastle: Tyne Tees TV for Channel 4.

Baird, C. (1993) _35 Plates_. San Diego, CA: Dawnsign Press.

Baker, C. and Battison, R. (eds) (1980) _Sign Language and the Deaf Community_. Silver Spring, MD: National Association of the Deaf.

Baker, C. and Cokely, D. (1980) _American Sign Language_. Silver Spring, MD: TJ Publishers.

Baker, C. and Jones, S. (1997) _Encyclopaedia of Bilingualism and Bilingual Education_. Clevedon: Multilingual Matters.

Baker, C. and Padden, C. (1978) _American Sign Language: A Look at its Story Structure and Community_. Silver Spring, MD: T.J. Publishers Inc.

Baker, A., van den Bogaerde, B. and Crasborn, O. (eds) (2002) _Cross Linguistic Perspectives in Sign Language Research – Selected Papers for TISLR 2000_. Hamburg: Signum Press.

Barringer, F. (1993) Pride in a soundless world: Deaf oppose a hearing aid. _New York Times_ (16 May).

Barthes, R. (1975) _The Pleasure of the Text_. New York: Hill Wang.

Barwiolek, A. and McKinney, C. (1993) CHALB Productions: Deaf culture through theatrical performances. _Deaf Studies_ III. Washington, DC: Gallaudet University.

Batson, T.W. and Bergmann, E. (1976) _The Deaf Experience_. South Waterford, CT: Merriam-Eddy.

Bauman, Z. (1973) _Culture as Praxis_. London: Routledge and Kegan Paul.

Bauman, Z. (1978) _Hermeneutics and Social Science_. London: Hutchinson and Company.

Baynton, D, (1996) _Forbidden Signs – American Culture and the Campaign against Sign Language_. Chicago: University of Chicago Press.

Becker, H. (1963) _Outsiders – Studies in the Sociology of Deviance_. New York: Free Press.

Becker, G. (1983) _Growing Old in Silence: Deaf People and Old Age_. Berkeley CA: Univeristy of California Press.

Bell, A.G. (1883) _Memoir Upon the Formation of a Deaf Variety of the Human Race_. New Haven, CT: National Academy of Sciences.

Bell, A.G. (1884) Fallacies concerning the deaf. American Annals of the Deaf 29.

Bennett, T. Martin, G., Mercer, C. and Woollacott J. (eds) (1981) _Culture, Ideology and Social Process_. London: Batsford.

Beresford, Q. and Omaji, P. (1998) _Our State of Mind – Racial Planning and the Stolen Generations_. South Fremantle, WA: Fremantle Arts Centre Press.

Bergmann, E. and Bragg, B. (1981) _Tales From a Clubroom_. Washington DC: Gallaudet Press.

Bernard, Y. (1993) Silent artists. In R. Fischer and H. Lane (eds) _Looking Back_. Hamburg: Signum.

Berthier, F. (1984) The Deaf before and since the Abbe De L'Epee. o.d. 1840. In H. Lane, and F. Philip (eds) _The Deaf Experience_. Cambridge MA: Harvard University Press.

Bertling, T. (1994) _A Child Sacrificed to the Deaf Culture_. Wilsonville, OR: Kodiak Media Group.

Bezagu-Deluy, M. (1993) Personalities in the world of Deaf Mutes in 18th century Paris. In R. Fischer and H. Lane (eds) _Looking Back_. Hamburg: Signum.

Bhabha, H. (1994) _The Location of Culture_. London: Routledge.

Bhabha, H. (1995) _Signs Taken for Wonders_. In B. Ashcroft, G. Griffiths and H. Tiffin (eds) _The Post-Colonial Studies Reader_. London: Routledge.

Bienvenu, M. (1991) Can Deaf people survive 'deafness'? In *Perspectives on Deafness*, (21–8). Silver Spring MD: Nationl Association of the Deaf.

Bienvenu, M. and Columnos, B. (1986) *An Introduction to American Deaf Culture* (videotext). Maryland: Sign Media.

Bienvenu, M. and Columnos, B. (1989) *Language, Community and Culture* (videotext). Durham: University of Durham Deaf Studies Research Unit.

Biesold, H. (1993) The fate of the Israelite Asylum for the Deaf and Dumb in Berlin. In R Fischer and H. Lane (eds) *Looking Back*. Hamburg: Signum.

Binford, L. (1968) Post Pleistocene adaptations. In L. Binford and S. Binford (eds) *New Perspectives in Archaeology*. Chicago, IL: Aldine.

Blauner, B. (1987) Problems of editing first person sociology. *Qualitative Sociology* 10, 46–64.

Blume, S. (2001) Reflections on bioethics from a Deaf viewpoint. In L. Leeson (ed.) *Looking Forward* Coleford: Doug McLean Books.

Bobovius (1679) Serrai enderum. In C. Magnus (ed.) *Quanto di piu Acurioso . . . Turchia (Parma)*.

Bohannan, P. (1995) *How Culture Works*. New York: Free Press.

Booth, T. and Potts, P. (eds) (1983) *Integrating Special Education*. Oxford: Blackwell

Boudon, R. (1980) *The Crisis in Sociology*. London: Macmillan.

Bourdieu, P. (1990) *In Other Words: Essays Towards a Reflexive Sociology* Cambridge: Polity Press.

Bourdieu, P. (1992) *An Invitation to Reflexive Sociology* (ed. P. Wacquant and L. Wacquant). Chicago: University of Chicago.

Bourdieu, P. (1993) *Sociology in Question*. London: Sage.

Bourdieu, P. and Passeron, J. (1977) *Reproduction in Education, Society and Culture*. London: Sage.

Bourdieu, P. *et al.* (1991) In B. Krais (ed.) *The Craft of Sociology*. Berlin: De Gruyter.

Boyce, T. (1996) *The Leeds Beacon*. Feltham: British Deaf History Society.

Brake, M. (1985) *Comparative Youth Culture*. London: Routledge and Kegan Paul.

Branson, J. and Miller, D. (1992) Linguistics, symbolic violence and the search for word order in sign languages. *Signpost* (Summer). University of Durham: ISLA.

Branson, J. and Miller, D. (1993) Sign language, the deaf and the epistemic violence of mainstreaming. *Language and Education* 7, 1, 21–41.

Branson, J. and Miller, D. (1994) Myth, history and genealogy among the Australian Deaf Community. Monash: Unpublished paper. Monash University Anthropology and Sociology Department.

Branson, J. and Miller, D. (1995) Sign language and the discursive construction of power over the Deaf through education. In D. Corson (ed.) *Discourse and Power in Educational Organizations*. Cresskill: Hampton Press.

Brien, D (1981) Is there a deaf culture available to the young deaf person? Paper from the National Council of Social Workers with the Deaf Study Weekend, Loughborough.

Brien, D. (1991) Is there a Deaf culture? In S. Gregory and G. Hartley (eds) *Constructing Deafness*. London: Pinter Press.

British Deaf Association (1994) *Policy on Cochlea Implants*. Carlisle: British Deaf Association.

British Deaf Association (1996) *The Right to be Equal*. London: British Deaf Association.

British Deaf Mute (1892) Edition of chat. Vol. 2, p. 25. Leeds

British Deaf Mute (1893) Vol 2, p. 23. Leeds.

British Deaf News (1985) Cochlear implants – Oralism's final solution? (November, p. 1). Carlisle: British Deaf Association.

Brydon, D. (1995) The White Inuit speaks. In B. Ashcroft, G. Griffiths and H. Tiffin (eds) _The Post Colonial Studies Reader_. London: Routledge.

Buchanan, R. (1993) The _Silent Worker_ newspaper and the building of a deaf community, 1890–1929. In J. Van Cleve (ed.) _Deaf History Unveiled_. Washington DC: Gallaudet University Press.

Bulwer, J. (1648) _Philocophus: Or the Deaf and Dumbe Mans Friend_. London: Humphrey Mosley.

Burch, S. (1996) History misinterpreted: Deaf history 1917–1953. _Deaf Studies IV – Visions for the Future_. Washington, DC: Gallaudet University.

Busch, C. and Halpin, K. 1993 Incorporating Deaf culture into early intervention. _Deaf Studies III_. Washington, DC: Gallaudet University.

Campbell, H. (1985) _Rasta and Resistance_. London: Hansib.

Capra, F. (1976) _The Tao of Physics_. London: Fontana.

Carmel, S. (1987) Deaf folklore in the United States. _Proceedings. X World Congress of the World Federation of the Deaf_. Helsinki: World Federation of the Deaf.

Carmel, S. (1997) _A Study of Deaf Culture in an Urban Deaf Community_. Ann Arbor, MI: University of Michigan

Carmel, S. and Monaghan, L. (1991) An introduction to ethnographic work in Deaf communities. _Sign Language Studies 73_. Silver Spring MD: Linstok Press.

Carter, S. (1991) _Reflections of an Affirmative Action Baby_. New York: Basic Books.

Caulfield, P. (1973) Culture and imperialism: Proposing a new dialectic. In D. Hymes (ed.)_Re-inventing Anthropology_. New York: Random House.

Chambers Encyclopaedia. (1862) Deaf and dumb. London: Chambers.

Chough, S. (1998) The fascinating Asian/Deaf cultures in America. _Deaf Studies V – Towards 2000, Unity and Diversity_. Washington DC: Gallaudet University.

Chrisman, R. and Allen, R. (eds) (1992) _Court of Appeal_. New York: Ballantine Books.

Christiansen, J. and Meisegeier, R. (eds) (1986) _Papers From the Second Research Conference on the Social Aspects of Deafness_. Washington DC: Department of Sociology and Social Work, Gallaudet College.

Churchill, W. (1994) _Indians are Us? Culture and Genocide in Native North America_. Monroe, ME: Common Courage Press.

Clark, W (1982) _The Indian Sign Language_. Lincoln, NE: University of Lincoln Press.

Clay, R. (1993) Do hearing devices impair Deaf children? _Monitor_, July. American Psychological Association.

Clifford, J. and Marcus, G. (eds) (1986) _Writing Culture: The Poetics and Politics of Ethnography_. Berkeley, CA: University of California Press.

Clifford, J. (1997) Diasporas. In M. Guibernau and J. Rex (eds) _The Ethnicity Reader_. Cambridge: Polity Press.

Coates, J. (1996) _Women Talk_. Oxford: Blackwell.

Cohen, A. (1985) _The Symbolic Construction of Communities_. London: Tavistock.

Conrad, R. (1979) _The Deaf School Child: Language and Cognitive Function_. London: Harper and Row.

Conrad, R. and Weiskrantz, B. (1984) Deafness in the 17th century: Into empiricism. _Sign Language Studies 45_. Silver Spring, MD: Linstok Press.

Cooper, D. 1968 _The Dialectics of Liberation_. London: Pelican.

Corazza, S. (1993) The history of sign language in Italian education of the Deaf. In R. Fischer and H. Lane (eds) _Looking Back_. Hamburg. Signum.

Corfmat, P. (1990) _Please Sign Here_. Worthing: Churchman.

Corrigan, P. (1989) *Schooling the Smash Street Kids*. London: Macmillan.

Cowan, J. (1990) *Dance and the Body Politic in Northern Greece*. Princeton, MA: Princeton University Press.

Craw, J. (1993) A Deaf man's viewpoint through the years. In *DAIL Magazine* 84, p. 13. London: Disability Arts in London.

Crawford, J. (2000) *At War with Diversity – US Language Policy in an Age of Anxiety*. Clevedon: Multilingual Matters.

Crean, E. (1997) *Breaking the Silence*. Dublin: Irish Deaf Society.

Daly, M. (1979) *Gyn-ecology*. London: Warrens Press.

Darwin, C. (1871) *The Descent of Man and Selection in Relation to Sex*. New York: The Modern Library.

Daunt, W. (1992) Editorial. *British Deaf News*. Carlisle: BDA

Daunt, W. (1995) *Under the Lamp-post* (videotext). Derby: Chase Video Productions.

Daunt, W. and Hanafin, J. (1995) *Sign Me a Story. The World of Animals* (videotext). Derby: Chase Video Productions.

Davidson, B. (1992) *The Black Man's Burden – Africa and the Curse of the Nation-State*. New York: Times Books.

Davis, L. (1997) *The Disability Studies Reader*. New York: Routledge.

Deaf Studies III (1993) *Conference Papers*. Washington, DC: Gallaudet University Press.

De Certeau, M. (1984) *The Practice of Everyday Life*. Berkeley, CA: University of California Press.

De Comte, A. (1822) *Plan of the Scientific Works Necessary for the Re-organisation of Society*.

De Comte, A. (1838) *Cours de Philosophie Positive*.

de Ladebat. L. (1815) *A Collection of the Most Remarkable Definitions of Massieu and Clerc*. London: Cox and Baylis.

De Land (1922) A.G. Bell, an ever-continuing memorial. *Volta Review* 24, 418.

De L'Epee, C. (1984) The true method of educating the Deaf confirmed by much experience (o.d. 1776). In H. Lane and F. Philip (eds) *The Deaf Experience*. Cambridge MA: Harvard University Press.

Deloria, V. (1988) *Custer Died for Your Sins – An Indian Manifesto*. Norman, OK: University of Oklahoma Press.

Deninger, M (1983) Managing cultural conflict in schools for the deaf: Focus on the organisational level. Paper presented at the Convention of American Instructors of the Deaf, Winnipeg, Manitoba, Canada, June 26–30.

Denmark, C. (1991) British Sign Language Tutor Training Course. In S. Gregory and G. Hartley (eds) *Constructing Deafness*. Milton Keynes: Open University.

Denmark, J.C. (1981) A psychiatric view of the importance and early use of sign language. In B. Woll, J. Kyle and M. Deuchar (eds) *Perspectives on BSL and Deafness*. London: Croom Helm.

Depledge, I. (1994) An investigation into the position regarding cochlear implants in the USA. In *Policy on Cochlea Implants*. Carlisle: British Deaf Association.

Derrida, J. (1991) *A Derrida Reader: Between the Blinds* (ed. P. Kamuf). London: Harvester Wheatsheaf.

Desloges, P. (1984) A Deaf person's observations about an elementary course of education for the Deaf. (o.d. 1779). In H. Lane and F. Philip (eds) *The Language of Experience*. Cambridge MA: Harvard University Press.

Deuchar, M. (1984) *British Sign Language*. London: Routledge and Kegan Paul.

DHSS (1988) *Say it Again*. London: Department of Health and Social Security.

Dickens, C. (1971) *Christmas Stories* (Everyman's Library). London: Dent.

Dimmock, A.F. (1994) Letter to *British Deaf News* (October). Carlisle: BDA.

Dodds, J. (1998) They said it could never happen. *The Voice* 1, 1. London: Federation of Deaf People.

Dolnick, E. (1993) Deafness as culture. *Atlantic Monthly* (September).

Downes, D. (1966) *The Delinquent Solution*. London: Routledge and Kegan Paul.

Du Bois, W. (1903) [1961] *The Souls of Black Folk*. New York: Premier Editions.

Du Bois, W. (1989) *The Souls of Black Folk*. New York: Bantam.

Duran, E. and Duran, B. (1995) *Native American Postcolonial Psychology*. Albany, NY: State University of New York Press.

During, S. (ed.) (1993) *The Cultural Studies Reader*. London: Routledge.

Early, G. (ed) (1993) *Lure and Loathing – Race, Identity and Assimilation*. New York: Viking Penguin.

Edwards, V. (1979) *The West Indian Language Issue in British Schools*. London: Routledge and Kegan Paul.

Edwards, V. and Sienkewitz, D. (1991) *Oral Cultures Past and Present: Rappin' and Homer*. Oxford: Blackwell

Eickman, J. (forthcoming) The role of Deaf sport in developing Deaf identity. Doctoral thesis presented to the University of Bristol.

Emmerick W. (1995) Poëzie in *Gebarenthaal I*. Amsterdam: Theater 't OOG.

Erikson, W. (1992) Deaf culture: In search of the difference. *American Deafness and Rehabilitation Assocation (ADARA)* 26 (3), 47–50.

Erting, C. (1985) Cultural conflict in a school for Deaf children. *Anthropology and Education Quarterly*, 16, 225–43.

Erting, C., Johnson, R., Smith, D. and Snider, B. (eds) (1994) *The Deaf Way – Perspectives from the International Conference on Deaf Culture, 1989*. Washington DC: Gallaudet University Press.

Fanon, F. (1968) *The Wretched of the Earth*. New York: Grove Press.

Fanon, F. (1986) *Black Skin, White Masks*. London: Pluto Press.

Farrah, A. (1923) *Arnold on the Education of the Deaf. A Manual for Teachers*. London: National College of Teachers of the Deaf.

Featherstone, M. (1990) Global culture: An introduction. *Theory, Culture and Society* 7 (2/3), 1–14.

Federation of Deaf People (2000) *The Voice* Vols 3 and 4. Darwen: Federation of Deaf People.

Fischer, R. (1993) *Language of Action*. In R. Fischer and H.Lane (eds) *Looking Back*. Hamburg: Signum.

Flynn, J. (1999) Some aspects of the development of post-school organisations of and for Deaf people in Australia. Unpublished MA thesis, La Trobe University, Victoria.

Foley, J. (1988) *The Theory of Oral Composition: History and Methodology*. Bloomington: University of Indiana Press.

Fortes, M. (1953) The structure of unilineal descent groups. *American Anthropologist* 55, 17–41.

Foucault, M. (1972) *The Archaeology of Knowledge*. New York: Harper Colophon.

Foucault, M. (1979) *Discipline and Punish*. New York: Vintage Books.

Foucault, M. (1980) *History of Sexuality, Vol 1*. New York: Vintage Books.

Fowler, D. (1998) In *'Sign On'*, *Deaf Nation 1:1*. Newcastle: Tyne-Tees TV for Channel 4.

Frake, C. (1980) Some reflections on methodology in cognitive anthropology. In *Language and Cultural Description: Essays Selected by Anwar S. Dil*. Stanford, CA: Stanford University Press.

Freeman, R., Carbin, C. and Boese, R. (1981) *Can't Your Child Hear?* Baltimore, MD: University Park Press.

Freire, P. (1986) *Pedagogy of the Oppressed*. New York: Continuum.

Gannon, J. (1981) *Deaf Heritage*. Silver Spring, MD: National Association of the Deaf.

Gannon, J.R. (1989) *The Week the World Heard Gallaudet*. Washington, DC: Gallaudet University Press.

Garfinkel, H. (1967) *Studies in Ethnomethodology*. Englewood Cliffs, NJ: Prentice-Hall.

Garretson, M. (ed.) (1992) *Viewpoints on Deafness*. Silver Spring, MD: NAD Press.

Garretson, M. (1993) *Deafness, 1993–2013*. Silver Spring, MD: NAD Press.

Gates, H. (1993) In G. Early (ed.) *Lure and Loathing*. New York: Viking Penguin.

Gates, H. (1997) *Thirteen Ways of Looking at a Black Man*. New York: Random House.

Gee, J. (1989) Two styles of narrative construction and their linguistic and educational implications. *Discourse Processes* 12, 287–307.

Gee, J., Michaels, S. and O'Connor, M. (1992) Discourse analysis. In M. LeCompte, W. Millroy, and J. Preissle (eds) *The Handbook of Qualitative Research in Education*. San Diego: Academic Press.

Geertz, C. (1973) *The Interpretation of Cultures*. London: Hutchinson.

Geertz, C. (1983) *Local Knowledge*. New York: Basic Books.

Geldof, B. (1986) *Is That It?* London: Penguin Books.

Gilroy, P. (1993a) *Small Acts*. London: Serpents Tail.

Gilroy, P. (1993b) *The Black Atlantic: Modernity and Double Consciousness*. London: Verso.

Gleick, J. (1997) *Chaos*. London: Minerva Press.

Goodenough, W.H. (1957) Cultural anthropology and linguistics. In P. Garvin (ed.) *Report of the Seventh Annual Round Table on Linguistics and Language Study*. Washington DC: Georgetown University Monograph Series. Language and Linguistics 9.

Goodenough, W.H. (1971) *Culture, Language and Society*. (McCaleb Module in Anthropology). Reading, MA: Addison-Wesley.

Gordon, L. (2000) *Existentia – Understanding Africana Existential Thought*. New York: Routledge.

Gordon, M. (1947) The concept of the subculture and its applications. *Social Forces* (October).

Gouldner, A (1971) *The Coming Crisis of Western Sociology*. London: Heinemann.

Gramsci, A. (1971) *Selections from the Prison Notebooks*. London: Lawrence and Wishart.

Gramsci, A. (1981) *Culture, Ideology and Social Process*, ed. T. Bennett, G. Martin, C. Mercer and J. Woollacott. London: Batsford.

Gramsci, A. (1985) *A Gramsci Reader*, ed D. Forgacs and G. Nowell-Smith. London: Lawrence and Wishart.

Grant, B. (1993) *The Deaf Advance*. Edinburgh: Pentland Press.

Grant, B. (1993) Francis Maginn (1861–1918.) In R. Fischer and H. Lane (eds) *Looking Back*. Hamburg: Signum.

Gregory, S. and Hartley, G. (eds) (1991) *Constructing Deafness*. London: Pinter Press.

Griggs, M. (1998) Deafness and mental health: Perceptions of health within the Deaf community. PhD dissertation, University of Bristol.

Groce, N. (1985) *Everyone Here Spoke Sign Language*. Cambridge, MA: Harvard University Press.

Grosjean, F. (1992) The bilingual and bicultural person in the Hearing and Deaf world. *Sign Language Studies 77*, 307–20.

Gross, B. (1973) Indian control for quality Indian education. *North Dakota Law Review* 49 (2).

Guha, R. (1982) On some aspects of the historiography of colonial India. In R. Guha (ed.) *Subaltern Studies I*. Delhi: Oxford University Press.

Guibernau, M. and Rex, J. (eds) (1997) *The Ethnicity Reader*. Cambridge: Polity Press.

Hairston, E. and Smith, L. (1983) *Black and Deaf in America*. Silver Spring, MD: TJ Publishers.

Hall, E. (1959) *The Silent Language*. New York: Premier Books.

Hall, E. (1981) *Beyond Culture*. New York: Anchor/Doubleday.

Hall, E. (1994) Deaf culture, tacit culture and ethnic relations. In C. Erting, R. Johnson, D. Smith and B. Snider (eds) *The Deaf Way: Perspectives from the International Conference on Deaf Culture, 1989*. Washington DC: Gallaudet University Press.

Hall, S. (1989) Train-Gone-Sorry: The etiquette of conversations in American Sign Language. In S. Wilcox (ed.) *American Deaf Culture – An Anthology*. Silver Spring, MD: Linstok Press.

Hall, S. (1966) Class and the mass media. In R. Mabey (ed.) *Class: A Symposium*. London: Blond.

Hall, S. (1983) The problem of ideology: Marxism without guarantees. In B. Matthews (ed.) *Marx 100 Years On*. London: Lawrence and Wishart.

Hall, S. (1993) Culture, community, nation. *Cultural Studies 7* (3), 349–63.

Hall, S. and Jefferson, T. (eds) (1976) Introduction. In S. Hall and T. Jefferson (eds) *Resistance Through Rituals*. London: Hutchinson.

Hall, S., Lumley, B. and McLennan, G. (1977) Politics and ideology: Gramsci. *Working Papers in Cutural Studies 10*, 45–76. Birmingham: University of Birmingham.

Hammersley, M. (1990) *Reading Ethnographic Research – A Critical Guide*. London: Longmans.

Hammesley, M. (1992) *What's Wrong with Ethnography?* London: Routledge.

Hammersley, M. and Atkinson, P. 1983 *Ethnography: Principles in Practice*. London: Routledge.

Handtheater (1997) *De Man, de Stad an Het Boek*. Amsterdam: Handtheater/Theater 't OOG.

Hannerz, U. (1992) *Cultural Complexity: Studies in the Social Organisation of Meaning*. New York: Columbia University Press.

Harris, J. (1995) *The Cultural Meaning of Deafness*. Aldershot: Ashgate.

Hawksworth, A. (1989) Knowers, knowing, known – feminist theory and the claims of truth. In Malson *et al.* (eds) *Feminist Theory in Practice and Process*. Chicago: University of Chicago Press.

Henry, C. (1990) *Culture and African-American Politics*. Bloomington, IN: Indiana University Press.

Here and Now (1996) *Cochlear Implants Controversy*. 26 November.

Herskovits, M. (1958) *The Myth of the Negro Past*. Boston, MA: Beacon Press.

Higgins, P. (1980) *Outsiders in a Hearing World*. Newbury Park, CA: Sage.

Higlen, P. *et al.* (1988) *Self Identity Model of Oppressed People – Inclusive Model for All?* Atlanta, GA: American Psychological Association.

Hillery, G. (1974) *Communal Organisations*. Chicago: Chicago University Press.

Hindley, P and Kitson, N. (eds) (2000) *Mental Health and Deafness*. London: Whurr.

Hirayama, H. and Cetingok, M. (1988) Empowerment: A social work approach for asian immigrants. *Social Casework* 69 (1), 41–47. Family Service America.

Hobsbawn, E. (1962) *The Age of Revolution: Europe 1789–1848*. London: Weidenfeld and Nicholson.

Hochschild, A. (1976) The sociology of feeling and emotion: selected possibilities. In R. Millman and R. Kanter (eds) *Another Voice: Feminist Perspectives on Social Life and Social Science*. New York: Octagon Books.

Hodgson, K.W. (1953) *The Deaf and Their Problems*. London: Watts Press.

Hoggart, R. (1958) *The Uses of Literacy*. London: Penguin.

hooks, b. (1989) *Talking Back*. Boston, MA: South End Press.

hoobs, b. (1995) *Killing Rage – Ending Racism*. New York: Holt.

Hough, J. (1983) *Louder Than Words*. Cambridge: Great Ouse Press.

Humphries, T. (1977) Communicating across cultures (Deaf/Hearing) and language learning. PhD dissertation, Union Graduate School, Cincinnati, OH.

Hurst, J. (1992) Memorandum to Task Force Report on American Sign Language and Deaf Studies. Unpublished. Washington, DC: Gallaudet University.

Hymes, D. (1974) *Foundations in Sociolinguistics: An Ethnographic Approach*. Philadephia PA: University of Pennsylvania Press.

Hymes, D. (1981) '*In Vain I Tried to Tell You*': Essays in Native American Ethnopoetics. Philadelphia PA: University of Pennsylvania Press.

Ihimaera, W. (1998) (ed.) *Growing Up Maori*. Auckland: Tandem Press.

Inglis, F. (1993) *Cultural Studies*. Oxford: Blackwell.

Jackson, B. and Hardiman, R. (1983) *Racial Identity Development*. NTL Institute.

Jackson, B and Marsden, D. (1962) *Education and the Working Class*. Harmondsworth: Penguin.

Jackson, P. (1986) *The Allan Hayhurst Research Fellowship Report*. n/p.

Jackson, P. (1990) *Britain's Deaf Heritage*. Edinburgh: Pentland Press.

Jacobs, L. McMillan, J. and Yates, P. (1993) The use of ASL/Deaf culture principles for effective communication in the classroom. *Deaf Studies* III. Washington, DC: Gallaudet University.

James, M. (1994) Letter. *DAIL Magazine* 86. London: Disability Arts in London.

Jankowski, K. (1997) *Deaf Empowerment – Emergence, Struggle and Rhetoric*. Washington, DC: Gallaudet University Press.

Johnson, R.E. and Erting, C. (1989) Ethnicity and socialization in a classroom for Deaf children. In C. Lucas and C. Valli (eds) *Sociolinguistics of the Deaf Community*. San Diego, CA. Academic Press.

Johnson, R.E. and Erting, C. (1989) (with Liddell, S.). *Unlocking the Curriculum*. Gallaudet Research Institute Working Papers. Washington, DC: Gallaudet Research Institute.

Johnston, T. (1994) Comment on Turner. *Sign Language Studies* 83. Maryland: Linstok Press.

Jones, J. (1995) Making the transition to being Deaf. *Deafness* 11 (1), 4–7. Carlisle: Alliance of Deaf Service Users and Providers and the British Deaf Association.

Jones, L. and Pullen, G. (1992) Cultural differences: Deaf and hearing researchers working together. *Disability, Handicap and Society*, 17 (2), 23–46.

Joyce, J. (1960) *Portrait of the Artist as a Young Man*. London: Penguin Books.

Kannapell, B. Inside the deaf community. *Deaf American* 34 (4), 21–27.

Kannapell, B. (1974) Bi-lingualism: A new direction in the education of the deaf. *Deaf American* 26, 9–15.

Kannapell, B. (1982) Inside the Deaf community. *Deaf American* 34 (4).

Kannapell, B. (1989) Syllabus for 'The Deaf Community: A Cultural Perspective'.

Kannapell, B. (1992) Materials for 'Culture and Communication Colloquium, Washington, DC: Gallaudet University. n/p.

Karacostas, A. (1993) Fragments of 'glottophagia'. Ferdinand Berthier and the birth of the Deaf movement in France. In R. Fischer and H. Lane (eds) _Looking Back._ Hamburg: Signum.

Karenga, M. (1993) _Introduction to Black Studies._ Los Angeles, CA: University of Sankore Press.

Katz, C. (1993) _Vishma and the Child: Personal Mythology of the Deaf._ Fremont, CA: California School for the Deaf (in manuscript).

Katznelson, I. (1981) _City Trenches._ Chicago: University of Chicago Press.

Keesing, R. (1974) Theories of culture. In B. Siegel (ed.) _Annual Review of Anthropology,_ 3, 73–97. Palo Alto, CA.

Keesing, R. (1981) _Cultural Anthropology: A Contemporary Perspective._ New York: Holt, Rhinehart and Winston.

Kendon, A. (1988) _Sign Languages of Aboriginal Australia._ Melbourne: Cambridge University Press.

Kleinjams, E. (1975) A question of ethics. _Exchange_ X (4), 20–5.

Klima, E. and Bellugi, U. (1979) _The Signs of Language._ Cambridge, MA: Harvard University Press.

Krausneker, V. (2001) Sign languages of Europe – future chances. In L. Leeson (ed.) _Looking Forward._ Coleford: Forest Bookshop.

Kroeber, A. and Kluckhohn, C. (1963) _Culture: A Critical Review of Concepts in Definition._ New York: Vintage Press.

Kuhn, T. (1962) _The Structure of Scientific Revolutions._ Chicago: University of Chicago Press.

Kroeber, A.L. and Kluckholm, S. (1952) Culture-critical review of concepts and definitions. _Papers of the Peabody Museum of American Anthropology and Ethology_ 47, (1), 23.

Kymlicka, W. (1997) Ethnicity in the USA. In M. Guibernau and J. Rex (eds) _The Ethnicity Reader._ Cambridge: Polity Press.

Kyle, J. (1991a) The deafness of psychology. In P. Arnold (ed.) _Monographs in Deafness._ Manchester: Manchester University Press.

Kyle, J. (1991b) The deaf community. In _Being Deaf._ Unit 2. Milton Keynes: Open University Press.

Kyle, J. and Allsop, L. (1982) _Deaf People and the Community: Final Report to the Nuffield Foundation._ Bristol: Centre For Deaf Studies Press.

Kyle, J. and Pullen, G. (1985) _Young Deaf People in Employment._ Bristol: Centre for Deaf Studies.

Kyle, J. and Woll, B. (1985) _Sign Language._ Cambridge: Cambridge University Press.

Ladd, P. (1979) Making plans for Nigel. In G. Montgomery _The Integration and Disintegration of the Deaf in Society._ Edinburgh: Scottish Workshop Publications.

Ladd, P. (1985) _What is Deaf Theatre?_ Privately circulated discussion paper.

Ladd, P. (1988) The modern deaf community. In D. Miles (eds) _British Sign Language._ London: BBC Books.

Ladd, P. (1991) _You Can Lie Through Your Teeth, But You Can"t Lie Through Your Body_ (Signed Song Video). London: BBC: See Hear programme.

Ladd, P. (1992) Deaf cultural studies. In M. Garretson (ed.) _Viewpoints on Deafness._ Silver Spring, MD: NAD Press.

Ladd, P. (1993a) Deaf consciousness. *Deaf Studies III.* Washington, DC: Gallaudet University Press.

Ladd, P. (1993b) The Deafhood papers, Volume One. In M. Garretson (ed.) *Deafness 1993–2013 AD.* Silver Spring, MD: NAD Press.

Ladd, P. (1994) Deaf culture. In C. Erting, R. Johnson, D. Smith and B. Snider (eds) *The Deaf Way: Perpectives from the International Conference on Deaf Culture 1989.* Washington, DC: Gallaudet University Press.

Ladd, P. (1996) Deaf futures – Towards a national deaf renewal. Paper given to conference, Central Lancashire University. [n.p]

Ladd, P. (1996) Report to the RNID from the Deaf BSL-Users Committee. [n.p.]

Ladd, P. (1999) The importance of deaf culture. Paper given to World Federation of the Deaf. Congress, Brisbane, Australia. [forthcoming]

Ladd, P. (2001) 2001 – The voyage out. Paper given to the Western Australian Association of the Deaf, Perth, WA. [published in conference proceedings in CDRom]

Ladd, P. (2002) Sign linguistics – Time to locate the big picture? In A. Baker, B.van den Bogaerde and O. Crasborn (eds) *Cross Linguistic Perspectives in Sign Language Research.* Hamburg: Signum Press.

Laing, R. (1965) *The Divided Self.* Harmondsworth: Penguin.

Landry, B. (1987) *The New Black Middle Class.* Berkeley, CA: University of California Press.

Lane, H. (1984) *When The Mind Hears.* New York: Random House.

Lane, H. (1991) Why the Deaf are angry. In R. Lee (ed.) *Deaf Liberation.* London: National Union of the Deaf.

Lane, H. (1993a) *The Mask of Benevolence.* New York: Random House.

Lane, H. (1993b) The medicalization of cultural Deafness in historical perspective. In R. Fischer and H. Lane (eds) *Looking Back.* Hamburg: Signum.

Lane, H. (1994) The cochlear implant controversy. In *Policy on Cochlear Implants.* Carlisle: British Deaf Association.

Lane, H., Hoffmeister, R. and Bahan, B. (1996) *A Journey into the Deaf-World.* San Diego, CA: DawnSign Press.

Lane, H. and Philip, F. (eds) (1984) *The Deaf Experience.* Cambridge, MA: Harvard University Press.

Lather, P. (1986) Research as praxis. *Harvard Educational Review* 56 (3), 257 –77.

Lawson, L. (1981) The role of sign in the structure of the deaf community. In B. Woll, J. Kyle and M. Deuchar (eds) *Perspectives on British Sign Language and Deafness.* London: Croom Helm.

LeCompte, M., Millroy, W. and Preissle, J. (eds) 1992 *The Handbook of Qualitative Research in Education.* San Diego, CA: Academic Press.

Lee, A.M. (1945) Levels of culture as levels of social generalisation. In *American Sociological Review* (August).

Lee, R. (ed.) (1991) *Deaf Liberation.* London: National Union of the Deaf.

Lentz, E. (1995) *The Treasure.* California: Motion Press.

Lester, J. (1991) What price unity? *Village Voice* 17, 9.

Levine, L. (1977) *Black Culture and Black Consciousness.* New York: Oxford University Press.

Lincoln, E. and Guba, E. (1985) *Naturalistic Enquiry.* Beverley Hills, CA: Sage.

Llewellyn-Jones, P., Kyle, J. and Woll, B. (1979) Sign language community. Paper given to the International Conference on Social Psychology of Language, Bristol.

Loeb, G. (1993) Letter to the Editor. *Atlantic Monthly* (December).

Lorde, A. (1984) *Sister Outsider.* Trumansburg, NY: Crossing Press.

Lucas, C. and Valli, C. (eds) (1989) *The Sociolinguistics of the Deaf Community*. San Diego: Academic Press.

Lucas, C. and Valli, C. (eds) (1992) *Language Contact in the American Deaf Community*. San Diego: Academic Press.

Lunde, A. (1956) Social factors in the isolation of deaf people. In W. Stokoe, *Sign Language Studies: An Outline of Visual Communication Systems of the American Deaf*. University of Buffalo Occasional Papers No. 8 of the Studies in Linguistics Series.

Lynas, W. (1986) *Integrating the Handicapped into Ordinary Schools*. London: Croom Helm.

Lysons, K. (1963) Some aspects of the historical development and present organisation of voluntary welfare societies for adult deaf persons in England, 1840–1963. MA dissertation, University of Liverpool.

Lysons, K. (1978) The development of local voluntary societies for adult deaf persons in England. *British Deaf News* 11, 214–17.

Lysons, K. (1979) The development of local voluntary societies for adult deaf persons in England. *British Deaf New* 12, 34–6.

Mackinnon (1982) Feminism, Marxism, method and the state: An agenda for theory. *Signs* 7 (3), 515–544.

Mair, L. (1965) *An Introduction to Social Anthropology*. Oxford: Clarendon Press.

Mally, G. (1993) The long road to self confidence of the Deaf in Germany. In R Fischer and H. Lane (eds) *Looking Back*. Hamburg: Signum.

Mannion, M. (1997) Genetic cleansing. *Irish Deaf Journal* 11 (41), 12–13. Dublin: Irish Deaf Society.

Marable, M (1981) *Blackwater*. Niwot, CO: University Press of Colorado.

Marable, M. (1992) *The Crisis of Color and Democracy*. Monroe, ME: Common Courage Press.

Marcuse, H. (1968) *One Dimensional Man*. London: Sphere Books.

Markovicz, H. and Woodward, J. (1978) Language and the maintenance of ethnic boundaries in the Deaf Community. *Communication and Cognition* 11, 29–37.

Marx, K. (1970) *The German Ideology*. London: Lawrence and Wishart.

Mason, C. (1991) School experiences. In G. Taylor and J. Bishop, (eds) *Being Deaf*. London: Pinter.

McCaskill-Emerson, C. (1993) Multicultural/minority issues in Deaf Studies. *Deaf Studies III*. Washington DC: Gallaudet University.

McDonnell, P. (2001) Deep structures. In *Deaf Education: Implications for Policy*. In L. Leeson (ed.) *Looking Forward: The European Union of the Deaf in the 21st Century* (pp. 100–116). Coleford: Doug McLean Books.

McDonnell, P. and Saunders, H. (1993) Sit on your hands. Strategies to prevent signing. In R. Fischer and H.Lane (eds) *Looking Back*. Hamburg: Signum.

McGuigan, J. (1992) *Cultural Populism*. London: Routledge.

McLuhan, M. (1964) *Understanding Media: The Extensions of Man*. New York: McGraw-Hill

McRobbie, A. (1986) Postmodernism and popular culture. In L. Apignanesi (ed.) *ICA Documents 4 and 5 Postmodernism*. London: Institute for Contemporary Arts.

McWhinney, J. (1991) Deaf consciousness. *Signpost* 2, 13–15.

Meadow, K. (1972) Sociolinguistics, sign language and the Deaf subculture. In T. O'Rourke (ed.) *Pschyolinguistics and Total Communication – The State of the Art*. (*American Annals of the Deaf*). Silver Spring, MO: National Assocation of the Deaf.

Meggers, B. (1971) *Amazonia, Man and Culture – A Counterfeit Paradise*. Chicago, IL: Aldine.

Merry, S. (1991) Law and colonialism. *Law and Society Review 25*, 889–922.

Merzenich, M. (1997) In *Do Hearing Devices Impair Deaf Children?* by Rebecca Clay.

Meyerson, R. (1969) *Sociology and Cultural Studies: Some Problems*. Birmingham: Centre for Contemporary Cultural Studies.

Miles, D. (1974) A history of theatrical activities in the Deaf community of the United States. MA thesis presented to Conneticut College.

Miles, D. (1983) *Aesop's Fables* (videotext). Carlisle: British Deaf Association.

Miles, D. (1988) *British Sign Language*. London: BBC Books.

Miles, M. (2000) Signing at the Seraglio: Mutes, dwarfs and jesters at the Ottoman Court, 1500–1700. *Disability and Society 15* (1), 115–34.

Miller, D. (1993) *Spivak and Postcolonialism: Literary Criticism and Political Action*. Unpublished paper. Monash University, Department of Anthropology and Sociology.

Millman, R and Kanter, R. (1976) *Another Voice: Feminist Perspectives on Social Life and Social Science*. New York: Octagon Books.

Mindess, A. (2000) *Reading Between the Signs – Intercultural Communication for Sign Language Interpreters*. Yarmouth, ME: Intercultural Press.

Mirzoeff, N. (1995) *Silent Poetry: Deafness, Sign and Visual Culture in Modern France*. Princeton, NJ: Princeton University Press.

Montgomery, G. (1976) Changing attitudes to communication. Supplement to *British Deaf News, June*. Carlisle: British Deaf Association.

Montgomery, G. (ed.) (1978) *Of Sound and Mind*. Edinburgh: Scottish Workshop Publications.

Montgomery, G. (1994) Comment on Turner. *Sign Language Studies 84*. Maryland: Linstok Press.

Moore, M. and Levitan, L. (1992) *For Hearing People Only*. Rochester, NY: Deaf Life Press.

Morrison, T. (1992) (ed.) *Race-ing Justice, En-gendering Power*. New York: Pantheon Books.

Mottez, B. (1993) The Deaf Mute banquets and the birth of the Deaf movement. In R. Fischer and H. Lane (eds) *Looking Back*. Hamburg: Signum.

Musgrove, F. (1974) *Ecstasy and Holiness – Counter Culture and the Open Society*. London: Methuen.

Myerhoff, B. (1980) *Number Our Days*. New York: Simon and Schuster.

Myers, R and Marcus, A. (1993) Hearing, Mother, Father Deaf: Issues of identity and mediation in culture and communication. In *Deaf Studies III*. Washington, DC: Gallaudet University.

Myhre, M. (1994) *The Culture of Deaf People: A Bibliography of Books, Artcles, Films and Videotapes*. San Francisco, CA: San Francisco Public Library Deaf Service.

Nader, L. (1973) Up the anthropologist – perspectives gained from studying up. In D. Hymes (ed.) *Reinventing Anthropology*. New York: Random House.

Nandy, A. (1983) *The Intimate Enemy*. Delhi: Oxford University Press.

National Association of the Deaf (1991) *Cochlear Implants in Children*. Silver Spring, MD: National Association of the Deaf.

National Union of the Deaf (1976) Wimbledon: National Union of the Deaf.

National Union of the Deaf (1977) *Blueprint for the Future*. London: National Union of the Deaf.

National Union of the Deaf (1982) *Charter of Rights of the Deaf*. London: National Union of the Deaf.

National Union of the Deaf (1992) _Deaf Liberation_, ed. R. Lee. Feltham: National Union of the Deaf.

Neisser, A. (1983) _The Other Side of Silence_. Washington, DC: Gallaudet University Press.

Neville, R. (1970) _Playpower_. London: Paladin.

Niparko, J.K. (1993) An update on cochlear implants. _Policy on Cochlear Implants_. Carlisle: British Deaf Association.

Oliver, M. (1990) _The Politics of Disablement_. Basingstoke: Macmillan.

Osborne, R. and Van Loon, B. (1996) _Sociology for Beginners_. Cambridge: Icon Books.

Padden, C. (1980) The deaf community and the culture of deaf people. In C. Baker and R. Battison (eds) _Sign Language and the Deaf Community_. Silver Spring, MD: National Association of the Deaf.

Padden, C. (1998) From the cultural to the bicultural: The modern Deaf community. In I. Parasnis (ed.) _Culture and Language Diversity and the Deaf Experience_. New York: Cambridge University Press.

Padden, C. and Humphries, T. (1988) _Deaf in America_. Cambridge, MA: Harvard University Press.

Padden, C. and Markowitz, H. (1975) Cultural conflicts between hearing and deaf communities. In _Proceedings of the VII World Congress of the World Federation of the Deaf_. Silver Spring, MD: NAD.

Parasnis, I. (1998) _Culture and Language Diversity and the Deaf Experience_. New York: Cambridge University Press.

Parsons, F. (1992) The pendulum since the Great Depression. In M. Garretson (ed.) _Viewpoints on Deafness_ (pp. 103–108). Silver Spring, MD: National Association of the Deaf.

Parsons, F. (1993) Education of the Deaf: A global look. In M. Garretson (ed.) _Deafness 1993–2013_. Silver Spring, MD: National Association of the Deaf.

Paulston, C.B. (1992) Biculturalism: Some reflections and speculations. In _Sociolinguistic Perspectives on Bilingual Education_. Clevedon: Multilingual Matters.

Peters, C. (1996) Deaf American literature: A performance-based minority literature. _Deaf Studies IV – Visions for the Future_. Washington DC: Gallaudet University.

Philip, M. (1987) Deaf culture and interpreter training curriculae. _New Dimensions in Interpreter Education_. Silver Spring, MD: RID Publications.

Philip, M. (1993) _Cross-Cultural Comparisons: American Deaf Culture and American Majority Culture_. Westminster, CO: Front Range Community College.

Philip, M. (1995) Response to Wallin. International Conference of Deaf Researchers n/p.

Pityana, B. , Ramphele, M. , Mpumlwana, M. and Wilson, L. (eds) (1991) _Bounds of Possibility – The Legacy of Steve Biko and Black Consciousness_. Cape Town: David Philip.

Plann, S. (1993) Roberto Fransisco Pradez. Spain's first Deaf teacher of the Deaf. In R. Fischer and H. Lane (eds) _Looking Back_. Hamburg: Signum.

Plann, S. (1997) _A Silent Minority – Deaf Education in Spain 1550–1835_. Berkeley CA: University of California Press.

Presneau, J-R. (1993) The scholars, the Deaf and the language of signs in France in the 18th century. In R. Fischer and H. Lane (eds) _Looking Back_. Hamburg: Signum.

Preston, P. (1994) _Mother Father Deaf_. Cambridge, MA: Harvard University Press.

Pryce, K. (1979) _Endless Pressure_. Harmondsworth: Penguin Books.

Quantz, R. (1992) Critical ethnography. In M. Lecompte, W. Millroy and Preissle (eds) *Handbook of Qualitative Research in Education*. San Diego: Academic Press.

Rancke, C. (1988) Letter. *TBC News 9* (December). Riverdale, MD: The Bicultural Centre.

Ramazanoglu, C. (1990) *Methods of Working as a Research Team*. London: Tufnell Press.

Redfern, P. (1995) Deaf professionals: A growing stream. *Deafness* 11 (1), 8–10. Carlisle: Alliance of Deaf Service Users and Professionals and the British Deaf Association.

Ree, J. (1999) *I See a Voice – A Philosophical History of Language, Deafness and the Senses*. London: Harper-Collins.

Reed-Danahay, D (ed.) (1997) *Auto/Ethnography – Rewriting the Self and the Social*. Oxford: Berg.

Reich, C. (1972) *The Greening of America*. London: Penguin.

Reilly, C. (1995) A Deaf way of education: Interaction among children in a Thai boarding school. PhD dissertation, University of Maryland.

Ridgway, S. (1998) The psychological health and wellbeing of deaf people in the community. PhD, Dept of Psychology, University of Manchester.

Robinson, K. (1995) The best of both worlds. *Deafness* 11 (1). Carlisle: ADSUP and BDA.

Roberts, H. (ed.) (1981) *Doing Feminist Research*. London: Routledge and Kegan Paul.

Rodney, W. (1982) *How Europe Underdeveloped Africa*. Washington, DC: Howard University Press.

Rodriguez-Gonzalez, M.A. (1993) *Fransisco Fernandez Villabrille (1811–1864) and 'el lenguaje designos'*. In R. Fischer and H. Lane (eds) *Looking Back*. Hamburg: Signum.

Rollwagen, J. (1988) *Anthropological Film-making*. Chur, Switzerland: Harwood.

Roszak, T. (1971) *The Making of a Counter Culture*. London: Faber and Faber.

Royal National Institute for the Deaf (1976) *'Hearing'* (magazine). London: RNID.

Royal National Institute for the Deaf (1996) Report of the BSL Advisory Group on Deaf Community Funding Priorities. Unpublished.

Rubin, L. (1976) *Worlds of Pain: Life in the Working-class Family*. New York: Basic Books.

Rutherford, S. (1985) *American Culture: The Deaf Perspective, Vols 1–4*. Berkeley, CA: D.E.A.F. Media Inc.

Rutherford, S. (1993) *A Study of American Deaf Folklore*. Maryland: Linstok Press.

Sacks, O. (1989) *Seeing Voices*. Berkeley, CA: University of California Press.

Said, E. (1978) *Orientalism*. New York: Pantheon.

Said, E. (1991) *The World, the Text and the Critic*. London: Vintage.

de Saint Loup, A. (1993) Images of the Deaf in medieval western Europe. In R. Fischer and H. Lane (eds) *Looking Back*. Hamburg: Signum.

Sardar, Z. and Van Loon, B. (1997) *Cultural Studies for Beginners*. Cambridge: Icon Books.

Schein, J. (1989) *At Home Among Strangers*. Washington, DC: Gallaudet University Press.

Schein, J. and Delk, M.T. (1974) *The Deaf Population of the United States*. Silver Spring, MD: National Association of the Deaf.

Schlesinger, H. and Meadow, K. (1971) *Sound and Sign*. Berkeley, CA: University of California Press.

Schultz. B. and Schultz, R. (1989) *'It Did Happen Here': Recollections of Political Oppression in America.* Berkeley, CA: University of California Press.

Schumann, J. (1988) *Hollywood Speaks – Deafness and the Film Entertainment Industry.* Urbana, IL: University of Illinois Press.

Schroder, O-I. (1993) Introduction to the history of Norwegian sign language. In R. Fischer and H. Lane (eds) *Looking Back.* Hamburg: Signum.

Scheurer, T. (1991) *Born in the USA.* Jackson, MS: University of Mississippi Press.

Seebohm, F. (1968) *Report of the Committee on Local Authorities and Allied Personal Social Services.* London: HMSO.

Seelye, H. (1992) *Teaching Culture – Strategies for Intercultural Communication.* Chicago, IL: National Textbook Company.

Shaw, R. (1987) p. 262 in Gleick. New York: Viking.

Showalter, E. (1987) *The Female Malady: Women, Madness and English Culture, 1830– 1980.* London: Virago.

Sicard, R-A. (1984) Course of instruction for a congenitally Deaf person. In H. Lane and F. Philip (eds) *The Deaf Experience.* Cambridge, MA: Harvard University Press.

Sign On (1998) *Deaf Nation* 1:1. Newcastle: Tyne Tees TV for Channel 4.

Silent News (1995) The brave new world of genetic planning. (January, p. 24).

Silver, A. (1993) Reframing Deaf art/De'VIA for the 21st century: New directions. *Deaf Studies* III. Washington, DC: Gallaudet University.

Simon, R. and Dippo, D. (1986) On critical ethnographic work. *Anthropology and Education Quarterly* 17, 195–202.

Sixty Minutes (1993) Cochlear implants – The new miracle. 29 April.

Skliar, C. (1997) *La Educacion de los sordos.* Mendoza: EDIUNC.

Skutnabb-Kangas, T. (2000) *Linguistic Genocide in Education, or Worldwide Diversity and Human Rights?* Mahwah, NJ: Lawrence Erlbaum.

Smith, D. (1988) *The Everyday World as Problematic: A Feminist Sociology.* Boston, MA: Northeastern University Press.

Soloman, A. (1994) Deaf is beautiful. *New York Times Magazine.* 28 August.

Spindler, G and Spindler, L. (1992) Cutural process and ethnography – an anthropological perspective. In M. LeCompte,W. Millroy and Preissle (eds) *A Handbook of Qualitative Research in Education.* San Diego: Academic Press.

Spivak, G. (1985) *'Race', Writing and Difference,* ed. H. Gates. Chicago: University of Chicago Press.

Spivak, G. (1987) *In Other Worlds: Essays in Cultural Politics.* New York: Methuen.

Spivak, G. (1990) *The Post-Colonial Critic: Interviews, Strategies, Dialogues,* ed. S. Harasym. New York: Routledge.

Spivak, G. (1996) *The Spivak Reader,* ed. D. Landry and G. Maclean. New York: Routledge.

Spradley, J. (1979) *The Ethnographic Interview.* Fort Worth: Holt, Rinehart and Winston.

Spradley, J. (1980) *Participant Observation.* New York: Holt, Rinehart and Winston.

Stewart, D. (1991) *Deaf Sport.* Washington, DC: Gallaudet University Press.

Stewart, L. (1992) Debunking the bilingual/bicultural snow job in the American Deaf community. In M. Garretson (ed.) *Viewpoints on Deafness* (pp. 129–44). Silver Spring, MD: National Association of the Deaf.

Stokoe, W.C. (1989) Dimensions of difference: ASL and English-based cultures. In S. Wilcox (ed.) *American Deaf Culture.* Silver Spring, MD: Linstok Press.

Stokoe, W.C. (1994a) Editorial. *Sign Language Studies* 83. Maryland: Linstok Press.

Stokoe, W.C. (1994b) Brief notices. *Sign Language Studies* 84. Maryland: Linstok Press.

Stokoe, W.C. (1994c) Comment on Turner. *Sign Language Studies* 84. Maryland: Linstok Press.

Stokoe, W., Casterline, D. and Croneberg C. (1965) *A Dictionary of American Sign Language on Linguistic Principles.* Washington, DC: Gallaudet College Press.

Street, B. (1993) Culture is a verb. In D. Graddol, J. Thompson and B. Byram (eds) *Language and Culture.* Clevedon: British Association for Applied Linguistics in association with Multilingual Matters.

Subaltern Studies (1982–7) Vols I–VI (ed. R. Guha). Delhi: Oxford University Press.

Supalla, S. (1992) *For a Decent Living* (videotext). San Diego, CA: DawnSign Press.

Supalla, T. and Newport, E. (1978) How many seats in a Chair? In P. Siple (ed.) *Understanding Language Through Sign Language Research.* New York: Academic Press.

Sutcliffe, T. and Sutcliffe, B. (1976) *Sign and Say, Book 1.* London: Royal National Institute for the Deaf.

Sutton-Spence, R. and Woll, B. (1998) *The Linguistics of British Sign Language: An Introduction.* Cambridge: Cambridge University Press.

Tannen D. (1986) *'That's Not What I Meant!' – How Conversation Style Makes or Breaks Relationships.* New York: Ballantine Books.

Tannen, D. (1990) *'You Just Don't Understand' – Men and Women in Conversation.* New York: Ballantine Books.

Taylor, G. and Bishop, J. (eds) (1991) *Being Deaf.* London: Pinter Press.

Taylor, G. and Gregory, S. (1991) *Issues in Deafness, Unit 1: Perspectives on Deafness: An Introduction.* Milton Keynes: Open University Press.

Taylor, G. and Meherali, R. (1991) *Being Deaf: The Other Deaf Community.* Milton Keynes: Open University.

Terstiep, A. (1993) Ethnicity, social theory, and Deaf culture. *Deaf Studies III: Bridging Cultures in the 21st Century.* Washington, DC: College for Continuing Education, Gallaudet University.

Thornton, R. (1988) In E. Boonzaeir and J. Sharp (eds) *Culture: A Contemporary Definition in Keywords.* Cape Town: David Philip.

Toure, S. (1974) A dialectical approach to culture. In R. Chrisman and N. Hare (eds) *Pan Africanism.* Indianapolis: Bobbs-Merrill.

Trompenaars, F. (1993) *Riding the Waves of Culture – Understanding Cultural Diversity in Business.* London: The Economist Books.

Truffaut, B. (1993) Etienne de Fay and the history of the Deaf. In R. Fischer and H. Lane (eds) *Looking Back.* Hamburg: Signum.

Turner, G. (1990) *British Cultural Studies.* London: Unwin Hyman.

Turner, G. (1994a) How is Deaf culture? *Sign Language Studies* 83. Silver Spring, MD: Linstok Press.

Turner, G. (1994b) Deaf Cultural Studies in an age of complexity. In *Sign Language Studies* 84. Silver Spring, MD: Linstok Press.

Tylor, E.B. (1871) *Primitive Culture.* London: Murray.

Urion, C. (1991) *Concept of Culture Applied to Deaf Culture.* ALEHI Convention, Calgary. (n/p)

Valentine, P. (1993) Thomas Hopkins Gallaudet: Benevolent paternalism and the origins of the American asylum. In J. Van Cleve (ed.) *Deaf History Unveiled.* Washington, DC: Gallaudet University Press.

Valli, C. (1995) *ASL Poetry: Selected Works of Clayton Valli*. San Diego, CA: DawnSign Press.
Van Cleve, J.V. (1993) The academic integration of Deaf children. A historical perspective. In R. Fischer and H. Lane (eds) *Looking Back*. Hamburg: Signum.
Van Cleve, J.V. and Crouch, B.A. (1989) *A Place of their Own*. Washington, DC: Gallaudet University Press.
Van Deburg, W. (1992) *New Day in Babylon*. Chicago: University of Chicago Press.
Van Gils, G. (1998) Surdophobia. *The Voice* 1, (1) 6–7.
Walby, S. (1990) *Theorising Patriarchy*. Oxford: Blackwell.
Walker, A. (2001) Deaf recollections of social interaction in mainstream schools. MPhil dissertation University of Bristol.
Washington Post (1994) Letter to the Editor. 15 November.
Wa Thiong'O, N. (1986) *Decolonising the Mind – The Politics of Language in African Literature*. Nairobi, Kenya: Heinemann.
Widell, J. (1993) *The Danish Deaf Culture in European and Western Society*.
Wilcox, S. (ed.) (1989a) *American Deaf Culture. An Anthology*. Silver Spring, MD: Linstok Press.
Wilcox, S. (1989b) STUCK in school: Meaning and culture in a Deaf education classroom. In S. Wilcox (ed.) *American Deaf Culture. An Anthology*. Silver Spring, MD: Linstok Press.
Williams, H. (1993) Origins of the St Petersburg Institute for the Deaf. In R. Fischer and H. Lane (eds) *Looking Back* (pp. 295–306). Hamburg: Signum.
Williams, H.G. (1993) Deaf teachers in 19th century Russia. In R. Fischer and H. Lane (eds) *Looking Back*. Hamburg: Signum.
Williams, H.G. (1993) The origins of the St.Petersburg Institute for the Deaf. In R. Fischer and H. Lane (eds) *Looking Back*. Hamburg: Signum.
Williams, R. (1958) *Culture and Society, 1780–1950*. London: Penguin.
Williams, R. (1975) *The Long Revolution*. London: Penguin.
Williams, R. (1976) *Keywords*. Glasgow: Fontana and Croom Helm.
Williams, S. (1992) Two words on music – Black community. In G. Dent (ed.) *Black Popular Culture*. Seattle, WA: Bay Press.
Willis, R. (1977) *Learning to Labour: How Working Class Kids Get Working Class Jobs*. Farnborough: Saxon House.
Winefield, R. (1981) Bell, Gallaudet and the sign language debate. Unpublished doctoral dessertation, Harvard University School of Education.
Winefield, R. (1987) *Never the Twain Shall Meet*. Washington, DC: Gallaudet University Press.
Winston, B. (1973) *The Image of the Media*. London: Davis-Poynter.
Wolff, J. (1990) *Feminine Sentences*. Oxford: Polity Press.
Woll, B., Kyle, J. and Deuchar, M. (eds) (1981) *Perspectives on British Sign Language and Deafness*. London: Croom Helm.
Woodill, G. (1992) Empowering adolescents through participatory research. Report presented to the Ontario Ministry of Health.
Woodward, J. (1972) Implications for Sign Language Study among the Deaf. *Sign Language Studies* 1 (1). Silver Springs, MD: Linstok Press.
Woodward, J. (1989) How you gonna get to Heaven if you can't talk with Jesus? The educational establishment vs. the Deaf Community. In S. Wilcox (ed.) *American Deaf Culture, An Anthology*. Silver Spring, MD: Linstok Press.
World Federation of the Deaf (1983) *Policy on Cochlear Implants on Deaf Children*. Rome: World Federation of the Deaf.

World Federation of the Deaf (1999) *The Blue Ribbon Ceremony* (videotape). Brisbane: Australian Association of the Deaf.

Wright, S. (1998) The politicisation of 'culture'. *Anthropology Today* 14 (1).

Wrigley, O. (1996) *The Politics of Deafness.* Washington, DC: Gallaudet University Press.

Young, A., Ackerman, J. and Kyle, J. (1998) *Looking On – Deaf People and the Organisation of Services.* Bristol: The Policy Press.

Zinn, H. (1980) *A People's History of the United States.* New York: HarperCollins.

Zwiebel, A. (1993) The status of the Deaf in the light of Jewish sources. In R. Fischer and H. Lane (eds) *Looking Back.* Hamburg: Signum.

Index

Authors

Subjects